# The Historiography of Psychoanalysis

Also by Paul Roazen

*Freud: Political and Social Thought*
*Brother Animal: The Story of Freud and Tausk*
*Freud and His Followers*
*Erik H. Erikson: The Power and Limits of a Vision*
*Helene Deutsch: A Psychoanalyst's Life*
*Encountering Freud: The Politics and Histories of Psychoanalysis*
*Meeting Freud's Family*
*How Freud Worked: First-Hand Accounts of Patients*
*Heresy: Sandor Rado and the Psychoanalytic Movement,*
with Bluma Swerdloff
*Canada's King: An Essay in Political Psychology*
*Oedipus in Britain: Edward Glover and the Struggle Over Klein*
*Political Theory and the Psvchology of the Unconscious*

Edited by Paul Roazen

*Sigmund Freud*
Walter Lippmann, *The Public Philosophy*
Louis Hartz, *The Necessity of Choice: Nineteenth Century Political Theory*
Helene Deutsch, *Psychoanalysis of the Sexual Functions of Women*
Victor Tausk, *Sexuality' War, and Schizophrenia:*
*Collected Psychoanalytic Papers*
Helene Deutsch, *The Therapeutic Process, the Self and Female Psychology:*
*Collected Psychoanalytic Papers*
Walter Lippmann, *Liberty and the News*

Paul Roazen

# The Historiography of Psychoanalysis

Routledge
Taylor & Francis Group
LONDON AND NEW YORK

First published 2001 by Transaction Publishers

Published 2017 by Routledge
2 Park Square, Milton Park, Abingdon, Oxon OX14 4RN
711 Third Avenue, New York, NY 10017, USA

First issued in paperback 2018

*Routledge is an imprint of the Taylor & Francis Group, an informa business*



Library of Congress Catalog Number:

Library of Congress Cataloging-in-Publication Data

Roazen, Paul, 1936-
The historiography of psychoanalysis / Paul Roazen.
p. cm.
Includes bibliographical references and index.
ISBN 0-7658-0019-5 (alk. paper)
1. Psychoanalysis—History—20th century. 2. Freud, Sigmund, 1856-1939. I. Title.

BF173 .R5513 2000
150.19'52'09—dc21 00-064757

ISBN 13: 978-1-138-51605-2 (pbk)
ISBN 13: 978-0-7658-0019-0 (hbk)

In Memory

of

Charles Rycroft

# Contents

# Foreword

Sigmund Freud's legacy seems to be as hotly contested as ever. It does appear that everything connected with him continues to attract fanaticism of one kind or another. It is even characteristic of various dissenting streams of thought, which may begin with the premise of his central significance, that they lay claim to being in exclusive possession of the spirit of the "true" Freud, though these different directions can vary widely from one another. And more or less official organizations can trace their genealogy back to his original guidance. Other groups also can lay claim to his inspiration, leaving newcomers more or less bewildered about the fractured nature of the psychoanalytic landscape. Impatient radicals have, unfortunately, wanted to abandon this whole area completely.

In good part, the heat of all the partisan battling has been due to the extent to which modern theories of the self have come to replace earlier religious and philosophic systems of thought. Controversies about psychology, including how the mind works as well as the processes by which emotions develop, involve the most intense kinds of disagreements that once might have been encountered in the sectarian wrangling associated with religious and ethical disputes.

One of the problems associated with most criticisms of Freud is the degree to which they proceed unaware of the whole history of the reception of his work. Right from the outset of his publications there were those who respectfully disputed the validity of what he proposed. Freud's aims were, I think, never restricted to the purely empirical world of verifiable propositions, which also helps to account for the passion of both his proponents as well as the detractors. It would be ahistorical if not falsely scientistic to expect Freud's ideas to fulfill today's standards of what scientific psychology should be like. And no one should be surprised if Freud was human enough to deceive himself about how objective his accomplishments were. The stories that he told, and encouraged others to communicate, gave meaning to people's lives, which is one reason why these explanations, even though flawed, proved difficult to give up.

An enduringly attractive feature to reflecting on the world Freud created is the extent to which he was proposing a fresh vision of what human beings might be like. Although he often expressed himself within the terminology of medicine, it should be evident that he had far more ambitious fish to fry than science itself. A central source of the controversies within psychoanalysis has been due to the existence of often unspoken rival conceptions about how life might best be lived. For example, socialists, Protestants, Bolsheviks, as well as conservatives and even reactionaries, have found something to feed off within psychoanalysis. And classical liberal thinkers were attracted, and sometimes repelled, by the implications of what Freud was proposing. He had tried to maintain his distance from competing branches of philosophy, and it is only fairly recently that we have found evidence about how well-educated he himself had been philosophically. In spite of his anti-philosophical pronouncements, I believe that Freud had tried to challenge the central tenets of traditional Western ethical thinking, and the reverberations of his novel ideas can still be disquieting.

It is, though, disheartening to see how lacking in perspective most of today's arguments about Freud still are. To have criticized him before he successfully made his mark, prior to World War I for instance, has to mean something special; and the early critiques were sometimes muffled with deference to his artistry. Even some of those who were highly dubious about Freud's initial propositions could herald him as a thinker of unusual distinction. But critics like Carl Jung and Alfred Adler tended to get swamped in the polemical legends that Freud set going about them. By the 1920s, when Freud's influence became genuinely worldwide, naïve propaganda flourished both for and against what he stood for. It has never been easy to find impartially minded assessors of what he contributed; even today proponents and antagonists seem separated by an impassable gulf.

Although Freud has been dead for over sixty years, there seems little sign of the old battlefields becoming recognized for the historical events they were. The confrontation between Freud and Jung, to take one example, has led to the growth of two separate schools more than to a reexamination of their original contrasting positions. To the extent that Freud's work has become an established part of the thinking of today's conventional wisdom, then it makes sense to continue pointing out the flaws in his approach. His impact has been so subtly pervasive that it is harder than one might imagine to discern how he has affected the ways in which we now think.

In some parts of the world, in eastern Europe and the former Soviet Union for example, Freud's approach seems novel, fresh, and liberating as we enter the twenty-first century. Stalinist pressures stifled psychoanalysis for over half a century, despite the striking affinities between nineteenth century Russian culture and Freud's own ideas. At the same time that Freud is being revived in Russia, with the backing of the political system, throughout mainland China traditional Confucian conceptions have so far barely been touched by the Freudian wave. The kind of individualism we are accustomed to in the West can appear in East Asia to be shocking. One has to wonder, thinking of big statistical studies in China and the relative scarcity of case histories, what the shape of our own healing professions would be like without the humanistic influence of psychotherapy as enriched by Freud. The competing claims of altruism as opposed to egotism, encountered in different cultural contexts, need to be reconsidered in the light of the experience that others have had in dealing with categories influenced by psychoanalysis. All ethical choices are inherently dependent, I believe, on psychological presuppositions of what it means to be human.

Throughout western Europe, and parts of South America as well, psychoanalysis has become closely allied with mainstream philosophy and literary criticism. In Buenos Aires psychology departments are headed by analysts, and thanks to Freudianism it is illegal in Argentina to spank a child. If Freud might be disappointed at the failure of his successors to confirm many of his so-called findings, he could be expected to be gratified at the transforming impact his ideas continue to have throughout contemporary moral and ethical thinking. In the Far East we may have barely begun to see the long-range effects that he has been capable of exerting.

Only in America, despite Freud's protests against what he viewed as new world barbarism, did psychoanalysis for a time sweep almost all before it. (The Netherlands, too, was quick to pick up on Freud before World War I, and the Dutch have been as notably receptive to psychoanalysis as Israelis have been resistant.) By the early 1960s, when I first became interested in the history of psychoanalysis, analysts held the leadership posts of all the major American psychiatric departments. Yet even then the general public could be patronizingly dismissive of what Freud had contributed; in those days the so-called neo-Freudians were being acclaimed for what they had added to Freud's achievements.

By now the situation has swung in an entirely different direction, partly as a result of the effects of the National Institute of Mental Health and the drug companies. Analysts today seem to have scarcely any psychiatric power in America, as psychopharmacology has become the predominant fashion. Yet outside of this country, where it is undeniable that the American claims of psychoanalytic therapy had once been widely over-sold, Freud has been continuing to gain in stature. Italian psychiatrists, for example, while apt to be dismissive of the approach of DSM-III and IV, are wary about repeating the earlier mistakes of American analysts who held out too long against the therapeutic possibilities of new medications. So Freud has now become popular almost everywhere except in America, where he once held such explicit sway and where his ideas have been imbedded in a range of fields from child-custody law to handbooks for child-rearing.

Despite the vagaries of the impact Freud has had over this past century, it has always made sense to ask, of Freud's defenders as well as opponents: "who benefits?" Trade union proponents of psychoanalysis, who stand to gain by the acceptance of his work, are bound to be insensitive to the concerns of independent investigators. Yet the history of ideas should teach us that power can be challenged in multiple ways. Anti-psychiatric advocates may no longer be in style, but they raised legitimate issues of enduring moral concern. High-handedly to reject Freud should imply the existence of superior alternatives whose full implications have been as thoroughly explored as Freud has been exhaustively studied.

Too many of the latest attacks on psychoanalysis are unaware of the unattractive tendencies within much of today's most fashionable practices. Biological psychiatry has had its own unexamined ethical dimensions. At what human sacrifice, for instance, do patients take certain medication? Ethical limits are still being explored about the necessary experimentation with new drugs. One has to wonder whether the diagnoses that psychopharmacology makes use of are really as clear-cut as it has often been presumed. (Jung used to say that diagnoses were only possible after the conclusion of treatment.) Cultural changes have their own force, as in the relatively new outlook in America on the psychiatric status of homosexuality. The official notion of "social phobia" is bound to mean something different in shame cultures like Japan and Korea than in the West.

Above all, I would contend that it is as easy to be authoritarian with the use of the latest categories of psychiatric thought as ever the old-line Freudians were capable of abusing their power. What kind of expert a psychiatrist or psychologist can be remains a contentious issue. To me, it is surprising how the most relentless of Freud's enemies today seem willing to allow to go unchallenged the approaches of those who think of themselves as having carved out a separate, supposedly impartial domain as opposed to the allegedly tilted psychoanalytic worldview.

It has been harder that one might have expected to get the study of the history of psychoanalysis onto the hopefully more neutral ground of scholarly inquiry. With all the existing controversial literature there has scarcely been an attempt to study Freud and his followers within the context of intellectual history, although that now seems to be changing in a more hopeful direction. Part of the excitement of this field is that it is still relatively easy for reasonably dispassionate observers to come up with thoroughly original material. In an era when psychiatry has been trying to go in such a different direction, at the same time that Freud's basic point of view is still attracting newcomers in areas of the world which have been relatively untouched by psychoanalytic influence, it can be all the more important to try to be clearer about both the strengths and limitations of his approach.

It is of course never possible to construct an account of the past that is without bias or preference. Even so, the goal of history-writing should be different from that of propagandizing; and the most elementary contributions should aim at the ideal of being correctable by the perspectives of future students of history. Although there can be no final, unchallengeable historical record about anything of real significance, there are degrees of disinterestedness as opposed to subjectivity. It has been my continuing hope over the last four decades to make an addition to the historiography of psychoanalysis, even though it is not possible to lay claim to the kind of scholarly authoritativeness that one might like.

So the essays that appear here were originally written for individual occasions, and never intended to qualify as definitive. I have revised them to minimize the possibility of repetition. It has been thoroughly enjoyable to witness the immense expansion of the substance of this field, and invigorating to see the growth of competing ideological alternatives. The body of work I have been able to come up with will, I hope, make it easier for others to go beyond me.

# Introduction

Although Sigmund Freud had many notable prescursors in the history of ideas, a broad consensus now exists that the distinctive set of doctrines known as psychoanalysis has passed its one hundredth birthday. No doubt there will be some legitimate disagreement about exactly when in the mid-to-late 1890s this unique approach, created by Freud, can be said to have begun. Some will perhaps choose the time when Freud initially used the new term for his special way of proceeding. Others will date its beginnings from the moment when Freud announced in a 1897 letter to his friend Wilhelm Fliess that he had abandoned the hypothesis that adult neurosis had its origins in childhood sexual seduction; instead, Freud began to believe in the powerful role that the fantasy life of patients can play in their irrational problems. Alternatively, one might propose that the most important turning point was when Freud substituted his version of free associations for the earlier therapeutic device of hypnosis. Finally, politically aware observers might want to argue that only in 1902, when Freud began formally to assemble a following around him, can psychoanalysis itself be said to be under way. As I see it, the fact that there can be fair-minded differences of opinion on such an issue is itself a sign that the study of this field has finally, after so many years of amateur endeavors and sectarian squabbling, come of age as a legitimate academic discipline.

Chosen dates in history influence, as well as reflect, rival interpretive stances. Yet it would be agreed by most that in some sense psychoanalysis was decisively under way by the time of Freud's publication of *The Interpretation of Dreams* (1900). Certainly, it has often been pointed out that throughout the twentieth century literature about all things psychoanalytic has multiplied at an ever-increasing rate. There are now more psychoanalytic journals than ever before, and the number of practitioners is still on the increase. The situation in France today can serve as an instructive example; they have some sixteen Freudian organizations functioning, and one of them in Paris alone forms the largest single component unit of the International Psychoanalytic Association, which was founded by Freud in 1910.

Although the story of the history of Freud's school ought to include much more than just himself, embracing those he quarrelled with as well as those who stayed with him through thick and thin, he continues to play a unique role in everything which has ever been written in connection with the system he created. Events since his death in 1939 have only seemed to heighten his stature. His continued dominance over the subject has to be traced to more than his own authoritarianism, which was a phenomenon of his culture and times as well as undoubtedly a special personal trait of his. I think it is telling how from his earliest writings he showed a sharp sense of history; he constantly introduced readers to the specific steps by which he had arrived at his ideas. Even with patients he could discuss his predecessors and early struggles. Freud had a powerful sense of the future; he was early on convinced of his destined triumph and therefore left no stone unturned to make sure of leaving behind something concrete that future historians could rely on. It is true that in 1885 Freud had written to his future wife about how he had undertaken to carry out "an intention which a number of as yet unborn and unfortunate people will one day resent." He went on to explain:

> Since you won't guess what kind of people I am referring to, I will tell you at once: they are my biographers. I have destroyed all my notes of the past fourteen years, as well as letters, scientific excerpts and the manuscripts of my papers. As for letters, only those from the family have been spared. Yours, my darling, were never in danger. In doing so all old friendships and relationships presented themselves once again and then silently received the *coup de grâce* (my imagination is still living in Russian history); all my thoughts and feelings about the world in general and about myself in particular have been found unworthy of further existence. They will now have to be thought all over again, and I certainly had accumulated some scribbling.
>
> But that stuff settles round me like sand-drifts round the Sphinx; soon nothing but my nostrils would have been visible above the paper; I couldn't have matured without worrying about who would get hold of those old papers. Everything, moreover, that lies beyond the great turning-point of my life, beyond our love and my choice of a profession, died long ago and must not be deprived of a worthy funeral. As for the biographers, let them worry, we have no desire to make it too easy for them. Each one of them will be right in his opinion of "The Development of the Hero," and I am already looking forward to seeing them go astray.[1]

It is telling about the passion of Freud's commitment to his work that even in the course of such an intimate letter, he described "the great turning point" in his life as the love between himself and his fiancée, and, on an equal footing, his own "choice of a profession." He had prefaced his remarks to his future wife by telling her that he had been browsing in Russian history, and perhaps this attention to historiography helped lead him to think of the need to tidy up some of his own.

Freud was doubtless writing partly tongue-in-cheek about his future biographers and his pleasure in the anticipation of misleading them. Still, from Freud's earliest letters as a young man we know something of his youthful convictions about his immortality. And it would seem that his mother in particular shared his ambition to be a world conqueror.[2] He kept this unusual sense of himself until the end of his life. In 1938, on his way from Paris to London on the boat-train at night, he dreamt he was landing at the same town in England as William the Conqueror. Although Freud was at that stage physically feeble, having had cancer of the jaw for fifteen years, this dream highlights how he had retained his inner identity of being a warrior of the spirit.

It is clear that Freud could be a skilful political leader on behalf of the cause he founded. But one significant component of his immense historical success, in addition to his considerable capacities in building an organizational structure which would long outlast him, was his prescience in understanding the importance of keeping control of the story of the early development of psychoanalysis. We may know virtually nothing about what Freud admired in his early reading of H. T. Buckle or W. E. H. Lecky, or even what he picked up from Nietzsche,[3] but he knew in his bones that shaping the past is a key instrument to becoming dominant in the future.

Freud was so astute about historiography that at the opening of his Clark lectures in 1909, he declared: "If it is a merit to have brought psychoanalysis into being, that merit is not mine. I had no share in its earlier beginnings. I was a student and working for my final examinations at the time when another Viennese physician, Dr. Josef Breuer, first (in 1880-1882) made use of this procedure on a girl who was suffering from hysteria."

Perhaps he was so extravagant about Breuer—with whom Freud had long since broken off all personal contact—because he wanted immediately to then give an account of Breuer's early treatment of the woman who has become famous as Anna O. But it is worth pointing out that not only has it been established that Breuer was not a success with Anna O., as Freud claimed at Clark, but that she ended up, after the cathartic treatment with Breuer, addicted to both morphine and chloral.[4] Equally striking is that by 1923 Freud added a footnote to his sentence declaring Breuer's priority in having "brought psychoanalysis into being"; for Freud then wrote: "See, however, in this connection my remarks on 'On the History of the Psychoanalytic Movement,' where I assumed the entire responsibility for psychoanalysis."[5] Freud cut Breuer as an old man when he passed him in a Vienna street, but when Breuer died in 1925 Freud sent a condolence letter to the Breuer family and published an obituary notice.

Freud's polemical "On the History of the Psychoanalytic Movement" (1914) was written after the series of difficulties he had with Alfred Adler, Wilhelm Stekel, and Carl Jung. Freud remained furious with them all, as well as their various supporters, and in order to distinguish his own ideas from their dissenting views he let himself go in public in a way that was rare for him. James Strachey's splendid edition of Freud's works in English might have succeeded in highlighting just how upset Freud was, if Strachey had consulted more than the printed versions of Freud's published texts; the original manuscript of "On the History of the Psychoanalytic Movement" shows Freud to have been even freer with his partisanship than in the published version.[6] It seems to me extraordinary that Freud was so sure of himself as to have considered psychoanalysis, at such an early date, to be entitled to have a history. After all, there were then only a relatively small number of practicing analysts, and Freud's influence was in those days far overshadowed by existing alternatives to psychoanalysis.

Equally surprising is that once Freud had launched his invective against his backsliding supporters, none of them shared Freud's own sense that something needed to be put into the history books. Freud's version of what had happened in those now epic pre-World War I struggles triumphed partly by default. Jung, for example, felt traumatized by what had happened between himself and Freud; and for years thereafter he bitterly complained in private how the Freudians had for a time succeeded in wrecking his clinical practice. Although he lived long enough to write an obituary of Freud, which was on the appreciative side, and discussed his difficulties with Freud in the autobiographical *Memories, Dreams, Reflections*,[7] by then the historical die had been cast. For those who had momentously differed with Freud it would always be an uphill battle to combat the account of things which Freud had put into the history books in a way which went unchallenged. Most subsequent controversies in psychoanalysis, long after Freud's death, have been too readily assimiliated to the models of what happened before World War I. Not only was Freud stylistically the greatest writer among twentieth-century psychologists, but his decision to recount his own side of these now famous quarrels proved politically a key move on his part.

Part of today's wave of revisionist scholarship is able to thrive on showing how unbalanced was the account of what happened that flowed from Freud's own pen, an account too credulously accepted by outsiders. Freud's disciples shared his own keen sense of the significance of keeping the record straight from his own point of view. If independent observers have unwittingly been apt to adopt Freud's own viewpoint, rather than appreciate how pupils of his struggled to develop ideas of their own, even if it meant crossing swords with Freud, these dissenting ex-students of Freud's did little to help their own cause historiographically. Not only did those Freud stigmatized as heretics do little publicly to fight back, but their supporters did not have the same sense of history as Freud and his own loyal friends. Even now, after all these years, the Jung family for example has yet to authorize an official biography; and so there are important personal Jung archives still to be explored. We do not even have decent scholarly editions of Jung's works. Tiny papers of Freud's appear with a considerable scholarly-seeming apparatus, while huge books of Jung's have been allowed to appear without even the semblance of decent editorial attention.

I am not suggesting that any of the so-called dissident figures in psychoanalysis can compare in stature with Freud as the first psychoanalyst. But as we know, there are many thousands of Freud's letters still to appear in print, which can be counted upon to continue to alter our view of him. As that striking passage from Freud's letter of 1885 about his future biographers going astray indicates, Freud's prose remains unmatched within all twentieth-century psychology. I believe Freud's unusual literary skills help account for the power his ideas still retain.

Through the creation of the psychoanalytic situation, Freud was also able to exert an unparalleled degree of influence. When Erik H. Erikson once suggested that Freud's recommended therapeutic technique amounts to "an exquisite sensory deprivation experiment,"[8] he was identifying one means by which Freud could create converts to his cause. The relative absence of sights and sounds has specific psychological consequences, as does any use of the couch. By 1910, Freud's critics were complaining that Freud was not fully aware of the element of old-fashioned suggestion which was built into his own treatment procedure; he instead chose to think that psychoanalysts were capable of confirming what he ambitiously thought to be his findings. We still have naïve people regularly talking about Freud's "discoveries," instead of more modestly accepting the idea that in actuality what he was doing was forwarding a special way of looking at things.

It is one part of the story that the ideas of Freud's dissenting former students have been relatively neglected, although fine recent biographies of Wilhelm Reich, Otto Rank, Karen Horney, and Melanie Klein, for instance, have helped remedy the situation. But legitimate criticisms of psychoanalysis, written from completely outside Freud's fold, have scarcely ever been given enough of a hearing. A mythology has been allowed to thrive in which Freud is viewed as a wholly misunderstood genius unfairly maligned by an uncomprehending opposition. If, however, one examines reviews of Freud's works which appeared while he was still alive, the ones that are least worth reading today are those parrot-like accounts composed by loyal apostles. The critiques offered by non-analysts, on the other hand, can be both insightful and respectful. Much that appears within the psychoanalytic literature today, which is supposedly an advance on previous professional thinking, turns out on examination to amount to reinventing the wheel.

I am not suggesting that what we confront in today's technical psychoanalytic literature can be considered unique. It has something to do with the ways in which classic authorities get cited in other fields as well. I am thinking, for example, of how the American founding fathers get quoted in Supreme Court decisions. It is sociologically important on behalf of national unity for people to believe they are living now under the same Constitution (with the acknowledged official amendments) which was written in the late eighteenth century. And so earlyAmerican thinkers are often cited out of proper historical context to answer contemporary needs of today. Two commentators on the way historians have made use of Alexis de Tocqueville's great study, *Democracy in America*, make a similar point:

> If one may be permitted to speculate generally on the uses of classic authorities, one notes that historians often use words from the classic authorities as aids in achieving

> intellectual legitimacy. They are means of making an author's ideas more palatable by conveying them through universal and universally acceptable symbols. Tocqueville's words have now become such symbols and are capable of evoking a mood of acquiescence toward the introduction of ideas quite remote from the context in which their creator originally used them. They reassure the reader that the new formulation is linked to the mainstream of intellectual endeavor.[9]

Whatever desirable social purposes such mythologizing may accomplish, the creation of such false continuities is a central obstacle against which intellectual historians are obliged to struggle.

The situation is unusual within psychoanalysis in that we have so many publications by practicing clinicians who have neither the leisure nor the training to perform academic research. Nor is it in their interest to promote impartial scholarship. So we have many journals which exist essentially for trade-union purposes. Independent research which in any way rocks the boat can not only become a threat to the way clinicians and their patients have ideologically organized their thinking, but also be perceived as a menace to their essential modes of being. I would not want to underestimate the way economic livelihoods could also be endangered. And so there are piles of psychoanalytic publications, each of which regularly cites Freud, but which instead of adding anything to the genuine history of the discipline is essentially using his words as "classic authorities," making its own contemporary ideas "more palatable" by linking them to isolated sentences that Freud once wrote. The body of Freud's work is so extensive that it is easy to place tortured constructions, useful for today, on what he originally penned. Freud's broad influence has been such that a Marxist like Herbert Marcuse could adapt psychoanalysis to serve his own ideological purposes, and even trained historians have so credulously accepted conventional psychoanalytic teachings as to allow themselves to become partisan propagandists.[10]

It is a commonplace in the history of ideas that a great writer has to be understood in the context of those against whom he was writing. As Hugh Trevor-Roper once put it, "St Augustine, St Thomas Aquinas, Descartes, Locke, Marx, all built up their systems against now forgotten adversaries." It is my conviction that Freud does rank as a giant in intellectual history. Although I am myself citing that sentence from Trevor-Roper as a classic authority for my own argument, I do not want to be guilty of what has come to be known as Jesuitical reasoning by omitting his very next sentence: "Vulgar disputants die with the disputes which have nourished them."[11]

The problem for me with Trevor-Roper's second sentence is that it is apt to sound too much like Whig history, or history written on the side of the big battalions. The fact that Freud succeeded against his rivals, or that his early critics are now forgotten, says nothing about the merits of any of the arguments in which they were then engaged. Mikhail Bakunin scored a number of telling points against Karl Marx, for example, and yet even graduate students specializing in the history of socialism are in my experience unlikely to be familiar with Bakunin's thought. I am not suggesting that he was in any way Marx's equal as a theorist, but there is something obviously wrong in history-writing which is obsessed by success. Marx won out within the first Socialist International, and the history of the twentieth century was uniquely influenced by him. We necessarily have to rely on the crude standard of survival in order to evaluate why any thinker deserves to be studied. But entirely aside from the advantage of understanding a writer in terms of the opponents he felt obliged to combat, it is notorious how some writers—such as Giambattista Vico—were unduly neglected in their own time.

If psychoanalysis were merely an aspect of the history of science, then it would make more sense to ignore those other figures who have fallen by the wayside. We are apt to think of science in connection with progress, and it follows that we should pay special attention to theories that win out as opposed to those that are discarded. Yet as intellectual historians we should be obliged to understand the Ptolemaic conception of the universe as well as the Copernican, and the phlogiston theory makes an interesting tale in the development of modern chemistry.

If one were to weigh Freud's concepts only in the cold light of science, however, I think his standing would seriously suffer. Whatever may be the case in France today (which has only belatedly caught up with the psychoanalytic revolution), in America, Freud's doctrines, popular even before World War I, are now under a medical cloud. While three decades ago psychoanalysts regularly ran American psychiatric departments all across the country, today it would be rare to have any hospital departments making such an appointment. Old-fashioned psychiatrists all along vigorously objected to the sectarianism among the psychoanalysts. And while these non-Freudian holdouts may have seemed anti-humanitarian, and sometimes been too tolerant of techniques like electroshock or even psychosurgery, they were fundamentally convinced that more was at issue, at least in the case of the great mental illnesses, than the purely psychological angle that most of the Freudians wanted to pursue. The gains made over the last generation in developing new and efficient drugs have given what is now known as biological psychiatry a standing which has, at least in America, eclipsed the analysts medically. Unfortunately, often in the history of ideas the baby gets tossed out with the bath-water, and the danger of over-medication as well as slighting the interaction between patient and therapist are still with us.

Freud himself believed that there were what he called constitutional bases to the psychoses, although he was belated in even distinguishing between neurosis and psychosis. He warned his followers in the 1920s that they had better hurry in their psychological research lest the development of new treatment made it impossible to study problems which might soon be too easily curable. But again, it has not been fashionable to see the extent to which Freud's commitment as a scientist could be at odds with his efforts as a therapist. And to the extent that he made his stand on purely scientific grounds, modern developments have left some of his work high and dry. He may in the long run have contributed something unique to the attention that ought to be paid to the relationship between therapist and patient, but surely that would have struck Freud as paltry compared to the grandiosity of his aims.

It is only by putting Freud back in context that it will be possible to appreciate precisely what he achieved. It is not simply that in his own time the great mental diseases were even more mysterious than by and large they remain today. In addition, he was trying to introduce an element of humane attentiveness to human troubles that will always rank, I think, as a significant accomplishment. It may be that some of his disciples were so aloof from the need to bring about therapeutic improvements that in effect they imitated the therapeutic nihilism of the most benighted of Freud's contemporary rivals. In the face of pressing human dilemmas, psychoanalysts—including Freud himself—could miss the wood for the trees, concentrating on abstract problems deriving supposedly from early childhood while overlooking distressing day-to-day difficulties, including the special setting of psychoanalytic treatment.

The truth of the matter is complicated in that Freud did not behave as a clinician at all in accord with his recommended techniques for his future disciples. Here an element of hypocrisy has crept into the history of psychoanalysis. Those who were intimate with Freud's own clinical practices knew perfectly well that he did not himself act as a so-called orthodox analyst is supposed to do. He talked, at least when he had his health, a great deal; he recommended specific marriage choices; he treated addicts, and even those whom he acknowledged to be schizophrenics; and he gave his views on political and moral matters. Quite apart from his conscious intentions, the unique treatment situation he had arranged had an immense impact all of its own. Looking at photographs of Freud's consulting room it is hard to believe that any patient could have been in it without feeling the impact of Freud's own idiosyncracies.[12]

In part, Freud made his rules about how analysts were supposed to behave for the sake of beginners. Those technical papers were devised for the purpose of letting others know where he himself had originally gone wrong in his own practice. But even if allowances are made for the contrast between what Freud said and how he behaved, it is hard not to think that there was something phony about the way some of his followers disguised the liberties he took. Surely the fact that he personally analyzed his own daughter Anna,[13] which was once a closely guarded secret, was as "wild" a bit of analysis as anything Freud could have condemned in those former pupils of his whom he refused to recognize as legitimate psychoanalysts. If it was a matter of heresy to treat a patient sitting up, instead of lying on a couch, what did it mean to analyze one's own child? Perhaps one sentence of Freud's about Paul Schilder, whom despite Schilder's brilliance among Viennese analysts Freud came to disapprove of, can illustrate how arbitrary Freud could be. Freud wrote of Schilder in 1936: "I must declare him unsuited to teaching psychoanalysis, quite regardless of whether others are more or less suited than he."[14]

The Freud-Schilder difficulties remain to be explored. But even the most celebrated controversies in the history of psychoanalysis ought not to be looked upon only as scientific disputes, or even intellectual disagreements; they did of course contain differences of ideological approach, and the confrontation between Freud and Jung represents for me one of those enduring clashes between alternative temperaments and points of view. Just as Diderot and Rousseau were at odds about something more than a personality clash, Freud and Jung represented lastingly different outlooks in the history of ideas. For example, while Freud saw religion as in principle neurotic, though in practice sometimes acknowledging the legitimate and valuable functions religious beliefs could provide, Jung thought neurosis arose from a fundamental absence of meaning, and he sought in religion that form of belief which he thought could help rescue patients from the distress of an unduly barren era lacking in significant alternatives.

The history of psychoanalysis has to be seen not just as a series of personal squabbles, although human differences could readily get blown up into theoretical proportions. What has been at stake, and kept the fires of conflict burning for so long, are rival worldviews. If one wants to appreciate the quality of the differences between contending factions in the history of psychoanalysis, then the quickest way would be to pick up a book about the wars of religion in the sixteenth century.

Psychoanalysts in training in different organizational contexts rarely appreciate the terminology or techniques of alternative approaches. The movement known as self-psychology, for instance, initiated by Heinz Kohut in Chicago, has in many quarters of North America become the most fashionable example of psychoanalytic revisionism. Yet Kohut (who was subsequently criticized in private as "anti-psychoanalytic" by Anna Freud) would not have dreamt of acknowledging Franz Alexander as a legitimate precursor, since Alexander had once been the leader among Chicago analysts and subsequently denounced as a deviationist. Jung is probably the single most seemingly sinister figure in the list of psychoanalytic iconoclasts, and although his notions about individuation ought to be more acceptable within the context of self-psychological thinking, he is still regarded as too much of a renegade to appear in orthodox psychoanalytic bibliographies.

Karen Horney, thanks to the successful impact of the feminist movement over the last generation, has reappeared within the so-called mainstream. And Melanie Klein, even though Freud loathed most of what she stood for, has also won a surprising degree of acceptance. The changes that do take place are likely to be accomplished slowly; the life of any effective organization means that the discipline provided by doctrine has to be changed only gradually and with deliberation. Psychoanalysis became a church whose unity had to be guarded against the threat of schism. And although claims have often, especially recently, been made for the existence of pluralism within psychoanalysis,[15] I think that ideological broad-mindedness remains more the exception than the rule.

Psychoanalysis has had its Ayatollahs, and even though I have never been a practicing analyst, my own research has at times been deemed subversive enough to have called forth thundering anathemas.[16] Heresy-hunting is not something that only happened in the distant past of psychoanalysis; it has also taken place within my own lifetime. The power of mythology ought never to be underrated; independent historical research has to be threatening, since social unity rests on the power of unquestioned consensus. Psychoanalysis has no official Index of Prohibited Books, but the informal means of social control are every means as powerful.

The problem of myth-making is hardly peculiar to psychoanalysis. Mikhail Gorbachev and Boris Yeltsin may have successfully introduced many changes into Russian life; but as yet Leon Trotsky has not been fully rehabilitated. Some might say that whether or not Trotsky's ideas are now debated is a relatively trivial issue; but I think that one should never underestimate the power of ideology. After all, psychoanalysis itself rests on the basic conviction that how we think profoundly affects how we behave.

Trevor-Roper, who has written so tellingly about the Renaissance and Reformation, has conjectured about how formal ideologies come to lose their power. Such weakening of conviction takes place almost imperceptibly. "To give precise dates to major intellectual changes is impossible. Intellectual systems are not destroyed intellectually by mere disproof; they are tied to social structures which, if themselves healthy, are prompt to repair local damage and to re-fortify weakened positions." Trevor-Roper is worth listening to, I believe, since he is writing without any explicit interest in a doctrine like psychoanalysis, although I suspect that his studies of sixteenth and seventeenth-century Europe owe more than a little to his knowledge of the fate of Marxism in this past century. He argues that even when grand philosophic systems of thought "have been discovered to be socially irrelevant, they do not dissolve at once; they live on in the minds of those habituated to them and only perish when that generation has disappeared, and a new generation, in different circumstances, proves immune to their appeal. Even then, their decomposing relics may linger on in corners and perhaps, in time, generate new heresies."[17]

It is beyond my competence to explain all the social sources of support for psychoanalytic thinking during the past hundred years. An examination of what has kept Freud's work so alive would require a comparative cultural analysis. For the Freud who succeeded in America is unlike the Freud that is currently flourishing, at long last, in France; and the English strand of psychoanalysis is unique, not to mention how other cultures have picked and chosen from within the broad doctrine that Freud first laid down.[18] Any generalizations about the sources of social support for psychoanalytic thinking would have to be linked to the specific circumstances of different national traditions.

Freud himself lived long enough to preside over the cross-cultural dissemination of his ideas. He selected disciples to carry on his calling in a variety of places, and even when he made misjudgments of character he persisted in his belief that, ultimately, he would triumph throughout the world. Even though he himself confessed to having little understanding of eastern religions, for example, he wrote letters to followers in both India and Japan. One of his favorites, Marie Bonaparte, undertook to finance anthropological field research by Geza Roheim in Australia. Freud himself stayed wedded to nineteenth-century convictions about how modern societies had evolved from so-called primitive cultures, and he never appreciated the requirements of modern field-work. Like Marx, he put forth his ideas with the conviction that they were universals.

Despite his self-confidence about his ultimate victory, he was not willing to leave things to chance. And so when the first biography of him was published in 1924, written by an early member of his Vienna circle, Fritz Wittels, Freud did not let the occasion simply slide by. Freud wrote the author a detailed letter based on an advance copy of the book; and in Freud's library in London there is still a copy of his annotated edition of Wittels's study. Wittels reprinted, with Freud's permission, extracts from Freud's letter to him. Later, Wittels was not only readmitted to the Vienna Psychoanalytic Society, but also published an article recanting his earlier candor.[19] A second book of Wittels's about Freud proved far less interesting. Wittels subsequently became a defender of psychoanalytic orthodoxy, and he was one of those analysts who helped drive Karen Horney out of her teaching position at the New York Psychoanalytic Institute.[20] A close examination of Freud's detailed markings of his copy of Wittels's first biography would amount to an essay in its own right; but then one would have to take into account not only what Freud objected to, or approved of, but some striking passages which he chose not to comment on or challenge.

Wittels was sympathetic to Stekel, but Freud never forgave Stekel for what Freud deemed an unpardonable act of betrayal. And his unremitting capacity to bear grudges extended to a host of people he regarded as his enemies. Freud once approvingly quoted a passage from Heine that bears on his intransigence, which extended to the outlook he adopted to his position in history. "A great imaginative writer," Freud wrote in 1929, "may permit himself to give expression—jokingly at all events—to psychological truths that are severely proscribed." Thus Heine (as quoted by Freud) confesses:

> Mine is a most peaceable disposition. My wishes are: a humble cottage with a thatched roof, but a good bed, good food, the freshest milk and butter, flowers before my window, and a few fine trees before my door; and if God wants to make my happiness complete, he will grant me that joy of seeing some six or seven of my enemies hanging from those trees. Before their death I shall, moved in my heart, forgive them all the

> wrong they did me in their lifetime. One must, it is true, forgive one's enemies – but not before they have been hanged.[21]

While on holiday in the summer of 1931, Freud had "composed what he called a 'hate list' of seven or eight people."[22]

This story about the construction of a hate list was told by Ernest Jones, who became Freud's authorized biographer. Jones commented that "one would dearly like to know what names were on it," and regretted that only one of the identities could be reconstructed. It is typical that Jones was so closely identified with Freud's side of things that he did not seem to realize how lacking in charity he had made Freud seem. All of us who have studied the history of psychoanalysis are deeply indebted to Jones's research; he was permitted to see documentation that remains even now restricted. Jones was himself not lacking in the capacity to hate, and one does wonder sometimes whether his own personal version of Freud left out too much of Freud's unique generosity and outgoingness.

It is unfortunately characteristic of almost everything that has ever been written about Freud that it has been partisan. Freud himself had not wanted an official biography, but the Freud family came to feel that so many critical studies were coming out that it would be a wise act of statecraft to put them all in their place by depositing in Jones's hands the mass of documentary material they had at their disposal. While some of Freud's children had their reservations, in the end it was Anna Freud, the only one to have followed in his footsteps as an analyst, who overrode the natural objections that any family is entitled to have about a biographer invading their privacy.

One of the oddities of the choice of Jones as authorized biographer was that although he had been angling for the job for years, he made it sound in print as if he had been reluctant to undertake the task. Furthermore, he and Anna Freud were hardly on the best of terms. Jones had since the mid-1920s been sponsoring the work of Melanie Klein, Anna's bitter rival within child analysis. Both Anna and her father thought that Klein was attacking Anna as a vehicle for getting back at Freud himself. Jones, then, was no personal favorite of either Anna or her father, although they both felt indebted to him for helping them escape to England after the Nazis occupied Austria in 1938. Only after Anna had read drafts of the first volume of Jones's biography did she decide to turn over in an unrestricted way the papers she had in her possession. Although Jones graciously dedicated his three-volume study to her, she remained privately lukewarm about what he had accomplished. Still, she and her allies knew that his version of things was good for the "cause" they all championed.

Jones's books were successful not just in propping up a picture of Freud which was desirable from the orthodox psychoanalytic position, but in swamping almost all other writers by virtue of the authentic detail to which he alone had access. A few notable but isolated dissenting voices rose in protest. Erich

Fromm, for example, wrote his short *Sigmund Freud's Mission* in an effort to show how Jones's own material could be used for different, "revisionist" purposes.[23] And Bruno Bettelheim was courageous enough not only to review Fromm's essay favorably, but to publish his own separate critiques of Jones.[24] Among professional psychoanalysts, however, Jones carried the day. The orthodox Robert Waelder, for instance, made sure that he contributed an extended critique of Fromm's position,[25] while the liberals within the movement by and large did not seem to appreciate the power which creating a historical record could give. A notable exception to this generalization was Clara Thompson's book *Psychoanalysis: Evolution and Development.*[26]

Within the literary community as a whole Jones was to go unchallenged for an extraordinary period of time. Insiders within psychoanalysis knew, for example, that Jones's account of Sandor Ferenczi's last days was heavily biased: essentially, Jones had accused Ferenczi of having had a mental illness which explained his difficulties with Freud, even though Freud's own obituary of Ferenczi had mentioned the physical disease of pernicious anaemia. But outsiders could be rougher on the "dissidents" in psychoanalysis than even Jones. Perhaps the most telling example of non-analysts being even more partisan than the most fierce of the Freudians was how the eminent literary critic Lionel Trilling could allow himself, with no basis in evidence, to exaggerate what he found in Jones. Trilling wrote in a review in the *Sunday New York Times Book Review* of Ferenczi and Rank: "Both men fell prey to extreme mental illness and they died insane."[27] Even Jones was surprised at the length to which Trilling had taken Jones's own various diagnostic labels.

The stage was then set for the next generation of historians who, almost inevitably, have been branded as debunkers. Once Jones had finished rounding out Freud's version of his life, identifying completely with Freud's own side of a career filled with controversy, then any attempt to correct the idealizations that Jones had publicized was bound to appear like the work of detractors. Jones aspired to be definitive, and Anna Freud too wanted nothing further after Jones. Her desire for control was such that, at the British Psychoanalytic Society, she rose to take exception to the forthcoming John Huston movie about Freud, starring Montgomery Clift, even though the original screenplay had been written by Jean-Paul Sartre.

The results of Jones's orthodox historiography were not what he had anticipated. The excellence of his narrative served to attract even more researchers, but increasingly their allegiances would be to impartial scholarship as opposed to doctrinal loyalty. It is true that orthodox analysts continued to cite Jones as the last word; and other members of Anna Freud's party, such as Max Schur, could be counted upon to present a picture that she would find attractive.[28] Jones himself died shortly after the appearance of the final volume of his biography, but where power (and patronage) are concerned there are always those willing to pick up the mantle of the defence of the orthodox faith. In my opinion Peter Gay's recent work, including his *Freud: A Life for Our Time*, has been designed to launch a Counter-Reformation in Freud studies.[29] (Since then Frederick Crews has been citing historical literature for the sake of the most disparaging kinds of remarks about Freud and what the whole upshot of the psychoanalytic influence amounts to.[30])

Anna Freud, right up until her death in 1982, watched over everything that appeared about her father. It is a safe generalization that she liked nothing that came out, not even Schur's book, apart from one notable exception: she thought that an article by Kurt R. Eissler about her father was splendid.[31] Starting with an attack on Franz Alexander, a particular battle that Anna Freud was still carrying on in one of her last publications,[32] Eissler became the official watchdog on behalf of psychoanalytic orthodoxy. He and Anna Freud worked together harmoniously. Even while Freud was still alive, Anna had been capable of exaggerating his dislikes; but after his death she was able to pursue her own agenda unchecked. She admitted to Jones once in a letter, while he was writing his biography, that she could be jealous of other women in Freud's circle. Basically she resented anyone whose link with Freud did not go through her. As the years passed she built up her own following, almost all of whom she personally analyzed at least briefly. "Miss Freud," as she came reverentially to be known, became so powerful as to intimidate almost anyone who tried to write about her father.

One brouhaha in the history of psychoanalysis was the direct responsibility of both Eissler and Anna Freud. They took it into their heads that a youngish Sanskritist, Jeffrey M. Masson, who had graduated from the Toronto Psychoanalytic Institute, should succeed Eissler in charge of the Freud Archives in New York City. Eissler had set up the Archives, with Anna Freud's half-hearted support, shortly after World War II. As time passed, and no doubt the advantages of tax deductions began to sink in, she gave the Archives her full backing. The idea was that people would donate material to the Archives, and then the Archives would in turn give items to the Library of Congress in Washington, D.C. That way the Freud Archives became the official donor, and could place whatever restrictions it chose on the material it deposited at the Library of Congress. The dates embargoing items were wholly arbitrary; patient confidentiality was not a central consideration; and just as Anna O.'s real name, despite her family's objections, had been revealed by Jones, so Eissler felt free, after the death of Freud's famous patient "The Wolf Man," to indicate his real identity as well.[33] Because of the arrangement under which the Library of Congress first agreed to accept the donation of Freud's papers, it remains helpless in the face of the partisanship that continues to this day to govern the operations of the Freud Archives.

The oddness of the choice of Masson in 1980 to be placed in charge of the Freud Archives was that he had had for years a bee-in-his-bonnet about the sexual seduction of children. Neither Eissler nor Anna Freud could detect

Masson's obsession with this theme; all they could see was that he was apparently bent on maintaining the glorification of Freud. He succeeded in charming them both. The fat was in the fire by 1981, within a year of his appointment, when he announced at a psychoanalytic meeting, and worse still to a *New York Times* reporter, that Freud had lacked the courage of his early convictions when he gave up the hypothesis that neurosis arose from childhood sexual abuses. Masson alleged that Freud had invented his theory of the Oedipus complex, and the significant role of fantasy, to curry favor with the Viennese medical establishment. Eissler then got the Board of the Freud Archives to fire Masson; Masson filed a legal suit, and an out-of-court settlement was finally agreed upon.

Eissler was subsequently eased out of his position at the Freud Archives; Anna Freud herself died in 1982; and one might have thought that the situation of psychoanalytic historiography would be radically transformed. It is true that no one now has to fear the force of Anna Freud's wrath, which could be considerable. For example, in my own case I did not realize how much at the time she had done behind the scenes against me because of her intense dislike of my second book, *Brother Animal: The Story of Freud and Tausk*, which first came out in 1969.[34] Only when I went through her papers at the Library of Congress in the summer of 1989 did I learn the full extent of her manipulations exerting pressure on publishers, reviewers, and other psychoanalysts. She participated in a shared fanaticism whose power extended to some of the most famous philanthropic foundations.

Although it would be unwise to be prematurely confident about the waning of cultism, in the face of renewed assaults on Freud's reputation, it does seem to me that over the last years the history of psychoanalysis has shown more signs of becoming a subject which can be studied in universities with something like the objectivity which one can expect of similar topics. It is still true that too many people remain fiercely attached to fixed ideological positions. The power of therapeutic transferences is such that those who have been analyzed by members of one school of analysis or another are apt to be irrationally attached to positions which cannot be defended on normal academic grounds. Still, I see real indications that the history of psychoanalysis is today being critically weighed by university scholars in a way in which it has never been before.

The past ideological wars mean that, as compared to almost any other academic endeavor in the history of ideas, it is strikingly easy to be original in this area. All one has to do is to maintain a modicum of impartiality and thereby cut through literature which has been written by clinicians with no real idea of normal standards of scholarship. In addition, with the continued withholding of primary data, such as Freud's numerous correspondences, there is plenty of time to assimilate new material. It will be years before all of Freud's letters finally appear. We are obliged to cross our fingers and hope that when these correspondences are finally accessible, people will be able competently to weigh the meaning of the feelings and events that are described there.

One danger in the current literature is that the pendulum may swing excessively in a scientistic direction. Practising clinicians have gone unchallenged for so many years that serious students of the history and philosophy of scientific methodology are able to make mince-meat out of most of the existing psychoanalytic literature. Freud can be seen, when judged by the severest standards of modern science, to appear naively ignorant of the need to verify his propositions.

Although Freud could undoubtedly deceive himself about how much of his work had been independently confirmed, at the same time I think there is a problem with importing into this field standards which are needlessly positivistic. Of course Freud's dream theory needs revision now; advances in biochemistry alone make many of his convictions seem elementary and misguided. Jung's theory of dreams, an alternative to Freud's, should have alerted people earlier to different possibilities that were available. It is impossible to make sense of what happened in the early days of psychoanalysis without taking seriously the various criticisms which were advanced against Freud by a wide variety of contemporary thinkers.

It should go almost without saying that by now we know much more about the nature of good psychotherapy. There is nothing sacred about the fifty-minute hour, and the use of the couch may, as some of Freud's earliest critics contended long ago, be inadvisable. Sophisticated therapists today are far more wary of artificially inducing regressions in patients than has been the case with orthodox psychoanalysis.

Nevertheless, all Freud's theories have to be seen in the context of his times. It would be anachronistic to look at him only from the perspective of what we now think to be true. We can better understand what Freud was doing with his patients thanks to the hindsight which the past century has given us; but we have to beware of the distortions which an exclusively present-minded orientation would impose on us. We should neither be appealing to Freud for ways of supporting the practices of orthodox analysis today, nor searching for ways of making Freud seem foolish and misguided by standards which were not accessible to him.

The aim of studying the history of psychoanalysis ought to be to take us out of ourselves, and to provide a fresh perspective on some of our own least examined ways of thinking. Freud was laying down some fundamental challenges to traditional Western ethics. This is not a subject on which one can be either right or wrong in a way which is strictly verifiable. He created through his works a world which was different; he attracted articulate and sophisticated people who tried their best to make sense of some of the most fundamental issues in human experience. Freud was trying to say something lasting about the nature of both love and hate, and even though the subject is in principle an inexhaustible one, the ideas he proposed were memorable and telling.

I am not making a plea for apologetics about Freud, which are in any case unnecessary. Both as a thinker and writer he is capable of withstanding the closest scrutiny. The people Freud attracted and repelled make for fascinating intellectual history. The fact that many of his supporters were on an unacknowledged religious quest helps make them appealing since their search for salvation meant that they were soul-seekers. This religiosity also led to an unfortunate degree of intolerance, which has been an obstacle in the path of scholarship. But the length of time it has taken to breach the defences of credulous believers and unreflective skeptics means that now the study of the history of psychoanalysis may have come of age.

## Notes

1. *Letters of Sigmund Freud 1873-1939*, ed. Ernst L. Freud, tr. Tania and James Stern (London: Hogarth, 1961), pp. 152-53.
2. Paul Roazen, *Freud and His Followers* (New York: Knopf, 1975; reprinted New York: Da Capo, 1992), pp. 39-46.
3. Paul Roazen, "Nietzsche and Freud: Two Voices From the Underground," *Psychohistory Review*, Spring 1991, pp. 327-49.
4. Henri Ellenberger, "The Story of 'Anna O.': A Critical Review with New Data," *Journal of the History of the Behavioral Sciences*, 8 (1972), pp. 267-79.
5. Sigmund Freud, "Five Lectures on Psychoanalysis," *Standard Edition*, Vol. 11, p. 9.
6. Sigmund Freud, *Selbstdarstellung*, ed. Ilse Grubich-Simitis (Frankfurt: Fischer, 1971), pp. 141ff.
7. Carl G. Jung, *Memories, Dreams, Reflections*, recorded and edited by Aniela Jaffe, translated by Richard and Clara Winston (New York: Random House, 1965).
8. Cf. Paul Roazen, *Erik H. Erikson: The Power and Limits of a Vision* (New York: The Free Press, 1976; reprinted Northvale, NJ: Jason Aronson, 1997), pp. 70-72, 182, 191.
9. Lynn L. Marshall and Seymour Drescher, "American Historians and Tocqueville's *Democracy*," *The Journal of American History*, 55, 3 (December 1968), p. 516.
10. Paul Roazen, *Encountering Freud: The Politics and Histories of Psychoanalysis* (New Brunswick, NJ: Transaction, 1990), pp. 121-24, 13-16, 263-64.
11. Hugh Trevor-Roper, *Renaissance Essays* (London: Fontana, 1986), p. 104.
12. Paul Roazen, *How Freud Worked: First-Hand Accounts of Patients* (Northvale, NJ: Jason Aronson, 1995).
13. Roazen, *Freud and His Followers, op. cit.*, pp. 436-46.
14. John C. Burnham, *Jelliffe: American Psychoanalyst and Physician* (Chicago: University of Chicago, 1983), p. 269.
15. Victor Tausk, *Sexuality, War, and Schizophrenia: Collected Psychoanalytic Papers*, ed. Paul Roazen (New Brunswick, NJ: Transaction, 1991), pp. 1-28.
16. Roazen, *Encountering Freud, op. cit.*, Ch. 6. Paul Roazen, *Meeting Freud's Family* (Amherst: University of Massachusetts Press, 1993).
17. Trevor-Roper, *Renaissance Essays, op. cit.*, p. 192.
18. Roazen, *Encountering Freud, op. cit.*, Ch. 2.

19. Fritz Wittels, "Revision of a Biography," *Psychoanalytic Review*, 20 (1933), pp. 361-74.
20. Susan Quinn, *Karen Horney: A Mind of Her Own* (New York: Summit, 1987), pp. 337-40.
21. Sigmund Freud, "Civilization and Its Discontents," *Standard Edition*, Vol. 21, p. 110.
22. Ernest Jones, *The Life and Work of Sigmund Freud*, 3 volumes (New York: Basic Books, 1953-1957), Vol. 3, p. 159.
23. Erich Fromm, *Sigmund Freud's Mission: An Analysis of His Personality and Influence* (New York: Harper, 1959).
24. Bruno Bettelheim, *Freud's Vienna and Other Essays* (New York: Vintage, 1991), pp. 39-56.
25. Robert Waelder, "Historical Fiction," *Journal of the American Psychoanalytic Association*, 11 (1963), pp. 628-51.
26. Clara Thompson, with the collaboration of Patrick Mullahy, *Psychoanalysis: Evolution and Development* (New York: Grove, 1950).
27. Cf. E. James Lieberman, *Acts of Will: The Life and Work of Otto Rank* (New York: The Free Press, 1985), p. 400.
28. Roazen, *Encountering Freud, op. cit.*, pp. 215-18.
29. Paul Roazen, "Book Review of Gay's *Freud: A Life For Our Time*," *Psychoanalytic Books*, 1 (January 1990), pp. 10-17.
30. Frederick Crews, *The Memory Wars: Freud's Legacy in Dispute* (New York: New York Review of Books, 1995); Frederick Crews, ed., *Unauthorized Freud: Doubters Confront a Legend* (New York: Viking, 1998).
31. Kurt R. Eissler, "Mankind at Its Best," *Journal of the American Psychoanalytic Association*, 12 (1964), pp. 187-222.
32. Paul Roazen, "Book Review of Sandler, Kennedy, and Tyson, *The Technique of Child Analysis: Discussions with Anna Freud*," *Journal of the History of the Behavioral Sciences*, 27 (1991), pp. 281-83.
33. Paul Roazen, "Psychoanalytic Ethics: Freud, Mussolini, and Edoardo Weiss," *Journal of the History of the Behavioral Sciences*, 27 (1991), pp. 366-74.
34. Paul Roazen, *Brother Animal: The Story of Freud and Tausk* (New York: Knopf, 1969; reprinted with new Introduction, New Brunswick, N.J: Transaction, 1990).

# Part 1

## Varieties of Discipleship

# Introduction to Part 1

A central part of the impact Freud had came from how he inspired a special kind of following. As a thinker, he created a band of pupils who were inclined to treat his work as the equivalent of holy scripture, and many felt forced to rebel against the leadership of this self-proclaimed heretic in Western thought. A resolution of these conflicting messages through either loyalism or "deviance" could be equally unsatisfactory; imitation, as well as rebellion, proved easier than genuine independence. A secular era reproduced many of the same sorts of phenomena which earlier had appeared in strictly religious movements. As bent as Freud was in creating a neutral science, he also was insistent on the public adherence of his pupils to certain fundamental axioms which he thought distinguished his work.

It is too simple to see Freud only in our own terms, although it is impossible not to do so at least partially. To use contemporary standards in looking over the complex materials of his life and accomplishments would be to deprive ourselves of the diverse richness which the past offers us. He was inevitably a man of his culture: at the same time he created a system of thought which retains its vitality into the twenty-first century. Although it may seem desirable in the short-run to reduce Freud in stature to what we might prefer him to have been like, either in order to serve the needs of today's professional organizations or as a whipping-post for our own frustrations, the tolerance achieved through distance is the most desirable point of departure. It will not be long before our own time has been succeeded by other central concerns, and the broader a perspective one brings to the history of psychoanalysis the more likely the future will respect our own outlook.

The patterns by which psychoanalysis gets handed down from one generation to the next are unlikely to change radically from what has been true until now. Generosity toward all past contending factions is not guaranteed to be successful in the face of the closed-mindedness that many have needed to cope with the uncertainties connected to dealing with depth psychology, but charity remains a central value by which I have tried to guide my own research. Believing in the ability of the truth to survive in the face of even the worst ideological fanaticisms is an ultimate liberal faith that all good historians of ideas share.

# 1

# Was Freud a Nice Guy?

To ask the question whether Freud was a nice guy is to elicit several different types of answers. To start off with a response in the form of another question: why on earth should we expect, or want, anybody born as long ago as 1856 to match standards that are anything like our own? One essential job of a historian should be to enable people to go back to an era unlike that in which we live today. We should proceed on the premise that the past is necessarily relevant to contemporary life, without at the same time steam-rolling all the differences between then and now. It would be essentially anachronistic to expect anybody from history to fulfill our own expectations about what we might approve of in our own time. And yet it is somehow typical of recent trends to be present-minded and unhistorical, stripping the past of what makes it most distinctive, compelling, interesting, and instructive.

While the past has to be different from us, great thinkers are somehow also our contemporaries. They reach out to us over the centuries; what they said and thought still challenge us; it is their ideas that succeed in keeping them alive. The liveliness of a historic writer does not mean that we have to accept everything that person had to say; we should retain the right to pick and choose that which we want to accept for ourselves. Unless we suspend a certain amount of disbelief, extending our imaginations as generously as possible to encompass others, we will be unable to hear the central questions asked by preceding thinkers in earlier centuries.

But beginning by placing a theorist in some cultural context at least makes less likely certain cheap tricks by which we are inclined to assert our own alleged superiority over the past; for some do proceed simply by means of the sleight-of-hand involved in presuming that our own contemporary standards of opinion are inherently superior to those of our predecessors. The present has all the advantages of hindsight. It does not limit an earlier figure that he or she did not know ahead-of-time what course events would take. Earlier times confronted complex social conditions and invoked values which may seem unusual to ourselves; studying history should mean a broadening of our horizons, stretching our sense of the possible.

Social prophets do exist who have foretold the future. A few heroes did accurately predict the possibilities of racial and sexual equality. Moral insight led some to proclaim the progressive changes that have taken place in at least some countries over the last century-and-a-half. In an earlier time Edmund Burke, a great conservative, predicted the course the French Revolution would take. Burke's antagonist, Tom Paine, may have defended democratic ideals about the public which sound attractive today, but few would deny the unusual depth and prescience of Burke's thinking. A pamphleteer like Paine lacked the complexities of someone like Burke, even though Burke's arguments may seem less immediately attractive. He did unquestionably foresee the full violence inherent in the French Revolution itself.

The history of the last century has hardly been moving solely in the direction of enlightenment and ethical enlargement that Paine was trying to promote. The twentieth century was one of the bloodiest on record, from its wars to the crimes of Hitler, Stalin, Pol Pot, Mao Tse-tung, and other tyrants. Freud saw the beginnings of the worst of what would happen. In the middle of World War I he realized that nineteenth century ideals of self-government were going to be submerged in the realities of brutal modern warfare, which would extend to civilian populations and include the success of mass propagandizing. And in the spring of 1933, when the Nazis first burnt Freud's books, he is reported to have ironically commented: "What progress we are making. In the Middle Ages they would have burnt me; nowadays they are content with burning my books."[1]

Freud had a predominantly grim, stoic outlook on mankind. He quoted at least once the ancient maxim *Homo homini lupus* ("Man is a wolf to man").[2] He was skeptically convinced that humanity was capable of doing some terrible things. His whole concept of the unconscious, which he made so central to all psychology, hinged on the presence in each of us of a kind of hellishness. So Freud ranks as a great unmasker, someone who was not easily taken in by the mere espousal of high-sounding principles. Pious intentions can after all lead to some of the worst social cruelties.

Assuming that it would be correct to say that Freud was not one of the obvious lovers of mankind, is that conclusive about him one way or another? If we begin with the question of whether he was "a nice guy," I think it is easier to see that it would be wrong to judge him by our own conventional standards of right and wrong. But it may be hard, and not in the self-interest of some, to absorb the full force of how Freud sought to undermine preceding ethical convictions. Some of our perfectionist ambitions may be threatened. Again, we do not necessarily have to agree with Freud. But I think it is necessary to see the daring spirit built into what he was after.

Let us take for granted that Freud was a so-called realist, one who did not readily share traditional lip-service to high-minded pieties. I think that that is by no means the end of the matter. He was, I believe, a deeply subversive thinker, and that capacity to undermine has to rank as part of his contribution to intellectual history. He was throwing down a gauntlet, among other things, to Christianity, not just as institutionalized in organized religion but in its essential precepts. And more than once he challenged in print the maxim "Love thy neighbor as thyself."[3] (His letters, which someday when finally completely published will exceed in length the works that appeared in Freud's lifetime, also reveal in subtle ways the scope of Freud's moral intentions.) His critique of an essential component of the Sermon on the Mount may have been misguided, and remain one that we do not need to accept; but I believe we are missing out on what he stood for in Western thought, and part of what made him so remarkable, if we ignore the degree to which he was taking deadly aim at some of the most cherished ethical ideals of human thought. His concept of unconscious homosexuality was another example of his troubling capacity to pull down ethical objectives. He was implying that psychoanalysis would be able to come up with some new moral standards.

I accept Freud as a debunker, and not a shallow one at that. He was pointing out some of the most disturbing aspects of human nature. He was saying, among other things, that human beings are capable of surprising and disappointing things. He liked to quote Hamlet's lines, "There are more things in heaven and earth, Horatio, Than are dreamt of in your philosophy."[4] Freud was trying to expand our conception of what people could be like, and inevitably this meant that he would be emphasizing sides to people's nature that most of us would prefer not to acknowledge. He took a dim view of the possibilities of equality, and saw the potential for violence, jealousy, and all the other sins that human beings are capable of displaying. He secularized sinfulness, substituting instead symptomatology; his was not a vision which would win agreement among those who are comfortable mainly with Sunday sermons.

To take a slightly different tack: it is not established that the most humanitarian-seeming thinkers are the best long-run friends of mankind. Thomas Hobbes in the seventeenth century had some pretty rough things to say about human nature, which has not diminished his stature in the history of ideas; and he also implicitly took for granted an extent of rationality and conscious self-direction which may seem outstanding even by today's standards. Also, we still read Machiavelli not only in spite of how shocking he can be, but just because he defies our standards of moral reasoning, and anticipated more conflicts between public and private moralities than we might like to imagine. Hobbes perceived fresh sources of social disunion, and Machiavelli dwelt on his own idea of the necessities that he thought eternal. To move on in the history of social philosophy: Jean-Jacques Rousseau, when he proposed "forcing" men to be "free," stood in the line of other avowed emancipators who may have inadvertently led to tyranny. The Jacobins chose to quote humane-sounding Rousseau, not the "pessimist" Hobbes. And when Lenin relied on Karl Marx, surely the Bolshevik was finding something real in Marx that got used to support a terrible form of enslavement. The concept of a dictatorship of the proletariat acquired real flesh and blood when invoked by some of the leaders of the old Soviet Union. Marx was at least as tough-minded about human motives as Freud, and neither men were easy for their contemporaries, or even their colleagues, to get on with. But the fact that Marx endorsed certain humanitarian ideals was not enough to settle the question of what his impact on history would amount to.

It is at least arguable that those who set out with the most idealistic objectives about changing people are the ones who end up enchaining the most. (Freudianism, when embraced for the finest of objectives, could itself tragically backfire.) I do not believe it is only the skeptics about human motives who have contributed to the prevalence of suffering and misfortune. Thinkers who begin with limited goals are perhaps the ones less likely to mislead people. If one starts out to transform human nature wholly, there may be a hidden license justifying acts that lead toward the most cruel social conclusions. Among the American founding fathers it was James Madison who insisted that "men are not angels," as he drew political and social consequences for the American federal system from that beginning premise.

I am not advocating misanthropy, nor would it be fair to link Freud with only the worst expectations of what human nature can be capable of being like. It is true that he can be quoted as having said some utterly harsh things about the human condition. When he invoked notions such as "trash," "riff-raff," or "good-for-nothings," he was expressing an outlook common to his social class as well as part of his profession as a psychoanalyst. And his sour observations about certain individuals, especially those he was acutely disillusioned with, can be read as literary savagery. Yet at the same time, he was an enormously hard-working physician, someone who spent most of the working hours, six days a week, trying to help people therapeutically. He was appealing to the capacities of people to overcome their limitations through the use of reason and self-knowledge. His activities as a practicing analyst by and large took into account practical limits on what patients could become. And he had to respect the human dignity of those he worked with if he was to hope to have any practical success.

Here, there is an inevitable difference between what Freud could be like as a theorist, and how he behaved clinically. In certain almost breath-taking sentences he could be damning about mankind as a whole, or at least certain parts of it. And yet he could also be exceptionally charitable in a way that is perhaps less easy to detect. I am thinking, for example, of a psychotic patient in the 1920s whom Freud saw for years in analysis, even though Freud had (like others) diagnosed him as a schizophrenic. Freud could get on with such a person better than contemporary practitioners, whatever their theories may sound like. Although in principle Freud, according to his own concepts, should not have been analyzing such a person, Freud was in better human touch with him than others. He wrote reassuringly to the patient's mother in America that she should try not to worry too much about her son—on the grounds he was of the type of Jean-Jacques Rousseau. Presumably the parent was well-educated, and knew as well as Freud how difficult in life Rousseau had been to his contemporaries. (I am thinking here of Denis Diderot, who once commented on the evening of their last meeting: "he makes me uneasy, and I feel as if a damned soul stood beside me....I never want to see that man again; he could make me believe in devils and Hell."[5] Rousseau did shock people by his ideas. For example, he had refused to maintain that "man's freedom consists in doing what he wants, but rather in never doing what he does not want to do."[6] That sort of outlook on freedom, built on a conception of a divided soul capable of self-torment, could be appalling; and late in life Rousseau acknowledged that his notion of freedom had scandalized his contemporaries. Friends of liberty in the twentieth century were to continue to be alarmed by the authoritarian implications of the paradox of "forcing" people to be free.)

Partly, Rousseau's quarrelsomeness was the problem, but he was right in thinking that his whole theoretical approach was one that his friends found horrifying. On a 1776 rumor of Rousseau's death (he did not actually die until 1778) the great Voltaire laconically wrote: "Jean-Jacques really did the right thing by dying."[7] Edmund Burke thought that Rousseau was pathologically sensitive, metaphorically lacking in human skin. And Friedrich Grimm wrote Rousseau personally objecting both to Rousseau's "horrible apology" and his "monstrous system....I shall never in my life see you again, and I shall deem myself fortunate if I can banish from my mind the recollection of your behavior...."[8]

Rousseau, whose *Confessions* amount to one of the world's great autobiographies (as does Freud's *The Interpretation of Dreams*), was obviously too much to take; and only from a great distance in time can we recognize his genius. But his intense search for purity, his quest for authentic human communication, rendered him not only terribly hard to get on with, but a theorist who has been accused of writing in behalf of modern inquisitions. (The Church had tormented people not out of sadism but in behalf of salvation beyond bodily existence.) Once Rousseau had legitimized splitting the human self, separating out false feelings from genuine intentions, he had given an intellectual basis for those who sought to search for human purposes beyond those consciously acknowledged. Rousseau can be defended on the grounds that ultimately he stood for self-mastery, not a new form of slavery, but critics always thought that he had handed the enemies of humanity a fresh means of being tyrannical. Freud would be viewed similarly as a professed liberator who ended up inventing a new set of chains.

Now Rousseau was only one of Freud's precursors, and Nietzsche[9] was another; yet both Rousseau and Nietzsche were in their lifetimes far more isolated than Freud himself. He was a cultured, urbane gentleman, married and the father of six children; although only a modestly successful middle-class physician,

Freud could afford six in help. He once rejected the idea that he was a genius on the grounds that he was not difficult enough to live with in order to warrant that accolade. As much as Freud's creation and championing of psychoanalysis would be filled with controversy after controversy, in his everyday life he dealt with different people all day long. He was not a cloistered scholar alone with books, but a therapist who regularly saw on a daily basis over half a dozen patients analytically and also conducted consultations.

One of the means of Freud's success was his sharing in a kind of Central European manners which, from an American straight-shooting perspective, may look like hypocrisy. It is true that Freud was able to say separate things, on the exact same subject, to different people. All charm can involve white lies; and representatives of old Vienna were among the most mystifyingly misleading of Europeans. In connection with an Italian psychiatrist (Enrico Morselli) who had written about psychoanalysis in the 1920s, Freud wrote to one of his disciples there to maintain that Morselli's work is "completely without value, the only value is its undoubted proof that he is a donkey." Freud was requesting that his pupil write an extended book review: "I ask you not to spare him any unpleasant truth." Freud was happy to leave the public polemics to another. So to Morselli himself Freud wrote in a different way, praising his book as an "important work." Freud's reproaches were expressed only in cautiously qualified terms:

> I noticed with regret that you cannot accept our youthful sicence without great reservations, and I have to comfort myself with the divergence of opinion in such difficult topics as well as with the certainty that your book will contribute a great deal towards arousing the interest of your compatriots for psychoanalysis.

Freud was engaging in a kind of public relations, as he praised one of Morselli's other writings "without any mixed feelings, with unreserved approval." To Freud's student in Italy (Edoardo Weiss), whom Freud had known for over a decade, Freud wrote with a kind of candor that could illustrate Henry James's conception of the contrast between European and American sensibilities. For Freud was pleased with the critical review that his Italian disciple had come up with: "I am glad you have shown yourself to be courageous and honest, as always." And in a letter a few months later, Freud used invective against Morselli that contemporaries of our own are apt to wince at: "it would be humanly interesting to learn whether he has always been such a bum or whether he has permitted himself to become that way only under the influence of senility."[10]

That Freud could use *schmaltz* in writing directly to Morselli can be easily misunderstood now, and it should be remembered when reading other of Freud's correspondences. He had a cause to promote, and in its behalf he would be hard and unrelenting, as well as devious; as long as Freud could count on somebody else tearing Morselli's book apart, Freud could write charmingly to Morselli. I do not think Freud can be simplistically accused of being two-faced, as long as one remembers the over-riding long-term purpose he had in mind: promoting the goal of psychoanalysis. Reading any of Freud's letters, and his published texts as well, one has to listen for the often subtle tones, the music that can lie behind the strict use of words. Freud's communication with Morselli fit into a larger plan that Freud had in mind.

Freud could be so unscrupulous sometimes as to sound like a humbug. For example, in a contribution to a collection in honor of Romain Rolland, Freud wrote in 1926:

> Unforgettable man, to have soared to such heights of humanity through so much hardship and suffering!
>
> I revered you as an artist and apostle of love for mankind many years before I saw you. I myself have always advocated the love of mankind not out of sentimentality or idealism but for sober, economic reasons: because in the face of our instinctual drives and the world as it is I was compelled to consider this love as indispensable for the preservation of the human species as, say, technology.[11]

In spite of how glowingly Freud could write for publication, knowing Rolland was a Nobel Prize winner, for years Freud had been treating the love of mankind as a sublimation of homosexuality. And one suspects that Freud, in this instance, did not think the sublimated feelings very far from their instinctual roots, ones he looked on with disfavor. In his *Civilization and Its Discontents* (1930) he would make no bones about why he thought the love for humanity was both unrealistic and undesirable. In a way, Freud had given away his true sentiments even in his letter to Rolland, when he put the love of mankind on the same level as the necessity for technology, which Freud like other Europeans of his time looked on with at best mixed feelings.

Americans have always had difficulty accepting Freud's continental ways, and they are apt to think in terms only of his having been duplicit with Morselli. To a European, though, Americans seemed like wild Indians; it would have struck Freud as barbarism to tell a stranger anything like the same thing as to a trusted intimate like Weiss. Americans have rarely shared the European distinction between public and private lives. In the course of Freud's one trip to America in 1909, he acquired an enduring conviction about the Americans as barbarians; there are a seemingly endless list of reproaches Freud had against America. Evidently, on his trip they addressed him by his first name, sat him on the ground for charcoal grilled meals, and asked him about the evidence he had for this theories. He was already fifty-three years old and did not see those he encountered as his equals. He presumed the appropriateness of a kind of distance between himself and others that the enthusiastic Americans did not share. So it may be no wonder that William James concluded that Freud was a man obsessed with "fixed ideas."[12] A Viennese analyst I knew once imagined that an American meeting Freud could be so crass as to ask him about his sisters (who were nonintellectual). Although Freud might have been expected to find American candor refreshing, he also minded any presumptuous intrusiveness about his work—not to mention his life.

The American reaction to Freud was always more positivistic and pragmatic than he liked. He felt that he was stooping to conquer when he discussed in his 1909 lectures in America practical matters like therapy and the utility of studying dream life. To Freud these issues were more properly understood within a broader context of the whole conceptual outlook he was proposing. Although I doubt Freud would have been anything like entirely pleased with what Jacques Lacan later did with psychoanalysis in Paris, the whole post-1968 French reaction to Freud has been in keeping with his implicit intention to keep psychoanalysis linked to the most ancient problems of moral and ethical thought. It is not easy to follow what Freud's purposes were, since he was apt explicitly to reject philosophizing as a legitimate part of psychoanalysis, and he often disclaimed his standing as an ethical theorist.

But if someone like Lacan, and many other theorists, could think they were being loyal to Freud's genuine intent, I think they were correct in putting in perspective the more down-to-earth concerns of the practically-minded Americans. Freud to be sure wanted therapeutic gains in treatment, but at the same time he sought not to allow his teachings to rest on the success or failure in therapeutic practice. The American reaction to him always seemed in his mind too immediate, ill-considered, and not sufficiently abstract. The current 1990s level of Freud-bashing in the States might only have confirmed Freud's earlier distrust of the initial welcome his ideas had received there.

It can be confusing to follow Freud's thought because so many of the people attracted to his movement were motivated by a humanitarian idealism that he did not necessarily share. As a young man engaged to marry he wrote his bride-to-be, while under the "talkativeness" of "the bit of cocaine" he had just taken, how Josef Breuer, Freud's mentor then, had discovered that "under the surface of timidity there lay in me an extremely daring and fearless human being." Freud went on: "I had always thought so, but never dared tell anyone. I have often felt as though I had inherited all the defiance and all the passions with which our ancestors defended their Temple and could gladly sacrifice my life for one great moment in history."[13] Freud was a passionate fighter who attracted others like himself to the field he went on to create.

I would like to take the death of Victor Tausk as an example of someone in Freud's life that I have thought a lot about. Freud was, as leader of the psychoanalytic movement, to arouse the most intense kinds of emotions, often on the part of people drawn to his field because of their own unresolved difficulties. Tausk was someone who sought, and received, Freud's assistance, as Tausk went to medical school to prepare himself for being an analyst. Tausk was one of the first analysts to be interested in extending Freudian insights to the psychiatric area of the psychoses. Despite the stature Tausk had earned, by late 1918 Freud, after many years of turning back Tausk's requests for a personal analysis, finally sent him to an analytic newcomer, Helene Deutsch, whom Freud had recently started to analyze.

The whole tangle between Freud, Tausk, and Helene Deutsch is one which in the end probably exaccerbated Tausk's problems, but one can give Freud the benefit of the doubt and think that he was trying to do his best, at a safe distance, with this troubled follower of his. We now know that throughout Frued's career as an analyst he often got himself into situations which were so intimate and close that one wonders how he could have been so ambitious to think he could ever be successful in being able to sort things out. Other groups of modern intellectuals have been also inclined to exchange intimacies in a way which seems almost inhuman (if not obscene). I am thinking of the circle around Jean-Paul Sartre and Simone de Beauvoir which she put into fictional form in her novel *She Came To Stay*.[14] (The Bloomsbury group in England was rather similar.) For people sleeping with one another to share with close friends the details of their arrangements does not differ much from Freud's having in analysis with him Helene Deutsch, the analyst of Tausk.

One can easily think, in the whole history of psychoanalysis, of other such sticky-seeming situations: (1) Freud's analyzing his daughter Anna; (2) Freud's analyzing Sandor Ferenczi as well as Ferenczi's step-daughter, with whom he was in love; (3) Freud's analyzing Ruth Brunswick, her husband Mark, and her brother-in-law David; and (4) Anna Freud's analyzing the children of her most intimate friend Dorothy Burlingham. The list can be extended almost indefinitely, and would include Erich Fromm's analyzing the daughter of his lover Karen Horney. The early history of psychoanalysis is strewn with such examples of the violation of "normal" therapeutic boundaries. Whatever rules of detachment and neutrality Freud may have tried to lay down for others, for himself and his chosen favorites he seems to have thought they were somehow beyond the confines of conventional good and evil.

The arrangement between Freud, Helene Deutsch, and Tausk had not worked out, and Freud instructed her either to break off with himself or with her patient, who was grief-stricken over his rivalry with Freud. (She, after filling her analytic hours with Freud with news of Tausk, had taken it to be an order on Freud's part.) A few months later, just before killing himself, Tausk sent Freud a suicide note in which he was at peace with Freud:

> I thank you for all the good which you have done me. It was much and has given meaning to the last ten years of my life. Your work is genuine and great, I shall take leave of this life knowing that I was one of those who witnessed the triumph of one of the greatest ideas of mankind.

Tausk's devotion to Freud, and the sacrifice of Tausk's life, was a tragic testimony to the toll of the success of Freud's teachings. Tausk's analyst friend Paul Federn, who had a seemingly unlimited view of what psychoanalysis might accomplish, even treating psychotics, was moved at the time privately to blame

Freud for Tausk's death: "The motivation was Freud's turning away from him." As Federn wrote his wife of Tausk,

> I was so terribly sorry about him....If Freud had shown him a human interest, not simply recognition and support, he might have continued to bear longer his martyr-like existence...But *he* was *not* kind as little as Freud is kind, i.e. Freud possesses so much love for people that he can be kind, but in his old age he became increasingly harder....That we could not keep Tausk is our shame.

(A literal translation, instead of the word "kind" in Federn's letter, would be "good.") Freud's reaction to Tausk's death shows that he was fully involved in a human tragedy, which should elude the tendency to blame. Tausk's self-destruction was the central act in a tale that had been building for years; Helene Deutsch's evasion of her own therapeutic responsibility, as well as Freud's own incapacity to react to Tausk's death except with relief that he was gone, are peripheral parts of the story. But it is still striking how Freud wrote to Lou Andreas-Salomé, once intimately involved with Tausk (as earlier with Nietzsche and Rilke): "I confess I do not really miss him; I had long taken him to be useless, indeed a threat to the future."[15] These words were originally censored from the correspondence between Freud and Lou, and only reinstated after I had put them in print.

In Freud's formal obituary of Tausk he was flattering: "He is sure of a honorable memory in the history of psychoanalysis and its earliest struggles." What was Freud doing, writing in public praise of Tausk (with expressed reservations about some of his work) at the same time that he wrote with such apparent coldness about Tausk to Lou Andreas-Salomé? People had been saving Freud's letters for years, Freud had joked about it as a good idea in his adolescence, and in Lou's case she even saved the drafts of some of her letters to Freud. Freud could write publicly in honor of Ernest Jones's fiftieth birthday at the same time indicating in private his dislike of Jones; and Freud's obituary of Ferenczi was at odds with his private note to Jones about Ferenczi's last days. Freud was part of a world in which such layers of different meaning were to be expected, even if we find it hard now to follow the discrepancies.

In Tausk's case, and in that of other calamities in Freud's career, a human life was lost on the way to Freud's historic "triumph." It is, I think, in the nature of tragedy that the participants be unable to act other than they did, at the same time that they blind themselves to the consequences of their own acts. Tragedy may not be "nice," or a part of what William Dean Howells called the "smiling" part of life, but tragedy remains an inherent aspect of human experience. Shakespeare is the acknowledged master of such painful experiences. It was harsh for Prince Hal to reject Falstaff on the way to becoming king. Lear moves us because of the inherent drama of his plight. And it is the same with *Othello*, *Macbeth*, and so many other tragedies.

Freud not only participated in such tragedies in his own movement, but embraced the inevitability of tragic conflicts in life. People are subsequently apt to reject the dilemmas he dwelt on. Freud was saying that we pay a price for each of our achievements, and that attainments rest on losses. Americans, on the other hand, are especially inclined to think that all good things must hang together, and without moral expense. The Declaration of Independence proclaimed the goals of life, liberty, and the pursuit of happiness, and our national ideals seem inherently coherent.

So that when a Freudian like Helene Deutsch wrote about a conflict between motherhood and sexuality, that seemed offensive to those arguing in behalf of the possibilities of female emancipation. A European is more likely to see how values conflict with one another. Contemporary enthusiasts for the achievements of psychopharmacology are prone to understate the human costs involved in pill-taking. Freud is always telling us that, morally, there is no such thing as a free ride.

For those who want to emphasize only the continuities with the past, and none of the disjunctions, it may seem easier to put Freud aside. He makes for complications that can be hard to absorb. When, for example, he recommends certain patients as especially "worthy," justifying attention to their treatment, logically that implied that there were some patients he considered as good-for-nothing, worthless. The Christian principle about the preciousness of every individual soul did not attract Freud, and he had his decided preferences about those he chose to work with. He was not proposing that psychoanalysis was equally good for all, but rather that it suited the superior few who he thought would be mankind's models.

The system Freud was advocating was elaborately put together, forming an attractive intellectual structure; it is up to us to respond to it, selecting what we like and rejecting the rest. Freud was imposing himself on the future in a single-minded way, though he could be more modest about what he had achieved than some of his most fanatical disciples. Melanie Klein, for instance, was at one time recommending that every child be psychoanalyzed, and she proposed that it was desirable for patients to re-experience psychoses in their analyses. Freud was reserved about the field of child analysis, and more skeptical than others about what psychoanalysis could accomplish therapeutically or prophylactically. When it came to understanding, though, Freud thought he had created a science of the unconscious, one that might not be immediately palatable but which in the long run would win out.

If we look on his claims with the dispassion appropriate to the study of the history of ideas, true believers are likely to think we are engaged in unspoken debunking. But intellectual historians have the special job of recreating a world unlike our own, for the sake of broadening our horizons and enriching our conception of what might be humanly plausible. To look on Freud without putting him in context, as he is apt to be quoted for example in so many contemporary psychoanalytic journals, is inevitably to distort things. To cite him in the midst of our own preoccupations, without being aware of all the complexities involved in reading him, contributes to a false kind of idealization.

No doubt he could be ruthless in behalf of the cause of promoting his life's work. Solzhenitsyn's *Lenin in Zurich*[16] seems to me a splendid account of how focused a spiritual revolutionary can be. The world does tend to reward such centered tunnel-vision. The more cautious and broad-minded souls, at least in the history of psychoanalysis, have tended to be more readily forgotten. According to one popular American saying, attributed to Leo Durocher, nice guys come in last.

Freud's kind of intolerance was not inconsistent with his being capable, on a day-to-day basis with patients for example, of unusual patience, tact, and understanding. But he was bent on establishing his system in history. Other great men, in the world of politics, people like Churchill or de Gaulle for example, were also determined to transform the world in a special direction. Freud had his own concentrated vision in the realm of ideas; and at the same time he coordinated an enduring school of his followers, one which succeeded in securing his accomplishment.

Outside of the context of the society Freud lived in he cannot engage us as much as if we see him in perspective. He remains, I think, abidingly challenging, as he surely aimed to be when he cloaked himself in diabolical-sounding sayings; each of the volumes of his letters as they appear add to the fascination of the complexities of understanding him. It does him no service to censor out of his letters (by translating tricks if not omissions) even the most startling thoughts he might have had. He could be as self-aggrandizing as any other great leader. And alongside his detached irony, he could also be utopian; for when he condemned as superstition the whole of organized religion and denounced the belief in God as a needless neurotic crutch, he was holding out an ideal of what the world might be like without such illusions. "By withdrawing all their liberated energies into their life on earth, they will probably succeed in achieving a state of things in which life will become tolerable for everyone and civilization no longer oppressive to anyone."[17] That strain of utopianism has continued to attract a certain kind of passionate following, such as the work of Herbert Marcuse and others.

Another side of Freud, where he is caustic if not bitter, is apt to seem to our contemporaries as less "nice." It may ultimately be a question of taste or personal preference which thinkers one chooses to adopt as heroes. In terms of American Supreme Court history, it is not obvious to me that Louis Brandeis, warm in his idealism, should be considered superior to the far more dour Oliver Wendell Holmes, Jr. In Freud's case, I would argue that the question of his stature is partly settled by the extent of his influence. Nobody has had a greater effect on our thinking, and the contentiousness that still surrounds his name means to me that he has proved an enduringly important writer.

A less austere man might well have been less successful; and a more intellectually amiable one would almost surely have allowed his insights to dissipate into a desire to be agreeable. As it is, Freud continues to provoke controversy, and this trait is partly attributable to his hardness. His almost cosmic defiance, which helps account for his deeming the traditional ban on speaking ill of the dead as a superstitious fear of retaliation, went into making him the conqueror he became. The history of ideas has had to accommodate itself to such great system-builders. And if we decline to share in some of Freud's ferocious self-conviction, that only underlies our distance from what it can take to be a pathfinder like him.

Talking about Freud's toughness, and the darkest sides of his message, does not mean that he could not also have modest moments. But perhaps the best balance to any otherwise harsh picture of Freud comes from remembering his altogether remarkable sense of humor. Patients reported on how frequently Freud used Rabbi stories to illustrate various human dilemmas in the course of his analyses. His book *Jokes and Their Relation to the Unconscious*[18] is one of the most complicated ones he ever wrote, and attracts little attention nowadays. That text is littered with examples of the worldly wisdom which can be communicated through jokes. Freud's dry cynicism was frequently reported. We know a bit about how much he appreciated Mark Twain's public appearances in Vienna. Like all complex figures Freud had his multiple contradictions, but they were harnessed by him into making the great literature he left which is still capable of enlivening debates today. It remains for the future to determine whether Freud will in the end succeed in ranking with thinkers like Machiavelli, Hobbes, Rousseau, and others who disturbed the sleep of the world.

## Notes

1. Ernest Jones, *The Life and Work of Sigmund Freud*, Vol. 3 (New York: Basic Books, 1957), p. 182.
2. Freud, *Civilization and Its Discontents, Standard Edition*, Vol. 21, p. 111.
3. Freud, *Civilization and Its Discontents, op. cit.*, pp. 109-110; "Why War?" *Standard Edition*, Vol. 23, p. 212.
4. Freud, "Leonardo Da Vinci and A Memory of His Childhood," *Standard Edition*, Vol. 11, p. 137.
5. Cf. George Sabine, *A History of Political Theory* (New York: Henry Holt, 1950), p. 575.
6. Jean-Jacques Rousseau, *Reveries of the Solitary Walker* (London: Penguin, 1979), p. 104.
7. *Rousseau's Political Writings*, ed. Alan Ritter and Julia Conaway Bondanella (New York: Norton, 1988), p. 194.
8. Arthur W. Wilson, *Diderot: The Testing Years* (New York: Oxford University Press, 1957), p. 298.
9. Paul Roazen, "Nietzsche and Freud: Two Voices from the Underground," *The Psychohistory Review*, Spring 1991, pp. 327-49.

10. Paul Roazen, *Freud and His Followers* (New York: Knopf, 1975; New York: Da Capo, 1992), pp. 501-502.
11. *Letters of Sigmund Freud*, ed. Ernst L. Freud, translated by Tania and James Stern (London: Hogarth, 1961), p. 365.
12. Roazen, *Freud and His Followers, op. cit.*, p. 372.
13. *Letters of Sigmund Freud, op. cit.*, p. 215.
14. Simone de Beauvoir, *She Came To Stay*, translated by Yvonne Moyse and Roger Senouse (London: Flamingoo, 1984).
15. Paul Roazen, *Brother Animal: The Story of Freud and Tausk* (New York: Knopf, 1969; second edition, with new Introduction, New Brunswick, NJ: Transaction, 1990), pp. 127, 153, 140.
16. Aleaxnder Solzhenitsyn, *Lenin in Zurich*, translated by H. T. Willetts (New York: Farrar Straus & Giroux, 1976).
17. Freud, *Future of An Illusion, Standard Edition*, Vol. 21, p. 50.
18. Freud, *Jokes and Their Relation to the Unconscious, Standard Edition*, Vol. 8.

# 2

# A Reconsideration of *Freud and His Followers*

It has to be sobering to write now about my *Freud and His Followers*, which originally appeared in English in 1975. Almost as daunting as the recent expansion of knowledge about Freud and his circle is the realization that this is a book on which I worked for over ten years. Looking back now, it seems that *Freud and His Followers* is still alive because of special features that went into its construction. I had had the good fortune to interview during the 1960s a large number of people who had known Freud personally; so that my writing about the history of psychoanalysis was informed by personal acquaintance not just with those who had been familiar with him but also with many who had themselves played a key role in the development of that momentous change in how we think about ourselves which has come to be known as the Freudian revolution in the history of ideas.

Entirely aside from the access I had to speaking with people who are now all long dead, my research was open-ended. I was determined to avoid past sectarian squabbling, and not to examine Freud only from the way he viewed things. The reader will find extensive discussions on Jung, Adler, Stekel, Klein, Rank, and Reich. I refused to accept the mythology that these "heretics" had betrayed the "cause" and therefore played no rightful place in the story of the development of psychoanalytic ideas. Someone like Edoardo Weiss, the founder of psychoanalysis in Italy, came to be out of favor with Freud's daughter Anna, and he has been relatively neglected; but Weiss was one of my important sources of information, and gets cited in the text.

Curious silences have grown up around certain figures from the past Although when I wrote two chapters about Ruth Mack Brunswick, for example, almost no mention of her appeared in the literature, despite her key importance to Freud, even now I have come across almost nothing that alters what I originally put into print.

Or let us take the example of Anna Freud. I first alluded to her having been analyzed by her father in my *Brother Animal: The Story of Freud and Tausk*. But in *Freud and His Followers* I went more at length into what Freud might have thought he was doing by contravening his own rules in treating his youngest child, and how she herself may have colluded in this unusual form of therapy. Yet, since the appearance of my work, I have never seen an article by an analyst in a professional journal discussing what was going on between Freud and Anna during her analysis. I had not thought what I was writing was definitive, and I supposed that clinicians would have something unique to add.

The biggest single difference between the literature now and when I first undertook my work is the appearance of a number of fine biographies about the early analysts. And we now have more volumes of Freud's correspondence in print. Since Freud was such a great letter-writer, the forthcoming volumes of his correspondences over the next generation promise to be the greatest single source of knowledge about the creator of psychoanalysis still to come.

Yet there are still taboos about Freud that are hard to breach. Unlike with other giants in the history of ideas, special problems are associated with looking at him with unblinkered eyes. For people seem to attach special transferences to Freud. Trying to evaluate him with normal scholarly dispassion can threaten the way people have reorganized their souls in the light of their own psychoanalytic encounters. To speak of Freud with detachment often seems to some as lèse majesté. At the same time, others disillusioned with what psychoanalysis can accomplish as therapy, or offended by the idealizations about Freud that still exist, have reacted to him with debunking intentions. So that the literature about him has fallen into the extremes of being excessively reverent or too hostile.

These general reflections bear on the climate of opinion in which *Freud and His Followers* was conceived. At the time I undertook my initial inquiries, the written material about the history of psychoanalysis was even more marred by cultism than it is today. The authorized biography of Freud by Jones was still rarely criticized and therefore securely established, and many people in those days were apt to treat it as the authoritative last word. So that part of my argument, given what was then the received conventional wisdom, had to be directed to showing in what ways Jones had camouflaged the truth about Freud. If some readers misinterpreted my book as an effort to belittle Freud, it was because of the nature of the historical evidence at the time I was working on *Freud and His Followers* mandated that I proceed as I did.

Inevitably there are parts of *Freud and His Followers* that I would look on with different eyes now. At that time, psychoanalysis in the United States was still riding high within departments of psychiatry; unlike today, when there are so many critiques of Freud that have become fashionable, in the 1960s he was looked upon as a kind of totem figure about whom it was impious to think critically. Instead of his being taken then as a model of innovation and daring, at the time he was looked upon as providing the basic rationale that lay behind the powers-that-be within the American psychiatric profession. I wish I had approached Freud's ideas more tolerant of the way he could legitimately distort reality for the sake of artistically hightening our capacity to see something new. And I would take today's critics of Freud more seriously if they simultaneously trained their guns on some of the excesses of biological psychiatry, which too often is given a free ride now. Lord Acton's maxim about power corrupting, and absolute power tending to corrupt absolutely, is as pertinent today as ever, and relevant to the authoritarian abuses inherent in the latest diagnostic categories.

I think it was, in addition, naïve of me not to have known that Freud's written texts already told one everything—provided one knew how to read between the lines. I found that those personally acquainted with Freud automatically filtered out that which they deemed subjective or distorted. In his work he accomplished a great autobiography; he also contributed to the advancement of science; but in the long run he will last as a genius regardless of which particular recommendations may or may not be viable. The man Freud, with all his frailties, is more worthy of emulation that the petrified god which some people need to support their idealizations of the founder of psychoanalysis.

It is still, even today, difficult to become well educated in the history of depth psychology; and I did not know at the outset that faults in Freud were well-known even at the time he first wrote. Contemporary criticisms, published while Freud was still alive, were often respectfully sound and perceptive, even though they are too often neglected in our own time. Psychiatrists in training now, for example, are rarely assigned Jung's essays on short-term psychotherapy which appeared in the 1920s and 1930s. He was one of the deepest critics Freud ever had. Few professionals appreciate that Jung was the first to insist, before World War I, that infantile material when it arises clinically may be used defensively, as an evasion of the present. And he took an orientation towards both dream-life and symptoms which was different from Freud's own approach.

I recall the disbelief with which Dr. Rene Spitz, a loyal Freudian and at the time prominent in the field, recounted how Jung had once claimed the responsibility for having invented the idea of requiring training analyses for future analysts; yet later I found that Freud had in print credited Jung with that proposal. Some have subsequently questioned the merits of the institution of training analyses; Edward Glover in England, and Jacques Lacan in France, both criticized the authoritarian consequences of the training practices which became customary within psychoanalysis. I am not sure that Freud was so keen on training analyses. When the idea was first broached at an international congress of analysts in 1918, both Tausk and Rank opposed it, and I doubt either of them would have taken such a stand without Freud's silent acquiescence. So Jung's idea may turn out to have had serious flaws—I do not believe he was more perfect than any other figure in the history of modern psychotherapy—but he remains currently neglected within much of world psychiatry.

One of the key pieces of good fortune that befell me, and provided a documentary source of independence, was stumbling across Jones's papers in London. With no specific purpose in mind other than talking with anyone I could find who was possibly a good informant about early analysis, I was told during the summer of 1965 that Jones's papers were deposited in the basement of the British Institute of Psychoanalysis. I will never forget the joy of pouring over these documents; everyone in academic life deserves at least one such reward for all the frustrations of the scholarly calling.

I do not know why no one had then taken the trouble to go through Jones's papers. Autobiographies inevitably contain what can uncharitably be called lies, but here one found chapter and verse of what Jones, in cooperation with the Freud family, consciously intended to evade or disguise. Evidence of Jones's double-dealing also cropped up. Dr. A. A. Brill was warm-hearted and good-natured, so he could in New York turn his proxy over to Jones to cast an extra vote on issues connected with the doings of the International Psychoanalytic Association. Nonetheless, Jones could take advantage of Brill's gullibility, and letters exist which demonstrate Jones's double-crossing Brill.

When I first wrote *Freud and His Followers*, I had to feel pretty tough about what Jones had succeeded in accomplishing with his Freud biography. By now, however, it has become widely known how partisan Jones was. The wheel of fortune has turned so far that people are apt today to forget just how indebted we all are to what Jones, whatever his biases, revealed to us, and how much his books did to forward our understanding of the history of psychoanalysis. His own tortured private life, once it became known to me, made him seem more sympathetic. So that even today there are other biographical studies of Freud, which often claim to be more even-handed than Jones, which are now the main obstacles to an accurate understanding of the past.

Biographers and the families of their subjects are inevitably in an adversarial relationship. It is all the more amazing that representatives of the Freuds ever thought they could get away with publishing tendentiously edited volumes of Freud's letters. They often censored Freud's writings without indicating that gaps had been introduced. Incompetent censorship is worse than publishing even the most potentially damaging material. Unless one is willing to destroy primary documents, doctored manuscripts in the end call more attention to what has been initially left out than would ever have been the case if an unedited version had been allowed to become public.

The Freud family has deposited in the Library of Congress in Washington, D.C., a vast collection of Freud's writings, as well as taped reminiscences about him. After the year 2000, the bulk of this material will start to be open for inspection. But what is one to make of a system of classification which restricts one of Freud's letters to his eldest son Martin until the year 2013, and another until 2032? One can only marvel at the precision with which it is possible to avoid indiscretion. Josef Breuer must have had something interesting to say, hopefully, for a bit of material of his to be sealed until 2102.

The problem of the existence of documentary evidence, elusive although it has to be in gaining access to it, still succeeded in enriching all my own later interviewing. The fact that an orthodox research project, even though under lock and key, already existed served to sanction in a way my own proposed work. No matter how old and famous any of the people I saw, I found that despite their reputations the aged are in need of recognition like anyone else. I did not begin with any hostile intent; my curiosity kept me going. It is true, however, that my great respect for the role in history I thought these early analysts had played did sometimes lead to disillusionment. When I saw Dr. Willi Hoffer in London, for example, he was suspicious that my traditional Harvard University green book-bag might contain a hidden tape-recorder. After awhile he got over his initial attitude toward me, but I could not erase from my memory a couple of his earliest, barbed questions: "So, you want to know what is not in the books? And maybe what we do not want in the books?"

Hoffer was a member of the Freudian establishment, and one of Anna Freud's circle of confidants; but it is telling that so-called deviants could be just as cautious. For example, Dr. Sandor Rado once ordered me not to write something down; and he was an exceptionally gifted psychologist. (He had analyzed people ranging from Mary McCarthy and Leonard Bernstein to Benjamin Spock.) Although Rado had long been deemed an outsider, he could still be fearful of psychological extinction at the hands of the most orthodox analysts. Being a "traitor" to the "cause" was an inner burden to him, and he forced himself to be discreet about what he considered the special features to Freud's own neurosis. Rado declined, for instance, to offer his own interpretations of specific dreams Freud had autobiographically written about, although Rado was willing to summarize his conclusions as to the inevitable limitations inherent in Freud's personality.

On the whole, analysts outside New York City, where Rado lived, were likely to be fairly outspoken. And in those areas or countries where analysis was not widely accepted, medically or intellectually, people were capable of being less guarded in what they were willing to talk about.

I confess my way of proceeding could lead to concrete kinds of mistakes. For example, I understand now some of the ways in which I went astray in writing about Ruth Brunswick. As I said earlier, in the course of my interviews it became apparent that one special favorite of Freud's in his last years, Dr. Ruth Mack Brunswick, had seriously been left out of the history books. She, as well as her husband and brother-in-law, were simultaneously in analysis with Freud, at a time when he took five regular analytic cases. (In order to appreciate the significance of this complicated arrangement, one has to realize that for Freud at his clinical best every patient was an exception.) The story of Ruth's involvement with Freud was suppressed due to the sad circumstances surrounding her last years. One analyst did not remember having written an obituary of her, which stood out since references to her in the literature were so rare. (That I then had to rely on obituary notices is an index of the low level of the historical state of the discipline; by now Freud scholarship is at a more sophisticated stage.)

In the course of my work I found out that a trunk-full of Ruth's papers was in the possession of her old friend Dr. Marianne Kris. Yet there was going to be no opportunity for me to get access to any of the "hard" data that historians ideally want to work with. On the other hand, I interviewed David Brunswick, as well as his brother Mark, Ruth's former husband. I found Mark Brunswick, a musician and composer, a true artist; he was free and open to all my questions.

Mark's second analysis, back in the States, had gone much better than the many years he had spent with Freud. Evidently, his later analyst made constructive use of any negative feelings Mark had about Freud. Mark's first wife Ruth had been an important source of American patients in Vienna; her father, Judge Julian Mack, was a rich philanthropist and a friend of President Franklin D. Roosevelt's.

When I interviewed Mark, I naturally wondered what he had lived on in Vienna. Yet I felt too inhibited to ask in effect, "Were you living off your wife?" Instead I inquired whether he had been related to the Brunswick bowling family. No, Mark told me, but he wished he had been and at some point Mark made fun of how rich he and Ruth had seemed to the Viennese analytic community. Now historians concerned with methodology regularly ask: "what is a fact?" I proceeded to write a version of Ruth and Mark's involvement with Freud to the best of my ability. I went ahead knowing that my chapters could not be definitive, but that it was all I could manage under difficult circumstances. Better an incomplete account, I reasoned, even if some errors crept in, than to leave things as blank in the history books as they were now.

In the summer of 1976 I received a letter from a former Viennese bookseller (a profession for which one then studied) who had been given an affadavit in 1938 by the Brunswicks, a copy of which he enclosed, so he could enter the U.S.; he had read my account of Ruth and Mark, and offered to meet me in New York. Looking over that affadavit, I was astounded to learn how rich Mark had been. As I was told when I interviewed the bookseller they had befriended, Mark had been related to the Brunswick record family, which had gone out of business before my time. Yet during the winter of 1990-1991 I finally got to meet the daughter of Ruth and Mark, who had still a different version of such matters. Mark's money came from a separate family business, not the record company, and anyway she thought that neither Mark nor Ruth had been as rich as one might expect, compared to the princess Marie Bonaparte for example.

Oral history is an uncertain line of endeavor; I had tripped up on an important point in *Freud and His Followers*, and doubtless there are more corrections to come. (A French source indicates that I misidentified a few of the people in the photograph of the Oxford Congress; the hats that women wore then make it hard for even Ruth Brunswick's daughter to be able confidently to pick out her own mother.) I made some further mistakes, some of which were obvious to me immediately. For example, in speaking with Wilhelm Reich's first wife, then an analyst in New York, I made two key blunders at the outset. Too early in our chat

I asked her about having once been a patient of her husband's. I had not realized how sensitive a point her having married her analyst was going to be. Furthermore, I did not anticipate how she would bridle over my asking about Reich's Communist affiliations. She preferred the term Social Democrat to Communist, and stressed that others in the Viennese analytic group had similar interests. I would have thought that Reich's efforts to integrate Marx and Freud were one of his main achievements, and that she did not need to underplay his involvement with Marxism. However I may have temporarily stumbled with Annie Reich, she was gracious enough so that it did not wreck the interview itself.

One source of anyone's interviewing strength, to shift away from weaknesses, is attentiveness to nonverbal responses. I had been told that Dr. Max Schur, Freud's physician at the time of his death, had been resentful of how long the suffering had been allowed to go on. I did not bring the subject up until well into our interview. When I finally got up enough courage to ask my point-blank question, his immediate response was a gulp; he then said Yes, if it had been up to him the morphia would have been administered weeks earlier. I still do not understand the implications of his answer for what was going on within the Freud family at that stressful period, but Schur's swallow was as telling as his formal answer. Incidentally, skepticism about oral history should extend to the written word as well; if one examines Schur's book on Freud one might never guess how important Ruth Brunswick, Schur's own analyst and that of his wife, was in Freud's last phase.

It may be hard to get new ideas into history books, but unfortunately once anything gets established there it is at least as difficult to dislodge. For a series of reasons Freud had the fixed idea that his chief Italian disciple had direct contact with Mussolini. Weiss vehemently denied that anything of the sort ever existed, and there is reason to believe him. Nonetheless, Jones repeated Freud's version, and at least two books have now reported that Weiss had personal audiences with Mussolini in Freud's behalf. An interesting correspondence between Freud and Weiss exists, and nothing in it lends credence to the story which Jones and others have perpetuated.

Freud's letters to Weiss are particularly interesting in that they primarily deal with clinical issues. Too much of the extant Freud correspondence presents him as a thinker rather than the hard-working therapist that he was. On the other hand, just because Freud wrote something in a letter one day does not excuse us from the responsibility of weighing, in the light of other material about Freud, just how much that comment should count.

In connection with Freud's letters to Weiss it is worth noting how hard it can be to please living people whom one writes about. Weiss had told me that he had a letter in his possession in which Freud discussed his analysis of his daughter Anna. The issue was so sensitive in Weiss's mind, and so fearful was he of any further trouble with certain powers that then existed in orthodox analysis, that he would neither tell me the date of the letter nor show me the contents.

So when I first mentioned in print Anna's analysis by her father, I excluded Weiss's name among my sources of information. I sent a copy of my book to him, but among his remarks to me afterwards was the complaint that I had failed to mention Freud's letter to him about Anna's analysis. In contrast to his earlier caution he now sent me a xerox of the key letter. All of us in debt to Freud labor under inhibitions of one sort or another. Yet historians insist on the relentless asking of questions, with the confident belief that whatever mistakes get made will ultimately be self-correcting.

To conclude: Freud's personal vitality and high energy level lie behind not only the quality of people he was capable of attracting, but also help explain the life his ideas have had. Whatever some of his concepts might imply about his own personal puritanism, and how he proposed that reality contrasts with fantasy, his example proves that play and work can reinforce each other. I would contend in general that Freud the man is much better than any of his theories. When all is said and done, what I gained most from meeting these people was not any particular insight here or there, but rather I acquired a feel for what the people in the circle around the great man were like.

While some of Freud's accounts of the aetiology of human troubles cannot be defended today, his life will remain a monument of fascinating contradictions and anomalies. With any great figure in intellectual history one wants to move from the work to the life, and then from the life to the work. Because of the many legends woven around Freud's life, I thought it necessary to go in the direction of the work to the life. But in the end, one needs a well-travelled street between life and work. It is an essential psychoanalytic proposition that an understanding of the past leads to a greater control of the present and the future.

The world of Freud's Vienna is long gone. For the historian, however, seeing how different Freud was from ourselves makes him an especially valuable object of study. History teaches the most when, through its broadening, it offers us alternatives to life as we already have experienced it. And therefore Freud, to the extent that we can begin to understand him in the context of a world so alien to our own, becomes both more interesting and useful in emancipating us from preconceived notions of how life might possibly be lived.

# 3

# Transmission: Tausk, Erikson, and Helene Deutsch

Within the general field of intellectual history there has long been agreement that it is extremely difficult to establish the ways in which one thinker has an influence on another. To the extent, for example, that any genius like Freud has to create a world anew, it becomes hard for such a figure to acknowledge genuine precursors in the history of ideas. Therefore, the relationship between Freud and an obvious predecessor like Nietzsche has to remain obscure.[1] The literary critic Harold Bloom has proposed that there is a general "anxiety" of influence, inhibiting any writer from acknowledging those to whom debts are owed.

Now that psychoanalytic doctrines have become part of history, we have had to learn not just what Freud taught, but also that which others within the field have contributed, both while Freud was alive and in the years since his death. The cultural background of old Vienna, if only in providing some of the foils against which Freud and other reacted, is a necessary part of the full story. No matter how complicated the saga of psychoanalysis, with its various struggles and factions, somehow a tradition has grown up which gets passed on to new generations of students.

Still, there are special oddities to how psychoanalysis has been transmitted, and the problem of transmission has been of special interest in France. I would contend that every country has received Freud's teachings in accord with its own national needs and traditions of thought. When I first started out working on Freud in the early 1960s, I was fascinated, for instance, with the comparison and contrast in how he had been accepted in Great Britian and the United States; I found there were differences both within medicine and general popular culture. After I had spent only one academic year studying in England, it was apparent to me that there was a gulf between psychoanalysis there and in America. And the more I have learned since, about different national communities and the way Freud's ideas get taught around the world, the easier it becomes to spot some of the striking aspects to each country's response to psychoanalysis.

In my own research on Freud and political theory I stumbled upon the story of the struggle between Freud and Victor Tausk. This was first communicated in my *Brother Animal*, and I have ever since its first publication in 1969 tried to keep track of the literature about Tausk which has continued to come out.[2] Although the tale of Tausk's problems with Freud had been unknown until I wrote about them, it seems to me that France was unusual in its special response to my reconstruction of Tausk's life and death. France was the first country where a collected edition of Tausk's psychoanalytic writings were brought out; and at last, many years later, I succeeded in publishing these papers in English, too.[3] The fact that it took me until 1991 to find a publisher willing to print Tausk's writings for the English-speaking world should say something about how threatening the story connected to him remained for the powers-that-be within international psychoanalysis.

When I got interested in Tausk, it was because of my fascination with historiography, and how an aspect of the past could get dropped out. My concern with Tausk was part of my effort to show how haphazardly history can get written. I came to conclude that because of magical fantasies that people had about Freud, attributing to him the power of life and death, those close to him were apt to exaggerate Freud's part in Tausks's suicide, and therefore they maintained a secrecy around Tausk's difficulties with Freud. Tausk's technical papers, and in particular his essay on the "influencing machine," succeeded early on in becoming a secure part of the psychoanalytic literature. Jean Laplanche and V. N. Smirnoff had translated that paper into French as early as 1958.

It so happened that when I was doing my original research on Tausk I lived in the same small city, Cambridge, Massachusetts, as Erik Erikson and Helene Deutsch. Dr. Deutsch was a great help to me in all my work on Freud, and I regularly brought her material as I gathered it. I would see Erikson, too, on an irregular basis, sometimes just in passing on a street-corner or at a coffee-shop, and I sat in on one of his faculty seminars.

As my interest in Tausk awakened, I naturally mentioned it to Erikson, who had graduated from the Vienna Psychoanalytic Society's Training Institute. Tausk had first attended meetings of the Vienna Psychoanalytic Society in 1909 and was a regular participant until his death in 1919. Erikson entered Freud's circle in 1927, and yet he knew nothing whatever about the story of the problems between Freud and Tausk. In so short a time history had closed over Tausk, eliminating the particulars of his life and tortured death. Erikson knew of course about the influencing machine paper, but as far as I can recall that was the extent of Erikson's knowledge. I can remember Erikson's teasing me about Tausk, referring to him as "St. Tausk," as if I were about to engage in an idealization of Tausk's life.

It turned out that Erikson, who had coined the notion of the "identity crisis," was unaware that Tausk had been the first in psychoanalysis to introduce the concept of identity. In his autobiographical reflections Erikson did acknowledge that Paul Federn's special ego psychology had been an important influence on Erikson's own work.[4] But Erikson was unaware that Federn, an intimate friend of Tausk's, credited Tausk with having originated the concept of "ego boundaries," for example, among other of Tausk's innovations.

I am citing these discontinuities in the way psychoanalytic history has been re-told in order to illustrate how hard it can be to establish a full account of the development of psychoanalysis. Of course every history has to be biased, and only in the mind of God could all aspects of reality get recorded; yet even on the assumption that every historical reconstruction is inevitably limited and selective, still there seems to me to be unique problems associated with how psychoanalytic knowledge has been communicated.

When I first knew Erikson, he was on his way to becoming famous, at least in America; for a time he was the most well-known psychoanalyst in the United States. By now his reputation is rather in eclipse, partly I think because he did not seek to found a separate school of his own, nor to perpetuate his teachings through having disciples.[5] Yet I think it worth noting that when I was doing my field research in the mid-1960s, Donald Winnicott said to me that the one analyst in the world whose books Winnicott envied not having himself written were those by Erikson. By now Winnicott's stature has soared, and he is more apt to be cited than Erikson; books about Winnicott have been published in which one cannot even find Erikson's name mentioned. So Erikson is now in danger of suffering, at least temporarily, something resembling the original fate of Tausk.

In France I do not think Erikson has yet succeeded in earning the recognition that his work deserves. The French have chosen to lump a variety of different ego psychologies together, dismissing them as an aspect of the Americanization of psychoanalysis. In certain circumstances Erikson does get mentioned, and yet I do not think the full impact of his ideas has yet been taken into account in France. Jacques Lacan once cited Erikson's paper on Freud's Irma dream, but on the whole Erikson's work has gone undiscussed and unappreciated. It is true that Erikson lacked the sense of tragedy that Lacan so properly underscored within his own psychoanalytic writings. But Erikson brought a breath of fresh air into psychoanalytic thinking, and it would be shortsighted to ignore what his contributions add up to.

Erikson, like Winnicott, sought to get away from the negativism in Freud's thinking. It is odd, at least to me, that Winnicott should be so admired in France without Erikson also coming in for his share of praise. In London, when I last visited the British Psychoanalytic Institute there, I was startled to find a large bust of Winnicott staring out at future students of psychoanalysis. Winnicott was a charming pixie of a man, and I cannot imagine a more inappropriate person to so embalm into stone. The creator of the squiggle now looks like some sort of powerful political leader. Such are the tricks which events play on us as psychoanalysis gets passed along.

If Erikson has gone relatively unrecognized in France, I think that nothing like that can be said for Helene Deutsch. Her reputation, at least in connection with the psychology of women, has been under a cloud in the States ever since the 1960s when the women's movement first started to attack Freud, and Helene Deutsch in particular, for allegedly sexist biases. In France feminism has been more sophisticated than on the other side of the Atlantic; and that may account, I think, for the vitality Helene Deutsch's ideas have retained in France. Of course, Simone de Beauvoir did rely on Helene Deutsch in *The Second Sex*; and Lacan, too, seems to have appeciated the special status Helene Deutsch had. She was, for example, early on interested in conflicts women have between motherhood and sexuality; and Helene Deutsch cited Balzac in support of her thinking. I have already touched on how Americans, however, are more apt to want to believe that people can have every good thing all at once; and America's feminism has shared in a naïve kind of utopianism which has characteristically been blind to the tensions women experience as both mothers and sexual partners.

I would not want to make it appear that I think gaps in the history of psychoanalysis fail to appear in North America, too. I believe we have been remarkably slow in picking up the significance of Lacan's teachings and the general standing of the so-called French Freud. For example, only in Paris does one find senior analysts willing and open to discuss the need to abolish the institution of the requirement of training analyses. I have come across similar thoughts on the part of at least one leading German psychoanalyst; but it would, in the United States and Canada, be considered heretical publicy to challenge the legitimacy of training analyses. Although there has been concern in North America with counteracting the authoritarianism increasingly acknowledged to be implicit in psychoanalytic education, a solution like doing away with training analyses has not made any sort of headway here.

In private Helene Deustch certainly wondered in my presence about whether training analyses had been a good idea or not. She herself instituted various reforms in an effort to make sure that the freedom and autonomy of students get protected; in Vienna she devised the notion of a continuous case seminar, as part of her handling the difficulties posed by Wilhelm Reich's technical contributions within the Vienna Psychoanalytic Society. Later she spoke about supervised psychoanalysis as an aspect of psychoanalytic training, although her paper on "control" analyses lay unpublished until, after her death, I arranged for its appearance.[6]

Discipleship has played a large role in the history of psychoanalysis, and the reputation of Helene Deutsch, like that of Erikson, has been harmed by their both being uninterested in promoting fanaticism on their own behalf. In almost every field I can think of it is the true believers who exercise the greatest amount of weight. So that the gentle skeptics, as both Erikson and Helene Deutsch were, tend to have to take a backseat to those thinkers who were more intolerantly sure of themselves.

Right now in America, for example, it is the self-psychologists, following the lead of the late Heinz Kohut, who are in the vanguard of promoting change within psychoanalysis. And in Britain, despite the efforts of Anna Freud and Edward Glover to check the influence of Melanie Klein, by today her terms are widely accepted within English psychoanalytic circles. It even seems now to be forgotten that it is precisely because Glover feared the suggestive impact of training analyses, some fifty years ago, that he tried so hard during World War II to stop the influence Klein was already exerting.[7]

I can remember once trying to talk to Erikson about Klein; it seemed to me, as an intellectual historian, that there were parallels to how Erikson and Klein were adopting a religious-seeming perspective on human psychology. Erikson, in an autobiographical piece, once mentioned that his use of play constructions with children had appeared, within the Vienna Psychoanalytic Society, alarmingly similar to Klein, and that the response he got then, which amounted to his being charged with betraying his own analyst, Anna Freud, was one of the reasons for him having decided it would be better to leave Vienna entirely.[8]

But when I spoke to Erikson about Klein, he wanted to hear nothing at all about her work. His view of children, and of the human condition in general, was so different from Klein that he simply brushed her aside. I certainly failed to get him to reconsider his views about her; I am inclined to think, based on my own limited contact with Kleinian doctrine, that Erikson, like Winnicott, was on the right track. But Erikson and Winnicott relied on others around them to place their work within the history of psychoanalytic concepts; neither had, I think, minds which were comfortable making conceptual distinctions. Winnicott, living in Britain, could not evade coming to terms with Klein's ideas, and felt stimulated by them; Erikson, on the other hand, could go his own way without having to pay attention to Klein's contributions.

It would be unfair to think that individual personalities fail to play their role in the development and transmission of psychoanalysis, entirely aside from the impact which training analyses can have. For I think that Masud Khan, an advocate in behalf of Winnicott in France, for example, played a key role in promoting his ideas on the continent. Khan was also an admirer of Erikson's epigenetic model of the life cycle, and Khan edited a volume of Helene Deutsch's psychoanalytic papers. Now that Khan has, for a variety of reasons, gone into disgrace within psychoanalysis, I think it would be unfortunate if his special role were to be forgotten.[9]

At the same time, we must keep in mind the larger forces that have been at work. I have never quite understood, for example, the French interest in Edgar

Allan Poe. Poe is not by any means America's greatest contribution to world literature, but there does seem to be a special interest in him in France, entirely aside from Marie Bonaparte's psychoanalytic study of him. Lacan and Jacques Derrida have also continued a French interest in Poe, which seems to have started with Baudelaire's translating Poe into French. So I come back to my earlier point: the significance of national traditions in the way ideas get received and accepted. Each country has the Freud it needs, and takes possession of special aspects of the history of Freud's doctrines.

It is my own conviction that French intellectual life has a special sophistication. And that whereas in the United States one encounters almost no criticisms of Anna Freud's writings, in France she has been, partly due to her role in excluding Lacan from the International Psychoanalytic Association, subjected to the most searching kind of scrutiny. Her ideas almost never have been challenged in America, where some of her concepts, for example about child custody, have made their way, scarcely with any critical examination, into the legal system. And yet in France the extent of the transgressions committed by Freud and his immediate circle, in violation of his written technical recommendations, have failed to become widely known; the whole tangled tale of Anna Freud's involvement with her friend Dorothy Burlingham's children makes for a story all its own.

Someday, perhaps in France ahead of any other country, psychoanalysis and its history will become a secure part of academic life. And then historians can be free to study whatever they choose without the fears associated with being charged with heresy or disloyalty. If that time does succeed in arriving, then there may be fewer limitations to the transmission of psychoanalysis. Yet I would not want to conclude on a utopian note, which would be a reflection of my own national origins as an American. Perhaps it is also a part of my American upbringing that I have not been afraid to speak my mind, even when it has meant contradicting powerful forces within orthodox psychoanalytic thinking. Admitting some of my own biases would be in keeping not just with what Erikson proposed in connection with what he called "psycho-history" but with the humility that I hope I picked up, thanks to my contact with meeting the early Freudians, from Freud himself.

Psychoanalysis should always, I think, remind us how little we know, not how much. The concept of the unconscious should not be a license for arrogance but set limits on what we think we can assert. It is that side of Freud's spirit, communicated to me from people like Erikson and Helene Deutsch, that I would like now to commemorate. These three psychoanalysts, Tausk, Erikson, and Helene Deutsch, are inextricably linked to one another; not only was Tausk Helene Deutsch's first psychoanalytic patient, but Erikson told me that Helene Deutsch was his first instructor in psychoanalysis at the Vienna Training Institute. It is my hope that my research succeeds in repaying them the debts I owe them as teachers of mine. As one tries to spell out the sources of influence on one's own thinking, it becomes more evident than ever how hard it can be to trace securely the means by which ideas in general get transmitted in intellectual history.

## Notes

1. Paul Roazen, "Nietzsche and Freud: Two Voices from the Underground," *Psychohistory Review*, Spring 1991.
2. Paul Roazen, *Brother Animal: The Story of Freud and Tausk* (New York: Knopf, 1969; second edition, with new Introduction, New Brunswick, NJ: Transaction Books, 1990). Cf. also *Encountering Freud: The Politics and Histories of Psychoanalysis* (New Brunswick, NJ: Transaction, 1990).
3. Paul Roazen, editor, Victor Tausk, *Sexuality, War, and Schizophrenia: Collected Psychoanalytic Papers* (New Brunswick, NJ: Transaction, 1991).
4. Paul Roazen, *Erik H. Erikson: The Power and Limits of a Vision* (New York: The Free Press, 1976; reprinted Northvale, NJ: Jason Aronson, 1997), p. 21.
5. Paul Roazen, "Erik Erikson As A Teacher," *Michigan Quarterly Review*, Winter 1992.
6. Paul Roazen, editor, Helene Deutsch, *The Therapeutic Process, the Self, and Female Psychology: Collected Psychoanalytic Papers* (New Brunswick, NJ: Transaction, 1992), Ch. 20.
7. Paul Roazen, "The Freud-Klein Controversies," *Psychoanalytic Books*, Fall 1992, pp. 391-98. Cf also Paul Roazen, *Freud and His Followers* (New York: Knopf, 1975; reprinted New York: Da Capo, 1992), pp. 478-88.
8. Roazen, *Erikson, op. cit.*, pp. 6-7.
9. Paul Roazen, "Book Review of Khan's *The Long Wait*," *Psychoanalytic Books*, January 1991, pp. 19-25.

# Part 2

## Freud Studies

# Introduction to Part 2

Although Freud's work has been intensely studied at psychoanalytic training institutes since their being established in the early 1920s, it is still usual to find him an insecure part of university education. All too many people seem to feel confident that they know what Freud stood for, yet considerable uncertainty remains on what sort of basis that self-assurance rests. Practitioners are apt to have a narrow focus on what seems to suit the needs of immediate clinical practice, even though these practical demands change from decade to decade. Psychologists are likely to view Freud's work as too incapable of scientific validation. Philosophers are still not sure what to make of the notion of unconscious motivation. Different social sciences have had a shifting interest in the relevance of psychoanalytic thinking. Intellectual historians are probably in the best position to be able to evaluate Freud's contributions, as well as his limitations. But any such attempts at being dispassionate are beset by the polemicism that seems to be permanently attached to the system of ideas Freud created. The various separate academic disciplines have imposed their special professional viewpoints on the field of knowledge that Freud started.

In my essay here on Eva Rosenfeld, I will be trying my hand at exploring the subject of historiography within the context of the tale of the development of Freud's school. It is, I think, easy even for sophisticated academics to go astray in writing about the history of psychoanalysis, and an examination of some methodological considerations may help make plain where I think it has been possible for even well-meaning observers to go wrong.

# 4

# Appraisals and Reappraisals

By now the relevant scholarship on Freud should be far advanced. It is today widely known how much original documentation about Freud is still sealed up at the Library of Congress at the request of the Freud Archives in New York. Still, the state of interpretive writing on the history of psychoanalysis ought not to be as primitive as it is at present. Practicing analysts use Freud for their own purposes, and in most professional journals passages from Freud are cited anachronistically; little effort goes into trying to understand Freud in his own time, but rather isolated words of his are bandied about in the context of today's therapeutic concerns.

It is in the midst of this regrettable state of affairs that the three volumes edited by Paul E. Stepansky are noteworthy.[1] The various writers included here, only a few of whom are clinicians, seek to understand Freud impartially as an object of historical inquiry. Although the essays inevitably suffer from flaws, taken as a whole they represent an admirable shift toward the professionalization of Freud studies. The authors cannot be accused of writing to defend organizationally vested interests. Nor, on the whole, do they echo many of the most sectarian past shibboleths about the history of psychoanalysis. The authors seem genuinely fair-minded.

Although I do have a series of criticisms to offer, scholarship stands to gain from the normal give-and-take of historical inquiry. Sixty years after Freud's death it makes little sense to invoke paens of praise as if it were novel to recognize his genius. I take it for granted that Freud was a momentous figure in world intellectual history, and there is no doubt in my mind that he can withstand the most careful examination. However, it is still true that almost anything can be written about him without being certain to encounter the critical standards that are customary for the usual subjects in university life. Because I have been publishing on Freud for over thirty years, and would like to see the development of the psychoanalytic movement become part of general intellectual history, I am insisting here on some pretty high objectives. (It may seem a small point, but I want to get it out of the way at the outset: the Index to each of these volumes is inexcusably bad. Often in books it proves hard to keep track of all the concepts that get discussed, but here not even the names of people are properly collated and cited.)

The highpoint of Volume 1 is Peter Swales's essay on Anna von Lieben, the Baroness Anna von Todesco, who was called by Freud "Frau Cäcilie M." in *Studies on Hysteria*.[2] Swales has done a remarkable amount of sleuthing around Freud's patients from the 1890s, and there is no question that future historians will be indebted to him for all that he has succeeeded in unearthing. It is impossible to encapsulate the details Swales came up with, but I assume his account will go substantially unchallenged. Despite my admiration for Swales's detective-like reconstructive efforts, I do wish that Paul Stepansky had succeeded in exerting more traditional editorial control over his contributor. It does not serve to establish Swales's credibility to allow him the self-indulgence of so many notes, and in particular a passage where he announces the relevance of "a forthcoming autobiography" that he is working on; nor should the sentences, where he explains that he is not a psychiatrist or even a psychoanalyst, but "simply my own person," have been allowed to survive in a note.

Volume 1 also contains a valuable piece by Edwin E. Wallace, IV, a psychiatrist and historian of medicine, on "Freud As Ethicist." At the same time Freud was both supportive of traditional Western values as well as antithetical to them, and Wallace pursues this critical problem with tenacity. For example, he notes "perhaps a subtle antinomian irony implicit in Freud's reference to the neurotic...as suffering from the 'negative' of the perversions, in the sense that the latter had traditionally been subject to the severest moral judgments."[3] Wallace is right in saying that "as early as 1900 Freud was using psychogenetics as an instrument to demolish man's moral pretensions...."[4] Freud was indebted to Nietzsche's influence, and there is indeed a "sardonic, levelling tone"[5] in Freud. Wallace appropriately quotes Freud writing: "Most of our sentimentalists, friends of humanity, and protectors of animals have been evolved from little sadists and animal tormentors."[6] But when Freud termed Dostoevsky a "sadist," Freud then went on to explain that meant Dostoevsky was "the mildest, kindliest, most helpful person possible." One minor error in Wallace's piece reflects a more general misunderstanding: Wallace writes that "although the simplistic 'strangulated affect-catharsis' theory of pathology and therapy was discarded well before 1900, its vestiges remained until 1926, when Freud formulated his structural theory of anxiety."[7] In fact, I learned from one of Freud's patients in analysis for years in the 1920s and 1930s that, in practice, Freud never gave up his earliest conviction about the significance of "dammed up libido," whatever changes Freud made in his theory of anxiety in 1926.

Volume 1 also contains Barry Silverstein's "'Now Comes a Sad Story': Freud's Lost Metapsychological papers." Silverstein, a professor of psychology, was writing before a manuscript of Freud's "Overview of the Transference Neuroses" got discovered in a trunk of Sandor Ferenczi's papers; subsequently it appeared in print entitled *A Phylogenetic Fantasy*.[8] The imposition of the title *A Phylogenetic Fantasy* instead of going along with Freud's own choice of "Overview of the Transference Neuroses" seems to me in keeping with the general need the current psychoanalytic establishment has to present Freud in a way that supports today's thinking. The true Freud, however, was radical and shocking, and even if some of his ideas do not serve the purposes of the 1990s establishment, it does his memory in intellectual history no service to cut him down to a lesser size than he was.

Silverstein provides an invaluable background to Freud's metapsychological articles, but it does seem to me awfully late in the day for Silverstein to refer even in passing to "the defections of Adler and Jung." Whatever the merits of the case in their growing disagreements with Freud, it is also true that he threw out both Adler and Jung. As Silverstein states at one point, Jung "who entered the relationship with Freud pleading to be accepted as a son, left the relationship demanding to be treated as an equal."[9] That seems to me a pretty fair summary of what happened. Freud did, as Silverstein says, jealously guard "his theory from violation by his male disciples as if that theory were his woman."[10] Silverstein rightly emphasizes the degree to which Freud's work has to be understood in terms of his quarrels with former disciples. He is also correct to say that in "creating the concept of the superego, Freud was continuing the battle with Jung begun in *Totem and Taboo*."[11]

The "brief contributions" to Volume 1 are not outstanding. Patrick J. Mahony, a practicing analyst as well as a literary critic, has elsewhere been more boldly original than in his "The Oral Tradition, Freud, and Psychoanalytic Writing." Paul Stepansky's own "Feuerbach and Jung as Religious Critics" is noteworthy mainly for the seriousness with which he treats Jung's ideas, which foretells some of the most interesting parts of Volumes 2 and 3. John E. Gedo's "On the Origins of the Theban Plague" is an unfortunate place on which to conclude this volume. It is extraordinary how Gedo, who considers himself "an amateur historian," can be so insulting to Frank Sulloway's work,[12] which is that of a professional student of the history of science. Gedo lambasts Sulloway, along with Jeffrey M. Masson,[13] and Swales. (Stepansky, as editor, should have struck out Gedo's numerous exclamation points.) In general, Gedo is not trustworthy as a summarizer of Freud, at least when it comes to Jung. In connection with the Sabina Spielrein story,[14] Gedo is naturally startled, but he has not kept the tale straight. "Jung apparently replied that the family would have grounds for complaint if he had continued (!) to receive payment for his professional services. And he offered to break off the affair if the family resumed tipping him!"[15] Gedo is too polemical, although I also was shocked by Jung's letter to her parents saying that they could expect the proper medical discretion if they paid the usual fees. Gedo concludes writing on the Spielrein affair with a comment which should appear dubious to outsiders: "By then, Switzerland had clearly suffered a great decline in public morality as a consequence of centuries of democratization."[16]

Volume 2 opens with an important "major essay" by Peter Homans, who teaches at the University of Chicago's Divinity School; the piece is unfortunately entitled "Disappointment and the Ability to Mourn: De-Idealization as a Psychological Theme in Freud's Life, Thought, and Social Circumstance, 1906-1914." I do not care how fashionable in certain circles the term "de-idealization" may have become, it is a barbarism. Such neologisms do nothing to establish the "scientific" status of psychoanalytic thinking. Homans is clearly writing under the influence of the work of Heinz Kohut, and Homans tells us that "de-idealization refers to the pre-oedipal line of development, the figure of the mother more than the father, and to issues of unconscious self-esteem, merger, and self-cohesion, grandiosity, and the loss of ideals."[17] Homans has publishd a book about Jung, and Homans maintains that he continues to "accord Jung a powerful influence denied by analytic biographers and historians alike."[18] Over eighty-five years have passed since the falling-out between Freud and Jung, and now at last the issues are being treated with the scholarly concern they deserve. Erich Fromm, who himself underestimated Jung, had ideas about Freud and the pre-oedipal that deserve more recognition. I trust it will not take a comparably long number of years after the publication of *Escape From Freedom* (1941),[19] for which Fromm was so unfairly excoriated by analysts, before his work gets regularly cited in professional bibliographies.

Homans is sensitive to the differences between Jung and Freud:

> Jung was attached to bourgeois European society as Freud was not, and he identified with the regnant ideals of European Christian humanism as Freud could not. Freud, knowing this, consciously wished for, and unconsciously dreaded, the expansion of analysis beyond his Jewish-Viennese "circle."[20]

Homans proposes that psychoanalysis "emerged as the mirror image, so to speak, of its Jewish surroundings."[21] Homans admires Sulloway's book and cites two quotations from it, one from Hanns Sachs and the other from Max Graf about the sect-like character of the movement. Sulloway had, however, relied on my own *Freud and His Followers* for those passages, and one would feel more secure about the success of Stepansky's books in getting the subject of Freud onto the proper academic level if the citations to Sachs and Graf were made in the usually accepted scholarly way. It does not detract from my admiration for Homans's essay if I point out a couple of queries. Quite suddenly, we are told of Freud that "London was...the city of his reality sense."[21] That seems to me a bit of romantic nonsense. Homans makes a more important error, however, when he writes: "in 1930, when he was vacationing in Frankfurt, Freud's mother died in Vienna."[22] Freud was in Vienna then himself, and it is significant because, as Homans writes, "Freud was unable to feel a strong current of grief. He did not attend the funeral, instead sent Anna."[23]

The other "major essay" in Volume 2 is Richard E. Geha's "Freud As Fictionalist: The Imaginary Worlds of Psychoanalysis." Geha, a practicing clinician, goes too far, I think, in the direction of accepting the significance of narrative coherence in therapy. Geha does not mention the logical possibility of lying; Frank Cioffi once published a combative-sounding article in 1975 entitled "Was Freud A Liar?"[24] It is too easy to accept Freud's own all-or-nothing line of reasoning; as Freud wrote, "either the analysis based on the neurosis in his [the "Wolf Man's"] childhood is all a piece of nonsense from start to finish, or everything took place just as I have described it above."[25] I cannot buy Geha's own "criterion of truth": coherence. Geha is right that Freud himself had a "philosophical commitment to a naïve realism,"[26] but the epistemological quagmire of relativism is not the only alternative. Geha correctly points out that Freud "kept repeating the same mis-adventure, delving into history for the ruins of the 'real thing' even after the ground of childhood seductions had evaporated into thin air."[27] Freud might have endorsed what Geha calls "simplistic realism," without it being necessary to go quite so far in the opposite direction of holding that "construction is the essence of psychoanalytic history…and constructed history has nothing at all to do with realism or with a correspondence theory of truth."[28] Geha's outlook might license irresponsible fantasizing.

Geha wisely highlights the disjunction between what Freud professed and what he did, and legitimately entertains "the question of Freud as an artist in disguise."[29] Geha, however, holds that "no such things as 'facts' or facts in themselves exist,"[30] but he does not adequately contrast his own position with Freud's beliefs on the matter. Philosophers have long debated the issue of what is a fact. Geha would do well to consult Otto Rank as a student of Nietzsche. But Geha's perspectivism is curiously at odds with Swales's paper in Volume 1: Geha argues that "No Wolf Man ever existed *out there* as the genuine article or thing-in-himself. Any such 'thing' maintains only a fictional existence."[31] If that were true, then what would be the point of tracking down clinical records and historical documentation? Because history is not scientifically objective does not mean we should allow propagandists a free rein.

Volume 2 closes with a fine "brief contribution" from Patricia Herzog, a philosopher. In her "The Myth of Freud As Anti-philosopher" she points out how puzzling "Freud's ostrich-like attitude" toward Níetzsche was. She acknowledges Jones's "monumental biography" of Freud at the same time she argues that "Jones's antipathy to philosophy blinds him to the fact that Freud's antiphilosophical remarks are not monolithic in character."[32] She shrewdly pursues the significance of Brentano's impact on Freud. As far as I know she is right in thinking that Freud "was in no doubt as to the philosophical nature of his goal…."[33] And I think she is also correct in suggesting that "it is fair to say that the myth of Freud as anti-philosopher was created by Freud himself…."[34]

The most interesting essay in Volume 3 is a lengthy piece by John Kerr, as a Ph.D. candidate in clinical psychology: "Beyond the Pleasure Principle and Back Again: Freud, Jung, and Sabina Spielrein." Under the influence of his thesis adviser, Robert R. Holt, Kerr continues, along the lines followed by Homans and Stepansky, to take Jung seriously as an important figure in intellectual history. Stepansky is wrong, however, in thinking that Freud's *Beyond The Pleasure Principle* (1920)[35] was "perhaps even the denouement of Freud's continuing preoccupations with Jung and the theoretical revisions of the Zurich school."[36] Even as late as Freud's *Moses and Monotheism* (1939)[37] Freud was concerned with the issues that preoccupied him with Jung.

Stepansky cites Quentin Skinner's brilliant work on the methodology of intellectual history, but it seems to me that more plain old-fashioned homework is still needed on the history of psychoanalysis. Kerr is centrally concerned with Freud's concept of the death instinct. But a close reading of my own work would have made it impossible for Kerr to use the term "Thanatos," because I have provided the reasons Freud himself never once used it. Kerr writes about Freud's concern with defecting students and his anxiety over priorities; Kerr also comments on Freud's personal association of death with the uncanny. Yet Kerr wholly ignores how Freud told Helene Deutsch that Tausk had made an "uncanny" impact on him, and Kerr neglects the following paragraph from *Brother Animal*:

> There really was something uncanny in the relationship between Freud and Tausk. For as if in continuation of their tie, at the time Tausk killed himself Freud was beginning to formulate the concept of a death instinct. In the very same letter to Lou telling of Tausk's suicide, Freud alludes to stumbling across a new aspect of the "death theme," "an amazing idea hailing from the instincts." Freud had been intrigued by the psychology of death for some time, as had a whole tradition within German literature. But his explicit postulation of an instinct of primitive destructiveness came simultaneously with Tausk's suicide. One can only wonder whether Tausk had heard—or intuited— anything about it from Freud. Could Tausk have been acting out Freud's newest, or even just burgeoning idea? Or perhaps the notion of a death instinct represented another way for Freud to deny any responsibility for Tausk's suicide.[38]

I am willing to concede that my suggestion about the relevance of the particularly violent and unexpected suicide of Tausk was off-base, although I would like to see some argument to that purpose. It seems to me, however, impermissible for Kerr to proceed without at all taking into account the hypotheses I raised; and I am hoping it does not seem self-indulgent of me to cite this particular example in behalf of the general cause of a more professional historiography of psychoanalysis. Intellectual history does proceed by one writer's work being checked and corrected by a later set of interpretations. It appears unfortunately unique to the history of psychoanalysis that texts can be silently passed over as if they had never been published. Kerr knows how crucial the years 1918-1919 were for Freud's adoption of the death instinct; but he claims, ignoring the whole story of Tausk's death, that "the biographical material...provides little help in understanding the timing of the later innovation."[39] Kerr then turns away "from any aspects of Freud's character" toward "the exigencies of theory construction."[40] It seems crude to me to suppose, in contrast to the obvious shock of Tausk's gruesome suicide, that Kerr can be right that Freud "hit on the idea of the death instinct" while re-reading a 1911 book by Wilhelm Stekel. All the evidence indicates that Freud never re-read any of the works of his ex-disciples.

Kerr proceeds to discuss Spielrein's work, mistakenly thinking that "phylogenesis" was "another favorite Zurich subject," as if Freud himself were not as fascinated by it as Ferenczi or Jung. Kerr is probably right in seeing Paul Federn's 1913 review of Spielrein's text as representing the then current "party line," without Kerr showing any adequate awareness of the need to acknowledge as well what might be today's corresponding conventional wisdom. Kerr is good at interpreting Spielrein's paper. Kerr's insight that "there is no such thing as a death instinct in Spielrein's paper"[41] might have led someone less devoted to textual exegesis to examine more of the biographical evidence in Freud's life. In Jung's *Symbols of Transformation* (1952),[42] he too credits Spielrein with the idea of a death instinct. Oddly enough, without mentioning *Brother Animal*, Kerr tells that in 1911:

> Victor Tausk in particular seems to have grasped what she was driving at. The following spring...he would present a similar theory, and she would respond by supporting him. Evidently her theory was more readily understood by those who, like Tausk, were ready to erect an ego psychology on the basis of an instinctual dualism.[43]

The strongest point in Kerr's article is the seriousness with which he takes Jung's texts. "Jung, like Adler and others, had grown disenchanted with the interminable interpretation of infantile wishes."[44] Jung's perspective was that "the sexuality of the unconscious is not what it seems to be; it is merely a symbol...."[45] Kerr is more patient in untangling Jung's writings than some of the Jungians have been. Kerr thinks that by the time of Jung's Fordham lectures, "all the various hints and suggestions that were scattered around the earlier work were now integrated into a single, coherent, and unequivocal system."[46]

> According to Jung, the patient produces infantile sexual material not because it is causative of the neurosis, but because it is constitutive, part of a regressive fantasy life brought on by the patient's flight from reality. In this view, the established analytic technique, by fostering the production of these fantasies, only strengthens the regressive process.[47]

Despite Freud's opposition at the time, Kerr believes that "the idea of adding a 'prospective' or 'ethical' or 'functional' dimension to psychoanalyis was quite possibly the most popular innovation in the theory of interpretation since the idea of transference."[48]

Kerr's essay, despite its defects, seems to me the most important one in Volume 3, although we have another bit of Swales's detective work, this time about the brief case of Katharina. It is a bit odd that Stepansky includes this piece without making any reference to how it contrasts with the "fictionalist" point of view of Geha. But Swales has once again told us so much about one of Freud's earliest patients that it is hard to believe that it can be bettered in the near future. Swales maintains that "Freud remained blind to a nonsexual understanding of the girl's condition,"[49] which would be in keeping with the general critique of Freud that Kerr outlines in his piece on Jung. (Once again, I wish Stepansky had succeeded in suppressing an amateur-sounding sentence in Swales's notes: "Am I not the only true Freudian?"[50])

Volume 3 concludes with another "brief contribution," this from Robert R. Holt, "Freud's Adolescent Reading: Some Possible Effects on His Work." Holt reports on Büchner, Feuerbach, and Strauss. I do wish that Holt had also commented on Buckle and Lecky, for although they are two works of history, having "relatively less to do with religious, moral, and philosophical issues,"[51] I would have been intrigued to learn more about them. Holt is, of course, wise in objecting to the "true believers (like Jones) in Freud's Athena-like, total originality...."[52] Holt knows that "to discover antecedents of a great thinker's formulations in books he read is more a work of homage than detraction, or at least it should be."[53] Holt's enlightened point of view makes a solid ending to Volume 3, which, unfortunately, is to be the last in Stepansky's series, *Freud, Appraisals and Reappraisals.*

## Notes

1. *Freud: Appraisals and Reappraisals: Contributions to Freud Studies*, edited by Paul E. Stepansky. Vol. 1 (Hillsdale, NJ: The Analytic Press, 1986); Vol. 2 (Hillsdale, NJ: The Analytic Press, 1987); Vol. 3 (Hillsdale, NJ: The Analytic Press, 1987).
2. Freud, *Studies on Hysteria, Standard Edition*, Vol. 2.
3. Stepansky, ed., Vol. 1, *op. cit.*, p. 89.
4. Ibid., p. 91.
5. Ibid.
6. Ibid.
7. Ibid., p. 109.
8. Sigmund Freud, *A Phylogenetic Fantasy: Overview of the Transference Neuroses*, ed. Ilse Grubich-Simitis, trans. A. Hoffer and P. Hoffer (Cambridge, MA: Harvard University Press, 1967).
9. Stepansky, ed., Vol. 1, *op. cit.*, p. 163.
10. Ibid., p. 164.
11. Ibid., p. 186.
12. Frank Sulloway, *Freud, Biologist of the Mind: Beyond the Psychoanalytic Legend* (New York: Basic Books, 1984).
13. Jeffrey M. Masson, *The Assault on Truth: Freud's Suppression of the Seduction Theory* (New York: Farrar, Straus, & Giroux, 1984).
14. Aldo Carotenuto, *A Secret Symmetry: Sabina Spielrein Between Freud and Jung* (New York: Pantheon, 1982).
15. Stepansky, ed., Vol. 1, *op. cit.*, p. 257.
16. Ibid.
17. Stepansky, Vol. 2, *op. cit.*, p. 12.
18. Ibid., p. 17.

19. Erich Fromm, *Escape From Freedom* (New York: Holt, Rinehart & Winston, 1941).
20. Stepansky, Vol. 2, *op. cit.*,p. 47.
21. Ibid., p. 85.
22. Ibid., p. 87.
23. Ibid.
24. Frank Cioffi, "Was Freud A Liar?" *The Listener*, February 7, 1975, pp. 172-74.
25. Freud, "From the History of an Infantile Neurosis," *Standard Edition*, Vol. 17, p. 56.
26. Stepansky, Vol. 2, *op. cit.*, p. 114.
27. Ibid.
28. Ibid., p. 115.
29. Ibid., p. 118.
30. Ibid., p. 132.
31. Ibid., p. 140.
32. Ibid., p. 179.
33. Ibid., p. 184.
34. Ibid.
35. Sigmund Freud, *Beyond the Pleasure principle*, *Standard Edition*, Vol. 18, pp. 7-64.
36. Stepansky, Vol. 3, *op. cit.*, p. xiv.
37. Sigmund Freud, *Moses and Monotheism*, *Standard Edition*, Vol. 23, pp. 7-137.
38. Paul Roazen, *Brother Animal: The Story of Freud and Tausk* (New York: Knopf, 1969; reprinted, with new Introduction, New Brunswick, NJ: Transaction, 1990), p. 143.
39. Stepansky, Vol. 3, *op. cit.*, p. 16.
40. Ibid., p. 17.
41. Ibid., p. 29.
42. Carl G. Jung, *Symbols of Transformation*, in R. F. C. Hull, trans, *The Collected Works of C. G. Jung*, Vol. 5, pp. xxiii-494 (Princeton, NJ: Princeton University Press, 1974).
43. Stepansky, Vol. 3, *op. cit.*, p. 42.
44. Ibid., p. 44.
45. Ibid., pp. 45-46.
46. Ibid., p. 48.
47. Ibid., p. 58.
48. Ibid., p. 62.
49. Ibid., p. 121.
50. Ibid., p. 154.
51. Ibid., p. 168.
52. Ibid., p. 188.
53. Ibid., p. 189.

# 5

# Patients: First-Person Accounts

The controversies associated with Freud's work are sufficiently unusual to deserve special scrutiny. The contentiousness surrounding his standing has followed partly from the way he presented his ideas, for he was convinced early in his career as a psychoanalyst that he had "discovered" a series of remarkable truths about human nature. The metaphor of a discovery implied that he had come upon something radically new that could be verified scientifically, rather than that he simply was proposing a fresh way of looking at things. Freud put forward his "findings" with the utmost conviction, and he systematized them into a framework that lent added credibility to his contentions.

Freud in fact was proposing a thorough revision of how psychology had developed up until then. The more we know about the history of ideas, the easier it becomes to situate his thinking in relation to that of other giants in intellectual history; and all his work has to be understood within the context of the last days of old Vienna. To approach Freud in the same way as any other subject of historical investigation does not detract from what he accomplished. But those who come to the study of his concepts ought to absorb the full implications of how he undertook to appeal to the individual human experience of his readers. He was putting his case, then, on humanistic grounds as well as scientific ones, and those who practice his profession have always been divided about what portion of psychoanalysis is art rather than pure science.

The personal immediacy of the way in which Freud presented his theses, sometimes explicitly relying on his own autobiography, meant almost inevitably that right from the beginning there would be those who challenged his manner of proceeding. Even though his close friend Wilhelm Fliess had been remarkably involved in Freud's working out *The Interpretation of Dreams* (1900), not long after its publication Fliess was questioning the extent to which Freud was reading his own thoughts into the minds of his patients and thereby projecting his personality into his theories. Freud bitterly resented Fliess's accusation, which doubtless played a part in their falling out.

Throughout the first decades of Freud's presenting his new ideas and developing the special therapeutic approach he was recommending for neurotic patients, skeptics continued to doubt the validity of Freud's claims. Amid the storm Freud evoked he went on undeterred. If one examines the reviews of his works that came out while he was alive, for example those that appeared in the first decade of the twentieth century,[1] one finds that some of the most basic questions about his ideas were being raised with sympathy and respect. Freud himself did not appreciate how he was being received and scarcely paused to answer any of these original articles. I believe he already sensed what a special source of power he had created in the psychoanalytic treatment setting itself. Although he does not seem to have understood the role that old-fashioned suggestion was capable of playing, he knew that his method of working was attracting loyal converts and disciples. By the end of the first decade of the century, it was apparent that Freud had succeeded in inaugurating a new school, or at least that is how it looked to outsiders.

However monolithic a movement Freud might seem to have founded, he did not feel obliged to consolidate his following, by a clear exposition of his own special therapeutic technique, until after his pre-World War I difficulties with Alfred Adler, Wilhelm Stekel, and Carl Jung. It was in connection with Freud's efforts to differentiate his own form of psychology from that of Adler, Stekel, and Jung that Freud spelled out his recommendations for what he regarded as proper psychoanalytic technique. Other means of psychotherapy, however much they may have borne similarities to his own, ran the risk of being dismissed by him as examples of so-called wild analysis.

In the context of these conflicts with Adler, Stekel, and Jung, Freud wrote his famous case history of the Wolf Man.[2] Earlier, with Dora (1905),[3] Little Hans (1909),[4] the Rat Man (1909),[5] and Schreber (1911),[6] Freud had sought to explicate psychoanalytic doctrine by relying on individual case histories. The Wolf Man was the only one of Freud's five great case histories that was written with an eye to the objections of knowledgeable skeptics. For Freud to have to confront the reservations of an uncomprehending, hostile outside world was one thing: Freud's earlier case histories can all be read as part of Freud's campaign to win the acceptance of his ideas. But once Freud had serious troubles within his own camp of psychoanalysts and felt he had to expel "deviations" like those which Adler, Stekel, and Jung represented, then he had to address himself, as in the Wolf Man, to the most subtle possible reservations about his work. With the Wolf Man he therefore sought to show the primary significance of childhood emotional problems, in order to rebut the contention that infantilism was primarily a defensive maneuver available to adults.

As I have watched the literature about Freud grow over the last four decades, it has been hard for me not to be bemused. For in the mid-1960s it was my good fortune to interview twenty-five people who had once been in analysis with Freud. Although I think I always appreciated the special status that Freud's five published case histories had attained, at the same time I also knew, from my own personal contact with these twenty-five former patients of Freud's, how completely different he was in practice from how he sounded in writing about his clinical conduct. Freud theoretically advocated all kinds of specially recommended techniques, yet in actuality he performed as a therapist in surprising, even contradictory, ways.

Relatively little attention is paid even now to Freud's actual clinical activites. Partly this has to be a question of the unavailability of reliable data, there being no hard-and-fast ways of determining how Freud did, in fact, approach his case material. One must be dubious as well even about written material, for merely being entrusted to paper does not guarantee veracity. Indeed, I have found that there was a good deal of professional smoke-and-mirrors at work, which accounts for what succeeded in being published. Plenty of insiders in his time knew that Freud had frequently violated his own central recommendations about technique. Many seemed to assume that the best way to proceed would be to cover up how Freud had behaved, in the interests of promoting an "ideal" image of how he should have acted.

One does not have to endorse the historical disingenuousness of some of Freud's closest followers, or be an apologist, in order to point out that the contractual terms on which he saw patients were unique. He had no difficulty, for example, in immediately mobilizing transference reactions. Patients who came to him usually were already well stocked with fantasies and expectations of an irrational sort. Plenty of emotional juices flowed from them without any special effort on his part. As a matter of fact, it is likely that Freud underestimated the extent to which he had facilitated the kinds of stories he was told. It was easy for him to think that the tales he encountered were in fact being revealed in the context of a neutral, laboratory-like clinical setting.

From a contemporary perspective, however, it is obvious that Freud had really constructed an environment for his patients that was hardly a level playing field. For example, the world is now familiar with photographs of the antiquities collection that filled his consulting room; yet almost nothing has been written about the effect that these objects had on Freud's patients or what they revealed about him to them. And I never met anyone who knew Freud who did not assume the smoke and smells from Freud's constant cigar-smoking; although he did not approve of addictions in others, he had this one of his own.

Freud ignored many of the precepts he laid down for others to follow. In keeping with Central European custom, Freud shook hands before and after each analytic session—and he could gaze inquiringly or sympathetically into a patient's eyes. When he was irritated (or bored) patients could feel that, too. He sometimes treated patients free of charge, especially when there was someone else in the family who had been financially generous to Freud's "cause"; he also had an eye out for who might be able to help his movement in the future. When he felt like it, Freud would accept presents. And he could get up from his chair in the middle of an analytic hour to check something in an archeological dictionary.

One reason Freud's disciples could be so secretive about the early history of psychoanalysis was precisely that they knew that Freud's behavior might not be good for the propaganda they had tried to put forward. For instance, Freud demanded of others, such as Sandor Ferenczi, who were technically innovative, that they make public what their practices were like. He himself admitted, in a now famous letter to Edoardo Weiss,[7] the analysis of Anna. So even though his most loyal followers might try to keep secret the story of her analysis, he had himself provided the world with the evidence that he had allowed himself a liberty that he might have criticized in another. Of course other early analysts went on to observe, and even analyze, their own children, too; but I cannot believe that any of this took place without the conviction that they were merely following Freud's own footsteps.

Part of what is so confusing about the literature on the history of psychoanalysis is the extent to which commentators have ignored how Freud's special tact and discretion, as well as his conception of what properly constituted science, shaped the clinical material he chose to present to the public. The job of the generation of analysts which came after Freud's death was seen to be one of stabilizing and making more teachable that which seemed so ephemeral and hard to pin down in Freud himself. And so the degree to which Freud could, by his own standards, behave waywardly was to be soft-pedalled.

Jones's authorized biography of Freud was an important vehicle for displaying an "orthodox" view of Freud's career. Despite our debt to Jones, at no point do we learn from him that the most significant single event in Freud's life as a practicing analyst was his getting cancer of the jaw in 1923. Among those I met who had been in analysis with Freud that event constituted a genuine watershed, and I have been advised by one translating expert that even Freud's handwriting changed. Significantly, he never wrote another case history after falling ill. Increasingly, he turned his attention to social, political, and philosophical issues. At the same time he sought to systematize all his thinking so that, for example in *An Outline of Psychoanalysis*,[8] left unfinished at his death, we have a highly abstract restatement of his position. I believe that after 1923 he was more withdrawn within his own family and altogether less outgoing than before in his clinical practice. It now hurt Freud to talk. Although the earliest patients of Freud's that I interviewed were in treatment with him before World War I and, therefore, had experiences with him prior to his getting sick, by and large most of those I spoke with were analyzed during Freud's final, declining phase, which lasted until his death in 1939.

Almost as soon as one makes generalizations about Freud as an analyst it is necessary to stop to state some appropriate qualifications. For although I think it is true that Freud did change after 1923 and became much less able to respond to each patient as a full human being, to the end of his days he remained unique in his practices. Having said that, I feel it is necessary to add a further complication. From the little I know of how Jung conducted himself, I am inclined to think that there were more similarities, couch or no couch, to how Freud and Jung approached their clinical work than there are between how Freud behaved and the ideal of psychoanalytic detachment and neutrality that at least some of his prominent adherents came to espouse.

Oddly enough, I believe that the idea of a technique that was both scientific and teachable took root especially among his American followers. The bulk of Freud's American students entered his world after he was already ill; they came in naïve search for a means by which personality structure could be rebuilt. Freud found these New World disciples eager to think that he had succeeded in creating a technique that was independent of the character of the individual practitioner. But, as Freud once said to the Princess George, Marie Bonaparte, "more important than what one does is what one is."[9] His conviction would be shared by someone like Jung, although as far as I know neither Freud nor Jung ever acknowledged how alike their procedures remained despite their epic disagreements before the first World War.

The question of who Freud was takes on key significance. In a partial attempt to answer the question of what Freud was like in practice, I have selected from my files a fraction of the interview material I accumulated about the Brunswicks—Ruth, Mark, and David. Ruth had been the first of them to go to Freud and was the only one of the three to have psychiatric training. Her future husband Mark was a musician and composer, and her brother-in-law David, although he later became a practicing analyst back in the States, had no such intention at the time he first saw Freud.

It would never have dawned on me to try to pursue the story of the Brunswicks if I had not been alerted to the special significance Ruth had attained within Freud's circle. For example, I once asked an exceptionally intelligent analyst, personally treated by both Jung and Freud: who around 1930 was the most important pupil in Freud's circle? I got the unhesitating answer: Ruth Mack Brunswick. Yet there was, at the time I began my work, almost nothing about her in the literature. When I interviewed Marianne Kris and discussed Ruth with her, Dr. Kris mentioned in passing, as I have reported, that she still had a trunk-full of Ruth's papers in her possession. Any historian's mouth waters at the prospect of so much primary material surviving. By now I am confident that all of it has disappeared into the hands of either the Freud Archives or the restricted portions of the Freud Collection at the Library of Congress.[10]

But even after I had published in 1975 certain key aspects of the tale of the Brunswicks in Freud's circle, almost nothing appeared about them. Instead, we have gotten continuing reconsiderations, for example, of those five famous clinical case histories that Freud published. Writers exercise their ingenuity in talking about the cases Freud chose to push to the forefront. And clinicians continue to cites passages in Freud that sustain the needs of contemporary psychotherapeutic practice. Yet an example like that of the Brunswicks remained poorly understood and not widely known; and as long as that sort of blind spot continues, we will not have succeeded in looking at the past in anything like its own terms.

All three of the Brunswicks were for some time in analysis with Freud simultaneously. I mention this to highlight right away that Freud did not, when he was actively concerned with helping, abide by his own technical advice against simultaneously analyzing different members of one family. He did not in general like Americans, but then he was always making clinical "exceptions." He took to Ruth and Mark Brunswick in particular and extended himself for them. Nonetheless, I gathered from both Mark Brunswick and his brother, David, whom I saw at separate times and in locations several thousand miles apart, that in the end each of them thought that Freud should not have taken either of them in treatment along with Ruth. Mark and David both went to analysts after seeing Freud and found that the creator of psychoanalysis could be deficient as a therapist in ways that his successors were not.

I think it is important to emphasize Freud's personal involvement with the Brunswicks because it is so odd how history tends to get written. As far as I can tell, for over a decade Ruth and Marie Bonaparte were the most significant female disciples in Freud's world; Freud's daughter Anna was at the time much less significant, although she played a crucial role as Freud's secretary, guardian of his time, and nursemaid for his health. But despite Ruth's own importance, she has received almost no attention in the literature about Freud. Her name does regularly come up in connection with the Wolf Man, since she did publish a case history about him after Freud had referred him to her for treatment.[11] (A second case history of hers about the Wolf Man remains unpublished and presumably will someday emerge from the interdiction of the officials at the Freud Archives in New York, which to repeat still retains control over everything that once passed through its hands on the way to the Library of Congress.) But Ruth's importance to Freud is certainly evident in his entrusting the Wolf Man to her care. Freud knew that there would be something to write up about her treatment of this memorable case. Anything she came up with would be an addendum to his own case history and therefore a permanent part of the professional literature.

Ruth Mack Brunswick is not the only early analyst to be overlooked in the most popular accounts of the history of Freud's school, which is why I have done my best to try to revive the figure of Victor Tausk, who disappeared from the psychoanalytic stage after he committed suicide in 1919 following a frustrating struggle with Freud.[12] Chance does play its part in how history gets written: Ruth Brunswick was not a therapeutic success of Freud's, and also she failed to deliver on her professional promise. Tausk's suicide was by itself enough to stifle interest in him among devout adherents of the "cause" of psychoanalysis as a movement.

But history ought not to be conceived from the perspective of the big battalions I mentioned in my "Introduction." Among historians, an exclusively success-oriented approach is known as "Whig" history, and such Whiggery is nowhere an admired form of proceeding. Yet in a recent widely popular biography of Freud, for example, the name of Wilhelm Reich does not appear even once.[13] Reich was of immense importance to Freud and his circle. Since Reich's death his books have been so appealing that they have sometimes appeared in unauthorized, pirated editions. Reich's last years were spent outside of organized psychoanalysis, since he was expelled from the official bodies that certify practitioners. But it would be odd, in reconstructing the story of Freud's life and struggles, to treat a historical figure as if he had never existed simply because one does not approve either of his ideas or his unfortunate last period.

Reich is so immensely well known if solely because some of his notorious practices landed him in an American federal prison cell where he finally died in 1956. It is necessary only to point out his omission from a historical account to establish quickly the untenability of an establishmentarian bias.

But what of those who for a variety of reasons wrote only a little or failed to attract a school of disciples? It is much harder to establish who in recorded history played a more subtle part. History is colored partly by success itself; and those who, for whatever reasons, are sidetracked, or who seem like "losers," can easily be forgotten. That historical memory can be so unreliable is all the more reason for us to be conscientiously on our toes.

Ruth Mack Brunswick, who was relatively unknown in the mid-1960s (as she is apt to be still), was throughout the 1920s and 1930s one of the key people in Freud's immediate circle and a special channel for his influence on his followers in the United States. She was also an analyst who made a memorable written contribution to the history of the discipline; her writings on the so-called preoedipal phase are sometimes cited today. Everyone who was in analytic training in Vienna at the time has attested that she was a special favorite of Freud's, in fact one of his last adoptive daughters in psychoanalysis. And yet almost nothing has been published, even now, about her.

Early on in my interviews with Freud's followers, it became apparent to me that although much had been written about certain of them, others had been neglected. My interest in this imbalance was not aroused by antiquarianism. Once one understands the full role of sectarianism in modern psychiatry, and how controversial the history of psychoanalysis has been, then when the neglect of a person or subject is pointed out, responsible inquiry demands that special attention be paid. For example, Paul Schilder, a Viennese analyst, was an important figure in twentieth-century psychiatry, yet because he was "on the outs" with Freud, virtually nothing exists in the literature about him.

With regard to Ruth Mack Brunswick, I knew early on that her story merited discussion. A close attention to the available literature would reveal how genuinely important she once had been. That Karl Menninger chose her as his own analyst is but one indicator of her standing in the field. William Fliess's son, Robert, was also her patient (as was the actress Myrna Loy and the literary critic Diana Trilling).

As I pursued Ruth Brunswick's career in the literature, I uncovered a "secret" about her which nobody had yet written or discussed publicly. Ruth Brunswick then became in my mind a historical underdog: she had been unnecessarily left out of the history books, and I made a point of following up on the matter by inquiring about her. Once I had put portions of her tale in print, however, a new sort of rewriting of history took place. It turned out that a central reason for literary reticence about Ruth Brunswick was the extent to which, under Freud's care, she had become addicted to drugs; at one point in Vienna she even put herself in a sanatorium to help overcome her dependency. Freud grew wholly disillusioned with Ruth, but not until his last months, when his capacities had become severely taxed by the approach of his death. Until then, he had not moralistically distanced himself from her problems but instead had tried to help her.

Thus Freud was again demonstrating how different he was in practice from his own stated theories. Supposedly, psychoanalysis was designed to treat a narrow group of exclusively neurotic patients. Addicts, like perverts, were in principle deemed to be outside the scope of neurosis, and therefore inaccessible to psychoanalytic influence. Nonetheless, in blatant contravention to the principles he had set down, Freud not only continued to treat Ruth, long after her addiction was well-established, but he worked with other such patients as well. Freud, who was trained as a neurologist and had little contact with psychiatric problems, even undertook to treat for years patients whom he knew to be far more troubled than neurotics. Curiously enough, Freud could be in good touch with such people, and some of them did better in his hands than with earlier or subsequent therapists.

History is constantly being rewritten; and Freud's school keeps transforming its record. When I started out to do research on Brunswick, there was no mention at all in the literature about her problem with drugs. Amazingly, later on, when Karl Menninger was asked by a historian whether he had known of her difficulty while he was being treated by her, Menninger claimed that it had been evident to him at the time.[14] Now however much Menninger may in old age have wanted to appear omniscient, it is inconceivable that anyone of his sophistication and stature would ever have knowingly put himself in the therapeutic hands of a drug addict. Freud, however, knew of Ruth's ongoing problems, and that he continued to refer patients to Ruth says something about her special niche in his world.

As I look over my detailed interview notes, I am jolted to find that in fact I had interviewed David Brunswick, Ruth's brother-in-law, before Mark, Ruth's second husband. I am not sure now at what point it finally dawned on me that all three of them had been personally analyzed by Freud. But Mark Brunswick has always stood out in my mind as a strikingly informative interview subject. Many times in the years since his death in 1971, I have wished I could have asked him even more questions, since I found him one of the most unusually open-minded and generous-spirited people of all those I met in the course of my interviewing work. His conception of Freud was rich, complicated, and realistic. Mark Brunswick remains one of the highlights of my interviewing.

David Brunswick, whom I interviewed before Mark, was by then a practicing analyst in Los Angeles, and I interviewed him in his office there and also at a luncheon. He had been, he told me at the outset, in analysis with Freud in Vienna from 1927 to 1930. At the time I saw him, I was also meeting other analysts in the Los Angeles area, and so inevitably I got their views on him as well. David was correctly described to me by one reliable source as an unusually "modest" man; in spite of his long and direct association with Freud, he had not assumed any airs. I found him to be straightforward and unpretentious, a bit on the colorless side, certainly pale in contrast to how I remember his brother, Mark. One old Viennese woman, the widow of the analyst Edward Hitschmann, strikingly said to me of David Brunswick that he was "hardly a human being," meaning that he was that boring. I learned some key things from him, though in retrospect it is understandable that in my memory he was overshadowed by Mark.

Although David's three-year analysis with Freud was by no means a short one, David informed me right away that his brother, Mark, and his sister-in-law, Ruth, were in Vienna even longer with Freud. (Freud's analyses before he got cancer were all characteristically shorter than afterwards.) I take it from my detailed notes that I was not then fully aware of the familial connections between David, Ruth, and Mark. Keeping things straight became even more complicated when Ruth's father, after his first wife died, married David and Mark's mother. (Ruth's father, Judge Julian Mack, was a famous jurist.) Even before then, David and Mark had been distantly related to Ruth; in fact, Mark as a young man had been present at Ruth's first marriage to a prominent physician, Herman Blumgart.

David told me that he had heard about Freud from Leonard Blumgart, a New York psychoanalyst who had been analyzed by Freud shortly after the conclusion of World War I. A small group of New York psychiatrists went to Freud then for further training since psychoanalysis seemed the wave of the future. Leonard Blumgart was, David said, a first cousin of his mother's; it was because of Mark Brunswick's link to Ruth's first husband that Mark came to be present at that wedding.

From David's point of view it was essential to explain to me at the outset that Mark and Ruth were already with Freud before him. But no matter how unusual the situation might have been, or how "unorthodox" it struck me then, David explained without defensiveness that analytically Freud had "done" them all at once. Supposedly, analytic therapy presupposes distance between the analyst and his patients; Freud had even made sure, right from the beginning of psychoanalysis in the 1890s, to have a separate entrance and exit for his office so that patients could be allowed to retain their anonymity. Yet in the cases of David, Mark, and Ruth, Freud was treating three people who were intimately acquainted with one another, and it would be impossible for any of them not to know something of what was going on with Freud in the analysis of the others. Freud had, for instance, discussed in great detail everything about Mark's first analysis with Ruth. At the start of Mark's second analysis, undertaken after a break of a few years, Freud said that that had been a mistake and he would not repeat it. (Before World War I, during Freud's analysis of Jones's common-law wife, Loe Kann, Freud had written extensively about her clinical case to Jones.) Throughout his analyses of Ruth and Mark, Freud saw a good deal of them both socially (but not David).

According to David, his treatment with Freud had not been "a good analysis." By the time I interviewed David, I was already pretty well informed about Freud's possible failings as a therapist; at least I knew that many of Freud's former patients were capable of joking among themselves about some of his clinical inadequacies. None of this skepticism was inconsistent with a shared reverence for Freud, or his immense personal significance in their lives. But David Brunswick may have been the first of Freud's former patients to be so blunt with me about where Freud had gone wrong with him.

According to David, Freud "should not have taken him" into analysis at the same time as his sister-in-law and brother. It did not seem to me that David was being abstract about where Freud had gone wrong; I did not think that David was making a generalization about how analytic therapists ought not to deal with too many members of the same family at one time. True, I had never before heard of Freud's so obviously violating his own recommendations about detachment and neutrality. Subsequently, I have known of psychoanalysts who analyzed married couples—sometimes at the same time, more often not—and who reported sometimes good success and sometimes bad results.

David stressed to me that when he went to Vienna, Freud was in a different stage than in his earlier work. At one time, Freud had been in favor of relatively quick analyses, which lasted only a matter of months; but this was no longer the case, David pointed out, by the late 1920s. According to his version of things, the "interference" with his analysis came more from Freud and his "countertransference" to David, than from David's own so-called resistances. In David's judgment, Freud had been "prejudiced" against him; and David attributed this emotional problem on Freud's part to his having been told about David "beforehand" by both Mark and Ruth.

According to David, Freud knew the proper way for an analyst to behave, and yet he did not do it himself. At the outset of the analysis, Freud indicated that he thought that David should become an analyst. David had no intention of doing so. He expected that when he got back to the United States he would go into business. But Freud told him, "You must go to medical school." Freud's reasoning was that in America, despite his own views on the matter, one needed to be a physician in order to be an analyst. So in Vienna, on Freud's instructions, David started to go to medical school, only to drop out as he had already earlier done in America. David had no doubt that there were "neurotic reasons" behind his inability to go through with becoming a physician, but he also thought Freud had given him mistaken directions.

Once David had returned to America and moved to Los Angeles, he was urged by one of the members of the small psychoanalytic study group to become an analyst himself. At that time David wrote to Freud about his decision to become an analyst. In reply, David received a letter in Freud's German script, which was difficult to read; like some others that I talked to, David had been so unable to decipher it that he had to ask someone else, a professor, to translate it. When I asked David whether Freud had known that he could not read Freud's script, David answered "yes." Freud's written English was excellent, and he used it, for example, with his American relatives and even often Ernest Jones.

The letter from Freud turned out to be his acceptance of David as a practitioner: "That you have become an analyst is the right punishment for you." But David did not seem to enjoy any of the irony in Freud's communication. Surely Freud had known about David's dissatisfaction with how the analysis itself had gone; after Freud, David saw for further analyses Ernst Simmel, Otto Fenichel, Mrs. Deri, and finally Freud's daughter Anna in London. David was unhappy enough about the experience he had had with Freud to be unable to see any humor at all in Freud's joking about what course his career finally took.

I was interested in finding out whether Freud had conducted the analysis in English. David said that he could read German but could not understand spoken German. They started the analysis in English, later went to using German, and then switched back to English again. The idea of David's speaking German, like the suggestion that he go to medical school, was to him an aspect of Freud's punishing attitude. "If he said you must go to medical school, I went!" But he protested to me that he "did not need to be punished." In his view he had been "punished enough as a child."

Perhaps this fragment from David Brunswick's account of his analysis will be enough at least to awaken the reader's interest in the first-hand accounts of other patients about their contact with Freud. David Brunswick actually gave a recorded interview to Kurt R. Eissler for the Freud Archives, but that, like so much else, has been locked up; David's interview is not scheduled to be unrestricted until the year 2013. I assume that Eissler's interviewing of David elicited a different set of responses from my own. I think, though, that a transcript of David's interview with Eissler is likely to be as misleading as any other written document if it is detached from the full human context of both David's own relation to Freud and Eissler's position as a defender of orthodoxy.[15]

I am not sure I could begin, in the limited contact I had with David, to untangle the sibling rivalry between David and Mark; they also had a sister being analyzed in Vienna. But Mark, who was by far the more artistic of the two brothers, really struck my fancy as well as, I presume, Freud's. (Freud had declined to analyze Ruth's distinguished first husband, instead giving him the names of three alternative analysts.) Mark said that at the outset of David's analysis, Freud had complained to Mark: "What have you and Ruth done to me? Your brother is the most boring person!" Mark somehow thought that this comment of Freud's had not been good for his own analysis; on the other hand, it might have been viewed as an indiscretion that flattered Mark.

Mark certainly knew how significant it was that Freud had been an official witness at the wedding ceremony for his marriage to Ruth in 1928. The wedding took place after his first analysis was over and marked a special occasion in the history of psychoanalysis. Mark spoke with me relatively freely about his problems, including his symptoms, which he put into the context of his marriage to Ruth and his professional life. Freud started to write up a disguised version of Mark's case history shortly after Mark left Vienna just before Hitler annexed Austria.[16] Mark went on to be a professor of music at the City College of New York. Ruth died tragically in 1946 after finally being divorced from Mark; they had divorced once before in Vienna, and then, to Freud's displeasure, been remarried.

The Brunswick story is a complicated one, and I cannot pretend to have by any means thoroughly explored its implications. I am presenting it now because its complexities have held me back from adequately being appreciative of what some others have been doing in this field by examining Freud's published case histories. If Freud was capable of behaving this exceptionally with the Brunswicks, then what should one make of his written recommendations for others? Surely one cannot accept them as the unshakable rules some have taken them to be. One has to wonder, I think, about the status to accord the practices Freud rejected under the heading of so-called wild analysis. I am not sure myself whether how he worked with the Brunswicks was, in fact, mistaken or whether he was not doing better than other therapists of the day might have done. The story of the Brunswicks at least highlights Freud's dedication to helping, even after he had fallen ill. At the same time, it also demonstrates the hollowness of approaching Freud's work in terms of his own stated ambitions to become an abstract scientist.

I also want to point out that the fragmentary case history about Mark that Freud succeeded in writing up bears little resemblance to the man I met or to the problems that he thought were really troubling him. He might have had his marital and career difficulties, but these were not the parts of the case that Freud chose to highlight. Freud was fascinated with aspects of the case that another person might never have noticed. Of course, Freud did not complete much of a case history on Mark, and he was already extremely old; but he did leave it for posterity, and it has found its way into Freud's collected works.

I think I know enough about the mystery of human motives to remain nonjudgmental about Freud's treatment of the Brunswicks. His relationship to them has to be seen in historical perspective. Ruth's unfortunate decline was, of course, solely her own responsibility, even though Freud may have erred, as Mark thought, in first being too close to her and then trying to become distant. I am presenting this material about the Brunswicks in order to flesh out an account of what Freud was actually like in his conduct of analyses.

To write about Freud's five famous case histories in a vacuum would be, I think, a historiographical error. Dora's prematurely ending treatment, for example, makes me wonder if Freud really might not have wanted to rid himself of her as his patient. Freud may have been fascinated with what he thought he could make out of Dora's tale, but at some point he may have been through with her. In contrast to any rejection of Dora, Freud had been specially attracted by Ruth's intellectuality, and some in her family thought Freud liked working with her too much. Whatever Freud's errors with her, they arose, Mark thought, out of good will and "outgoingness."

I do not want to overdo the significance of the first-person accounts Freud's patients gave me. Freud's ideas do matter, and his texts are worthy of being looked at as literary works of art. But his writings need to be evaluated within the human and social context in which they originated. It was in keeping with Freud's own methodology that I started out in the mid-1960s to look for and learn from his former patients. I tried to listen even for the most unexpected material. I have stuck to this enterprise even for follow-ups with the children of Freud's former patients. I did not meet the daughter of Ruth and Mark until 1991; physically she looked just like the pictures of her mother, and she wore the antique ring that Freud had bestowed on her mother.

Silence has played a special and unfortunate part in the history of psychoanalysis. Over thirty years have passed since I first publicly disclosed Freud had analyzed his own daughter, Anna. Then again in 1975 I discussed the whole matter at greater length.[17] I knew that I was violating a taboo by opening up this issue, but I never realized that what Freud had done would still be so seldom mentioned. Until an official biography of Anna Freud appeared, there had never been any extended discussion of the matter of her analysis.[18] My own discovery of Anna's analysis by her father is pointedly ignored in her authorized biography, as is everything else I have written on the subject. Instead, Freud's analysis of his daughter is handled with kid gloves.

In this connection I would like to repeat a point I made in 1975. (Reviewers of books in this field sometimes claim to object to repetition, but in actuality there is no other way of getting across one's ideas since ideological considerations seem to drown out originality.) Of the many reasons for Freud's analyzing his own daughter, I would like to single out one: he was afraid of the damage that another analyst might do to Anna. I do not know whether it violates any current taboo to suggest that analysis might do harm, but I daresay any experienced psychoanalyst would agree that it can. I am not trying to defend Freud's violation of his own principles, but I think it worthwhile bringing up this matter once again.

The field of the history of psychoanalysis will receive academic acceptance only when past sectarianism has been laid to rest. All ideas, whatever their sources, deserve consideration; and the implications of Freud's encounter with the Brunswicks, as well as his analysis of Anna, need more attention. We need not fear that somehow Freud's stature will be diminished if he is looked at without the constraints of pious blinders. No loyalty barriers, nor considerations of trade unionism, should be part of research.

But we still have a long way to go before reaching ideal scholarly objectivity. As far as I am concerned, it is still too early, or too late, to approach Freud's work as pure science.[19] There are so many other matters to come to terms with that I am uninterested in looking at him through only the lenses of scientific methodology. He was struggling with the most intimate aspects of human loves and hates. And his greatness surely lies in his heroic attempt to try to say something noteworthy about the nature of human emotions. I think there is still a great deal more to be recounted and absorbed before we begin to judge the validity of Freud's work as seen from the dispassionate and detached perspective of "modern science." Freud was torn between being an artist and a scientist, and he dealt with that struggle in himself prophetically when he wrote his book about Leonardo.[20] For me, the strength of Freud's approach lies in his willingness to bring a profoundly humanistic bent to bear on empirical problems. Psychoanalysis will continue to attract interest because it has entered the ancient debate about how we ought to live. And it is on behalf of that quest for the good life that I think the first-person accounts of Freud's patients are of vital importance.

## Notes

1. Paul Roazen, "Review of Kiell, *Freud Without Hindsight: Review of his Work (1893-1939*), *Journal of the History of the Behavioral Sciences* (1990), pp. 197-202. See also below, pp. 429-434.
2. Freud, "From the History of an Infantile Neurosis," *Standard Edition*, Vol. 17, pp. 3-133.
3. Freud, "Fragment of an Analysis of a Case of Hysteria," *Standard Edition*, Vol. 7, pp. 7-122.
4. Freud, "Analysis of a Phobia in a Five-Year Old Boy," *Standard Edition*, Vol. 10, pp. 5-149.
5. Freud, "Notes Upon A Case of Obsessional Neurosis," *Standard Edition*, Vol. 10, pp. 155-318.
6. Freud, "Psychoanalytic Notes on an Auto-biographical Account of a Case of Paranoia (Dementia paranoides), *Standard Edition*, Vol.12, pp. 3-82.

7. Edoardo Weiss, *Sigmund Freud As A Consultant* (New York: Intercontinental Medical Book Corporation, 1970; with a new introduction by Paul Roazen, New Brunswick, NJ: Transaction, 1991), p. 81.
8. Freud, "An Outline of Psychoanalysis," *Standard Edition*, Vol. 23, pp. 141-207.
9. Celia Bertin, *Marie Bonaparte: A Life* (New York: Harcourt Brace Jovanovich, 1982), p. 176.
10. Paul Roazen, "The Freud Archives," *New York Review of Books*, November20, 1986, p. 59.
11. Ruth Mack Brunswick, "Supplement to Freud's 'History of an Infantile Neurosis,'" in *The Psychoanalytic Reader*, ed. Robert Fliess (New York: International Universities Press, 1948), pp. 65-103.
12. Paul Roazen, *Brother Animal: The Story of Freud and Tausk* (New York: Knopf, 1969; with new introduction, New Brunswick, NJ: Transaction, 1990). See also Paul Roazen, ed., *Victor Tausk, Sexuality, War, and Schizophrenia: Collected Psychoanalytic Papers* (New Brunswick, NJ: Transaction, 1991), pp. 1-31.
13. Paul Roazen, "Review of Gay, *Freud: A Life For Our Time*," *Psychoanalytic Books*, 1, pp. 10-17. See also below, pp. 245-247.
14. Lawrence Friedman, *Menninger* (New York: Knopf, 1990), p. 86.
15. Paul Roazen, "Reading, Writing, and Memory: K. R. Eissler's Thinking," *Contemporary Psychoanalysis*, 14, pp. 345-53; Paul Roazen, "Review of Eissler, *Freud As An Expert Witness*," *Contemporary Psychology*, 33, pp. 213-214; Paul Roazen, *Encountering Freud: The Politics and Histories of Psychoanalysis* (New Brunswick, NJ: Transaction, 1990), pp. 95-119; Paul Roazen, "Review of Eissler, *Three Instances of Injustice*," *The Forum*, American Academy of Psychoanalysis (Winter 1995).
16. Freud, "The Splitting of the Ego in the Process of Defence," *Standard Edition*, Vol. 23, pp. 275-78.
17. Paul Roazen, *Brother Animal*, *op. cit.*, p. 100. Paul Roazen, *Freud and His Followers* (New York: Knopf, 1975; New York: Da Capo, 1992), pp. 438-40. Cf. Also Paul Roazen "Freud's Analysis of Anna," in *The Death of Psychoanalysis: Murder, Suicide, Or Rumor Greatly Exaggerated*, ed. Robert Prince (Northvale, NJ: Jason Aronson, 1999.)
18. Paul Roazen, "Review of Young-Bruel's *Anna Freud: A Biography*," *Academy Forum*, 1990, pp. 22-23.
19. Paul Roazen, *Encountering Freud*, *op. cit.*, pp. 228-32.
20. Freud, "Leonardo Da Vinci and A Memory of His Childhood," *Standard Edition*, Vol. 11, pp. 59-137.

# 6

# What is a Fact? Eva Rosenfeld

The problem of evidence has to be of central concern for each kind of historian. As a field, history has been more receptive to psychoanalysis than other of the social sciences: since every narrative has implicitly to assume certain conceptions of human nature, and what might be plausible to suppose about motivation, historians have been sensitive to the existence of psychological systems of thought.

Often historians have been put off by excessive speculative claims made on behalf of psychoanalytic interpretations. Freud, and the early analysts, thought in terms of "applying" their work to history, as if the truth had been revealed and it were a secondary matter of high-level public relations to explain how these teachings could be applicable outside a clinical setting. At the beginning, psychoanalytic reasoning was marred, from the historical point of view, by a tendency reductionistically to highlight the more unsavory motives people might have. But at least in the second half of the twentieth century others, such as Erik H. Erikson, sought to concentrate on the higher aspects of ego functioning which organize, synthesize, and adapt our inner world to outer realities.

Although from the earliest analysts were interested in how their ideas could benefit outsiders, it has been rarer for the history of psychoanalysis to be itself subjected to critical scrutiny. Here, I will be trying to discuss the question of "What Is A Fact?" within the context of the history of analysis. There are quasi-philosophic issues connected with every attempt to reconstruct the past. Analysts of course are used to working clinically with the lives of patients, and necessarily become practicing historians of private life. Freud, however, got off on an unfortunate footing when he tried to divorce his work from philosophy itself; and he was repeatedly tempted to argue that he had unearthed facts, so-called discoveries, which were provable. (Carl Jung reasoned likewise about the status of his own work, although Jung, like Horney and Fromm, was not afraid to engage in explicit philosophizing.) To the extent that others could use Freud's ideas to reach conclusions that he would have repudiated, we can say that he had success in creating a science. Yet inevitably theoretical expectations shape the perception of facts. And it has taken many years since Freud's death in 1939 for analysts to feel comfortable with looking on interpretations in a more relational or relativistic light, as the product of an interaction between analyst and patient under given circumstances of a possibly transitory nature.

There are solid reasons for believing that this whole matter of facts, and how they can be established, should be of concern not only to scholars but to citizens as well. For history-writing, although ideally it should be undertaken in as dispassionate a spirit as possible, also inevitably serves partisan purposes. Strictly political history has sometimes encouraged the down-trodden and those who would combat oppression; and yet works of historical imagination have also been used to reinforce the powers-that-be of the status quo. Within psychoanalytic history I have tried to write on behalf of neglected figures, which has meant running afoul of various organizations' viewpoints. (In terms of my own profession of political science to be interested in Freud at all is to have committed a kind of heresy.) It makes sense that the past gets explained for the benefit of the present and the future, without one ever being licensed to turn into an agent of mere propaganda.

Freud was savvy about the power to be gained from formulating narratives about the development of his work and the various struggles he encountered in implementing his innovations. He put a considerable amount in print about not only the official opposition that he encountered, from within psychiatry for example, but he also retold frequently the tale of how he had been abandoned by a series of faint-hearted supporters. Starting with his mentor Josef Breuer, but including obviously students like Alfred Adler, Jung, and Otto Rank, Freud felt deserted by those he once helped and came to rely on. A whole mythology developed about these so-called defectors, and this legend served to underlie the "mainstream" of Freud's cause, binding together loyalists on his side. Freud's critics for their part rarely provided their own version of what had gone wrong between themselves and Freud, and cas I touched on in my "Introduction" Freud's own sharp polemics went comparatively unanswered.

Freud's account of the various controversies he became enmeshed in has continued to find echoes which reflect his own point of view, and the dissenting voices with the perspective they offer still represent a minority outlook. (Jungians feel they have to read Freud, but Freudians rarely know much about Jung, even though followers of his are now at the top of American best-seller lists.) Unfortunately it has remained true that people prefer to approach Freud in an all-or-nothing frame of mind; so even though Freud-bashing has hardly ceased to be fashionable, neither has professional credulity about the nature of the more famous psychoanalytic quarrels.

At the outset I should make plain my commitment to the old-fashioned belief in the existence of facts. The reality of the significance of such phenomena comes up, for example, each time a new volume of Freud's correspondence appears, and the publication of these texts is going to continue to take place over at least the next generation. Each of the books needs to be read with an eye cocked to the editorial apparatus accompanying the letters. For no matter how conscientious the editing is, and it has generally improved over the years, unfortunate errors seem to be inevitable. Given the youthfulness of both editors and translators, none of the people who crop up in Freud correspondences is likely to be known to contemporaries today. At least personal familiarity might put a check on certain kinds of mistakes. But as things stand foul-ups do continue to take place, and the problem is that once they occur they are likely to proliferate in the future.

To take just one small example, in Volume 1 of the Freud-Ferenczi letters we are told that in April of 1909 Freud was travelling with his younger brother Alexander and his sister-in-law Minna.[1] In reality Freud had simply written that he was on holiday with his brother and sister-in-law, and because of all the publicity that the supposed liaison between Freud and his wife's sister Minna has gotten, it can be too easily forgotten that Freud had a second sister-in-law, Alexander's wife Sophie. Alexander had gotten married in February 1909, and it would seem common sense to presume that by April he was travelling with his new wife and not the now more famous Minna. Each such presumed factual error may not in itself seem more than small potatoes, but cumulatively it can be unsettling to find out how many such erroneous propositions appear in print . I cannot hope to prove with whom, besides Alexander, Freud was holidaying in 1909, but the editor who authored the note in question has readily conceded that the likelihood is that it was Alexander's wife Sophie after all.

Any supposition that Freud was travelling with Minna in 1909 would help lend support to the whole conjecture that Freud was erotically entangled with her, a notion that I have not been able to share. But I would readily concede that it is the historian's job to sort through facts, deciding what is relevant as opposed to that which can be discarded. Such decisions, even if taken implicitly and without forethought, can require exquisite judgment-making. Amy delicate evaluations have to follow from beliefs and values which serve to make sense of facts. Raw evidence itself can never instruct historians in how to order it, and selection can be an almost artistic choice which defies simple rationalistic procedures which are easy to follow. The principles that historians invoke to make the past meaningful are part and parcel of preconceptions which are often moral, ethical, and political, if not down-right intuitive and incapable of being fully justified.

In the case of psychoanalysis, history-writing serves many sorts of unspoken purposes. If for example one were set on blackening Freud's reputation, the more of an involvement with Minna that can be shown the darker the picture would become. For by the social and religious standards of Freud's world, he would have been engaged in gratifying an incestuous temptation. It is not necessary to underestimate how significant a person in his life Minna was to draw a line between an actual physical relationship as opposed to a genuine emotional dependence.

A similar-seeming issue arose in the course of my interviewing Dr. Edith Jackson in 1966. Thirty years earlier she had had a lengthy analysis with Freud, and went on to be a psychoanalytic psychiatrist. Before seeing her I had been told in passing that she had had an affair with Freud's eldest son Martin. I could not bluntly bring up the issue with Dr. Jackson, but I talked around it, mainly by inquiring about the Freud family and Martin, so that she grew distinctly chilly in that context about what I might be implying.

My indirect line of questions, after discussing many other matters connected with her analysis, did elicit the firm memory that Freud had forbidden her to have sexual relations during the course of the treatment. She always remained unmarried, and appeared spinster-like in demeanor; but she claimed to have been resentful at the restriction Freud imposed on her, one which I never found reported by any of the other patients of Freud's that I met.

In 1969, without mentioning Dr. Jackson's name since she and Martin were still alive, I put in print that there had been an affair between a Freud patient and a Freud son.[2] D. M. Thomas in his *The White Hotel* (1981) built his novel around the existence of such an unusual situation. Whether or not the relationship was really a consummated one may never be known. But Anna Freud, his youngest child, was deeply offended by the book of mine in which that issue of a Freud son being erotically involved with a patient of his father's came up, and she wrote a lengthy private critique of my text as a whole. But she did not choose to comment on the possibility that her Don Juan brother might have been romantically involved with someone whom she had to have known was Dr. Jackson. She also did not object to my having said, in the same book of mine, that she had been analyzed by her father, an analytic secret which subsequently has been confirmed by abundant independent evidence. By my writing while such people were still alive, I was consciously sticking my neck out in the hope that living witnesses could refute or corroborate what I said; if I had waited until everyone were dead there would be less chance of getting any kind of feedback from the participants concerned.

In order to investigate further the problem of facts I would like to turn to the specific historiographical problems associated with the life of Eva Rosenfeld (1892-1977), and how it might be possible to use a series of different perspectives, from an unusual variety of sources, in order to follow her career. One recent book, written by two distinguished British intellectuals, goes so far as to maintain: "Among the Vienna-based women who moved in Freud's and Anna's orbit, Eva Rosenfeld was, next to Ruth Mack Brunswick, Freud's undoubted favorite."[3] Such a position, put forward by Lisa Appignanesi and John Forrester, might be capable of being sustained, although since we know so little about Ruth Brunswick it can seem secondary to be moving on to Eva Rosenfeld. Helene Deutsch was far more productive than either of the other two women, but she was independent enough to try to steer at a relative distance from Freud's most immediate circle, and, unlike Eva and Ruth, Helene never received the gift of a signet ring from Freud. Eva was a remarkable woman, and I found her to be especially frank and outspoken in the course of interviews, so it should be important to keep straight, as best we can, what her standing was vis-à-vis Freud.

Let me begin by quoting from a letter Freud sent to Eva when she had written him about the possibility of her having a further analysis, following ones under Freud and also Felix Boehm, with Melanie Klein. (Eva's son dates the letter from 1937,[4] but Appignanesi and Forrester place it in 1936.) Eva was a practicing analyst living in London by then, having moved from Berlin in 1936; Klein was in those days much sought after as a clinician, supervisor, and theoretical guide. For years, however, Klein had been involved in a heated controversy with Anna Freud over the practices and theories of child analysis; and Freud was convinced that Klein's work represented a disguised assault on himself. Since by today Kleinianism has become a central part of British analysis, it is not easy for most analysts there, and the academic community friendly to them, to want to acknowledge just how heretical Freud found Klein to have been.

Appignanesi and Forrester had been in touch with me prior to the publication of their book, and asked me what I made of Freud's letter. It was conscientious of them to inquire about my views, and I wrote back as best I could. It had been through the intercession of her intimate friend Anna Freud that Eva had first been analyzed in 1929 (and off and on a bit later), so Eva's choice of Klein as an analyst was a serious matter. Evidently, Eva was considering either a four-week analysis back with Freud or one with Klein. Appignanesi and Forrester, writing with my own information silently in mind, observed: "Although certain commentators have implied that Freud resentfully cut her off when she decided on Klein, his letter to her reads rather more like an attempt to allow her to think the matter through clearly for herself and points her in the direction of Klein, a direction, he suggests, she has already decided on. It is a telling reminder of Freud's impartiality, at least towards some of his friends and former patients."[5] Since I think this conclusion, as well as the chain of reasoning, is all wrong, I will first quote the letter of Freud's that is in question, and then explain why I disagree that it means anything like how it has been described in print.

> There are other aspects of the matter to consider, one that could prove disagreeable to you, another that could prove disagreeable for me. You know what my attitude toward Melanie Klein's work is. I too think that she has found something new, but I don't know if it means quite so much as she believes, and I am certain that she has no right to use it to place theory and technique on a new basis. Our four weeks would naturally attempt critically to unravel what you have found in yourself to confirm the Kleinian theories. It is possible that I might bring you to another judgment of these things. Then you would go back to London and find youself in opposition to the circle and direction

> of work when you would manifestly prefer to stay in tune with both. On the other hand, it wouldn't be possible for you to hide from the English group the influence that you have experienced through me, and that would kindle an antagonism I have gone out of my way up until now to avoid.
>
> The other possibility, that in four weeks you would convince me of the fundamental significance and correctness of Kleinian findings, I do not really think is a probable outcome. I think then that the piece of inner work that is now thrust upon you, the resolution of your intellectual allegiance as well as of your father and mother influence, is something that you will have to sort out without help, at least without mine. Because as always I take a lively interest in your destiny, I am naturally unhappy that such a problem should have posed itself, particularly for you.[6]

Freud, in turning aside Eva's request that she once again come into analysis with him over a holiday, was replying with patience and tact. He assumes she already knows that he would try his best to undermine the bases for her interest in Klein's "findings." He allowed himself so many words, in refusing Eva, that it can be possible to miss his central thrust in the midst of his Viennese manners. Freud could at times, when he wanted to, be brutal in turning a supplicant aside; he rejected the entreaties of seeing someone like Herbert Silberer,[7] or analyzing Victor Tausk,[8] and both men, for different reasons of their own, ended up as suicides. Eva was not of the intellectual rank to match Silberer or Tausk, but she was an unhappy and troubled former patient of his, and above all an old friend of his daughter Anna. Freud was trying to let Eva down carefully, and one has to read between-the-lines as to his real meaning. Others may disagree with my reasoning, but I want to present it in contrast to Appignanesi and Forrester who do not seem willing or able to acknowledge just how much Freud "loathed" (to quote from one of my interviews with Eva) Klein and what she stood for.

At the same time, Freud was politic enough not to want to risk alienating the British supporters analysis had attracted. When Freud broke with Jung, it had meant the loss of almost the whole of analysis in Switzerland. British analysis was under the leadership of Ernest Jones, a long-standing ideological ally of Freud's who happened to be most sympathetic to Klein's point of view. From Eva's perspective she had reason to share Freud's desire for peace; to cross him (or Anna) absolutely would threaten her professional practice. Jung complained he had been clinically ruined by Freud for years.

Freud was, at length to be sure, saying No to Eva; he did not want to analyze her again, and he was putting that in a hand-written note as opposed to dictating a letter to be typed-up by Anna, who had long been acting as his secretary. It was widely known how during the past years Klein had been making Anna Freud's life unpleasant, both in print and at conferences. Freud turned eighty years old in 1936, and was weakened by a thirteen-year-old struggle with his cancer of the jaw. By then he was more dependent than ever on Anna's care and attention. He was as closely identified with her standing as she with his. Freud felt protectively about Anna, wanting to ensure her future within analysis after his death; yet he did not want to encourage any open polemics with Klein, since he felt too feeble for ideological battling like he had once engaged in. Both Adler and Jung, for instance, had turned – in his view – against himself; Freud's personal affection for Rank was such that Freud rarely answered him by name. Freud had learned not to enhance anyone's reputation by denouncing them. In Klein's case it was possible for Freud to evade an outright confrontation with her.

Freud was making of Eva's interest in Klein a question of "allegiance"; he was also finding an emotional, psychoanalytic matter when he contrasted the "father or mother influence." In his view, her interest in Klein was psychologically motivated by her problem with men, which he had attributed to her bad relationship with her father. He was making an *ad hominem* point about her attraction to Klein's theories being based on unresolved inner conflicts. Freud's silence about what Eva's turning to Klein had to mean to Anna herself is in itself notable, although reasoning from the absence of evidence can be notoriously misleading. One wonders what Anna's response might have been if Eva had been instead writing to her for another analysis.

Appignanesi and Forrester, in their account of Freud's rejection of Eva's request, are in my opinion unsound. They observe: "If Freud seems altogether sanguine here, and more concerned about Eva than about psychoanalytic politics, then it is more than possible that Anna, on the other hand, took her decision to begin a Kleinian analysis as a sign of betrayal."[9] How on earth do these scholars think that it can be possible to drive such an interpretive wedge between what Anna felt and how Freud reacted? These two people had developed an almost symbiotic tie, and it is far-fetched to think that if Anna considered herself betrayed, Freud did not respond in her behalf similarly.

Not long after Freud's death the so-called Controversial Discussions broke out within the British Psychoanalytic Society, and Klein's local enemies thought that with the support of the Viennese analysts who had emigrated to London it might be possible to curb her power, and the influence she was threatening to exert on future analytic training.[10] Eva did stay back, as Appignanesi and Forrester note, from the worst of the quarrelling. But if the Viennese Willi Hoffer could ever, in a passage they do not document, have gotten into "an attack of fury" against whatever Eva had been saying, he, as an ally of Anna's, must have felt the presence of Eva's Kleinianism. (In 1962 Eva published the official obituary of Hoffer's wife.) That Klein herself did not accept Eva as an apostle of her own only means that Eva's moderation had not succeeded in appeasing Klein's need for strict adherents.

These early analysts, following Freud's lead, were engaging in theologically tinged differences. It is, I think, no disrespect to any of these analysts to contend that they were battling over rival conceptions of how the good life ought to be lived. Just as Adler represented one moral approach, and Jung another ethical perspective, so did both Rank and Wilhelm Reich. In the case of Klein, one needs to plow through the pages of the Controversial Discussions to see just exactly how rare were the clinical examples that ever got brought up. Klein had an almost messianic fervor that she was being more royal than the king, following up Freud's principles more strictly than the founder himself. Reich, in his own work, shared a similar belief, although he was going in the direction of sexual emancipation and family reform.

I do not want to give too central a place to that one letter of Freud's to Eva, but an understanding of it, in contrast to Appignanesi and Forrester's version, does pave the way to the different sorts of pieces of evidence that have accumulated. A volume of Anna Freud's letters to Eva has been published, and that correspondence bears directly on the problems we have been talking about. It makes sense when the editor tells us that in their later years (1946-1977), the letters on the part of Anna were confined "to brief and/or business-like communications, while Eva continues on a largely unrequited quest for their former intimacy." The extent of Anna's own commitment to analysis can be inferred from her having written Eva in 1929, when she was about to begin her analysis with Freud, that "being good and being in analysis finally amount to the same thing."[11]

Eva's son could openly write how the "one great gash, deliberately—some would say provocatively—inflicted by my mother was her ripening friendship with Melanie Klein." In 1929 Anna had been capable of writing Eva: "you are I and I am you and any part of me that you can use, you must always take, because you have a right to it." In 1947 Eva wrote to Anna in an allusion to her going to Klein; Eva referred to "how much I hurt you in 1938."[12]

Still another source of information, in addition to Freud's own letter and the correspondence between Anna and Eva, has to be the hundreds of pages of an unpublished autobiography that Eva undertook. Scholars have grown used to treating such explicit self-disclosures with caution, whereas we are tempted, I think, to believe that letters are a private form of communication that rank ahead of formal publications. As Freud's various correspondences come out, it will be increasingly tempting to think of them as at least as authoritative as what he saw into print during his lifetime.

Eva's autobiography communicates a lot of information about her background and conflicts, but she only glancingly touches on the sensitive matter of her having turned to Klein for analysis. "I inflicted on myself a horrible wound—I felt that my interest in Melanie Klein's teaching estranged me from Freud in the eyes of the analytic world, and I felt an outcast." Eva went on diplomatically: "it is due to Anna's dignified and human attitude toward me that I never was made to feel that I lost her friendship." I find it hard to believe, knowing the story up to now and how relatively distant Anna held herself from Eva, that we should not take these words of Eva with the proverbial grain of salt. Eva concluded what little she had to say about this incident by admitting: "But I lost a position and that is the lot of many independent persons."[13]

Eva added autobiographically that before she had started analytically with Klein, Eva had written "about my problem to Professor Freud. He wisely thought, since I would not convince him in Mrs. Klein's favor, I had better solve this problem myself. I did in the course of many painful years." Eva tried to limit the scope of her defection, and she quoted Mrs. Klein as having said to her once: "You have sacrificed your analysis to the friendship with Anna Freud."[14]

Still a further source of evidence consisted in my series of interviews with Eva, which took place in the mid-1960s, at the same time I was seeing people like Edith Jackson and Anna Freud. (Eva told me she had seen Kurt Eissler for the Freud Archives, and that he had been interested in finding out Freud's views of Klein; this material remains sealed until the year 2008.) It is awfully hard to pin down exactly what one learns from any such interviewing experience, aside of course from getting to know her as a person. I read to Eva, late in our contact, the then unpublished letter of Freud's addressed to Lou Andreas-Salomé following Tausk's death. This letter was new to me, and still seems startling in its lack of compassion. Eva chimed in that Freud had once been through with her, too, meaning as a result of her going to Klein.

Freud's real feelings may have been muffled in the generous-sounding way that he wrote to Eva, yet she was in no doubt what she had lost. She continued to see him on occasion after he moved to London in 1938, but the former intimacy was affected. He even saw Melanie Klein, all the while he was telling someone like Edward Glover that it was the first time a so-called deviant had been able to be held within the analytic movement. Within a short time Glover, who had once been influenced by Klein's ideas, had joined with Anna Freud in doing battle against Kleinianism within the British Psychoanalytic Society. To repeat a point made earlier, today's British analysts are apt to feel uncomfortable acknowledging just how standoffish Freud was about Klein's work. He might have cited her, but those who knew him were aware how he really felt about what he regarded as psychoanalytic heresy. But here I have to rely on my own interviewing of Glover, which once again cannot be made fully demonstrable. As I hope to have shown, the written word has its own ways of being misleading.

I feel confident that Eva's letters to me tell a different aspect of the story I have sought to try to communicate. After my *Freud: Political and Social Thought* came out in 1968, I sent Eva a copy, and she responded in accord with her enthusiastic nature. She was of course pleased that I had quoted her at one point; her technical papers, the few she published, would of course make another source for biographical evidence. It is worth noting that she had told me in interviews that when she had shown Jones what she had written about Freud, quoting him from her analysis when she was living with him in the same house on holiday, Jones had insisted that she take out the fact of her residence with the family. Jones also did not approve of Eva's interpretation of Freud's childhood nanny, and how it might bear on Freud's later anti-religious beliefs, since Jones was the kind of atheist who did not find anything lacking in Freud's own approach to religion.

In 1956 Eva had given a talk about Freud, on the occasion of the centenary of his birth, for the British Broadcasting Corporation. I could find nothing that Anna might have objected to in what she said, when I read a copy of the transcript years later at the Library of Congress, but then it is impossible to predict the subtle sensitivities of family members. Eva's son, fully loyal to Anna, realized that his mother, "talkative and indiscreet," was "a threat" to Anna. "And she had intimate knowledge of family matters quite apart from the letters. In a broadcast talk Eva gave for BBC she reminisced harmlessly about the Freuds. Anna's wrath was quite disporportionate to the offense and suggests deeper apprehensions: if anecdotes today, why not letters tomorrow?"[15]

Based on my knowledge of what Eva was like, I would guess that Anna knew how frank (and disloyal) Eva could be. Eva's going to Klein for that analysis must have been the culmination of years of frustration; Dorothy Burlingham had displaced Eva as Anna's most intimate friend, and Eva's treason-seeming act (likely not the first) was one that Anna could never forgive. Eva might outwardly maintain her links with Anna, and she was on excellent terms with Anna's older sister Mathilda; but in the course of what Eva told me about Anna she was uninhibited and strikingly irreverent.

Eva was nonetheless shocked by the 1969 appearance of my *Brother Animal: The Story of Freud and Tausk*. She wrote me at length about it in 1970. I believe the timing of her contact with me was occasioned by the news of the birth of my first child. After congratulating me, she moved on to the problem of my new book:

> It is excellently written and very well argued, but why did you write it while the family of Freud is still alive? It is both embarrassing and misleading to those who read it today and feel glad to put their knife into the old man. For myself I must say that if you had told me that you intend such a book when we had our confidential talks, I would not have provided you with the material I did.

In reality I had broken off the story of Tausk while engaged on the writing of my *Freud and his Followers*, which only appeared in 1975. If I had not separated the Tausk tale it would have threatened to assume too large dimensions over my larger study of Freud's circle.

Eva claimed to have specific grounds for objecting to *Brother Animal*:

> Not because there is anything wrong in a great man having his faults and angers, but because it amounts now to just a scandal story which only unpleasant people will relish. You must forgive me for being so frank with you, I consider you a friend and I would blame myself if I did not tell you the echo that this book will have. A book about Tausk would have been interesting, even though you could not have known him and also his family are still alive, but the title as a story of Freud and Tausk is really most unpleasant.

Today's readers should remember that that book had come out before the wave of revisionist scholarship which followed in the next decades, and prior to the appearance of Henri Ellenberger's *The Discovery of the Unconscious* in 1970. *Brother Animal* could be read at one long sitting, while Ellenberger's encyclopedic-like text changed people's minds in a different and slower way. I had been hoping that *Brother Animal* would be understood as an expresion of my interest in historiography, as I had been trying to put Tausk back into the history books. To Eva, however, who doubtless by then knew Anna Freud's own horror at the book, I had failed completely.

Eva could not restrain herself from psychoanalytic inquiry:

> One must ask oneself: what was really your purpose, we are all much too well informed about the storms of a person's life as to need to be told it once again in the shape of a man who disliked quick intuition and intelligence because he found it ruinous to scientific progress. In a sense that was his greatness. I did not admire his personality, but you had to admire his work and there is time enough to criticise him when all those who knew him will not read your book any more. I suppose you will get many angry letters. I hope also admiring ones, because your penetration into the subject is, of course, admirable.

Eva welcomed me to see her once again "so to make sure we are still friends." I replied to Eva not as someone who had been of historical importance, but as a human being who had helped my research yet seemed blinded by Freud idolatry. I wrote her, in a passage later quoted in the book of Anna Freud's correspondence with her, that "a great man is all of a piece, the good with the bad, one cannot have the one without the other."[16]

Eva replied pursuing her understanding of the problem with my book. "Yes, the title is misleading." (I had taken "brother-animal" from an eloquent passage about Tausk in Lou Andreas-Salomé's diary of her stay in Freud's Vienna.)

> In German the word "Brudertier" means something close and almost tender. The translation into English transforms it into a nasty word, meaning "we are both no better than animals." I would have called the book "Tausk, the..." and then some important word giving him his due. But the two names and the pictures shown together like in a correspondence (see Freud-Zweig) is journalistic and whets the appetites of gossipmongers.

Eva was obviously having second thoughts about what she had written to me at first.

> I regret that I wrote to you: "I did not admire, etc. etc." What I meant was, there is never a complete identity between a man and his genius, that is why we need not admire his person whilst having the greatest admiration for what he gave and will give to the world. Had you delved into the tragedy more of Freud's loneliness and Tausk's torment, then you would have written a history of an unavoidable struggle of a genius manqué, i.e. Tausk the psychotic (?) and Freud the inexorable, and we would have learned once again what we have known all through history (see Beethoven, Durer etc. etc.) that those are not loved who follow their inner tyrant.

*Brother Animal* described what then seemed to me an unusual form of human enmeshment, as Freud had rejected Tausk for an analysis but sent him instead to a newcomer, Helene Deutsch, who was herself in analysis with Freud. It was a few months after Freud gave Helene, one of my prime sources, the choice between ending her own treatment or dismissing Tausk that he committed suicide. Eva, as an analyst, tried to put her own professional understanding to work:

> Have you—may I ask—experienced analysis from the inside? If so you will know—and if not you cannot know what final destruction an analysis with Freud would have brought to Tausk. The only hope was for someone else to undertake the task, and H. Deutsch was probably as good as anybody. It is more true to say: at least Freud must have felt that he still keeps an eye on this promising but daemonic fellow.

My argument was that the Tausk-Deutsch-Freud set-up had helped worsen Tausk's considerable problems even if it provided Freud a measure of control.[17]

Eva was obviously stung by other aspects of *Brother Animal*:

> Whether Freud analysed his daughter or whether I lived in their house in Grundlsee is not relevant to the story of Tausk, it is only incomprehensible to the young generation who has not our stamina, cannot imagine how *free* we were in spite of vicinity and that of course rules are made for the *masses* not for *individuals*.

Eva was arguing that Freud's special technical licenses, at odds with his written therapeutic recommendations, ought to be tolerated; in the context of those years then I thought it important that these exceptions had never been publicly revealed before *Brother Animal*.

Tausk's death bothered Eva, as it did others, but she somehow spared the founder of psychoanalysis from any share in the tragedy:

> Tausk's suicide was only insofar connected with Freud as he probably murdered Freud within himself, but to come home from the War penniless, engaged to be married, yet tied to wife and children is plenty of reason in reality. In my eyes it was a very clever solution!

Eva was not the only analyst to want Tausk to vanish. The problem for orthodox Freudians was that if Tausk had been psychotic, Freud and Helene Deutsch should not have treated him that way, but if he was only neurotic he should not have killed himself.

At the time I wrote the book I had worried that Helene Deutsch would react badly to the paragraphs in which I described her own unwitting involvement in Tausk's undoing, but she responded, as Eva did too, with concern over how I might have damaged Freud's reputation. Eva continued:

> Freud was a simple and shy human being, he did not surround himself with the aura of greatness, admirations embarrassed him, the aura of his shy lonely simplicity was often mistaken for the opposite.

> I knew him well. I observed him closely when he was old. He fought for analysis, but he did not grant us the pleasure of admiring "a great man."
>
> And now goodbye and good luck. Please don't quote me as saying "I did not admire…" he did not wish any admiration.

(That sensitive passage from her letter to me appeared first in the 1992 edition of Anna's letters to Eva.)

By June Eva was intrigued to know more about what my research had come upon. I must have alluded in letter-writing to Ruth Brunswick:

> Do you mean to say that Ruth committed suicide? I never heard that. Was *she* your first analyst? I only heard that she had a fall, an accident in her bathroom. I never questioned this. It happened the night before the Princess Bonaparte was due in New York. Do please tell me what is rumour and what fact!

Despite how Eva had reacted to *Brother Animal*, her own appetite for information had been aroused. And, however much she disapproved of the way that book had presented its material, she still trusted me enough to ask about the circumstances surrounding Ruth Brunswick's early death at a time, incidentally, when I was a young boy.

In September, Eva was thinking about writing on Frederick the Great and his France-loving son: "to write about dead people is so rewarding. They can't tell us that we are wrong; it is as if we put them under an anaesthetic and then we can cut about and they don't feel anything." Eva thought that Voltaire's late book on Frederick the Great, "his erstwhile friend," was "a little bit like" my *Brother Animal*: "One cannot help regretting that he wrote it. So there you get scolded again," as she closed with "cordial greetings." I had evidently asked how others had responded to *Brother Animal*, and Eva replied:

> You asked me whether nobody like the book "Brother Animal." I must sincerely answer that nobody did. Now I wonder very much what the next one is about, but I shall not take up your time by asking you to give me advance information. I shall wait patiently until it appears and I only hope that my name has vanished in case it is a book about Freud. You cannot well imagine what an unimportant little speck of dust I am in that circle.

To Appignanesi and Forrester, Eva was hardly a "little speck of dust." And whatever Eva and the oldest group of analysts in London might have thought, some of my reviews in England were absolutely excellent.

Kurt Eissler had in 1971 published the first of two books criticizing *Brother Animal*, and I sent Eva a 1972 reply[18] that I finally found a journal brave enough to be willing to publish.

> Your article is of course very well thought out and I hope you understand that there must be zealous people like Kurt Eissler. There must be non-belligerent souls like me, but I think, I *still* think that the role you took upon yourself in writing "Brother Animal" was to your disadvantage as well as that it gave us "dismay." It is not unusual that an

> unhappy man will commit suicide, but nobody needs to get the blame for it explicitly. That was not wise of you to imply, because it means that you expect somewhere "perfection". I don't and never have.

"As a punishment" for my "misdeeds" she talked about sending me her autobiographical memoirs, but she specified that they were about herself, not Freud.

In 1973, when I was finishing my *Freud and His Followers*, I needed help in identifying some of the people in the group photograph of analysts taken at the 1929 Oxford Congress. Eva agreed to help me, although she was not able to "guarantee" to be right about who was who. "In any case do *not* use my name, the Freud ladies would be *very* angry with me." Eva was alluding to Anna and Mathilda. Eva could not help wondering whether I might be up to "some mischief." I suspect that Eva must have written something nice about me to Anna, who at the time was throwing up roadblocks in the form of the Freud Copyrights to prevent me from getting the right to reprint photographs – unless I were willing to show them the manuscript prior to publication. It was, I think, in this context that Anna wrote Eva in 1974: "All I can say is that Roazen is a menace whatever he writes."[19]

The contact that I had with Eva (and Anna's 1974 letter) is a source of some pride to me, and I am happy that Eva gave me enough material about her analysis with Freud to include her in a chapter in my 1995 *How Freud Worked: First-Hand Accounts of Patients*.[20] If I had succeeded with Eva, despite how she reacted to *Brother Animal*, I would like to think that my own respect for her combined with her own qualities as a peacemaker to lead to that happy outcome. I always thought that my own natural deference to these elderly analysts was a help in overcoming what reticences they might have had about being interviewed. Henry James's "The Aspern Papers" is a nightmarish reminder of how biographical sleuthing can miscarry. In James's short story the narrator has been in quest of documents possessed by the former mistress of a great poet; only towards the end did he come close to his booty, but she foiled him finally. The passage when she fully realized what he had been after has to be permanently sobering for historians to think on:

> her hands were raised, she had lifted the everlasting curtain that covered half her face, and for the first, the last, the only time I beheld her extraordinary eyes. They glared at me; they were like the sudden drench, for a caught burglar, of a flood of gaslight; they made me horribly ashamed. I shall never forget her strange little bent white tottering figure, with its lifted head, her attitude, her expression; neither will I forget the tone in which as I turned, looking at her, she hissed out passionately, furiously: "Ah you publishing scoundrel!"[21]

It was Eva who first taught me that Freud had had in mind that psychoanalysis be "a moral medal," and she was convinced that he harbored ethical purposes alongside scientific ones. I was in part attracted to psychoanalysis because of its great bearing on the age-old questions concerned with how we ought to live. Eva herself was sensitive to the legitimacy of religious questions;

and one of her papers was on the problem of Moses, and she returned to the theme of Freud as a Jew in a 1956 essay.[22] I suspect that Eva knew that this was a side to the creator of psychoanalysis that Anna would not have appreciated being explored. (Klein had a religious dimension to her thinking, communicated by her concept of the "depressive position," that had helped to attract Eva in the first place.) According to the early view, psychoanalysis was a neutral body of knowledge detached from cultural influences. And if Freud's Jewishness was a problem for some of his first disciples, more recently Jacques Lacan's Catholicism has been a troubling issue for the French psychoanalytic community.[23]

The historian then has an awesome task: similar to Flaubert's conception of the artist, who was supposed to be like God, present everywhere yet visible nowhere, historians aim for the greatest degree of detachment. In my own case, having been so involved in research with the help of people like Eva, it would be phony to try and pretend to be exempt from inevitable personal bias. Yet at the same time I did struggle, I hope, to be as objective as humanly possible. I remain committed to the importance of the ideal of impartiality, no matter how difficult it may be to succeed.

Goethe is supposed to have maintained that "every fact is a passion," and people do perceive reality in the light of special expectations and values. As a result, history gets written in a way that is bound to become capricious. Yet at the same time there has to be a line differentiating partisanship from the pursuit of truth. One should be obliged to explain the different kinds of sources one has relied on, and something about one's own relationship to the way in which material has been accumulated. Even if omniscence may be humanly impossible, at the same time the ideal of objectivity remains a worthwhile one.

I have tried to suggest how one goes about ordering the different set of sources about Eva. It is hardly a scientific process by which one weighs every bit of historical factuality as part of the competing possibilities of interpretation. I hope to have helped establish that publications can be at least as misleading as oral testimony at its most unreliable. I have reason to suspect that Eva may have been even more upset with *Brother Animal* than she wrote me. But I am presenting this collection of material in order to show how it is inevitable that contrasting evidence does not automatically fit together without requiring judgments to make sense of the past.

George F. Kennan, in a beautiful little 1959 paper on "History As Literature," gave an example from his own work. On the concluding page of the second volume of his study of Soviet-American relations, he described the departure of one of the last American semi-officials from Soviet territory in 1918. He and his companion were stopped for awhile on a railroad bridge to Finland. Kennan used extraordinary literary talent in reconstructing the scene, which included the presence of "a tethered nanny goat, indifferent to all the ruin and all the tragedy," who "nibbled patiently at the sparse dying foliage...."

In reflecting on what he had done, Kennan wrote:

> I confess that if I were asked whether I could prove that the goat was actually there, the answer would be that I could not. I never saw such a scene in Russia *without* a goat...It was the last of a thousand pages on this subject, and the chafing of three years of academic restraint may have inclined me, I fear, to a brief fling of scientific indiscipline.[24]

Kennan was right in supposing that written history is a form of literature at the same time that it retains unique canons of its own. As the historian Carl Becker once put it, "to set forth historical facts is not comparable to dumping a barrow of bricks."[25] The issue of Eva Rosenfeld's perceived disloyalty to Freud can be taken, in Kennan's terms, as my modest goat. Betrayal and desertion have to be understood in the special light of the conflicts in the history of psychoanalysis. By my supplying various perspectives in connection with Eva Rosenfeld I am trying to make it possible that future researchers will be able to make use of my own work for achieving different results, at the same time that I am attempting to say something about the nature of historiography itself.

## Notes

1. *The Correspondence of Sigmund Freud and Sandor Ferenczi*, Vol. 1, ed. Eva Brabant, Ernst Falzeder, and Patrizia Giampieri-Deutsch; trans. by Peter T. Hoffer (Cambridge, MA: Harvard University Press, 1993), pp. 52-53.
2. Paul Roazen, *Brother Animal: The Story of Freud and Tausk* (New York: Knopf, 1969; New Brunswick, NJ: Transaction, 1990, with new Introduction), p. 41.
3. Lisa Appignanesi and John Forrester, *Freud's Women* (New York: Basic Books, 1992), p. 380.
4. Peter Heller, *Anna Freud's Letters to Eva Rosenfeld*, translated by Mary Weigand (Madison, CT: International Universities Press, 1992), p. 45.
5. Appignanesi and Forrester, *op. cit.*, p. 383.
6. *Ibid.*
7. Paul Roazen, *Freud and His Followers* (New York: Knopf, 1975; New York: Da Capo, 1992), pp. 338-41.
8. Roazen, *Brother Animal, op. cit.*
9. Appignanesi and Forrester, *op. cit.*, p. 383.
10. Paul Roazen, "Book review of King and Steiner, eds., *The Freud-Klein Controversies*," *Psychoanalytic Books*, Fall 1992. See also Paul Roazen, *Oedipus in Britian: Edward Glover & The Struggle Over Klein* (N.Y.: Other Press, 2000).
11. Heller, *op. cit.*, pp. ix, 112.
12. *Ibid.*, pp. 44, 116, 182.
13. Eva Rosenfeld, *Recollected in Tranquillity* (unpublished), Ch. 24.
14. *Ibid.*
15. Heller, *op. cit.*, p. 46.
16. *Ibid.*, p. 71. Cf. Also Peter Heller, "Trois lettres d'Anna Freud a Eva Rosenfeld," *Revue Internationale d'Histoire de la Psychanalyse*, Vol. 6 (1993), p. 490.
17. Paul Roazen, "Presence de Victor Tausk dans la correspondance Freud-Ferenczi," *Etudes freudiennes*, September 1993.
18. Paul Roazen, "Reflections on Ethos and Authenticity in Psychoanalysis," *The Human Context*, Autumn 1972; Paul Roazen, *Encountering Freud: The Politics and*

*Histories of Psychoanalysis* (New Brunswick, NJ: Transaction, 1990), pp. 95-108.

19. Paul Roazen, *Meeting Freud's Family* (Amherst: University of Massachusetts Press, 1993), p. 201.
20. Paul Roazen, *How Freud Worked: First-Hand Accounts of Patients* (Northvale, NJ: Jason Aronson, 1995), Ch. 8.
21. Charles Neider, ed., *Short Novels of the Masters* (New York: Rinehart, 1948), p. 370.
22. Eva Rosenfeld, "The Pan-Headed Moses," *International Journal of Psychoanalysis*, Vol. 32 (1951), pp. 83-93; Eva Rosenfeld, "Dream and Vision," *International Journal of Psychoanalysis*, Vol. 37 (1956).
23. Paul Roazen, "Lacan's First Disciple: An Interview with Lacan's Brother," *Journal of Religion and Health*, Winter 1996.
24. George F. Kennan, "History As Literature," *Encounter*, April 1959, p. 14.
25. Carl L. Becker, *Everyman His Own Historian* (New York: Appleton-Century-Crofts, 1935), p. 251.

# Part 3

## Letters

# Introduction to Part 3

It would be hard to overemphasize just how important, and yet potentially misleading, letters can be. They provide an immediate-seeming window into a writer's life and thought, and Freud was as passionate as anybody in intellectual history with his devotion to his correspondences. It still remains an open question how in any particular instance one should weigh these private reflections. We need to ask to what extent these letters were intended for the recipient alone, for posterity, or for a combination of both. Freud's personal relationship with each of the recipients of his letters was a different one, and these ties could change over the passage of years. Letters are of course more apparently personal than publications, yet it does often seem that Freud was writing with an eye cocked to future historians.

At the same time Freud's published works, all his essays and books, still have their own ways of being misunderstood. I am not suggesting that there is ever any hard-and-fast rules by which Freud can be interpreted. But the more we understand him as a writer, and he did seem to keep up his correspondences at least partly as a way of staying fit as a stylist, the better we will be able to follow the subtleties of his most famous texts. When I reread Freud, it can be difficult going, for instance, since to my mind he can be doing so many things at the same time in the course of any one sentence.

At any rate, for a long time in the future scholars will be welcoming the appearance of new volumes of Freud's letters. None of us now alive may see the ultimate publication of all Freud's correspondences. So far, it seems to me that each of them have provided fresh layers of meaning to what we thought we already knew. It should require all our critical faculties to evaluate and assess these collections of letters. It is my hope that my observations on these books of Freud's will help others in the future who will be lucky enough to be around when the "definitive" texts of Freud's correspondences see the light of day.

It is in keeping with my general interest in the history of psychoanalysis that I am including here my examination of books made up of letters by people like Karl Menninger and Heinz Kohut. I am also adding in my assessments of the letters from Anna Freud to Eva Rosenfeld, as well as the correspondence between James Strachey and Rupert Brooke, since it is my conviction that these texts have enriched our understanding of the development of psychoanalytic thinking.

# 7

# Freud-Silberstein

*The Letters of Sigmund Freud to Eduard Silberstein, 1871-1881*[1] forms a part in a long series of volumes of Freud letters. Earlier there was a 1954, and then a complete 1985, edition of his correspondence to his close friend Wilhelm Fliess, a Berlin physician, and a general collection of Freud's correspondence came out in 1960. The other books, containing both sides of exchanges of letters, were with students and disciples; that with Oskar Pfister appeared in 1963, the one with Karl Abraham in 1965, that to Arnold Zweig in 1970, the one with James Jackson Putnam in 1971, and that to Lou Andreas-Salomé in 1972. Perhaps the high point of them all was when the Freud/Jung correspondence was published in 1974; Freud's letters to Edoardo Weiss had come out as a book in 1970.

It has long been known how in 1937 Freud's analysand the Princess George (Marie Bonaparte) paid a German bookseller the equivalent of some $500.00 for Freud's letters to Fliess. When Freud heard about it, he was cross with Fliess's widow for having sold the letters; in fact, Mrs. Fliess was afraid that unless they went to a bookseller they would not get out of the country and survive. In an effort to exert some control over the fate of his Fliess letters, Freud offered to share in Marie Bonaparte's expense; she declined for fear of what he might want to do with them, but carefully saw that the correspondence was safeguarded on the continent throughout World War II. Freud's friendship with Fliess had taken place during the critical years of Freud's creation of the central doctrines of psychoanalysis, and they have been generally considered of key historical significance. So it is a sign of the growth (or inflation) of Freud studies that this new batch of Freud's letters, written to a Romanian school friend and unconcerned with Freud's ultimate professional work, should have fetched over twenty years ago the sum of $100,000.

It is worth starting off with this financial point since such a significant detail nowhere appears in the introduction or the two prefaces to *The Letters of Sigmund Freud to Eduard Silberstein.* Although we now have a small shelf-full of books of Freud's letters to go along with the twenty-four volumes of James Strachey's

*Standard Edition* of Freud's psychological works (the neurological texts are appearing separately), it is still the case today that the great bulk of Freud's correspondence remains unpublished. The most important new information about Freud will come from the huge quantity of letters still to come. Since the editing of almost all the Freud letters has been up to now highly questionable, and it looks as if this unfortunately may continue to remain the case, I would like to highlight the general problem associated with our understanding of Freud as a letter writer by looking more closely at the background to the appearance of these letters to Silberstein.

Some three decades ago a batch of Freud's letters to Silberstein were published in an obscure Israeli psychiatric journal. They did not then seem especially remarkable, and rather less significant than comparable bits and pieces of Freud's correspondence that were appearing in other more prominent periodicals. More recently, the attention of experts has been concentrated on the well-known larger sets of Freud's professional letters, some of which—such as those to Ernest Jones and the ones to Sandor Ferenczi—have editorially been in the works for years. For some curious reason Freud's letters to his fiancée have been, except for use by his official biographer Jones, completely closed to outsiders.

I had known that Freud's daughter Anna was very keen about these early letters of her father's to Silberstein. In itself this was remarkable since Anna was so possessive about everything connected with him. Despite all her horror at what she regarded as the invasion of her family's privacy by historians and biographers, not to mention the damage she feared to the practice of psychoanalysis, she personally transcribed these letters to Silberstein. (Once again, we get nothing of this in *The Letters of Freud to Silberstein.*) She was also closely involved in the arrangement by which Kurt Eissler, in behalf of the Freud Archives in New York City, paid all that money for the Silberstein letters. (It remains unclear whether the money went to a dealer, or perhaps even to the Silberstein granddaughter who contributed an important little set of biographical notes to this volume.)

At this point it is necessary to be clear about the various organizations, often involving the same people, that have been in charge of Freud's letters. The Freud Archives is now famous if only because of Janet Malcolm's two celebrated 1983 pieces in *The New Yorker*; she was fascinated with the rise and fall of Jeffrey Masson, who was Eissler's chosen successor, as Projects Director of the Freud Archives, for a year. (Masson's libel suit—for ten million dollars—against Malcolm, *The New Yorker*, and Alfred A. Knopf, Inc. got considered by the Supreme Court. He had contended that she invented words of his to put within quotation marks, while she claimed to have relied on the spirit of tape-recorded interviews. The Supreme Court was unanimous in reinstating his lawsuit against Malcolm for having concocted libelous quotations and attributed them to him. According to the holding in *Masson v. New Yorker Magazine*, the

Constitution does not guarantee free speech for fabricated quotations which materially change the meaning of what was actually said. After two widely publicized lower court trials, Masson proved unsuccessful in winning money from Malcolm.)

The Freud Archives, for whom paradoxically Jungian money had at first been a key resource, became the main conduit by which Freud material wound up at the Freud Collection at the Library of Congress in Washingon, D.C. The Archives' status as the official donor of most of the Freud Collection has meant that the Library of Congress, although publicly funded, has had to abide by any restriction on access that the Archives has seen fit to impose. That situation remains true today.

Nobody has ever offered any evidence that the weird dates by which items at the Freud Collection become accessible to inspection by scholars are the product of anything but Eissler's eccentric protectiveness about Freud—some material has been restricted until the twenty-second century. Even people who gave the Archives Freud letters were later unable to retrieve copies of them from the Freud Collection without the express permission of the Archives. Although ultimately Eissler fell from power at the Archives because of his curious choice of Masson, and Eissler's handling of the public controversy connected with him, until he died in 1999 Eissler still commanded some control at the Freud Collection—as Anna Freud's personal representative—over a sizable chunk of material she gave, before her death in 1982, directly to the Freud Collection.

A third institution to keep in mind is the Freud Museum on Maresfield Gardens in London. Freud lived in that house for a bit over a year after being driven into exile from Vienna. He died there, and it was only open to the public in 1986. I would not have thought it necessary to bother singling out the Freud Museum, even though it possesses much of Freud's library, photographs, and documents as well; it has also had trouble keeping a director ideologically satisfactory to orthodox sponsors. But the Supreme Court in the factual summary of its decision completely muddled up the Freud Archives with the Freud Museum.

Finally, the Freud Copyrights in London exists to monitor the use of Freud's writings, and also to make money for Freud's literary heirs. Here a provision in Freud's final will bore directly on the trouble connected with getting the Silberstein letters in print. Freud, much to Anna Freud's annoyance, left the royalties on his works to his grandchildren. This decision on his part, which she claimed was owing to pressure from two of her brothers, meant years of added tension between herself and her nephews and niece, for it set up a conflict of interest between them over the future publication of Freud's letters. The Freud Copyrights, and therefore the grandchildren, stood to gain from any such new books, while Anna Freud had her own agenda for protecting what she regarded as the dignity of her father's "cause."

It is a sign of the taboos that still exist in the field that until I decided to put Freud's last will into print in an article in the *Journal of the American Academy of Psychoanalysis* in 1990 it had remained unpublished.* There has been a laughable amount of chaos about "secrets," so that while the copy of the will at the Freud Collection was sealed until the year 2007 (Eissler came up with that date, and once it was established, his successors maintained it), the document has been on public record in London ever since it was first probated after Freud's death in 1939.

To bring this background to bear on the Silberstein letters, the Freud Archives had laid out all that money, and then naturally wanted some share of the proceeds from the publication of the volume. However, books of letters, even those by Freud, do not usually sell well. Eventually a compromise was agreed on, so that there would be a fifty-fifty division of proceeds between the Archives and the Freud Copyrights.

Now, the Freud Archives has never had much in the way of funds itself. So that when Masson decided to sue against his dismissal, he included in his legal case his former supporter Muriel Gardiner, a New Jersey analyst. Gardiner may be best known publicly as the supposed model for Lillian Hellman's "Julia"; Hellman denied it, but her capacity for telling tall tales was notorious. Gardiner herself had her own ideological agenda that could lead her, too, to tailor the truth. One of her avocations was keeping track of Freud's famous patient the Wolf-Man (Gardiner was analyzed by Ruth Mack Brunswick); and Gardiner always did her best, whatever the Wolf-Man himself may have said, to put Freud's handling of that case in the best possible light. She was immensely rich and sent the Wolf-Man regular funds. (She was also for years the financial angel behind *Dissent* magazine.) Gardiner was so much a member of Anna Freud's faction that she set up a foundation to buy Freud's London house, where Anna lived, so that it could eventually be made into a museum. Masson's including her in his lawsuit was practical; she had been involved in enabling him to be hired at the Archives, and so it was her money that also went to pay for the Massson out-of-court legal settlement.

Further, Muriel Gardiner had made possible the purchase of the Freud letters to Silberstein. Finding the right editor was a problem, but at no time did anybody involved seem to think that it might be appropriate to go outside the immediate psychoanalytic family. One German woman analyst (now in charge of publishing the more than one thousand letters from Freud to his future wife) declined the job; anyway, Anna Freud complained about working with her. And then Masson—even when he was being trusted before the publicity over his obsession with the idea that the sexual seduction of children accounts for the origin of neurosis, and that Freud had cowardly retreated from his early tenets—seemed unsuitable. Apparently Masson had wanted to dissect the letters

*See Part 9 of this book, New Documents, pp. 447–452.

through the use of modern psychoanalytic theories about adolescence, and Anna Freud thought such a procedure approximated textual sacrilege.

She was convinced that the letters to Silberstein were unique, the best biographical material ever available about Freud, even though she wanted assurances that after publication no more of Freud's letters would appear for years. It is a safe guess that she would not be happy about the course that events have recently taken. For a new organization, the Freud Literary Heritage Foundation, has now been set up, originally once again with Eissler in charge, which has undertaken to raise funds in order to bring out complete editions of Freud's letters with friends and colleagues, as well as family members.

Muriel Gardiner is now no longer alive, but for a time it had seemed natural, once Masson was out of the picture, that she herself edit the letters to Silberstein. She was already old and sick, and every time she put her mind to working on the Silberstein correspondence her blood pressure went up precipitously. She could not forgive the way Masson had, she felt, taken financial advantage of her; so in the end, on medical grounds, she bowed out of the editorial job.

At last in 1991 we got the letters to Silberstein, edited by Walter Boehlich. I know nothing about him except that he has chosen to ignore the complex history behind the appearance of this correspondence. He tells us only that "thanks to the initiative of Dr. Kurt R. Eissler and a donation from Muriel Gardiner, the Sigmund Freud Archives were able to acquire the originals at the end of the 1970s." He himself "relied mainly on photographs." It is to me alarming to find him, among his many acknowledgments, singling out for thanks "the esteemed Kurt R. Eissler," even though for more than half a century Eissler remained the main guardian of psychoanalytic orthodoxy.

One does not know what to make of it, but a number of letters to Silberstein appear to have vanished. This is most striking in connection with the fact that Silberstein's first wife came from Romania in 1891 to consult Freud in Vienna psychotherapeutically. It turns out that she committed suicide by throwing herself from the fourth floor of Freud's apartment house. Boehlich tells us merely that she killed herself "without having seen Freud." Yet in an appendix to this book we are informed by a Silberstein grandchild that the woman had become "mentally ill, was treated unsuccessfully by his friend Sigmund Freud, and threw herself from a window in Freud's apartment building. This tragedy was corroborated by Anna Freud." And a 1928 letter of Freud's, after Silberstein's own death, says that Freud "once had occasion to attend to his first wife." There are no letters here more directly connected with the death of that wife.

I would think that Silberstein himself might have done away with such letters for the sake of his own privacy and that of his wife; there is no sign of any later reproach in him against Freud. As of 1910, Silberstein was evidently still recommending further patients to Freud. Perhaps Freud was unhappy with the capacity of Silberstein (then some sort of businessman) to pick diagnostically patients who were suitable. In any event, Freud wrote back in 1910, at a time when he did not, as in later years, have his time filled with pupils from abroad: "the patients you mention are welcome to call; I shall refer them to my many pupils, who will treat them as I suggest, but I myself cannot take on anything more this season."

I do not suspect Anna Freud, or someone in her behalf, of having deliberately done away with evidence pertaining to the suicide of Silberstein's first wife. If Anna had found something in the correspondence that put her father in any kind of bad light, she would presumably not have been enthusiastic about bringing out the letters in the first place. True, her historical vision was clouded by filial piety, but by the 1970s she must have been on her toes about the significant issue of suicide among psychoanalytic patients. (She did, however, remain strangely unremorseful when her intimate friend Dorothy Burlingham's older daughter, who had been in analysis with Anna since early childhood, killed herself in 1974 while staying at Anna Freud's house, where Dorothy lived too, in London.) Anna facilitated the acquisition of these letters, with money from Muriel Gardiner, because, I think, she admired them so much.

Yet, for years Anna Freud had felt free to pencil out anything she chose in Freud's published correspondence. In spite of this arbitrariness, somehow the historical fraternity has not succeeded in challenging Anna Freud's almost unquestioned North American public standing. I first brought up the issue of the censorship of Freud's letters in a couple of footnotes to a 1968 book of mine; no reviewer, even in professional journals, took notice of what I had said. Then with my book *Brother Animal* in 1969, I gave an appalling example of an excision from a Freud letter in connection with Victor Tausk's suicide. After that there was no more such tampering with Freud letters. Previously, passages could be dropped without even the presence of the appropriate marks indicating a deletion. That is why "complete" editions of Freud's letters to Abraham, Pfister, Zweig, and Andreas-Salomé, for example, are now necessary, for the earlier ones are all chopped up in ways that are historiographically incomprehensible.

But starting in 1989 we have had to worry about missing Freud letters. For once his correspondence to his sister-in-law Minna became unrestricted, a mystery started about how some of them from a key period could have vanished. People have had a curious prurient interest about Freud and Minna. She was important both emotionally and intellectually to him, but—although this seems unfathomable in our age of sexual preoccupation—I still think he relied on relaxing with her at card-playing.

As long as Freud letters continue to come out under the auspices of the same narrow orthodox psychoanalytic faction, then independent observers have every right to remain on their guard. Partisanship can take multiple forms, including of course the alternatives that exist for translations. One wishes that before signing contracts university presses would submit these manuscripts to the normal channels of outside readership; those who choose to endorse the editing of such texts would then be publicly quotable and could be held to account for their advice. Since the editing of Freud's letters is still not in impartial hands, scholars cannot rest assured that the best possible job has been undertaken.

The circumstances surrounding the publication of the Freud-Silberstein letters are so significant because they turn out to be remarkably interesting. Some people have been tempted to allow themselves to think that everything important about Freud has already essentially been known, and now along comes a set of letters that presents us with a Freud we have not encountered before. He is only fifteen years old at the beginning of this correspondence, and the letters last until more than nine years later. Freud was in the full tide of his youth, and one can be grateful that there is nothing here of the acrimony that one so often finds in his later years.

It is true that Freud and his friend Silberstein had set up between them a secret society, the Spanish Academy, of which they were the sole members; and they even had a seal made for their "society." (Freud jokes about their being entitled to have a historian.) They often wrote to one another in Spanish, taking their signatures from two dogs in one of Cervantes's tales. Here is a Freud who was altogether more warm and outgoing than he usually sounds in later years.

For example, after a trip to relatives in England in 1875, Freud was moved to reflect on his aim as a "scientist" to "reduce or wipe out some of the ills that afflict our body." England, he thought, would be "just the place" where "a respected man, supported by the press and the rich, could do wonders in alleviating physical ills, if only he were enough of an explorer to strike out on new therapeutic paths." In his autobiographical reminisences as an old man, Freud would claim that he had never had such humanitarian hopes. At the same time, we do get intimations here of how harsh Freud could be. In 1877 we find him writing a letter at the age of twenty-one in

> a kind of crisis intended to rid me of morbid matter. I wish for all the rabble found on this earth to be struck down by heavenly thunder and the world to become so depopulated that one would encounter just one human being every three miles. If this wish remains unfulfilled, posterity will rue the day. A certain number of scoundrels is quite acceptable, for it helps people to grow hot under the collar, but too many are unhealthy.

If there is one single overriding aspect to Freud in these letters, it has to be in connection with just how absorbed with philosophizing he was as a young man. The editor has done nothing significant to help us compare Freud's youthful involvements with Ludwig Feuerbach, Franz Brentano, and Nietzsche in relation to Freud's mature convictions. It is startling to find Freud, who in later years claimed to have always abhorred philosophy, here so preoccupied with it.

In some of Freud's earliest remarks to Silberstein he is mainly concernd about what letter writing itself means to him. For the rest of Freud's life he remained remarkably anxious, as here, to get word from correspondents. Freud said he had a special "need for communication," at the same time that he felt it had to be by means of a secret code. (Freud and Silberstein agreed on disguised terminology; for example, "principles" turn out to have meant "girls.") Freud characteristically cursed "the invention of postcards," which robbed him of some deeply sought letters from Silberstein: "The world grows more prosaic at every new invention; in the end, letters will fall into disuse and be replaced by telegrams. Then we shall be able to correspond with a friend for a decade without so much as catching a glimpse of his handwriting." (E-mail fits into a technological pattern Freud disliked already.) Even in later years, Freud stuck to his own difficult script rather than rely on a typewriter, and only on the rarest occasion is he known to have received a telephone call.

We now have a record of Freud falling in love for the first time, and how it also involved his feelings for the young woman's mother. Freud was more devoted to humanistic studies than one might have imagined, although Silberstein does get teased for his commitment to being a social democrat. Freud tells about enrolling in swimming classes, and increasingly discusses his reading of books. Although I have given my reasons for being dubious about the overall editing of this volume, Boehlich has been extraordinarily conscientious in filling the reader in on obscure literary allusions.

At times Freud may sound sententious: "A letter demands a degree of composure, or artistic calm, a letter is nothing if not an exercise in the so-called liberal arts in which one can take pleasure only when the din of the daily round and cares has been silenced." Freud was eighteen at the time he wrote this. Within a year his friendship for Silberstein was such that Freud could write him:

> I really believe that we shall never be rid of each other; though we became friends from free choice, we are as attached to one another as if nature had put [us] on this earth as blood relations; I believe that we have come so far that the one loves the very person of the other and not, as before, merely his good qualities; and I am afraid that were you, by an unworthy act, to prove quite different tomorrow from the image I keep of you, I could still not cease to wish you well.

Not one single line of Silberstein's, to Freud or anybody else, seems to have survived. Natural writers like Freud have to throw things out, while others like Silberstein were left saving Freud's letters. Freud's correspondence to Silberstein grows more and more interesting the further one gets into it, and the letters whet the appetite for what is to come in the future. If only university presses would self-respectingly stand their ground, and refuse to be merely agents of the ancien régime in psychoanalysis, we should be better able to appreciate the scale of Freud's genius.

## Note

1. *The Letters of Sigmund Freud to Eduard Silberstein, 1871-1881*, edited by Walter Boehlich, translated by Arnold J. Pomerans (Cambridge, MA: Harvard University Press, 1991).

# 8

# Freud-Jones

The world of university scholarship remains at too great a distance from the teaching of psychoanalysis, and therefore when a book like *The Complete Correspondence of Sigmund Freud and Ernest Jones 1908-1939*, edited by R. Andrew Paskauskas,[1] appears one is left more than a little uncertain how to begin describing it. Students in training read certain key papers by Freud, and then a batch of texts usually written by analysts who are chiefly notable by virtue of their being geographically or nationally familiar. The work of intellectual historians is too rarely considered relevant to understanding the analytic past. If one travels around the world, visiting various centers of analytic training, it is possible to sense just how parochial the educational situation is apt to be.

There is also the special problem of Freud-baiting. Trying to understand Freud's work in its historical context, or even reading his writings in the light of the various enemies he was trying to contend with, can lead to being tarred with the dread brush of being stigmatized as "anti-psychoanalytic." To outsiders, for example within the increasingly powerful world of biological psychiatry, this sort of persistent sectarianism has been held responsible for holding back the development of analysis as a science. Polarizations about Freud are as bad now as ever, and the world is too readily divided between those who are friendly toward him as opposed to his enduring enemies.

University life has its own special problems. For example, Freud's popularity right now is riding high within literary and philosophical circles, but it is hard to get such people to realize the kinds of clinical concerns that a practicing analyst like Freud necessarily had. Intellectuals are capable of coming up with some of the most tortured readings of Freud imaginable, without understanding either the underlying continuities or the central controversies that have taken place in the past. The study of the history of analysis has not yet gained legitimization either within academic departments in universities or inside analytic training centers. As a result there is a regrettable degree of amateurish writing that appears in print.

With all that has already come out about Freud, it is going to be a surprise to many how little we know about the creator of analysis. Some twelve books of Freud's letters have appeared in print so far, but this only scratches the surface of what ultimately will get published. A dispute exists about just how many thousand letters by Freud have survived, but the most conservative estimate seems to be that he wrote something like 20,000 of them. In the end, although it may take another generation if not more, the bulk of Freud's various collections is going to be greater than the existing *Standard Edition* of his works.

That sort of productivity on Freud's part makes it easy to forget that almost all of his professional time was spent treating patients psychotherapeutically six days a week. Freud did his writing only in the evenings, on Sundays, and sometimes over holidays. He was such a prodigious letter-writer that his family took it for granted, and did not comment among themselves unless he was specifically embarked on a project intended for publication.

Unfortunately, many of the earlier volumes of Freud's correspondences have been expurgated, so that when the Freud-Jones letters are entitled *The Complete Correspondence* this is intended as a signal that no hanky-panky has been associated with the present editorial process. We now have untendentiously selected letters of Freud to Wilhelm Fliess, Carl G. Jung, and Eduard Silberstein; further, the first two volumes of Freud's letters to Sandor Ferenczi have appeared uncut. But other editions of Freud's letters (such as those to Karl Abraham, Lou Andreas-Salomé, Arnold Zweig, and Oskar Pfister) are going to have to be redone some day. Thousands of Freud's letters have never been published at all. The problem of compromising the confidentiality of former analytic patients has not been nearly as significant as the defensive idealizations about Freud, which have led to an unnecessary degree of secrecy.

It does not necessarily follow that because Freud expressed something by letter we are necessarly getting a "truer" picture of how his mind worked than by reading what he wrote for contemporary publication. It is one of the complications of the story of Freud's life that from an early age he knew that his letters were being preserved. On many occasions he could write differently on the same subject to a range of correspondents, just as sometimes he would virtually repeat himself word for word. Freud was a great letter-writer not just in terms of the quantity of what he was able to toss off, but the way he could express his ideas in memorable and idiosyncratic ways.

Interpreting Freud's letters is going to be a lot harder since virtually all the recipients of what he wrote are no longer alive and able to comment on what he might have had in mind. It is too late now, but it would have been desirable if Freud's letters had been widely circulated years ago, so that those who knew him would have been in a position to help us make sense of what he was doing. It is so easy for academics, for example, to go wildly astray in interpreting Freud's correspondences, since he was great enough as a writer to be able to succeed in muffling some of his most characteristic preferences. The manners of old-world culture are bound to be misleading to our own contemporaries.

Analysts are going to find it daunting once they realize how limited an aspect of Freud's writings can be found in a wonderful set of books like the *Standard Edition* edited by James Strachey. Yet the generations that get to see the full, untendentiously edited volumes of Freud's letters are certain to have trouble recreating the human circumstances under which he was working. The more time passes the greater the likelihood that the society of old Vienna is going to seem a universe that has long vanished from human understanding.

Although there are legitimate grounds for complaining about various features to the *Complete Correspondence of Sigmund Freud and Ernest Jones*, we are now clearly in a fresh phase of scholarship. A major turning point started with the 1974 publication of the Freud-Jung letters. As late as 1969 Freud's correspondences were still coming out in bowdlerized form. An immense percentage of his letters then had been silently truncated; he was a great enough letter-writer not to need any such crutch.

The huge volume of the letters between Freud and Jones has been eagerly awaited, although its length turns out to be intimidating. As Riccardo Steiner points out in his Introduction, "the more than seven hundred letters exchanged by Freud and Jones cover a longer period between Freud and any of his other collaborators of the first generation." I doubt that this book will attract many general readers, but it should be of keen interest to specialists. Even then, I wonder if more than a handful will read every word of it from beginning to end. In the hope that my remarks here might help improve the quality and usefulness of books of Freud's letters in the future, I want to let out a howl about the miserable state of the Index to the *Complete Correspondence of Freud and Jones.*

In a book of letters, and especially one of such substantial length, any interested reader is apt to turn first to the Index to look up people (or even subjects) of some special interest. With the Freud-Jones correspondence, I was at first disappointed to find that a shortcut had been adopted of having the Index refer only to the correspondence numbers, instead of the pages themselves. That device necessarily complicates the student's task, since many of these letters are lengthy and the correspondence numbers are not at the top of the page as they are in the Freud-Jung letters. But the state of the Index itself turns out to be slovenly, and the publisher should be ashamed of itself. I found myself having to work out my own hand-to-mouth provision for referencing.

For example, I happen to have a special interest in Sandor Rado. Although his name does not appear in the Index, I found thirteen instances in which it comes up in the text of these letters. The philosophers G. W. F. Hegel and F. W. Nietzsche do not get listed in the Index, nor is Henri Bergson, although the names of all three men appear at one point or another in the book itself. It is irritating that Felix Deutsch merits one citation in the Index, even though I counted his name coming up three different times in separate letters. Two references to Edward Glover were missed; and two mentions of Edoardo Weiss go unlisted. It is maddening that the indexer did not know that Ruth Blumgart and Ruth Mack Brunswick were one and the same person married to different husbands; moreover, four references to her were missing from the Index. Herman Blumgart, referred to in the letters only as "Herman B.", did not succeed in making it into the Index; nor did Victor Tausk, who comes up in the text twice —although without editorial help in connection with his dates of birth and death.

James Strachey has nine citations in the Index, but I counted eighteen times that references to him were missed; and I came across eight omissions to his wife, Alix. The Index contains no mention of John Maynard Keynes, who crops up once in the text, nor to Lytton Strachey, who appears twice; yet those writers are of outstanding significance to intellectual history. According to my calculations, Horace W. Frink's name goes unrecorded four times. The Index also omits mention of Kata Levy. Further, I detected one missing reference to Carl Jung, one to Alfred Adler, two to Freud's eldest son Martin, one to Siegfried Bernfeld, one to Gregory Zilboorg, and one to John Rickman. All these observations of mine represent only a spot-check of the Index; there are almost certainly further deficiencies that I failed to note.

A university press should be aware of its responsibilities to the scholarly community. A volume of such letters is bound to have a special appeal to future researchers, and I have already found myself hunting around in order to reread certain passages. It is elegantly satisfying to be able to find out, as we are in this volume, whether a letter was initialed by Jones and underscored with a characteristic scribble (a symbol standing for his younger sister), or merely initialed by Jones but not so underscored, or simply signed by Jones. It is of course critical to be told when Jones and Freud were writing in English, and when, on those rare occasions, Freud used Gothic instead of Latin characters in writing Jones. But all the exquisitely admirable paraphernalia of the text to *The Complete Correspondence of Sigmund Freud and Ernest Jones*, which tells us even when Jones's signature does not appear but his name was signed and initialed by a secretary, or when a word was crossed out, becomes secondary to such a sloppy job of indexing, which will always hamper the use of this book. One would like to think that the Freud Copyrights in England care about such a matter, but I suppose until a real foul-up occurs they have little reason to be on their guard.

To turn to evaluating the correspondence itself, and what we learn that we did not know before, I think that on the whole these letters are a mild disappointment. Part of the problem is no doubt purely linguistic. As Freud wrote Jones in 1926:

> I find it very difficult to write German in Latin script, as I am doing today. All facility—inspiration is reserved for greater matters—deserts me at once. But you have often told

> me that you cannot read Gothic script, thus leaving me with only two means of communication, both of which interfere with one's intimacy: either to dictate a letter to Anna on the typewriter or to use my clumsy English.

Freud's handwriting could be very difficult for his recipients to decipher. In fact, the human gulf between Freud and Jones, in spite of their long association, may be one of the central lessons to be learned from reading this volume; Jones was never one of Freud's special favorites.

Sometimes Freud's English has a special charm, as when he refers to Abraham's "Prussianity," in a letter unlisted in the Index. Jones claimed in his authorized biography of Freud to have left Freud's English unaltered or unimproved, but that turns out to have been a falsehood. Only on rare occasions does one come across here the kind of mordant irony that was so intrinsically a part of Freud's thinking; for example, he wrote of himself in English after the end of World War I: "it is no relief to have his sympathy placed on the winning side if one's well being is staked on the losing one." Since the main difficulty seems to be that for a variety of reasons Freud never took to Jones personally, these letters are less revealing of Freud's mind that one might have hoped. In 1910 Jones wrote to him:

> The originality complex is not strong with me; my ambition is rather to know, to be "behind the scenes," and "in the know", rather than to *find out*. I realise that I have very little talent for originality; any talent I may have lies rather in the direction of being able to see perhaps quickly what others point out....Therefore my work will be to try to work out in detail, and to find new demonstrations for the truth of ideas that others have suggested. To me work is like a woman bearing a child; to men like you, I suppose it is more like the male fertilisation.

The first years of the relationship between Freud and Jones produced exchanges that are so flat as to be almost alarming about what the rest of the book would be like. Many of these are essentially business letters; and if one has kept an eye on the scholarly ball, over the years bits and pieces of the juiciest parts of this correspondence have appeared in the literature before. The book itself would have seemed even more immense and off-putting but for the generously large pages on which the letters are printed.

When it comes to such famous controversies as that over Adler within the Vienna Psychoanalytic Society, Freud confided so little in Jones that we learn next to nothing about what happened. And even though Jones knew Jung, I do not believe that the difficulties between Freud and Jung are especially illuminated by what can be found here. (The one letter of Jung's to Jones that I have read, written during Jones's writing his biography, hopes that bygones could be left as bygones, and seemed to me most telling in contrasting Jones's grudge-holding with Jung plea for toleration.) Jones backed Freud down the line against Jung, and certain passages here are apt to read sychophantishly. Even when it comes to the loss of Otto Rank from Freud's world, we learn nothing from these letters of how anguished or tortured Freud must have felt. Jones had for years been struggling with Rank over detailed publishing matters; Jones, as head of a press and *The International Journal of Psychoanalysis* in London, was perhaps bound to come in conflict with Rank, who was Freud's chief assistant in Vienna. Writing to others, Freud could be open about how he thought Jones had helped to make a bad situation worse, but with Jones himself Freud maintained a proper form of diplomatic distance. For years Jones had approached Freud with the most detached sort of reverence; for example, it took six years before Jones was able to take the liberty of addressing Freud as simply "Professor" instead of "Professor Freud."

And yet such caution on Jones's part was consistent with his being almost stupefyingly obtuse, as when in 1927 he casually remarked about Anna Freud's first volume: "It is a pain to me that I cannot agree with some of the tendencies in Anna's book, and I cannot help thinking that they must be due to some imperfectly analyzed resistances; in fact I think it is possible to prove this in detail." Jones's striking capacity for being tactless bears repeating. When he was living in Canada before World War I, he wrote about his hosts:

> The people are 19 parts American, and one part Colonial, therefore they are very insulted if called Americans.... They are a despicable race, exceedingly bourgeois, quite uncultured, very rude, very stupid and very narrow and pious. They are naïve, childish and hold the simplest views of the problems of life. They care for nothing except money-making and sport, they chew gum instead of smoking or drinking, and their public meetings are monuments of sentimental platitudes. They are horror struck with me because I don't know the date of the King's birthday, for they take their loyalty like everything else in dead seriousness and have no sense of humor.

One can well believe that wherever Jones was he was well-hated; but it still takes my breath away that he could write so brazenly to Freud about his youngest daughter. The editor refers the reader only to a pious 1988 discussion of Freud's analysis of Anna but omits any reference to what I myself—or others subsequently—wrote about the matter earlier.[2] It seems to me still an open question whether Jones then knew for sure that Freud had been Anna's analyst; but Freud's reply to Jones was typed, almost certainly dictated to Anna, and a model of studied patience:

> I will make only one comment on the polemical part of your letter. When two analysts have differing opinions on some point, one may be fully justified, in ever so many cases, in assuming that the mistaken view of one of them stems from his having been insufficiently analyzed, and he therefore allows himself to be influenced by his complexes to the detriment of science. But in practical polemics such an argument is not permissible, for it is at the disposal of each party, and does not reveal on which side the error lies. We are generally agreed to renounce arguments of this sort....

A few months later, after an international symposium on child analysis, Freud, in a handwritten German letter, criticized Jones further:

> In London you are organizing a regular campaign against Anna's child analysis, accusing her of not having been analyzed deeply enough, a reproach that you repeat in a letter to me. I had to point out to you that such a criticism is just as dangerous as it is impermissible. Is anyone actually analyzed enough? I can assure you that Anna has been analyzed long and more thoroughly than, for example, you yourself.

In his next letter to Jones, again handwritten, Freud mentioned that he thought it "inexcusable" that Jones could have allowed the "reproach, which is not customary and offends against all good practice, that she was not analyzed sufficiently—put forward by you publicly and in private...." At least one other British child analyst had written as much about Anna in Jones's journal. Jones made no effort to continue the debate and failed to deny Freud's charge that Jones had brought the issue up "publicly." If Jones knew or suspected who Anna's analyst had been, then that might help account for his feeling free to so transgress against what one might have thought was a taboo with Freud. (Some day analysts will feel free to write about the significance of Freud's analyzing Anna: were they, I wonder, protecting one another?)

These letters do provide concrete evidence for how strongly Freud disapproved of Melanie Klein's work. (The Index is again unreliable about exactly where Klein comes up.) Freud knew that Klein had been treating Jones's children. One has to know something of Freud's style of differentiating his ideas from what he regarded as heresy when we find him writing in 1927: "Mrs. Klein's view of the ego-ideal in children seems quite impossible to me and is in contradiction to all my postulates." When Jones wrote to inquire what Freud found so "heretical" in Klein, Freud replied:

> Naturally I criticize her for denying half the facts, while the other—what you call "the phantastic part"—is alone proclaimed; incidentally, in an excellent way. This makes her viewpoint "heretical," contains an unfortunate similarity to Jung's, and, like his, is an important step toward making analysis unreal and impersonal....All our apostates always grasped part of the truth and wanted to declare it as the whole truth.

One would be mistaken to underestimate the extent of Freud's loathing for what he saw taking place within British analysis, even if his health were not up to any more public brawling. He believed that "Melanie Klein is on the wrong track and Anna is on the right one." When Freud in 1932 was referring to his disputing "Kleinian interpretations," the ground was already laid for the controversy that would wrack the British Psychoanalytic Society after Freud's death. Those who sought publicly to brand Klein then for treason were carrying out Freud's privately expressed convictions.

Aside from the relevance of Freud's letter-writing thinking to what later became a full-scale public debate, these letters are interesting in what they tell us about Freud as a clinician. There is, for example, the case of Loe Kann, whom, when she lived with Jones, he described as his "wife." I found in Freud's efforts to deal with her morphine addiction similarities to his later attempt to cope with Ruth Mack Brunswick's problems. Freud, incidentally, attended the weddings of both Loe and Ruth, though none of his own children. Freud could be indiscreet with Loe, a former patient of Jones's, about Jones, and also reveal material about Loe to Jones. Freud does sometimes sound, in dealing with patients, as if he were openly interested in converting them to his own special way of looking at things.

Throughout *The Complete Correspondence of Sigmund Freud and Ernest Jones* there are many editorial points that one might question, as an issue of legitimate differences of opinion. But one glaring bit of unfairness that I came across concerns the last period of Ferenczi's life. Senior British analysts I once knew thought that Jones never forgave Ferenczi for having briefly been his analyst. (Ferenczi was once such an intimate friend of Freud's that one passage in the first volume of their correspondence was startling enough for me to deliver a short paper on it.[3]) When Jones, in the third volume of his biography of Freud, made Ferenczi sound mentally ill in his last period,[4] marked by difficulties with Freud, a generation ago one dared not suspect that Jones might have been relying on Freud's authority.

In a letter to Jones (again not included in the Index) Freud referred to "the slow process of destruction to which he [Ferenczi] fell victim. During the last two years it expressed itself organically in pernicious anemia...." In Freud's 1933 obituary of Ferenczi he mentioned the pernicious anemia, but it is noteworthy that in private he regarded that illness as an expression of something else. In Jones's biography, however, he suppressed all mention of the pernicious anemia. I should add that an editorial note cites me for suggesting that Jones had "concocted" allegations of mental sickness against Ferenczi. In truth there were plenty of Hungarian, Viennese, and British sources who took issue with Jones's published account, and it reads lamely now to be told that "in fact Jones felt he had corroborating evidence supporting his position, and not just from Freud." When Michael Balint, for example, challenged Jones, Jones claimed to be relying on a witness, but Freud in Vienna would hardly qualify for reporting what had transpired in Budapest. The editor here is unable to solve the mystery of that so-called witness.

The Introduction to *The Complete Correspondence of Sigmund Freud and Ernest Jones* reminds us that in 1908 Jung wrote to Freud about Jones that he was "an intellectual liar (no moral judgment intended!) hammered by the vicissitudes of fate and circumstances into many facets. But the result? Too much adulation on one side, and too much opportunism on the other." And we are also told about Freud's having earlier written to Jung:

> Jones is undoubtedly a very interesting and worthy man, but he gives me a feeling of, I was almost going to say, racial strangeness. He is a fanatic and doesn't eat enough. "Let me have men about me that are fat," says Caesar, etc. He almost reminds me of the lean and hungry Cassius. He denies all heredity; to his mind even I am a reactionary. How, with your moderation, were you able to get on with him?

No mention is made in the Introduction, however, of how in 1927 Freud wrote to his disciple Max Eitingon, a colleague of Jones's:

> I don't believe that Jones is consciously ill-intentioned; but he is a disagreeable person, who wants to display himself in ruling, angering and agitating, and for this his Welsh dishonesty ("the Liar from Wales") serves him well. Riviere claims that he chased her into her position, congratulated her on the telephone for her theoretical propositions, and then betrayed her when he told me that he had tried unsuccessfully to tone her down.

In 1922 Freud had mentioned to Jones "the fact that accuracy and plainness is not in the character of your dealings with people." It is not a simple matter trying to sort out how to evaluate that which Freud wrote in private as opposed to what he put in print. When it came to Jones, for example, both in public and private Freud could be lavish with his praise, despite all the reservations we know Freud to have had about Jones. So in 1929 Freud not only published a notable tribute to Jones, on the occasion of his 50th birthday, but also Freud wrote him:

> Much that I could have written in reply to your letter must...be left unsaid. Not, however, the assurance that I have always counted you as one of my closer family members, and will continue to do so, which indicates—beyond all the discords that are seldom lacking within a family and have also not been lacking between us—a fund of tenderness that one can draw on time and again. I believe it began when I accompanied you once to the train station (in Worcester?) To be sure, I am not in the habit of expressing such affection freely, so that I can easily seem indifferent, but my family knows better.

Historians who remain confused about Freud's relationship to Jones may well wonder about the "accuracy and plainness" of both men. We know that Freud could publish praising obituaries alongside correspondence, which he knew was being saved, indicating very different feelings, leaving the future in a muddle about what Freud was ever doing.

Most people now realize that Jones single-handedly, even if autocratically, was responsible for creating the British Psychoanalytic Society. For those interested in the development of the historiography of psychoanalysis, Jones's work has to play a pivotal role. To be sure, fair-minded observers have long been aware of the element of bias that Jones interjected into his account of Freud's school, even though the volume of their correspondence may be an unlikely place to expect the fulfillment of anything approximating an impartial evaluation of Jones's contribution.

At one point in these letters it dawned on me that correspondence from Jones's Viennese wife to Freud was not included here. Freud's own wife, from whose pen so little exists, also wrote Jones, but that is not here either. Loe Kann's letters to Freud, now at the Freud Museum in London, were also excluded. Loe sounds spicey and engaging. As she wrote Freud shortly after World

War I, "It is all very well threatening me with your old age, but if you dare to leave this crazy world before we have met several times more, I'll pray God that all cigars in Heaven may be squashed and damp and rank! So there." Around the same time she also wrote to Freud about Jones: "I wonder why he is such an incorrigible fibber (to put it politely!)." Although in 1910 Jones wrote Freud from Toronto that "the government" had "forbidden" his asylum bulletin to appear any more, an editorial note here points out that "there is no significant break in the regular issues" of the quarterly journal.

Toward the end of this book, when I realized how often Jones had written to Anna Freud with the knowledge that her father would be made privy to anything he wrote her, I was grateful that this already huge body of material was not made even more difficult to finish reading by correspondence so concerned with the politics of the psychoanalytic movement.

Evidently, it was at Anna Freud's suggestion that Freud's English in his letters to Jones was sometimes altered for the sake of Jones's biography. To repeat, in print Jones explicitly denied having "ventured to amend" Freud's "grammar; if one started making such improvements one would end by defacing the original style."[6] *The Complete Correspondence of Sigmund Freud and Ernest Jones* has, in contrast to Jones's earlier practice, stuck to the most honest renderings of the original manuscripts. Jones's lack of truthfulness in writing about what he supposedly failed to change in Freud's English for the biography does seem flagrant.

It is a shame that it has taken so long for the full correspondence between Freud and Jones to have come out. People have unnecessarily suspected the existence of some shameful secrets which were being deliberately hidden from public scrutiny. For those with an interest in the growth of the psychoanalytic movement during Freud's lifetime these letters are essential reading. The Introduction was supposed to be written by the editor, Paskauskas, but the Freud Copyrights did not approve of Paskauskas's draft, and Riccardo Steiner was put in as a pinch-hitter. Steiner does a serviceable enough job, but no one was left to worry about the Index. Paskauskas deserves to be congratulated for the tremendous amount of hard conscientious work that went into creating the editorial apparatus that has made possible *The Complete Correspondence of Sigmund Freud and Ernest Jones*.

This set of letters is more about the politics of the psychoanalytic movement than an exchange of abstract ideas, or even a discussion of clinical matters. Nonetheless, it makes for fascinating reading, and it will be a required part of the primary data for future students of the history of psychoanalysis. There is material here about Frink and Freud's view of America, and Freud's attitude toward Strachey as his translator, that should prove immensely rewarding to scholars later on. For those with a special interest in the development of analysis in Britain, there are unique insights here which are impossible to find anywhere else. Jones ran British psychoanalysis with a firm hand, and it is inconceivable to detach his personality and convictions from the early tale of Freud's reception in Britain.

## Notes

1. *The Complete Correspondence of Sigmund Freud and Ernest Jones,* edited R. Andrew Paskauskas, with an introduction by Riccardo Steiner (Cambridge, MA: Harvard University Press,1993).
2. See Paul Roazen, "Freud's Analysis of Anna," in *The Death of Psychoanalysis: Murder, Suicide, or Rumor Greatly Exaggerated*, ed. Robert Prince (Northvale, NJ: Jason Aronson, 1999).
3. Paul Roazen, "Presence de Victor Tausk dans la Correspondence Freud-Ferenczi," *Etudes Freudiennes*, 37 (1993), pp. 1-7.
4. Ernest Jones, *The Life and Work of Sigmund Freud*, Vol. 3 (New York: Basic Books, 1957), Ch. 4. Cf. Paul Roazen, *Freud and His Followers, op. cit.*, Part VII, Chs. 6-7; and Paul Roazen, "Elma Laurvik, Ferenczi's Stepdaughter," *The American Journal of Psychoanalysis*, Vol. 58, No. 3 (September 1998), pp. 271-86.
5. Ernest Jones, *The Life and Work of Sigmund Freud*, Vol. 2, *op. cit.*, p. xiii.

# 9

# Freud-Ferenczi

After the first volume of the Freud-Ferenczi correspondence,[1] it will take two more full texts to complete the fascinating storehouse of letters that helps flesh out the story of the relationship between Freud and his chief Hungarian disciple. Since by one (perhaps high) estimate there could be as many as 35,000 Freud letters that have survived, only a small fraction of which have appeared, it will be a long time before all of Freud's correspondence gets published. It is likely that these letters are going at least occasionally to show sides of Freud that his most politic defenders would want to minimize.

The Freud-Ferenczi letters are exceptionally interesting, at least as important as the earlier edition of Freud's letters to Fliess, or the Freud-Jung correspondence. When Volume I of the Freud-Ferenczi letters appeared in 1992 in France, it caused a literary sensation. Some 7,000 copies were sold in a couple of weeks, and the literary dailies there were full of interest in Freud and Ferenczi. The French have only belatedly come to recognize Freud's stature, especially since the late 1960s; still, the reception of the first installment of the Freud-Ferenczi correspondence was a cultural event in Paris.

It is generally well known to professionals that, around the time of Ferenczi's death in 1933, his relationship to Freud was highly strained. Despite Jones's allegation that at the end of Ferenczi's life he had been mentally ill and that this sickness accounted for the difficulties with Freud, over the years a consensus has grown up that Jones had been malicious, however much he may have relied on Freud's opinion in an irritated mood at the time of Ferenczi's death.

It is now generally agreed that Ferenczi had been a pioneer in adjusting the "classical" use of the psychoanalytic situation in order to encompass types of patients who were less likely to thrive under Freud's recommended way of handling people. Ferenczi's posthumously published 1988 *Clinical Diary*,[2] originally written in 1932, had in it some stinging criticisms of Freud. By today, Ferenczi has come to symbolize all the therapeutic alterations with which loyal followers of Freud tried to experiment. Unlike Carl G. Jung, who cleanly broke with Freud (or was expelled) to set up his own independent school,

Ferenczi remained securely within the "mainstream" of psychoanalytic practitioners who were faithful to Freud's cause. So it is impossible to read Ferenczi out of the tale of the development of Freud's school. Ferenczi knew that the analyst necessarily remains, even when aloof, an active participant in the clinical encounter.

Andre Haynal, a Hungarian psychiatrist who practices in Geneva, has been helping (under Judith Dupont) to oversee the whole Freud-Ferenczi correspondence with a team of editorial allies. In his introduction to this volume, Haynal has written an interesting and informative account of the steps by which this immense body of letters finally succeeded in being published. In the mid-1960s, when I was fortunate to meet the surviving early analysts, I brought to Dr. Michael Balint, then Ferenczi's literary executor, a publishing offer from the Massachusetts Institute of Technology Press. Haynal finds it surprising that Balint should have "suddenly" written to one of the key players in the drama, Ferenczi's step-daughter Elma. In fact, I was actively interviewing all these people at the time, and, if only from me, Elma and Balint had to understand that eventually the full account of the emotional involvement between Ferenczi and Elma would get told. Relying on documents I had seen among Jones's papers, and which I asked Balint and later Elma about, I could not fathom exactly what had been going on between Ferenczi and Elma, although in the 1950s Balint had demanded that Jones never allude to it. Anna Freud, who was in charge of her father's side of the letters, had her own long-standing objections to releasing the Freud-Ferenczi correspondence, and it seems that she thought in terms of their eventual "partial" appearance.

The central tangle of the first volume revolves around Ferenczi, Elma with whom he fell in love, and Elma's mother, Gizella Palos, with whom Ferenczi was engaged and whom he eventually married. Gizella's first husband may have taken his life on the day of the wedding ceremony. Ferenczi had already analyzed both Gizella, who was older than he, and Elma; then Ferenczi sent both Elma and Gizella to Freud to get his judgment. Ferenczi later underwent a personal analysis with Freud. To make matters more complicated, Freud entrusted Jones's analysis to Ferenczi. Freud himself analyzed Elma for a few months, after which she went back into treatment with Ferenczi in Budapest. Eventually Ferenczi decided, on Freud's advice, against marrying Elma.

Haynal's introduction makes the point that clinically "many indiscretions" were committed by Freud and Ferenczi, although such a characterization seems to me too mild to fit the human complexities in which Freud and Ferenczi had become engaged. All these early analysts seem to have felt themselves beyond the constraints of customary morality, for they thought of themselves as creating new standards of good and evil. Freud may have been acting out of the best and most generous intentions and at times appreciated the dangers of the corruption of power, but he allowed himself to go ahead anyway. It is now some thirty-five years since I first learned that Anna Freud had been analyzed by her own father, and however wild and hair-raising such a procedure had to be, I think we can now see how it fit into a series of other practices in which early analysts behaved as if they were exempt from the restraints that civilized life has traditionally relied upon.

Freud and Ferenczi wrote back and forth more than once a week, over a period of many years. They could count on mail delivery between Vienna and Budapest taking about a day. Right from the start Freud aspired to have Ferenczi found a separate psychoanalytic group, but that ambition was not finally to be fulfilled until 1913. The Hungarian analysts always maintained their own characteristic tendencies, at least up until Ferenczi's death. Ferenczi's warmth and humanity inspired a whole group of practitioners who were not as naïve as North Americans about the implications of the written recommendations Freud published on how he thought beginners should go about avoiding mistakes. In 1910, for example, Ferenczi reported as Freud's "newest principle...that technique has to direct itself according to the uniqueness of each case," which might seem to undermine Freud's whole pretense at having any general "technique" to offer.

Since this is only the first of three large volumes, it is necessary to be tentative on what we will understand about the central people at a later date. But my own impression is that in this correspondence with Ferenczi we have Freud writing at his most unguarded. Often it has been easy for commentators to be misled by Freud's capacities as a stylist. He could beguile and entrance his readers, all the while holding himself back at a considerable human distance, as with Jones. In writing to Ferenczi, however, Freud let his hair down and trusted him, so that we find here passages that are historically fascinating.

For example, Lou Andreas-Salomé wanted to come visit Ferenczi for a few days in 1913, after completing a stay with Freud. Freud writes of her: "Her interests are really of a purely intellectual nature; she is a highly significant woman, even though all the tracks around her go into the lion's den but none come out." An editorial note reminds us of Aesop's fable in which the lion, lying ill in his den, asks the fox why he doesn't come closer; the fox replies: "I would certainly come in if I didn't see that so many tracks go in but that none come out." Lou was already well known as Nietzsche's expositor and a woman of letters, and there is an abridged volume of the correspondence that she and Freud exchanged. She ended up a practicing analyst, an intimate friend of Anna Freud's, and Freud wrote an obituary of her after her death. But I was fascinated to find Freud also writing, in the same letter introducing her to Ferenczi, of her liaison with Tausk, a local analyst about whom Freud had highly ambivalent feelings. Freud communicated to Ferenczi: "She has become very friendly with Tausk and is very vigorously championing his cause, which is becoming difficult for me. If you see her, ask her about it and arrive at your own opinion so that we will have a point of departure as to how we should relate to him." A subsequent letter from Ferenczi to Freud reports that he did try to "find out about

Tausk from Frau Lou," but left it for a visit of Ferenczi's to Vienna to report what little he was able to learn.

All specialists on early psychoanalysis will find important nuggets of information in these letters. My own special interest in the relationship between Freud, Lou, and Tausk has been a long-standing one, but I would never have thought that Freud would have written so freely to Ferenczi. The Freud-Ferenczi correspondence is an extraordinarily intimate human document, and one awaits the further volumes with the greatest interest.

One central complaint comes to mind about the way Freud letters are being presented to the public. The Freud Copyrights in London, in behalf of the Freud heirs, decides which texts are next to come out, and, in the case of the Harvard University Press, it seems eager to be cooperative. As fine as the translations appear to be (the German texts are still not available), and as conscientious as the editing has been, I am sorry to report that I found no fewer than a dozen editorial errors. For example, we are told that "Freud's sons all emigrated to London and died without returning to Vienna." In fact, Oliver Freud, the middle son, came straight from Europe to America, where he eventually died. And Sandor Rado was definitely not "the brilliant young patient" Ferenczi was hoping to rely on in 1910; Rado became editor of the *Zeitschrift* in 1924, not 1942. A note tells us that "in 1934" Anna Freud "took over from Helene Deutsch as director of the Training Institute of the Vienna Society"; but the true date of Helene Deutsch's resignation from her position was 1935, and the functions she had performed were then split between Anna Freud and Edward Bibring. And despite what a note tells us, it is not true that Freud "kept a Busch album in his waiting room"; such a text was reported to be there before World War I, but not by the 1920s. Further, it seems to me extremely dubious to think that René Spitz was anything like Freud's first patient for a training analysis. Also, Edoardo Weiss never emigrated from Italy to England, but instead came directly to the United States. The general reader need not be concerned with these or other slip-ups that I came across.

But is is generally instructive, if frightening, to think that once a mistake gets into print how much scholarly effort will be necessary to shake it out. I can immediately think of at least half a dozen people, and actually there are a good deal more, to whom a university press should be circulating drafts of edited volumes of Freud's letters. It would then be a simple matter to minimize the possibility of unnecessary errors arising, especially since the Freud-Ferenczi correspondence is so important.

One paragraph, sent from Ferenczi to Freud in 1910, does stand out, leaving me more bewildered than ever about what these people thought they were up to. Ferenczi sent Freud what he calls "a personal observation":

> I never have sexual intercourse at *night*—only in the morning. But one is "sober" in the morning; the compulsion-like urge (i.e., a part of the libido) is missing in the act. But if

> one still lets oneself be enraptured to moderate excesses, one becomes almost incapable of work during the day because of neurasthenic parasthesias, headache, heaviness in the legs, etc. I.e., the act had the character of masturbation. The satisfaction, as well as potency, was *incomparably greater*, and in fact, devoid of the slightest pathological reaction, if the act was carried out without exception in the late afternoon.

In the midst of all the bizarre-seeming exchanges between Freud and Ferenczi, and granted how idiosyncratic sex can be, this passage seems to me almost dotty. There is not any answer on this particular point from Freud, although Ferenczi had been expressing himself within Freud's conceptual framework. Perhaps I have concentrated too much on a few editorial howlers, in a text which is otherwise superbly edited, because I am still so uncertain what in the long run one should make of the whole story of Freud and Ferenczi, or of all the psychoanalytic changes in the history of ideas that they both did so much to forward.

Freud's correspondence with Ferenczi, which stretched from 1908 until 1933, would appear to have been the most extensive of Freud's life, and these letters could not have been incorporated in any one book. Yet there are reasons why publishers are traditionally wary of multivolume editions on the grounds that people are unlikely to purchase books that follow an initial text. Reviewers, too, cannot usually be expected to pay as much attention to a series of volumes as they do to an initial one, and Volume II of *The Correspondence of Sigmund Freud and Sandor Ferenczi*[3] has not attracted, at least in the United States, anything like the amount of reviews that Volume I achieved.

Part of the problem for the reader is that Volume II appears to cover a lull between storms. Volume I was shocking in that it gave the exact details of how enmeshed in other people's lives Freud allowed himself to become. The details bear reiterating. Ferenczi had been in love with a married woman, Gizella Palos, since 1900. Ferenczi first analyzed Gizella, and then in 1911 she asked him to analyze her daughter Elma. Ferenczi undertook the analysis, Elma's lover killed himself, and Ferenczi became emotionally involved with Elma. Freud had seen Gizella, accepted Elma for an analysis, and subsequently analyzed Ferenczi also. (After the analysis with Freud, Elma had returned to being analyzed by Ferenczi.) By the end of Ferenczi's life he was reproachful of Freud for having advised him against marrying Elma; Ferenczi minded the impossibility of having children with Gizella, who was eight years older than he. Ferenczi developed a passion for recommending that therapists be far more empathic than Freud was willing to countenance. Freud thought that Ferenczi had become disloyal and a "dissenter" like Carl Jung before him.

One of the enduringly attractive features of these early analysts is the extent to which they found human meaning in their mutual dedication to the "cause" of psychoanalysis. That shared militant commitment, a religious kind of devotion, meant an immense amount of self-scrutiny and soul-searching. Contemporary readers are likely to feel more than a little uncomfortable as

Ferenczi unburdens himself of all kinds of sexual as well as strictly medical confessions.

Freud does not seem to have been suitably appalled at Ferenczi's capacity for becoming infantile, and Freud was not adequately aware of the degree to which he was personally responsible for bringing out some of Ferenczi's less attractive traits. Freud could evade responsibility by attributing Ferenczi's regressions to what can be expected in a therapeutic analytic situation. In the end, Freud felt licensed by his cause to discard Ferenczi despite how wounded Ferenczi was bound to have felt; for years Ferenczi had suffered from various hypochondriacal-sounding ailments and then finally succumbed to the ravages of pernicious anemia. Personal bitterness and sectarianism had to be an essential part of the lives of these pioneers, even as they felt exhilerated by their path-breaking work. Outsiders at the time could not be expected to share in the spiritual gratifications that Freud and his followers experienced. They thought of themselves as in possession of deep "truths" that the world had not yet acknowledged. Today the pendulum has swung so far away from psychoanalysis that it is fashionable, in America for example, to find little of scientific merit in what Freud had proposed. But for a time, in the 1950s and 1960s for instance, Freud's teachings were professionally dominant in the United States.

In contrast to the surprising drama of Volume I and the intense struggles that can be expected to mark the final parts of Volume III, the reader may find it hard, as I did, to get into Volume II. The first half of the book is taken up with Ferenczi's tortured vacillations about marrying Gizella and Freud's shifting attempts to promote the marital union. Only in the latter part of Volume II, especially after Ferenczi has finally decided to give Elma up, do the letters get away from Ferenczi's private torments and move on to more general matters like the psychoanalytic movement itself. (Incidentallly, we learn virtually nothing here about Freud's own marriage, since there was no such give-and-take between himself and Ferenczi.)

Even if parts of Volume II make for slow reading, we do have an authentic record of the kind of transferential dependencies that Freud allowed. Because of Ferenczi's later contributions, he has become a major stalking horse in behalf of the advantages of therapeutic flexibility. (The introduction to Volume II seems to yearn nostalgically for the formal ideals of neutrality and abstinence, despite how the substance of the story of Freud and Ferenczi flies in the face of such artifacts of psychoanalytic theorizing.) Within psychoanalysis, Ferenczi's work has come to symbolize how it can be possible to repudiate Freud's conclusions while remaining loyal to psychoanalyis itself. It is historically not possible to read Ferenczi out of the tale of Freud's circle since, unlike Jung, Ferenczi remained on close terms with the master and never publicly repudiated him.

Volume II covers the era of World War I when Freud is substantially isolated in Vienna, and the supporters Freud had captured before the war are now scattered and sometimes inaccessible behind enemy lines. It took Freud's special intransigence for him to continue to believe that his school could triumph. These were the years when Freud delivered and then wrote his *Introductory Lectures* as well as a composed a series of famous metapsychological papers. Throughout Volume II Ferenczi is still providing Freud with the most friendly, if not slavish, echo. His theoretical differences with Freud about the most desirable therapeutic technique have not yet begun to emerge.

On the whole, Volume II seemed to err on the side of under-editing. Although the triangle between Freud, Ferenczi, and Gizella may seem old hat by now, toward the end of this book we confront an entirely new emotional tangle: one of Freud's Hungarian pupils, rich but married, had fallen in love with a married Hungarian analyst. Both Freud and Ferenczi felt entitled not only to treat the man, who is in acutely bad physical health, but they also use therapy on both the woman involved and her husband.

Whatever we may now think of how naïve the early analysts were in venturing to get involved with many human dilemmas that are apt to look like so many cans of worms, it was in keeping with the messianic spirit Freud inspired that commonsense caution was thrown to the wind. Psychoanalysis went on to become a profession that relies on its organizational defenders. But at this stage one wishes the Freud Copyrights could cut loose from the ideologically partisan past and ensure that the publication of Freud's various correspondences be used only for the purposes of the advancement of scholarship.

It should be exciting to see exactly what the final volume of the Freud-Ferenczi correspondence has to teach. Volume II illustrates Freud functioning without challenge. With Ferenczi, at least in these years, Freud was unusually relaxed and at ease. He did not even need to fear the effects of his dry irony. For example, Freud wrote Ferenczi in 1916: "One must be able to decide whether one loves a woman or not even with stuffed-up nostrils." In the end Freud was asked by Ferenczi to make the marriage proposal to Gizella, and that letter is included here, as is Freud's eloquent note of marital congratulations. Intellectual historians should find the early days of psychoanalysis, as recounted in these volumes of letters, rich with ideas.

## Notes

1. *The Correspondence of Sigmund Freud and Sandor Ferenczi*, Vol. I, *1908-1914*, ed. Eva Brabant, Ernst Falzeder, and Patricia Giampieri-Deutsch, translated by Peter T. Hoffer, with an introduction by Andre Haynal (Cambridge, MA: Harvard University Press, 1994).
2. *The Clinical Diary of Sandor Ferenczi*, ed. Judith Dupont, translated Michael Balint and Nicola Zarday Jackson (Cambridge, MA: Harvard University Press, 1988). Roazen, "Review of *The Clinical Diary of Ferenczi*," *The American Journal of Psychoanalysis*, December 1990.
3. *The Correspondence of Sigmund Freud and Sandor Ferenczi*, Vol. II, *1914-1919*, edited by Ernst Falzeder and Eva Brabant, with the collaboration of Patrizia Giampieri-

Deutsch, translated by Peter H. Hoffer, with an introduction by Axel Hoffer (Cambridge, MA: Harvard University Press, 1996).

# 10

# Anna Freud-Eva Rosenfeld

Anna Freud ended up as her father's leading disciple. By the time of her death in 1982, no one was able to challenge the extent to which she had come to symbolize the profession of psychoanalysis. She had not only continued to live in the house Freud died in—which has now become the Freud Museum, in Hampstead, England—but she exercised special power by virtue of her control over Freud's literary remains.

Anyone from the world of scholarship had to feel intimidated in "Miss Freud's" presence. Yet early photographs of her from before she entered her father's world as a clinical practitioner, and even at the time of her first seeing patients in the early 1920s, show a more vulnerable and shy woman than the side she later displayed to the outside world. Once Sigmund Freud fell ill with cancer of the jaw in 1923, his youngest child, Anna, had all sorts of new responsibilities thrust upon her. Under the burden of statecraft she changed, growing into a formidable force.

*Anna Freud's Letters to Eva Rosenfeld*[1] record a private aspect of her which I had beforehand only heard of from others, and to which I was never able myself to bear witness. She is here writing to her intimate friend Eva Rosenfeld. The most passionate part of Anna Freud's attachment to Rosenfeld took place before the time Dorothy Burlingham had supplanted the latter as the former's closest friend.

Rosenfeld was demonstrative and outgoing, far less withdrawn as a person than Anna, and close enough to her that Anna undertook to arrange for an analysis with Sigmund Freud for Rosenfeld. But Rosenfeld could not hide the fact that she felt hurt by the place in Anna's affections that Burlingham ultimately attained. (Letters from Anna to Burlingham exist, and are housed now at the Freud Museum.)

Rosenfeld, as we have seen, later went on to become an analyst herself, and in England she chose to go to Melanie Klein for a further analysis. This step on Rosenfeld's part had to represent a slap in the face to her friend Anna, since Klein headed a rival school of child analysis. Rosenfeld somehow saw herself as a mediator between Sigmund Freud's theoretical position and that of Klein, but as we have already discussed Freud himself would have nothing of it and did not want to hear about Klein from Rosenfeld. Freud viewed Klein as not just a heretic but also an enemy of his daughter, and it is remarkable how these people managed gently to skate over the hurt feelings that took place. Manners in old Vienna were sophisticated, and sometime hypocritical, but this complicated side of things has not often enough been explored.

Peter Heller's edition of these letters is wholly admirable, although he has decided here not to include all the letters between Eva Rosenfeld and Anna, some of which are accessible at the Library of Congress in Washington, D.C. Heller was as a child a patient of Anna's, went to the school that Dorothy Burlingham created in Rosenfeld's backyard, and later was married for a time to one of Burlingham's daughters. I cannot imagine anyone better able to understand these letters than Heller. He is, in addition, a serious scholar in Central European intellectual history, and he approaches this correspondence with a unique kind of knowledgeability and yet with the detachment that befits his place within academic life.

Rosenfeld's son Victor has provided a valuable memoir here about his mother. She wrote a lengthy autobiography (alluded to earlier) that has not yet appeared in print, but on the basis of what we have in these letters, it will now be much easier to understand her place in the history of psychoanalysis.

All Heller's commentary and editorial notes bear rereading; he is an immensely subtle interpreter and has become the most interesting authority on Anna Freud that I know. Previously, he published *A Child Analysis with Anna Freud*,[2] which is an account of the case history about him that Anna kept; that earlier book should be supplemented by Heller's powerful essay "Reflections on a Child Analysis with Anna Freud and An Adult Analysis with Ernst Kris."[3]

The history of psychoanalysis has been dogged by the sectarianism associated with the animosities fueled by personal and ideological rivalries. Heller's scholarship is impeccable, and a welcome sign that future students of this field will have the wherewithal to approach their work without the blinders that have marred so much earlier research in this area.

## Notes

1. Peter Heller, *Anna Freud's Letters to Eva Rosenfeld*, translated by Mary Weigand (Madison, CT: International Universities Press, 1992).
2. Peter Heller, *A Child Analysis with Anna Freud* (Madison, CT: International Universities Press, 1990). See Paul Roazen, "Review of Heller's *Child Analysis with Anna Freud*," *Journal of the History of the Behavioral Sciences*, April 1991.
3. Peter Heller, "Reflections on a Child Analysis with Anna Freud and an Adult Analysis with Ernst Kris," *Journal of the American Academy of Psychoanalysis*, Winter 1992, pp. 48-74.

# 11

# Karl Menninger

Karl A. Menninger played so important a role in the history of twentieth-century American psychiatry that he seems almost an institution rather than a man. In 1920 he founded, with his father, the Menninger Clinic in Topeka. They had a sanitarium by 1925, and a school for disturbed children was opened the next year. For years now, the Menninger Clinic has been a central training facility for young psychiatrists as well as for those with primarily research interests. Dr. Karl's first book, *The Human Mind* (1930), was a best-seller that sold some 200,000 hardcover copies. He published a number of other notable texts, contributed countless columns for magazine readers, and generally became identified in the public mind with the progressive effort to use psychiatric knowledge for humanitarian purposes.

I will be examining Menninger's specific contribution to psychoanalysis as illustrated in a selection of his correspondence.[1] It is worth noting at the outset that by and large the distinctively American analysts have been relatively little written about, compared with those European figures who had training contact either with Freud or with his immediate disciples abroad. Evidently, Menninger early on felt resentful of the kind of reception the European emigré analysts were getting in the States. As he wrote in 1943, "some of them came over with a very authoritative, eloquent attitude as if they were about to instruct the benighted American savages in the highlights of European science." I could not help being amused by a passage from a 1936 letter of Menninger's about Helene Deutsch, who had then only recently arrived in America:

> As for Helene Deutsch, I personally wish you would cancel the [speaking] invitation. It makes me so damn mad at these foreigners who act as if they were privileged characters who didn't need to answer letters and telegrams, etc. As far as I am concerned, I don't want to hear Helene Deutsch and I'm telling you right now I won't come to hear her when you do get her to Chicago. She told me in Boston that she was coming on down to Topeka and if she wants to do so I will come in and listen to her but I think we ought to put a stop to this adulation of the Europeans just because they speak a broken English...

(According to what Erik Erikson told me, Helene's German—she was Polish—was as cracked as her English.)

These letters of Menninger's are all lively and colorful, and sometimes combative; none of them is short. According to one letter Dr. Karl wrote in 1939, he averaged about eighty letters a week; the editors cite this mathematical figure in their introduction, so presumably that means that he kept up some such pace over the years. *The Selected Correspondence of Karl A. Menninger, 1919-45* covers only a fraction of his career; one presumes, then, that the archives at the Menninger Clinic must constitute a rich mine of information about the leading issues and personalities that Dr. Karl tried to come to terms with.

In the early letters Menninger was a buoyant combatant spreading psychiatric knowledge, but he soon underwent a thorough "conversion" to the specific addition that psychoanalysis could make. By 1921 he could write: "I am head over heals into this psychoanalysis business." His own first analysis was brief but with a fascinating leader in psychosomatic medicine, Smith Ely Jelliffe. Next, Menninger tried to get analyzed by Albert Polon, who had been analyzed by Freud (evidently Freud thought ill of Polon); this again was a short effort. Then, during 1930-1931, Menninger had an eighteen-month analysis with Franz Alexander, who at the time was the leading figure at the new Chicago Institute of Psychoanalysis. Dr. Karl saw Freud at a meeting with him in 1934, but the occasion was unsatisfactory since Freud chose to spend time with Alexander and kept Menninger waiting. (Freud always had disdain and contempt for his success in America, all the more so since his American patients were the most lucrative source of his analytic practice, and he disliked the dependency this involved.)

Menninger went to New York City in 1939 for a further analysis with Ruth Mack Brunswick, which lasted a year and a half. As we have already seen, she is still an almost unknown figure in the history of analysis, largely owing to the unfortunate circumstances connected with her struggle against drug addiction; the editors misleadingly claim that "complications of mycocarditis caused her untimely death at 48." As we have dicussed, for years she was a favorite of Freud's (he sent the Wolf Man to her for a second analysis), and a bridge between the Vienna and New York Psychoanalytic Societies. I have traced Menninger's analytic lineage, following the information in this book, since, as with all psychoanalytic pioneers, geneology has to be a critical aspect of the story. Transferences, suggestion, and old-fashioned personal influence have played a larger part in the history of analysis than in most other fields; and therefore the issue of who trained whom has always, I think, to be paramount.

Menninger came to analysis with not only a secure native self-confidence, but a relatively established position in Topeka. Thus, even though one has to make note of his analysts, it is mainly for historical accuracy and also to provide the names of those against whom he reacted. For he came to struggle with his mentors, and in particular Franz Alexander, without losing his essential faith in the efficacy of analysis as therapy and its significance as science. The editors tell us of a key 1985 personal communication from Menninger to them: "I think now Alexander was on the right path and might have saved [us from] the decline of psychoanalysis."

Through much of the book, however, Menninger is tough on Alexander—not for being weak toward the most orthodox forces in analysis, as Abram Kardiner and Sandor Rado thought, but for Alexander's being too tolerant of those independent spirits who were trying to pursue their own paths in analysis. Menninger does write in 1935 of Alexander that "there can never be any doubt in the world about his essential friendliness, kindness, and bigheartedness." But Menninger minded that Alexander "always had a tendency to be a little patronizing and depreciatory toward American psychiatry in general...."

Worse still, Alexander was, in Menninger's 1940 view, "too kind to Horney," in writing a professional article about her work. "Does one," Menninger asked Alexander, "have to be disagreeable and attack Freud in order to be taken seriously by his colleagues?" Menninger (then in analysis with Ruth Mack Brunswick) continued, "Freud did not treat me very nicely, as you know, but nonetheless, I think his ideas, his grasp, his formulations are so infinitely ahead of anything else that has been proposed, that I have nailed my banner to his mast, and I'll defend it against assault for the rest of my life." Menninger could not agree with Alexander that "the opposite of anti-Freudianism is an emotional dependence upon Freud." Writing to Alexander, Menninger objected to "the bastards or fifth columnists of psychoanalysis...I think you feel that you are tolerant in this respect, and I feel it is a weakness on your part, a neurotic complacency...." Menninger said he was against "appeasement": "I still think you are terribly wrong when you recommend tolerance as an attitude toward rascals...." Menninger was objecting to what he called "the psychoanalytic traitors and exploiters." To John Dollard at Yale Menninger observed of Dollard's work, "There are some traitors to psychoanalytic convictions and principles who will welcome your book...." Dollard aptly replied, "Why is it treacherous to quote Freud correctly and not to agree with him?"

It may be that some of Menninger's stridency to Alexander about Horney had a personal basis: Horney had analyzed Menninger's first wife. On the whole, though, even while Menninger may later say he thinks Alexander was basically on the right track, Menninger threw himself then into defending an orthodox analytic position. So if he has to be credited with promoting psychoanalysis in America, both within psychiatry and in the popular culture, Menninger also has to be held partly responsible for what he himself spoke of as the current "decline" in the field. Alexander at the time was trying to initiate some interesting changes in analytic psychotherapy, but Menninger seems to have ignored these proposals and instead allied himself firmly with Freud's daughter Anna in London. In later years, the *Bulletin of the Menninger Clinic* was even constrained in how it reviewed books, since Dr. Karl kept an eye out for what was and what was not likely to be deemed offensive by "Miss Freud." The record is still not clear which of them was the better at raising foundation money, but I suspect that they both turned to similar sources. (Dr. Karl told me he thought that Ruth Mack Brunswick and Anna Freud bore a physical resemblance to each other; most others have emphasized the complicated and ambivalent love-hate relationship between the two women.)

At least as historically interesting as the intra-psychoanalytic ideological differences that come up in *The Selected Letters of Karl A. Menninger* are the bits and pieces that one can glean about non-Freudian psychiatry. In order to evaluate the contribution that psychoanalysis made to intellectual history, it is necessary to take a serious new look at figures like Adolf Meyer and others who are today relatively forgotten among the educated reading public.[2] Why did they hold out, and on what grounds did they criticze the psychoanalysis of their day? My hunch is that if Menninger came to think that Alexander was "on the right path," many of the well-meaning criticisms on the part of the old-line psychiatrists are going to have to be taken seriously now.

For example, Menninger was so enthusiastic about psychoanalysis that he, along with others, helped contribute to the overselling of psychiatry that has in recent years provoked a substantial anti-psychiatric backlash. It seems to me good-natured, but fallacious, for Menninger to have believed that "anti-Semitism is one very poignant symptom of a widespread social disease." Prejudice is not the same as illness. Menninger had a particular (and I think naïve) interest in extending psychoanalysis into the law, but he also thought that the public could benefit from political leaders being subjected to psychiatric profiles before being allowed to govern. His faith in what so-called experts could accomplish was part of a strongly felt American conviction that knowledge could lead to almost unlimited possibilities of social improvement. Freud himself was highly skeptical about progress, and had—at his best—a secure sense of the limits on what psychoanalysis could accomplish.

The editorial apparatus of this book has to be considered unfortunate. There is, for openers, an inexplicable lack of an index; and we are told in the acknowledgments that the "photographs" are "courtesy of the Menninger Foundation Archives," but the book contains no photographs. The editors admit that they "complied" with Dr. Karl's "request that a few letters be excluded from the book and that portions of perhaps a dozen others be deleted." Historians, however, need a completely free hand in such matters. The compromised nature of the editors' position perhaps explains some of the defects of the footnoting. Often these are sins of omission. For example, when Horace W. Frink's name comes up, they describe him but leave out the historically significant tragic encounter he himself had with Freud. We are told though that Frink paid one "visit" to Freud, and then a second "visit," whereas in fact he was twice in analysis with Freud. The editors also assert that Ernest Jones's life of Freud "remains the definitive biography," flying in the face of all the research of the last generation. And Alfred Adler supposedly simply "resigned" from the Vienna Psychoanalytic Society "to establish his own school," without having first been excommunicated. Kardiner and Rado[3] are also said to have led a "defection." I had the general impression that in the footnotes the deck was ideologically stacked, but not in keeping with Menninger's supposedly belated recognition that Alexander's thinking might have been the better path to have taken.

Moreover, the notes are full of howlers in terms of the history of psychiatry. When one of Menninger's correspondents refers to "Kretchmer" and "the whole subject of constitution," the editors identify him as Herman Kretschmer, a Chicago urologist instead of the obviously right person, Ernst Kretschmer, the famous German psychiatrist who wrote about body types. The editorial notes contain so many little (but important) mistakes—first names wrong, places of birth incorrect, and people completely misidentified—that it would be easy to despair for the future of the history of psychoanalysis. A text like this, published by a famous university press, might well be thoughtlessly considered authoritative.

The book does not have enough scope to be able to begin successfully to evaluate Menninger's contribution to modern psychoanalysis. He did take Freud's death instinct theory very seriously and tried to elaborate the consequences of destructiveness instead of being tied to Freud's notion of libido: "it is probable," Menninger maintained in 1935, "that no one is made seriously sick by his sexual impulses, no matter how forbidden they are or how deep or how close to consciousness." Menninger over the years has swung in many different directions; late in life he even wrote approvingly of Thomas Szasz's general approach. But each of Menninger's phases has always been interesting in his vehemence. Perhaps *The Selected Correspondence of Karl A. Menninger* will be the beginning of a long overdue reassessment of the seminal accomplishments of this pioneering figure.

## Notes

1. *The Selected Correspondence of Karl A. Menninger, 1919-1945*, ed. Howard J. Faulkner and Virginia D. Pruitt (New Haven, CT: Yale University Press, 1988).
2. Paul Roazen, *Canada's King: An Essay in Political Psychology* (Oakville, Ontario: Mosaic Press, 1998), Ch. 2 especially.
3. Paul Roazen and Bluma Swerdloff, *Heresy: Sandor Rado and the Psychoanalytic Movement* (Northvale, NJ: Jason Aronson, 1995).

# 12

# Heinz Kohut

Chicago has an unusual history within the tale of Freud's reception in America. Some of Carl Jung's most influential patrons were from Chicago, but little is yet known about the sorts of Americans who went to Zurich, although the literature about Freud and America would seem to be abundant. Yet there are some striking gaps in what we know about Freud's impact on the States. And Chicago is one of the main blank spots. The Institute of Psychoanalysis there was founded by Franz Alexander in the early 1930s; he had come from being a star in Berlin, and with an academic family background he sought to make a university-like atmosphere for analysts in Chicago. Until he left for Los Angeles in 1956, Alexander was the life and soul of the Chicago Institute. He became centrally interested in psychosomatic medicine, but his range was enormous; he wrote about the history of psychiatry and proposed changes in therapeutic technique. Alexander (already famous) became notorious as an enemy to orthodox analysis by proposing the advantages of a "corrective emotional experience" in treatment.

It may seem hard to believe today, but the fanatics within psychoanalysis denounced Alexander for heresy. And for many years now there has scarcely been a sound about Alexander emanating from within Chicago psychoanalysis. Heinz Kohut, who in the 1970s developed the system of ideas known as "self psychology," rarely saw his work in relation to Alexander, and as others then and now avoided the dread of being associated with Alexander's legacy as a kind of renegade. Yet Kohut was a genuinely original spirit in psychoanalysis, and it is a pity that the fear of "dissidence" is so great, the terror of being torn apart from the so-called mainstream so enduring, that neither Kohut, who died in 1981, nor his followers have sought to put his ideas in proper historical context. Kohut was, as Alexander himself, unwilling to explore such predecessors as Jung; Kohut even steered clear of the work of someone as relatively uncontroversial as Erik H. Erikson, whose ideas Kohut once admired. And so young analysts today are apt to associate conceptions of the self exclusively with Kohut, who succeeded in creating a movement of his own, and one which has resisted being stigmatized as heresy. Yet the costs of achieving innovation have been considerable.

*The Curve of Life: Correspondence of Heinz Kohut 1923-1981*,[1] admirably introduced by a professional historian, Geoffrey Cocks, serves as an excellent beginning for those interested in exploring Kohut's ideas further. Kohut's most well-known texts are difficult to read, as he introduced much new technical jargon. For anyone who expects clear prose his sentences can be daunting. One has to wonder whether Kohut's unconscious fear of going too far in upsetting the status quo in psychoanalysis did not, at least at the outset, hamper the clarity of his expression. In the end, just as his books began to sell, he wound up offending the powers-that-be in orthodox psychoanalysis. So that when Anna Freud, in her last years, pronounced Kohut as "antipsychoanalytic," that fearful excommunication was echoed by some of her most powerful allies in New York City. They also had their influence within Chicago analysis, and Kohut found himself criticized and embattled. He managed in the end to enable his self-psychology movement to become a progressive force within analysis, but he never had to acknowledge how his ideas fit into the work of those earlier pioneers who had challenged Freud's conceptualization even while he was still alive.

*The Curve of Life* is refreshingly well-written; none of the letters here are as awkwardly written as some of Kohut's published prose. (One would have thought, though, that the title of the book would be related to Erikson's concept of the "life cycle.") It would seem that Kohut was sadly in need of the confirmation of the applause of the outside world. As he said at a dinner in his honor in 1978, "I have always felt I wanted very much to have a childhood like the other children. And I tried very much to do all the right kinds of things. However, in the long run, I couldn't. I grew up not quite like the other children. I continued to ask all the kinds of questions which annoyed the other 'fathers' that I had." In the end he seems to have found some sort of peace with having disturbed his elders, but it came at an unnecessary price.

Reading these letters one has to be impressed, I think, how relatively late Kohut was in reading Freud. Even though Kohut was a native Viennese, and analyzed first in Vienna, he seems to be discovering Freud in the 1950s. From his earliest years, Kohut was interested in music and literature, subjects which were not high on Freud's own agenda. Only in 1981, according to these letters, did Kohut acknowledge, despite his "respect" for Freud, that he "doesn't seem to have been exuberant enough for my taste—no pleasure in music really, and a bit stuffy about modern art...."

Kohut's contribution was to expand Freud's concept of narcissism (which had been originally designed to counter Jung) and then move on to expound a full-fledged theory of the self. But the up-shot was to reinterpret the Oedipus complex: as he once asked, "Is it not the most significant dynamic-genetic feature of the Oedipus story that Oedipus was a rejected child?" Many of the pages of this book are taken up with Kohut's entangled enmeshment with Anna Freud and her allies; initially he basked too much in her enthusiasm for him, and he cooperated in publicly distancing himself from Kleinian thinking. But the politics of the international psychoanalytic movement meant that Kohut failed to get elected to the presidency of the International Psychoanalytic Association.

Too much of Kohut's energies went, I think, into trying to make his conceptual angels dance on the head of an orthodox psychoanalytic pin. Yet he did succeed in getting the so-called mainstream of psychoanalysis to think beyond the drive psychology it inherited from Freud. It remains for future students to place Kohut's work within the history of ideas, at a time when there can be no danger of his being excommunicated as a heretic. For now, though, Kohut will seem a master of convoluted ambivalence; as he writes here, "Over the years I've analyzed many colleagues who know me well and with whom I remain in (scientific and professional) contact. The unrivalled achievement in this realm is of course Freud's analysis of his daughter Anna—a masterstroke which even appears to me to have gone too far." To independent outsiders, however, the analysis of Anna by her father seems a good deal less than a "masterstroke," and one cannot help thinking that Kohut should have known better. As it is, we will have to wait for students of intellectual history to put Kohut's considerable contribution in historical perspective, which should entail the rehabilitation of a whole host of pioneering thinkers with whom in his lifetime Kohut was uncomfortable being associated.

## Note

1. *The Curve of Life: Correspondence of Heinz Kohut 1923-1981*, ed. Geoffrey Cocks (Chicago: University of Chicago Press, 1994).

# 13

# Strachey-Brooke

*Friends and Apostles: The Correspondence of Rupert Brooke and James Strachey, 1905-1914*[1] records a moving love story. Rupert Brooke and James Strachey first met as boys of ten at Hillbrow School. Brooke was the son of a housemaster at Rugby, while Strachey was a member of one of England's most illustrious literary families. Strachey's older brother Lytton became a leading figure in the Bloomsbury group. Both Brooke, who attended King's College, and Strachey, a member of Trinity College, were elected to Cambridge's famous society called "the Apostles." I can still remember my shock at discovering that the Apostles, described so eloquently in moral and intellectual terms in one of the volumes of Leonard Woolf's autobiography, was also programmatically homosexual. Brooke and Strachey were eighteen years old when they renewed their acquaintance at Cambridge, which marks the beginning of this collection of letters. Shortly after Strachey's death in 1967, his wife Alix sold the correspondence to the Berg Collection of the New York Public Library.

Brooke, who died of blood poisoning in 1915 on his way to fight for the British at Gallipoli, is known mainly for his patriotic poetry. I would have called him a minor poet except for a talk Brooke gave in 1906: "People who speak disparagingly of minor poetry are either stockbrokers and lawyers and rich practical people who don't understand, or reviewers in the Press, who are always young men fresh from a university with souls so stuffed with intellectual pride that they might as lightly speak of minor roses or minor sunsets." My central interest in the Brooke-Strachey letters was elicited by Strachey's having become Freud's main translator into English; Freud picked him as one of his translators during the time when Freud was analyzing both James and Alix in Vienna following their marriage in 1920. (One reliable-sounding story I heard dated the occasion for the marriage by the way it eased the Stracheys getting a visa to Austria after World War I.) At the conclusion of World War II, at a time when a committee might have been struck in London to undertake translating *The Standard Edition* of Freud's works, Anna Freud and others were relieved when Strachey volunteered to take charge of the whole project himself. That set of translations remains Strachey's real claim to fame. The editorial apparatus he constructed has been taken over by the Germans for their own edition. In France, despite more interest in Paris about Freud than almost anyplace else in the world, a committee is still in the early stages of bringing out its edition of Freud's writings.

We have known for some time that Strachey could be an unusually pithy writer, although of course his brother Lytton is the one who wrote the justifiably famous books. When James saw the results of the biography of Lytton that James had authorized Michael Holroyd to undertake, James was unhappy, and Holroyd made the brilliant decision to publish James's acid-sounding comments as footnotes on the pages of the text. It should not detract from all that Holroyd succeeded in accomplishing if I say that James's testy objections helped liven up the text. Then a volume of the letters exchanged between James and Alix, while they were temporarily separated during 1924-1925 when Alix went for a second analysis in Berlin, came out as *Bloomsbury/Freud* in 1985.[2]

Although James and Alix were obviously deeply attached to one another, there was plenty of suspicion about the extent of their heterosexuality. Alix Strachey put some restrictions on the early appearance of these letters, and Brooke's literary trustee Geoffrey Keynes (John Maynard's brother) not only dragged his heels about the release of these letters to Strachey but tried to deny the homosexuality of Brooke.

Nothing prepared me for the immensely touching human encounter to be found in *Friends and Apostles*. Until about 1912 the letters do make for some difficult going. At least I found all the studied archness on the part of both Brooke and Strachey difficult to take. Of course they had some fascinating friends and acquaintances. Virginia Woolf, one of the greatest of them, wrote about the Strachey family in her diary that she found "an air, a vapour, an indescribable taste of dust in the throat, something tickling & irritating as well as tingling & stimulating." But all the cultivated cleverness, especially on James Strachey's part, seemed to me off-putting. He was so cerebral about sex that it is hard to imagine that he could have enjoyed it much; he kept using the word "copulating" as if he were writing about another species, and I can almost see the wry smirk on his face. These letters give a picture, I hope, not of homosexual attachments so much as those specific to the British upper classes at the turn of the twentieth century. I could not help being reminded of the way that D. H. Lawrence had loathed the whole Bloomsbury set.

After Brooke has some sort of nervous breakdown in 1912, the letters change. For years Strachey had been the adoring pursuer, and Brooke standoffish. But with Brooke's collapse his letters grow almost out of control in length, and Brooke comes to doubt his own sanity. In a note to Virginia Stephen (not yet married to Leonard Woolf) Brooke wrote about how he hated "the healthy unimaginative hard shelled dilettanti" like James. Strachey stuck by Brooke, and financed at least one trip to the continent. Brooke wrote a letter to Strachey concerned with an acquaintance of theirs (Denham Russell-Smith) who had just died, and whom Brooke had seduced in 1909; Brooke provides all the details of the night's encounter in which he lost his virginity, which reminds us just how inexperienced these people were. James, in the midst of Brooke's collapse, was still trying to encourage Brooke's writing talent; but also Strachey revealed something of his own sort of thinking when he wrote to congratulate Brooke on the letter: "It seemed to give the whole of that sort of copulation so completely. They say there's another sort, that I know nothing about—with people one's in love with. Is that really quite different? I've always thought it must be....Well, one way or another you've immortalized Denham." For some reason the editor, Keith Hale, who has done an extraordinary amount of conscientious work identifying the people in *Friends and Apostles* and providing an editorial apparatus that would have pleased Strachey's own exacting standards, finds this letter about Denham "in many ways the most fascinating...written by Brooke."

Yet within weeks of Strachey's own response to this letter Brooke is acknowledging his own "dreary flippancy" toward Strachey. Two days later Brooke lowers the boom on Strachey. "Listen. Men and women neither 'copulate' nor want to 'copulate': men have women: women are had by men. Listen. There is between men & women, sometimes, a thing called love: unknown to you. It has its laws & demands. It can be defiled: poisoned: & killed...All these sentences—there's the point—are entirely meaningless to you. I might as well write in Assyrian. You'd just twitter on...." The next day Brooke continues: "I've changed, not you. I suppose if I got better; or if you grew up; we could manage it again."

After that Hale tells us that "Brooke all but disappeared from Strachey's life...." Brooke started to refer to the Stracheys "in the plural, as a disease." To a friend, Brooke acknowledged that James was "less dirty" than Lytton, and "so defenceless that it is no sport kicking him." To Brooke, James did not "understand about the only important things." "He's far too selfish & minor to be hurt ever. He's precisely as he always was: with his brilliant sense of humour, & his liking for contemptuous criticism; which keeps him happy." Brooke, as one of their friends commented, "yearned for marriage but not a wife." Brooke was romantically interested in several women, one of whom would later have a long extra-marital liasion with Strachey. Brooke wrote her: "Really the unrelieved *sordidness* of that man's career—loving me for nine years and you for the rest of his life! I sometimes think God has been a little *too* hard on him, dreadful as he is." Yet Brooke could also write of Strachey: "he's a very fine person extraordinarily honest and trustworthy, very intelligent, and meaning well (which is important)."

In 1913 Brooke wrote James that he had "no sense of what are to me the most important things in the world. Perhaps one day you'll grow up; or I shall have got down to your level. No doubt, both motions are in process. But I wish you well." Brooke had been responding to a note of James's in which he had written "I hated you, dear, a good deal a few months ago....But that's gone now, I think, I love you (and don't care if you laugh at me for saying so) and I believe I've loved you all the time." Brooke found this note "dreadful," and Strachey did mind Brooke's sharp response. Strachey defended himself: "it seems rather a pity that your sorrows should have turned you into a prig. And aren't you a bit uncharitable too? But I suppose that goes with self-righteousness." The mood, Strachey serpentinely wrote, of Brooke's last letter made Strachey "foam a good deal. But like all the troubles of babyhood, ça passes, ça passe. I feel, and always felt, infinitely benevolent towards the mysterious worries of these perplexed grown ups at whose feet I crawl—I'm placid even when they tread on my fingers. My good Rupert, I've got one great advantage over you. You can't prevent my being fonder of you than of—well, of almost anyone else in the world."

Brooke and Strachey stayed in touch until Brooke's death in 1915. Brooke enlisted in the war-effort, while Strachey stayed a pacifist. In one of his war sonnets Brooke was probably referring to Lytton Strachey among the "half men." W. B. Yeats had considered Brooke "the handsomest man in England," and thanks to Brooke's poetry he became at his death a national hero. Henry James, on hearing of Brooke's death, was reported to have wept. Strachey had been fired from his position at the *Spectator* because of his position on the war. After James and Alix married, they honeymooned in Vienna. Hale suggests that "it is likely that Strachey's desire to understand both his own sexuality and Brooke's strange behavior partially accounts for his being drawn to Freud." Strachey's last quoted comments on Brooke came in someone else's 1964 review of a Brooke biography: "Rupert wasn't as nice as people now imagine; but he was a great deal cleverer." (But Brooke had been unable to follow a 1909 reference of James's to *Middlemarch* and thought that the world of Chekhov was one of "tired children.")

Brooke had actively sought the oblivion of death in the great campaign of World War I; Strachey had the common sense, however unrequited his adoration of Brooke, to be a survivor. Strachey did not set out, like Brooke, to destroy his closest friendships. One wonders whether the poetic intensity of Brooke was not too much for the commonplace world to endure. Strachey never did, in Brooke's terms, grow up, but he lived to have the last word. (Lytton Strachey had written to Virginia Woolf about James that he was "either incredibly young or inconceivably old." One of my British analytic friends once commented about James that in his old age he had "grown into" himself.) The publication of the letters in *Friends and Apostles* may lead us to wonder again about the nature of love, and how it struggles to fulfill itself. Especially because of the exchanges between Brooke and Strachey dating from 1912-1913, *Friends and Apostles* becomes a poignant record of the tragedy of unfullfillable human affection. Intellectual historians do not usually come across in non-fiction the makings of poetry and fiction. I cannot speak for experts on modern British literature or Brooke, but I am certain that students of the history of psychoanalysis will now have a fresh picture of James Strachey.

All these letters, starting with those by Freud to Silberstein, and including his exchanges with Jones and Ferenczi, as well as the volumes connected with Anna Freud, Menninger, Kohut, and James Strachey, illustrate how rich and complex a heritage has been left for intellectual historians to examine.

## Notes

1. *Friends and Apostles: The Correspondence of Rupert Brooke and James Strachey, 1905-1914*, ed. Keith Hale (New Haven, CT: Yale University Press, 1998).
2. *Bloomsbury/Freud: The Letters of James and Alix Strachey, 1924-25*, ed. Perry Meisel and Walter Kendrick (New York: Basic Books, 1985). See Paul Roazen, *Encountering Freud* (New Brunswick, NJ: Transaction, 1990), pp. 24-26.

# Part 4

## Interviews

# Introduction to Part 4

My work on Freud arose from my good fortune in having met and interviewed over seventy people who knew Freud personally, including twenty-five of his analytic patients. My interviewing was largely conducted in the 1960s, but over the years I have continued to meet people who have played a part in the history of psychoanalysis. To the extent that I have been able to succeed in making an original contribution to this field, it has been largely due to my contact with these pioneers. Yet it is not easy to reproduce just what this sort of personal field work has been like. What I learnt has to be partly a consequence of that which I brought to the interviewing itself. There is, alas, no clear way of codifying how I proceeded. I was not after that which could be easily reproducible—my quest was impressionistic yet disciplined by all my prior academic interests, as well as whatever human experience I may have brought to these encounters.

It is almost certain, even as I have attempted to write up a few of these interviews, that I am overlooking features to these encounters which might be easy for outsiders to comment on. Still, I did the best I could, in an area of human knowledge which seems to remains as contentious as ever.

And perhaps this is as it should be; for to the degree that psychoanalysis has involved contrasting conceptions of the good life, it will be possible to evaluate the upshot of these interviews only from different moral and social perspectives. I feel that the best of what I picked up was the living examples of what the early analysts were like as people. And even though it is not a simple matter to put that learning experience down now, I have felt spiritually rejuvenated each time I have reflected back on these precious human contacts. I will always remain deeply indebted for the unusual conscientiousness with which my inquiries were met.

# 14

# Michael Balint

It is both easy, as well as at the same time extremely difficult, to try to reconstruct the interviews on the history of psychoanalysis that I conducted with Dr. Michael Balint on July 22, 1965 and November 8, 1966. I did keep detailed working notes of the time I spent with Balint, and also certain key aspects of the interviews stand out in my mind independently of any written record that I saved. But although I was proceeding then with the hope that everything I was accumulating about early analysis might one day be publishable, as a scholar I did not keep track of the kind of exact details which are apt to make a written account seem journalistically vivid. Unfortunately, I did not write down physical details connected with the setting of my talking with Balint, although I suspect that such material would be helpful for the purposes I have undertaken now.

So the reader will have to make the effort of an imaginative stretch if the following remarks are going to be historically useful for future research. Above all, perhaps the central challenge I face now is attempting to explicate what conditions were like in the field over thirty years ago, which is bound to be at odds with the way the same subject matter appears today. To take only one obvious starting point for explaining the circumstances I was laboring under at the time, Anna Freud was not only still alive and working in the same city, London, England, as Balint, but she was for both Balint and myself, as well as any researcher then, an intimidating presence inevitably over-shadowing my discussions on the history of her father's field. (When, some years later and following her death, I once gave a presentation before a group at the British Psychoanalytic Society, I found a photograph of her smiling face on the wall more alarming that the rather severe shots of either her father or Ernest Jones.) At the time I first met Balint, Anna had, thanks to my introduction to her through her old teacher, Dr. Helene Deutsch, been fully welcoming to me, and I had been invited that summer to sit in on weekly case conferences at her Hampstead Clinic for treating children, which has now been renamed the Anna Freud Center.

My first two sets of notes to myself can help establish the setting which surrounded how I got on with Balint. "A wonderfully Hungarian house —really something to see," was how I had started out the record of our interchange. Balint, who was living then near Regent's Park, had been unable to fit me into his schedule earlier, when I had first arrived in London in late June, but I had succeeded in setting up an appointment when it proved possible for him to spare the extra time. By then, however, I had gotten used to various British consulting rooms, which made the contrast to Balint's central European furnishings all the more striking. As I recall it, he saw me in his living room, or at any rate I remember some spacious atmosphere which was beautifully decorated.

My second recorded remark for myself was: "very clever man." I was at the time dealing with a lot of pioneers in the history of analysis, all of whom were highly intelligent and interesting sources of historical information, so my reaction to Balint must have been exceptionally favorable. My own way of assessing people had to do with how much they had to teach me, and I recall at dinner sometime shortly thereafter with the anthropologist-writer Geoffrey Gorer (an old friend of people of the stature of George Orwell, Margaret Mead, Lucien Freud, W. H. Auden, and the Sitwells), as Gorer was helping me absorb what I was learning from interviews, that he remarked on how positively I seemed to have reacted to my first encounter with Balint.

Right at the outset, Balint and I had gotten onto discussing the Freud-Ferenczi letters, which Balint then had in his physical possession (there were four sets of copies), although at the time the originals were still sealed at the Freud Collection at the Library of Congress in Washington, D.C. (Somehow Balint also had the Freud-Otto Rank correspondence as well.) Balint explained that fifty years after Freud's 1939 death, Balint would have the legal right to publish whatever he wanted of the Freud-Ferenczi material, since by then it would have become "public property." I assume we both took for granted that Balint was Ferenczi's literary executor. It was hard for me to absorb at the time how extensive the Freud-Ferenczi letters were, since only snippets of them had been used in Jones's authorized biography of Freud. According to Balint, there were some 2,500 letters, which were "not" of momentous "scientific importance" but amounted to something of "great personal significance." (We now know that Balint repeatedly was apt somehow to double the number of Freud-Ferenczi letters in existence.) Freud and Ferenczi had been, Balint told me, "very close," and I never doubted the truth of this proposition.

Ferenczi's wife Gizella was a woman to whom Freud had given one of his antique stones to be made into a ring, and at the time I had thought there was only one such female to whom Freud had made such a present. At any rate, the gift was enough to establish something of how intimately involved with Freud both the Ferenczis had been. Ferenczi had had, according to Balint, "a long courtship" with his future wife, although he said there were many "neurotic complications" to be taken into account.

I tried contrasting Freud's relation with Karl Abraham to how the creator of analysis had gotten on with Ferenczi, but that line of inquiry did not lead anywhere. (The same summer in London I had been able to read through the page proofs of the book of Freud's letters to Abraham, although at the time I was only partly aware of how truncated a version of the full correspondence the text amounted to. James Strachey, for example, alerted me to how certain angry letters by Freud, just before Abraham's death, had been omitted. By today a whole new edition of the Freud-Abraham correspondence has been undertaken to be an uncensored version. The initial English translator, Eric Mosbacher, had been so upset with the wordings that Abraham's analyst daughter Hilde had insisted on that Mosbacher refused to have his real name appear on the book itself, and instead relied on the pseudonym of "Bernard Marsh." Although I put a note in the back of my 1975 *Freud and His Followers* about "Bernard Marsh" as a false translator's name, it is only now, as the new edition of these letters are being prepared, that anyone has noticed what I naively had thought was going to be a striking scholarly point.)

Balint showed me how he was then wearing the antique-stone ring which Freud had once given Ferenczi as part of his being a member of the now famous Committee, founded before World War I, to safeguard the future of analysis. Balint seemed delighted to hear from me that Jones's own ring had been lost. (When I had once told Erik H. Erikson about Jones's loss of that precious ring, Erikson hypothesized that Freud himself might never have forgiven Jones for such an oversight.) Balint thought that Jones was "the best hated man in London," even though he was "respected." When Jones was writing his biography of Freud, Balint said that he had kept back some of Ferenczi's own letters to Freud, in which Ferenczi had had some "very harsh" things to say about Jones, an analysand of Ferenczi's. Because Jones had been a "scoundrel" toward Ferenczi did not, in Balint's view, justify advertising the unflattering things Ferenczi had had to say about Jones. Balint insisted that Jones had copied out some wrong dates for the Freud-Ferenczi letters, since none existed where Jones claimed there were some; that sort of inexactitude would fit what Strachey had told me about Jones's volumes.

Since, in going through Jones's unsorted papers in the basement of the British Psychoanalytic Society, I had come across the fact that in 1923 Freud had had a "Steinach operation," a rejuvenatory procedure on his testicles in a bizarre attempt to overcome the death instinct by mobilizing the forces in behalf of life, I mentioned it to Balint. (Cancer of course thrives on the host.) He seemed already to know about the surgery (perhaps from the Freud-Ferenczi correspondence), considering it "nothing special." He thought that Paul Federn had once given a paper, perhaps at the Innsbruck Congress, in which a clinical illustration was offered of a patient having had, after a Steinach procedure, an increase in anxiety dreams because of the presence of more libidinal strength; according to Balint's rendition of Federn's argument, that showed the proof of

Freud's theory that anxiety is itself linked to the damming-up of libido. (Although I had thought that Federn's paper must have been collected in the edition of his works edited by Edoardo Weiss, I never could find the appropriate citation that Balint alluded to.) Balint believed that "everyone" had known that it was "Professor" (which is the way all Freud's immediate pupils still referred to him) Federn was talking about.

Balint was very specific and outspoken that "they," meaning the Freuds and their official spokesmen, had built up a "myth" about him. (I had found Balint's letters to Jones eloquent and most interesting.) Balint was explicitly informing me that I could never hope to publish the full truth—not as it might exist as a metaphysical entity, but what was already believed to be the case. He was gently warning me that my preferred way of proceeding would lead to professional consequences that were too damaging to bear, and he was not referring to any questions of medical discretion. "They will attack you!" he predicted at one point. I tried to reply: "But what can they do to me?" Balint and I both agreed that in his biography Jones had "idolized" Freud, but Balint also exclaimed: "You are going to say that!" His acknowledgement of my intentions did not stop him from continuing to cooperate with me. My relative knowledgeability was misleading to other worried informants; for not being an analyst myself, but a student of intellectual history, I could not be subject to excommunication, or any of the worst privations that "deviancy" can entail.

According to my notes, right at the outset and "rather aggresively at that" Balint had wanted to know who had analyzed me. It seemed to me not a surprising question, and we were speaking in private; subsequently, on other occasions I have been challenged on that point in public, even though that seems to me an improper intrusion. Having had a personal analysis ought to be an asset, and at least in the 1960s should have been no more surprising in the circles I moved in than that one had had biological parents. Although Helene Deutsch had not analyzed me, Balint somehow felt reassured that she would "not permit" me to use "gossip." To use the English expression of the carrot and the stick as forms of control, if Helene Deutsch was the carrot then Anna Freud would be the stick, and Balint warned me of the possibility that she would "destroy" me if I got out of line. (I had no knowledge then of any possible tensions between Balint and Anna Freud, although I knew that he was not a member of the separate group led then by "Miss Freud." Jones had allowed Balint, unlike some other continental analysts, to move to England, but it was some time before he was able to live in London itself.)

Balint proceeded, doubtless thinking of Ferenczi's own difficulties within orthodox analysis, to run through the troubles that a line of so-called troublemakers in analysis had had. Rank, for example, had supposedly had "a paranoid spell" while he was in America in the 1920s, and Freud had spent "hours and hours" with him "trying to get him straightened out." Before World War I Rank had been "a boy," and Freud had seen to his education. Then, while Rank was serving in the military stationed at Cracow, he had been the editor of an army journal and been given some special responsibilities, which turned him, according to Balint, into becoming "a man."

Sandor Rado, a Hungarian who became guilty of psychoanalytic "treason," was in Balint's view an "awful person" whom "no one" liked at the Columbia Psychoanalytic Institute Rado had founded during World War II. (I found Rado to be unusually brilliant, and felt Balint was too harsh; in 1995 I helped publish *Heresy: Sandor Rado and the Psychoanalytic Movement.* Having once been heterodox, by then the Columbia Institute seemed to lean over backwards to orthodoxy.) Hanns Sachs, an early apostle of Freud's who at one point collaborated with Freud but never organizationally, like Rado, set up his own independent school, was known to Balint as another one of the leading teachers at the Berlin Psychoanalytic Institute in the 1920s. Sachs and Rado were prominent in Berlin when Balint was then in training. But Balint never knew that Sachs was a divorced man, as I told Balint that I had in fact interviewed Sachs's former wife. Balint was very surprised to hear that Sachs had ever been other than a happy bachelor, and Sachs seemed to have had a string of very attractive lady friends. Max Eitingon, also in Betrlin, was "the least significant" of Freud's Committee, yet "very cultured"; his wife returned to Europe from Palestine, where they had fled from the Nazis, after Eitingon's death.

Although we often drifted away from Balint's central role as Ferenczi's spokesperson, and talked about a variety of issues connected with writing about the history of analysis as a whole, it was never long before we came back to Ferenczi himself. Balint claimed that the reason he had not protested even more strongly to Jones about the way Jones attributed Ferenczi's falling away from Freud to Ferenczi's supposed slumbering psychosis was Jones's final illness when he wrote the final volume of his biography. Balint said he had known that Jones was then dying and with only a few months to go.

When I first saw Balint he said he was "planning" to publish the Freud-Ferenczi letters, with the qualification that he had to wait for Anna Freud to agree to the project. "Otherwise" Balint maintained that he would go ahead and just publish Ferenczi's own letters. Balint was looking for financial and publishing help to assist him with all the translating work that would be involved in such an undertaking. I mentioned the suggestion that Harvard University (where I then taught) had a press that might undertake such a commitment, but Balint mainly seemed concerned that he needed the help of a grant that would pay him while he did the necessary editing. (In the end it took a whole team of people on the continent to take charge of the Freud-Ferrenczi correspondence.)

It was inevitable, since I was interviewing the most eminent Hungarian in the British Psychoanalytic Society, to talk about other Hungarians in analysis, such as Anton von Freund, whose sister, Kata Levy, was still alive and allowing herself to be interviewed by me. Balint pointed out that it was von Freund, an exceptionally "charming" man, whose idea it was to have training institutes, although originally it had seemed like "a pipe-dream." The von Freunds were a very rich family, and it turned out that shortly after Anton's untimely death the Berlin Institute opened its doors to students in training. Balint mentioned that there had been a family upheaval after von Freund's death, since he had left some money to a mistress, an analyst who was still alive in Budapest, and his family tried to fight the bequest.

Kata Levy told me that her husband Lajos had been the one who first gave Ferenczi a copy of Freud's *The Interpretation of Dreams*, and although Jones had brushed aside Kata's story, Balint thought it "may well" have been true. Balint said that at first Ferenczi had not liked Freud's teachings. Ferenczi had gone to medical school in Vienna during 1899-1900, which was when he claimed Freud was already lecturing there; yet Ferenczi had never heard Freud then. Balint kept alluding to how "original" a thinker Ferenczi was, especially in contrast to someone like Jones. (Rado, too, thought Ferenczi had been a "poet" as opposed to how Jones seemed to be merely a "sargeant.")

Ferenczi was supposed to have gotten interested in psychoanalysis when someone told him it was possible to measure human thoughts with the help of a stop-watch. Jung had proposed the use of such association experiments, and Ferenczi had gone "all over" Budapest trying out Jung's technique. In those days Ferenczi was still unmarried and "he lived in cafes." Years later, when Balint went to these cafes himself, he found that the older waiters always remembered Ferenczi fondly from those Jung association experiments.

Lajos Levy, one of the few founding members of the Hungarian Psychoanalytic Society, was in Balint's view "an unhappy man" because of his relationship with his wife. He was, though, good for patients "who needed a certain kind of reassurance." The Levy son had to live away from home, with the Aichhorns in Vienna, because of the difficulties between his parents. I already knew that after her brother Anton von Freund had been treated by Freud, Kata (and later Anton's second wife) were also both in analysis with Freud. Balint claimed to know who had told Jones about Ferenczi's final, supposedly paranoid, days. Although it was not until later, at our second interview, that Balint explicitly blamed Lajos Levy, at the time I suspected that perhaps Anna Freud herself was responsible. At this first interview all Balint would say was that Jones had resorted to "an unreliable witness." (It never dawned on me, as an example of the kind of taboos about Freud it was possible to labor under then, that Freud might have been Jones's direct source; yet the newly published letters between Freud and Jones would appear to make that the most likely possibility, although it may have remained unknown to Balint himself.)

A. A. Brill was another Austrian who became prominent in the analytic movement, and Balint cited Brill as an example of how Freud could "play favorites." As a translator of Freud into English, when Brill for example got to a difficult paragraph in *Totem and Taboo*, Brill just omitted it entirely, yet Freud did not mind what Brill had done. (Balint seemed not to know that Brill sometimes—

as in his influential Modern Library collected edition of Freud—was trying to protect Freud's copyrights, and intentionally put into print less than Freud's full texts in order not to endanger the sale of Freud's individual books.) According to Balint, "the Freuds" had always had such "favorites." Yet, when I told Balint a story from Helene Deutsch, about how Freud had asked her to pick out a present in his behalf for Brill when she first came to the States in 1930, Balint acknowledged that Brill had not been so great a favorite after all. (Brill's papers are still, even after all these years, not available to scholars until the year 2000, and should prove richly interesting; it is my conviction that Brill's reputation will do better once researchers realize how naively good-natured he could be, at least in terms of the politics of the analytic movement as a whole.)

In contrast to Brill, Rank had—like Ferenczi—meant trouble to Freud, and Balint thought that the reason was that Freud could not tolerate others having had "really original ideas." (Here Balint was disputing one of the central contentions of Jones's biography.) Rank only started to practice as an analyst after World War I, at which time he "discovered" the clinical "importance of the mother." Ferenczi and Georg Groddeck were, like Rank himself, pursuing an identical course in emphasizing in the early 1920s the significance of mothering.

When I asked point-blank what had been the most distinctive about the Hungarian Psychoanalytic Society, Balint replied with emphasis: "Ferenczi!" He had been "so inspiring to people." No other analytic society had anybody so central to its existence. Balint thought that throughout Ferenczi's lifetime the Hungarian group of analysts remained "very small," with a membership "at the most" of about thirty-five.

Somehow I mentioned the French writer Anatole France, since I was puzzled over Freud's interest in him. Balint told me that Ferenczi had in fact once written an article on France, who was once a very fashionable figure in the literary world.

By the summer of 1965 I was aware that the Freud-Bullitt collaborative work on President Woodrow Wilson not only existed but was scheduled for early publication, and I was eager to find out whatever references to that manuscript might exist in the Freud-Ferenczi letters. Balint, however, understandably considered it too much trouble to try to look through the huge correspondence he had to watch out for any mention to Wilson; the date 1930, by which time a version of the manuscript was completed, became "a critical year" in the relationship between Freud and Ferenczi, which made it all the harder for Balint to find what might be needed on Bullitt and Wilson. At the same time, Balint was maintaining that he could not believe I could write about Freud and his followers without access to the Freud-Ferenczi letters. (Since they did not start coming out until 1992, that would have been a long time for me to have had to wait. Whatever interviewing errors that I may have made were in my view more than made up for by the fact that I was publishing while those were still alive who were able to challenge what I wrote.)

Balint remained very discreet, actually I thought cagey, about the existence of Ferenczi's wife's children, since I knew, from examining the Balint correspondence with Jones, that Balint had been determined that Jones steer-clear of mentioning Ferenczi's private life. Jones had even used the word "intimacy" in connection with Ferenczi's step-daughter Elma, and I was not yet aware of Jones's colossal tactlessness; Balint had replied rather hotly to Jones that when he handed over the "whole" correspondence between Freud and Ferenczi to Jones, Balint had stipulated that as long as Elma and Magda were still alive nothing from those letters could be publicly disclosed about them or their mother.

This exchange between Balint and Jones had taken place after they had tried to sort out their differences in published letters to appear in the *International Journal of Psychoanalysis* about the specifics of Ferenczi's mental condition at the time of his death. Although Balint had wanted there to be a sentence included in which he mentioned that both Jones and he had been analyzed by Ferenczi, with the implication that therefore each of them might have biassed interpretations, Jones had insisted that that passage be pencilled-out for purposes of publication.

Knowing what little I did about Elma, Gizella, and Ferenczi, I thought it natural to inquire from Balint about the existence of Ferenczi's children. To repeat, Balint never mentioned them, until I raised the issue as I was leaving the interview. Balint maintained that Ferenczi had never had any children, at which point I corrected myself and spoke about his step-children. At that point Balint did acknowledge that indeed there were such possible sources of information. I did not get to interview Elma in New York City until 1967 (her sister had married one of Ferenczi's siblings), but that makes a separate story in itself.

On April 25, 1966, Balint wrote me, in response to my getting in touch with him once again, this time not in connection with the manuscript about Wilson but the possible references in the Freud-Ferenczi letters to the death of Victor Tausk. Balint said he would do what he could, but specified that he would need the permission of the Freud family before communicating anything to me. At that time Balint informed me that "a decision" had been made to prepare about 400-500 of the letters in existence, which would make one volume, and then a second book would be an account of the relationship between Freud and Ferenczi based on the full correspondence. Anna Freud and Balint would be jointly in charge of the first book, and Balint alone would undertake the second.

Three days later Balint was writing a similar letter to Elma in New York City, except that here Balint went into the delicate problem of the relationship between Elma and Ferenczi. As he put it to her, "a certain number of people know (by heresay) an approximate version of that history, and if the official biography were to remain silent on this point, it would give rise to fresh gossip and new rumors." Elma wrote back to Balint in May, asking how many and what sorts of people knew about the tie between herself and Ferenczi.

Then, in the late fall of 1966 and before Balint and Elma had come to any final resolution about how they would proceed (Balint himself only lived until December 1970), I went back to see him among others in London. As early as the winter of 1963 I had read his *Thrills and Regressions*, and he had given me some reprints to take along; but it was years before I fully appreciated the scope of Balint's international reputation. In 1966 I was bringing him a publishing proposal from the editor-in-chief of Massachusetts Institute of Technology Press. At that time I had yet to publish any book of my own, and most of the stipulations of my friend in charge of the MIT Press were well over-my-head, but Balint, who was experienced at such contracts, seemed to understand what was at issue. I was simply doing my best to facilitate the appearance of the Freud-Ferenczi letters, and I do not think that Balint took it in any way amiss that I was bringing such a proposal along with me.

My notes about this second interview with Balint are rather sketchier than those from my first encounter with him. At this point my interviewing in general was dwindling, as I had a clearer idea what I wanted to proceed to write about. So I boldly started off by raising with Balint the names of early analysts who for one reason or another had been left out of the history books—Ruth Mack Brunswick, Tausk, and Herbert Silberer. (Trotsky's attitude toward losers, consigning them to the "rubbish heap" of history, was not at all my own.) It turned out that Balint knew nothing directly about Ruth Brunswick except her historical importance. Balint thought that Tausk had been "very difficult to reach and had a depression," but Balint wanted to see a copy of Paul Federn's letter that I mentioned, which was written immediately after Tausk's suicide and highly critical of Freud's role. Although Balint was a little unsure about the correct date of Silberer's own suicide, Balint maintained that "the unconscious is always right," meaning that he knew there was a close parallel between these two incidents of direct self-destruction, Tausk's and Silberer's.

Balint was clearly most expert on Ferenczi, who Balint thought was unduly unsuspecting about clinical regressions. (Balint also considered that Freud could be too intolerant of them.) Balint himself chose to distinguish between what he called benign and malignant forms of regressive phenomena. Someone like Rado, who had his own innovations in clinical practice, was said by Balint to have been on "bad terms" with Ferenczi, as Rado had been supposedly with everyone within organized psychoanalysis. (Yet Rado wrote an obituary of Ferenczi which was so warm and appreciative as to offend Anna Freud. And Rado stayed close friends with Franz Alexander.) I asked whether Ferenczi had been a threat to Freud, and Balint replied that he had "never" thought of that. Balint, thinking back over my earlier set of questions, seemed to remember having heard from Ferenczi some remarks about Tausk—that he was "impossible"—and Balint proposed that all these people had been like "children" in their demands on Freud. When I cited Freud's letter to Lou Andreas-Salomé after Tausk's death, in which Freud declared that Tausk had been both "useless" and a "menace to the future" of analysis, Balint said that he seemed to recall having heard something like that from Ferenczi himself, who "no doubt" got it from Freud. Balint asked me to remember that "there is a grain of truth in everything Freud ever said." Freud had "created his own world – and we must be grateful for it." But Balint also acknowledged that Freud was capable of kicking people out of the movement, as he supposedly did with Groddeck.

Balint now maintained that he was sorry that he had ever cooperated with Jones. On this occasion, Balint insisted that Jones had gotten it from the Levys about Ferenczi's last days, since "there was no one else." In hindsight today I believe that Balint was ignorant of Freud's own direct communications with Jones, which Freud asked to be kept private. (Jones, in writing to Balint, remained silent about his alleged witness.) Balint was proceeding to blame the Levys on the principle that Lajos Levy had been Ferenczi's doctor. Balint said that Anna Freud had asked him to cooperate with Jones, and therefore Balint had "complied." I naturally, in this context, asked why Lajos had mattered to Freud. Balint said that he was exceptionally "brilliant," and wrote "wonderful" articles for a prominent Hungarian medical journal. Yet Lajos was "a terrible therapist." As for "understanding a case" one could not be better, but in treating the patient Lajos was awful. When I asked if this were rather like Freud himself, Balint answered "Yes." It was Lajos's "superior mind" which marked him in Freud's estimation.

This time in seeing Balint I was more outspoken in asking about the tie between Ferenczi and Elma. Balint said that there was "no sexual relationship" between them, although they were "very deeply in love." Elma had gone to Freud for an analysis before World War I, and then "shortly thereafter" married an American, but it had not lasted. As Balint presented me with the moving personal tale of Ferenczi, Elma, and Freud, I made up my mind to see her when I got back to the States. The whole story was, according to Balint, to be found in the Freud-Ferenczi letters. Balint thought that there were so many versions which were "worse" than the truth that it was better to have it all in the open with the publication of the correspondence.

Balint made the general point, in terms of the history of analytic theory, that the concepts of transference and the role of mothers really first became important in Hungary in the early 1920s. Balint had just finished blaming the Levys for the allegation that Ferenczi was psychotic at his death. (Kata Levy stoutly denied to me that Ferenczi was suffering from anything except pernicious anemia, but in the published literature it is Erich Fromm, as early as 1958, who deserves the credit for first attempting to correct Jones's account of Ferenczi.) Balint went on to recall how Kata had gotten up at a meeting of the Hungarian Society to ask whether they were a scientific discussion group or a "Freud Society"? Balint, like Rado too, was appalled at the way Freud succeeded in creating such credulous disciples. Balint considered that Freud had had unusual success with women followers, in that he could keep them in a strikingly dependent relationship with him. Freud had been great at "seducing" people into his movement.

Since the problem of plagiarism and priorities of discovery had, by the time I saw Balint the second time, become so central a theme in many of the difficulties Freud had with his pupils, I asked Balint directly about the matter. (Lacan, too, was especially preoccupied with these sorts of issues, although at the time I had no special knowledge about French analysis.) It turned out that on a few occasions Ferenczi had raised the issue of priorities against Freud, but Freud had never done so against Ferenczi. Ferenczi was able, according to Balint, to cite "chapter and verse" of where Freud had taken ideas and not acknowledged them; according to Balint, Freud had never denied such charges levelled by Ferenczi.

Balint helped me understand a problem that worried Kata Levy, namely how Ferenczi had succeeded in detaching himself from the association in Hungary between psychoanalysis and Communism. Balint specified that there had been two revolutions in Hungary after World War I, and it was during the first "bourgeois" one that Ferenczi had been appointed as a professor of psychoanalysis; it was only during the brief Communist regime that his appointment took effect, which explains why he was able to escape serious recriminations later on.

My notes indicate that Balint wound up the interview with a story about Helene Deutsch and the termination of her analysis with Freud. According to Balint, she had wanted to continue further, but Freud had felt that he had told her everything that he had to say. It is true that she went for a second analysis in Berlin with Abraham, but Balint's version of the ending of Helene's analysis did not seem to tally with what she had told me herself, and I tended to discount his tale as second-hand. (She had her own stories about him from Wilma Kovacs, once his mother-in-law.) I might of course have been wrong, but on the other hand I thought then, and now too, that Balint was in an exceptional position to be able to help me specifically on the history of analysis in Hungary, and on Ferenczi's role in particular. This is a chapter in the history of ideas which still remains unsettled, and even after the publication of all the volumes of the Freud-Ferenczi corespondence there will be plenty of room for historiographical disagreement about the implications and meaning of this key phase of the growth of modern psychotherapy.

# 15

# Philipp Sarasin

On November 30, 1966, I interviewed Dr. Philipp Sarasin in Basel, Switzerland. At that time, I was concluding my interviews with all those I could find who had directly known Freud, either as his patients or his students. In Sarasin's case, I knew he had once held high offices in the International Psychoanalytic Association, and that he had also been in analysis with Freud. So he seemed obviously someone I should try to see.

As it happened, my contact with Sarasin was facilitated by Dr. Edward Glover; my hunch is that Sarasin would have been willing to see me anyway, but Glover had written me to recommend that I interview Sarasin. Glover had been a valuable and independent source of information to me; he had joined up with the Swiss Psychoanalytic Society (as had Anna Freud temporarily) after he resigned in 1944 from the British Psychoanalytic Society. I found Glover a free-thinker, and an extremely gentle, nice man; my personal impression of him was wholly at odds with the bitterness with which the Kleinians continued to look on him, because of his role in the "controversial discussions" within the British Society toward the end of World War II. In America these contentious issues were either unknown, or else Glover was approvingly cited as a defender of orthodoxy; his having sided with Anna Freud against Melanie Klein, and his combativeness against Carl Jung, would have been enough to have endeared him to the American psychoanalytic establishment. In fact, however, Glover was very much his own man, and capable of writing critically about the ideas of such different thinkers as Franz Alexander, Heinz Hartmann, Sandor Rado, and Edith Jacobson.

Glover gave me his advice in a letter of September 21, 1965: "It occurs to me that if you are pursuing your researches amongst those who knew Freud fairly intimately in the old days, I would suggest writing to Dr. med. Philipp Sarasin." According to Glover, I "would of course have to submit a list of specific questions" to be answered by Sarasin, as Glover had asked me to do with him. Glover suggested that I mention his name to Sarasin, adding a bit of color of his own about his old friend: "I knew him well; he had a voice like a brass band but very nice and helpful." (A Polish analyst friend of Helene Deutsch's, Dr. Salomea

Kempner, had had a long-standing relationship with Sarasin but did not survive the war. They visited Freud together once in 1935.)

As it happened, Sarasin agreed to see me in a letter (November 19, 1966) written "%American Express, London, England," where I was once again undertaking more of my interviews on another trip of mine to Europe. Sarasin was most cooperative when I arrived at his house; in order to make the interview easier, he arranged for a niece of his, who spoke English readily, to act as an interpreter for us. As I reconstruct the interview now, I am relying on the detailed notes I took at the time, and amended slightly in the light of how I later came to reflect on what he had told me.

It turned out that he first came across psychoanalytic ideas in 1912, when he was studying medicine in Munich, Germany; it was before his degree, and in his first clinical semester. Sarasin then had some personal analysis with Hanns Sachs in Switzerland; and subsequently Sachs recommended him to Freud. It was at the Hague Congress (1920) that he first met Freud, and Freud agreed then to accept Sarasin for an analysis. The analysis began in the spring of 1923 and lasted two whole years.

At the beginning of Sarasin's analysis with Freud there was already tension between Freud and Otto Rank. Rank could supposedly make "acid" comments about Freud. During the winter of 1923-1924, Freud brought a quotation from Schiller which was not quite correct, and Rank straightened it out. (The implication was that Rank had been impudent.) But what really happened between Rank and Freud was for Sarasin an "obscurity," and that controversy remained "completely in the dark." As far as the difficulties with Rank went, Freud was "discreet."

Sarasin could not comment about what he thought of Jones's biography of Freud since Sarasin said he did not like to read Jones. It was a "hopeless" undertaking on Sarasin's part since he was "so involved" in the material; similarly, Sarasin said that he did not like to read his own autobiography. Sarasin had met Freud's wife once in a garden, and found her an "amiable and nice person." But he did not know any members of the Freud family; even Anna Freud he met only at psychoanalytic meetings.

I asked directly about Herbert Silberer, a Viennese analyst who had committed suicide in 1923. Sarasin thought him "very striking, interesting, and intense," an "explosive" person. At the beginning of the analysis Freud had asked him whether he had "noticed tensions within the Vienna group." (I knew that Freud had asked another of his patients in the late 1920s, Dr. Irmarita Putnam, a similar question.) As a matter of fact Sarasin had not detected any such group difficulties. Freud was sixty-nine, according to Sarasin (actually Freud was sixty-seven); and Sarasin himself was thirty-four then.

Although I inquired about Freud's interest in telepathy, he had never mentioned it to Sarasin. And Jung was already "not existing" within Freud's world, so Sarasin was "ignorant" of any problems between Freud and Jung. According to Sarasin, Freud had "scotomized" both Jung and Alfred Adler. (A "scotoma" meant an active withdrawal of attention, or disavowal.)

Since I was already interested in Victor Tausk, I inquired from Sarasin about him. He was dead by the time Sarasin came to Freud. Freud did tell Sarasin that Tausk had wanted to come to Freud for an analysis, but that Freud had refused to have him. If I took Tausk into analysis, Freud explained, it would have been impossible to publish anything without Tausk's thinking that it had come from him. Tausk was, according to Sarasin, "enormously intelligent but a difficult personality." He was "crazy"; when I tried to explore what Sarasin meant by that term as applied to Tausk, Sarasin reasoned that Tausk had after all killed himself, and what more does one need to say about him?

After the analysis with Freud was over, Sarasin was not in Vienna very much, although now and again he went there. It was notable, and Sarasin remarked on it, that Freud had gotten sick with cancer while Sarasin was in analysis with him. But Sarasin had not taken any special notice of the illness. (This was also true, I found out in other interviews, for the English Roger Money-Kyrle as well, who was analyzed by Freud at the same time.)

Freud was "like a father who tried to make peace within the Vienna group." Herman Nunberg once said that when Freud spoke it was like the evening being lit by light. Nunberg was completely devoted to Freud, and it was the same for Isidor Sadger and Paul Federn. In contrast to this sort of admiration, Rank had become oppositional. In this connection Sarasin referred to "the Tausk catastrophe."

In reply to a question of mine as to whether Sarasin had ever received any patients who had already been in analysis with Freud, the answer was "no." But Sarasin, who knew I had been spending interviewing time with Helene Deutsch, remarked that she had gotten such patients from Freud. He quoted her as having said that the patients she received from Freud fitted her "like a glove," in that they were perfectly prepared for analysis with her. (I knew that this was untrue about Tausk, but I did not pursue the point.)

Sarasin paid Freud 40 Swiss francs an hour; the standard analytic fee would be, as of 1966, 96 francs an hour. Freud gave Sarasin little receipts for the payments; the custom was that Sarasin see Freud analytically six times a week. In answer to a direct question of mine whether Freud had ever given him a photograph of himself, it turned out that at the end of the analysis he got the famous one with Freud holding his cigar. Sarasin brought the photo to Freud and he signed it.

"With a good analysis," Sarasin quoted Freud, "one forgets everything. The goal of analysis is to forget!" (Freud was wryly playing on the early psychoanalytic recommendation of patients becoming better by remembering the past.) After the analysis was over, Freud sent Sarasin some books on Goethe for a paper Sarasin was working on, which eventually came out in Volume 15 of Freud's journal *Imago*.

It turns out that only "much later" did Sarasin ever hear of Anna Freud's having been analyzed by her father; Sarasin did not know anything about it in Vienna. And "even now" Sarasin said he did not know "for certain" that it ever took place.

During the analysis, Sarasin always went to meetings of the Vienna Society. Freud was "extremely human in his technique." By that Sarasin meant that Freud "always" included "conversation about himself" in the course of the treatment. Freud could remark: "Did I say that? An old man is loquacious." Freud could be quite astonished at himself. He "chattered" in the analysis. So it was not difficult for Sarasin to speak with Freud. Sarasin had the conviction that it was "impossible for anything bad to happen to him there"; that was how he summarized the atmosphere of the treatment setting. It was not "silent torture," but rather like being at home.

Emil Oberholzer always had difficulties between his Swiss Society and that of Oskar Pfister's. Freud supported Pfister, Sarasin, and Hans Zulliger against the group run by Oberholzer. (Sarasin referred me to the Freud-Pfister letters, which unfortunately are still seriously incomplete.) In the controversy between those with a medical as opposed to a purely psychological conception of psychoanalysis, Oberholzer took the medical viewpoint. (That means that his group did not recognize lay analysis.) Nonetheless, Freud spoke "very generously" about Oberholzer. His group lasted in Switzerland up until World War II; then some in Oberholzer's group came back to Pfister's Society. According to Sarasin, Oberholzer's Society had not been acknowledged by the International Psychoanalytic Association. (Oberholzer later died in New York City.)

As far as Sarasin could tell, Freud had a "good" relation to his mother and a "natural" one with his father. For Sarasin Freud's theories were "very personal," while Sarasin held that Freud's therapeutic "technique was admirable." Among the personal theories of Freud's Sarasin included the libido concept and the death instinct. But Sarasin did not want to conjecture about the origins of Freud's theories being in his personality. "Who knows the unconscious of Freud?" Freud was, according to Sarasin, only satisfied with ideas if they were dualistic—that was a personal conception of Freud's. Life against death would be an illustration of a dualism in Freud. Lou Andreas-Salomé discussed the dualistic orientation, even though she felt like Freud did. That was, in Sarasin's view, a "secret" to Freud's thinking—it was Jewish and oriental. Freud was against Leibniz's "monads." All such theoretical matters are "a question of taste," and Sarasin held that it was "impossible to discuss it."

Freud was "utterly correct" with patients. He also demanded "correctness" from his patients. Someone might say to Freud: "If I want to be honest, I would think etc." and Freud would get "furious." His attitude was that people must be "honest." Nothing like such a confrontation had happened between Sarasin and Freud! I asked whether Freud would be intolerant of patients who were unable to be honest, and Sarasin commented that Freud did not work with them. I asked: "How could he tell?" Sarasin thought Freud would "notice it at once."

When I inquired who Freud had esteemed among the Americans, he agreed that Freud liked A. A. Brill; but, Sarasin reminded me, Brill was originally an Austrian.

It was important for Sarasin to emphasize to me that Freud had come to psychoanalysis from neurology, not psychiatry; and that Freud had had no real experience with psychiatric cases.

Sarasin said he had himself had many French patients. He practiced six hours a day, five days a week. And he also did many "controls" for supervision. Besides formal psychoanalysis, Sarasin also practiced psychotherapy, and not always with the use of the couch. He found that something "always remained in him of the physician," interested in therapeutic improvement, and that he was not "fanatical" about psychoanalysis.

Sarasin concluded the interview by giving me a copy of an article written about his experiences with Freud, and touching on Freud's attitude toward lay analysis. Here he again described how his analysis with Freud had provided an atmosphere of "protection and security." If I did not pursue with Sarasin any of Jones's characteristic hobby-horses against Ferenczi, it was probably because Sarasin had a much more relaxed attitude toward patients than was implied by Jones's approach; with those former patients of Freud's like Sarasin there seemed no special necessity of inquiring into the pioneers advocating humanity in analytic technique. (The reader might like to know that in 1999, while I was finishing a little book on Edward Glover, it appeared that all Sarasin's files failed to survive as historical documents. While that has to be discouraging, young researchers can look forward to the day when the seventy-odd boxes of Edward Bibring's remains get catalogued and opened to inspection. Ives Hendrick's papers are at least in the process of getting catalogued, and someday Franz Alexander's files will be accessible.)

# 16

# Donald W. Winnicott

Every interview I conducted with any of the early psychoanalysts always succeeded in teaching me something special. While many of those I saw, during my most intense field work in the mid-1960s, were either relatively obscure then or have been generally forgotten (such as Philipp Sarasin), Donald W. Winnicott is an outstanding exception to any such generalization. For, rather to my amazement, his stature has continued to grow, so that by now his writings have been widely translated into French, Spanish, and doubtless other languages as well. With the passage of time his reputation has eclipsed many of those who were once considered leading representatives of the profession.

It is true that at the time I proposed to see Winnicott in September of 1965, he had already been recommended to me by someone as reliably intellectual as Dr. Charles Rycroft as "the genius of British analysis." Rycroft went through a volume of Winnicott's 1958 *Collected Papers: Through Paediatrics to Psychoanalysis* in order to help tutor me about which articles I ought to read in what order. By now, following Winnicott's death in 1971, more by him has appeared in print than while he was alive.

At the outset of my contact with Winnicott he indicated that he had heard about me from Masud Khan, and that I was reportedly "an assiduous reader." Khan was in those days in charge of Jones's papers at the British Psychoanalytic Society, and Khan had given me the green light to inspect material there, even though Khan himself underestimated the significance of what I could find in Jones's raw files. I gathered that Khan, who had a picture of Winnicott in Khan's impressive apartment, was on close personal terms with Winnicott. I heard that Khan helped Winnicott with compiling Indexes to his books, and I supposed that Khan did other editorial chores for Winnicott as well. But I admit that it never dawned on me that Khan might still then be in analysis with Winnicott, although that now turns out to have been the case. Khan seemed already so senior a figure within analysis that at the time the thought that he might have been a patient of Winnicott's never crossed my mind. As far as I can tell Khan, a vocal Francophile with many important friends in Paris, was personally responsible for helping to introduce Winnicott in France. (There was also some correspondence between Winnicott and Jacques Lacan.) In Khan's controversial last book, *The Long Wait: And Other Psychoanalytic Narratives* (published in Britain as *When Spring Comes*), there is a plausible-sounding account of how Winnicott behaved with patients.

My own response to Winnicott was that he seemed very much like a pixie; he was full of an extraordinary kind of whimsical, child-like charm, and I found him disarming and wonderful to spend time with. Yet he also had a rather weak grasp of theory and the history of analytic concepts, which is where I assumed Khan could help him. Winnicott was strikingly unlike someone as original as Erich Fromm, who had what I considered a Germanic concern for system. While Fromm's standing is now relatively marginal (although probably no analyst's writings are as accessible to browsers at airport bookstores), Winnicott still seems gaining in ascendancy; a book of his letters has come out, his papers are widely studied, and the literature about him continues to grow.

The examples of both Winnicott and Fromm should prove that it is possible to go beyond Freud, using his methods to reach conclusions that he might have found abhorrent; such writers deserve, I think, to be considered an important part of the thinking of psychoanalysis as a whole. Freud did develop his ideas out of his own autobiographical understanding; and therefore all the historical fascination with his life, which shows no sign of slowing down, is fully justified. But in the end it is possible to emerge from his work with a variety of different points of view, without being guilty of some "treason" to his basic "cause."

I saw Winnicott only that once in London. We spent an afternoon together in his consulting room, where he also served me an impromtu meal. When he reported what he had heard about myself as a reader, he was volunteering that it was not true of himself. (I suspect now that he was a good deal more cultured than he was inclined to let on.) He had started off as a pediatrician before specializing in the psychoanalysis of children, and he used to work with them by means of their drawings (what he called "squiggles"). One organization formed since his death to advance his ideas was appropriately known as the Squiggle Foundation. Almost at the outset of our time together he handed me a marvellous sketch-book to use as a writing pad to support my note-taking. He claimed to have originally been an inhibited Englishman, with few outlets in fantasy except for music. I found him a wonderfully free and open person.

He mentioned how similar to Freud's impact on him Charles Darwin had once been; a new world was revealed to him by both men. "What a release it was!" He had been surprised to discover, when he got to Cambridge as an undergraduate, that there were such beings as Darwinians. He himself had come from a religious background, as had a number of other early British analysts; a book he came across by Oskar Pfister, an analyst as well as a Swiss pastor, had helped him initially to read through Freud.

Winnicott said that he had had "a disturbed adolescence." He had been "very normal" until he was nine years old, and then suddenly he could not remember his dreams anymore. Being cut off from his dreaming was disturbing to him. Later he therefore asked a librarian what she could recommend on dreams. She gave him a book by the French philosopher Henri Bergson, which was "no help," and then another text, until finally he came to Freud's *The Interpretation of Dreams*. Subsequently, Winnicott happened to have a medical student friend who was already personally in analysis, and Winnicott decided that it was "for him," too.

Winnicott went to see Ernest Jones, who gave him a list of names of possible psychoanalysts, which was of "no use" since Winnicott did not know what to do with these references. Jones had proceeded to "reel off" not only the symptoms that Winnicott was already aware of, but those that came up during his analyses later. Jones had been "absolutely right," and Winnicott considered him quite a "show-off."

Winnicott chose to go to James Strachey for an analysis that lasted almost ten years. Strachey was about as bookish as it is humanly possible to be, and I find it hard to imagine what kind of therapist he could ever have been. He seemed at a special sort of distance from usual human contact. A 1924 letter of Strachey's to his wife in Berlin implies an absence in Winnicott of a sexual interest in the wife he continued to be married to for years; a lack of "normal" masculinity might unfortunately fit his fascination with children. Because of his clinical work with youngsters, Winnicott became interested in the ideas that Melanie Klein was working on. Strachey was by no means anti-Klein, but he said that he could not teach Klein to Winnicott in analysis, so Winnicott went to her directly to learn about play therapy. He did so by bringing her a case of his. He got on well with her, and finally finished his analysis with her disciple Mrs. Joan Riviere. (Both Winnicott's analysts were non-medical and had been analyzed in Vienna by Freud.)

As far as Winnicott was concerned, Freud's technique was ideally suited for the psycho-neurotics, which "one sees so rarely nowadays," largely due to the fact that people can read for themselves widely circulated texts "like the Pelican editions of Freud's works." Clinically, Winnicott said he saw so-called borderline cases all the time, like those in Freud and Breuer's *Studies on Hysteria*. (The term "borderline" seems to me to have become as much a wastebasket category as the concept "neurosis" once was.)

I think that what first charmed me about Winnicott was his early emphasis in our talk on "the danger of sanity in psychoanalysis"; he proposed that the "flight to sanity" was "quite a problem," which I found in refreshing contrast to the dull-as-dishwater conception of normality that one tended to get in North American ego psychological thinking. As Winnicott once wrote, "we are poor indeed if we are only sane."[1] According to Kleinian theory, psychosis is closer to health than one might guess; paradoxically, neurosis is less apt to be self-healing. This whole line of thinking implies that symptoms can be both constructive and self-healing, a point of view that the British analyst R. D. Laing would make widely popular in the 1960s. (Jung had proposed it far earlier.)

Edward Glover, who had once been Jones's second-in-command, gave me many hours of his time in 1965-1966. Glover is, I believe, one of those analysts who has gotten a raw deal in being relatively forgotten, or at least undervalued now. (The most orthodox Kleinians blamed Glover for the split between Klein and her daughter Melitta.) Like Winnicott, Glover too had said to me that there is much sanity that has a symptomatic quality. (Winnicott thought it "a pity" about Glover's leaving the British Psychoanalytic Society,[2] which he would himself head twice as president, since Glover had such a "good head." Khan told me how ineffective he had been in trying to lure Glover back into teaching British analysts. Glover, however, may not have reciprocated Winnicott's compliments, since Glover once wrote to Anna Freud after World War II that one of Winnicott's presentations had been "moonshine.") Fromm, too, was critical of normalcy as part of his distrust of conformism. But Fromm never mentioned Winnicott to me, and I would doubt that Winnicott had ever read much Fromm.

Winnicott had consciously benefited more from Jung's ideas than Fromm had. Winnicott had written a long, appreciative review of Jung's published autobiography.[3] *What kind of reaction did the review provoke*? (I have underlined each of my exact questions.) One of the leading Jungians in London, Dr. Michael Fordham (whom I had met), thought "very well" of it; the review was what he "would have liked to have written, except that he was too close to it." *Was the contrast between Freud and Jung that of a man with a self at odds with a man still in search of a self*? "Yes," but for Winnicott the question remained: "Was Freud's self a false one?" (The distinction between true and false self was one which had so many traditional philosophic overtones that I am pretty sure Freud would have disapproved of it, since he sought to make his psychology scientific in an empirical sense; but it echoed for me the issue of authenticity, raised for example by Fromm.) Winnicott said he had once mentioned Jung's name at a meeting of the British Psychoanalytic Society, but the hush was so striking that he dared not repeat the exercise. Winnicott was proud of how the British Psychoanalytic Society had remained unified and not split, despite all the ideological differences of opinion that coexisted.

Since I was seeing Winnicott at a time when Freud's work was under sustained assault from feminist critics, and even earlier Fromm as well as Karen Horney had made a great deal out of the inadequacies of Freud's conception of femininity, that seemed a logical line to pursue. *Did Freud err about female psychology*? It is certainly true that in Freud "one finds only women who want to be men, never men envying women." In order to get at the more serious disturbances, no matter how normal on the outside the patient may appear, the patient has to go through a psychosis in the analytic consulting room. (This proposition, which many other analysts as well as non-analysts would consider highly dubious, followed from Klein's thinking that the infant is psychotic, and that it is therapeutic for patients seriously to regress.) Freud himself "could not accept" the maternal in himself, because he was so strong a paternal head of his family. "Yet the maternal is inextricably linked to the infantile." And therefore Winnicott thought he could explain why Freud would have been personally blocked from adopting a less rationalistic approach to therapy. Freud could tolerate, indeed was "attracted by," his feminine side, as long as it was located outside in Sandor Ferenczi or other followers like him.

*What about Freud's addiction to smoking? How would it affect his clinical practice?* The smoking was not just a question of nicotine, but also hinged on the psychology of being able to put something in his mouth. The issue is not just the presence of repressed homosexuality, although it is that "of course." But on a deeper level the smoking has to be related to an attempt on Freud's part to "recapture and make up for the loss of the experience of omnipotence." Some people never have the experience of omnipotence at all. But the smoking can be seen to present a form of "control over the mother"; she is incorporated yet not swallowed, and then the loss is made up.

*What about Freud's fainting fits with Jung?* It means, Winnicott supposed, "a feminine identification." It is characteristically Jewish, after all, not to be able to tolerate "an iota of femininity" in oneself, or one's eldest son. Freud's difficulties here help explain why he remained at bottom "blind to pre-oedipal" problems. Freud wanted to leave the mother and the feminine out, and reserve it all to nurse-maids and such. But in spite of these striking defects in his thinking, Winnicott thought that "Freud's supreme achievement was the development of his technique."

*Were Jones's own analytic contributions rather slight?* He was "not terribly original." Certainly he had proceeded to apply Freud's "discoveries" all over the place. Jones's symbolism article was important (Glover had thought so too), as is Jones's notion that annihilation anxiety has to be considered deeper than neurosis, psychotic in fact. In those early days the fear everybody was obsessed with was the castration anxiety that Freud thought so central to neurosis.

Although Winnicott was not trained in psychiatry, he was notable for being more open to the significance of psychosis than the traditional Freudians; it was related, I think, to Winnicott's special interest in the psychology of children. *A dream may be structurally like a psychosis, as Freud thought, but does it not function very differently?* Patients who have psychotic experiences often say that it was exactly like they were having a dream. The big trouble, though, is that they were awake; in a sense they could not get properly asleep. "It makes all the difference in the world."

*Would Freud have failed to recognize the positive, ego-integrative functions of the dream?* He saw dreams in terms of release, which is different from fulfillment. The idea of the constructive uses of regression comes much later in psychoanalytic theory. (In reality I think that Jung had this concept first, although it was developed later among orthodox Freudians by Ernst Kris.) When Freud terms a dream as being like a psychosis, nobody would say that nowadays. A certain kind of dream does not even need to be analyzed "at all"; it just means that the analysis has gotten so far. Winnicott had those kinds of dreams after he was out of analysis. It is terribly important to be in contact with one's dream life, and to be able to talk about it to one's analyst. The specific interpretation that gets offered "really matters much less." (At this point I could better understand how Winnicott had lain on Strachey's couch for so many years; Winnicott was so full of his own ideas as probably to have been relatively impervious to an uncomprehending analyst, even if that is a somewhat forlorn view of the human condition.)

Winnicott tried to arrange his consulting room carefully for his patients. They could get in "a tremendous row" with him sometimes over the arrangement of the room. It is an entirely non-verbal aspect of the situation, yet it acts like an interpretation, even though the analyst has been completely silent. "The important thing is that the analyst does not die, and that he does not retaliate," no matter what happens in the patient's life or what he says. The analyst's job can sometimes be just to sit there and be a "bad" analyst for the patient.

Being "a bad analyst" was what Winnicott thought that Wilhelm Fliess had done for Freud. (It seems to me unfortunate how, like Glover and others, Winnicott understood Freud's friendship with Fliess on the model of the analytic encounter.) Maybe Freud did not "ever read" Fliess's letters. (That cannot have been literally true, but I took Winnicott to be saying something important about the inevitable self-involvement of all creative activity.) Obviously Fliess was "an idealization" for Freud, which had to lead to disappointment. No real evidence exists that Fliess had any idea of the "discoveries" that Freud was coming up with.

Winnicott had a love for psychological paradox that I found especially engaging; for example, he maintained that it is easier for a man to analyze the maternal components in his patients, "precisely because the analyst does not have breasts." With female patients there is no danger of homosexual involvement, and with males it means that they will not get stuck at that early stage, for they can "get out of it." Yet the practice of analysis puts "a great strain," Winnicott held, on a male analyst.

Winnicott was struck by the example of how John Rickman had gone to Freud with a particular infantile memory; but Freud could not make anything out of it at all. Freud told Rickman he was "psychotic" and had "best get out of being an analyst." The memory was how Rickman as a small child was lying in his cot with pneumonia, thinking he was going to die. He saw this round object at both ends of the curtain rod. On one side, the round object started to turn; he knew it was not really turning, and yet it was so for him. Apparently, this was a very disturbing memory and it was what he took to Freud for his analysis. But Freud was "not able to help him at all."

When Rickman's mother died, he recounted to Winnicott how he had held her ashes in an urn, and turned it about. "Now I have you in my control"; that is what he thought at the grave. Rickman felt that now he could tell her what he really thought of her. Winnicott did not connect the two things, the urn and the infantile memory, until after Rickman's death; Winnicott had wanted to"burst into tears" at the story of the graveside. Rickman always remained "bothered" by the same memory from early childhood. It hinged, according to Winnicott's interpretation, on Rickman's projection of himself onto his mother's breast, in order to keep control of her. (Klein was responsible for the symbolic standing of the breast for British analysts.) Freud had, however, been unable to do anything with that memory of Rickman's supposed identification with his mother's breast.

Rickman had lots of good stories about Freud; for instance, they used to smuggle cigars into the crates of the psychoanalytic press being shipped to Vienna. Winnicott also shook his head, sadly, about the obsessional notes Rickman had kept on patients, which proved of "no use" to anyone later after his death. Rickman had evidently been planning some study of Freud's concepts. In his writing Rickman "dramatized" things; those examples in his book with Geoffrey Gorer on Russia[4] are not "strictly true." The illustrations were drawn from several individual instances, but they were "dramatically true."

Winnicott thought Rickman's early troubling memory was a model for what had needed to be done in changing psychoanalysis as Freud had left it. Like Edoardo Weiss and others, Winnicott thought the problem of psychosis could not be left in the outer darkness that Freud had tended to assign it. And Winnicott himself had become especially interested in defenses against the loss of the experience of omnipotence. Cigar-smoking, for example, means that the cigar is not lost, incorporated but not swallowed. Of course this was a line Freud himself, with all his own smoking, could not have pursued. But Winnicott was convinced that Freud had done quite enough for one man; his self-analysis went so far, and really far enough. "If he had been able to go further, he would not have been capable of making the original contributions."

Winnicott saw himself as someone who was moving psychoanalysis beyond how Freud had left it, and he felt indebted to Melanie Klein's thinking. She had felt that when Anna Freud came over to England she was menaced; it was, Winnicott thought, to be the end of the "happy, productive" period of British analysis. Of course "Mrs. Klein was not at all a scientist." But she was "very original and creative." Whether or not it was a reality that Anna Freud was such a threat to her, or even if it were "a delusion," it is impossible to say. Anyway, Klein withdrew, and set up her own system with her followers. Glover then, "as people usually do," proceeded to enter into her dread of enemies. "It had been such an exciting and prolific period; and then she shrank back, and it was over."

After World War II Winnicott felt ready to do some lecturing. Yet neither Mrs. Klein nor Miss Freud would have him on their different training schedules. Fortunately he had "other irons in the fire." Mrs. Klein proceeded to build up "a closed system." There is even an introduction of Mrs. Riviere's to one of Mrs. Klein's books where she implies that "there is nothing new to be discovered."

Like other analysts who became unusually creative, Winnicott remembered how taken in by psychoanalytic thinking he had at first been: "What a pest I must have been to my friends around 1926!" His new knowledge of the unconscious meant that he was led to insist on pointing out to others that various things in everyday life "meant" such and such. Winnicott was then using Freud "all over the place." He thought such an excess was really a phase-appropriate stage. (Part of Winnicott's attractiveness later as an analytic theorist was that he did not communicate the spirit of being a know-it-all.)

*Did he ever meet Freud*? No, although he could have done so in 1938-1939 after Freud had emigrated to London. But Freud did not want to see new people, and Winnicott did not desire to be "cruel" about it. *How central a flaw was Freud's outlook on women*? Freud thought they were just like men, except they are not; and therefore Freud considered them as "frustrated men." Freud had his own female "anima." (That was one of the rare occasions on which I encountered a specifically Jungian term being used to understand Freud. The feminist critique of Freud was then too fresh for me to have had the necessary distance to see the anachronistic side of some of their charges; not only did women thrive in psychoanalysis as a profession, but in the context of his own times Freud can be seen as a progressive force. For example, he insisted over opposition within the Vienna Psychoanalytic Society that women be admitted to full membership.)

Winnicott had a patient then that bore on the issue of male homosexuality that he was trying to write about. The issue Winnicott wondered about was: what has stopped the patient from engaging in homosexual practices? Winnicott thought that the patient "unconsciously knew" that he was a woman, although he also knew that it was not true; he did not want his unconscious conviction to be disproved. (This was an example of Winnicott's playfully topsy-turvy sort of thinking.) Male homosexuality, for Winnicott, could not just be explained on the basis of feminine identifications.

Winnicott was already well known enough to have done guest-lecturing in the States, so I tried to ask what he thought of people we knew in common. *What did he think of the people he met in Boston, Mass.*? He was not very impressed. He had stayed with Elizabeth Zetzel. (I knew from Glover that he considered her Jones's "pet".) Winnicott called her "clever" and "a restless spirit," and hoped she might turn out to have "a very original mind." (I found her admirably tough-minded; her whole face brightened at the mention of Winnicott, as if he were in a unique category; she died prematurely, reportedly a suicide, in 1970.) He also remembered having met Beata ("Tola") Rank, and he "quite liked her." (Winnicott thought that Otto Rank had done "good work" after proposing his theory of the birth trauma. By chance Winnicott, with his first wife, had been on the Forbes's island in Massachusetts; Winnicott knew that Malcolm Forbes had killed himself, but I am not sure Winnicott was aware how closely linked Rank had been with the Forbes family.) Only very late in the 1930s, and it was Winnicott's doing, could one say in the British Psychoanalytic Society that one "liked" somebody. Anna Freud had "picked it up" from him.

Winnicott asserted that Anna Freud had been very generous in citing him. Yet it seemed "rather ridiculous" how all American students read one article of his, on "transitional objects," because of her having used it in her bibliographies. "Obviously" they had not read anything else by him, since they always cited the article from the *International Journal of Psychoanalysis*, where it originally appeared, and not from his book of collected essays.

Winnicott thought that "one cannot get properly analyzed in America." Americans were more orthodoxly Freudian than the British, partly out of their great deference to Anna Freud. But in America if an analyst tries to meet a patient's needs in a regression during a session, then the analyst is being naughty, "wild." The best people in America seemed to him preoccupied with maintaining training "standards"; psychoanalysis did spread "awfully fast" there. But his own experiences as a child analyst made him much less concerned about fulfilling any of the traditional analytic proprieties; he was unconcerned about whether the patient was on the couch or on the floor. Once upon a time he would have been terribly worried about being a proper analyst or not, a concern expressed by other analysts in talking about having had the same early anxieties.

*What did he think about Erikson's ego psychology*? Winnicott wished he were the author of Erikson's books—this was said with the utmost conviction, even though later on, in Phillips's *Winnicott*,[5] the name Erikson never appeared. Winnicott told me that Erikson was the only one in analysis he felt that way about. Winnicott himself claimed to be "no good" at theory. When Erikson had been over in London once, and saw patients at a children's clinic, he could spot something positive in each of them; "he was not making it up either." Winnicott, who had recently been asked to write a review of a revised edition of Erikson's *Childhood and Society*, asked me to send Erikson his best greetings. (Winnicott also thought that Heinz Hartmann was "a giant" with "really tremendous clinical experience." Hartmann's ego psychology was supposedly "a help" in treating psychotics.) I already knew about Erikson's tortured relationship to Anna Freud; Winnicott not only talked about Martin James's struggle to disengage himself from "Miss Freud," but Winnicott was aware of the inhibitions Jones worked under doing his biography of Freud because of her position in London. Like others, Winnicott thought Jones had been brave in going to Vienna to rescue the Freuds in 1938, and also courageous in finishing his biography of Freud despite the onset of serious ill-health.

*What about Paul Federn's ideas on psychosis*? Despite Weiss's efforts in behalf of keeping Federn's work alive, and Erikson's acknowledgement of how important Federn had been to his own development, Winnicott did not know about him at all, even in connection with what Federn had written about the self. (Winnicott did understand that the biased story of Sandor Ferenczi's relation to Freud, as promoted by Jones, needed to be told properly.) I gave Winnicott a citation to a case of Freud's that Weiss had told me about: an agoraphobic, under analysis, had turned into a schizophrenic, and then the patient had been "cured" by a reimposition of the agoraphobia through hypnosis. Winnicott was eager to have me write down the proper source for this case, since it fit Winnicott's thinking that a psychotic condition could emerge from the removal of a neurotic symptom. Winnicott was operating on the explicit assumption of a psychological basis for mental disorder; for him, psychosis was a result of early maternal failure. When he rejected the traditional view of Freud that psychotics cannot "transfer" in therapy, and therefore are inaccessible in treatment, I thought this position was part of Winnicott's psychological optimism; he pooh-poohed the possibility of a biochemical basis for psychosis. Nor did he think much of the power of the hereditary element in schizophrenia. (Here other analysts were to be more prescient; Sandor Rado, for instance, had notably insisted on the significance of genetics for psychiatry.)

When Winnicott got wind of all my own historical interests, he said with emplatic encouragement: "It is going to be possible to write volumes and volumes on the intellectual history of psychoanalysis." It seemed to me unusual, and extraordinarily nice of Winnicott, that after he had given me so much time that we spent hours together, he turned before I left and genuinely thanked me for the discussion. I had never encountered anyone more gracious, and spontaneously so, in helping me with my research.

## Notes

1. Quoted in Adam Phillips, *Winnicott* (London: Fontana Press, 1988), p. 81.
2. Paul Roazen, "Book Review of *The Freud-Klein Controversies 1941-1945*, ed. Pearl King and Riccardo Steiner," *Psychoanalytic Books*, Fall 1992, pp. 391-98. See also Paul Roazen, *Oedipus in Britian: Edward Glover & The Struggle Over Klien* (N.Y.: Other Press, 2000).
3. D. W. Winnicott, "Book Review of Jung's *Memories, Dreams, Reflections*," *International Journal of Psychoanalysis*, Vol. 45 (April-July 1964), pp. 450-55.
4. Geoffrey Gorer and John Rickman, *The People of Great Russia: A Psychological Study* (New York: Norton, 1962).
5. Phillips, *Winnicott, op. cit.*

# 17

# Franz Jung

Interviewing can be an uncertain and sometime perilous undertaking, and in my experience it is possible for people to agree to be seen who then turn out to be uncooperative and even downright hostile. Although such unfortunate encounters have been for me exceptional, that they can happen at all leaves one with a degree of trepidation about any work like that in the future. Far more likely, instead of a negative reaction from one's interview subject, is the possibility that central problems may stem from the interviewer's own inadequacies. I am putting aside the whole matter of how lacking in knowledgeability any outsider is bound to be, as well as the difficulties in explaining what is taken for granted among scholars. For those who have lived through events of historical interest it requires a special effort to understand what historians need to know, yet it can be an immense challenge to communicate the special perspective beginners bring. An insider's point of view, especially when family history is an essential part of the story, almost inevitably has to be at cross purposes with the outlook of a researcher.

Even more troubling is how in the course of attentive listening it is easy to become naively credulous, and tempting to accept too much of what one has been told. Such a mood of identifying with one's host makes it all too conceivable that the ideal of objectivity can be lost sight of, and hard questions evaded for the sake of social amiability. It can be easier, at least for me, to object to something in writing a book (or a review) than to confront someone face-to-face. But in spite of all the flaws that are possible in this sort of undertaking, and how easily one can be misled, I have found over the years that extraordinary enlightenment can come from having once been in direct personal contact with the pioneers in depth psychology as well as their surviving family members. Such human familiarity can be a precious resource in hoping to understand what has appeared in print.

So when I knew I was going to be giving some lectures in French-speaking Switzerland in late May of 1995, I wrote ahead to Jung's only son Franz in order to try to arrange a meeting with him. The then president of the International

Association for Analytical Psychology, Dr. Thomas Kirsch, agreed to put in a good word for me. It has rarely been my practice to rely on a tape-recorder, since my objective has usually been to learn as much as humanly possible within the interview itself, and any recording device is bound, I think, to make the situation even more artificial than it necessarily has to be. (A highly eccentric British analyst, in an effort to account for my degree of success in keeping documents straight, maintained in a letter that I had supposedly relied on secret photographic and tape-recording equipment.)

I was going to see Franz Jung not for the sake of coming up with a document whose exact transcription might be helpful to future historians; such transcripts like that as I have come across them have their own special ways of being misleading. I had ambitions which were less grand, or perhaps in a sense more so, in that I was hoping to be able to establish enough of a rapport with Franz Jung so that I could carry away an impression which would be of enduring general significance for the further work I might do on the history of psychoanalysis. I had already written a few chapters about Jung and his psychology, but usually only in relation to Freud. (In 1969 I had published, in passing, the news that Jung had had an extramarital affair with one of his pupils, and when I later asked one of Jung's biographers whether that revelation had assisted or hurt the willingness of the family to facilitate the work of biographers, I was pleased when Barbara Hannah wrote me that it had helped.)

I came to Franz Jung, once he had graciously written back to me agreeing to be seen, with the conviction that the break between Freud and Jung had been of central significance in Freud's career. Jung put in print some of the central interpretive lines at odds with Freud's whole system, even if he is not often enough today credited with having been so far-seeing. Much of the psychological writing within Freud's own school, even before his death in 1939, can seem like reinventions of the Jungian wheel; and many of the issues that had most bothered Jung in Freud have been coped with by changes in psychoanalytic thinking that might well have seemed gratifying to Jung. His own ways of thinking were far less familiar to me than Freud's, but that only added to the interest I had in being able to learn something new. To those most loyal to Freud's point of view, the term "Jungian" has remained about the most dreadful accusation that it is possible to hurl at anybody, and even the boldest of analysts (including Winnicott) have been reluctant to trace their intellectual lineage to anything Jung might have had to say. Organizational rivalry, and the fear of losing therapeutic business to another camp, only partly accounts for the acute sensitivities that still persist about Jung. Some analogies hailing from how different religious groups feel about one another would be needed to account for the standing Jung has today among Freudians.

One historical perplexity I carried in the back of my mind had to do with why Freud had in 1938, once the Nazi occupation of Austria made it imperative that he leave, ignored the possibility of moving from Vienna to Switzerland.

Instead he agreed to take his family to London. But in England his daughter Anna was sure to have professional problems with her opponent in child analysis, Melanie Klein, by then securely established there. As a partial explanation for Freud's not choosing Switzerland, it is worth recalling that before World War I virtually the entire Swiss psychoanalytic group had resigned from Freud's International Psychoanalytic Association to go along with Jung, and I have to suspect that Freud always continued to view Switzerland as Jung territory. Even though the physicians in Switzerland were top-notch, and Freud's health precarious, in thinking of how reluctant he was as an old man to move at all one has to conclude he stayed dangerously too long in Vienna. By putting himself first he had endangered not only relatives (four sisters died during World War II) but pupils who had been reluctant to leave without him.

I have come to surmise that Freud would have resented ever being in Jung's wake, even if there was the compensation of being close to his old doctors in Vienna. Switzerland was also expensive to live in, and if some of Freud's students might have been able to help him financially, Freud would have resented being dependent on them for such assistance. So England, which he had visited as a young man and where his half-brothers had been long settled, represented an attractive compromise. America, given all Freud's old-world prejudices against the whole of the North American continent, was out of the question. (Freud was fortunate that arrangements for Holland had not worked out, since the Nazis so readily swept through there.)

Franz Jung had been living in what had once been his parents' house in Küsnacht, which is located outside Zurich. Küsnacht, literally meaning "kiss-night," is on Lake Zurich and was the setting in Schiller's *William Tell* for the swearing of a famous oath of allegiance. It is also noteworthy for having been one of the richest parts of Switzerland. Before Thomas Mann left for the States prior to World War II he had lived there, too. (Many central Europeans feared the possibility that Switzerland might be invaded by the Nazis, which also might help account for Freud's going to London.)

My objective in seeing Franz Jung was to try and slice through what had appeared in pre-existing books, and to succeed in getting as much knowledge as possible. I believed I was going not to snoop but rather to encounter Jung's son in the family home; above all perhaps, I wanted to have a look at the house itself. It has been my conviction that where people choose to live can be extremely telling about the historical inhabitants themselves.

I was only partially successful as far as the house went, since there were still so many Jungs living in it that most of the quarters were closed off to me. I sat with Franz Jung in his father's old study, which was one flight up from the ground floor. It seemed a huge house, set right on the lake, and family members were living both upstairs and downstairs from where I met Franz Jung. But I started learning things on the long drive up to the house itself, which was set on beautiful grounds. Unlike in Vienna, where I visited Freud's old apartment in

1965 although my cab-driver remained ignorant of where we were, the Zurich taxi-driver recognized whose house he was taking me to. One approaches Jung's home from the land side, away from the waterfront. There are some 800 meters of land on the property, and when the large house was constructed in 1908-1909 there were still peasants living on either side. The area was less built-up then, and altogether more rural; most of the trees were planted later. Since the old house does face onto the lake it retains its magnificence. Freud visited Jung's Zurich flat in 1908, and may or may not have seen the remarkable location of the proposed house. (Although one might think that Jung's move there would come up in their correspondence, all we have is the fact that Jung wrote to Freud on June 2, 1909 from the new Küsnacht address.)

Jung's good-sized writing-desk was at the side of a window, so evidently he did not find it a distraction if he happened to turn his head and look out at the water. The chairs at the writing-table struck me as surprisingly small and delicate, considering how large a man Jung was. Franz assured me that the chairs were the same original ones. He himself, at the time aged eighty-six, had never grown as tall as his father.

I was of course intrigued by the sight of all the books that lined the walls. (I had found Jung's writing hard to follow because of his frequent citations to texts, often with untranslated classical references, which were obscure to me.) The library had lettering indicating which parts of the alphabet were associated with the books residing on each shelf. Early on Jung could find exactly what he wanted, without any such artifical aid, but in his later years someone helpfully put the letters there. Like other intellectuals, Jung's equanimity could be temporarily shaken in the uncertainty that existed without such lettering. Not being able to put his fingers on a book, just when he wanted to, could be a real strain. Everyone who writes can appreciate something of that same feeling.

I also saw the consulting room where Jung met his patients. There seemed little possible place for a couch, but I felt sure that before the falling-out with Freud there must have been one. (I am no longer confident about this point, and it remains for Jungian scholarship to establish whether he did work extensively with a couch.) In the 1920s Jung wrote some memorable words about the disadvantages to using a couch in psychotherapy, since Jung believed it led to encouraging too much clinical authoritarianism on the analyst's part. (Among Freudians not using a couch was for years taken as a sure sign of treason.) There were three beautiful stained-glass windows which had to be in the patients' sight. It was a small room, much less spacious than the study, and I would guess that the size helped ensure intimacy and a measure of reciprocity between Jung and his patients. (I knew he was also capable of taking a client on a day-long sail, just as Freud could go on long walks with patients.) The old waiting-room was gone, but must have been relatively large; it had been transformed into Franz's kitchen, where he liked to cook.

One of Franz's sons had died, due to cancer; he did not wince at the view of a remarkable photographic shot of him. I spotted other family traces around the library. Another son, Peter, was a psychiatrist living nearby. When Franz changed the waiting room into his kitchen he left the old wooden door intact; filial piety came through every inch of Franz.

I talked a bit about my own two sons, for I was in the presence of a proud father who was full of gratitude for his own childhood. I took no notes during the interview, but wrote up a draft the next morning. Thirty years earlier, when I had seen Anna Freud in London, I headed to a tea-shop right afterward and wrote everything down; by 1995 I trusted my unconscious better, and hopefully the reader will get some idea here of the Jung family.

We sat in front of a fireplace, and Franz offered me something to drink. (Jung's teacher Eugen Bleuler had been a teetoteler, and the issue of the use of alcohol had been part of Jung's difficulties with Freud, leading to one of Freud's fainting episodes.) Sherry seemed perfect for the occasion, and I sipped a bit throughout the interview; Franz himself needed no such supportive steadying.

If I got the drift of what Franz thought his father had done correctly, it was to treat each child separately, giving them all physical and emotional space. Franz quoted a few examples of how his father could guide without stifling by means of a few brief words. He had built things with his father, although I did not get to see anything. A large stove had been an opportunity for wood-chopping.

Jung had had five children in all, and Franz made a point of emphasizing that there had been no divorces. (Freud's middle son Oliver got divorced, but on at least one occasion Freud curiously seemed to suppress the memory of this first brief marriage of Oliver's.) I thought to myself that Jung was so boldly emancipated in his private life that it might have helped ensure that his own children kept to a pretty straight path. The Freud family had been notoriously protective about his personal life, and cooperated in all kinds of tendentious editing of his correspondences for example; the Jung family was similar. By 1995 they had still not allowed an authorized biography to appear. Jung's hundredth birthday twenty years earlier should have been the occasion for such a work. The Jungs may have waited too long, from the point of view of vibrant history-writing, since those who might once have added human interest to the story are no longer alive. The Freudians had a better sense of history, and annotated his works far better than Jung's ever were. (Jung had even waited years to begin to reply to Freud's 1914 attack on him.) When I asked Franz point-blank about the existence of a second installment of Jung's autobiography, which I have been told by Sonu Shamdasani was suppressed from publication, Franz denied that there was such a text. Perhaps he did not think of it as an autobiography, or at any rate must have disliked it intensely, for such additional material is authoritatively reported to exist.

Franz had eight grand-children of his own, and I felt he had every right to be as proud of them as he was. The American divorce rate of one out of three marriages seemed to both of us a sign of cultural barbarism. Franz knew little about Freud's own family life, and nothing about Freud's philandering eldest son. (Franz laughed over the story of how Martin Freud had collected photographs of his various women friends, a volume of which happened to fall into the hands of his estranged wife.) Franz had only met Freud's youngest son Ernst, at the time when they struck the deal about the publication of the Freud-Jung correspondence. Ernst was already sick with heart trouble, and Franz was moved by meeting him; they were both professional architects.

When I told Franz that I did not think that Freud had ever gotten over the loss of Jung, Franz proposed that it had been true for Jung, too. (They had been in contact for some six years.) For four years after the falling-out Jung could not write and function as usual with patients. Then, using this space of time to recover, and stepping back into his own "shadow" side, Jung had been able to come up with his momentous book on psychological types.

Freud and Jung shared much in common, although they came from such completely contrasting backgrounds—nationally, religiously, and professionally. I pointed out to Franz how they both had liked oriental carpets, which obviously added to the beauty of Franz's home. These rugs were on the staircase as well as in the study. (In Freud's house in London, when he moved there in 1938, some of the original rugs had been subsequently damaged by Anna Freud's dogs; a relative had apparently supplied the carpets, and they were used on table-tops as well as the floors. Freud had wisely invested mainly in his collection of ancient art objects, but Jung's study had no such antiques.)

I could not help thinking more than once that the property at Küsnacht must have reinforced Freud's conviction that Jung deserved to be Freud's "crown prince," a term he used for him in a letter of April 19, 1909. The exquisite taste, style, and setting of the high-ceilinged house (with four servants) might well have added to why Freud thought that Jung deserved to be his successor. Freud was to grow conflicted about Jung's talents, and minded that Jung was altogether the larger man physically. Franz reported that his father had had alternating anger and affection toward Freud, and Franz agreed that the word "ambivalence," coined by Bleuler, was the one that covered Jung's emotions about Freud.

Midway through the interview I spotted a drawing of Franz's mother, Emma, as a relatively young woman. (She had originally had the money in the family, but I believe under old Swiss law a husband was automatically entitled to a large share in it.) "Determined" was the way I described the expression I saw portrayed in her face, and Franz agreed with that characterization. She had had the fortitude to deal with Jung, and withstood his sexual liaisons. The best letters in the Freud-Jung collection were, I honestly believed, those written by Emma to Freud, in which she pleaded that he allow her husband growth and autonomy, and Franz shared my assessment.

Emma Jung had had little formal education, and there are not many documents from her hand which have survived. (Exactly the same is true of Freud's wife Martha.) Franz explained how much Emma had been given by his father; her "vision" had been expanded. When I asked about it, he said that she often did not travel with him, although sometimes she did. I knew that Jung had treated her psychotherapeutically at some point, but I did not think to discuss what sort of therapist she herself became; nor did I dare to raise the issue of Jung's lady friends.

I would have learned nothing from such tactlessness. If Jung needed to skate so close to danger, like extramarital sex and perhaps madness too, it can be understood as having been for the sake of his creativity, and he had the immense good fortune to have a wife who understood him. The inner demons that Jung had to struggle against were probably tougher than what Freud had to deal with. It seems that Freud was more normally neurotic, and found it easier to keep his equilibrium; also he was beloved by the gods in having had a doting mother, whereas Jung's mother is known to have been mentally sick.

The German Swiss are very special culturally, yet rather like the Canadians I had known since 1971; formality on the outside can go along with great inner imagination. Perhaps that helps explain why Canadians were so relatively eager to respond warmly to Jung's teachings. It took longer for Jung to become secure in America, and his work never attained the psychiatric impact that Freud's once did. I am convinced that Jung's unfortunate politics in the 1930s, another subject Franz and I did not touch on, held back the American reception of Jung's thinking.

Franz told me that he had destroyed some love letters to himself, and I took that to mean that when Toni Wolff, Jung's co-worker and his former mistress, instructed at her death that Jung's letters be returned to him, that he too destroyed these documents. Although historians are not apt to see it that way, for Jung to have saved them would have been a form of exhibitionism.

Franz said that he had in the house transcripts of many seminars of his father, few of which had appeared in print. They were taken down in short-hand, and could become a little scholarly industry of their own someday. (At least that has been the fate of Jacques Lacan's own seminars.) Franz also had the appointment books of his father, although that seemed to me relatively unusual for such confidential information. The families of other clinicians have shredded such material.

But Franz said he had no intention of allowing biographers to get their hands on intra-family letters. I tried my best to encourage Franz to cooperate fully with Deirdre Bair, an experienced biographer (of Samuel Beckett, Simone de Beauvoir, and Anaïs Nin) whom I had encouraged to work on Jung. But Franz seemed to balk at her name when I raised the subject of her on-going work. And he clearly implied that he intended to do away with certain family documents rather than allow them to come into the hands of outsiders. In spite of my own biographical interests, as a person I had to respect Franz's desire to retain the family's privacy. He spoke approvingly of Linda Donn's published work, but research which is complete is less likely to be threatening. I have to wonder how any biographer on Jung could know enough to handle properly Swiss standards of propriety.

After several hours together Franz volunteered to drive me to the nearest train station. I found he had an earthy sense of humor, as his father too is reported to have had. He said that Tom Kirsch was stepping down as president of the international society of analytic psychology at the next Congress, although Kirsch had not mentioned that to me when I had seen him recently in San Francisco. So Franz was up-to-date on events within the Jungian movement, as well as the growing literature about his father. He mentioned that Richard Noll's recent book (*The Jung Cult*) was "full of errors," which he thought surprising since Princeton University Press, which has published so much of Jung, might not be expected to bring out such a harsh view of Franz's father.

We talked a bit about William McGuire, who had formerly been editor-in-chief at Princeton University press. Franz had relied on McGuire, who did a superb job of editing the Freud-Jung letters at a time when such scholarship was rarer than now. Franz did not know that McGuire had been analyzed by the orthodox Freudian Kurt Eissler, or that Bollingen foundation money, often associated with Jungian projects, had gone to help start the Freud Archives that Eissler set up after World War II. (Eissler had been embarrassed that Jung's letters to Freud surfaced in Anna Freud's house at the time of Jones's biography, but had earlier, when the Jung family offered to share Freud's letters, been found to be missing.) To this day there is a world-wide alliance among orthodox Freudian analysts, still particularly strongly established, for example, between Germany and the United States.

As a relatively young man I had been impressed by finding in the files of Ernest Jones a letter from Jung in which, having answered some queries of Jones, he tried to encourage Jones, in writing about old quarrels, not to let old quarrels be perpetuated. Jung was being naïve about Jones's commitment to legend-weaving. It would be hard to over-emphasize the significance of family for either Jung or Freud, even though such commitments, in a world in which families are now lucky even to eat together, may seem rare. I cannot comment as knowledgeably about Jung, but Freud certainly made his whole movement into a kind of extended family. He explicitly thought of Jung as one of his prime ideological sons.

In the back of my mind, while I was talking with Franz Jung, I suppose I had been wondering what it had been like to be the son of such a great man. I had failed to be specific, and that question remained a hidden agenda on my part. My general impression, for what it is worth, would be that for Franz it had not been a hard experience, although others would be in a better position to pursue the subject in the future.

Only after I had completed a draft of this paper did I discover that Franz Jung had died on June 29, 1996.

# Part 5

## Neglected Stories

# Introduction to Part 5

History is inevitably written mainly by the victors. And each era asks questions of previous times in terms of its own special preoccupations. Yet such biases inherent in historical inquiry require us to be vigilant about those people and events who inevitably have been left out of the received written record. It is not necessary to be driven to idealize historical victims to take the patience to try to ensure that as best we can the goddess of success does not become our sole guide.

My initial interest in the life and work of Victor Tausk was aroused by my conviction that lacunae were bound to arise; and yet he was intimately associated with such important people as both Freud and Lou Andreas-Salomé. My historiographical concern with Tausk was evidently easy to be misunderstood as an effort to besmirch Freud rather than to appreciate the full roundedness that the study of the past has to offer. I now think, though, that the lack of therapeutic boundaries in the case of Tausk (he was analyzed by Helene Deutsch while she was in treatment with Freud) was only the tip of the iceberg for what much of the rest of the history of psychoanalysis was like.

The historian is inevitably a story-teller, and naturally one is likely to think in terms of good-guys as opposed to bad-guys. As far as I am concerned, the best people are those who are least understood, and at times this includes Freud himself. Trying to correct misconceptions or imbalances in the record should not be confused with being unduly biased. One should write, I think, for the sake of promoting the cause of better understanding.

In addition to Tausk, Otto Rank's wife "Tola" also seemed to me someone in danger of being forgotten, for a wholly different set of reasons. Whereas Tausk's struggle with Freud, and then Tausk's suicide, put his tale off-limits for half-a-century, a separate set of considerations arose in connection with the standing that Tola Rank could hope to have. And the specific question of Felix Deutsch's contact with the Federal Bureau of Investigation during the McCarthy period represents another aspect of the past which was in danger of being neglected.

We impoverish ourselves to the extent that we fail to study those who even temporarily have lost out in terms of the construction of the historical record. It is my own belief that absolutely nothing guarantees that merit is sure inherently to win out. The only historical inevitability that I recognize is that of our personal responsibility for what we make of the past. I believe that we triumph when we see as many sides of things as possible.

# 18

# A Curious Triangle: Freud, Lou Andreas-Salomé, and Victor Tausk

When Lou Andreas-Salomé came into Freud's circle in 1912, she was bound to represent an acquisition for Freud personally, as well as for psychoanalysis. As Nietzsche's friend and expositor, she came to Freud with the aura of past European culture. Lou was still on close terms with Rilke, whose lover she had been and whose development as a poet she had assisted; together they had taken a trip to Russia, where they made Tolstoy's acquaintance. (Lou introduced Rilke to Freud in 1913, and Freud once wrote a paper about the meeting.[1])

Freud was fifty-six and Lou fifty-one when she came to Vienna in 1912; she regarded it as "the turning point" in her life.[2] Perhaps not entirely by chance, Freud also later wrote that 1912 had been "the very climax of my psychoanalytic work."[3] Before entering the Viennese psychoanalytic scene, she prepared herself by reading everything Freud had written. She came with the intention of eliciting Freud's interest in her, and succeeded completely in her aim.

Lou fits the genre of women who have a knack for collecting great men. Madame de Staël in the eighteenth century and Alma Mahler in the twentieth illustrate the type. In Lou's case beauty was not her main attraction; whatever her earlier good looks, she now had to rely on her psychological resources to arouse the attention of any potential conquests. Vibrantly responsive to ideas, Lou possessed an extraordinary talent for identifying with men, and especially with creative intellectuals often subject to inner uncertainties. So of course she would have read all of Freud before approaching him. Lou was useful to her series of great men, but as men fell in love with her, they eventually discovered that she had not truly given of herself; she had mirrored them, had helped in their creative needs, but had withheld herself as a person. Her great men all needed her, but each of her lovers ultimately realized how she had eluded them.

Many years later Freud wrote that he had admired Lou immensely and been very attached to her, "without a trace of sexual attraction."[4] Puritanical by temperament, and head of a family of six children, for Freud a physical relationship was out of the question if only because he could never have tolerated the degree of disorder such an affair would entail. Freud was always moved by the great charm of what he called narcissistic women. Through Lou, Freud was in touch with the spirit of Nietzsche and much of the best in German cultural life. Freud later began to honor his favored pupils by presenting them with an antique stone to be made into a ring; although he never did this for Lou, he took her into his confidence to an extraordinary degree. In his letters of later years he discussed with her the emotional problems of his daughter Anna. For a time in the 1920s Lou became Anna's psychoanalytic therapist. Freud asked Lou to help loosen Anna's ties to him; but Lou refused.[5] They discussed Anna together almost as if his wife did not matter at all, and Anna were their child instead. Lou responded with all her devotion, later dedicating one of her books to Anna Freud.

Freud certainly had no special fondness for women with a checkered sexual past. But in 1912 he courted Lou. Her *Journal* records him sending her flowers, and walking her home at 2:30 in the morning. These attentions are all the more noteworthy from a man who husbanded his time jealously. Lou succeeded in making Freud fall in love with her, although in a sublimated way. When she missed a lecture of his, he felt uneasy. Freud had immediately grown used to speaking for Lou; as he wrote to her, "I have acquired the bad habit of directing my lecture to a particular person in the audience, and yesterday I stared as if spell-bound at the vacant chair reserved for you...."

In these pre-World War I days, before his cancer and all the disappointments with his pupils, Freud was at his most inspiring. In addition to the regular members of his Society, some well-known people came to meetings. At the height of his powers, Freud was constantly reformulating his ideas; he flourished on contacts with richly endowed human beings. Lou noticed that Freud did not care for cats or dogs. When we consider how in his old age he turned to chows for emotional sustenance, her observation suggests how much more open to human communication he was at this earlier time. He would go to cafes after scientific meetings, amplifying the issues of his lectures in discussion, always exploring possibilities.

Lou was in a special position to understand Freud and his whole circle. For she had actively set out to seduce Victor Tausk, whom she ranked "the most prominently outstanding" among Freud's students. Tausk was a dashing Slav whose dynamism and good looks won the hearts of a whole series of women, yet his marriage had ended in failure and successive love affairs came to grief. A man of great versatility, a poet and a writer, a lawyer as well as a physician and psychoanalyst, Tausk was ultimately overwhelmed by his contact with Freud. In 1912, however, Tausk was the most brilliant of Freud's pupils in Vienna. He was handsome, with blond hair, blue eyes, and a moustache. At thirty-three he was eighteen years her junior, and to his friends it was strange, if not offensive, to see him involved with a woman so much older.

Lou came to Vienna flaunting her attractiveness to great men as a vehicle by which present lovers might liken themselves to the famous ones in her past. While she was in search of talented men to identify with, Tausk could hope that being accepted as Lou's lover might help make him to psychology what Nietzsche was to philosophy and Rilke to poetry. One would think that Tausk, so enormously attractive to women, could have easily found a younger and more single-mindedly devoted woman; but Lou's very self-sufficiency, her skill at pulling out of love affairs at the opportune moment, was a special source of her attractiveness to him. Afraid of being depended upon and loved, Tausk need never feel guilty about Lou.

Lou and Tausk shared many interests in common. Tausk got her into a clinic to observe some cases. He brought her a collection of Serbian ballads he had translated, and she accompanied him on his visits to his two sons, who lived with their mother in Vienna. But on Tausk's part his love for Lou ended in physical revulsion and distaste.

For the year 1912–1913, however, Freud, Lou, and Tausk established a triangle which had advantages for each. Lou had recurrently had two men in her life simultaneously. She married Friedrich Carl Andreas after he threatened to kill himself; but she slept only with other men. Before Lou married she had used another man against Nietzsche (Nietzsche's sister considered her a devil). Lou, Rilke, and Andreas travelled to Russia as a threesome. And now she had a physical relation with Tausk, alongside her deep involvement with Freud.

For Freud the arrangement had frustrations as well as satisfactions. He was jealous of Tausk's opportunity to have an affair with Lou. Tausk was much younger, more virile, and altogether a larger man physically; Freud had already acquired his scholar's stoop. When Freud stared spellbound at Lou's vacant chair, she may well have been with Tausk. On the other hand, Lou could give Freud information about Tausk, and she could help keep this potentially troublesome student under control.

Meanwhile, Tausk had taken Lou at least partly out of identification with Freud; Tausk was certainly glad to play the role of the great man who was currently her lover. Just as Freud was jealous of Tausk's relation to Lou, so Tausk envied what Freud could mean to her. Lou could serve as a channel from Tausk to Freud, raising Tausk's importance in Freud's eyes. For both men she was a buffer.

The Viennese psychoanalytic group was beset by competiteness for Freud's admiration, and petty jealousies and backbiting are bound to arise in any hothouse atmosphere. To be an analyst then meant to be a pariah in psychiatry. Having given up the quest for approval in the external world, Freud's pupils needed his favor in exchange. Freud provided the inspiration, and more mundanely, the patients. These apostles gave all their devotion to Freud and turned their hostilities onto the outside world. His believers followed whatever Freud was then working on, without daring to stray very far from the legitimate borders he defined. The Psychoanalytic Society had an air of secrecy. Political or religious imagery can best convey the atmosphere of those early meetings. As Tausk put it, "Darwinism...was a scientific religion, just as psychoanalysis is."[6] If Freud reigned as God, it was his students who made his word law.

Freud, to be sure, encouraged the absolute devotion of his students. Hated and maligned, he was entitled to entice followers by exaggerating the degree to which his supporters were an embattled minority. Freud gave regular lectures before heterogeneous audiences at the university on Saturday evenings, to which his students came with spouses or lady-friends; he limited his audiences by requiring them to get his express permission to attend beforehand. But still Freud preferred speaking in his small group of dedicated followers. He was so self-critical about his ideas that he very much needed a "yes" from the outside world. Since this recognition did not yet come from the world at large, or even from Vienna's intelligentsia, approval had to come from his own little Society.

So Freud collected able people who would in effect be yea-sayers; they were the audience for which he wrote. He wanted them to mirror back his ideas, to help him see his concepts in a slightly different light; but he did not want to be jolted out of a line of thinking already embarked upon. Even if original ideas were brought by others as a sign of their positive relation to Freud, these might seem to him like a hostile attack. "What he wanted was to look into a kaleidoscope lined with mirrors that would multiply the images he introduced into it."[7]

As a woman, Lou would arouse none of Freud's feelings of rivalry; for such an old-fashioned man, women simply did not exist as competitors. He wanted corroborators rather than collaborators, and Lou fitted perfectly into such a passive role. She could flatter him while believing everything she said; and as a woman she could take a special delight in pleasing this man. A woman can more easily dissociate her sense of self from her professional work, so to give Freud what he wanted in no way compromised her integrity.

Freud's demand that his students identify with him would eventually mobilize rebellion in men. For a man really to be like Freud meant finally for him to be original, yet originality ended his usefulness to Freud. On the other hand, for a woman like Lou to reflect Freud's ideas back to him fitted in perfectly with the feminine ability to identify with creative men. But for one man to flatter another can be corrupting, and the best of Freud's male pupils left because the atmosphere was too narrow and ultimately dispiriting.

Some have likened Freud and his circle to a reigning monarch with a court, an obvious comparison for those who lived under the absolute monarchy of the Hapsburg Empire. Freud certainly had this much significance for them all. His pupils were his subjects, owing fealty to him alone; they performed tasks, wrote articles, expounded his ideas. And yet often Freud did not respect them because they lacked independence. Another image which has been used by analysts who lived through those days is that of a large and extended family, with Freud as the unquestioned head. In these terms Freud needed his pupils as adopted sons, to escape isolation and to establish his immortality. Both images imply that if the pupil were not respectful toward the leader and his ideas, he would be in danger of being ousted. Very often the followers were more stringent than Freud in interpreting the permissible range of thinking.

Lou captured this whole atmosphere in one tiny vignette in her diary; her involuted sentences repay the closest attention. Early in her stay she reported a meeting at which Freud tried to counter Jung's influence on psychoanalytic thinking. Freud argued that Jung's term "complex" was unnecessary. ("Complexes" then referred to what we now call "emotional conflicts.") According to Lou, Freud

> showed a subtle and ingenious bit of malice in his attempt to make the term "complex" superfluous, pointing out how it had insinuated itself into the terminology out of convenience, without having grown up on psychoanalytic soil, just as Dionysus was artificially exalted from being an exotic god to becoming the son of Zeus. (At this, Tausk, who was sitting or standing next to Freud, and was still in the white doctor's smock he wore coming from the psychiatric clinic, did not quite stifle a chuckle.)[8]

Both Lou and Tausk obviously understood the undercurrents of Freud's comment. He was likening himself to an immortal god capable of conferring divine favors or withdrawing them from an artifically created son.

If Jung were not to be Freud's successor, then Tausk might yearn for recognition. Even if Tausk did not expect to be accepted quite yet as Freud's most beloved son, he might well have seen himself as the future recipient of royal favors once the defecting barons were driven out. Supporting Freud in his quarrel with Alfred Adler, Tausk displayed a degree of malice that Lou considered excessive and unfair. And at the height of Freud's public battle with Jung, Tausk thundered against Jung's heresy. "Clever and dangerous," Lou reports Freud saying about Tausk, "he can bark and bite." Tausk had indeed an aggressive mouth; his beautiful teeth were a prominent part of his face, especially when he smiled. And in these verbal battles Tausk was at his best, though in his articles he could also be truculent and polemical. As Freud commented in an obituary praising Tausk, "his passionate temperament found expression in sharp, and sometimes too sharp, criticisms...."[9]

In listening to Tausk lecture on psychoanalysis, Lou had the impression "not only of classical Freudian theory but also of an unusually loving and reverent approach to the essential discoveries of Freud...." She objected only that Tausk was "*too* precisely Freudian; in any case, he is never likely to be reproached with the contrary." Lou felt that for Tausk's own good his identification with Freud should not descend to imitation. The first to give lectures on psychoanalysis for the lay public, Tausk could repeat Freud word for word. Freud himself was a great orator; but the more Tausk felt impelled to ape Freud, the less of a personality in his own right he became.

Lou felt with the lightest possible touch just exactly the sources of tension between these two men. Tausk had only been in Freud's circle for a few short years before he became a rival in Freud's eyes. Ellen Delp, a woman of doubtful sexual allegiance who was an intimate friend of Lou's, looked on Tausk as "a genius of Freud's own stature bearing up loyally under Freud's jealous provocation."

What put Freud off? Lou reported that in a discussion after one of Tausk's papers, "Freud's rejoinders were more severe than usual and yet no other person presents his papers to him with such evident reverence. I think that Tausk is of all the most unconditionally devoted to Freud...."

In a few areas Tausk was forging ahead of Freud. For example, he wanted to extend psychoanalytic thinking to the psychology of the artist. He delivered an early paper on sublimation, focusing on the role of inhibitions in artistic creativity. This would one day be considered a perfectly legitimate subject among analysts, but in 1912 Freud felt that "with the persistent calumny of our whole movement on the part of official science, we should not dare to move so boldly into new territory leaving the rear so exposed, and confirmation of earlier discoveries needs to be made again and again...." After this meeting Lou noted Freud's conflict with "independent, or temperamental characters."

Freud characteristically wished to transcend all previous limits of knowledge. Yet when it came to Tausk, Freud thought he was seizing problems ahead of their time. In his obituary, Freud noted Tausk's gift for exploring the philosophic implications of psychoanalysis. Once again, though, Freud hesitated. "Perhaps the time was not yet ripe for laying such general foundations as these for the young science of psychoanalysis." Tausk, according to Freud, had "an impetuous urge for investigation."

When Freud was submerged in following a theme of his own, he would push aside anything that interfered with it. As his earliest biographer (Wittels) noted, "he finds it a nuisance when lights other than his own are thrown athwart his path, or when others try to push him forward or to divert him from his chosen course. Whenever necessary he erects outworks to cut off inconvenient crosslights." Tausk's interests were disturbances to Freud. Tausk pursued fields where Freud thought the way would be blocked, and under those circumstances he soon lost interest.

In contrast to Tausk's universalistic aspirations, Freud believed in the single-minded pursuit of research. The only way to make important discoveries, he thought, was to "have one's ideas exclusively focused on one central interest."[10] In part Freud was reacting to the diversity of his own youth. He recorded in his autobiographical study how "In complete contrast to the diffuse character of my studies during my earlier years at the University, I...[developed] an inclination to concentrate my work on a single subject...." Freud admitted his contribution to psychology was one-sided: he claimed only to have unearthed the importance of unconscious motivation, other motives being commonplace. Defending his own narrowness, Freud thought that he "must have needed this one-sidedness in order to see what remains hidden from others."[11]

Tausk's work irritated Freud, and a good part of the problem was Tausk's originality. Lou and Freud talked it out repeatedly, while she was still engaged in her affair with Tausk. In her diary Lou mentioned having supper at Freud's: "Earlier in the living room he turned the conversation to Tausk and we talked a lot about him, the same later in his study and it was nearly half past one when he took me home...." On another evening Lou wrote that "before supper, and then again later, Freud talked readily and at length about the Tausk problem. At the end he spoke kindly and tenderly...." Evidently this spiritual *ménage-à-trois* arrangement was accepted quite naturally by them all.

Tausk's independence disturbed Freud. He recognized brilliance; admired creativity, but in his immediate circle he needed passive receptacles for his concepts. At this stage Freud was still trying to keep his best students. He hoped to reconcile psychoanalysis's need for first-rate adherents with his own manner of working out his ideas. But Tausk's talents upset Freud's inner harmony. Lou reported after one of the Society's meetings that

> Freud acts with complete conviction when he proceeds so sharply against Tausk. But...bearing in mind Tausk's original neurotic disposition...it is also clear that any independence around Freud, especially when it is marked by aggression and display of temperament, worries him and wounds him quite automatically in his noble egoism as investigator, forcing him to premature discussion....[12]

Freud resented Tausk's intellectual ambitiousness, preferring men like Otto Rank who, according to Lou, was at that time "a son and nothing but a son." Of Rank, Freud said to Lou: "Why is it that there can't be six such charming men in our group, instead of only one?" As Lou shrewdly noted, in Freud's wish for half-a-dozen Ranks "the individuality of the man referred to is put in some doubt."

The crux of "the Tausk problem" was not just that he was a son striving to grow up; for Tausk's independence was partly a façade. His inhibitions in being fully creative made the situation with Freud acute. For worst of all, from Freud's point of view, was that at times Tausk stayed glued to Freud's own preoccupations. In an uncanny way Tausk seemed able to anticipate Freud's own formulations; hence Lou's reference to Tausk forcing Freud to "premature discussion." Freud felt uneasy with Tausk not just because he had a mind of his own, but also because he dared to use this talent on problems which mattered so very dearly to Freud himself. One passage in Lou's Journal conveys Freud's distress:

> In the afternoon after Tausk had finished the lecture...we drove to the meeting. I went on ahead and walked with Freud, who was waiting for me in the street, He was restless (on account of the closeness of the ideas to his own), questioning me during the lecture, passing a note to me: "Does he know all about it already?"[13]

Here lay the centre of Freud's difficulties with Tausk; and Freud's distress that Tausk might steal some of his ideas before Freud himself had quite finished with them also helps explain why Lou could be useful to Freud in relation to

Tausk. Freud could count on her to keep him informed about Tausk's work, just as he could be sure on whose side she would ultimately come down. Freud felt uncomfortable with someone like Tausk around, a man bright enough even to anticipate some of Freud's own concepts. Freud did not like the uncertainty that Tausk might have an idea before Freud himself, and it bothered Freud to have to acknowledge Tausk's contributions.

The situation, however, never got beyond Freud's control. Ultimately, Freud could afford to brush Tausk off completely. But for Tausk the whole conflict with Freud touched close to the centre of his being. Lou was sensitive enough to see it all from the perspective of Tausk's inner difficulties:

> Only now do I perceive the whole tragedy of Tausk's relation with Freud: that is, I realize now that he will always tackle the same problems, the same attempts at solution, that Freud is engaged in. That is no accident, but signifies his "making himself a son" as violently as he "hates the father for it." As if by a thought transference he will always be busy with the same thing as Freud, never taking one step aside to make room for himself.

Lou knew enough about Tausk to understand how much he was one of those psychoanalysts who "stand themselves in practical need of the method they profess." However, she greatly exaggerated the degree to which Tausk could only follow in Freud's footsteps; for at this time Tausk was already making thoroughly original contributions by pioneering the application of psychoanalytic insights to the understanding of psychoses. (Freud held himself at some distance from psychotic clinical problems, restricting his work to the less severely disturbed, to neurotics.) Lou was right, however, that Tausk was self-absorbed and introspective, excessively ambitious and yet passionately loyal to Freud. The situation was in fact such that Tausk could place all the blame on Freud for their mutual difficulties.

Lou recognized the extent to which Tausk's troubles came from within his own discordant soul. "What he wants is his blind and dumb self-expression, suffering so greatly as he does under the burden of himself." Tausk clung to Freud partly out of his own lack of inner resources. No matter how brilliant and independent he might be, somewhere he did have a "gap in creativity," which became "filled by identification with the other (son-ship) which constantly begets the illusion of having attained the anticipated position." Tausk could be profound in his psychological understanding of others as a displacement of "his own longing to be analyzed himself," and so at times be as self deceptive as anyone.

Lou loved in Tausk his helplessness before his inner being, his tortured struggle to use his intellect to master his passions. He was demanding, but his capacity to have illusions made him lovable. His self, however, remained the prisoner of the past. In Tausk, she wrote,

> there still remain those irreconcilable contradictions between that which Freud calls the "beast of prey" (which at least helps him in the practical management of life) and his

> own over-sensitivity to the point of self-dissolution. It is all so painful to behold that one would like to look the other way and run away. In the long run no helpful relationship is possible; there can be none when reality is cluttered by the wraiths of unabreacted primal reminiscences. An impure tone resonates through everything, buzzing as it were with murmurings from within.
>
> Yet from the very beginning I realized it was this very struggle in Tausk that most deeply moved me—the struggle of the human creature. Brother-animal. You.[14]

Tausk went on to do creative work as a psychoanalyst; later both Erik H. Erikson and Bruno Bettelheim, for example, were to build upon Tausk's prior contributions to ego psychology. In his quite original work with psychotic patients, Tausk was the first to formulate the important concept of "ego boundaries"; and he was also the first to introduce the term "identity" into psychoanalytic literature, in his paper on the "influencing machine" in schizophrenia. But the first World War uprooted Tausk from his medical practice, and when he came back from the war seeking Freud's help, the master put him off with finality. In 1919, six years after his affair with Lou and after being decisively rejected by Freud, a lifetime's troubles came to fruition in Tausk's decision to kill himself.[15]

Lou, already embarked as a practicing analyst, exchanged letters with Freud about Tausk's sudden end. Regrettably, as in the case of all Freud's correspondences until finally the publication of the Freud-Jung letters in 1974, selected passages were initially censored from the published version of their final comments on Tausk. Freud wrote the official obituary, the lengthiest he ever penned, in honor of Tausk: "No one...could escape the impression that here was a man of importance."[16] But the immediate circumstances of Tausk's death, including a suicide note to the master, were electrifying to the members of Freud's inner circle. To kill oneself after a quarrel with Freud was to enact one of the most fearful expectations of Freud's followers: to cross Freud meant to run the risk of being destroyed, of having the candle snuffed out and the book slammed shut.

In Tausk's instance he was historically extinguished. The closing sentence of Freud's obituary became ironic, for he had proclaimed that Tausk was "sure of an honorable memory in the history of psychoanalysis and its earliest struggles." Neither Lou nor Freud ever wrote of Tausk again; and the rest of Freud's circle, trying not to think about what had happened to their fallen friend, certainly did not.

By 1969 Victor Tausk continued to be an almost completely forgotten figure, with scarcely a place in history books. (Kurt Eissler's criticisms of my work on Tausk, combined with my attempts to defend myself,[17] probably amount to what became one of the more extensive discussions of any figure besides Freud in the history of psychoanalysis.) Entirely aside from the polemics that Eissler engaged in, I still think that Tausk's tale can help us understand many of the other controversies in Freud's life, as the same pattern of conflicts recurred several times between Freud and his leading male pupils. The story also powerfully illustrates the timeless theme of how a man's struggle to liberate himself can end in his own undoing.

## Notes

1. Freud, "On Transience," *Standard Edition*, Vol. 14, pp. 305–07.
2. Lou Andreas-Salomé, *The Freud Journal*, translated by Stanley Leavy (NY: Basic Books, 1964), p. 131.
3. Freud, "An Autobiographical Study," *Standard Edition*, Vol. 20, p. 72.
4. Ernest Jones, *Life and Work of Sigmund Freud*, Vol. III (NY: Basic Books, 1957), p. 213.
5. Rudolf Binion, *Frau Lou* (NY: Princeton, NJ: Princeton University Press, 1968), pp. 372–73.
6. *Minutes of the Vienna Psychoanalytic Society*, ed. Herman Nunberg and Ernst Federn, Vol. II, translated by M. Nunberg (NY: International Universities Press, 1967), p. 467.
7. Fritz Wittels, *Sigmund Freud* (New York: Dodd Mead, 1924), p. 134.
8. Andreas-Salomé, *The Freud Journal*, op. cit., p. 134.
9. Freud, "Victor Tausk," *Standard Edition*, Vol. 17, p. 275.
10. Hanns Sachs, *Freud, Master and Friend* (Cambridge, MA: Harvard University Press, 1945), p. 69.
11. *The Letters of Sigmund Freud*, ed. Ernst L. Freud, translated by Tania and James Stern (London: Hogarth Press, 1961), pp. 97–98.
12. Andreas-Salomé, *The Freud Journal, op. cit.*, pp. 97–98.
13. Ibid., p. 114.
14. Ibid., pp. 167–68. The concept "beast of prey" comes from Freud's essay "On Narcissism," *Standard Edition*, Vol. 14, p. 89.
15. The why, wherefore, and how of this decision is discussed in my *Brother Animal: The Story of Freud and Tausk* (NY: Knopf, 1969; New Brunswick, NJ: Transaction, with new Introduction, 1990).
16. "Victor Tausk," *op. cit.*, p. 275.
17. See Paul Roazen, *Encountering Freud: The Politics and Histories of Psychoanalysis* (New Brunswick, NJ: Transaction, 1990), Ch. 6. Paul Roazen, "Reading, Writing, and Memory: Kurt R. Eissler's Thinking," *Contemporary Psychoanalysis*, April 1978.

# 19

# Tola Rank

Although I cannot say that I have any special competence in the history of women, I do have a commitment to writing about people who have been misunderstood or left out of the recorded past. Voltaire was only one thinker to have been appalled by how unreliable historical knowledge can be. It was he who memorably said, "History is nothing but a pack of tricks which we play on the dead."[1] As I look back on those few events in my own experience that have mattered enough to get covered in the press, or even to appear in books, my skepticism about how history gets written has to be enhanced.

After my own interviews with twenty-five of Freud's psychoanalytic cases in the mid-1960s, it is hard for me now to be, like so many others, particularly interested in reconstructing the Freud of the 1890s. Critically important though that period was for the history of analysis, it was a time for which no one I ever met could offer any first-hand evidence. The distortions that exist about what I think I know best are so grievous that I scarcely can conceive how to begin to handle the more remote past. If I now have picked Tola Rank as the subject of this essay, it is out of a general concern with historiography in general, and with underdogs. For she is in real danger, I believe, of being forgotten, even though she should rank among the pioneers in psychoanalysis.

Yet I also think that if she were to be securely established in history, it would be better if instead a woman were writing about her. The current climate of opinion is such that women writing about other women have far more persuasive power. The problem is that I think it unwise to rely on someone else to do what needs to be done, since for one reason or another our culture remains committed to an ideology of success. The fact that Tola Rank had so hard a life means she is not apt to attract the interest of writers; it seems to be much easier to insure an audience with the retelling of tales celebrating known achievements. Yet Tola Rank played a historic role, if only in taking part in the falling out between her husband Otto and Freud. Because of this conviction of mine that she is important though largely unknown, I am now exploring her historical position.

Freud himself could share a special respect for failure, which helps explain the attention he gave to those problems accounted for by his concept of neurosis. Defeat doubtless has a kind of romance attached to it, and antiheroes are said to have a notable contemporary appeal. Alix Strachey, married to Lytton Strachey's brother James, once told me that she had had to argue with Freud, in the course of her own personal analysis with him, about Queen Elizabeth I, a woman who Freud somehow told her was "a bad queen." When Alix vigorously protested at this characterization, Freud amended his criticism; anyway, he said, she was "a bad woman." Alix said she was "furious" about his attitude toward Elizabeth, and disdainful of the romantic attachment people are apt to have for Mary Queen of Scots. To Alix, Elizabeth was an exceptionally good queen who at one point had even sheltered Mary Queen of Scots.

In Tola Rank's life she ended up with the short end of the stick on so many counts that an air of defeat rather than triumph hangs over her story. I would like to help try to rectify the situation at least as far as insuring her place in history books. Obviously many others knew her far better than I could, though so far no literature about her has begun to accumulate. By all accounts she became, between the time of her first arrival in Boston in 1936 and her death in 1967, the most important child analyst in the city; she trained everyone in the field there. Her accomplishment was all the more remarkable since she had had no formal higher education, not to mention any medical background, and one would expect Boston to be conservative on such issues. (It is true that analysts like Hanns Sachs and Erik H. Erikson also flourished in Boston, and they too were without M.D.s) When Tola Rank was chair of the education committee, a real center of power, at the Boston Psychoanalytic Institute, it has been reliably said that everyone there adored her; Tola's need for love was temporarily fulfilled. For years she had been known for running a salon in Cambridge, where she had her house; people like the well-known critic Bernard DeVoto, for instance, liked discussing literature with her.

My own personal contact with her was restricted. I saw her for the first time in the summer of 1963. I was talking briefly with Dr. Felix Deutsch, who at the time was old and ailing. Mrs. Rank dropped by the house to speak to his wife Helene (both women were originally Polish), and popped in for a minute to say hello to Felix. He had himself been a psychoanalytic pioneer, a leader in psychosomatic medicine and interviewing technique, and president of the Boston Psychoanalytic Society. He had also been Freud's personal physician at the time he first contracted cancer. Yet as she left the room, he turned to me with his eyes widening: "Do you know who that is?" She had mentioned her name to me in passing as she seemed to bounce in and out of the room. Felix's question inquired not whether I had caught the name, but whether I recognized her stature.

She of course had been Otto Rank's wife while he was in Freud's circle of followers. For someone like Felix Deutsch this association inevitably lent her a special magic. For years Rank had been a special personal favorite of Freud's. Rank's significance to Freud sunk in for me in a new way when I first saw a copy of one of the editions of *The Interpretation of Dreams* in which on the title page Rank's name appears directly under Freud's. Shortly after Rank and she married in November 1918, Freud wrote disparagingly about Tola, whom he had just met, to his disciple in Berlin, Karl Abraham. But in public Freud welcomed her to the psychoanalytic movement by thanking her for an idea in a footnote to his 1919 essay "The Uncanny." The meaning of such a reference to "Frau Dr. Rank"[2] could not have been lost on any of Freud's disciples then. She was the same age as his daughter Anna, and both of them had the honor of taking dictation from him. (In 1923 her translation into Polish of Freud's *On Dreams* came out.) After the Rank's daughter was born in August 1919, she was received in the Freud family like a new grandchild.

When in 1964 I began to interview as many of Freud's early students as I could, it was out of immense admiration on my part for that cultured surviving set of early analysts. I was then living in Cambridge, too, and Mrs. Rank was an obvious person for me to try to consult. The hitch was that Helene Deutsch soon became a key aspect of my research, and precisely because she and Tola were such intimate friends I felt I had to be careful in how I approached seeing Mrs. Rank. (Because of her extensive publications Helene Deutsch was always in my mind "Helene"; only her oldest friends knew her by the diminutive of "Hala." If I refer to Mrs. Rank as "Tola," even though her given name was "Beata," it is not due to any lack of respect on my part for her professional accomplishments; everyone then talked about her as Tola, and only those who did not know her at all could think of her as Beata. In the hundreds of hours I spent with Helene Deutsch, Mrs. Rank's name naturally came up as Tola.)

My interviewing routine with Helene Deutsch settled into my seeing her every Saturday morning for several hours. After our morning's work I would usually drive her to Mrs. Rank's house, not far away, where Helene would spend the afternoon, and perhaps longer. I do not remember Helene ever indicating to me whose house she was heading for, even though I knew perfectly well it was Tola's. Cambridge's intelligentsia was small. It seemed to me impolitic, since Helene was so much the greater figure in the history of ideas, to threaten my relationship with her by going elsewhere quite so close to home. Doubtless I was too cautious, and I later found out from Mrs. Rank some of the points in my work that Helene had talked to her about. When Helene gave a dinner party for my studies (Victor Tausk's elder son had come from abroad), Tola naturally heard about it. But it was only after I had succeeded in seeing other early analysts across America, and throughout Europe, that I brought up with Helene my desire to interview Tola. By then Mrs. Rank had already had a spell of bad health, and as I recall it was Helene who spoke to Mrs. Rank in my behalf.

I first saw Tola at home in February 1966; it was, for a single person, a grand house on a nice circular road just off Brattle Street. Although Helene's house was probably worth more money, and certainly better maintained, it gave off an impression of being small, whereas Mrs. Rank's house communicated the opposite illusion. Tola's furnishings were along traditional Central European lines, whereas to me Helene's taste was more modern; at Mrs. Rank's I remember oriental rugs on the tops of tables, and an abundance of books in view. Tola's living room was strikingly beautiful, although many of the pieces turned out to be on loan.

I knew that Mrs. Rank had written little, as for that matter had Dr. Grete Bibring, at the time another power in the city's psychoanalytic group. But while Helene was a world famous analyst, and Grete Bibring had been head of a prominent psychiatric department at an important hospital, Mrs. Rank remained known as Otto's widow. It is true that Tola had some papers to her credit on "atypical" development in children, and Helene had cited more unpublished articles of Tola's in her *The Psychology of Women*, but Tola was worth my interviewing mainly for the sake of the key personal role she had played in the history of analysis. (I do not care how often Tola's pieces may get cited in volumes of *The Psychoanalytic Study of the Child*, or elsewhere, she, like most other psychoanalytic writers, cannot be considered as a major thinker.)

By the time I met Tola with my set of questions I was shocked at how terrible she looked; I could scarcely believe she was the same person I had seen at the Deutsches', only two-and-a-half years earlier. She was suffering from circulatory disturbances; earlier one foot of hers had frozen. Even though she was not yet 70 (Helene was already in her early 80s), Tola did not seem to have much time left. She was conscious of the need to husband her "available energies," as she put it, and I was supposed to keep that in mind when I approached her for another interview.

She chose to think of herself as having been the hostess of the Vienna psychoanalytic group. I knew about at least one Christmas party she had given for Freud's foreign patients in Vienna, and Helene told me of how Tola had once given Freud a dinner party to welcome Lou Andreas-Salomé back to town. According to Tola, Freud had asked her to be the hostess rather than his own wife, and it seemed natural for her to accept even though the Ranks had small living quarters. Tola also talked to me about another dinner party she had given for one of Freud's most prominent English analysands. (The Freuds, who had plenty of guests, gave no parties since they disliked them.)

We talked about many issues, for example, how Andreas-Salomé had analyzed Anna Freud while living at Freud's apartment. Mrs. Rank said that if Anna were to deny it (as I knew she had to a New Haven analyst), then Anna could "get out of it" by saying it was "not a proper analysis." I also knew, but did not mention to Tola, that Anna was capable of trying to deceive another Viennese analyst I met about ever having been analyzed by her father. Tola and I discussed the evidence I had come up with for Anna's having been analyzed by Freud, since Tola said she was not certain it had happened; those were the days before I had first put the matter into print. Mrs. Rank was concerned for me to be clear that she knew for sure that Andreas-Salomé had also analyzed Anna.

In the period after the Ranks were first married, Otto would go off to the Freuds for dinner on Wednesday; afterwards the two men went to Freud's study to talk, and then, every other week, there would be the meeting of the Vienna Psychoanalytic Society. (Rank had started taking the *Minutes* of the proceedings in 1906, and the practice was not interrupted until World War I; the four volumes are now in print.) Otto was so devoted to Freud, who had done so much to encourage him, that according to Tola her husband was not at all aware in himself of any ambivalence or feelings of rivalry.

Mrs. Rank could not say for sure whether it was World War I that changed him, as Ernest Jones alleged, or Freud's getting cancer, as Helene and other friends had thought, but Tola said that Otto was terribly afraid of Freud's death once he fell ill in 1923. According to her, Otto reacted to Freud's sickness by denial of the loss. (The notion of denial as a defense mechanism was first introduced into the literature by Rank.) The disruption between Freud and Otto took place over a number of years, and for a time Freud analyzed him, Tola said. Whether it was a formal analysis, with a couch, remains doubtful. We do know that Freud gave Otto dreams of his own to interpret. After a reconciliation between Rank and Freud proved impossible, Tola moved to Paris with Otto in 1926, even though in the end it turned out that she sided with Freud, "the father."

Mrs. Rank was not at all angry about Jones's account, even though it claimed that a slumbering psychosis on Rank's part helped to divide him from Freud. Jones's contention was completely groundless; Tola volunteered to me that Jones was "one sided," but she said she was aware of "how hard it is to be objective." Jones could not, she said, have written otherwise than he did without making it come out ringing false. He had his "views," and "to suppress them would have been a mistake." (Her daughter, who lived in California, later told me that she herself thought it odd, when the Jones books first came out, that her mother was not more offended, and suggested that perhaps she had not read them. The daughter said that Tola never wanted to talk much about the falling out between Freud and Otto, and was as vague about it in the 1950s as with me.)

After the Ranks had moved from Vienna to Paris, Tola used to return to Vienna for visits every year. Freud once asked her a question about her and Otto, which she said to me she could not recall, but which was "personal and harsh." Tola's reply, which seemed characteristic of her, was to say to Freud, "Why do you ask me that, you know how I think and feel, why do you make it more difficult for me?" According to her it was the only time he had done something like that. When Freud was difficult, she reminded him that she was "loyal to her companion of many years," and that she had a child. In behalf of Freud, on the other hand, she had tried to remind Otto of all Freud had once done for him.

Tola remained a member of the Vienna Psychoanalytic Society until its members were scattered by the Nazis in 1938. She had joined it, she said, the same year as Anna Freud, although the records indicate that it was in the following year. Mrs. Rank reported that Freud had told her that she could not go to meetings without being a member, and she said he had proposed her name. He also informed her that according to the conventions of the time she would have to give a paper. In May 1923 she spoke about "The Part Played by Women in the Evolution of Culture," and was elected a member. Her talk was subsequently published in *Imago*, a journal she helped her husband to edit. At some point Tola was analyzed in Switzerland by a former patient of Freud's, Dr. Mira Oberholzer, a fellow Pole who became an intimate friend; when I interviewed Tola she still wore a ring Mira had given her.

Since Tola had lived in Paris for ten years, I thought of her as a source for information about early psychoanalysis in France. Even though I was uncertain when she had started clinically to practice, certainly not while in Vienna, inevitably it would have been the case that she knew everybody of significance in the field. Her name comes up in the diaries of Anaïs Nin, in connection with Henry Miller and the other people around Otto Rank in Paris.

During our interview, I read her a passage from Freud's (1939) *Moses and Monotheism* that a pupil of her husband's, whom she respected for his truthfulness, had pointed out to me as Freud's formal explanation for Rank's so-called defection:

> A young man whose fate it was to grow up beside a worthless father, began by developing, in defiance of him, into a capable, trustworthy and honorable person. In the prime of life his character was reversed, and thenceforward he behaved as though he had taken this same father as a model.... at the beginning of such a course of events there is always an identification with the father in early childhood. This is afterwards repudiated, and even overcompensated, but in the end establishes itself once more.[3]

Rank's own father was known as a good-for-nothing, and Rank had abandoned his family name of Rosenfeld for one chosen out of Ibsen. (Theodor Reik had reminded me of the Dr. Rank in *A Doll's House*, an odd character for Otto to identify with.) Tola listened to the quotation from *Moses and Monotheism*, and quietly said that it fit in with "Professor's way of thinking." I had not heard anyone speak of Freud as "Professor" with anything like the same sort of reverential awe since I had been in the circle around Anna Freud in London. Yet at the same time, it was striking to me that Tola was able so easily to distance herself from such a passage in Freud, even though she herself had become a practicing orthodox analyst. Freud was, in my experience, more apt to be definitive to those who did not know him than to those who did.

When I asked her which of her husband's original ideas she thought had been confirmed by time, she really had not a clue. His *Trauma of Birth* in 1923 was designed to highlight the significance in early childhood of mothering, and what he implied about the problems of anxiety and guilt in separation and individuation has been followed up by many writers since Freud's death. Despite what Freud wrote about Rank in *Moses and Monotheism*, for years Rank had been insisting that fatherhood, and for that matter masculinity, were not the central subject matter of psychology. Tola had a complicated, subtle mind, but she was considered someone mainly interested in feelings rather than the intellectual material that is apt to interest academics. Yet her husband had been one of the most erudite and philosophically inclined of all the early Freudians. Even though she might sometimes speak with incomplete sentences, and people said her diction and pronunciation were hard to understand, I found her insightful in a particularly delicate manner.

Late that August I saw her again, this time in a nursing home. Once again Helene had set things up since Tola's health was now so variable. Earlier one might have simply said that Tola had prematurely aged, but now she looked like she had again gone sharply downhill. We talked once more about her having been a hostess in Vienna; she thought she was even more so in Cambridge, and was proud of it. Repeatedly she had trouble with English and German, and found French easier.

After fifty minutes or so she asked me to take her out for a cup of coffee, she wanted the drive more than anything. On the way back her eyes filled with tears. In our first interview she had told me she had the complete text of the Freud-Rank letters, but said she was awaiting word from the Freud family before trying to publish them. I now tried to encourage her to see about getting them in print. (They are today still not out, but already announced in Paris.) "Could we talk about something else? I was hit so hard." (She was referring to the divorce from her husband as well as his falling out with Freud.) Of course I felt like a first-rate heel. Tola said she had received many "demands" for the publication of those letters, and implied that it would happen after her death. I tried to apologize, and just at that point it turned out that someone else had come to visit her, and her whole demeanor so brightened by the transforming effect on her of old friendship that I could leave without feeling too bad.

She told me one incident connected with Freud that I had not heard before. Once in Vienna she had had pneumonia, been in the hospital, and Freud had come to see her. (Tola being who she was meant that rumors of suicide attempts were always associated with her, both while she was alive as well as after her death.) It was at the beginning of Otto's detaching himself from Freud, sometime after Rank had returned from a trip to America. Tola said that her hospitalization had been at the outset of the crisis between Rank and Freud, and perhaps Otto had guilty feelings. She reported that Professor had come, on his daily walk, almost every day to see her in the hospital, and suggested that Otto sleep over "to reassure her of his love." The Rank marriage was such that, according to Tola, she and Otto scarcely spoke of the problem with Freud. (Helene Deutsch once remarked that she never found out whether her husband Felix preferred light or dark chicken meat.) Tola knew, even at her bedside, that

Freud was "bitter" about Otto, and also that Otto realized that he had disappointed Freud, "not just as a pupil." Tola was familiar with the whole Freud family; Freud had been closer to Otto than to any of his own three sons. She said it had been Freud's "*confiance*" in Otto as a young man that had meant so much to his aspirations.

Now the one issue that Tola never mentioned, and I failed to raise with her, was that Freud had blamed her for the rift between himself and Rank. "It's her fault, his increasing need of money and importance." Helene quoted that sentence to me from one of Freud's conversations with her in such a way that it sounded like an exact report of Freud's conviction. It would be in keeping with Freud's initial disapproval of Tola as Otto's wife. In a letter to Jones from Anna Freud, I found that she, like her father, had initially dated "the first personality change" in Rank from his marriage, and thought that it had been Tola's fault, though Anna later decided that Tola had been a "victim."

Nothing has ever been written in order to find patterns in Freud's relationships to the spouses of his disciples, when he had not been the instigator of the match. Freud, who often transmuted current conflicts into speculative hypotheses about past ones, once proposed of his childhood relationship with his nephew John that this early tie had become

> the source of all my friendships and all my hatreds.... All my friends have in a certain sense been re-incarnations of this first figure.... My emotional life has always insisted that I should have an intimate friend and a hated enemy. I have always been able to provide myself afresh with both, and it has not infrequently happened that the ideal situation of childhood has been so completely reproduced that friend and enemy have come together in a single individual—though not, of course, both at once or with constant oscillations, as may have been the case in my early childhood.[4]

Most impartial historians have used this autobiographical confession to help explain how Freud could turn so sharply against, say, his friend Wilhelm Fliess or his pupil Otto Rank, but the psychology Freud describes in himself might also help account for the contempt he heaped on Fliess's wife, and how in the 1920s Freud could blame Tola for Otto's "heresy." Intimate friend and hated enemy could coexist for Freud within a single couple.

As best as I could reconstruct, Tola always did have, as Edward Hitschmann's widow put it to me, certain Polish extravagant ways about money. It never really mattered to her, and she spent money without especially seeking it. In the nursing home she was unrealistic about being able to afford to keep her house, which she still wanted to be able to return to even if parts of it had to be closed off. Money can be a complex emotional issue, and the finances of the early psychoanalytic movement have never been adequately described. Money would certainly help explain how certain people managed to become important in Freud's eyes, as well as within the movement as a whole.

One accusation against Rank at the time of the break with Freud was that by advocating shorter analyses he was promoting a get-rich-quick scheme; yet his defenders thought that the real way to make money, without too much trouble for the therapist, was by keeping patients in long and extended analyses. In Paris Otto was able to scoop up American patients who might otherwise have been on their way to Freud in Vienna. Freud despised his own dependency on New World wealth as his practice became almost entirely American. Freud criticized Rank in print, but only obliquely, he did not let himself go as he had against Alfred Adler and Carl Jung before World War I. Therefore it took years for the falling out between the two men to sink in publicly and professionally. I would be surpised if Freud had not used the written word "*gonif*" for Rank, since that is how he verbally described him and remains the implication behind many of the other terms (like "rascal," "roguish boy," and "mountebank") that have made their way into print in his letters.

We know that as late as November 1925, Tola was lending money to Freud's psychoanalytic press. Perhaps this background can help explain why in the 1950s Tola could tell Kurt Eissler in interviews for the Freud Archives (which are supposed to be sealed until after the year 2000) about an instance of Freud being callous with her about money in 1928. It sounds to me from the description that this must be that same time she told me about when Freud had been "personal and harsh" with her about Otto. While she was visiting Freud in Vienna he had informed her about someone then in his waiting room who had once long ago advanced Otto money for his education, and she said that Freud thought she should ask her husband to repay him. According to the Eissler interviews, Tola was off-guard and taken-aback; she did not know whether the man was there by accident or design, and she felt she could not visit Freud again. Otto himself quietly resigned from the Vienna Psychoanalytic Society in 1929.

Otto had married Tola while he was geographically separated from Freud because of World War I. On his own he had, it was said, grown into manhood. Tola's immense admiration for Freud may have helped encourage Rank's initial strivings to emancipate himself from Freud; Rank was trying to be more like him. Doubtless it seemed especially necessary once Freud's health was threatened. At first it had been thought that Freud would not survive the jaw cancer, but after he had done so, Rank had more or less adjusted to being on his own. One interpretation would be that Rank prematurely grieved for Freud, and that this was partly responsible for the ultimate separation; such a line of thought would seem more generous than seeing Rank as a rat fleeing from a sinking ship, which is how Freud once described him. Freud cannot have been pleased to read an American newspaper story saying that he was slowly dying and that Rank was the chosen successor. Both on trips to America and in Paris the Ranks had a circle around them that put their life in sharp contrast to the restricted circumstances of their Viennese days. One New York analyst told me that in Vienna Rank had worn patches on his pants; in Paris the Ranks lived in luxury. Tola became a patron for artists, yet her husband never seemed able to earn enough money to support their new ways. When Rank and Freud both died in 1939, Rank left an estate of less than $3,000, while Freud bequeathed over 16,000 British pounds. A year earlier Freud (with his younger brother) had also provided his four sisters in Vienna, who had been left behind, with Austrian currency worth $20,000.

The breakdown in the Rank marriage has remained obscure. On most of Otto's trips to America Tola preferred to remain in Paris. She had attended Anna Freud's seminar on child analysis in Vienna, and apparently had started to work with children therapeutically in the mid-1930s. By then Otto was helping to found a school of social work at the University of Pennsylvania. He went to Nevada for the divorce in 1939. Tola's own mother had been divorced in an era when marital breakdowns were even rarer. In Paris Tola had a psychiatrist (a certain unsavory-sounding Dr. Glass) in her life for a period, and Otto was briefly, for three months, remarried before his sudden death in October 1939. In a letter afterwards to Felix Deutsch, Helene had written that Tola had returned from Otto's funeral "profoundly broken, for she still loved him."[5]

In Boston Tola succeeded professionally. She, with Dr. Molly Putnam, had helped found the James Jackson Putnam Center for preschool patients. Merrill Moore's widow told me that the early cases were largely babysitting problems; neighbors made up symptoms to get rid of their kids temporarily. Soon Tola moved from supervising to training, and ultimately she was to have some famous figures from academic life in analysis with her, such as Robert J. Lifton, Jerome S. Bruner, and Lester Grinspoon. One of Tola's students was a Freud grandchild who lived locally. In the profession of analysis she found an outlet for her artistic creativity. Freud had, at his best, treated every patient as an exception, and she too could be technically unorthodox in her practices.

Otto Rank does now seem to be coming into his own as a thinker and a writer. A superb intellectual biography of him by E. James Lieberman, *Acts of Will*, appeared in 1985.[6] Yet in it Tola does not succeed, as far as I am concerned, in coming alive as a person. Perhaps it seems to me to fail on this score only because Lieberman refers to her throughout as "Beata." But entirely aside from the interesting concepts, especially about artists and creativity, that Otto Rank originated, Tola ought not to be forgotten or ignored.

I have written as much as I can about Tola; I hope that her friends will do more on her behalf. As far as I know I pressed her furthest about her husband and Freud. In retrospect she does look like a tragic figure, always seeming to be in a jam. In Anaïs Nin's diaries she wore black dresses, which is how she was remembered from her earliest days in Boston; the color was an expression of both her elegance and some depression. To the extent that she was successful as a Boston analyst, it may be attributable to the influence of her peer group.

How history gets written remains mysterious. What worries me is that when the letters between Freud and Rank finally become public, Tola might scarcely appear in them, and literal-minded historians may take that as a sign of the insignificance of her role. I do not want to sit back while one of the tricks Voltaire wrote about gets played on the future. Most history may be in some sense false, but there are degrees of failure and unreliability. If what I have written means that someone as relatively inarticulate as Tola, at least when she is compared with the other early psychoanalytic pioneers, gets remembered, perhaps people will know more surely that the past is a construct for which we are responsible.

## Notes

1. C. Vann Woodward, *American Attitudes Toward History: An Inaugural Lecture* (Oxford: Oxford University Press, 1955), p. 3.
2. Sigmund Freud, "The 'Uncanny'," *Standard Edition*, Vol. 17, p. 230.
3. Sigmund Freud, *Moses and Monotheism, Standard Edition*, Vol. 23, p. 125.
4. Sigmund Freud, *The Interpretation of Dreams, Standard Edition*, Vol. 5, p. 483.
5. Paul Roazen, *Helene Deutsch: A Psychoanalyst's Life* (NY: Doubleday, 1985; New Brunswick, NJ: Transaction, with New Introduction, 1992).
6. E. James Lieberman, *Acts of Will: The Life and Work of Otto Rank* (New York: The Free Press, 1985; Amherst: University of Massachusetts Press, with new Preface, 1993).

# 20

# Felix Deutsch and the FBI

J. Edgar Hoover's Federal Bureau of Investigation kept surprisingly extensive dossiers on many people whom one might never have expected to have been put under surveillance. Psychoanalysts might seem as unlikely a group as any to be subjected to FBI scrutiny. The right now to invoke the Freedom of Information/Privacy Act, even if that has become a cumbersome procedure involving many delays, has turned up many unanticipated files. Sometimes this material has been already explored by historians, as for example the large amount of information collected by the FBI in connection with Wilhelm Reich and the trial that followed his difficulties with the Food and Drug Administration.

Yet one also gets the impression that almost any European immigrant was in principle looked on with suspicion by Hoover. Although it might make sense that the FBI kept tabs on Reich, it does seem strange that an equally huge amount of material should have been accumulated in connection with the social philosopher Herbert Marcuse. (He did once work for the government.[1]) Marcuse's file, however, so far as I know has not attracted any scholarly interest. Nor have the approximately six hundred pages that the FBI compiled on Erich Fromm been subjected to outside scrutiny. One irony is that Marcuse and Fromm had become ideological enemies, and they publicly argued with one another.[2] But from the point of view of the FBI they must have simply seemed European Marxists of influence currently residing in the United States. At the time of Fromm's death in Mexico in 1980, a CIA report (still classified) got filed. Marcuse was for a time in the 1960s a political figure of some significance; but Fromm remained a fairly isolated thinker, and what impact he had was largely spread by books that have been widely popular. The circumstances of his death and burial would not seem of concern to American national security.

It is fairly easy now to make considerable fun of the FBI's suspiciousness. They wasted resources keeping an eye on people who can scarcely be thought of as in any way dangerous. Usually the files are filled with innocuous material including newspaper clippings. And huge portions are often blacked out by today's FBI censorship; although it is possible to appeal such blocking-out of dossiers, there is a limit to how dogged one can be in following up on files that are less than earth-shaking in their implications. An appeal to the federal court system is not likely to be worth the money and effort. The FBI insists on the right to protect its sources, as part of its national mission, but the world of scholarship is correct to dismiss most of what they collected as trivia unworthy of serious attention.

In the case of the polical thinker and columnist Walter Lippmann, one of the American writers most influential in the twentieth century and an early advocate of the significance of Freud for political and social thought, Lippmann's file has remained unexplored until recently largely because it never occurred to students of politics that J. Edgar Hoover could have kept tabs on someone so powerful.[3] According to some reliable sources, Hoover left certain of his most highly explosive dossiers to be immediately destroyed by a faithful colleague once Hoover himself had died.

Although the psychoanalysts who emigrated from Europe to the United States were primarily clinicians, and not particularly politically active, it turns out that the FBI monitored many of their activities as a matter of course. In the case of one of Freud's sons, Oliver, who came to the States during World War II, the material the FBI compiled is in fact a great service to historians, since their interview with Oliver gives an excellent account of how that particular member of the Freud family made his way out of Nazi-occupied Europe.

Yet the various Red scares that have afflicted the United States this century were part of a preceding history of ideological intolerances, and did not just touch the powerful and the famous. Oliver Freud would have been less likely to be of interest to the FBI had it not been for his famous father, and the powerful political allies who tried to help Oliver once he arrived in the States probably only ensured that the FBI would be more vigilant in following up his case than might otherwise have been likely.

It is too easy to forget what sort of intimidating impact the FBI surveillances had on those who were not mighty, but nonetheless fell within the sights of government investigation. I have picked Felix Deutsch's file because it seems to me a poignant example of how anti-Communist hysteria could sweep up and complicate the lives of unexpected people. Although some might have felt invigorated by such lengthy inquiries, I would suspect that the chilling effect of FBI investigations would be far more common.

Felix's wife Helene was more important in the history of ideas, and she played a part in Freud's movement that over-shadowed in prominence that of her husband. She was also probably the more politically active of the two, and had once been involved in Polish socialism[4]· yet in the context of her busy professional life as a psychoanalytic psychiatrist in America, she cannot be taken to have been all that political. Felix Deutsch's FBI file can be used as a symbol of how anti-Communism could affect the lives of ordinary people, although to be sure Felix Deutsch was an exceptional individual, for a brief period Freud's personal physician, and he made important contributions to the modern practice of psychotherapy and psychosomatic medicine. The circumstances by which he came under governmental scrutiny, rather than his more famous wife, can exemplify just how wayward and capricious the FBI's practices could be.

From a cultured European perspective the Americans had long seemed crude and intolerant. Freud's own notoriously anti-American sentiments can be linked to his trip to the States in 1909, but the story is more complicated than that.[5] Other European intellectuals, such as Virginia and Leonard Woolf from Britain, never needed to come to America—despite the lure of commercial considerations—out of their anti-American prejudices. In early 1935, Felix Deutsch, knowing that his wife was planning to emigrate from Vienna, went to the States to see what he could manage professionally for himself. Although he was a member, like her, of the Vienna Psychoanalytic Society, he was an internist, not a psychiatrist, and less mobile than his more established wife. Still, he could help her, and their son, in problems with immigration authorities. As he jokingly wrote Helene from Boston on March 17, "I have already sworn not to be an anarchist, not to engage in polygamy, etc."[6]

Although Helene had an appointment at the Massachusetts General Hospital (one of the most ancient and prestigious) waiting for her when she first arrived in Boston in the fall of 1935, on the whole she tended as the years passed to withdraw into her private practice. For a time she had been a leader of the Boston Psychoanalytic Society, but for a variety of reasons she felt that her training activites ought to be minimized. Felix, however, really only came into his own as a psychoanalyst in Boston; while in Vienna he had not been a practicing analyst but in Boston he became a famous teacher. (Ironically, the feminist interest in Freud's patient "Dora" has meant that to many Felix is now only known for the short piece he once published about his brief contact with her.[7] It is not uncommon to find that an unnamed informant of Felix about Dora's last years, who described her as "one of the most repulsive hysterics" he had ever met, gets confused with Felix's own impression of her.[8]) A relatively minor appointment of Felix's, starting in 1947 as a consultant with a veterans hospital, was the occasion for a 1953–1954 loyalty inquiry into his background.

Felix had been a consultant in psychiatry at the Cushing VA Hospital in Framingham, Massachusetts. As of 1952, he had shifted to the VA Hospital in Jamaica Plain, Massachusetts, and that was apparently the occasion for the November 1953 FBI request for loyalty data about him. It should be pointed out that by then some of the worst excesses of McCarthyism were apparently over. Dwight D. Eisenhower had been elected President a year earlier, and the anti-Communist hunt was no longer such a partisan party matter. The Army-McCarthy hearings were so to undermine Senator Joseph McCarthy's position that by the fall of 1954 the Senate voted to censure him. But in contrast to difficulties that J. Edgar Hoover had under Harry Truman's presidency, "Hoover often said that the two terms of the Eisenhower administration were 'the best and happiest years he ever had.'"[9]

The FBI's investigatory activities continued unabated. The November 5, 1953 loyalty request listed Felix Deutsch's naturalization number, his place and date of birth, as well as the details of his marriage to Helene. It was noted that he was affiliated with the Boston Psychoanalytic Society and Institute, as well as the Boston Neurology and Psychiatry Society, and also the American Psychoanalytic Association. The FBI was so tightly run that Hoover was himself being kept informed about this inquiry. It was reported that Felix had once been an associate professor at Washington University in St. Louis. John C. Whitehorn had been, before later going to head the famous Phipps Clinic at Johns Hopkins, creating a neuropsychiatry department at Washington University. Although Whitehorn had formerly been a patient in training with Helene, no mention of that got made by the FBI; nor did the FBI show any interest whatsoever, at least in connection with Felix Deutsch, in the doings of his son Martin, a nuclear physicist who worked at Los Alamos during World War II and whose political commitments, at least in Europe, had been more left-wing than that of either of his eminent parents.

The FBI was interested in interviewing doctors who also had been employed at the Neuropsychiatry Department at Washington University, and who may have been acquainted with Felix Deutsch. Although Whitehorn's name, like that of others, is blacked out in the file which exists now for inspection, I have to suspect that Whitehorn was consulted for an interview by the FBI since a Baltimore source gets repeatedly mentioned.

One source of the FBI advised that this appointee, Deutsch, had once been involved in a committee to aid immigrant physicians from about 1936 until 1941. The FBI was informed that "people originally interested in this group had no Communist influence," and that Deutsch was not an officer and may not have been an official member.

At this point the FBI was conducting a "preliminary inquiry" as opposed to "a full field investigation." The study was supposed to be sufficiently complete to resolve the question of Deutsch's loyalty. One detail, on a page titled "top secret," indicated that the FBI had been advised that both Felix and Helene had "accepted an invitation to attend a reception given in honor of Dr. L. K. Barsky, National Chairman of the Joint Anti-Fascist Refugee Committee in July, 1942," an organization to aid the victims of Franco Spain.[10] That particular engagement of the Deutsches seemed to be enough to arouse serious FBI misgivings, since the Joint Anti-Fascist Refugee Committee, along with the North American Spanish Aid Committee, had both been designated by the Attorney General as coming "within the purview of Executive order 10450," which also applied to the Communist Party. Felix Deutsch was reported to have been a member of the Progressive Citizens of America in 1947, and his name was said to be on the mailing list of the North American Spanish Aid Committee in 1942. Since people like Deutsch under FBI study were not directly informed of the nature of the allegations against them, there was no way of them rebutting anything.

The 1942 party in honor of Barsky was held on his return from Mexico. although nothing specific was reported about Barsky, the geographical change had a sinister sounding air. (Members of the atomic spy ring associated with Julius and Ethel Rosenberg had used Mexico as an escape hatch.) It turns out that Barsky, so far as I have been able to ascertain, was "a New York surgeon who had saved many heretical lives as head of a hospital near Madrid."[11] Barsky had been cited for contempt in 1946 by the House Un-American Activities Committee because he failed to give names of others, and he was sentenced, along with the novelist Howard Fast, to some months in jail. Both Felix's name, and that of Helene, appeared on a list of people "who helped in connection with the holding of the reception" for Barsky in 1942.

Pages stamped "top secret" (some are still deleted and unavailable for inspection) report Felix's employment at the VA hospitals in Framingham and Jamaica Plain. One of Felix's VA colleagues "advised that the employee was used on a consultant basis approximately once every few weeks" and since the FBI source was not personally "engaged in the practice of psychiatry, he had very little contact" with Felix. That informant "did not feel qualified to comment upon the employee's character, reputation, associates or loyalty to the United States of America."

Another souce at the VA hospital in Jamaica Plain confirmed, based on a review of Deutsch's personnel file, the details that the FBI already had accumulated about his record of employment in the United States; this informant "added that the employee's record contained no information that would reflect unfavorably upon his character, reputation, associates or loyalty to the United States." One additional source at the Jamaica Plain Hospital was unable to comment on Deutsch.

Others at the VA hospital, obviously psychoanalysts, were able to endorse Felix's character and political commitments. One, for example, "advised that he has been associated with the employee since approximately 1947. He stated that he is in contact with him at the VA, at the Boston Psychoanalytic Society and Institute, Inc., and had visited the employee's home on a few occasions." This analyst said that Deutsch was "a person of sterling character, scrupulous honesty, irreproachable associates and unquestionable loyalty to the United States. He stated that he has never heard anything of an unfavorable nature concerning Dr. Deutsch."

Another analyst, who too knew Felix at the VA hospital and the Boston Psychoanalytic Society, "stated that he has also been at the employee's home and had met his wife." Felix was described "as a charming person of excellent character and reputation; that his associates are beyond reproach and his loyalty to the United States unquestionable." He added that "the employee has very little social life and very few friends and acquaintances other than those connected with Psychiatry, as he has no other interest outside his work." Felix was reported to have stated "that the United States is a wonderful country and he considered himself very fortunate to be here." (Since this source is described later as having been involved in "writing a book" with Felix, I am assuming it was William F. Murphy since they co-authored a two-volume study, *The Clinical Interview*.[12])

One other of Felix's professional colleagues endorsed him in similar words; and still a further source states, having spoken admiringly of him, that "it is conceivable that inasmuch as the employee is Jewish he was forced out of Germany [sic] during the Hitler regime and as a result of this had strong anti-Nazi feeling." It was proposed as "conceivable that the employee may have unwittingly joined some organizations which he thought were interested in opposing Nazism and that some of these organizations could have been later declared as subversives." The blacking out by today's FBI censors was not always perfectly successful, and one can just detect the name of a further analyst, Dr. John Murray, as having known Felix "intimately" since 1929 when he met him in Vienna. Murray stated that he had "seen the employee under all circumstances," and he advised that he was "a person of unquestionable character, reputation, associates and loyalty to the United States."

The "top secret" report on Felix also included questioning people in the posh Cambridge, Massachusetts, neighborhood where Felix and Helene lived. One woman had been a neighbor since 1942, but "just had a speaking acquaintance with him." This person "informed that the employee and his wife do not associate with people in the neighborhood and are always busily engaged in the practice of Psychiatry. She stated that she could only say that she had never heard anything of an unfavorable nature concerning the employee or his wife and did not feel that any other neighbors could provide any further information." Another neighbor had known him since he moved onto the street in 1937, "but has just had a speaking acquaintance with him and his wife." This woman "said that they are respected people in the neighborhood and she has never heard anything which would reflect unfavorably upon their character, reputation, associates or loyalty to the United States." A Mrs. Sturgess somehow escaped having her name blacked out; she spoke along similar lines, although she had lived on the street for only four years; she affirmed that both Felix and Helene were "rather famous people and excellent neighbors," and echoed the views of the others. To me it is appalling, knowing how suspicious and gossipy even under the best circumstances neighbors can be, to think of having FBI agents going around to interview people who lived near the Deutsches.

FBI sources who were "in a position to know some of the Communist activites in the Greater Boston area...were unable to provide any additional information pertinent" to Felix. The credit rating of Felix and Helene was found to be sound, "one minor traffic violation" of Felix's turned up, and the Boston office of the FBI contemplated no further investigation.

Nothing derogatory turned up at the Hotel Commander, where once Felix stayed, as Helene had lived there briefly, too. The FBI checked at its New York office, and its "confidential informants, of known reliability, who are familiar with general Communist activites in the NY area, advised that they do not know the employee and possess no information concerning him." Although a few passages are blacked out on the file, on the whole this preliminary investigation seemed rather repetitiously to endorse Felix's political reliability. One Albany source "said that he knew Deutsch to be a refugee from Austria and in 1939 and 1940 there was no doubt in anyone's mind as to whether or not Deutsch was pro-American." Felix "seemed to have very personal convictions concerning" the matter of Hitler, and Felix was said to be "a very pleasing and responsible person of real integrity."

One central source was obviously John Whitehorn. He advised that "the employee and his wife are both physicians who came to the United States from Austria in the early 1930s [sic] because of unsatisfactory conditions there." Whitehorn described Felix as "a very charming, cultured, intellectual type person of good character and reputation. He stated that from his knowledge and association with the employee, he does not believe the employee was a fanatical or crusading anti-Nazi, but came to the United States to get away from the Nazis, and has always regarded the United States as a wonderful country." Whitehorn reported that Ferlix "had also been helpful in getting friends of his into this country from Europe."

A March 5, 1954 document restates the request for a preliminary inquiry on Felix, although the reasons for this are partly blacked out. The information about Felix having been a member of the Progressive Citizens of America in 1947, his name appearing on the mailing list of the North America Spanish Aid Committee of 1942, and the acceptance "reportedly" of an invitation to attend the 1942 reception for Barsky get cited. "Although no substantive disloyal data was developed, it is felt that additional investigation is necessary so that the question of employee's loyalty can be resolved and so that a Security Hiring Board may properly adjudicate this case." All FBI offices were therefore instructed to convey their investigation into a "full-field inquiry."

A closer scrutiny of Felix's career only amplified what had already been turned up. The FBI questioned people at Washington University, and at the hotel where Felix lived in St. Louis. Someone who had known Felix in St. Louis, but now was at the Walter Reed Hospital in Washington, "advised that he regards Dr. Deutsch as a very stable citizen of this country and does not think that he is the type of person who would want to get 'hooked-up' with any organizations of a subversive nature." This source stated that "he would regard Dr. Deutsch as conservative but not a reactionary and advised that he is the type of fellow who would perhaps not be in the same camp with everyone in the Republican Party but that on the other hand, he feels that Dr. Deutsch's thinking would follow very closely the pattern and expressed desires of President Eisenhower." It was pointed out that Felix had "considerable property in this country, that he has a farm and a large town home and both were decorated in conservative colonial style...." This was considered relevant since he "feels it is indicative of the conservative and orderly pattern" of Felix's existence.

Felix was said to be "very generous with respect to donations...." He was reported to be "timid of manner," "extremely anxious to make friends and if he had been approached by someone with regard to [sic] donation for an ambulance he, in all probability, would not hesitate to make the donation." Felix was supposedly "extremely naïve with respect to politics and political organizations and could readily find himself the victim of alleged involvement with some organization, although, in fact, his only act with respect to same...was the making of a donation to a cause which appeared on its face to him to be a worthy one." This person affirmed that "he would be very much surprised to hear that Dr. Deutsch had ever taken any active stand with respect to anything left of center and that he was not acquainted with any activites on the part of Dr. Deutsch which would cause him to question his loyalty and felt that Dr. Deutsch's associates were above question."

Lest the reader think that this file was accumulated without the support and encouragement of the FBI head himself, there is a February 10, 1954 directive, signed "Hoover," which confirms that the investigation has been, as of February 5th, converted into a "full field" one.

This more extensive inquiry looked at Felix's academic appointments with more detail but nothing striking turned up. An "acquaintance" of Felix's examined the entry about him in the 1950 edition of the American Psychiatric Association Directory, and read off details connected with Felix's European background and training. Felix had held some appointments in the United States, such as at the Smith College School of Social Work, which had not come up earlier, and he was a member of a few other professional organizations than those itemized in the preliminary investigation. The House Committee on Un-American Activities, "CSC," State Security Office, and the CIA all reported an absence of information about Felix. A memo from Hoover, dated March 30, 1954, to Warren Olny, assistant Attorney General, seemed to announce the conclusion of the FBI's investigation. Hoover directed the "confidential" memo to Olney so "that consideration may be given as to whether any Federal laws have been violated...." Another confidential memo, of the same date, from Hoover to the Chief of the Investigations Division, U.S. Civil Service Commission, announced the closing of the full field inquiry.

Out of the sixty-six pages that the FBI reviewed for me, under my Freedom of Information Act request, sixty-four pages were released. To get hold of the two withheld pages would have required an appeal and a delay. (Five further pages later got sent on to me.) I think we can presume that a fairly reliable account of the FBI investigation can be gleaned from this extensive existing report. To me it does read like a nightmarish inquiry. Although nothing incriminating turned up initially, it did not deter the FBI from pursuing the matter further. One can only guess what it must be like to have professional colleagues and neighbors questioned about one's loyalty and political beliefs, not to mention the search for credit ratings and a possible criminal record.

I presume that Felix might have known, from friends, the kinds of questions the FBI was asking, yet I doubt anybody could guess that so many pages could be taken up with inconsequential material. Being a European psychoanalyst was not that rare, and Felix only atracted the FBI's special attention because of his VA appointment, one which did not in fact take up much of his time. One does have to wonder about people who were less well defended than Felix, with fewer allies and supporters. Any such climate of opinion has to have been especially threatening. The FBI material on Felix provides, I think, a special glimpse of American history that none of us can be proud of. It seems to me a bureaucratic accident that all this file has survived, and it can serve as a concrete warning about a spirit of ideological fanaticism which has repeatedly afflicted this country.

In recent years we have had other instances of the federal government intruding into private lives and careers. Justice Louis D. Brandeis issued a prophetically memorable warning in a dissenting opinion from the Supreme Court in 1928:

> The makers of our Constitution undertook to secure conditions favorable to the pursuit of happiness. The recognized the significance of man's spiritual nature, of his feelings and his intellect. They knew that only a part of the pain, pleasure and satisfactions of life are to be found in material things. They sought to protect Americans in their beliefs, their thoughts, their emotions, and their sensations. They conferred, as against the government, the right to be left alone—the most comprehensive of rights and the right most valued by civilized men. To protect that right, every unjustifiable intrusion by the government upon the privacy of the individual, whatever the means employed, must be deemed a violation of the Fourth Amendment.... The greatest dangers to liberty lurk in insidious encroachment by men of zeal, well-meaning but without understanding.[13]

Strangely enough, a rough contemporary of Felix's, Dr. Henry A. Murray, turned out to have a far smaller FBI file. Murray, one of the founders of the Boston Psychoanalytic Society and Institute, led the Harvard psychological Clinic throughout the 1930s, and during World War II went to work for the military to help the Office of Strategic Services devise some testing devices for selecting secret agents; During World War II there were Soviet spies operating in Washington, D.C., such as Marcuse's close friend Franz Neumann who was working for the government[14]. the reality of espionage highlights the contrast between Felix's and Murray's files.

In an August 1941 report Hoover wrote that Murray's family dated "back to colonial times and he is married to [sic] prominent Boston socialite." Murray was rich, well-connected, as well as an anti-Fascist; and he was not born abroad. Murray's long standing extramarital liaison did not come up.[15] Another August 1941 report indicated that "Murray says one of his forbearers was the last Tory Governor of Virginia. He is married to a Rantoul woman of Boston, and the Rantoul family is a very prominent Salem and Boston family, people of considerable means, dating way back to pre-revolutionary times. Murray's daughter made her debut this year. He is well fixed financially and does not have to work for a living."

Even though Murray participated as an expert witness in behalf of Alger Hiss at the trial which ended in his being convicted of perjury,[16] Murray's dossier remained slim and unlike that collected about the psychiatrist Dr. Carl A. Binger (like Felix a Jew), who also testified at the same time in Hiss's behalf. Murray's social credentials were evidently especially protective, while Binger, like Felix Deutsch, had also to be scrutinized in the mid-1950s because he too did some VA work. (Binger's wife was an old friend of Hiss's wife.)

It may shock, or even amuse some, to find out how extensive a record the FBI kept on someone like Felix Deutsch. It would be beyond my competence to hazard a guess how many eminent people were similarly hounded by the FBI, or had their careers and lives cramped or damaged by this sort of file-gathering. In contrast to Henry Murray, there is no evidence that Felix was ever given a chance to be interviewed himself, or to comment on any of the material Hoover's organization collected. He could have been asked to challenge why his name appeared on the Barsky guest list, assuming it was any sort of serious matter. At the same time perhaps Felix ought to have felt honored by the FBI's attention. It is now possible to get only one hundred pages the FBI kept on Thomas Mann, and he won a Nobel Prize.[17] Freud used to like to quote the saying "many enemies, much honor," which could be appropriate to this FBI file on Felix Deutsch. It was governmental inquisition, not private malice, which was the source of Felix's problem.

So far no decent study has ever been written about Felix Deutsch's contributions to the history of psychotherapy; in all fields the impact of a great teacher can be too ephemeral. His wife was more successful as a writer and she has continued to attract scholarly attention.[18] It is only in connection with the FBI that Felix came out ahead of her. When I asked the FBI for Helene's file, I got twenty-five pages about some Hungarian, obviously the wrong Helene Deutsch. Belatedly the FBI sent me another eight pages about the correct Helene Deutsch; her name only appeared on an extensive "confidential" 1967 list, well after Felix's death, of Cambridge intellectuals opposed to the Vietnam War. It may be questioned in hindsight who, the FBI or the Deutsches, can be considered truly politically naïve.

## Notes

1. Barry M. Katz, *Foreign Intelligence: Research and Analysis in the Office of Strategic Services* (Cambridge, MA: Harvard University Press, 1989).
2. See *Sigmund Freud*, ed. Paul Roazen (Englewood Cliffs, NJ: Prentice-Hall, 1973; NY: Da Capo, 1987), p. 15.
3. Natalie Robins, *Alien Ink: The FBI's War on Freedom of Expression* (NY: Morrow, 1992).
4. Paul Roazen, *Helene Deutsch: A Psychoanalyst's Life* (NY: Anchor Press/Doubleday, 1985; second edition with new Introduction, New Brunswick, NJ: Transaction, 1992).
5. Paul Roazen, *Freud and His Followers* (NY: Knopf, 1975; NY: Da Capo Books, 1992), pp. 372–89.
6. Roazen, Helene Deutsch, *op. cit.*, p. 281.
7. Anne E. Thompson, "The Ending to Dora's Story: Deutsch's Footnote As Narrative," *Psychoanalysis and Contemporary Thought*, Vol. 4 (1990), pp. 509–34.
8. See Felix Deutsch, "A Footnote to Freud's 'Fragment of an Analysis of a Case of Hysteria,'" reprinted in *In Dora's Case: Freud-Hysteria-Feminism*, ed. Charles Bernheimer and Claire Kahane (NY: Columbia University Press, 1985), p. 43. See Part 8, "Dora," pp. 363–69.
9. Richard Gid Powers, *Secrecy and Power: The Life of J. Edgar Hoover* (NY: The Free Press, 1987), p. 313.
10. Herbert Mitgang, *Dangerous Dossiers: Exposing the Secret War Against America's Greatest Authors* (NY: Donald I. Fine, 1988), p. 270.
11. Cedric Belfage, *The American Inquisition 1945–1960* (NY: Bobbs-Merrill Co., 1975), p. 56.
12. Felix Deutsch and William F. Murphy, *The Clinical Interview*, Vol. I *Diagnosis*, and Vol. II *Therapy* (NY: International Universities Press, 1955).
13. Quoted in Mitgang, *Dangerous Dossiers, op. cit.*, pp. 20–21.
14. Allen Weinstein and Alexander Vassiliev, *The Haunted Wood: Soviet Espionage in America—The Stalin Era* (NY: Random House, 1999), pp. 249–51.
15. See Part 6, "Murray," "Christiana Morgan" pp. 257–65.
16. Allen Weinstein, *Perjury: The Hiss-Chambers Case* (NY: Random House, 1997), pp. 437–40.
17. Mitgang, *Dangerous Dossiers, op cit.*, p. 80.
18. See Janet Sayers, *Mothers of Psychoanalysis: Helene Deutsch, Karen Horney, Anna Freud, Melanie Klein* (NY: Norton, 1991); Brenda S. Webster, "Helene Deutsch: A New Look," *Signs*, Vol. 10, No. 3 (Spring 1985), pp. 553–71. Also Paul Roazen, ed., Helene Deutsch, *Psychoanalysis of the Sexual Functions of Women* (London: Karnac, 1991), and Paul Roazen, ed., Helene Deutsch, *The Therapeutic Process, the Self, and Female Psychology: Collected Psychoanalytic Papers* (New Brunswick, NJ: Transaction, 1992).

# Part 6

## Biographies

# Introduction to Part 6

Biographies of early figures in the history of psychoanalysis, and full accounts of the lives of those who played an important part in the development of the psychoanalytic "movement," have been appearing at a steady pace over the last three decades. One of the key reasons why we are in a more subtle phase of historical understanding can be directly traced to the existence of a series of invaluable biographical studies. When one considers that in the early 1960s almost the only available documents on the history of analysis were Freud's own polemics and Jones's three-volume authorized biography of Freud, then it becomes clear just how recent is the genuine historiography in this area. The early pioneers in analysis were a remarkable group of people; they chose their career as a spiritual calling, and pursued their occupation with a rare degree of devotion. Compared with most practitioners of our own time, the early analysts were an admirably cosmopolitan group of people; they came from a wide variety of walks of life and often brought an unusual cultural range to this new "profession."

All recorded history has to be heavily dependent on biographical knowledge. And I think that the general reading public picks up much of what it knows about the past by its reading of biographies. But the history of psychoanalysis has been unusually indebted to the biographical form. Fritz Wittels published the first biography of Freud in the early 1920s; and although Wittels was not a professional historian, his personal knowledge of Freud, combined with considerable artistic talent, meant that he was able to write a book that would be permanently interesting, and still in print today. And then Helen Walker Puner, a freelance journalist, had the courage following World War II to come up with her own iconoclastic biography of Freud. Jones's three-volumes on Freud temporarily overwhelmed almost everything else in the field, and that was pretty much the situation when I first came to learn about psychoanalysis in the early 1960s.

By now, however, the limitations of Jones—even though he made a permanent contribution, and I cannot think of any set of books about Freud I have consulted more often—are fairly well-established. Above all, these last four decades have seen an outpouring of biographical studies about other early analysts, and these largely excellent books have I think done more to move this field in a professional direction than any other single factor. Even a relatively minor figure like Adrian Stephen, who wrote only a handful of psychoanalytic papers but was also Virginia Woolf's brother, has been accorded a full and interesting biography. I feel confident that we have not seen the last of the biographies of psychoanalysts, and hopefully some of the early figures will also be reexamined in the future by writers with fresh ideological perspectives.

# 21

# Charcot

Biography-writing is a distinct literary form, a craft as well as an art. The biographer's aim should be evocative—to bring to life and revive people and places long since extinct. Although ours may be a time which seems often excessively present-oriented, biography-reading has become part of our popular culture.

Catherine Drinker Bowen, the author of half-a-dozen well-known biographies (including books on Justice Holmes, John Adams, Sir Edward Coke, and Francis Bacon), made a profession of being a biographer and should be well-qualified to tell us something of her calling. Relatively few good books exist about the writing of history, and almost none about the problem of biography. Miss Bowen's *Biography: The Craft and the Calling*[1] is a joy to read, a real treat. It is a very short book, filled with lively examples for each of her points.

Miss Bowen is concerned with technique, ways and means of expression. "People like to say that writing cannot be taught. If they mean that talent cannot be taught they are correct of course....But where technique is concerned, surely it is as teachable as any art." She includes chapters on plotting the biography, the opening scenes, the biographer's relationship with his hero, how individuals looked and techniques of revealing the hero's thoughts, as well as many other topics of interest to writers and readers of biographies. The final chapter is a wise one on greatness, entitled "A Few Words About Talent."

Particularly in the social sciences, biographical research has been a neglected subject for far too long. In recent years a host of new devices have evolved for data collection and interpretation, so that students of society and politics have been tempted to try to do without the more old-fashioned means of understanding.

Yet, in the last analysis people make history and suffer as individuals from the unintended consequences of their actions. Human motives and feelings are entitled to as much dignity and attention as the externals of human behavior. As scholars reflect over the past, they run the danger of structuring the sequence of events so that no one who lived through the period would ever recognize it as his own.

Miss Bowen reminds us to try to retain the quality of uncertainty and the element of surprise, which can play as fateful a part in the lives of others as in our own. Professsionals tend to write solely for each other – historians for historians, lawyers for lawyers, psychiatrists for psychiatrists, political scientists for political scientists. Miss Bowen's work should reassure us that the ability to communicate with people need not be a sign of being unscientific or lacking in seriousness of purpose.

Her special talent for expressing herself in good writing provides no grounds for suspecting her scholarship. Her early book on Justice Oliver Wendell Holmes, Jr., for one, will long endure, even though recent scholarship of a more "definitive" sort has already been written.

* * *

A jointly authored study of Jean-Martin Charcot[2] is remarkable, thoroughly conscientious and engrossing at the same time. Little has been known about Charcot and his place in the development of nineteenth-century neurology, apart from the appreciative essay which Freud wrote following Charcot's death in 1893. Charcot had an impact internationally, and Freud was only one of the many foreign students who came to Paris to study with a man who stood out as a leader of a neurological school all his own. Although the Salpètriere did not manage to maintain its role as the Mecca of international neurological study following Charcot's own death, he did succeed in setting up some of the major classifications which still endure in modern neurology.

*Charcot* is really an intellectual biography, and an examination of his private life is largely undertaken in a chapter appearing late in the text. We are, however, given at the outset an account of Charcot's education as a physician. Charcot's social background was what could be called the lower middle class, but he married a wealthy widow and ended up living in immense luxury. His career built up gradually, and his first efforts to get a professorship were unsuccessful. Charcot's name may now be most closely associated with the modern concept of hysteria, and relatively late in his life he did focus on hysterical phenomena, but he maintained his earlier major neurological interests in progressive muscular atrophy, locomotor ataxia, spinal cord localization, multiple sclerosis, Parkinson's disease, cerebral localization, and aphasia.

Charcot's influence was exerted by his immense personal charisma, a steady flow of publications, teaching, a large private practice, as well as travels abroad. It took a substantial amount of time for Charcot's reputation to get established. And he started off as a professor of pathological anatomy. Only in 1881 did he get elected to the chair in diseases of the nervous system for which he is now best known. While in Germany comparable medical research took place in laboratory settings, Charcot always worked within the context of clinical interests. He delivered lectures, wrote them up, and they appeared in several volumes, many of which were translated abroad. Charcot's work with patients could be harshly criticized by opponents for being suggestive and not adequately scientific, yet he remained convinced that medicine had to remain an art as well as a hard science. From his earliest years he made drawings as part of his research, and *Charcot* has many illustrations about the neurologist's life, as well as by him, which add notably to the success of the text.

Charcot was working within a rich native neurological tradition, and France has every right to be proud of its national success in this area. Charcot had his French predecessors, and he kept abreast of work that was being done abroad. He steered clear of the domain of psychiatry, and made his mark within neurology itself. He was therapeutically an activist, and followed some of his patients for decades.

In terms of his personality, Charcot seems to have been on the authoritarian side, and he was not ashamed to have photographs of him taken with Napoleon-like poses. In his lifetime he had many students and proteges, but they did not succeed in keeping his school alive after his death. Although Pierre Janet studied with Charcot and eulogized him after his death, Janet's work proceeded independently of Charcot's central concerns.

*Charcot* concludes with a valuable essay on the historiographical sources connected with the biographical subject. The authors, two neurologists and one historian, have succeeded in collaborating seamlessly, and each of them is responsible for writing three of the nine chapters.

## Notes

1. Catherine Drinker Bowen, *Biography: The Craft and the Calling* (Boston: Atlantic Little Brown, 1969).
2. Christopher G. Goetz, Michel Bonduelle, and Toby Gelfand, *Charcot: Constructing Neurology* (New York: Oxford University Press, 1995).

# 22

# Breuer

Albrecht Hirschmüller's *The Life and Work of Josef Breuer*[1] first appeared in Germany in 1978, and ever since then it has enjoyed a special status as the for now standard discussion of Freud's teacher and former collaborator. The excellence of Hirschmüller's book makes one's mouth water for the author's forthcoming study of the period Freud spent in Theodor Meynert's Viennese psychiatric clinic.

We have long known that Freud and Breuer had a serious falling out by the spring of 1896; in letters to Wilhelm Fliess, Freud bitterly complained about Breuer. Freud resented his earlier dependency (financial and otherwise) on Breuer and blamed Breuer, among other charges, for speaking ill of him to Fliess's wife. Otto Rank once suggested that when Freud reported the upheaval in himself supposedly occasioned by the death of his father, Freud was really using a distant event to camouflage his distressed feelings over the loss of Breuer.

Despite the fact that they saw each other no more, Freud was still capable in 1909 of writing extravagantly about Breuer's critical role in the creation of psychoanalysis. Years after their quarrel, when Breuer was an old man walking in Vienna with his daughter-in-law, he spotted Freud "coming head on towards him. Instinctively, he opened his arms. Freud passed, professing not to see him." Others have confirmed the reports of the intransigence of Freud's anger.

One of the many peculiarities to this story is that in his Clark Lectures Freud had credited Breuer with the successful treatment, through the method of catharsis, of his early patient "Anna O." (Ernest Jones, much to the displeasure of Anna O.'s family and friends, revealed in his biography of Freud that she became a famous German social worker, Bertha Pappenheim; she was also a social acquaintance of Freud's wife Martha, and wound up being commemorated on a postal stamp.) Also claiming success, Breuer had written about Anna O. for the *Studies on Hysteria* on which he and Freud collaborated. Yet Carl Jung was maintaining in the 1920s that Freud had told him that Anna O. had not been a therapeutic triumph but, rather, a failure. Henri Ellenberger substantiated Jung's assertion, and on the basis of medical records that Ellenberger unearthed he proved that she had wound up, after being seen by Breuer, addicted both to morphine and chloral.

Hirschmüller's book carefully documents not just the story of Anna O. but the whole of Breuer's full career, including his family background. *The Life and Work of Josef Breuer* is a tribute to the tradition of Germanic scholarship. According to my count, there are some 1,846 notes at the back of the book. The biography itself takes up only about half the total text; the remainder of the book consists of primary documents and letters.

Hirschmüller argues that "for a Jew in Vienna around 1860 the chances of securing an academic appointment were limited." Public service as a career was still practically impossible: "The best opportunities were in the fields of medicine and the law. Medicine was a traditional profession amongst Viennese Jews."

Breuer's specialist studies began in 1859, "the heyday of the second Viennese school of medicine, the period of those men who restored to the University of Vienna the reputation of possessing one of the leading medical faculties in Europe...." Breuer did not enroll for the course in psychiatry, but acquired "a certain breadth of medical knowledge." In 1873 Breuer, then a docent in internal medicine, "published his sensational discovery of the function of the semicircular canals in the labyrinth of the ear." Like Freud later on, Breuer found his further academic advancement at the University of Vienna blocked. According to Hirschmüller, "true to their different temperaments, they responded in different ways to the inevitable failure. Freud, the fighter, finally managed to wrest professorial status." Freud gradually withdrew from the university and founded his own independent school. Breuer became a member of Viennese high society and occupied a large house in a central part of the inner city. He was Brahms's physician during the last months of the composer's life.

Hirschmüller hypothesizes that Breuer, who continued in his later years to treat cases of hysteria and was aware of the role of sexuality as a clinically disturbing influence, saw in the case of Anna O. "no connection between the severe neuralgia and the rest of her symptoms, and therefore assumed that he had been completely successful in eliminating the element in the hysteria that was accessible to psychotherapy." Breuer remained a dedicated physician. According to Hirschmüller, "unlike Breuer, Freud used the occupation of physician as a mere expedient."

Although Hirschmüller is aware of the controversies over scientific priorities in Breuer's life and Freud's own troubled desire to establish his fame, Hirschmüller makes no mention whatever of later controversies in psychoanalysis over the issue of alleged plagiarism or of Freud's difficulties, for example, with Victor Tausk. A usually reliable informant reports that Kurt R. Eissler had undertaken his own study of Breuer, which might be taken to be a tribute to Hirschmüller's achievement since it seems that Eissler wanted to challenge the authoritativeness of this first biography of Breuer.

Breuer not only pioneered with his cathartic method but directed attention to the psychological meaning of the symptoms of his hysterical patients. His case history of Anna O. when she was hospitalized at Binswanger's Bellevue Sanatorium in Kreuzlingen in Switzerland is included as an Appendix to *The Life and Work of Josef Breuer* and is a noteworthy document.

## Note

1. Albrecht Hirschmüller, *The Life and Work of Josef Breuer: Physiology and Psychoanalysis* (New York: New York University Press, 1989).

# 23

# Wagner-Jauregg

Magda Whitrow's biography *Julius Wagner-Jauregg (1857-1940)*[1] is an extraordinary achievement. The author, whose scholarly credentials are unknown to me, has revived a figure who has become unduly forgotten. And she has done so with such scrupulous attention to primary sources, as well as human tact, as to make one want to urge her immediately onto another such project.

What little I once knew about Wagner-Jauregg came largely from bits and pieces that Helene Deutsch, who once worked under him before going to Freud, chanced to tell me. Although these conversations with Helene Deutsch took place some three decades ago, I did not doubt that what I was told, even as an aside, was worth recording. And so I worked this information into various of my publications. But only now, on reading this full-scale study of Wagner-Jauregg, do I realize how important an impression had been conveyed to me.

The drawings and photographs are striking and memorable. Even the quotation at the outset of the book, where Wagner-Jauregg describes why he is writing some reminiscences, gives a feel for the strength of his character and his integrity. The Foreword, by Professor Peter Berner, reminds the general reader of Wagner-Jauregg's claims to fame. He studied in three fields where his reputation deserves to be lasting: the role of cretinism and goitre prophylaxis, the reform laws concerning the insane, and of course malaria therapy. It was for his research on malaria that he won his Nobel Prize in 1927. Wagner-Jauregg's work preceded the development of other means of somatic therapy for psychiatric problems, even if the discovery of penicillin made malaria therapy unnecessary. In contrast to other Viennese psychiatrists, Wagner-Jauregg was not content to try to relate diseases to hypothetical brain lesions. Wagner-Jauregg's anti-Semitism is a sensitive matter, and the only issue about which I think the author might have done more homework.

It has been well-established how skeptical of psychoanalysis Wagner-Jauregg remained, and the letters between him and Freud require the closest possible scrutiny in order to untangle the sensitive ways these old-world gentlemen communicated their genuine feelings. To Wagner-Jauregg Freud seemed too abstract and ambitious, a generalizer.

In an era afflicted with AIDS, we tend to forget what a scourge the general paralysis of the insane could be, even if the treatment Wagner-Jauregg succeeded in coming up with is no longer used because, according to Whitrow, "this late stage of syphilis is hardly ever seen now as antibiotics can prevent that dreaded disease." Tough as Wagner-Jauregg was, he did go about relieving human suffering.

Although little is known about Wagner-Jauregg's childhood, Whitrow has done her best to unearth the available evidence. (It is spooky to me how, although he was a year younger than Freud, he only managed to survive him by a year; Freud, of course, had had cancer for many years, and was forced to die abroad where the physicians were unfamiliar with his case.) Wagner-Jauregg was Catholic and came from Austrian peasant stock, and like Freud he considered the possibility of forwarding his career by emigrating. Also like Freud he, too, lived with his parents for an extended time. Apparently Wagner-Jauregg had never thought of becoming a psychiatrist until a chance professional opening came up. Unlike Freud, who was a born writer, Wagner-Jauregg took no special joy in writing. For years he remained interested in the relationship between infectious illnesses and mental sickness, which still may someday bear fruit.

First Wagner-Jauregg succeeded Richard von Krafft-Ebing as the professor of psychiatry in Graz, then the second largest city in Austria. From 1889 until 1893 he worked in Graz, where he married his first wife who was Jewish. His private life was unhappy, although Whitrow does a great deal to clarify the specifics of his problems. Wagner-Jauregg returned to Vienna, even if it took some time for him to consolidate the power which he later achieved at the University there. Eventually he was elected Dean of the Medical Faculty. About half the medical students were Jewish, and Wagner-Jauregg always had Jews on his staff. When he retired from his Chair in 1928, he was succeeded by a former assistant, Otto Poetzl.

It was news to me how Wagner-Jauregg had been so preoccupied with forensic psychiatry, and he allowed himself to get embroiled in some nasty journalistic squalls. Wagner-Jauregg could suffer from the same sin of over-ambitiousness as Freud, even if in a different realm. Wagner-Jauregg "argued forcibly and vehemently against the competence of a lay jury to decide on whether a person ought to be certified," without acknowledging the possible abuses of psychiatric power.

The specific struggle between Freud and Wagner-Jauregg, which took place at the end of World War I over the treatment of military mental illnesses, must have wounded Wagner-Jauregg terribly. It would have seemed to Wagner-Jauregg utterly presumptuous for psychoanalysis to claim to be better able to treat war-neuroses than the available physical therapies.

The chapter on Wagner-Jauregg's contribution to the study of cretinism is a model of following the scrupulous steps of a genuine scientist. Thyroid tablets from Burroughs Wellcome in London played a beneficial part. Wagner-Jauregg's campaign for goitre prevention through iodized-salt proved less successful in the short-run, and he was only vindicated in his efforts to improve the health of his nation after his death.

The chapter on fever therapy comes late in the book, and is inevitably the high point. Wagner-Jauregg only started with malaria therapy in June 1917, but the news of his successful efforts was to spread around the world so that by 1923 an editorial in the *American Journal of Psychiatry* was urging that observations on the effects of malarial infection be made on the progress of paresis.

The years of Wagner-Jauregg's retirement make for sad reading. But he stoutly opposed public shows of hypnotism, suggestion, and telepathy. Unfortunately, he also thought that criminals were sick people. (Oddly enough Freud shared some of this proclivity.) Wagner-Jauregg had made a second marriage, to a much younger woman, but continued to live alone though not childless. I am not competent to assess how much of a German nationalist and conservative he was. We are told here that "he disliked Jewish jokes for which he had no understanding," although he himself could be very witty. I wish Whitrow had done more to establish whether it is really true that Wagner-Jauregg joined the Nazi party.

An appendix to this book reminds us that in 1913 more than 8 percent of new admissions to mental hospitals under the London County Council were diagnosed as suffering from general paresis of the insane (GPI). Wagner-Jauregg deserves to be generally honored in our memory even if some of the medical particulars of his achievement seem no longer pertinent.

## Note

1. Magda Whitrow, *Julius Wagner-Jauregg (1857-1940)* (London: Smith-Gorden, 1993).

# 24

# Sigmund Freud

Sigmund Freud continues to attract biographical interest. But the subtitle to Peter Gay's biography[1] ("A Life For Our Time") betrays its central flaw. For despite his being a historian, Gay has committed a central sin of the profession —presentism. Gay has written as if Freud, although he was a European born in 1856, were somehow our contemporary; and therefore Gay has flattened out or ignored the central differences between the genuine Freud and ourselves. He has missed the chance to hold up the example of the real Freud, who was inevitably a man of his time, hard though it may be to reconstruct. Gay has neglected to present a vision of how life might be lived differently from our own conventions.

To take one startling example, Gay writes that by 1905 Freud felt able to criticize "his fellow psychiatrists." Any beginning university student should be taught that Freud was not a psychiatrist at all, just because it is a point not immediately obvious today. In Central Euorpe of that era, in contrast to our own North American practices, a gulf existed between psychiatry and neurology. Freud was trained as a neurologist and remained an outsider to Viennese psychiatry headed by his former classmate Wagner-Jauregg. This professional isolation meant that Freud lacked clinical experience with psychotics, the most severely ill mental patients. Freud waited until the 1920s to draw a distinction between what he was familiar with, the neuroses, and those mysterious illnesses known as psychoses. Fair-minded observers have often remarked that Freud's early diagnoses often ignored signs of psychosis, and the organic basis to mental suffering. It would be impossible to understand either the respectful criticisms of Freud that were made in his own lifetime, or the changes that have taken place within psychoanalysis since Freud's death, if one were not aware of the fact that Freud created his own discipline of psychoanalysis and cannot possibly be described as having "fellow psychiatrists." Gay mixes things up more by erroneously referring to Wagner-Jauregg as a "great neurologist," and such confusion means that Gay cannot hope to account for the special attraction which Carl G. Jung, a trained psychiatrist, had for Freud.

Gay glides over such a central historical issue, fixing Freud up in what he sees as the best possible contemporary light. A good deal of religiosity has already accompanied the retelling of the story of psychoanalysis. There has been such abundant criticism of the most partisanly orthodox accounts of Freud's struggles that Gay tries to incorporate some of the so-called revisionist historiography. But essentially, Gay's book is a dogmatic Freudian wolf in sheep's clothing. It makes minor concessions to recent scholarship for the larger purpose of prettifying Freud for today.

Gay writes with a readable style, but all these hundreds of pages should not obscure the fact that at bottom he has not allowed himself to reconsider Freud's theories. He presents Freud's account of dreaming, worked out in the 1890s, without any attention to the interesting neurological work on dreams that has been done within the last couple of generations. Even while Freud was alive, people such as Jung questioned Freud's outlook on dreams; Gay mentions no alternatives to Freud's point of view.

The book contains many of the most standard quotations from Freud, and repeats accepted cliches in the language of today's higher journalism. Gay notes that he spent more than two and a half years writing the book, which may seem a lot, but is too brief in the light of the pretension the book makes to being conclusive.

The bibliographical essay at the back of the book presumes to pass judgment on nearly everyone who has ever written on Freud; but Gay commits sloppy scholarly howlers alongside his pontificating. For example, he praises one multi-volume translation of Freud by a "brilliant" early analyst; the problem is that although Gay credits her with being "mainly" responsible for the translation, an exact examination of the text reveals that she translated only 7 percent of that edition of Freud. The presumed superiority of the translation is thereby not only in question, but one does have to wonder how carefully he has done his homework.

Gay's book does have authenticity in that he has chosen to cite as sources primary documents themselves rather than any of the secondary works that are responsible for bringing evidence to our attention. It is to Gay's credit that, perhaps because of his known loyalty to certain current powers-that-be in psychoanalysis, he was allowed to quote from some hitherto unused Freud letters. But one has to know all this material intimately to realize how equally important is what Gay has chosen not to cite.

The whole book reads as though he had immersed himself without preconceptions or indebtedness. But facts never speak for themselves. Just as it is tendentious to suppose that Freud, as Gay would have it, worked with patients without preconceived ideas and empirically induced his findings, so it is misleading of Gay to make it seem like his own work derives simply from an examination of the available Freud manuscript material.

Gay selectively omits awkward circumstances that might complicate an idealization of Freud. It is unbelievable, given Wilhelm Reich's stature within

Viennese psychoanalysis and his importance to the history of ideas, that this book contains not a single reference to him; and this is so even though Freud wrote his *Civilization and Its Discontents* against Reich, a text that Gay discusses.

Gay has written "a life for our time" and, in that pursuit, he ignores a host of little-known figures. At the same time, Gay wholly overstates Anna Freud's standing based on the stature she ultimately achieved. Freud did go to considerable effort to build his youngest child up, in order to ensure that after his death she would have a livelihood and career. But Gay has not tried to reconstruct the story of Freud's life as it was lived, which would have meant contradicting preconceptions about him that arise from the very different society in which we exist.

Although Gay complains that the literature about Freud is growing "almost out of control," this irritation reflects Gay's own ambition, not unlike Jones's, to put a stop to further inquiry. But Gay's own thinly veiled partisanship will be almost sure to encourage an even greater avalanche of new Freud studies.

The first biography of Freud appeared almost seventy-five years ago; it was written by Fritz Wittels, a Viennese analyst who had temporarily fallen out with Freud, and it was remarkable enough that it is still in print today. On more than one occasion Freud expressed his disdain for biography-writing, feeling strongly that the story of his life ought not to overtake the tale of his creating the theory and practice of psychoanalysis. Contrary to his skepticism about the validity of biographies, all along Freud had been using illustrations from his own experiences to support his innovations. After his death in 1939, one path-breaking biography by freelance journalist Helen Puner, alluded to earlier, proved so commerically successful as to upset the Freud family and their loyalists. It was then decided that the time had come to override Freud's known objections to an official biography. That was the occasion for authorizing Jones to write his three-volume biography, which appeared in the 1950s to coincide with the 100th anniversary of Freud's birth. Jones's work may have been partisan, but it was also full of necessary details, and it remains for all its unevenness an essential source. In 1980 Ronald Clark published an unusually objective biography, followed eight years later by Peter Gay's largely defensive portrait of Freud.

After only ten years since Gay's popular biography tried to put Freud's critics in their place, Paul Ferris was bold to have entered this embattled field so full of controversy. His book[2] is engagingly written, free of jargon and even-handed. He is neither out to write a work that will serve as promotional literature for the practice of Freud's profession nor is he a debunker. It is impressive how he has made use of a wide body of material without showing signs of partisanship. Ferris handles Freud's death, which came after coping with cancer of the jaw for more than sixteen years, with tact and dignity. His book contains no bombshells, but can be relied upon as an up-to-date and balanced survey of the Freud biographical literature.

*Questions for Freud: The Secret History of Psychoanalysis*,[3] by Nicholas Rand and Maria Torok, emerges from the world of French psychoanalysis. Freudian thinking has become the leading doctrine in Parisian intellectual life, and the bookstores there brim with new and interesting texts about the history of analysis. Rand and Torok begin with the endearing premise that psychoanalysis "in its classical form is indeed indefensible." They are not interested in promoting any orthodox party line, and feel free to point out various key contradictions in Freud's thinking.

For example, Freud proposed that a patient's free associations, every random thought that might pass through the mind, are essential to understanding dream reports; at the same time he alleged that he had uncovered universal dream symbols that were independent of patients' thoughts. With a keen ear for internal rifts within Freudian psychoanalysis, Rand and Torok wonder about the inconsistencies in how Freud came to repudiate his 1890s theory about the significance of the alleged sexual seductions of his patients.

Rand and Torok single out one of Freud's applications of his theories to a turn-of-the-century novella by Austrian writer Wilhelm Jensen, *Gradiva: A Pompeiian Fancy*. Rand and Torok use this case study to show how Freud could distort literature for the purpose of proving his theories. They also raise the problem of how the defenders of Freudian orthodoxy have censored Freud's letters. Such secrecy naturally encourages the suspicion that there is something damaging to Freud's reputation that it is necessary to hide.

Rand and Torok are partly licenced in their project of writing a so-called secret history of psychoanalysis by the defensiveness about Freud's documentary legacy. In particular, Rand and Torok are advocates of the analyst Sandor Ferenczi, that Hungarian favourite's of Freud's, who proposed in the early 1930s that Freud tended to overvalue fantasy at the expense of traumatic reality. Rand and Torok believe that Freud repudiated Ferenczi as a way of quelling his own self-doubts, a hypothesis about Freud's psychological make-up that Wittels first proposed three quarters of a century earlier to explain the pre-World War I battles within psychoanalysis.

Rand and Torok dwell on a family disaster that befell the Freuds in 1865, when Sigmund Freud was only nine. A brother of his father was convicted in Vienna of trying to circulate counterfeit ruble notes. The historical evidence also hints that the origin of this counterfeit money was in England, where Freud's two half-brothers had moved. We have long heard that Freud's father's hair turned grey in a few days because of this whole matter. But Rand and Torok are reductionistically determined to find in this family tragedy "the source of the theoretical, clinical, and institutional contradictions in Freudian psychoanalysis." Unfortunately, the open-mindeedness they bring to the history of psychoanalysis is undermined by their determination to find in this one childhood incident the key to all the many tensions in Freud's life. Such tunnel vision is bound to be distorting, and happily Ferris's biography has no such hobbyhorse.

John Forrester's *Truth Games: Lies, Money and Psychoanalysis*[4] also arises from a background in French psychoanalysis. But Forrester's collection of essays is marred by a different flaw from the one that afflicts the work of Rand and Torok. For Forrester never finds significant contradictions in Freud; instead, even the most controversial changes in Freud's thinking, for example his turning away from the seduction theory to his dogmatic belief in the Oedipus complex, get lamely characterized as "fruitful." Forrestal does not have a grasp of the more intangible implications of Freud, the music behind the words. He seems to be aiming at the metaphysics that underpin psychoanalysis, but is naïve in accepting Freud's writings at face value.

Whatever the drawbacks to the approach of Rand and Torok, *Questions for Freud* makes for a lively and challenging read. Forrester's *Truth Games* seems sterile, the equivalent of trying to count how many angels can dance on the head of a pin. When, for example, Forrester quotes Jacques Lacan, the single most important figure in French analysis, he exhibits the same lack of critical perspective that he brings to Freud himself.

Psychoanalysis has come under a medical cloud during this past generation, largely due to advances in psychopharmacology that have provided therapeutic alternatives in the form of a variety of new pills. But intellectuals will continue to be intrigued by the philosophical implications of Freud's work, accounting for its vitality on the continent of Europe today, and his life and struggles will attract still further historiographical inquiry.

With all the recent polemics surrounding Freud, attacking him both as a scientist and healer, it is a relief to find *Sigmund Freud: Explorer of the Unconscious*[5] appearing in a series called Oxford Portraits in Science. This short book is both readable and reliable, and serves to introduce a new generation to the basic contours of Freud's achievements. Of course there is far more to Freud than can be encompassed by his strictly scientific works, as he sought to transform Western ethics as a whole. But in the current climate of opinion, where Freud still tends to be either defensively idolized or tendentiously assaulted, it is welcome to have as even-handed an account as that provided by Margaret Muckenhoupt.

There are a few biographical details that could be improved on. While it is true that historians have never been able to follow what Freud's father lived on in Vienna, and the presumption is that he got help from his grown sons from his first marriage, who were living in England, it is worth pointing out that Jacob Freud had ruined himself in Moravia by bailing out their poor investment in ostrich feathers. Freud himself kept in close touch with his English relatives, and a volume of Freud's correspondence with Sam Freud has already appeared in French.

Muckenhoupt repeats the old story that Freud translated four essays by John Stuart Mill into German. A history of confusion about these translations started in a letter of Freud's to his future wife and was compounded by Jones's biography of Freud. Despite what Jones maintained, three of the pieces were by Mill himself, and only one was written by Harriet Taylor, whom Mill ultimately married.

It is a bit confusing for Muckenhoupt to write, "Breuer also treated one of Freud's most famous patients, 'Anna. O.'" Of course Freud never saw Anna O. in therapy, but made much of the supposed success of her treatment in his accounts of the history of psychoanalysis. Muckenhoupt repeats the old story that Anna O. had a hysterical pregnancy as part of her relationship with Breuer, but there is reason to believe that this whole legend might have been fabricated.

It would have been better, given the narrow scope of Freud's efforts to deal with neurosis, not to introduce the concept of "mental illness." It should be enough, as Muckenhoupt contends, that Freud introduced "a new vision of the mind."

The text of this book is clearly written and filled with photographs that, though all well known, enliven the process of introducing readers to Freud's accomplishments. Curiously enough, there is little effort to weigh Freud's theories about dreaming in the light of modern evidence or to question the reliability of Freud's therapeutic procedures. Even before Freud's death there were substantial challenges to his ways of proceeding. But to argue that Freud made a pack of original mistakes, many of which were subsequently corrected, to my mind only makes his work a more secure part of the history of science. Only fanatics, or the most callous skeptics, need to see in Freud's work an unchanging body of theories.

## Notes

1. Peter Gay, *Freud: A Life For Our Time* (London: Norton, 1988).
2. Paul Ferris, *Dr. Freud: A Life* (London: Sinclair-Stevenson, 1998).
3. Nicholas Rand and Maria Torok, *Questions For Freud: The Secret History of Psychoanalysis* (Cambridge, MA: Harvard University Press, 1998).
4. John Forrester, *Truth Games: Lies, Money, and Psychoanalysis* (Cambridge, MA: Harvard University Press, 1998).
5. Margaret Muckenhoupt, *Sigmund Freud: Explorer of the Unconscious* (New York: Oxford University Press, 1997).

# 25

# Jung

Carl G. Jung was not only a pupil of Freud's, but Jung became one of Freud's most searching critics. At first glance, Frank McLynn's biography of Jung[1] looked like the best one to date. Jung, who was born in Switzerland in 1875 and died there in 1961, has to be considered one of the central figures in twentieth century psychology. After he and Freud had their famous falling-out before the First World War, Jung went on to publish about as many volumes as Freud, and eventually founded his own school. I approached reading this book with anticipation, since so much of the Jung literature has been written for those already initiated into his work. McLynn is a biographer with several titles to his credit, but his book does not succed in making Jung's life more understandable. Within a couple of hundred pages, I was keenly disappointed with McLynn's efforts.

In retrospect I should have earlier spotted signs of potential trouble. There are no photographs and no use of primary material. Doubtless McLynn, once he came up with his derogatory theses about Jung's work and personality, could not ask for cooperation or permissions from the Jung family. It is a mystery to me why anyone would devote hundreds of pages to debunking someone like Jung, who has scarcely established himself among intellectual historians.

McLynn starts off dealing intelligently with Jung's complicated family background. His father was a Protestant pastor, and his mother often ill and away from home. At the time Jung chose to become a psychiatrist, the field was just becoming established on a modern basis. Jung had his apprenticeship at one of the best psychiatric centres in Zurich, so that, when he first got in touch with Freud, his experiences in psychiatry made him an attractive disciple. Freud's own background in neurology at that time meant as we have noted earlier that he had very little experience with the severest forms of mental distress. Jung also married an immensely rich woman, and a husband then had full access to his wife's money, making Jung a highly suitable "crown prince" for Freud to anoint.

We have known for some time now that, although it was Freud who made so much of sex in his theories, Jung led a far less restricted sexual life. Jung not only had five children, but a couple of well-known mistresses in Antonia Wolff and Sabina Spielrein, both former patients, and there may be more revelations to come.

At first, after the crisis of losing Freud over the issue of Freud's authoritarianism, Jung had a rough time of it emotionally, but he sought the supportive help of Wolff, not his wife. Neither man seems to have overcome the loss of the other. By chapter 12, we are told that Jung "could never cooperate with others or treat them as equals," at which point the cat is out of McLynn's bag. McLynn claims that Jung "deserted" Freud, a term which might be expected to come from a partisan on Freud's side, rather than from a biographer with no axes to grind.

Jung had plenty of savvy about raising money to establish his school; many wealthy American patients came after ther publication of such famous books as *Psychological Types* in 1921. But even before McLynn has adequately described Jung's most original ideas, we are being presented with harsh Freudian critiques of them. Jung became one of the toughest critics Freud ever encountered, but McLynn scarcely allows Jung's most characteristic points of view to get developed.

Although describing Jung in unattractive terms for his work with patients, McLynn acknowledges that for Jung psychotherapy meant a partnership, "a dialectical relationship between doctor and patient." Jung had the idea that, unlike in regular medicine, a diagnosis had to come at the end, not the beginning, of treatment. Jung proposed a theory of the stages of life, which later Erik H. Erikson, a famous Viennese analyst and patient of Anna Freud, would do so much to build on. Jung had clear prophetic aspirations, but who in the whole field of depth psychology, including Freud, did not?

McLynn is, I think, balanced when it comes to Jung's unfortunate contacts with the Nazis in the 1930s, when among other things he went to Germany to talk about the differences between "Jewish psychology" and "Aryan psychology." It would be hard to absolve Jung from the accusation of opportunism. Every now and then in his book, McLynn does allude to some of the pioneering points Jung made for psychotherapy, but there is too little of it for my taste. Jung had an altogether more positive view of religion than Freud did, and although he has been accused of having a "Christ complex," his favorite religion seems to have been Buddhism.

The worst single section in the book is Chapter 22, about Jung's final "settling of accounts" with Freud immediately after his death. Jung wrote an essay after Freud died in 1939, which McLynn finds marked by bitterness and hostility rather than by charity and reconciliation. But the reader gets no real feel for the grounds—the use of the couch, the demand of Freud's for adherence to his teachings—that Jung had for not continuing to practice therapy the way Freud did.

Deirdre Bair, who has published biographies of Simone de Beauvoir, Samuel Beckett, and Anais Nïn, is currently completing a biography of Jung. That will be the book to watch out for. McLynn missed a real chance to get Jung studies on a sound basis after the confusion and consternation caused by Richard Noll's recent *The Jung Cult* (1994) and by Paul Stern's *C. G. Jung: The Haunted Prophet* (1976).

Jung's autobiography, *Memories, Dreams, Reflections* has had a wide audience, and his *Answer to Job* was a bestseller. Barbarah Hannah's 1976 biography of Jung was written with affection, and Linda Donn's 1988 *Freud and Jung* seemed fair. I wonder whether any biographer with such distaste for Jung as McLynn has can possibly succeed in giving us a fair account of his life and work.

## Note

1. Frank McLynn, *Carl Gustav Jung* (New York: St. Martin's Press, 1998).

# 26

# Sabina Spielrein

Sigmund Freud and Carl G. Jung, unquestionably among this century's most eminent psychologists, came from widely divergent backgrounds. Freud was trained as a Viennese neurologist, and although he created the new discipline of psychoanalysis he had little experience to repeat an earlier point with hospitalized cases. Jung, on the other hand, held a prestigious position at one of the most famous psychiatric clinics in Switzerland.

Since Jung was a generation younger than Freud, and held out the hope of expanding the horizons of psychoanalytic influence beyond the boundaries of Freud's own clinical clientele, Freud picked this brilliant young man to be his professional heir and successor. In addition, unlike Freud who worried that his own origins as a Jew might expose his movement to the prejudices of anti-Semitism, Jung was the son of a Protestant pastor and eager to bridge the gulf between Freud's innovations and traditional Christian ethics.

The relationship between Freud and Jung—they collaborated with one another between 1907 and 1913—has long fascinated intellectual historians, since after the falling-out between them, Jung went on to set up the most significant alternative school of clinical psychological thinking to Freud's own. (For a variety of reasons Jung has had a special impact in Canada where, unlike in the U.S., he has long been acknowledged as far more than simply a "dissident" who broke away from Freud's influence.)

Almost twenty years ago we discovered that a key part of the tangled web of the human ties between Freud and Jung was played by an early patient of Jung's, the Russian-born Sabina Spielrein. Her name comes up in their correspondence, and she went on to develop some interesting ideas of her own. At least for a time she sought to bridge the different perspectives of Freud and Jung. She and her immediate family were killed early in World War II, during the Nazi invasion of Russia, and for a long time she disappeared from the annals of the history of psychoanalysis.

At some point in Jung's treatment of Spielrein, they became lovers. Jung was then a married man with small children. His indiscretion was communicated to

Spielrein's parents, perhaps by Jung's wife. Freud, too, was made privy to the scandal. Although at first Freud was tolerant of Jung's misdeed, after he and Jung had separated Freud held Jung's misconduct against him.

John Kerr's *A Most Dangerous Method: The Story of Jung, Freud, and Sabina Spielrein*[1] is an extraordinarily conscientious account of the direct links between Jung and Freud, showing how all their ideas intertwined. Kerr has sought to demonstrate how Spielrein was a pivotal figure in the break-up of the alliance between these giants in modern psychotherapy. In order to make his argument fully symmetrical, Kerr has adopted the thesis that Jung was aware of a hypothetical incestuous relationship between Freud and his wife's sister, who lived in the Freud household for years. According to Kerr's version of what happened, Jung and Freud each had something on the other, and Kerr traces the supposed evidence of these sexual triangles in their public and private writings.

My own understanding of what was going on is rather less straightforward than Kerr's. As far as I have been able to reconstruct what happened, Freud had a complicated emotional involvement with his sister-in-law, which may have been briefly distressing to her. Contrary to Kerr's thesis, Jung felt that Freud's inability to follow through by making his wife's sister into a sexual partner was a sign of Freud's own neurotic inhibitions, and testimony to Jung's own emancipated superiority in lacking Freud's supposed sexual hang-ups.

All these pioneering psychologists felt beyond the bounds of conventional conceptions of good and evil, as they sought to work out new ethical standards for the elite they considered themselves to constitute. Kerr may have gone too far in simplifying the problems between Freud and Jung by exaggerating Spielrein's importance, but no one has ever taken more pains to describe the exact steps by which these three people became entangled.

Kerr has also succeeded in permanently putting Spielrein on the map for her own independent contributions to the history of modern psychotherapy; she had a special theory of how sexuality and destructiveness can be fruitfully united. Among other of her accomplishments, she was the training analyst for the great Swiss psychologist Jean Piaget.

Kerr has also given the most careful rereading of the exchanges between Freud and Jung that have ever appeared in print, and his work will remain a permanent contribution to our understanding of the links between these two fascinating thinkers. Freud, who was suspicious of the unconscious, and Jung, who saw the constructive possibilitites in symptoms, represent an enduringly different set of psychological perspectives. Most subsequent thinkers in the field have been reinventing minor variations on the points of view Freud and Jung first articulated at the turn of that century.

## Note

1. John Kerr, *A Most Dangerous Method: The Story of Jung, Freud and Sabina Spielrein* (New York: Knopf, 1993).

# 27

# Murray

Jung's various disciples have attracted far less attention than those of Freud; and a surprising feature of growing older is that it turns out that people one has met in real life appear increasingly in books. I was acquainted with Henry A. Murray only slightly; but to everyone connected with the post-World War II interdisciplinary department of social relations at Harvard, Henry Murray was known simply as "Harry." Even as far away as the government department there, where I taught despite rooted prejudices against depth psychology, Harry was a charismatic figure. He came from such a wealthy background, I was reliably informed, that if the Psychological Clinic he headed ever needed any special funds he was able to dip into his own bank account to make up the difference. Murray was obviously outside the mainstream of university appointments and received tenure relatively late in life. His name was vaguely asociated with that of Jung, but Murray was not really a member of any given psychological school except perhaps his own.

I formally interviewed him a couple of times in 1965 in connection with my work on Freud and his followers, but each occasion was unstructured and transformed by Harry's innate informality. He had seen Freud once in Vienna and been a founding member of the Boston Psychoanalytic Society; he knew many of the early psychoanalysts, yet looked on them with a unique kind of detachment. I last saw him for dinner at his house in 1985, and I am glad to report that even in his early nineties he was able to hold forth and as host succeed in being the center of an evening's conversation at which many others were present. By then I had long since stopped taking notes in Harry's presence. In 1988 he died at the age of ninety-five.

I believe I already knew there was a more or less authorized biography being written about him; and when I saw a public notice from Forrest Robinson, looking for Murray correspondence, I sent along whatever I could find in my filing cabinets. As Robinson so well puts it, in the book[1] that ultimately appeared, Murray was "a great listener; you came away from an encounter with Harry feeling full and satisfied at the top of your personal form." My own early contact with Harry in 1965 had been enriching and stimulating. And my notes are as full of ideas he aroused in me as of specific bits of historical information he passed on. I had every reason to think that he was deserving of a full-length biographical study.

Murray was primarily self-taught as a psychologist and reported that in college he had never taken a psychology course; he felt proud to be in the humanistic tradition of William James. Like James, Murray was trained as a physician, with a specialty in surgery. He not only had been in formal analysis with Jung, partly conducted while sailing on the lake in Zurich, but also had gone to the Freudian Franz Alexander, who helped train a number of the earliest Boston analysts. Harry was, however, too broad-minded and eclectic to put up with the tiresome antics that were associated with what he told me were local professional orthodox Freudian "crackpots."

And so Harry went on to build up his own Psychological Clinic at Harvard, which had originally been founded by Morton Prince. He inspired a whole generation of graduate students. *A Study of Lives* (1963), edited by Robert W. White, was presented to Harry on his seventieth birthday "by students and colleagues past and present who will always remember with excitement and gratitude their sojourn in the high invigorating climate created by his infectious zest, wide-ranging awareness, bountiful powers of creation, and staunch fidelity to the increase of human understanding." *A Study of Lives* contains eighteen essays by such people as Nevitt Sanford, Kenneth Keniston, David C. McClelland, Leopold Bellak, Edwin Schneidman, M. Brewster Smith, Robert R. Holt, Silvan Tomkins, and Erik H. Erikson.

There never was any way of categorizing Harry through conventional academic pigeon-holes. Starting in the 1920s, he had been obsessed with studying the life and works of Herman Melville, at a time when the Melville literature was still scarce. Although in the end Harry failed to come through with a formal Melville biography, he did succeed, through a succession of influential essays, in helping to establish Melville's standing today. He was fascinated with Melville's family history and wrote an influential introduction to *Pierre*.

Harry also had early training, before turning to psychology, as a biochemist, and this left a permanent imprint on him in that he sought to put his theories of personality on a scientific foundation. The Thematic Apperception Test (TAT) is perhaps the most famous device associated with his name, along with that of his collaborator Christiana Morgan. The TAT was a means of drawing forth from people words and stories as a way of inferring important aspects of personality that the individual could or would not volunteer. His most famous single book, which was the outcome of collaborating with others at his Psychological Clinic, was *Explorations in Personality* (1938). He co-edited, with the anthropologist Clyde Kluckhohn, the influential book of readings, *Personality in Nature, Society, and Culture* (1948).

Robinson's *Love's Story Told: A Life of Henry A. Murray*[2] had the task of covering the story of a man born as long ago as 1893. Ninety-five years of life is hard to compress within the pages of any one book. Examining the notes to this text, it looks to me as if a great deal of the primary research was done in the early 1970s. Harry and his second wife, who still survives, cooperated in this project. The problem for his biographer, as I see it, is partly that Harry went on to live so long. He was recently widowed when I first met him, and he did not remarry until 1969. But almost twenty years of married life gets little attention in *Love's Story Told*, almost as if Robinson had written his book in the early 1970s and then put it aside pending Harry's death.

The result is, I regret to say, an unbalanced view, even if it hard for me to criticize a book that has been in the works for twenty years and that duly acknowledges my help. Rumor had long ago reached me that, while he was married to his first wife, Harry had maintained an important extra-marital relationship. A 1988 article informed us that his lover was Christiana Morgan, and essentially *Love's Story Told* is an account of that particular liasion. As I now write objecting to how much Robinson makes of the significance of Christiana in Harry's life, I can hear him protesting against my own Freudian puritanism. Robinson argues that for more than forty years Christiana had been "at the center" of Harry's life, and Robinson even details sadomasochistic practices. But it does seem to me that, though Harry's relationship to Christiana extended from the 1920s until her death in 1967, there is something unseemly about making so much about his tie to her.

Harry's first wife had died suddenly in 1962, and he made no effort then to marry the woman who had been his co-worker and mistress. She had long been drinking too much, and she died in circumstances that were at best accidental. They were on a holiday on St. John, Virgin Islands; she had drunk heavily, Harry got angry, fell asleep, and Christiana was found drowned in less than two feet of water. Harry seems to have felt guilt-ridden and suspected suicide. I have no doubt that he wanted the story of their relationship reported. Still, I do not think this book has done for Harry what he deserves. Reading it makes me want to recommend that, given how unlikely it is that any outsider is ever going to understand the most intimate parts of our lives, the safest procedure is to destroy all old love letters, divorce documents, and so on, in order to allow the work itself to come forth.

This may seem an extreme suggestion, but let me illustrate some telling aspects of how *Love's Story Told* goes astray. Surely an important part of Harry's life has to do with the formation of the social relations department at Harvard. The reader is given some names, such as Talcott Parsons and Clyde Kluckhohn, but nothing much further gets said about them. What was distinctive about Parsons's mark on modern sociology? Books have been written about his ideas, but one would not gather that from *Love's Story Told*. The social relations departrment has long ceased to exist, but we learn nothing whatever about what might have happened. Readers are also entitled to know more than a spare page worth about Harry's participation as an expert witness in behalf of Alger Hiss at the trial that ended in his being convicted of perjury.

And Clyde Kluckhohn—why does he matter? One would never guess the fecundity of his contribution to anthropology and social science, or that his *Mirror For Man*, written for the general public, was in its time immensely influential. Robinson does not address the question of whether Kluckhohn's ideas were right or wrong, or the extent to which they were sound, for it is as if he had no concepts to contribute. We are told on page 294 of *Love's Story Told*, in an explanation of the intimate friendship between Murray and Kluckhohn, that "Kluckhohn had his own carefully guarded secret life, which made him a sympathetic and trusted confidant." That's all the main text has to say about Kluckhohn's "secret," and I confess my mind did start whirling over stories I had once heard. The notes to *Love's Story Told* appear at the back of the book, and there is nothing to help explain the reference to the "secret" referred to on page 294. But on reading through all the notes, after finishing the book, I found a citation attached to page 230: "Kluckhohn's homosexuality was no secret to many in the Harvard community. He was truthful with Harry on this score and promised to respect his friend's very decided heterosexual orientation." The evidence here is an interview with Harry conducted in 1985, which again makes me wonder exactly when the main text got constructed. But is this any way to compose a narrative, so that a reader coming across a "secret" on page 294 has to find the solution in a note to page 230 maintaining that there was "no secret"? I cite this example about Kluckhohn since it, in a nutshell, shows how askew the book itself is.

Now that I have stuck my neck out and said that this book, written with Harry's cooperation, has such an awkward air to it, I want to make certain that I am not being misunderstood. If one opens *Love's Story Told* knowing how truly remarkable and emancipated a man Harry was, then the exaggeration of the relationship between him and Christiana may not seem so important. But I fear that a generation that did not know him is going to be inadequately drawn by the book to the ideas Harry had and to why as a teacher he was capable of inspiring so many serious graduate students.

True, the book is full of invaluable information that would be impossible to get anywhere else. For example, Robinson relies on a "carefully crafted autobiography" that Harry published as "The Case of Murr." Also, Harry's slight stammer is recognizable, and we learn about his Groton and Harvard rowing background. Dean Acheson was one of his roommates at Groton, and Robinson quotes him as having reported, in 1970, that Harry was the "outstanding" member of their class "in the sense of originality of mind, curiosity about everything, sympathetic personality, catholicity of taste, cultural breadth." I only wish that *Love's Story Told* communicated more of what Acheson had in mind, which also fits in with the man I, only slightly to be sure, knew.

Robinson does tell us how "one expanded in Harry's ample presence; one lifted gratefully toward his eminence. The patrician in him was never concealed, but it appeared in the midst of much else—intelligence, learning, discipline, generosity, creativity – that was more conventionally estimable." And we do get a report from a 1970 interview with Kenneth Keniston saying that his old teacher was "the most imaginative and creative person I've ever known."

But there is not enough in *Love's Story Told*, as far as I am concerned, to substantiate Keniston's judgment or any such claims of intellectual distinction that Robinson seems to take too much for granted. Robinson faithfully reports how Murray felt blocked and frustrated as a writer, not just in connection with the Melville project but in explaining his whole orientation toward human nature. But just how powerful Harry could be as a writer can be illustrated, I think, by an obituary of Freud he published in the *American Journal of Psychology* (1940). Murray referred to Freud as the "creator and dictator of psychoanalysis."

> Hardly had the International Psychoanalytic Association been founded in 1910 than it began to break up into factions; and within a few years the heretics, Adler, Jung, Rank, Stekel, unable to accept 'pansexualism' as a doctrine, were pursuing independent paths. But many followers were left and a host of others gained who knew better than, or not enough, to oppose a man who had staked his life on an idea.

Murray said he thought that Freud's book *Group Psychology and the Analysis of the Ego* "applied rather well to the state of affairs in the psychoanalytic society, as well as to the ideology of fascism." He wrote that "Freud knew that he had conquered" and that "innocent of the dread of being wrong, he did not hesitate to publish the most far-fetched conceits of speculation." Murray believed that "if Freud had been more of a scientist he would have pressed no claims to be one. Dogmatism is anti-scientific, and there are reasons to distrust a truth that forms a sect." Such comments, written over half a century ago and bound to have gotten Harry into all sorts of trouble at the time, do not appear at all in *Love's Story Told*.

If Robinson's book is the first of other biographical studies of Murray, then it should be possible to correct what I find unbalanced about it. But I fear that the concentration on the illicit love for Christiana is going to blind future students to Harry's love for his two wives and daughter, as well as the students he helped to encourage. Robinson reports, for example, that more than 600 people came to Harry's first wife's funeral, which I presume means she was no cipher. Harry was, Robinson tells us, fascinated by creativity, yet it is Harry's most creative side that is underemphasized in *Love's Story Told*.

In my reading, the book seems too much an account of self-indulgence and rationalization. Some will think that the whole transformation in ideas that Freud and Jung participated in has sanctioned old-fashioned selfishness. It is true that the married Jung, too, who offered himself in many ways as a model to patients like Harry, had for many years another woman besides his wife. Robinson quotes Lewis Mumford's review of Jung's autobiography, which faults the omission of any mention of Toni Wolff, and Robinson sees that as "symptomatic" in Jung of the "kind of self-absorption that Harry wished to avoid." Unknown to Mumford, and Robinson, is there that unpublished volume of Jung's autobiography, which the Jung family has not allowed out yet, which does explicitly describe Toni Wolff as well as others in Jung's life.

If Harry did, as Robinson thinks, believe that the relationship with Christiana was "a new religion," and that he and she "had been called as a couple to take a leading role in the history of the human spirit," then he was, as far as I can tell, sadly misguided. *Love's Story Told* reads to me like a tale of Harry having taken advantage of Christiana, which, even if it were true, would be at odds with his behavior in his second marriage, which gets all-too-brief attention here. There is abundant material in *Love's Story Told* about the combat between Harry and the most scientistic psychologists at Harvard in his day, but those struggles take a backseat to Robinson's theme of the tie to Christiana. Yet at the same time Robinson tells us that a central principle of Harry's had been to turn from the abnormal to the normal, from failure to success.

Biography is a perilous business, and perhaps Robinson's work, to those who knew Harry better than I, will seem more successful. Melville, may, under the circumstances, be an appropriate authority to cite in behalf of how only once Harry had died could a faithful narrative be constructed: "Biography, in its purer form, confined to the ended lives of the true and the brave, may be held the fairest meed of human virtue—one given and received in entire disinterestedness—since neither can the biographer hope for acknowledgement from the subject, nor the subject at all avail himself of the biographical distinction conferred."

## Notes

1. Forrest G. Robinson, *Love's Story Told: A Life of Henry A. Murray* (Cambridge, MA: Harvard University Press, 1993).
2. *Ibid.*

# 28

# Christiana Morgan

Serious studies of Jung are only now beginning to appear and can be expected to become a fascinating world all their own. Years ago we already knew a lot about Americans who went to Vienna to study with Freud and his pupils, but little has yet appeared about the different sorts of Americans who were attracted to Jung's thought and travelled to Zurich to get in touch with him. By and large Jung appealed to a higher social class than Freud did, and Jung's admirers were less likely to include Jews. The whole tale of Jung and his contact with America remains an important if largely unwritten chapter in modern intellectual history.

Claire Douglas's *Translate This Darkness*[1] is pathbreaking; it describes the life of Christiana Morgan, whom the book jacket describes as "the veiled woman in Jung's circle." She first arrived in Jung's world in 1926 and at the beginning saw Jung "several times a week for two-hour sessions, with an occasional visit to Toni Wolff." Although Christiana spent less than a year with Jung, with his encouragement she was able to enter trances that produced a series of visions that Jung found memorable. Christiana had had some formal training as an artist, and she compiled volumes of her visions that Jung later made the subject of several years of seminar work. Unfortunately, the Jung family has not released most of the correspondence between Christiana and Jung, so that what is known about them remains sketchy.

*Translate This Darkness* is not primarily concerned with Christiana as a Jungian or with Jung's circle as a whole. The book is instead an enthralling story of Christiana's life and how she succeeded in making her mark in modern psychology. In the end, as we know, she appears to have killed herself, drowning in shallow water while on a holiday in 1967 with her longstanding love Harry Murray, with whom she had for years collaborated. Claire Douglas has written an engrossing biography, the tale of Christiana's triumphant struggle to be creative, which finally resulted in tragedy and historical neglect.

Christiana came from a Boston Brahmin family that could trace its ancestry back to the Mayflower. Although she was a favorite of her father's, typically for a woman born in 1897 her family refused to take her seriously as a professional. Not only was a college education considered out of the question, but, Douglas believes, within her family circle can be detected that "subtle footbinding of Christiana's talents" which marred her whole life. *Translate This Darkness* recounts how Christiana and the circumstances of her time collaborated to render her a victim.

The after-effects of her having scarlet fever as a child weakened her health. And as a young woman she was treated for a depressive episode. Instead of attributing her problems to Christiana's restriction "in too narrow a sphere," the medical opinion was that she had been "improperly exciting her mind in a world too large for her." The remedy was that she "be closeted away from the world, to avoid stimulation, give up reading, and, above all, not use her mind." Winter depressions were recurrent.

During World War I Christiana did some nursing, but she still felt frustrated in her struggle to find meaningful work. She seems never to have had to earn her own living. Like "so many women of her generation," Christiana "believed she could and should live through her man." So in 1919 she married William Morgan after his return from serving on the Allied military frontlines. Sixteen months after her wedding, Christiana bore a son; then she had "a full-blown postpartum depression."

Christiana read both Freud and Jung and also allowed herself a couple of extra-marital affairs, one with Chaim Weizmann, who later became the first president of Israel. Christiana and her husband were social acquaintances of Harry Murray and his wife. Christiana shared Harry's interest in Melville, and they both responded to Jung's writings. In 1925 Harry went to consult with Jung about his attraction to Christiana, and Harry's wife subsequently blamed "Jung for much that was to follow." Jung had married someone rather like Harry's wife and succeeded in keeping Toni Wolff as well. Jung thought that Christiana could help inspire Harry. After Harry returned from Zurich, Christiana went to see Jung herself, as did her husband.

Douglas is a Jungian analyst, but she does not try to whitewash how Jung behaved. Seeing Christiana as a pioneering woman whose function was "to create a man," Jung seems to have put her into the background. "Though Jung could not have been more helpful to her in his interpretations and support concerning many of her problems, and although his warmth, interest, and liking for her were healing, the analysis faltered when Jung's own complexes and the cultural norms of the time interfered and became arbiters of psychological health." Christiana was capable of inspiring both Jung and Harry "but she got overlooked in the process."

Christiana assisted Harry in setting up the Harvard Psychological Clinic. Christiana and Harry also had a small apartment where they could meet in Harvard Square. For a time they were both members of the Boston Psychoanalytic Society, but their main interest was in creating their own center for humanistic clinical psychology. Christiana's most original work was in her helping Harry create the Thematic Apperception Test.

Alongside their professional collaboration, Christiana and Harry led a torrid-seeming private life. He gave her the money for building a tower like Jung's; it was to be an affirmation of the union between Christiana and Harry, which they fancied was going to be a model for future lovers. Although *Translate This Darkness* does not underplay Christiana's friendships with people like Alfred North Whitehead and Lewis Mumford, the book focuses on her affair with Harry. While, according to Douglas, Harry sought to destroy the record he kept of their sadomasochistic practices, Christiana's copies of certain passages meant that we know how whips, handcuffs, and cross-dressing were included in their quest for individuation, which took them beyond coventional ethics. Douglas proposes that "perhaps neither could bear the tawdry reality of being simply another married lover and his mistress…."

After Harry's wife died in 1962, he did not marry Christiana, but instead fell in love with another woman, with whom he later had a successful second marriage. Harry's work never fulfilled its promise; and although he succeeded in inspiring a whole generation of graduate students, he failed to complete the theory of personality he set out to construct. For years Christiana, who had blood pressure problems, self-destructively smoked and drank too much. Toward the end of his life Harry, who lived on until 1988, felt guilt-ridden about his relationship with Christiana. It is a tribute to Douglas that her biography restores Christiana to her rightful place in the history of ideas.

I worry, though, about Douglas's theme of victimization, and whether it can do justice to the full complexities of human experience. It should go without saying that men as well as women have sometimes not received their proper place in intellectual history. One accusation Douglas makes against Harry may well be not only groundless, but undermine Christiana's full stature. When their joint book on the Thematic Apperception Test reappeared, only Harry's name was on the cover. According to what I have been told, this was not because Harry was stealing the limelight, but for the reason that Christiana sensibly did not want to be bothered by the sterile academic letters that would arrive in connection with that text. So Christiana was not so powerless after all, and perhaps an equal amount of charity should go toward both these pioneers.

## Note

1. Claire Douglas, *Translate This Darkness: The Life of Christiana Morgan* (New York: Simon & Schuster, 1993).

# 29

# Menninger

The study of the history of psychiatry has been appallingly slack. Because medical schools are centrally concerned with the nuts-and-bolts issues of training future physicians, the history of medicine in general is apt to be neglected. Psychiatry poses special problems for sustaining the importance of the past because of the existence of rival schools of thought. Each of these factions, even when genuinely concerned with history, has been prone to ignore developments in neighboring quarters of thought. The result is, for example, that although the general public now knows a good deal about the story of Freud and his following, those figures not immediately associated with the creator of psychoanalysis have been left in scholarly limbo. Critics of early psychoanalytic thinking, even when their points are today silently acknowledged, go unremembered. Virtually no psychiatric literature exists about someone as important as Karl Jaspers, or even a member of Freud's Vienna Psychoanalytic Society like Paul Schilder. And Adolf Meyer, arguably the most important person in the history of twentieth century North American psychiatry, has yet to attract anything close to the attention he deserves.

Lawrence J. Friedman's *Menninger*[1] is an outstanding exception to the general state of neglect in this area. Friedman is a professional historian without any partisan ideological commitments. He was given free access to the files at the Menninger Foundation, although legal restrictions kept most patients' records out of bounds; Friedman also interviewed many people who once worked there.

Karl Menninger, known in his circle as Dr. Karl, died in July 1990. As an American he was relatively ignored by Freud's European disciples; worse, despite the significance of his role in promoting psychoanalytic thinking within American psychiatry, Menninger's writings have too often been ignored in authors' reference lists. Fortunately, although unbiased historical scholarship in this area is only in its early stages, Friedman's *Menninger* comes across as a scrupulously conscientious re-creation of the story of the founding and growth of today's Menninger Foundation.

The tale begins with Charles Menninger, Karl's father, also a physician, who shortly after marrying became a well-respected practitioner. Karl's mother, Flo, taught Bible study classes. She had "a proud and active career as a missionary reformer" but suffered from serious mood swings. Her struggles with depression were notable. Friedman, probably correctly, does not impose a retrospective psychiatric diagnosis on her, although I can recall one eminent psychiatrist explaining Karl to me in terms of his mother's having been "manic depressive." She recognized how much Karl was like her. I should think the hereditary link more probable than Alice Miller's unlikely theories about early child development that Friedman somehow chooses to cite in explaining Karl's psyche.

Karl studied at the University of Wisconsin and then Harvard Medical School. He was importantly influenced by Elmer Ernest Southard. At a time when custodial care had a higher priority than medical therapeutics, and when psychiatry itself stood at the bottom rung of the medical prestige ladder, Karl undertook to build on the nineteenth century boardinghouse tradition to create a family business that would be oriented toward curing mental patients. The Phipps Clinic had opened at Johns Hopkins in 1913, and Karl was keenly taken with what Adolf Meyer was doing there. At the time, only Sheppard-Pratt and the McLean Hospital were also interested in conducting research.

By the early 1920s the Menningers were running a Diagnostic Clinic in Topeka, Kansas. From the outset Karl was optimistically concerned with prognosis. Then in 1925 they set up a corporation that bought a farm-site for the twelve-bed sanitarium. Although there were private shareholders, "the family assumed control over all aspects of the hospital as well as the clinic." Karl's younger brother Will had also become a physician and proved an exceptionally able administrator. In 1930 Karl published his first book, *The Human Mind*, which became "the best-selling mental health volume in American history."

In Kansas the Menningers were devoted to "stressing the social environment as the primary area for psychiatric innovation." While reactionary thinking at the time saw everything in terms of heredity, the Menningers were determined, in the great American tradition of relying on self-help, to create a milieu that would in itself be conducive to producing good therapeutic results. Later on, by the time psychopharmacological drugs became available, the Menninger Clinic was still so tied to its earlier convictions as to be too slow in implementing these new methods of treatment. But at the time the Clinic was first created, the Menningers were in the forefront of humanitarian care, even if only for those wealthy enough to be able to afford their facilities.

From the outset, the Menningers were notable for their contributions to raising the level of psychiatric education in America. For years Robert Knight was their leading psychotherapist; David Rapaport also worked there. A list of those who studied at the Menninger Clinic, as well as their teachers, would make up a special honor role within American psychiatry and abroad. In addition the Menningers, even though later resentful of how the European analysts succeeded in getting all the literary attention, made a special effort to provide a haven at Topeka for refugees from the ravages of Hitlerism. The Menningers eventually made it possible for a separate Topeka Institute of Psychoanalysis to be established.

A surprisingly large portion of *Menninger* is taken up with the course of the tension and rivalry between Karl and his brother Will. This book is not a formal biography but, by intention, an organizational and family history; therefore, the struggles between Karl and Will form an essential constituent of the tale. Karl was a man of boundless energy; books, papers, and letters poured out of him. But he could be temperamental and his judgment erratic, and he preferred innovation to routine. Will was needed as a more down-to-earth balance wheel. For Will's services in developing U.S. army diagnostic terminology he "became the first American psychiatrist in the twentieth century to be promoted to general."

Although the Menningers promoted a policy of having an unmarried staff, both Karl and Will had extramarital affairs. This is a side to Friedman's book that I doubt the Menningers anticipated. He has written a straightforwardly honest book, and although his interest in the sex lives of these leading psychiatrists is not a prurient one, I cannot but wonder how they thought a first-class researcher like Friedman was not going to come across the evidence of their personal transgressions. Will shared his brother Karl's capacity for denial. When this hypocrisy was pointed out—that as hospital director he had "officially prohibited staff from dating while [Will was] having a relationship with the head nurse...Will would not listen."

Friedman has not produced a muck-raking book, even if Karl cannot have liked its appearing in his own last days. Karl had censored the editors who brought out a book of his letters, so that even portions of correspondence that he allowed to appear have been cut out. On one point Friedman, instead of being tough on Karl, is much too credulous. In interviews with Friedman, Karl claimed that when he was in analysis with Ruth Mack Brunswick he had some sense of her own morphine addiction. (I consider that pure hindsight on Karl's part.) Her addiction was a closely held secret. Though Freud continued to send her patients, no independently minded professional would have chosen to go to such an analyst for personal treatment.

Karl never had a personal association with Freud; they met once, when Karl was ushered in to see Freud at the tail-end of an exchange between Alexander and Freud. But Freud took an aloof and impersonal attitude toward Menninger, perhaps because of difficulties Freud was having with Alexander over the latter's going to the States from Berlin. Although Freud was an extraordinarily devoted letter-writer, he failed to respond to a couple of letters from Karl.

With Anna Freud, however, Karl succeeded in maintaining a successful tie. He had established the Southard School for children, and both he and Anna sought foundation support from similar sources. Karl would go to great lengths to affirm his loyalty to Anna, whom he emotionally identified with his analyst, Ruth Mack Brunswick. Long after he had been displaced from real power at the Menninger Clinic and was being kept on as a kind of show-piece, Karl and his second wife maintained control of the *Bulletin of the Menninger Clinic*.

Karl's theoretical writings are hard to categorize. In line with a strand in Freud's own thinking that most orthodox analysts failed to pick up, Karl elaborated the significance of the death instinct. Unlike Freud, however, Karl used the significance of aggression to downplay the importance of sexuality. And Karl differed from Freud in treating religion as a positive and enhancing aspect of human strength, instead of dismissing it as a neurotic crutch. For years Karl harried so-called traitors like Karen Horney and Erich Fromm; yet by the end of his life Karl, an advocate of the use of psychology instead of law, was writing Thomas Szasz about how ahead-of-his-times Szasz was.

Friedman notes in Karl a basic insecurity, and I think he hated to be left out of things. When the psychoanalytic tide was in the direction of orthodoxy, he rode it, and when it went in a pluralistic direction, he tried to take advantage of that, too. I do not mean to imply that Karl was necessarily behaving opportunistically so much as I think he did not like being isolated. One of his books, *Theory of Psychoanalytic Technique* (1958), was written in a conservative vein and, I think, amounts to a compendium of recommended therapeutic errors. A later book, *The Vital Balance* (1963), composed in a different spirit, may be his best one. Some of his selected papers in *A Psychiatrist's World* (1959) make required reading for a historian of twentieth-century American psychiatry. But all Menninger's efforts did not in the end win him acceptance by the European analysts who dominated the scene from New York City.

Probably the single most startling sections in *Menninger* concern the incestuous-like ways in which people in Topeka struggled to get psychoanalytic training. While Karl was succeeding in making the Menninger Foundation into "a national center for psychiatric education" that raised standards throughout the country, those in training in Topeka were divorcing spouses, remarrying, all within the tight circle of people who knew each other's private business intimately. Friedman is too generous in blaming Karl's own inclinations toward indiscretion on the similar behavior of Karl's own analysts.

Although Karl liked to think of himself as being in the progressive vanguard, it turns out that he did not want his staff involved in the landmark Brown v. Topeka Board of Education suit that ultimately resulted in the Supreme Court's declaring racial segregation in public schools unconstitutional. Also, Friedman provides evidence of how Karl "tolerated the anti-Communist hysteria of a post-war decade, especially from Washington and within the VA system."

Friedman thinks that toward the end of his life Karl "lacked intellectual vitality." That may be correct, but I think it remarkable that Karl remained an indomitable force for so long, as mercurial and as capable of charm as ever. The last time I saw Karl he was a spectacle. At the age of 90 (he lived on to be 96) Karl showed up in 1983 at the fiftieth anniversary of the Boston Psychoanalytic Society. I thought he stole the show. "They told me," he slowly and tellingly began his little talk, "not to speak too long." We all laughed at Karl's subtle triumphing over suspicions about his possible senility. It is still hard for me to imagine, even now, that he is really gone. To those immediately around him he must have been a holy terror; but that strength in him made an indelible mark on the course of psychiatry in our time.

## Note

1. Lawrence J. Friedman, *Menninger: The Family and the Clinic* (New York: Knopf, 1990).

# 30

# Karen Horney

It continues to be the case that the historiography of psychoanalysis contains certain underdogs who are in need of special attention. On the other hand, there is a growing number of books connected with those so-called deviants who at one time or another broke with the ranks of the orthodox "mainstream." Often, nobody can quite remember who the representatives of the "mainstream" might once have been, since they left so little in the way of memorable writings of their own. But everyone would agree that psychoanalysis has had its share of difficult people who were capable of becoming organizationally troublesome.

Karen Horney is in a special category all her own. For, although she once was humiliated by the New York Psychoanalytic Society and departed to form her own training facilities, by now some of her writings are increasingly apt to be cited among the necessary texts to be mentioned in connection with the early history of essays on female psychology. Thus, although listing citations to, say, Jung, Adler, Rank, Fromm, or Lacan would be almost sure to raise eyebrows among those in a position today to review most scientific papers, Horney now seems no longer an unacceptable forebear. On the contrary, analysts are likely to find in Horney's work ammunition to show that early psychoanalysis was not as dim-witted about the psychology of women as feminist critics have been trying to make it seem.

Bernard Paris, who became President of a short-lived International Karen Horney Society, has had the great merit to have ignored all stereotypes about Horney's work. His book[1] is a genuine contribution to intellectual history; he has sought to understand Horney's work in the round. He is not just interested in those of Horney's ideas which have found widespread acceptance lately, but he seeks to show us aspects of Horney's mature theory that we know too little about. Above all, he has interwoven her life and work in such a way as to use her biography to illuminate her writings; at the same time, he finds beneath some of her theorizing a glimpse of her own most candid self-revelations.

Horney (1885-1952) was one of the founding members of the Berlin Psychoanalytic Society and an analysand of both Karl Abraham and Hanns Sachs. Her private diaries (still only partially in print) record the nature of the emotional conflicts she had as a young woman and a beginning analyst. From the outset she seems unusual in her capacity to transcend conventional moral expectations. Although it would be unfair to minimize the psychological pain that her convictions caused her, she soon came to believe that "free love was morally superior to a marriage without love." She began to lead a Bohemian life and continued to do so even after her marriage to Oskar Horney; both husband and wife had discreet liaisons, and although finally separated in 1926 they did not get divorced until 1938. In addition to her professional duties, Horney also raised three daughters; even if reasonably successful by most standards in her mothering, Horney never was able to establish a permanent relationship with a male partner she considered an equal. One of the remaining mysteries to Horney's life has to do with the exact circumstances of her long-standing involvement with Erich Fromm, which ought to make up in itself a chapter in modern intellectual history.

How any of us interprets a life history is bound to be at least in part a subjective exercise, so I am trying to be cautious about what I learned here about Horney. But from what Paris's book tells us, I take it that she was not an easy colleague to work with. The nature of her quarrels with Abraham and Freud, for example, are even more complex than Paris sometimes understands. For instance, it was not necessary for Horney to attack certain papers of Helene Deutsch's, since both women were in fact concerned with similar sorts of insights; but Helene Deutsch was dressing up what she said with Freud's own chosen terminology, whereas Horney went out of her way to assert her independence. For Horney to challenge Deutsch was pretty much the same as Melanie Klein's criticizing Anna Freud. Although Deutsch was only a personal favorite of Freud's, and not as close as his beloved daughter, for a disciple like Horney to challenge the work of someone who was known to be so allied to Freud was in effect to be seen as a potential threat to the master himself.

In fact, during Horney's middle period she became a trenchant critic of Freud's whole system of thought. Paris is throughout fair and even-handed, and he spells out how Horney's *The Neurotic Personality of Our Time* (1937) and *New Ways in Psychoanalysis* (1939) amounted to a full-scale assault on key features to the Freudian worldview. By that stage of Freud's old age, he himself was not keen on dealing with any new "heretics," but unfortunately there were always others around, no matter how limited their own capacities, to defend the orthodox faith. Toleration as an ideal is incapable of flourishing in a context in which people are still convinced that such an entity as revealed truth exists; but by now, when, with the distance of time, it is apparent that none of the great crises in the history of psychoanalysis can be understood merely as the occasion for reaffirming the legitimacy of what was then the status quo, it behooves us to start thinking about where Horney had some thoroughly worthwhile theoretical and practical grievances against psychoanalysis as it was then understood.

For example, Horney "regarded the Oedipus complex as a culturally conditioned phenomena," and therefore she saw the origins of neurosis in different sources than Freud had proposed. As the world Freud took for granted has wholly ceased to exist, it is more than ever apparent that he was capable of assuming certain institutions and values as immutably part of the human condition. Once she set up her own organizations, however, Horney's groups were as subject to schisms as orthodoxy itself. Paris seems to agree, for example, that because of the prominence of Fromm's *Escape From Freedom* Horney "drove him away because she was threatened by the success of his book and his popularity with students."

Paris's study is, in contrast to other books about Horney that I have read, particularly strong on those later works of Horney's which were so original as to be "not reviewed in establishment journals." In *Self-Analysis* (1942), *Our Inner Conflicts* (1945), and *Neurosis and Human Growth: The Struggle Toward Self-Realization* (1950) Horney outlined both interpersonal as well as intrapsychic defenses that people adopt to cope with basic insecurities. Unlike the traditional Freudian model, which centrally looks back to early childhood experience, Horney proposed that we examine the structured way adults have of neurotically coping with conflicts. Her concept of an "idealized image" seems to me particularly useful for those trying to understand political figures and historical actors. Paris is exceptionally good at finding illustrations for Horney-like conflicts within the range of modern literature, and he succeeds in making a persuasive case that "her mature theory represents her most significant contribution."

Paris's *Karen Horney* will doubtless trouble those who had idealized Horney. It puts in perspective what her specific contribution to femininity amounted to in the light of her broader aims. She thought that to continue to write exclusively about problems of feminine psychology would detract from the larger questions of human self-fulfillment that came to concern her so much. Paris brings her ideas into the framework of "third-force" psychologies like those of Abraham Maslow. Paris's book should also remind the remaining smug defenders of the orthodox "mainstream" that for students of intellectual history the story of psychoanalysis remains a rich mine for understanding the life of the mind.

## Note

1. Bernard J. Paris, *Karen Horney: A Psychoanalyst's Search for Self Understanding* (New Haven, CT: Yale University Press, 1994).

# 31

# Dorothy Burlingham

Dorothy Burlingham's life has to be put in the perspective appropriate to the history of analysis. She came to Freud's circle only in 1925; by then the most creative period in Freud's life was past, and he was already in his last, dying phase. Although Dorothy wrote on blind children and helped on Anna Freud's Hampstead Index, she did not go on to introduce anything major to psychoanalytic thought, and she had, except for Tom Freeman, few notable pupils. But she did become, almost immediately after arriving in Vienna, Anna Freud's most intimate friend, and because of that alone she was closely tied to the history of the movement until her death in 1979, three years before Anna Freud's own end.

*The Last Tiffany*[1] is a curious book, and yet I think it is one of the best biographies in the whole history of analysis. From an academic perspective it has notable flaws. The Tiffany family history, with which the first 110 pages of the book are concerned, does not live up to the highest standards of history-writing; it is too anecdotal and informal, not sufficiently tied to the most sophisticated understandings of American history. Yet the book is always easy to read, and those first 110 pages, which I found myself studying as a duty, could perhaps have been written only by a family member. For the biographer, Michael John Burlingham, is a grandson of Dorothy Burlingham, and by the time we do at last get to her birth, the author has indeed successfully prepared us for her life story.

Dorothy's grandfather, Charles Louis Tiffany, founded the family fortune with his store Tiffany & Co.; and then her father, Louis Comfort, made his mark with his glass. In her family background, then, she had a notorious pirate for a grandfather, who would, she would later say, "do anything to make money," and an equally autocratic father who was able to cultivate an essentially artistic temperament. Dorothy's mother died when Dorothy was not yet thirteen, leaving her deprived of needed maternal attentions. Her future husband, Robert Burlingham, was a young medical student from a wealthy family that traced its ancestors directly back to five of the *Mayflower* Pilgrims; he and she were married in 1914, when she was about to turn twenty-three.

In a little less than a year, Dorothy gave birth to her first child. At about the same time, her husband, suffering Dorothy thought from the pressures of medical school, had his first breakdown. Dorothy's biographer uses the diagnosis "manic-depressive psychosis." Robert Burlingham was recurrently ill; he continued, however, to function in his medical career. Dorothy had four children in all; in 1921, just before the birth of her fourth, she left her husband. From the Burlingham family's point of view, Dorothy's action was intolerably selfish. As her biographer puts it, "Dorothy was abandoning a man in desperate need of her support," and he tells us that "the Burlinghams...could never understand how a woman could have left her husband under such conditions, and it was for this that they later condemned her."

According to *The Last Tiffany,* Dorothy "having had a father but no mother,...had created as if by way of compensation the opposite situation for her children." But once she got to Vienna she sought in Anna Freud a maternal helpmate in rearing her four children. Anna Freud was, I think, continuing her identification with her Aunt Minna, who had helped Miss Freud's own mother raise her and her siblings.

It is not entirely clear how Dorothy first heard of Freud and analysis, other than that by the 1920s the climate of opinion was such that Freud was becoming widely popular in America. One of Dorothy's cousins was planning to go to Ferenczi in Budapest for an analysis. Dorothy had "some kind of analytic experience" in Connecticut before she decided on settling in Europe. Her eldest child, Bob, was "angry at Dorothy for separating him from his father," and the boy "had becone unmanageable." In the meantime, Dorothy's husband's illness had "forced him to give up his private practice, a humiliation that he never truly got over." He began a new career in medical research, "which, unlike the art of surgery, could be structured around his breakdowns. Loyal friends and relations rallied to him, taking him in while he recovered from depression." Knowing how devastating her departure from America would be for her husband, Dorothy "left without telling him." Like her autocratic father, Dorothy now made a selfish choice and found in psychoanalysis a new form of morality that could be used to justify her decision. She later claimed that her "reason for going to Vienna was entirely because of" her eldest son, Bob.

From the point of view of the relatives in the States, Dorothy's problems helped account for the family tragedy; as a friend put it to Dorothy's mother-in-law, one of Dorothy's allies in Europe did not seem at all to realize that "Dorothy's eccentricities have had anything to do with Robert's illnesses...."; according to this source, Dorothy's ally in Europe evidently had "no idea that Dorothy has ever been at all abnormal...." According to *The Last Tiffany*, "Dorothy then had great difficulty in expressing her affection—to the children as well as to Robert, and this, presumably, together with her abandonment of him, provided the basis for the charge of abnormality."

Anna Freud arranged to take Bob Burlingham into analysis and for Dorothy herself to be analyzed by Theodor Reik; almost immediately, Anna also took into analysis Dorothy's next oldest child, Mabbie. These were the beginnings of child analysis, about which Freud said he knew little. As he put it in a letter at the time to a relative in England, "Anna is treating naughty American children."

Subsequently, Dorothy's other children would be treated by Anna as well; and they all went to a special little private school, founded by Dorothy and Eva Rosenfeld, which was for children in analysis or whose parents were in Vienna being analyzed. Dorothy "was no doubt relieved to surrender to Anna a share of her parental responsibility and authority." But between the two of them the situation could be overpowering for the children. (The dual authority of Freud's wife Martha and her intimate sister Minna had been a difficult power situation for Freud's own children.) Bob Burlingham's loss of his father had left him with an unappeasable longing, which was interpreted by Anna (who wrote about the Burlingham children in her early case histories) as a homosexual matter. Bob's first tutor was fired for being "too handsome." Anna Freud later would not allow the boy to go away to boarding school on the grounds that there was the threat of homosexual temptation there.

When Anna sent a book of hers, *Introduction to the Technique of Child Analysis*, to Lou Andreas Salomé, Anna was pleasantly surprised by Lou's positive response to her case histories. Anna wrote to Lou, "I was not at all sure that you would be satisfied, especially because they are children, whom I always want to change, while you prefer to leave as they are." Anna considered Mabbie Burlingham the "most successful" of the ten early cases. Anna had actively intervened in the child rearing of the Burlinghams; with Mabbie, for example, in behalf of the analysis Anna had shaken Mabbie's confidence in her nanny. In his foreword to his biography, Michael John Burlingham, a son of Bob's, mentions family "resentments" about his grandmother, who came to worship Anna Freud. The author's Aunt Mabbie, after years of analysis, eventually killed herself in 1975 while staying at Freud's house on Maresfield Gardens, where both Dorothy and Anna still lived.

Dorothy herself, however those around her were to suffer, immediately hit it off with Anna Freud. Freud himself was delighted that Anna had found such a good friend, and he was relieved also that her financial future would now be secure. (*The Last Tiffany* is unduly reticent about what became of Dorothy's money, but her biological descendants do not seem to have received much.) Dorothy stayed in analysis with Reik until 1927, when she switched over to being treated by Freud himself; she remained in analysis with him for twelve years, until his death in 1939. Freud described Dorothy in a letter at the outset of the analysis as "a quite congenial American woman, an unhappy virgin." (I thought she gave off the appearance of a nun-like chastity.) According to Freud, what became established was a "symbiosis," as he put it in a letter, "with an

American family (husbandless), whose children my daughter is bringing up analytically with a firm hand...."

Back in America Dorothy's husband was writing to his own father, "I think our attitude should be one of tender solicitude for Dorothy's condition, but at the same time we should make an iron stand on the question of no more psychoanalysis for the children, all four of them, and their return to me while Dorothy is getting the first care she has ever had...." Robert Burlingham came over to Vienna for a consultation with Freud, who was favorably impressed by him and made "a surprisingly positive diagnosis." But from the Burlingham point of view, Dorothy had "first driven him [Robert] 'over the precipice' and then starved him of his own children." Freud was himself a participant in the family tragedy to the extent that he helped maintain "an absolute barrier between husband and wife." When Freud saw Robert, the founder of psychoanalysis felt he had to be on guard lest anything he say be used against Dorothy in a custody suit.

The ethics of what Freud and Anna were doing requires some examination. Mabbie, for example, was, according to this biography, so characterized by "sensitive empathy" as to make "her a virtual ambassador of child analysis, a paradigm of the pedagogic analysis envisaged and practiced byAnna Freud." Even without knowing of Mabbie's subsequent suicide, it is disquietingly touching to read of her writing of herself as she floundered as a child in her encounter with the unconscious: "I with my many troublys [sic] and unknown reasons. Everything has an unknown reason. Oh, reason after reason, everything with its reasons. It nearly makes me mad."

It is perhaps too easy to forget that the circumstances of an analysis with Freud were unique; a clinical contract with the creator of analysis was unlike that with anyone else. But Dorothy's involvement with Freud while her children were in treatment with Anna does make the situation look far too close. John Michael Burlingham no doubt intends some irony when he describes Dorothy's children in Anna Freud's own words as analytically "protected." By 1940 Dorothy was able to write that the school she had helped found in Vienna had been "a mistake." But her overall confidence in her judgment remained immense. After Hitler came to power, the Burlinghams back in the States were more worried than ever; her father-in-law wrote her that she had "failed" to treat her husband "fairly and justly in the matter of the children. You observe that I leave the rest of us out. We adore the Four and you know how little we have seen of them." Dorothy and her children remained dependent on Anna Freud, who seems never to have reconsidered the grandiosity of her own aims. In 1938 Dorothy's husband, unable to sleep for days, killed himself.

During World War II, Dorothy and Anna ran their facility for children separated from their families. (By then her own children were back in the States.) For the first time, Anna Freud uncovered the role played by separation from the mother in the creation of symptoms. The 1950s and 1960s, "when psychoanalysis was at its height," became "the years of Dorothy's personal and analytic fulfillment." As this biography puts it, "Her Freudian orthodoxy had decisively stamped the family, and yet she was physically removed from it. Her grandchildren felt that distance, and not the sacrifice she had made of a family life."

In 1947 Mabbie returned to Anna Freud for more analysis, the first of what became annual summer analyses. According to Michael John Burlingham, "Anna Freud should not have been the one analyzing Mabbie, or Bob, or possibly any of Dorothy's children." Their spouses tended also to turn to analysts, such as Kurt Eissler in New York. Bob in particular found himself troubled by manic-depressive problems, but "Anna Freud continued to treat him from the psychoanalytic angle, despite the increased suggestion of a biochemical, genetic etiology." Bob continued to smoke in the face of asthma and emphysema and died of an asthma-induced heart attack in 1970 at the age of 54. Five years later Mabbie, after failing to succeed in an analysis with Anna Freud's friend Marianne Kris in New York, returned to Anna Freud in London where Mabbie killed herself. "Amidst the shambles, Bob's and Mabbie's children particularly found it hard to see Dorothy and Anna Freud in a positive light...psychoanalysis had been foisted upon them unnecessarily, and when dependent upon it, had not helped them." Pharmacology was not tried.

Different readers will doubtless come to contrasting conclusions about this book and the story it recounts. It is to me an instructive tale of professional success and private failure. Michael John Burlingham does not once mention the names of Horace Frink or Victor Tausk, to cite two other tragic episodes in the history of analysis; and the story of Ruth Mack Brunswick shares certain similarities. *The Last Tiffany* is an immensely moving human document. Michael John Burlingham has not written a book that aims to blame; instead, we have a tale that ought to be chastening for all who try to impose idealistic theories on fallible human beings. No one did anything out of ill will. One comes away from the book as from a good novel, with a deeper understanding of the complexities of human motives and how even the most brilliant people can retain the full capacity for self-deception.

## Note

1. Michael John Burlingham, *The Last Tiffany: A Biography of Dorothy Tiffany Burlingham* (New York: Atheneum, 1989).

# 32

# Anna Freud

Psychoanalytic liberals have a lot to answer for. Out of a spirit of tolerance, combined with an understandable distaste for controversy, they have neglected to monitor books on the history of psychoanalysis. And therefore academic authors eager to please the established powers–that-be in orthodox psychoanalysis have felt free to puruse their zealous cause without fear of reprisal from reviewers. Historiographic atrocities have been licensed not just by the encouragement of the defenders of "classical" analysis but by the reviewing silence of the free-thinkers within the field.

I believe that this background helps to account for Elisabeth Young-Bruehl's heavily biased biography of Anna Freud.[1] It is of course an official biography, authorized by Anna Freud's literary executor, Lottie Newman. And it is natural for every biographer—for whom the biographical subject is apt to assume overwhelming significance—to glamorize and exaggerate the life he or she has undertaken to describe. Writing a biography means choosing to live with a ghost; and however difficult it may be to get along with people of power in real life, in our imaginations it is pleasurably possible to conjure up beings of almost omnipotent stature. And so Anna Freud becomes, in Young-Bruehl's view, "her generation's most scientifically exact and wide-ranging theoretical and clinical contributor."

The means by which Young-Bruehl establishes Anna Freud's standing ought to be memorable, for they are telling about the general state of psychoanalytic literature as a whole. For example, Young-Bruehl simply abolishes the existence of many who might be thought of as plausible rivals to Anna Freud's stature. Young-Bruehl is capable of giving us three pages about Anna Freud's views on psychoanalysis and feminist thought, without once, anywhere in this whole book, mentioning the name of Karen Horney. Likewise, we are given three pages about a paper of Anna Freud's on six parentless children who survived a concentration camp; Young-Bruehl calls the essay nothing less than "one of the most unusual and fascinating papers in the history of psychoanalysis." Yet since not once does Young-Bruehl even mention the name of Bruno Bettelheim; her judgment looks to me highly questionable.

Erich Fromm's name also does not appear in this text. (Nor does Abram Kardiner exist for Young-Bruehl.) Even Young-Bruehl's bibliography omits any mention of Fromm. But entirely aside from Fromm's clinical and theoretical contributions, he wrote *Sigmund Freud's Mission* as a brief rebuttal to Jones's authorized biography of Freud. It should go without saying that nobody is required to agree with what Fromm had to say, although he did, I think, make a number of tellingly persuasive points. But Fromm took the trouble to try to keep track of the historical literature on psychoanalysis, even though in those days there was nothing like the flood of writings that are now appearing. I do not think that psychoanalytic liberals know the ferocity with which the orthodox historiography is proceeding to rewrite the past.

Since such matters go uncorrected in professional journals, how on earth are general readers going to be able to notice what is going on? They may pick up an unfairness here and there, but they are never going to be able to spot the kind of glaring omissions that I have tried to point out. Young-Bruehl's book is in my opinion lacking in fair historical judgment; yet its polemicism has gone almost unnoticed. Stalinist historiography successfully proceeded by leaving out of account important figures in the Soviet past; but although abundant revisionism has been underway ever since Gorbachev's regime, I see little sign of such progress within the history of analysis.

A significant part of this biography is devoted to Freud's analysis of Anna. Young-Bruehl not only makes no mention of my work in this connection, but she implies that I invented interviews that (supposedly) never took place. The evidence she offers is unthinking; it seems that once I started to publish, Anna Freud wrote around to her friends inquiring as to whether they had ever seen me. It would appear that some of them, according to Young-Bruehl, wrote back saying that they had not. If that is so, then they were trying to protect themselves from appearing to have betrayed Anna Freud. But the important point is that Young-Bruehl at no point made any effort to try to contact me directly before putting such a serious charge against me into print. In normal circles of history-writing such failure to check evidence would be considered scandalous. But as long as psychoanalytic liberals allow such practices to go unchallenged, writers are going to feel free to proceed as they wish in building up a picture to suit the needs of their particular ideology.

Young-Bruehl's book is full of sloppy mistakes, entirely aside its lack of fairness. It is rubbish to single out Freud's sister Dolfi as "the one he appreciated most," but this detail assumes significance when Young-Bruehl compares Dolfi, whose personality was sacrificed to taking care of Freud's mother, to Anna's own role in her father's life.

More importantly for the history of the discipline as a whole, Young-Bruehl tells us that "Freud had argued strongly for years that a personal analysis should be required of every psychoanalytic practitioner, and his Viennese colleague Herman Nunberg brought a proposal to that effect before the Budapest meeting in 1918." In fact it was Carl Jung who before World War I first proposed the idea that all future analysts be analyzed, and Freud himself in print credited "the Zurich school" with this innovative suggestion.

When a niece of Freud's commits suicide, the fact that she was in analysis, as well as the name of the analyst, get left out of Young-Bruehl's book. Throughout her text people who are nonentities get blown up far out of proportion to their intellectual importance (compared to those who have been ignored). When Anna Freud turned on Heinz Kohut and dubbed his work "antipsychoanalytic," Young-Bruehl passes along this assessment as if it were canonical. She also buys the wild idea that Ernest Jones had a "negative attitude" toward Freud. She presents without comment or criticism Anna Freud's suggestion that a "Defense League" of a few people be set up to "defend" her father's life, as if such an informal organization had not already long existed. A close reading of *Anna Freud* has convinced me that Young-Bruehl is not only a partisan in behalf of Anna Freud's viewpoint, but that Young-Bruehl has added her own distorted twist to things.

As the history of psychoanalysis becomes more a legitimate field of scholarly inquiry, professional practitioners should be obliged to help ensure the education of intellectual historians. As George Orwell knew, those who control the past have special power over the future. It behooves us to watch out that advocates of orthodox analysis do not succeed in making the past disappear down truth-holes.

## Note

1. Elisabeth Young-Bruehl, *Anna Freud: A Biography* (New York: Summit Books, 1988).

# 33

# Deutsch, Klein, Horney, Anna Freud

Janet Sayers's *Mothers of Psychoanalysis: Helene Deutsch, Karen Horney, Anna Freud, Melanie Klein*[1] is a miracle of a book. The author has woven together the intellectual biographies of four notable women from the early history of psychoanalysis, in order to link their individual ideas to their respective lives, and at the same time show us how they succeeded as a group in shifting the center of gravity of Freud's school. I have long suspected that Freud himself would not have published on female psychology in the 1920s if he had not felt that he had pioneering women in his movement who were about to jump the gun on this critical area of his subject. And so Freud ventured forth and was to provide critics with a notable stick by which they couild later beat all his psychological constructions. Each of these early women analysts in *Mothers of Psychoanalysis* were full of ideas about a wide range of clinical and theoretical subjects and helped promote work that is now widely accepted professionally.

Janet Sayers does not herself indulge in any of the political phrase-making that has, I think, marred so much of contemporary feminist thought. She has written a series of essays in intellectual history and successfully tied them all together. The book will seems dense at spots to some, and perhaps elementary to others in separate sections, but I consider it remarkable that Sayers can sustain such an extremely high level of discussion and do so evenhandedly. For not only is *Mothers of Psychoanalysis* without polemics or partisanship, but Sayers seems to me consistently balanced in her treatment of these four women.

I had to be especially touched by the cardinal role Sayers chose to give to Helene Deutsch, since I first in 1985, and then in a 1992 revision, published Deutsch's authorized biography. Since 1981 I have been publishing English versions of Helene Deutsch's uncollected papers. I had known Deutsch for some years before we undertook together that I write her biography, and I had a chance to go through her private files, as well as her published writings, in the course of interviewing her for my book. I set out to show how Deutsch's life was more complicated than one might guess from certain hostile feminist critics of her writings; in addition, by the end of my study I concluded that her ideas were in fact far more different from Freud's own than I had ever guessed.

Sayers has understood the proper center of gravity to Deutsch's life and work, and she proceeds to give a fair-minded summary and evaluation of her contributions. But I was equally impressed with how dispassionately Sayers could approach Karen Horney, Anna Freud, and Melanie Klein. These four women had complicated personal relationships with one another and often criticized each other's writings. But throughout *Mothers of Psychoanalysis*, Sayers never adopts any particular ideological slant and proceeds to describe the work in its best possible light. At the same time, she is not unaware of the criticisms that have been leveled at each of these thinkers and does pause to show she is up to date on the limitations to the approaches these women took.

Psychoanalysis has been a field notorious for a series of controversies that were more theological than scientific. People became analysts in the early days because they truly believed in the power of enlightenment, and they sought to save their souls through the secular profession that Freud had devised.

But the literature about the history of psychoanalysis is still impoverished because of the multiple biases that so many observers bring to bear in this area. Analysts who were the most fanatical, for example, formed their own schools with disciples and these apostles proceeded to disseminate the truth as they saw it. Among loyalists to Freud's memory, fanaticism took the form of a defense of orthodoxy, but all these intolerances grew on the soil of undissolved therapeutic transferences. The most unlikely ideas could get proselytized, while those analysts who were least interested in creating a special following of their own, like Deutsch, are apt to get neglected precisely because of their tolerance, broad-mindedness, and lack of sectarian ambitions. Erik H. Erikson's reputation is currently in a slump because of his failure to produce a group of acolytes. At the same time, the standings of certain orthodox analysts have been inflated by those who ignore the sweep of the history of ideas.

At no point does Sayers try to make any of her four thinkers look foolish. There were occasions when she might have challenged more forcefully some of the central convictions of these theorists. But I think she made the correct choice, at this stage of the historiography of psychoanalysis, to lay out the central different lines of thought that these analysts had in mind. The book will seem daunting as it is, yet I found it a triumph of clarity and generosity of spirit.

I hope that *Mothers of Psychoanalysis* will stimulate others to explore this neglected area of inquiry. In New York City, for instance, Horney's ideas may now be widely acknowledged to be in some sense central, but in England the figures who were dominant while they remained alive were Freud's daughter Anna and her chief rival in child analysis, Melanie Klein.

To my mind Deutsch was the one of these four most in need of being revived, since she did the least of them all to create a following in her own likeness. For Deutsch's ideas were subtle and complex, in spite of the stereotyped way her views were condemned for so many years by propagandists of one cause or another. Sayers is appreciative of Deutsch's sensitivity to conflicts over sexuality and self-esteem posed by maternity, and Sayers knows how Deutsch's work on narcissism underlies today's concern with "borderline" problems. There are a number of small points on which I would disagree with Sayers, but to go through such details would distract from what should be, I think, an overall objective of pointing out when a book is an unusual scholarly contribution.

Future students of the history of psychoanalysis may well want to use Sayers's book to ask more about Freud himself. For instance, what were his own relations to his mother, to his wife, as well as to mothers in his family and the psychoanalytic circle? Here again I think we should not fall back on any traditional cliches, which are too apt to be readily at hand, about what Freud was actually like. As the years pass, and more of his voluminous correspondence is published, I think it will become evident just how complicated a man Freud was and how much harder it is than one might think to account for the ways in which his ideas took shape.

Also, I suspect that it will not be too long before scholars, as opposed to clinicians who have had a narrow training in our current institutes, are going to take seriously the work advanced by those who for one reason or another left, or got thrown out of, the so-called mainstream of psychoanalysis. Although names like Carl Jung, Alfred Adler, and Otto Rank necessarily scarcely appear in *Mothers of Psychoanalysis*, each of them made important contributions to the issue of female psychology, and to modern psychoanalysis as a whole, which eventually should get examined and appreciated.

It is not possible yet to imagine a full-scale understanding of the history of psychoanalysis because of the delayed effects of so much ideological partisanship. Those like Sayers who work in universities are able to have the necessary independence of thought and spirit to approach this subject with the requisite kind of detachment and impartiality. A whole new group of scholars, like Sayers, will need to arise in order to get the study of the history of psychoanalysis out of the hands of the fanatics. Sectarianism often is most heavy-handed when it is least likely to be noticed; and silence toward "deviants" has been a deadly weapon by which thinkers have been relegated to the sidelines of the story.

For Sayers to have placed Helene Deutsch at the outset of *Mothers of Psychoanalysis* not only was in keeping with the tale of how the rise of mother-centered psychoanalysis took place, but also required courage on Sayers's part in defying the conventions of the discipline. I found Sayers's book consistently sound, unusually nonjudgmental, and I hope it has a great influence on how these four women are understood in coming years.

## Note

1. Janet Sayers, *Mothers of Psychoanalysis: Helene Deutsch, Karen Horney, Anna Freud, Melanie Klein* (New York: Norton, 1991).

# 34

# Erikson

Reading and then rereading Lawrence J. Friedman's *Identity's Architect: A Biography of Erik H. Erikson*[1] induced in me a mood of nostalgia. I had known him at Harvard throughout the 1960s, when he was an outstanding psychoanalyst who had helped breathe new life into all the social sciences. Erikson's close friends encouraged Friedman as a biographer, and Erikson's wife Joan was cooperative. *Identity's Architect* is comprehensively spacious as well as textured; thinking about the many biographies of psychoanalysts that have appeared over the past forty years, I cannot think of any that is better than Friedman's. The eighty-odd pages of "Notes" at the back of the book are in themselves a rich storehouse about the intellectual life of the last half-century.

It is unclear to me how Erikson's books appear now to those who never knew him. *Childhood and Society* (1950) has I think the status of a classic. But so does Erich Fromm's *Escape From Freedom*, published a decade earlier, and Fromm has long fallen out of fashion. While Fromm was able to reach the most general reading public through the power of his mind and his ability to popularize an important revision of psychoanalytic ideas, Erikson's appeal was more strictly confined to university audiences. He did however once make it to the cover of *Newsweek*. Erikson, who lacked the clarity of Fromm's conceptual powers, had the different strengths of his artistic background, and was uncomfortable in the role of being any kind of renegade in the history of psychoanalysis. So Erikson scarcely ever mentioned Fromm, although they both shared an interest in being moral prophets. Orthodox analysis continues to repudiate the significance of Fromm's contributions, while Erikson's writings are given at least peripheral standing by the powers-that-be among Freud's followers.

The slide in Erikson's public standing started in the mid-1970s, when a controversy first arose about whether he had been guilty of bad faith in having disguised his own entirely Jewish upbringing. Erikson's book sales have never recovered from what they were before. After that period Erikson proved unable to sustain his earlier productivity. There seems no doubt, although Friedman hesitates whether to call it senility or Alzheimer's, that Erikson's powers prematurely declined, and by the time of the years in the 1990s when Friedman worked on *Identity's Architect*, Erikson (1902-1994) was a pale shadow of his former self.

Friedman's success has been due to his thoroughness and even-handedness, and also his willingness to explore flaws in Erikson. Although Friedman does not ever explicitly use any such word as "vanity" in connection with Erikson, he communicates the spirit of the problem just the same. And even if I am hesitant how to bring it up, lest it be the central point readers take away, Friedman did succeed in unearthing a family secret known to only a tiny few of Erikson's associates. The Eriksons had had three children before a fourth, Neil, was born suffering from Down's Syndrome. The Eriksons immediately proceeded to institutionalize the child, and for a time they lied about Neil's dying to two of their kids; the Eriksons rarely saw Neil, then left him in California when the family moved to the East Coast. Neil died in his early twenties when the Eriksons were in Italy; they telephoned two of their children in California, who had by then been told about Neil's existence, to arrange for the funeral. Freidman does not, I think, over-do the significance of Neil's existence in Erikson's life and thought. Erikson once wrote about tragedy as a matter of developmental lag, an idea which had seemed incomprehensible to me until now but becomes more understandable in the light of Neil's existence. Friedman thinks that Erikson's commitment to his theory of the life cycle, on which Joan specially collaborated, reflects their continuing distress over the fourth child.

Erikson had himself been deceived in his own early childhood, since his mother and step-father conspired to keep him in the dark about the identity of his biological father. I had long suspected, on the basis of conflicting stories Erikson published about his own background, that he was in fact illegitimate, and Friedman amply confirms that hypothesis. Erikson liked to exaggerate the social standing of his apparently Danish and Gentile father, and never wrote about his own bar mitzvah. The German step-father (a pediatrician named Homburger) married Erikson's Danish mother when Erik was three. Homburger and Erik's mother were Jewish, and the couple emigrated to Palestine in the mid-1930s. This religious background becomes critical for understanding Erikson's work since he became a believing Christian, and one of his central contributions to psychoanalysis lay in his proposing an alternative to Freud's own anti-religious bias. *Young Man Luther* was one of Erikson's most tightly reasoned books, even if Erikson underplayed the anti-Semitism in Luther's thinking. And in *Gandhi's Truth* Erikson failed to highlight how Gandhi had once proposed that the Jews of Europe ought to commit collective suicide in order to object to Hitlerism; comments of Gandhi's about the creation of the state of Israel were controversial enough to remain still embargoed. Erikson chose his new last name when he first filed for naturalization as an American in 1938, and declared then that his "race" was "Scandinavian." Erikson had abundant personal reasons for advocating the significance of conflicts over problems connected with identity.

When I first in 1976 published my own most large-scale evaluation of Erikson's work, I had no idea of some of the health problems (operations for prostate cancer in 1974 and 1975) he was already suffering from. Erikson has had good fortune in his biographer, and *Identity's Architect* is generous-spirited without being partisan. Although Friedman has explored each of Erikson's writings within the context of the times and the influence of others, Friedman missed the opportunity of knowing the Erikson who justifies the book.

Erikson had a kind of magical intuitiveness and immediacy of expression which infused his work, and which I for one miss on a personal basis. A chance meeting on a street-corner or a coffee-shop elicited comments from him that I will forever treasure. Off the top-of-his-head during his seminars and lectures, Erikson could say things that others too seem to find momentous. Friedman gives as good an account as any I have read about what Erikson was like at his best, even if I do worry how well the books stand up without the personal aura of Erikson's magnetism and inner charm.

Still, there was an opportunistic side to Erikson that Friedman might have done more to explicate. For instance, Erikson's relation to his analyst, Anna Freud, became tortured. (It has to be oddly anachronistic for those of us who knew her as "Miss Freud" to find her in *Identity's Architect* as "Ms. Freud.") She had analyzed him in the late 1920s at a low fee, his psychoanalytic training became the main formal credentials he ever earned, and then she disapproved of his work as "sociology." But he continued publicly to trace his professional lineage to her, which was part of dedicating his *Insight and Responsibility* to her. When she did not even acknowledge this professed form of allegiance, she must have known how at that time his connection to the Freuds was helping establish his public role in America. One of Erikson's other teachers at the Vienna Psychoanalytic Institute, August Aichhorn, once harshly criticized in a letter Erikson's narcissism; Aichhorn was also an expert in adolescent waywardness, and technically there was something delinquent both about Erikson's accounts of his biographical background and his links to psychoanalysis.

No matter how Erikson stylized what not knowing his real father meant to him, it does seem to have been an early deficit that he could never wholly overcome. Other adopted children have similarly suffered, but Erikson was able to transmute that uncertainty about his origins into works which I think remain enduringly memorable. No one did more to keep alive the vitality of psychoanalytic thinking, even as Erikson quietly repudiated many of Freud's own clinical recommendations. As Winnicott observed, Erikson could spot strengths in patients without imagining things, and his conceptual outlook helped redress the negativistic imbalance in psychoanalysis as Freud left it. Erikson also illuminated the human sciences through the concreteness of individual life histories.

I hope it is a sign of my own enduring affection for Erikson that I found the twenty pages of the last chapter of *Identity's Architect*, dealing with Erikson's final years, almost unreadably long. In my mind's eye I would prefer to reduce those painful medical details to a couple of paragraphs, but doubtless Friedman's historian's judgment was sound. It may seem a bit bonkers that Erikson needed at the end to have a reminder of the Danish flag in his nursing-hospital room, but then everyone has their eccentricities. Friedman has woven that detail into the fabric of his tale in a way that is consistent with everything that has come before. Objectively, *Identity's Architect* will I hope amount to a celebration of Erikson's life and achievements, even if for me it also amounts to the tale of what we have lost.

## Note

1. Lawrence J. Friedman, *Identity's Architect: A Biography of Erik H. Erikson* (New York: Scribner's, 1999).

# 35

# Winnicott

Britain's Donald W. Winnicott (1896-1971) was one of the genuinely original thinkers in modern psychoanalysis. *D. W. Winnicott: A Biographical Portrait*[1] is the first installment of Brett Kahr's work on Winnicott; his "Preface" here tells us that he will shortly be publishing a full text on Winnicott's life and work, as well as a volume of essays to celebrate Winnicott's one hundredth birthday. Although Winnicott lived in a professional community beset by ideological rivalry between the adherents of Anna Freud as opposed to the disciples of Melanie Klein, Winnicott himself succeeded in avoiding sectarianism, at the same time as his work has been absorbed within the so-called mainstream of psychoanalysis.

It has proven difficult to reconstruct much about Winnicott's childhood in Plymouth. His father was a successful merchant, and for his various public services was knighted by King George V. Kahr seems to think that Winnicott's father was inadequately attentive to his only son, especially given Winnicott's mother's proclivity to depressions. Winnicott had two older sisters, both of whom remained unmarried. He himself was sent to boarding school in Cambridge, where he developed an interest in the natural sciences. Winnicott decided on becoming a medical doctor, even though that career in England lacked the social prestige it has acquired elsewhere. He specialized in pediatrics, and soon became a psychoanalytic child therapist.

In 1923 he married his first wife, and the marriage lasted for twenty-five years. The couple, however, was plagued by problems; she became emotionally unbalanced, and he appears to have been impotent. For some ten years Winnicott remained in analysis with James Strachey; Winnicott's buoyantly spontaneous charm contrasted with Strachey's skeptical intellectualism and aloofness. Since Winnicott was so interested in children, and Strachey had been partly responsible for getting Ernest Jones to invite Klein to London, Strachey encouraged Winnicott to turn to Klein for furthering his education. Winnicott spent about six years in supervision under Klein, from about 1935 until 1941. Klein rejected Winnicott as a patient on the grounds that she wanted to send him a son of her own for analysis; Winnicott took the case, but declined Klein's proposal that she supervise this analysis, too. Since Winnicott wanted further analysis, he went to Joan Riviere, a follower of Klein's, and this treatment went on for about five years. Somehow Winnicott had more difficulties with Riviere than with Strachey, although both of them in different ways were intimidating presences.

Winnicott's first book, *Clinical Notes on Disorders of Childhood* (1931) began with a typical Winnicottian sentiment: "This book proceeds from the heart of a clincian rather than from the brain of a library student; hence some of its merits and demerits." Winnicott took a healthy-minded approach to the development of children, and the Kleinians became angry at his interest in the environmental sources of emotional strength. Anna Freud's group found Winnicott's degree of involvement in Kleinian thinking incomprehensible, and disloyal to Freud's teachings.

In 1951 Winnicott remarried to a woman who herself became an analyst, and this union was a happy one. His professional productivity accelerated; as her husband he wrote six books before his death, and afterwards others assembled his various writings and lectures to make up an additional twelve volumes. Winnicott became one of analysis's most popular and engaging exponents, and was twice President of the British Psychoanalytic Society.

Even though concepts of Winnicott's, such as that of the "transitional object," became widely accepted, in 1968 he was so roughly received at the New York Psychoanalytic Society that he returned to his hotel room where he had a serious coronary attack that he spent months recovering from. (He had already experienced heart seizures, but the reception he got in New York was a shock.) Winnicott saw the relationship between the analyst and patient in terms which were too interpersonal for orthodox American analytic thinking then. Winnicott was willing to tolerate almost psychotic-sounding regressions in analysands for the pursuit of a "true self," yet he remained unusually constructive in outlook and exceptionally generous in supportiveness.

I would have thought no book could capture Winnicott's unique combination of puckish kindliness and intuitively original theorizing. But it seems to me that the genuine spirit of Winnicott's nature comes through in Kahr's biographical portrait. Winnicott proposed that psychological health could be defensive: "we are poor indeed if we are only sane." For Winnicott fantasy and illusion were enriching; he could be humanitarian without sentimentality. And he proposed that writers on psychoanalytic technique often missed the significance of the setting itself. Winnicott was apt playfully to turn every analytic concept on its head. He was paradoxical at the drop of a hat, and retained an enchanting childlikeness that stands in marked contrast to dry-as-dust theorizing. Kahr's book succeeds in bringing Winnicott's elfish nature back to life, and it will be a pleasure to await Kahr's further Winnicott publications.

## Note

1. Brett Kahr, *D. W. Winnicott: A Biographical Portrait* (London: Karnac, 1996).

# 36

# Khan

British psychoanalysis has had a distinguished history. Jones, for all his many flaws, deserves the credit for making a functioning organization of analysts in Britain. Of course, that means also that sometimes Jones kept out brilliant people whom he disliked, especially men with medical degrees; he felt far more at home with female physicians and lay analysts, although he could be curiously obedient to certain women analysts. Jones was stuck with the fact that many of those interested in Freud's work were Cambridge intellectuals; once Freud had accepted people like James and Alix Strachey for personal analyses, Jones could do nothing to block them from becoming full members of his society. Jones, a Welsh outsider, might envy superior social connections, but he was a good enough politician to ride out his many practical problems.

Never in British psychoanalysis has there been, however, anything like the scandal now associated with Masud Khan. Once a figure at the pinnacle of power, trusted and respected not only in Britain but throughout the world of official orthodox psychoanalysis, Khan ended up being defrocked. His final crime was not that of behaving in an admittedly sexually improper way with a patient, but for publishing anti-Semitic remarks. The details of his fall from grace are part of the center of the story of this fascinating book, *Speak of Me As I am: The Life and Work of Masud Khan,*[1] written by one of his former patients, Judy Cooper, who was in analysis with him between the years 1967 and 1973.

The book begins with a foreward by Eric Rayner, who has written about the so-called independent school of British analysts. That sets the stage for Cooper's account of how Khan succeeded in adding "a fresh voice to psychoanalysis." Khan was passionately Francophilic and helped introduce the writings of his mentor, D. W. Winnicott, in Paris. So the French today may know next to nothing about someone like Erik H. Erikson, but Khan and Winnicott are accorded special standing not just within French analysis but inside the intelligentsia of Parisian society.

Part One provides a biography of Khan, who lived from 1924 until 1989. Although it begins by calling Khan "fascinating," it makes for tough sledding, for Cooper minces no words about Khan's human failings. An official obituary of Khan by Adam Limentani, for the *International Journal of Psychoanalysis*, alludes to Khan's having gone to Balliol College at Oxford, yet Cooper establishes that Khan was never admitted to Balliol, nor is there any trace of him there. Khan's father was not a ruler of a state in old India that later became Pakistan, but he was rich and powerful; his father was 76 when he married Khan's mother, a woman of 17 who had a questionable past as a courtesan.

In writing this book Cooper had the full cooperation not only of the present powers-that-be in British psychoanalysis, but also of somone as brilliant as Charles Rycroft, an old friend of Khan's but someone who years ago quit the British Psychoanalytic Society out of boredom with the nonsense that could be taken seriously at professional meetings. Some of the best parts of *Speak of Me As I Am* come from passages in letters Rycroft sent Cooper. Khan spent most of his life, at least starting in 1943, undergoing analysis. Arriving in England after World War II, Khan started analysis with Ella Freeman Sharpe. Cooper criticizes Sharpe for having lacked later analysts' understanding of preoedipal layers. But then Cooper writes, "For instance, even when writing on Lear, she picked up on his obsessional neurosis but not on his paranoid psychosis." It might have been forgivable for Freud, or any other early analyst, to treat a Shakespeare character as a patient, but this is much too late to allow such a confusion between reality and art.

After Sharpe died, Khan moved on to John Rickman for another stint of analysis. Anna Freud was always in the background for therapeutic consultations. When I first met Khan, in 1965, he was married to a famous ballerina. I would not have believed it, but Cooper tells us that Khan's analysis with Winnicott lasted from 1951 until 1966.

What are nonanalysts to make of any of this tale? Did nobody in Britain accept the limits of what analysis can hope to accomplish? It is widely known that the so-called biological psychiatrists in Britain always held more power than in the States, but, reading this biographical account, one shudders at what outsiders are going to think about analysts who abuse authority. Pill-pushing is no good either, but somehow there should be a middle ground.

Thanks to Khan's capacities as a courtier, he had both Melanie Klein and Anna Freud as his supervisors, and he was qualified in child analysis, too. Khan's French associates, who now can speak most bitingly of him, included the leading lights of Parisian analysis (but excluded Jacques Lacan). Winnicott died in 1971 and Khan's mother did too; that year was the beginning of the end. Cooper never once, however, raises the issue of the abuse of transference, a point Jung discussed around World War I. Khan had problems with smoking and drinking, and in 1975 got cancer for the first time. His larynx and trachea had to be taken out. In 1975, the Training Committee withdrew Khan's right to train, and his practice seems to have almost vanished. In 1988 he was thrown out for the published anti-Semitism.

But what does it say about British analysis that nobody seems to have minded Khan's venomous anti-Americanism, although it never got into print? Prejudice against the New World still seems socially acceptable in Britain and elsewhere in the world as well.

Part Two deals with Khan as theory maker and clinician. Brillliant as Khan was, this biographical background has to make independent observers look on his writings with skepticism. I am not suggesting that everything Khan wrote should be ignored, but, for goodness sake, there is such a thing as common sense, even among psychoanalytically committed people. Cooper points out what I had not known before—that Khan believed that "every dream carries in it a demand for privacy and non-communication." But then Cooper, like so many others, proceeds to choose to quote Laplanche and Pontalis as if they had given us a new gospel. Like others in Britain, Cooper does not realize that the concept that countertransference can be utilized constructively was not invented by Paula Heimann in 1950 but was proposed by Helene Deutsch in 1926.

Winnicott was genuinely special, and Cooper correctly writes of him as remaining "elfin." But this wonderful pixie of a man, as I have already mentioned, now has a stolid bust in his honor at the British Psychoanalytic Society which is in contrast to everything Winnicott stood for at his best. I wonder whether in hindsight Winnicott can escape criticism for the way his attitude toward Khan allowed his imperiousness to persist, and how Khan subsequently deteriorated.

In my experience Khan was not, as Cooper thinks, "a real intellectual." For intellectuality means that in principle everything can be considered, whereas Khan, and his analytic friends, got sucked into the quagmire of transferential temptations. Lord Acton was correct enough to warrant reiterating: power corrupts and absolute power tends to corrupt absolutely.

Cooper presents thoroughly fair-minded critiques of Khan's work. That section of the book is worth the price of the whole text. But Khan fits into the history of psychoanalysis in a way that even Cooper does not appreciate. As wild as Khan became, old-fashioned, orthodox analysts may wield more hidden authority, by means of their adherence to so-called neutrality and its special suggestive effects, than Khan did by his outrageous overbearingness.

All analysts should study this book and learn from what Cooper's reliable tale has to recount. Janet Malcolm is wrong in preferring "a nebbish Rabbi Small" to "a dancing Prince Masud." I found Cooper's book impossible to put down. Cooper does not know there are letters between Khan and Anna Freud at the Library of Congress in Washington, D.C., which others should study and explore. Nor does she realize that people like Paul Federn and Carl Jung wrote about the self long before Khan did. But, then, this is an imperfect world, and Cooper has written a memorable book.

## Note

1. Judy Cooper, *Speak of Me As I Am: The Life and Work of Masud Khan* (London: Karnac, 1993).

# 37

# Bettelheim

Bruno Bettelheim was imprisoned for almost a year at Dachau and Buchenwald in 1938-1939, and first came to prominence because of a 1943 article he wrote about the psychology of concentration camps. At the time the public was not yet aware of such atrocities, and Bettelheim pioneered in describing the horrendous impact of Nazi incarceration. He tried to explain why he had had the good luck to survive, as opposed to others who deteriorated.

In 1944 Bettelheim became head of a small residential school for emotionally disturbed youngsters which the University of Chicago supported. Bettelheim's idea was that if the environment could be used destructively as at Dachau and Buchenwald, it ought to be possible to make a constructive therapeutic use of the outside world. For the next three decades he led a facility which sought to reconstruct the personalities of children who, as a condition of their treatment, had been taken from their parents. Bettelheim wrote a series of popular books about the treatment milieu he created, and became one of the world's most famous psychotherapists. He won a National Book award for a book on fairy tales, and played himself in Woody Allen's movie *Zelig* (1983).

Richard Pollak has written a disturbing book, *The Creation of Dr. B.: A Biography of Bruno Bettelheim*,[1] that records a scandalous story. For Pollak, whose younger brother attended Bettelheim's school and died in an accident that Bettelheim interpreted as suicide, has composed a life of Bettelheim concentrating on how he cooked all his evidence and was responsible for manufacturing his own legend.

Pollak begins with Bettelheim's background as a Viennese Jew, demonstrating that despite Bettelheim's claims to the contrary he never had any formal therapeutic training, only some personal analysis. Moreover, Bettelheim was himself similar to those concentration camp inmates he made himself sound superior to. After the Nazis seized Austria, Bettelheim was, like others, behaving as if it were business as usual, unable rationally to assess the danger he was in. And while he was a prisoner he was allegedly too tied to the disposition of his possessions back in Vienna. Thanks to bribery, connections, and good fate he managed to get released before the camps turned into extermination centers.

Once in the States, Bettelheim embellished his credentials in pursuit of an academic position. Pollak finds such story-telling at every step of Bettelheim's career. Bettelheim exaggerated the rate of therapeutic success at his school, and falsified his diagnoses. Furthermore, he succeeded in tyrannically dominating the school and its counselors. Although Bettelheim had accused others of behaving self-destructively in the face of Nazi terror, as a sick old widower he killed himself in 1990. Pollak has unearthed the suicide note to two of his children, which would be more touching if we did not know that he failed to address any words to his oldest child, Ruth, with whom he was on bad terms at the end.

No sooner was Bettelheim dead than former patients at his school went public about the abuse they had suffered there. Although Bettelheim had claimed he was against corporal punishment like spanking, his practices were at odds with his stated principles. So starting in 1990 Bettelheim's reputation collapsed like a house of cards. He was even accused of plagiarism in his work on fairy tales.

As we have touched on, psychoanalysis is not doing well in America, although elsewhere in the world it has become a mainstay of philosophical thinking. On this continent the interest in Freud's work was primarily therapeutic, and Bettelheim relied on the American hopefulness that through better parenting most childhood mental disorders could be alleviated. He appealed to the New World naivete about what psychological "experts" could hope to accomplish.

Pollak has a field-day exposing Bettelheim's weaknesses, and *The Creation of Dr. B.* makes for a depressing if compelling read. Although Pollak cites Bettelheim's first wife on how he was an intellectual, cultivated, and interesting man, this side of him scarcely comes through in the book. With reason the editors of *The New Yorker*, the *New York Review of Books*, the Sunday *New York Times Book Review*, and *Daedalus* turned over space for Bettelheim's writings. He became a powerful force, and was able to make an adversary look like a fool. But Pollak does not, in my view, talk enough about Bettelheim's independence, for example how outstanding was his early criticism of the orthodox biases in Ernest Jones's official biography of Freud.

*The Creation of Dr. B.* has an advance quotation referring to him as "a charlatan," and we do have to wonder how readers can have been so suggestible as not to have critically questioned Bettelheim's theses long ago. And yet by the mid-1970s he was being criticized for having maintained that concentration camp inmates had regressed to infantilism; it was proposed instead that survivors should be viewed as reminders not of human weakness but of evil circumstances that were objectively powerful. But Bettelheim had the tactical advantage of having been there as an eye-witness. It was not just the American public that was taken in; in France Bettelheim's name became a household word, and his book on autism sold some 100,000 copies in 1974.

Although Pollak may not have intended such a reaction, *The Creation of Dr. B.* made me feel sorry for Bettelheim. His relationships with wives, children, friends, and colleagues are dissected so thoroughly that it is hard to know how anybody could withstand such inspection. Bettelheim's depressiveness fed his exploitiveness and need for control, just as the public's craving for a miracle-worker helped fuel the illusions Bettelheim succeeded in propagandizing. It takes an effort now to remember how iconoclastic Bettelheim could be, and his provocative and challenging writings deserve to be evaluated on their own merits. Nina Sutton's *Bettelheim: A Life and Legacy* (1996) seemed to me more comprehensive than Pollak on the European years, and over-all better balanced in its critical assessments. It will take further books to put in perspective all the distressing aspects to Bettelheim's career.

## Note

1. Richard Pollak, *The Creation of Dr. B.: A Biography of Bruno Bettelheim* (New York: Simon & Schuster, 1997).

# 38

# Skinner

Some people have all the luck in the biographer they end up with. I could not have imagined a less philosophically attractive figure than B. F. Skinner, someone who was bent on denying not only the existence of the unconscious, but also freedom and dignity. His *Walden Two* presents a picture of human existence without conflict, suffering, or humor. Skinner's work, nonetheless, has been enormously influential, especially in America.

Now along comes Daniel Bjork, who presents Skinner in a thoroughly sympathetic light.[1] Skinner only died in 1990, but I never even thought of trying to meet him. Bjork described Skinner's early years spent in an unforgettable and attractively tortured manner. Who might have thought that the inventor of the Skinner box also loved Wagner, or could be on writing terms with Robert Frost? Skinner recalled that Henry Murray once called him "a romantic defending himself with science," a judgment which seems most sound. Skinner was attracted to behaviorism "not as a cold unfeeling nihilist, but as a sensitive, unhappy slightly cynical young man...." Skinner could criticize Chekhov's short stories, while praising Dostoevsky. Skinner even read *Ulysses* "in awe." One must be obviously persuaded by now to read Skinner's multivolume autobiography.

Alas, it is also true that Skinner did not believe that "the 'mind' existed." Despite having an apparently difficult personality, Skinner continued to prosper in his academic career. He was explicitly antipolitical, and this defect mars, I think, his whole argument in *Walden Two*. Although rats are certainly not people, Skinner worked on teaching machines and programmed instruction. Skinner had an abundance of critics, but by the time of his death the sales of *Walden Two* came close to 2.5 million. Bjork has written an unusually fine book, and no psychologist could want a more sensitive biographer.

### Note

1. Daniel W. Bjork, *B. F. Skinner: A Life* (New York: Basic Books, 1993).

# Part 7

# National Receptions of Freud

# Introduction to Part 7

One way of thinking about twentieth century intellectual history would be in terms of the different national receptions of psychoanalysis. Each country's reaction to a common body of doctrine is telling about how nationalities pick and choose what they need for their own special purposes. So the French Freud is as different as could be from what we know in North America, and there is a Russian and British Freud as well. Psychoanalysis was flourishing in Russia up until the time when Stalin managed to get rid of Trotsky; and now once again, after the collapse of the Soviet regime, interest in things psychoanalytic there is on the rise. Further, Argentina has been a special source of psychoanalytic influence throughout Latin America. Just as the English chose to emphasize certain elements in Freud's work, at odds with what happened in America, Mexico has picked up parts of psychoanalysis which are unlike those in Argentina.

In Buenos Aires, as in Mexico City, it is possible at ordinary street-corner kiosks to pick up, at an inexpensive price, a hard-backed edition of the first volume of the Spanish edition of Freud's collected works, packaged-together with Rousseau's *Social Contract*. In itself that seems to me to be a telling sign of Freud's triumph as a figure in intellectual history. At the same time, in Italy Freud's picture is used on large billboards for the sake of commercial advertising purposes. Although Freud always complained about his low standing within Austria, and the Vienna Psychoanalytic Society has been notably slow to thrive, his image does appear there on the 50 schilling bills.

# 39

# Russia

In his *Freud's Russia: National Identity in the Evolution of Psychoanalysis*[1] James Rice has done a remarkable job of exploring Freud's Russia. He begins with an account, new to me, of just how tied to Russia Freud was in terms of his ancestry and family background. Freud's mother retained many close relatives there. At the same time Rice perceives how acutely Freud felt his own "lack of a fatherland," in that a decent Viennese Jew had to be incapable of Austrian patriotism. Several of Freud's most prominent disciples were Russians, such as Lou Andreas-Salomé, Max Eitingon, and Sabina Spielrein. Rice proposes, not terribly persuasively I think, that the concept of a human instinct to destruction can be considered "a distinctively Russian contribution to psychoanalytic theory." But I believe that the notion of the death instinct can also be explored in terms of Freud's biography as well as in connection with German intellectual life.

Rice spends a good deal of time both on Freud's Wolf Man case history as well as on Freud's essay about Dostoevsky. It seems to me that Rice is most successful in writing about Freud and Dostoevsky, and that this section of the book will endure as a permanent contribution to the literature. Freud viewed Russians as unusually ambivalent, and both the Wolf Man and Dostoevsky were used to illustrate Freud's thesis. Rice gives a sustained treatment to the background of Freud's piece on Dostoevsky, and we learn about the Viennese Stefan Zweig's short story that Freud chose to cite there. Freud saw Dostoevsky as a hysteric, and even traced his epilepsy to the supposed murder of his father. Rice does a conscientious job of understanding Freud's thinking about Dostoevsky within the terms of the then available literature. We now know though that Dostoevsky's epilepsy was first medically diagnosed some eight years after his father's death, which was also two years before Dostoevsky was sentenced to be executed for his radical political activities.

Rice does also show how Freud's *The Future of an Illusion* should be related to Dostoevsky's legend of the Grand Inquisitor, although it would have been nice to have at least mentioned the other aspects of Freud's inspiration as well. (Freud's dialogue resembles in many ways a classic one by Arthur Schopenhauer.) In taking on religion as a neurosis Freud was, as in his Wolf Man case history, also settling an old score with Jung, who had repudiated Freud's attempt to dissolve religious belief through scientific-sounding dissection.

Rice is capable of the most subtle sorts of understanding Freud's thinking. For example, in discussing the Dostoevsky article Rice notes how Theodor Reik had skillfully complained about the "error in proportion" in how Freud had relied on Zweig's tale; Reik complained that it seemed "as though a medieval artist painting the Passion of Christ should place in the foreground of the picture the bishop of his native diocese." For all of Freud's cosmopolitanism, he remained a Viennese to his fingertips. Freud would have appreciated Reik's comparing him to the medieval artist, concerned with the central problem of the crucifixion; at the same time Reik's also suggesting that Freud had for local reasons made the Viennese Zweig too central to the universal theme that psychoanalysis was undertaking to deal with would have appealed to Freud's sense of incongruity, given his own skepticism about religion.

The issue of Dostoevsky's anti-Semitism also gets well treated in Rice's book; and that habitual prejudice, in the special form it took in Dostoevsky's writings, has to be understood within the broader context of Freud's own ambivalences about being Jewish. Reading *Freud's Russia*, though, I felt that Freud's irony was not highlighted as much as it might have been. For example, Rice quotes without comment a remarkable bit of 1933 sardonic reasoning on Freud's part about Marxist accounts of revolution: "I really believe that it was gunpowder and firearms that abolished chivalry and aristocratic rule, and that the Russian despotism was already doomed before it lost the War, because no amount of inbreeding among the ruling families of Europe could have produced a race of Tsars capable of withstanding the explosive force of dynamite." Implicitly, Freud was turning the tables on contemporary psychiatric accounts of the inbreeding which led to "nervous" difficulties which were said to be characteristically Jewish. And he was also offering technological change as an alternative to the Marxist theorem of the importance of class warfare.

Rice concludes with an authoritative account of the controversy over Max Eitingon, and whether this Russian favorite of Freud's could ever have been secretly working in the service of Stalin's regime. Oddly enough, the otherwise comprehensive book by Roudinesco on psychoanalysis in France, *Jacques Lacan & Co.*, does not cover an important Paris trial concerning Soviet spying at which Eitingon's name came up. The time may arrive when the accounts of the different national receptions of Freud's work will complement one another, but right now they are still too much like ships passing in the night.

* * *

Alexander Etkind's *Eros of the Impossible: The History of Psychoanalysis in Russia*[2] first appeared in Russian (1993), subsequently in French, and was eagerly awaited here. While high expectations might be expected to threaten disappointment, *Eros of the Impossible* makes for an exciting if demanding read. Etkind is a cultivated author who has produced a series of remarkable essays which flesh-out further the story of the reception of Freud's work in Russia.

One chapter deals with Lou Andreas-Salomé, her complicated psychoanalytic contributions as well as her relationship with her native land. The next deals with the symbolist movement and its similarities to psychoanalysis, helping to account for the initial Russian responsiveness to Freud. The third chapter is devoted to the Wolf Man. (The literature about him will expand once again after Freud Archive material becomes available.) The next section is on psychoanalytic activity before World War which was active enough to overshadow how Freud was at the time being received in most other countries. Sabina Spielrein (Jung's first analytic patient) is important enough to justify a chapter of its own: Etkind succeeded in interviewing some of her surviving relatives, and thereby helped to reduce some of the mysteries of her fate after she returned to the Soviet Union following her years in Central Europe.

In 1923 the thirty members of the Russian Psychoanalytic Society comprised a full eighth of the membership of the IPA. An analytic pediatric facility (attended by a son of Stalin) was attempted, and Etkind comes up with findings about not only how positively Trotsky viewed analysis, but the multiple ways in which he encouraged the movement. According to Communist thinking then, human nature was supposedly capable of being transformed, which partly explains why analysis flourished (until 1930) in the land of the Bolsheviks. The Russians had also tried in the 1920s to make a special study of childhood as part of applied education.

By the early 1930s analytic thinking was denounced as a deviation from the Party line. (Etkind does not address Harold Lasswell's suggestion that the turning point had come with a lecture trip Wilhelm Reich had made to the Soviet Union, and his contention that sexual reform and the continuation of family law changes were a prerequisite to the continuation of political liberalization for the Soviets; supposedly this seemed to Stalin the last straw, and began the end of psychoanalysis in Russia.) Totalitarianism ultimately destroyed analysis in Russia, although today once again there is a resurgence of Russian interest in Freud, relying on government support as well as old translations made either before World War I or during the 1920s. Those interested in the history of ideas will relish Etkind's book; among other points he examines the pros and cons of whether Eitingon was a NKVD agent; he also points out how one chapter in Bulgakov's famous novel *The Master and Margarita* was modelled on William C. Bullitt, a former patient of Freud's and President Roosvelt's choice as the first Ambassador from America to the Soviet Union. Etkind's study, along with that of Rice, has given us enough about the Russian situation to have made a memorable contribution to the growing literature on the comparative national receptions of Freud.

* * *

Martin Miller's *Freud and The Bolsheviks: Psychoanalysis in Imperial Russia and the Soviet Union*[3] is the third book on Russian psychoanalysis to have recently appeared. Miller's study is different and yet wholly fascinating. As a professional historian Miller provides a smooth narrative account, whereas the two earlier texts were each primarily thematic rather than chronological. While the first two books on Freud in Russia interestingly explored special topics on the subject that particularly interested the authors, this new study by Martin Miller undertakes to cover the entire sweep of the story of psychoanalysis in Russia, and he does so in less than 200 pages.

It is often forgotten that before the Russian Revolution there were psychiatrists and intellectuals in the Romanov Empire who took great interest in Freud's work. The 1904 Russian translation of *The Interpretation of Dreams* was the first to be made into any language. Although Miller does not choose to dwell on the way nineteenth century Russian literature prepared the way for Freud, it is clear than in no country was the national response more immediate than imperial Russia.

Once the Revolution took place, even more interest in Freud's work grew in Bolshevik Russia. Miller sensitively explores the issue of how ambivalent about psychoanalysis Lenin might have been. By the mid-1920s there was a full-scale debate about the difficulties of reconciling Marxism with psychoanalysis, a topic which interested some important Western thinkers as well. Trotsky's support was to prove a fatal sort of backing, and by the end of the 1920s psychoanalytic studies was considered heretical and the practice of Freudian therapy seems to have ceased. Regulatory legislation on marriage, divorce, and other such areas were pursued in an unenlightened spirit, at the same time that a Stalinist witch-hunt was undertaken against psychoanalysis.

A thaw started after Stalin's death, and accelerated throughout the 1960s. By the time of the collapse of the old Soviet Union in 1991, Freud had become a popular subject in Russia, even though easily confused with tea-reading and old-fashioned mediums. Even if Miller does not take the subject quite up to the present-day, it is the case that psychoanalysis is now, as in the early 1920s, supported by the Russian state, and Boris Yeltsin's 1996 decree made it a legitimate part of university education. So Freud is once again fashionable in Russia, and if only that tragic country has a bit of good luck it should have a secure future in the history of psychoanalysis over the coming century.

## Notes

1. James L. Rice, *Freud's Russia: National Identity in the Evolution of Psychoanalysis* (New Brunswick, NJ: Transaction, 1993).
2. Alexander Etkind, *Eros of the Impossible: The History of Psychoanalysis in Russia*, translated by Noah and Maria Rubins (Boulder, CO: Westview, 1995).
3. Martin A. Miller, *Freud and the Bolsheviks: Psychoanalysis in Imperial Russia and the Soviet Union* (New Haven, CT: Yale University Press, 1998).

# 40

# America

Nathan G. Hale, Jr., has brought an extraordinary degree of nonpartisan scholarship to bear on the contentious history of psychoanalysis in America. His 1971 *Freud and the Americans*,[1] now at last reprinted, carried the story until 1917, and has become a standard source for historians and other students of the reception of psychoanalytic doctrines in the United States. One way of judging a book is in terms of how often it has been necessary to use it over the years as a point of reference; on numerous occasions I have turned, each time with benefit, to look something up, especially about pre-Freudian psychiatry, in Hale's *Freud and the Americans*.

The strength of *Freud and the Americans* lies in its fair-mindedness and its extraordinary array of details; it concludes with a splendid bibliographical essay. By and large this first volume of Hale's lifework was a success story, as he showed how Freud's system displaced the relatively less enlightened thinking of his American predecessors. For my own taste I would have preferred it if Hale had been knowledgeable enough to put the American reaction to psychoanalysis within some comparative cultural framework. One can better understand America's take on Freud if one also knows something, for instance, of how he was faring at the time in Britain, Germany, or France. But Hale's strong point has been his close attention to the historical narrative, and it may be asking too much of him at the same time to be aware of the response to psychoanalytic theory and practice in different national contexts.

It has taken over two decades for Hale to complete the second volume of his study, which brings the reader down to 1985, but *The Rise and Crisis of Psychoanalysis in the United States*[2] seems to me an even better book than Volume I. Hale has searched through all kinds of manuscript collections and has also kept up-to-date on the secondary literature, which has proliferated since the original appearance of *Freud and the Americans*. In the years after Hale completed his first installment, psychoanalysis has encountered heavy weather, both medically and popularly. *The Rise and Crisis of Psychoanalysis in the United States* reflects the different climate of opinion that replaced the initial enthusiasm which got expressed implicitly in *Freud and the Americans*. The altogether more skeptical period in which Hale wrote Volume II is mirrored in the title change, and the key word now, in the general thesis Hale is advancing, is the term "crisis."

It is probably inevitable, in the course of such a lengthy book, that I was able to find a number of minor mistakes, and I hope it will not appear churlish if I point them out now. Von Freund, the man who first funded the psychoanalytic publishing house in Vienna, was named Anton, not Ernst, and the index omits him entirely. Freud never reviewed Walter Lippmann's *A Preface to Politics*, even though that legend has appeared before in the literature; in fact it was Ernest Jones who wrote the review in question. The early Boston analyst, Ives Hendrick, was not just "DIFFICULT," as Harry Stack Sullivan so strikingly maintained, but Hale should have been told that Hendrick was epileptic. Hale somehow believes that David Brunswick was "California's first trained analyst," when in reality Brunswick only had a personal analysis with Freud and as we discussed earlier had had no intention at the time of ever becoming an analyst. Horace W. Frink, whom Freud chose in the 1920s to lead American analysis, not only became psychotic "after" his analysis with Freud in Vienna but also in treatment with the founder of psychoanalysis. Felix Deutsch was indeed a member of the Vienna Psychoanalytic Society, but did not practice analysis until after coming to the States in the mid-1930s, so there seems something odd about describing his impact as "a Viennese analyst" on Flanders Dunbar, especially when Dunbar was analyzed in Vienna by Felix Deutsch's wife, Helene. Hale somehow has the idea that Heinz Hartmann was "invited by Freud to be his last trainee," and Hale maintains that Hartmann's papers were "seldom illustrated with case histories," when I would have thought a much stronger word than "seldom" would have been more accurate. To continue with a catalog of detailed flaws that I found, Hale has somehow completely omitted the controversy surrounding the publication of the Freud-Bullitt collaborative study of President Woodrow Wilson, which first appeared in 1967 and was for many years allowed by the Freud Copyrights to go out of print in English. Robert J. Lifton to my knowledge never completed psychoanalytic training, and I cannot recall his ever describing himself, as Hale would have it, as an analyst.

It is a hard matter to put my finger on, but somehow Hale has trouble distinguishing between the woods and the trees. At a number of points, for example, when he is discussing people like Hendrick or Lawrence Kubie or Karl Menninger, I found myself shaking my head in bewilderment, since Hale seems to have so little intuitive feel for these people as human beings. Hale has been so studious about looking through their papers, and none of these three men has been dead for terribly long, that I found it all the more odd that Hale does not seem to have known them as individuals, or at any rate that kind of knowledge does not succed in showing itself in his text.

Hale is very good at describing the trouble psychoanalysis came to encounter after the high point of Freud's popularity associated with his hundredth birthday in 1956. Somehow in *Freud and the Americans* I detected a lack of sympathy on Hale's part about the reasoning behind ego psychology's becoming influential in the United States, but by *The Rise and Crisis of Psychoanalysis in the United States* Hale seems open-minded about the need for a variety of revisions in psychoanalytic thinking.

In the Conclusion to *The Rise and Crisis of Psychoanalysis* Hale mentions the reception of psychoanalysis elsewhere in the world, and a few works on that subject do get cited. And at the very outset of *Freud and the Americans* Hale had asked the fundamental questions: "Why did America welcome psychoanalysis more warmly than any other country? What was there in the nature of psychoanalysis and what in American conditions that created this affinity?" By now there is a rich literature about Freud's fate in places like France, Argentina, and the Netherlands, to take only a handful of countries where psychoanalysis has had a strikingly important recent influence. But Hale's heart is simply not in comparative cultural analysis; he has instead mastered the available archival sources connected with American matters, even if he does not feel inclined to speculate about just why Freud himself entertained such a series of negative prejudices about America and the fate of his ideas there.

*The Rise and Crisis of Psychoanalysis* makes for an informative and enjoyable read, and the book will be a mine of information for future scholars. My own minor reservations, I hope, will not appear carping. It is frustrating to have errors appear in history books, since they tend to multiply without correction in other texts. Hale should be congratulated for bringing to splendid fruition his two-volume study. It will be a building block for those who want not only to explore the history of Freud in America further, but also to understand the unique nature of the reception of his work in this country, as opposed to the impact he had in different national cultures. The more studies we have like those by Hale, in distinct countries or regions, the easier it will be to specify why it is that the course of psychoanalysis has been so characteristic within each social context. Hale does not repeat Freud's own words in *On the History of the Psychoanalytic Movement*, in which he surveys the influence psychoanalysis had before World War I, but it is likely that Freud would have been interested in the record of how his work has spread and changed world thought.

The literature about Freud is by now really much better than anything that could be said about Carl Jung or Alfred Adler, for example, so Freud's success has been historiographical as well as otherwise. It would be intriguing to look into just what sorts of Americans turned to Adler and to Jung, as opposed to those who were attracted by Freud. But that suggestion of mine would open up an entirely different sort of inquiry from what Hale took as his own. It should not be any criticism of Hale if I suggest that in the future other researchers will ask a different set of questions than those Hale has so competently set out to answer.

* * *

Throughout this century Americans have developed a special romance with psychology, one that has become increasingly influential in the rest of the world. Wherever traditional religious faiths have waned, psychological convictions have been able to function as a replacement. Whereas once the concept of soul could be invoked without embarrassment, people on this continent now tend to feel more comfortable talking about "selfhood"; while competing notions about God were unashamedly discussed and disputed for centuries, psychology has popularly displaced the domain of theology. Even if religious dogmatism may appear to be hard to defend, at least among nonbelievers, it has been relatively easy to be attracted by the claims to certainties put forward by advocates of the so-called science of psychology.

Clinicians have often insisted that their work was morally neutral. But all the intense controversies throughout the history of depth psychology have been fueled, I think, by largely underground rival conceptions of how the good life ought to be lived. It seems to me unthinkable to try to imagine a clinical encounter taking place apart from an ethical context, even though it remains true that not much attention is paid to the moral dimension in the course of the work of training facilities. From the point of view of intellectual history, not only do ethics become relevant at the points where power might be abused, but all aspects of psychological thinking are (and should be) colored by an awareness of the possible options provided by differing standards of right and wrong.

Ellen Herman's *The Romance of American Psychology*[3] is a scrupulously dispassionate account of the public uses that psychology has been put to in America over the past fifty years. Starting with World War II, she describes how psychological knowledge could be successfully marshaled on behalf of various projects for mobilizing the war effort. Specialists in psychological morale not only investigated what was happening behind enemy lines, but also provided advice on domestic matters, such as how to deal with interned Japanese-Americans.

The concept of national character got a special boost from culture and personality proponents as anthropologists and sociologists, as well as a handful of emancipated political scientists and psychoanalysts, joined forces to try to understand the complexities of modern nations at war. The effects of strategic bombing were investigated, as well the psychology of American prejudice and the morale of minority groups. Foundation money, as well as government funds, were increasingly available as scholars took part in wartime psychological efforts.

An extraordinary number of potential soldiers during both world wars were either disqualified on psychological grounds or discharged from military service as invalids. A variety of diagnostic tests were devised to make the military more efficient, and to save the government postwar disability payments. Although, for some reason, Herman does not deal with traumatic neuroses and how this notion played a renewed prominent role in psychodynamic thinking during World War II, she does admirably succeed in providing the background against which one can place this particular issue.

As Freud once quoted Dostoevsky, psychology is "a stick with two ends," or as Constance Garnett translated the metaphor into English, "a knife that cuts both ways." In a broad-minded spirit Herman moves on to describe how psychological expertise continued to be used by the American government throughout the Cold War period. Defense spending proved beneficial to psychologists, even if too little attention was given to the political pros and cons of what they were doing. Social science research, which had been used on behalf of racial emancipation, as in Gunnar Myrdal's 1944 classic *An American Dilemma: The Negro Problem and Modern Democracy*, also proved helpful in dealing with "internal wars" in places like Latin America and Southeast Asia. Americans were characteristically naïve in failing to inquire into what sorts of experts psychologists could be, as we tended to hand over to outside "authorities" the making of value judgments. It would be in keeping with American national character to think that science could be a substitute for metaphysics or moral investigation.

Given how little attention had been paid to the nature of ethical inquiry about the ways psychology was willy-nilly coming up with substitutes for old-fashioned philosophizing, one can appreciate that the antipsychiatry movement could have had a relatively clear field. For the concept of mental health and the presumed benefits of being well adjusted had gone virtually unchallenged, so that critics were readily able to punch holes in the supposed humanism of partisans on behalf of all that psychologizing could hope to accomplish. Modern feminists were hardly alone in perceiving how morally biased psychology was capable of being. Writers as politically far apart as Thomas Szasz and R. D. Laing were able to expose the weaknesses in the theoretical underpinnings of much propagandizing for psychological knowledge. More than one book could be written about how American legal practices, as in child custody matters, have been influenced by special variants of psychological conjecturing that have too often gone unscrutinized in the courts.

Herman has performed a thoroughly scholarly piece of ground-breaking historical research as she surveys the wide area of how modern social science has been politically applied. The book is full of hard work, and she seemed to have no fixed ideology to promote. Until now, almost no professional attention has been paid to all the points of intersection between psychology and politics. In keeping with Freud's own efforts to divorce his work from ethical inquiry, most psychoanalysts have been insensitive to the moral implications of their ideas; academic psychologists too have not been eager to acknowledge the philosophic dimensions to their discipline. And political scientists have, for their part, wanted little to do with what they perceive as the "soft" areas like psychology. National crises should not be required to encourage interdisciplinary work. Native pioneers like William James knew that it is impossible to separate out these different strands of thought, and he remains a giant in philosophy and psychology who has had, alas, few followers. One hopes that the many lessons of *The Romance of American Psychology* will not be lost on the next generation of researchers and students.

* * *

The history of psychiatry remains, I think, in an appalling state. A complete outsider might naively be tempted to think, thanks to the current fashionability of the ideas of Michel Foucault, that psychiatry's history was in the forefront of contemporary academic life. But, without my going into the curiosities of the ideological attractions to French intellectual complexities among North Americans, it ought to be apparent and beyond dispute that the bread-and-butter work on the history of psychiatry remains to be done. One can go into any city throughout the world and find that primary historical documents in the field remain almost untouched.

The figure of Adolf Meyer is an outstanding example of how slowly research has proceeded in this area. Meyer was, even before his appointment in 1908 as the first professor of psychiatry at Johns Hopkins as well as the founding director of the Henry Phipps Psychiatric Clinic there, the leader of American psychiatry. By 1902 he had been dining regularly with John Dewey, James Harvey Robinson, and other prominent "progressives." Until Meyer's retirement in 1945, when he was seventy-five years old, he led the most powerful single school of psychiatric training anywhere on the continent (he did not die until 1950). Meyer was one of those people who saved everything; the collection of his papers now at Johns Hopkins is a historical gold-mine. As a Swiss-born physician who also studied in England, Scotland, and Paris, in 1892 Meyer emigrated to the United States at the age of twenty-six; but he also retained his links to his European origins, and his files contain fascinating exchanges with the great continental thinkers in the field. Ruth Leys, a co-editor of *Defining American Psychology: The Correspondence Between Adolf Meyer and Edward Bradford Titchener*,[4] has already published an important article on "Meyer's Dealing with Jones: A Chapter in the History of the American Response to Psychoanalysis."[5]

In 1909 Meyer not only got an honorary degree along with Freud and Jung from Clark University in Worcester, Massachusetts, but he preceded them to the podium. Although Ruth Leys tucks William James's reaction to Meyer at Clark in a note, it is worth highlighting: James, in a letter, observed: "That man has the levelest mind on psychological matters that I know! A splendid character!" (James was, in contrast, unhappy with how Freud seemed obsessed with fixed ideas, although Jung made a better impression.) As another testimonial to Meyer's standing, one which Ruth Leys correctly singles out, the considerable E. E. Southard, as president of the American Psychiatric Association, observed in 1919:

> No greater power to change our minds about the problems of psychiatry has been at work in the interior of the psychiatric profession in America than the personality of Adolf Meyer....I shall designate him as a ferment, an enzyme, a catalyzer. I don't know that we could abide two of him. But in our present status we must be glad there was one of him.

I believe any body of Meyer's correspondence would have substantial objective interest; but I was somewhat put off, or intimidated, by the other side of this letter-writing exchange; that is, the letters of Edward Bradford Titchener. Titchener (1867-1927) was English, studied psychology in Leipzig, and in 1892 went to Cornell University; from there he became one of the founders of modern academic psychology. Titchener was an experimentalist who relied on laboratory work. He wanted to make a science out of studying the mental processes of "normal" adults, as a result of what could be obtained through introspective analysis under the controls of experimentalism. Titchener also got an honorary degree at Clark in 1909, which was the occasion for Meyer and Titchener starting up their exchanges by letter.

Unfortunately, neither Meyer nor Titchener was a great writer, and some of their letters make for pretty slow going. Jung, in contrast to Freud, may sometimes in his correspondences sound like a windbag, but when Jung and Freud were writing to each other they maintained an extraordinarily high level of directness and charm. It is possible to debate some of the most serious issues without taking leave of being down-to-earth; at the same time the fascination of the Freud-Jung correspondence need not make us suspicious of their seriousness of purpose. Neither Meyer nor Titchener, though, had the literary talent to be both profound and enduringly interesting. But I found myself engaged enough by the differences between Meyer and Titchener, and what they meant for American culture, to be able to read through the entire volume with profit and pleasure.

The editing of *Defining American Psychology* is exemplary; the notes are a storehouse of information. Sometimes Meyer wrote marginal comments on his copies of Titchener's letters, and these get reproduced for us now. In addition to the primary data itself, *Defining American Psychology* contains an instructive essay by Rand B. Evans on "The Scientific and Psychological Positions of E. E. Titchener," and two dazzling pieces by Ruth Leys: "Adolf Meyer, A Biographical Note," and "The Correspondence Between Adolf Meyer and E. B. Titchener."

Meyer, shortly after the Clark University ceremonies were over, sought out Titchener in the hope they could come to some mutual understanding, and even shared ground. (It is a sad reflection on our own times that mail delivery was then so efficient that Titchener was able to start replying to Meyer one day after Meyer first wrote him.) At the time, Meyer was more favorably disposed to both Freud and Jung than Titchener himself, although Titchener was not unaware of Freud's stature; in later years Meyer would grow relatively disenchanted with all of psychoanalysis, especially its sectarianism. Meyer was generous and open-minded as a thinker, and pragmatically inclined; he kept siding with common sense and life, whereas Titchener remained committed to pure science. Titchener even thought (not unlike Freud) that philosophy was "quite irrelevant to our present discussion...." From Titchener's point of view Meyer was a teleologist; and in Titchener's view "the cardinal sin of the scientific writer is muddle."

In contrast to Meyer's conviction that the whole of human experience has to be brought to bear on psychiatric psychology, Titchener's science was supposed to have "nothing whatever to do with values." Meyer felt he had to defend himself against being a mere "reflector" of Freud and Jung. Meyer and Titchener's letter-writing had been broken off in 1909, and then resumed again in 1918; but their differences remained irreconcilable. Meyer, in the end, said his mind thought of "formulations oftener than definitions." But Titchener remained resolute: as he wrote Meyer, "in proportion as you find me strict and pedantic do I find you elusive and intangible...I don't at all mind being wrong, provided only I am clear....To be right, even in the midst of muddle, is (I take it) your notion of the biggest service an individual may render to the same cause." And so Titchener gently proposed that they stop writing "for a while."

One of the most interesting facets to the Meyer-Titchener exchanges comes up in connection with the behaviorist John B. Watson; this incident, for me, turns the tables on everything connected with the Meyer-Titchener relationship. Meyer was quick to recognize the links between Titchener's so-called Structuralism and Watson's own approach. Meyer was humanistic enough to repudiate Watson's account of sexual behavior on the grounds that it was mechanical and fatalistic, and suspicious that Watson's approach might justify irregular sexual conduct at odds with the strictest of social expectations. Nonetheless, Meyer invited Watson, who in 1908 was appointed to the psychology department at Johns Hopkins, to move his psychology clinic to Meyer's Phipps Clinic.

Then, in 1920 Clark University's G. Stanley Hall let Meyer know that Watson was carrying on an illicit sexual affair with his research assistant. A dreadful scandal ensued, partly because the woman came from a prominent local family. Watson's academic career was in the end destroyed. Watson refused to break off the extramarital affair, Meyer turned the matter over to the university authorities, and Watson was asked to resign. Titchener criticized Meyer:

> What makes me indignant...is that A. Meyer and the Clinic in general couldn't have used their arts to keep W. straight. They are so blamed keen on theory—in which they are after all only logical infants—that they forget that the business of the psychiatrist is to prevent and cure. A little decent advice (for W. is intrinsically a very decent and

eminently likable person) would have prevented the family tragedy. And it is the children who suffer most.

Meyer, however, had seen in Watson's adultery the logical consequence of Watson's theories. To Titchener, Meyer had objected that science depends to some degree on what we define to be factual; Meyer had broadened the taking of case histories (he invented the "life chart"), and sought to free psychiatry from excessive classification. Meyer refused to separate "facts" from "values," yet his humanism led him, in Watson's case, to be moralistically intolerant. (Meyer also had lacked sympathy for W. I. Thomas's forced resignation in 1919 from the University of Chicago for sexual misconduct.)

*Defining American Psychology* is a landmark in the field; it successfully revives both Meyer and Titchener, places their ideas in historical context, and hopefully prepares this whole area for further research.

* * *

Philip Cushman, the author of *Constructing the Self, Constructing America: A Cultural History of Psychotherapy*,[6] is a practicing psychotherapist with advanced degrees in psychology as well as American and family studies. He is in an excellent position to reflect on the unusual place that psychotherapy has taken in American life. Cushman is methodologically up-to-date, and he relies on the latest social scientific conceptualizations in an effort to come to terms with how psychotherapy has evolved in the United States.

Cushman has worked within the tradition of psychoanalytic psychology and is particularly concerned with how modern conceptions of the self, designed to get away from the instinctual orientation of Freud, may have special and unacknowledged inadequacies. So Cushman spells out the strengths of the work of people like Heinz Kohut and Donald Winnicott, but at the same time he is wary about the social and philosophical implications of their ideas. It may be understandable if America welcomed concepts that provide substance to the liberal value of individualism, but Cushman worries that without being aware of it, American practitioners have started advocating consumerism, or what Cushman calls an "empty self." Others before now have been inclined to think that conformism and adaptation were the real beneficiaries of the American embrace of the Freudian tradition.

*Constructing the Self, Constructing America* can do a lot of good in encouraging psychotherapists to be more aware of the political implications of their work. Even the most neutral-seeming therapeutic help necessarily has philosophical dimensions. Therapists, whether they are always conscious of it or not, are inevitably engaged to cope with moral and ethical dilemmas, presented to them in the concrete circumstances of the troubled lives of clients.

Although I admire Cushman's interdisciplinary objectives, I cannot help regretting that he did not push his whole argument a good deal farther. I wonder, for example, whether it is ever going to be possible to understand the American reception of Freud's school unless there is some sustained comparison with the way at least one other country responded to the psychoanalytic impact on the history of ideas. Different nations have characteristically taken what they wanted from Freudianism, and although Cushman cites British (but not French) texts readily enough, it does not seem to me that he succeeds in getting at demonstrating just how special was the American response to psychoanalytic psychology.

Cushman would also have benefited from broadening the psychoanalytic ideology he examines. Thinkers such as Carl Jung, as well as Otto Rank, although alluded to in passing, were both centrally concerned with selfhood and individuation. The problems such theorists encountered would have bolstered Cushman's argument about the more recent writers. Perhaps we should just be grateful for Cushman's having given moral discourse such an important role in the implications and practice of psychotherapy. Although he ignores the advances that have been made in biological psychiatry, that branch of medicine could benefit as well from philosophical critiques.

* * *

*The Idea of the Past: History, Science, and Practise in American Psychoanalysis*[7] is part of an interesting series edited by Leo Goldberger of the Department of Psychology of New York University; its author, Leonard Jonathan Lamm, once taught political theory and now practises clinical psychology. In this ambitious and unusually reflective book, L. J. Lamm seeks to reconsider how psychoanalysis looks at the past, and he relies on contemporary continental theorists like H. G. Gadamer in taking a humanistic approach to how we construct narrative accounts of personal history.

Ever since its beginnings, psychoanalysis has been linked to certain unfortunate turn-of-the-century convictions about causality. Lamm takes an attractive position as he tries to ensure that psychoanalytic theory absorbs the lessons of current hermeneutical thinking. He is in favor of "pluralism," a term which can mean a number of different things.

Lamm does a conscientious job of evaluating the work of recent thinkers like Roy Schafer, as well as some other contemporary writers; but one wonders why, when the whole system of ideas he is working with had its origins elsewhere, he decided to restrict himself to American psychoanalysis. Even Gadamer, whom Lamm cites approvingly, comes out of a European context.

Throughout the conscientiousness that pervades *The Idea of the Past*, I had the impression of an unnecessary degree of scholasticism: for example, someone like Schafer seemed to Anna Freud to have made unacceptable concessions in terms of orthodox theorizing, and she felt even more harshly about Heinz Kohut. I do not share Anna Freud's convictions about either Schafer or Kohut, but I think it would have been better for Lamm to acknowledge some of the reasons that innovation has been so difficult until now. I do not think it makes much intellectual sense to pretend that there are (false) continuities when in fact serious disagreements among analytic theorists have been notable.

In fact, I wonder why Lamm did not stand back and put American psychoanalysis in a more cosmopolitan perspective. The name of Erich Fromm does not come up at all, and Jung is mentioned only once; yet someone like Fromm knew quite a bit about what was missing in Freud's approach to causality, and Jung actually proposed, before World War I, that patients could use the past defensively as a smokescreen against current realities – which I think many would now accept as a possibility even though Jung is rarely credited with this original insight.

The notion that American psychoanalysis is some kind of independent entity seems to me an artifical construct. Naturally Freud's work has meant different things in other national cultures, but the United States has never had a thinker who founded a distinctive school of thought. It is in keeping with American pragmatism that Lamm is as committed as he is to the value of pluralism, but I would encourage him to go even farther in the direction he has already embarked upon. He might find that many of the choice ideas of recent thinkers have in fact been anticipated by earlier writers even though it may not yet be conventional to cite their works.

Karen Horney plays no role in *The Idea of the Past*, nor need she: but if it is currently legitimate to cite Horney, can it be logical to continue to exclude Fromm? Pluralism will have real teeth to it when it is no longer acceptable to exclude any thinker on grounds other than the merits of ideas themselves. Genuine toleration of diversity would be welcome to the next generation of students of psychoanalysis. My hunch is, for example, that Lamm would find the writings of Otto Rank directly relevant to the theses he wants to advance. I believe that pioneering figures like Fromm, Jung, and Rank, no matter how much they may have disagreed with each other, need to be wrestled with before one deals with the most recent psychoanalytic thinkers.

* * *

*Conflict and Compromise: Therapeutic Implications*, edited by Scott Dowling,[8] begins to make any kind of sense only after reading the entire text and getting the gist of its political agenda. It starts off, incomprehensibly, with three theoretical papers that have nothing to add to what has been known for years now among orthodox psychoanalytic theorists. It is difficult to understand why this monograph in the Workshop Series of the American Psychoanalytic Association should begin with a set of stale theories. We are told, for example, that "the history of the patient's neurotic conflicts is reenacted in" the analytic setting, as if no one has ever challenged the idea that psychoanalysis succeeds in becoming in reality a laboratory-like situation. Numerous modern workers have pointed out the multiple tilts introduced by so-called classical analysis in the relationship that develops between therapist and patient.

When clinical issues are raised in the first three chapters, they are barren of reports of sensitivity on the part of therapists to the role of the counter-transference reactions toward patients. There is one illustration of a clarinet-playing patient that is designed to illustrate the concept of sublimation, but it reads like a travesty of Freudian thinking dating from before World War I; the author reduces the musical accomplishment to a series of sexual conflicts without an adequate awareness that human achievements defy such belittling.

Chapters 4, 5, and 6 deal with case material, and they are as interesting as all reports of clinical encounters are bound to be. As with the early chapters, however, I felt increasingly uneasy about a lack of adequate material on what was most idiosyncratic about the therapists themselves, except perhaps that they felt secure in safely practicing a well-established science without need of any special justification.

The remaining half of the book is made up of "discussions," starting off with a piece by Charles Brenner, a leading orthodox psychoanalytic theoretician. After a second, unilluminating chapter, there follow two chapters that help explain, I think, the purpose of *Conflict and Compromise*. Here we find a section written by a Kleinian analyst and then a piece composed by a self-psychologist. Notice that these appear in the "discussions" rather than in chapters equal to those which begin the book. I found the self-psychology chapter potentially arresting, but it looks like it will be another generation until a Jungian gets allowed into the fold at such orthodox "workshops." One of the early theorists in the text tells us that "numerous psychoanalytic contributors have carefully built up this new knowledge during the past fifty years without much fanfare or polemic insistence on forming new schools" without seeming to be aware how smug such a sentiment sounds.

Once the Kleinian and the Kohutian have had their say, the book concludes with the responses of the original authors. I found a tone of weary superiority over innovative ideas, combined with self-congratulation about what has already been accomplished. The Kleinian and the Kohutian are very well behaved, and there is no sound here of the thunder of battle, or even the life of the mind. *Conflict and Compromise* is representative of the "decline" that Hale reported on.

Psychoanalysis cannot survive, I think, without a great deal more openness. *Conflict and Compromise* does not read like a workshop where people are genuinely testing out new ideas or groping for new formulations. Part of it sounds like a funeral dirge; and if the point of the exercise is to demonstrate so-called toleration toward a Kleinian and a Kohutian, then I think that the illusion of genuine debate can do damage in reinforcing the prejudices and preconceptions of the old establishment. A sound book might have given substantial conceptual standing to viewpoints other than the ones expressed in the bulk of the text. As it is, *Conflict and Compromise* will not change the way anyone thinks, although it may get added (surely unread) to the bookshelves of orthodox psychoanalysts.

* * *

Early psychoanalysis had a special commitment to the belief in the power of rational enlightenment. An essential constituent of Freud's program was the notion that scientific insight would lead to social reform and, in the long run, amelioration of human suffering. So Freud challenged traditional family customs and sought to free people from superstitions and illusions. Throughout Freud's career he retained the ambitions of a social prophet; as a therapist, however, he also sought to rely on the efficacy of insight. Through reconstructing the patient's early years by means of the analyst's relying on the technique of free association, Freud thought that patients could gain a key leverage over the past and be able to make more rational choices.

Freud sought to structure his theories so that they would form a body of knowledge which would fulfill the standards of scientific theory; he thought not only that his "findings" were capable of being verified but that he and his followers had brought solid evidence to support his hypotheses. In practice, Freud had considerable artistic powers and ranks as the greatest writer among twentieth-century psychologists. But he distrusted his own capacities for art and presented his conclusions as a scientific system. It was in this sort of rationalistic mood that Freud was capable of criticizing intuition as an illusion, a form of hocus-pocus produced by the need for wish-fulfillment.

Freud's critics within modern psychotherapy were unhappy with this aspect of his approach; they thought that much more had to be involved in helping patients than simply the analyst's offering them rational insight. Furthermore, critics often said that old-fashioned suggestion lay hidden behind the supposed neutrality of Freud's approach. By now there is some agreement that the whole concept of psychoanalysis as the quest for abstract truth implied that the analyst was capable of being ideally rational and that the patient was susceptible to all kinds of infantile strivings. Freud wrote about the existence and significance of the patient's emotional transferences, whereas he treated the analyst's counter-transferences as a potential interference in the laboratory-like clinical situations he believed he had created.

More recently, Freud's school of thought has been moving away from his own most scientific-sounding pretensions, and many of the points that his critics tried to establish are now being accepted in psychoanalysis. Alfred Margulies's *The Empathic Imagination* [9] is a touching and concrete account of a modern psychoanalyst's trying to come to terms with the demands of a clinical practice conducted with a humanistic orientation. Margulies is searching for light on the problem of empathy without making an effort explicitly to challenge the earlier psychoanalytic premium on insight. Margulies's outlook points to more of a burden on the therapist, since in principle the therapist, incapable of being omniscient, is only a working partner in an inherently troubled alliance with the patient struggling for help.

The result is that *The Empathic Imagination* relies on a broad range of sources. Margulies has broken with past sectarian orthodoxies and feels free to cite some of the ideas of Carl Jung, Otto Rank, Karen Horney, and Harry Stack Sullivan when he finds them relevant. Although Freud thought that psychoanalysis was capable of avoiding the traditional problems of philosophy, Margulies rightly tries to confront some of the central dilemmas of moral thought; he makes the whole problem of "world view" a central one clinically. And he is willing to tell us about at least one clinical occasion when he felt secure in prescribing a drug like lithium, in contrast to an earlier generation of analysts who frowned on using medication.

The self psychology of Heinz Kohut has been centrally responsible for a shift in psychoanalytic thinking over the last two decades, and Margulies—without being doctrinaire about it—relies on Kohutian terminology. Margulies is more catholic than most analysts in the list of thinkers he relies on, but I believe he still might benefit from going back for instance to the concept of a phenomenological self advanced by the early analyst Paul Federn. The work of Erik Erikson, although touched on in passing in this book, is also more unfashionable currently than it deserves to be for those eager to move in the general direction of emancipating analytic thinking from the constraints of scientistic reasoning.

Apart from all theoretical issues, Margulies is centrally concerned with the various functions of psychotherapy and how personality changes can be mobilized. Yet here I wonder whether he unwittingly is not too tied to past orthodox techniques. For example, he presents us with an extended account of one of his cases, an apparently regressed woman who has trouble coming to terms with Margulies's office renovations. But only in passing does Margulies mention his silences and the use of the couch. It is hard for me not to wonder to what extent his patient was reacting not so much to the exigencies of her own psychopathology as to the emotional deprivation of the setting of the classic analytic situation itself.

Margulies tells us how important in his own training was the example of the Boston psychiatrist Elvin Semrad and how Semrad concentrated on the analyst's special supportive functions. As a student, like Margulies, I also "experienced Semrad as magical," but I think it is time to try to decipher where even someone as extremely talented as Semrad might have been hobbled by the constraints of the theoretical concepts of his psychoanalytic era. Margulies has succeeded in going far beyond the conventional pieties that used to be customary at our best psychoanalytic training centers, but my impression is that if he continues along the road he has chosen he will find that others before him, even if they have not recently been fashionable to cite, have seen some of the main inadequacies of the excessive rationalism that we owe to early psychoanalytic thought.

## Notes

1. Nathan G. Hale, *Freud and the Americans: The Beginnings of Psychoanalysis in the United States. 1876-1917* (New York: Oxford University Press, 1995).
2. Nathan G. Hale, *The Rise and Crisis of Psychoanalysis in the United States: Freud and the Americans, 1917-1985* (New York: Oxford University Press, 1995).
3. Ellen Herman, *The Romance of American Psychology: Political Culture in the Age of Experts* (Berkeley: University of California Press, 1995).
4. Ruth Leys and Rand B. Evans, eds., *Defining American Psychology: The Correspondence Between Adolf Meyer and Edward Bradford Titchener* (Baltimore, MD: Johns Hopkins University Press, 1990).
5. Ruth Leys, "Meyer's Dealing With Jones: A Chapter in the History of the American Response to Psychoanalysis," *Journal of the History of the Behavioral Sciences*, 17 (1981), pp. 445-65.
6. Phlip Cushman, *Constructing the Self, Constructing America: a Cultural History of Psychotherapy* (Reading, MA: Addison-Wesley, 1995).
7. Leonard Jonathan Lamm, *The Idea of the Past: History, Science, and Practise in American Psychoanalysis* (New York: New York University Press, 1993).
8. Scott Dowling, ed., *Conflict and Compromise: Therapeutic Implications* (Madison, CT: International Universities Press, 1991).
9. Alfred Margulies, *The Empathic Imagination* (New York: Norton, 1989).

# 41

# France

Although psychoanalytic doctrine may sometimes look like a uniform system of thought, in fact different national societies, and even regions, have taken up and magnified disparate strands in Freud's work that peculiarly suited their own cultural moods. The story of Freud in America has to do largely with the medical need to find a new psychotherapeutic system; and the Americans also wanted to find in psychoanalysis a way of challenging traditional family life, overthrowing past norms of constraint.

The French Freud is a completely different creature. William James was reading Freud in the 1890s to understand what might be accomplished in practice through hypnosis; and even before World War I American psychiatrists were trying out psychoanalytic techniques on clinical patients. By 1914 Greenwich Village intellectuals were being introduced to the latest psychoanalytic formulations. In France, however, right up until Freud's death in 1939 psychoanalysis was viewed as an alien, if not German, ideology. All Freud's chosen disciples who worked in Paris had credentials that were viewed as somehow not thoroughly French enough. Even today there is still not yet an authorized, standard edition of Freud's works translated into French.

Yet by now there is no city in the world more abuzz with matters psychoanalytic than Paris. The bookstores there are full of fresh works about Freud and the history of his school. Something like 16 different Freudian institutions are functioning in France. One society in Paris has the largest number of members in the world of any unit affiliated with the International Psychoanalytic Association (IPA), first founded by Freud in 1910. Controversies about psychoanalytic issues have become central to the Parisian life of the mind: readers of *Le Monde*, *L'Express*, and *Le Figaro* have been exposed to learning about court battles between rival psychoanalytic factions. Although Freudian matters have largely been of concern to the Left in France, still I think it is fair to say that there is nowhere which can currently challenge the French national embrace of all things psychoanalytic.

Elisabeth Roundinesco's *Jacques Lacan & Co.*[1] reflects as well as recounts how this state of affairs could have come about. We are informed on the jacket-cover that it was a best seller in its French edition. Although *Jacques Lacan & Co.* is a huge book, more than 700 large pages long, it is only the second volume of a two-part study; the first volume, not yet translated into English, covers the years 1885-1925. Although I found *Jacques Lacan and Co.* a fascinating study, it is so detailed that I suspect only a handful of people will ever join me in having read every word of it.

Just because *Jacques Lacan & Co.* is apparently so encyclopedic it is necessary to notice its curious narrowness. For example, we find here absolutely no account of the legitimate criticisms to which Freudianism has ever been subjected. I find it impossible to believe that over the years since 1925 there have been no fair-minded objections to psychoanalysis advanced in France. The evidence in Vienna itself is that, even while Freud was still practicing, respectful and sympathetic reservations were being proposed. With all the careful attention that Roudinesco lavishes on Freud, almost nothing gets said about Carl Jung. Yet the conflict between Freud and Jung remains, I think, one of those central confrontations the implications of which we will always have with us. Ever since before World War I, Jung has remained Freud's most searching critic; and much that has appeared since then amounts to new labels for old ideas.

Even more striking is the omission in *Jacques Lacan & Co.* of any attention at all to Otto Rank, Freud's former favorite pupil, who lived in Paris in the 1920s and 1930s. Rank had for more than a decade in France a circle around him which included people like Henry Miller and Anaïs Nin. Yet we learn nothing about this from Roudinesco. There is even little here on Marie Bonaparte, the Princess George, who became an enemy of Lacan's; it seems as if not even Marie Bonaparte qualifies as adequately French. But we do learn the names of various personal family servants of Lacan's. Oddly, while Jean-Paul Sartre and Simone de Beauvoir were pioneers in introducing psychoanalysis, they play little role in *Jacques Lacan & Co.* (That the narrator to Beauvoir's *The Mandarins* was an analyst must have reflected something about the standing of Freud in France then.)

Even if Roudinesco is convinced of the unique superiority of Lacan to all other analysts after Freud, she should have been obliged to do more homework about the founder of psychoanalysis. It is shortsighted of her to argue that "The Freudian definition of 'normality' and 'deviation' excluded all blame or moral judgment." Freud had his definite value commitments which got communicated through his theorizing, and it is futile at this late date to try and deny the immense role which his ethical preferences played. At the same time it is in error for Roudinesco to write, when talking about Freud's refusal to see Andre Gide, that "Freud always refused to analyze artists…." For example, he treated the poetess called H. D. for some time, and she was not alone among the artists Freud saw. Roudinesco is also not as knowledgeable about her sources as she might be; for example, Ronald Laing was not analyzed by Donald W. Winnicott, as she supposes, but by Charles Rycroft.

The general problem with *Lacan & Co.* is that Roudinesco, not unlike Hale, has had trouble distinguishing between the largest problems and the more isolated ones. The book proceeds at a breathless pace as controversy breeds further contention. It is true that since psychoanalysis has become such a major component of contemporary French culture, all her attention to detail seems justified. But as she gives us, for example, an account of how the Lacanian movement has splintered since Lacan's death in 1981, one still has to wonder whether all her effort in *Lacan & Co.* is not too much a case of a mountain bringing forth the proverbial mouse.

Supposedly, Lacan is a hero because he refused to go along with the conformist thinking of the Anglo-American psychoanalysts. And Lacan made the term ego-psychology, which has especially flourished in America, into an uncontestably bad-sounding concept in Paris. Yet much of *Lacan & Co.* is taken up with Lacan's own conformist efforts to win recognition from the International Psychoanalytic Association; if he was a failure in preventing his excommunication, which was supported by Freud's daughter Anna, it was not for want of Lacan's trying. Roudinesco provides only a fancy rationalization for what she calls Lacan's "relentless pursuit of recognition by the IPA"; supposedly he sought to avoid becoming a master with his own school. When one fully realizes just what relative nonentities he was organizationally struggling against, then it does seem a poor show for him to have accused others of unnecessarily bowing to the weight of authority.

Lacan was right in thinking there were central authoritarian problems associated with psychoanalytic training. He himself ended up even dissolving his own psychoanalytic society. In the 1920s he occasionally participated in meetings of the Action française and supported monarchism supposedly to compensate for his loss of Catholic faith; by the 1960s, however, Lacan was allied with political Maoists. Roudinesco says he was "Spinozan when he assumed his banishment, de-Gaullian when he founded his school, and Maoist when he supported his red guards against his old friends in a concerted practice of divisiveness." Lacan seems to have wanted to promote an uninterrupted cultural revolution within psychoanalysis; he was in the vanguard of a cause that seemed in principle incapable of being institutionalized.

Therapeutically he was innovative in seeing patients for brief time spans; he could dismiss an analytic patient after ten or fifteen minutes. (His fees were not cut down proportionately.) Lacan was correct in thinking that there ought to be nothing sacrosanct about the 50-minute analytic hour; his son-in-law Jacques-Alain Miller, who has inherited Lacan's empire, gives appointments every 15 minutes, and occasionally functions without appointments. But all Lacan's experimentations with time were in the same direction of brevity. And it was not because he was wary of the impact of his personality being too great on his patients. Lacan was as high-handed as anybody in the history of psychoanalysis has ever been.

Although it still goes unrecognized in Parisian intellectual life today, ego psychology took root in America for legitimate therapeutic reasons. It is nonsense for Roudinesco to call a lightweight like Rudolph Loewenstein, I think simply because he was Lacan's own analyst, "the future founder of 'ego psychology.'" Freud's own practices as an analyst left much to be desired; after his death there was a problem of how to make teachable the arbitrary ways in which he had proceeded. Some of his concepts might sound intriguing, but at the same time be deadly from the point of view of successful therapy. His proposal of the existence of a death instinct was not just an aspect of Central European sophistication, but could in practice lead to a form of pessimism almost nihilistic in its implications. And a notion of Freud's like that of a so-called negative therapeutic reaction meant that patients supposedly got worse because of their own unconscious guilt feelings rather than any mistakes on the part of the analysts.

It is all well and good to admire how dazzling Lacan was capable of being in leading one of his famous seminars, and doubtless the American Freud has as many blind spots as the French Freud. Lacanianism was the functional equivalent to our own antipsychiatry movement. But any one country can ill afford to dismiss in a wholesale way what has been accomplished elsewhere. It is disquieting to be reassured by Roudinesco that "Lacan was never mad, although he was occasionally a megalomaniac." Freud left a body of thought which conscientious followers found unduly negativistic, and ego psychology was designed in particular to breathe a more caring and optimistic component into the body of thought Freud had bequeathed.

I would not want in any way, however, to detract from all the important labor of love Roudinesco has accomplished. Whatever my own reservations about Lacan, she has in *Jacques Lacan & Co.* successfully recreated a whole separate world. Nobody will ever be able to write about the story of Freud in France without relying on her pioneering work. I can think of no comparably comprehensive account of Freud's reception in any other national culture with the exception of Nathan Hale's *Freud and the Americans* and *The Rise and Crisis of Psychoanalysis in the United States*. Roudinesco is, I found, rather better at her institutional history than at explaining concepts; even after all these hundreds of big pages I doubt readers on this side of the Atlantic are going to be much clearer about just what Lacan did mean by a "matheme" or the intricacies of "*la passe*."

It is a tribute to what Roudinesco has accomplished that *Jacques Lacan & Co.* is bound to promote more interest in the French Freud; a synthetic view of the reception of Freud's work in different national cultures would almost amount to an intellectual history of the twentieth century. For example, with the end of the Cold War Freud's writings have once again, as in the 1920s, become best-sellers in the old Soviet Union. Studies on the Russian Freud, and the distinctive uses of psychoanalytic thought there or in France, will doubtless give us more insight into the multidimensional character of Freud's own ideas. It is a testimony to his seminal genius to have spawned so diverse a heritage.

## Note

1. Elisabeth Roudinesco, *Jacques Lacan & Co.: A History of Psychoanalysis in France, 1925-1985*, translated by Jeffrey Mehlman (Chicago: University of Chicago Press, 1990).

# 42

# Argentina

Psychoanalysis in Argentina plays an unusual role in the world today, and has fulfilled a unique place in the intellectual history of this past century. It would be hard to think of any nation in which the transformation in ideas which Freud initiated has had more impact than on Argentinian culture. Today it has to be striking not only how numerous psychoanalytic groups are in Argentina, but how widespread an influence varieties of the teachings espoused by Freudian disciples have succeeded in making. For an outsider it is remarkable how academic departments of psychology within universities (unlike in the United States) are aware of the significance of psychoanalytic doctrine; so that not just among therapeutic practitioners Freud became a powerful force, but throughout Argentinian life his work continues to attract the most intense kind of interest. A whole chapter of the life of the mind, at least since 1910 and long before Freud's death in 1939, can be taken up with how Freud's work was received by Argentinians.

Ever since the early 1940s Freud's writings have been organizationally welcomed in Argentina, as analysts started to get trained within international bodies entitled to certify psychoanalytic candidates. (For reasons I do not yet understand the work of Melanie Klein has played a special role in Argentina.) Following World War II, Argentina became a key to the transmission of psychoanalytic teachings throughout Latin America as a whole. By now Freud's ideas, amended and adapted to the needs of different national cultures, are flourishing throughout the Southern American hemisphere. (So much of the funding of the International Psychoanalytic Association comes from there that now the Presidency of the IPA rotates every two years between North America, Europe, and Latin America.) In spite of Freud's own personal ambivalences about social philosophy, since at times at least he claimed to want only to create a neutral scientific discipline, his theories were bound powerfully to shape our conceptions of what it is like to be human. His concepts have changed moral values and belief as well as empirical expectations about how people behave.

This past century has been more terrible than ever anticipated. Those who, starting in the Enlightenment and continuing through the Victorian era, looked confidently forward to social and political progress would have to be shocked by events that unfolded in our time. Hitler's coming to power in Germany should be impossible to forget. But too many choose to gloss over the fact that he succeeded by means that were pretty fair-and-square; he did not seize power illegally, but was democratically elected under a parliamentary system. To make matters worse, more worrisome to friends of the ideal of self-government, the Weimar constitution, which governed Germany after World War I until Hitler finally did away with it, had been drafted by some of the best minds in modern social science. Tyranny and state terror have not just beset someplace like Argentina, about which most of us know little, but have afflicted a culture like Germany that has been so central to the Western tradition. Freud, along with so many others at the time, missed seeing the impending catastrophe: "A nation that produced Goethe," he is reported to have observed, "could not possibly go to the bad."[1]

I would argue that the practice of psychoanalysis, and psychotherapy too, becomes impossible under conditions of a modern authoritarian political regime. Just as I believe that Germany under Hitler lacked a legal system, since the "law" was administered by courts for such arbitrary and evil purposes, so I think that under such political conditions it is indecent even to think of carrying on something like psychoanalytic therapy. Of course there is such a phenomenon as heroism, and it is possible for human nature to be capable of rising to extraordinary heights. But most people try to get on with their lives, as they adapt to outside reality; and it is all too easy to slide into collaborating in nefarious social practices.

I am suggesting that the problem of state terror and psychoanalysis is not something we can afford safely to keep our distance from. Just as it is agreeable to think that Hitler was a madman, alien to norman human nature, so it is too reassuring to suppose that what happened there is not directly relevant to our own society. Old-line Soviet psychiatrists, to cite another instance of tyranny in our century that has invaded the healing professions, may seem out of the way and alien to what we know in the West. But I do think that we all have to be on our toes about the extent to which we cooperate in social injustices within our own culture.

The old standard of analytic neutrality ought not to be misused in order to help countenance allowing political immorality in our own societies to go unchallenged. I am not recommending that psychoanalysts and psychotherapists should turn themselves into propagandists. And I do not think that patients should be burdened with problems that are alien to their own troubles. But Freud's profession is at least as much an art as well as a science, and moral values play an essential role in every single therapeutic encounter. I am reminded again of a comment Freud is reported to have made to Marie Bonaparte, a remark of his that I think has never been adequately absorbed within the profession. She noted in her journal of her analysis for 1926 that he had said to her: "More important than what one does is what one is."[2]

It is impossible to be a decent, civilized person and not espouse certain moral commitments. This expression of ethical views does not have to be verbalized, but it is most tellingly communicated through our very being. And so although it might be heartening to think that the problems of politics, and resistance to tyranny, can be confined to countries away from our own—to Argentina and Germany, Italy, Brazil, and Spain, for example—in reality these issues need to be brought closer to home. George Orwell once argued that everything was ultimately political, and although that memorable saying of his was an exaggeration, still it points toward a truth. We cannot afford to ignore the implications of moral philosophy, even if our training and education are not apt to equip us well in this connection.

## Notes

1. Quoted in Ernest Jones, *The Life and Work of Sigmund Freud*, Vol. 3 (New York: Basic Books, 1957), p. 151.
2. Quoted in Celia Bertin, *Marie Bonaparte: A Life* (New York: Harcourt Brace & World, 1982), p. 176.

# 43

# Great Britain

Although I have long found publishing to be a fascinating enterprise, intellectually stimulating and interesting, *Leonard and Virginia Woolf As Publishers*[1] is the first book about publishing, outside of Bennett Cerf's memoir *At Random*, that I can recall having read. My interest in the Woolfs was aroused because of the central role they played within the Bloomsbury circle of intellectuals, and in particular the part that the Hogarth Press, as Freud's English publisher starting in the 1920s, took in disseminating psychoanalytic ideas throughout the English-speaking world. I interviewed Leonard Woolf in 1965 in connection with his personal knowledge of Freud and relished each of the five volumes of Woolf's autobiography; he sent me some sales figures of Freud's pre-World War II texts.

Willis's book about the Woolfs is extraordinarily conscientious, and one would think definitive. He spent more than ten years reconstructing the records of the Hogarth Press from its inception in 1917 until Virginia Woolf's suicide in 1941; the documents managed to survive the London Blitz. Initially, the Woolfs did their own printing and binding in their dining room; the first texts of the Hogarth Press were hand-set by themselves. Even when the publishing house was at its most thriving, the offices were housed in the basement of their flat; printers and authors were interviewed in their sitting room.

The Woolfs at first drew on friends and acquaintances to flesh-out their list of authors. Eventually the Hogarth Press had a small staff, but Leonard (who had once been an Imperial civil servant) always kept a tight grip on the day-to-day operations. Virginia was the chief reader he relied upon for decisions about accepting fiction. Willis suggests, probably correctly, that one of the attractions of the Hogarth Press from Leonard's point of view was that it was a means of keeping Virginia's mental balance secure. The physical and mental labors functioned as an escape valve from her most imaginative creative efforts. Much as she might sometime bemoan the time the Hogarth Press took up, the couple seemed to enjoy the work.

Intellectual historians have to be impressed how early on the Hogarth Press helped through their contracts such writers as T. S. Eliot, Katherine Mansfield,

E. M. Forster, Christopher Isherwood, Vita Sackville-West, John Maynard Keynes, Henry Green, Robert Graves, and Herbert Read. The Woolfs also commissioned translations of the works of Rainer Maria Rilke, Italo Svevo, Ivan Bunin, Maxim Gorky, and Anton Chekhov. Ironically, Virginia had not approved of the first few chapters of James Joyce's *Ulysses*, and that rejection meant that the Hogarth Press forfeited the right to have the honor to introduce that modern classic; it took years for it to get into print, and the foreign printers in France introduced multiple errors into the text. Virginia seemed to grow more strongly antipathetic toward *Ulysses* as the years passed. Willis records how the Woolfs also rejected a translation of Andre Gide's *Straight Is The Gate*, Gertrude Stein's *Making of Americans*, Ivy Compton-Burnett's third novel, and an early story by Richard Hughes. It has been claimed that Saul Bellow and Jean-Paul Sartre also got rejection notices from the Hogarth Press. But the fact that such works got submitted to the Woolfs at all is testimony to how enlightened, compared to other publishers, they could be counted upon to be.

Even as late as 1965, when I met with Leonard Woolf, the Hogarth Press retained a wonderfully old-fashioned ramshackle appearance. I can never forget the narrow rickety stairs I climbed to reach Woolf's office; nor the special glow his face acquired, in the midst of our conversation, as he happened to glance over at something of Virginia's he was overseeing for posthumous publication. Leonard had, even before Virginia's death, taken an outside partner into the firm. According to Willis's painstaking reconstruction of the financial records, the Hogarth Press was always modestly profitable. Virginia's own books, and those of Freud and the psychoanalysts, were to be keystones to the business. At times Leonard, though not with me, exaggerated the risk he took in accepting Freud and the analysts as authors. In an era, even by 1965 standards, when publishing had become an overwhelmingly commercial undertaking, the Hogarth Press fulfilled the ideal of what a writer desires from a publishing house. (The Hogarth Press brought out the English edition of my first book in 1969, which also happened to be the year of Leonard's death; when they got sent galleys for my second book, *Brother Animal*, they were forwarded on to Anna Freud which meant a pack of trouble for me.) Any publisher who loves books was, then as now, a rarity, and the Hogarth Press deserves the kind of scrupulously careful treatment that Willis has accorded it.

The most successful publishers I have known, however, maintain that they are more or less at a loss at what it is that sells books. A central mystery would seem to lie at the heart of the publishing industry, not one of the world's most profitable business undertakings. Leonard and Virginia were never out to make a financial killing through the Hogarth Press. I am surprised to find how meticulous Leonard was as a financial manager, and Willis demonstrates that Leonard was difficult, and downright authoritarian, with the tiny staff he struggled to retain.

Willis breaks his general chronology to accord a special chapter to "Freud and the Freudians," but I found it not as novelly informative as I had hoped.

Woolf had explained to me how hopelessly amateurish the analysts had been as businessmen, printing up thousands of copies of texts, out of megalomania, which remained unsold for years. Books, because of the way they were kept in Vienna, were bound to have gotten soiled, and Leonard said that for ages he got complaints from British booksellers about the quality of what he handed on to them. It was James Strachey, according to what he told me, who first brought the proposal to Leonard that he publish Freud in England.

Strachey's translations have come in, partly at the hands of Bruno Bettelheim, for a good deal of recent criticism. Yet it is often forgotten how Strachey was functioning within an already preexisting confine of decision-making about how certain terms of Freud's were to be rendered in English. Freud's command of English was excellent, and I think he was lucky, once alerted by Ernest Jones, to have been perceptive enough to spot Strachey's special talents. Even when Strachey invented a term like "cathexis," Freud incorporated it into one of his own German texts. There is still to this day no comparable edition of Freud's works in French, for example, and the latest German edition of Freud's works relies on translations of Strachey's notes to the English edition. I have never seen any evidence pertaining to whether Strachey ever got monetary payment for what he undertook, but it surely did not explain, or adequately compensate for, the special labor of love that later went into what became the twenty-four volumes of his *Standard Edition* of Freud's psychological writings. Had Strachey, shortly after Freud's death in 1939, not volunteered to undertake the task, a committee would have been struck instead and the project inevitably postponed for years. As it was, Strachey, along with Alix and the cooperation of a few others, accomplished what has to be considered, I think, a special feat.

If Willis taught me nothing really new about the relationship between Freud and the Hogarth Press, he did succeed in putting that aspect of the history of the Woolf's publishing ventures into the context of their work as a whole. I had had no idea how Leonard, "in his lifetime obsession with details, prided himself on his book-keeping." Literally "he kept his finger on every penny and every shilling...." At the same time "Virginia, not Leonard the businessman,...handled the gritty matters of house hunting and lease signing for their various moves."

Still Leonard was the first reader for whom Virginia wrote; she always needed his judgment and reassurance on the initial completion of one of her texts. With the freedom and independence provided by the Hogarth Press, she needed no one else to please. Leonard's own political and social writings, part of his intense involvement, as editor and activist, in Socialist politics, bear testimony to his own creative capacities. I have long thought that Leonard, as the imaginative lesser of the two writers, has been unduly valued for what he brought to Virginia's life. But Willis's story of the Hogarth Press helps to keep straight not just the details of the collaboration between Leonard and Virginia, but amplifies an essential constituent to one of the twentieth century's most unusual marriages.

I cannot help wondering, given the advanced state of contemporary printing technology, whether even today two such people, "energetic consumers of books, readers with vast interests, professional reviewers and editors," could not reproduce their publishing achievement. When asked, Leonard certainly said he thought it could all happen again.

* * *

The subject of influence has always intrigued intellectual historians. Great thinkers conceive the world anew; they work within a culture's traditions of thought, and yet must of necessity conceive of ideas in their own terms. Nonetheless, although the impact of one writer on another is usually impossible to pin down, those of us within the academic world are naturally drawn to the problem of comparing and contrasting figures in the life of the mind. In Freud's case, for instance, it is impossible not to be intrigued by his relationship with both Nietzsche and Schopenhauer.

I accidentally happened to stumble on a hitherto unknown apparent link between Freud and the English biographer and moralist Lytton Strachey. The issue of the relationship between psychoanalysis and Bloomsbury intellectuals has become the subject of scholarly inquiry. Leonard Woolf, as Freud's English publisher, with his wife Virginia met Freud after he moved in exile to London. It had been James Strachey, Lytton's younger brother, who, as we have seen, had first put his friend Leonard Woolf onto the idea of bringing Freud's books out at the Hogarth press. Virginia Woolf's brother Adrian, and his wife Karin, both had become themselves psychoanalysts. And we know that early on in the analyses of both James Strachey and his wife Alix, who had originally gone to Vienna shortly after World War I to be analyzed by Freud, he acknowledged their literary talent and picked them then to start translating papers of his into English.

There has been speculation about the relationship between Freud and Lytton Strachey, since they had so many thematic and stylistic similarities. It is known for example that Freud enjoyed reading Strachey's *Eminent Victorians*, although it has been doubted that at the time Strachey first wrote that book he was yet influenced by Freud's teachings. Freud relished Strachey's debunking approach to religion. Strachey's great book on Queen Victoria ends with a famous paragraph in which, while she is dying, he enters into her mind after she has become speechless; he imagines that she lies in bed free-associating back to her earliest childhood. Strachey first wrote this stunning last paragraph, and only then proceeded to compose the rest of the book itself. I have long suspected that in Lord Keynes's *General Theory of Employment, Interest and Money,* which also concludes with an extraordinary and even more often-quoted last paragraph, and whose work has recently been investigated for its similarities to Freud's, Keynes had been competing with his old friend and rival Lytton Strachey to see whether Keynes too could draft a passage and then write a book to precede it.

According to James Strachey, the main example of his brother Lytton being consciously influenced by psychoanalysis came in his composition of his relatively late *Elizabeth and Essex*, a book which Lytton dedicated to James and Alix Strachey, who were then practicing analysts. A letter from Freud to Lytton discussed the problem of the psychology of Queen Elizabeth I.

Now I have come across an instance of an apparent reciprocal relationship between Bloomsbury and Freud. We have known that during James Strachey's analysis with Freud he lent his analyst a copy of Keynes's *The Economic Consequences of the Peace*. That is historically relevant, since Freud already disapproved of Woodrow Wilson, and Keynes's unattractive concept of Wilson fed Freud's political prejudices, which culminated in his later collaboration with William C. Bullitt on a study of the American president.

In addition, it seems that Freud might have quoted something from Lytton Strachey's work without acknowledging the kind of indebtedness that academic scholars are accustomed to. At any rate, there is a curious parallel that needs pointing out. In preparing Helene Deutsch's collected psychoanalytic papers for publication, I was faced with a sudden editorial dilemma on the page proofs. In a clinically important 1926 paper of hers on occultism, she discussed how an analyst's counter-transference can be a constructive source of intuitive empathy into patients' problems. Her paper has been often neglected in the literature as part of downplaying psychoanalysis and the occult. The whole subject of telepathy, Freud's fascination and repulsion over the matter, has for too long been a taboo subject among analysts. A paper of his from 1921 was deemed by some of his closest disciples to be so potentially troublesome that it was withheld from publication until 1941.

Oddly enough, he there discusses a patient he had referred to Helene Deutsch for analytic treatment, but she never noticed this mention, because she had not realized that Freud's posthumously published paper was actually anything new. I brought the clinical illustration to her attention in the course of my interviewing her. She had never bought Strachey's *Standard Edition*, since she was so confident she knew Freud's works by heart from much earlier German texts. Freud never specified in his published paper that one of the patients he was talking about was sent by him to Helene, but from her own prior description to me of patients she had gotten from Freud it was easy for me, when I came across it in re-reading Freud, to confirm with her that it was in fact the identical case we had already talked about. It was fascinating to see just how Freud had described in print, with disguises, a case that Helene herself knew about clinically and from a different perspective. (Ernst Falzeder tells me that an examination of the manuscript of the paper indicates that in Freud's text, in contrast to what got published, he specifically mentioned having sent the patient to Helene Deutsch.)

The problem with my editing Helene's own paper on occultism was that in the first published version she refers to works of Freud from a German edition; and in the only English translation of her essay, which appeared originally in

1953, Strachey's early *Collected Papers* is cited. I felt I had to scramble to put a proper reference for English-speaking readers to Strachey's later *Standard Edition*, and therefore I looked through everything Freud had written on telepathy to find the appropriate references. Although I left the wording of the quotation from the *Collected Papers* intact, I hunted for the appropriate modern page numbers in the *Standard Edition* since I assume that is the text most of us use now.

If I believed in telepathy I would think that the following coincidence was an illustration for it, for I had only just a day earlier been reading from Lytton Strachey's *Books and Characters*,[2] a collection of his odds and ends, dedicated to Keynes, which appeared in 1922. Although I had already read almost everything by Lytton Strachey, this book had escaped my grasp; he wrote with such clarity and wit that, even though I know how he could distort historical evidence, every essay is a joy for me to savor. One piece of his I had just read late at night; it was called "Madame du Deffand," and was based on the letters she wrote to Horace Walpole. The three volumes of their letters appeared first in 1912, and Strachey had written about them in 1913.

The relevant passage in Strachey's essay is as follows:

> Her famous "mot de Saint Denis," so dear to the heart of Voltaire, deserves to be once more recorded. A garrulous and credulous Cardinal was describing the martydom of Saint Denis the Areopagite: when his head was cut off, he took it up and carried it in his hands. That, said the Cardinal, was well known; what was not well known was the extraordinary fact that he walked with his head under his arm all the way from Montmartre to the Church of Saint Denis—a distance of some six miles. "Ah, Monseigneur!" said Madame du Deffand, "dans une telle situation, il n'y a que le premier pas qui coûte."

Roughly translated she had said: "in this situation, it is only the first step that counts."

The comparable though slightly different passage with which Freud concluded his 1921 telepathy paper reads:

> Perhaps the problem of thought-transference may seem very trivial to you in comparison with the great magical world of the occult. But consider what a momentous step beyond what we have hitherto believed would be involved in this hypothesis alone. What the custodian of [the basilica of] Saint Denis used to add to his account of the saint's martyrdom remains true. Saint-Denis is said, after his head was cut off, to have picked it up and walked quite a distance with it under his arm. But the custodian used to remark: "*Dans les case pareils, ce n'est que le premier pas qui coûte.*" The rest is easy.

A translation from the custodian might read: "in these instances it is only the first step that counts." James Strachey added the footnote: "the *mot* was Madame du Deffand's. See her letter to Walpole of June 6, 1767." In Freud's version it was no longer a Cardinal who told the tale, and the custodian both reports it and jokes about it.

Freud's use of irony has often been neglected. First, he had modestly restricted himself to the problem of thought-transference, in contrast to the whole area of the occult. And then, in proposing that in spite of such a restriction his contribution might amount to a "momentous step" nonetheless, his open-minded paper on the possibility of the existence of telepathy concluded on a note which implied his continuing suspicion that it ought to remain in the category of an aspect of human superstitiousness. Freud could not, given his own critical attitude toward religion, have retained the Cardinal as narrator; that would have gone too far and undermined the purpose of the paper, which was to express his tolerant acceptingness of the reality of thought-transference. But his inner doubts were enough that the paper never appeared in his lifetime.

Part of what intrigues me is the question of sources. According to James Strachey, Freud wrote the paper between August 2 and 6, 1921; then he presented it to a meeting of his closest international followers, who made up his "secret committee" in early September 1921. Strachey's splendid *Standard Edition* was mainly constructed out of an examination of Freud's printed texts. But since this paper was only published in 1941, an inspection of the original manuscript might shed light on whether Freud could possibly have added the passage about Saint Denis, after delivering the paper—a question for future scholars.

I am offering this tiny aspect of the history of ideas since it does seem to be a striking coincidence. At the least it shows how Freud could, with an anecdote, express a subtle reservation about something he had just carefully tried to argue; and it indicates he shared some patterns of thought in common with Voltaire, presuming Lytton Strachey was correct in thinking Madame du Deffand's comment was "dear" to Voltaire's heart. Also, it shows something of Freud's own taste for *bon mots*.

Additionally, Freud had omitted to name Madame du Deffand as a source; we know why James Strachey himself was familiar with the origins of the story, even though he failed to highlight any differences between his brother's version and that of Freud. A further question is whether Freud had been acquainted with the *mot*, or reminded of it, having been alerted (either in print or through personal contact with James and Alix Strachey) to Lytton's use of it. It can be established how Freud's artistic capabilities, as in how he shaped the account of Helene Deutsch's patient in the same essay, could enter his construction of a narrative. Freud's general use of quotations, and how he could alter them, would be a subject all in itself. Even if the multiple puzzles about the *mot* connected to Freud's slightly ironic "momentous step" cannot be resolved here, I think the parallel between Freud and Lytton Strachey an uncanny one. The Bloomsbury ties that Freud had become part of the whole general story of his relations with England, and the interconnections between his work and Britain.

* * *

R. D. Laing may not have been a great theorist or a reliable-seeming practitioner, but his books, especially *The Divided Self*, attracted an immense audience. Although Laing got a reputation for being something of a wild man, he was also a serious intellectual. It is easy to think that drink had been too much for him, and if only a portion of the rumors about him turn out to have been true, one can understand why the British psychiatric community has looked askance at the mere mention of Laing's name. At a time when the scientific evidence about the genetic and biological bases for schizophrenia was mounting, Laing's concern with the phenomenology of having a schizophrenic family member was bound to seem beside the point. To the extent that Laing can be interpreted to have meant that families are responsible for producing mental illness, that represents a position which would be a good deal harder to defend today than it was a generation ago.

Bob Mullan has put together a fascinating book. *Mad To Be Normal*[3] consists of transcripts from some of the tapes that Mullan made with the expectation that they would precede a full-scale biography. Mullan had received Laing's blessings to become Laing's official biographer, but after he died unexpectedly in August 1989 the executors of the estate could not agree with Mullan's continuing with his project.

One of the most interesting sections of the book consists of Laing's account of his family life. He grew up in Glasgow and as a Scot always remained an outsider. (Jones himself was Welsh.) Although Laing talks about more psychopathology in connection with his father than his mother, it seems clear that Laing had a distinctly odd pair of parents.

Since the culture Laing grew up in is so different from our own, I do not feel at all confident about anyone putting diagnostic labels on Laing's family members. But it is clear that he had, as an only child, a barren-sounding beginning; the apparent emotional impoverishment Laing suffered from was not enough to overwhelm his individuality, and Laing managed to make constructive use of his background.

Although Laing is insistent here that the loneliness of his childhood was not all that damaging, the enduring emnity between himself and his parents does make a somber tale. Laing reported that he went to his parents' funerals, but the maternal rejection he got sounds like something out of one of Laing's own books. (As if what she did during his childhood were not enough, his mother tried to make sure that her relatively small estate did not go to Laing. Scottish law disallowed her leaving everything to a next-door neighbor, so Laing in the end got half of her money.)

Laing had two wives, ten children, and an abundance of female lovers as well. It is of course not possible to evaluate fully what Laing had to say about his private life, and perhaps it is ungenerous to be skeptical. But nobody can be expected to be impartial about themselves, and Laing's life was tempestuous enough to support the notion that he was unusually difficult to get on with.

For me some of the most absorbing parts of *Mad To Be Normal* concern Laing's post-World War II psychoanalytic training in London, England. He had been an army psychiatrist, and after being demobilized he spent some time at the Tavistock Clinic. Laing was influenced by a range of continental existentialist thinkers, so his career in psychiatry was at arm's length from the central concerns of his psychoanalytic teachers. Laing's analyst, Charles Rycroft, was a member of the Middle Group, neither Kleinian nor Anna Freudian, and Laing himself rejected the two competing analytic ideologies which were most fashionable during his training.

Kingsley Hall was an experiment in living with mentally disturbed patients, and Laing may be best known for the attempt to deal with psychotics without the aid of medication or physical means of treatment. As Laing describes it here, Kingsley Hall did not take up too much of his time. It is striking how harshly bitter Laing sounds about all his co-workers, and it does not sound as if the Philadelphia Association, often linked with Laing's name, can be considered a legitimate offspring of his influence.

Parts of *Mad To Be Normal* are less accessible than others, and I found the last half of the book slower going. In 1971 Laing went to Ceylon, now Sri Lanka, but his encounter with Buddhism did not come alive for me. It is probably inevitable that in the nature of the case tape-recorded interviews would be repetitious, and Mullan as editor was not entirely successful in getting around that problem. It sounds a pity that Laing's premature death cut short his collaboration with Mullan, since that put an end to their projected work together.

* * *

There was a time in the history of psychoanalysis in Britian when intellectuals played a central role in the new discipline. Charles Rycroft, for example, was not only educated at Cambridge, but all his papers demonstrate his cultural sophistication as well as independence of spirit. For years he was not a member of the British Psychoanalytic Society, although he once served as an officer there; he found the meetings simply too boring to be worth attending, and he had the courage to go his own way.

Rycroft did not set out out to found a new cult, but one can appreciate his feeling of revulsion toward the game-playing and careerism that had been so much a part of twentieth century British psychoanalysis. While Melanie Klein and Anna Freud were alive there was a tense (though not always visible) struggle; so-called Middle Groupers like Rycroft pursued a hard course, without the support of the two financially well-endowed factions. Rycroft was an admirer of Donald Winnicott's thinking, but he drew the line at building Winnicott up posthumously to some kind of oracle.

*Viewpoints*[4] was the third volume of Rycroft's essays to be published; one of the valuable features of the book is that it includes a complete bibliography of Rycroft's writings. Rycroft had been publishing for what he called "the general reading public," but by that he did not mean a mass audience. Readers of the

*New York Review of Books*, *The Times Literary Supplement*, and a few other such exceptional publications found Rycroft congenial.

For years Rycroft went on saying fresh things, and *Viewpoints* will reward anyone who enjoys listening to an immensely civilized intellect reflect on matters psychoanalytic. The first chapter is on "Faith, Hope, and Charity"; the title alone should indicate how different Rycroft was, especially when one realizes that he wrote without an ounce of false sentimentality. There is a nice piece here on "Anxiety," and a thoughtful essay titled "Where Is Psychoanalysis Going?" Everything Rycroft wrote was in a non-sectarian spirit, and he did not need to lean on technical jargon. I particularly like the tone of an article called "Why Psychiatry is an Intrinscally Odd Profession."

In addition to relatively sustained pieces, *Viewpoints* contains some brief but compelling book reviews. For example, there is one discussion here of "Why Freud and Jung Could Never Agree." Rycroft also included a discussion of the friendship between Freud and Wilhelm Fliess, and also deals with "Masson's Assault on Freud." Rycroft could be counted on to be both fair and balanced, and sometimes cynically astringent. Anna Freud, he tells us, objected to Marilyn Monroe playing a leading part in John Huston's film *Freud*; but Anna Freud was willing to accept money for her Hampstead Clinic in London that came from Monroe's will.

Rycroft was no friend to conformist establishmentarian thinking, and he looked a bit askance at what he saw coming out of American psychoanalytic circles. He did think highly of the contributions of Erik H. Erikson, and he has elsewhere spoken well of Thomas Szasz's achievements; but in *Viewpoints* he points out, rightly I think, how Szasz is able to be "a sentimentalist about private practice psychotherapy."

A substantial section of the book is devoted to pieces which attempt to cope with the challenge of understanding the psychology of creativity. If Rycroft did not succeed in coming up with any synthesizing theory of the creative act, at least he never treated artistry with the belittling, reductionist spirit that still pervades too many psychoanalytic writings that purport to understand sublimation.

*Viewpoints* is a quiet, wise little book which will reward anyone who chooses to browse with leisure through its highly intelligent pages. Reading Rycroft does make one nostalgic for the older generation of British analyst, now alas almost all gone, who were at ease with the life of the mind.

## Notes

1. J. H. Willis, Jr., *Leonard and Virginia Woolf As Publishers: The Hogarth Press, 1917-41* (Charlottesville: University of Virginia Press, 1992).
2. Lytton Strachey, *Books and Characters: French and English* (Toronto: Goodchild, 1922).
3. Bob Mullan, *Mad To Be Normal: Conversations with R. D. Laing* (New York: New York University Press, 1995).
4. Charles Rycroft, *Viewpoints* (London: Hogarth Press, 1991).

# Part 8

## Intellectual History

# Introduction to Part 8

An examination of the different evaluations of Freud has become a subject all its own. It would be possible to write an intellectual history of the past century based on the varieties of reactions, in various literary, social, ideological, philosophic, and national contexts, to Freud's work. Although I have tried to survey almost everything that has ever come out, it is during the last four decades that I have most closely monitored the on-going literature on the history of psychoanalysis; the tale of what has appeared this recently on Freud is in itself a story worth examining. In the course of looking at what has been published, certain general issues stand out; and these central questions are likely to recur in the future as well.

One curious change worth noting has only recently occurred: a number of intellectual historians writing about Freud have decided to undertake full psychoanalytic training and become practicing clinicians. Ideally this should mean an enhancement of our appreciation of the history of psychoanalysis. But so far the well-known conformist effects of the training process have apparently undermined what otherwise might have been independent voices. It remains to be seen what the upshot of academics turning into analysts will be for the study of this field. But it is my own conviction that the world of scholarship, and the critical standards of social science, continue to have something unique to offer psychoanalysis. There remains a challenge here which one can only hope that analysts will not miss picking up.

# 44

# The History of Psychiatry

When one thinks of it, the situtation may be surprising, but it is only within the last few years that the history of psychiatry itself has started to become established on secure academic grounds. For many years medical history in general was more or less consigned to the concerns and hobbies of retired physicians; but lately it has been possible to conceive of people pursuing an interest in the history of psychiatry not only at the outset of their academic careers, but as a means of normal professional advancement. The journal *The History of Psychiatry*, which is only a few years old, has been a strikingly excellent supplement to more well-known quarterlies such as the *Bulletin of the History of Medicine*, the *Journal of the History of Medicine*, the *Journal of the History of the Behavioral Sciences*, and *Social History of Medicine*.

The Introduction to *Discovering the History of Psychiatry*,[1] by the two editors Roy Porter and Mark Micale, is especially fine and holds up a high standard for the rest of the text. Porter has been prolific in the past and published so many books, articles, and reviews, all of an exceptionally original character, that he has become a scholarly phenomenon in his own right. Micale is an unusually promising historian and an expert on the history of the concept of hysteria, and Porter is Associate Director of the Wellcome Institute for the History of Medicine in London. The subtitle of their introduction here is "Reflections on Psychiatry and Its Histories," which spells out the pluralistic tolerance of their perspective. They want this book "to explore the peculiar, complex, and powereful interplay between psychiatry, historiography, and social, cultural, and political ideology." Micale and Porter are sensitive to the existence of competing schools of thought that have been bitterly at odds with one another. And the editors are determined to ensure that the history of psychiatric medicine does not fall into any one partisan camp.

The editors are also keenly concerned to avoid the dangers of what has been commonly designated elsewhere as "Whig" history. The category of Whiggery, and evidently the point cannot be made too often, means that the past ought not to be looked upon solely through the telescope of our own moral preferences; of course, it is impossible to disengage ourselves entirely from our most cherished beliefs, but the job of the historian ought to be distinct from propagandizing in behalf of our pet preconceptions, since every generation is apt to consider itself as uniquely enlightened. "Whig" history would be an account of the past that is unduly oriented to the standards of what has up to now been a success. Any teleological thinking in historical studies is likely to be misleading, and we can be confident that the next generation will promptly conclude that our times were also sorely lacking in insight.

The first part of this book is concerned with "early development" and starts off with an excellent chapter by Otto Marx on the beginning of psychiatric historiography in nineteenth-century Germany. Marx is enormously learned and has been writing important articles for over a generation now. His thoroughly readable, ten-page essay has no less than forty-eight complicated notes. The other article in this initial section of *Discovering the History of Psychiatry* is by George Mora on early American historians of psychiatry from 1910 until 1960. Mora touches on the careers and contributions of people like Henry Mills Hurd, Smith Ely Jelliffe, Albert Deutsch, Gregory Zilboorg, Walther Riese, in addition to Walter Bromberg, Franz Alexander, Erwin Ackerknecht, and Jerome Schneck. It may seem hard to believe that the first person to receive a Ph.D. in medical history in the United States, the admirable Ilza Veith, was still active recently.

Part II of this book deals with Five Major Voices. Porter writes about the mother-and-son team of Ida Macalpine and Richard Hunter. Their extensive private library has been preserved and is available at Cambridge University. Macalpine and Hunter are notable for studies of Schreber's memoirs of his psychosis and the problem of George III's madness, as well as for a volume called *Three Hundred Years of Psychiatry*. Over the years Macalpine and Hunter became disenchanted with the uses of psychodynamic thinking in understanding past figures, and they ended up highly skeptical of armchair psychologizing. Edward Moran's essay concentrates on George Rosen's contribution to the history of mental illness, much of which appeared in Henry Sigerist's *Bulletin of the History of Medicine* at Johns Hopkins. Mark Micale, who has already edited a fine volume of Henri Ellenberger's previously uncollected papers, contributes an additional piece on *The Discovery of the Unconscious.*[2] Ellenberger's own archives are now housed at the Sainte Anne Hospital in Paris. Micale is right that it is remarkable how "during an era of psychiatric sectarianism, Ellenberger remained resolutely eclectic." So Ellenberger could be critical of Freud and show strengths in Jung, and Ellenberger also provided what "remains to this day the most comprehensive exposition of Janet's ideas in English." Fernando Vidal, a young Argentinian, now teaching in Germany, has an admirable piece on Jean Starobinski, who is a great man of letterts as well as a psychiatrist. I know of no single volume about Jean-Jacques Rousseau as psychologically outstanding as Starobinski's own, and he has also written notable books about Montaigne and Montesquieu. Vidal has provided an excellent overview of Starobinski's life work.

Part III, The Psychoanalytic Strain, unfortunately comes as a letdown. It begins with a chapter by Elisabeth Young-Bruehl purporting to be "A History of Freud Biographies." She jumps from Freud's 1914 *On the History of the Psychoanalytic Movement* to Freud's 1925 autobiography, and then to Freud's official biography by Ernest Jones. She makes a few cursory references to other titles and is especially savage about Helen Walker Puner's pioneering 1947 study of Freud, which had a foreword by Erich Fromm. Young-Bruehl writes: "The nadir of the history of Freud biographies was reached—one can hope—when Helen Puner's book was republished, with an introduction by Paul Roazen" in 1992. I suppose it might seem to some to be a back-handed compliment that Young-Bruehl holds me responsible for being involved with the "nadir" of almost 100 years of scholarly research.

I hope it will not appear partisan for me to point out that Young-Bruehl (now a practicing analyst) has strikingly failed to discuss at all the first biography of Freud, the one written by Fritz Wittels (1924)[3] which is still in print today. Porter and Micale, neither of whom has a special interest in psychoanalysis, evidently do not realize how amateurish Young-Bruehl's essay is bound to appear when subjected to ordinary scholarly standards. Wittels had had a falling out with Freud years earlier because of Wittels's allegiances to Wilhelm Stekel, but Wittels was not only journalistically talented but wrote with psychological subtlety. Freud took Wittels, a former member of the Vienna Psychoanalytic Society, seriously enough to write Wittels a lengthy letter challenging various of Wittels's points. Freud's marked copy of Wittels's book still exists at the Freud Museum in London; Freud's marginalia, and especially those aspects of Wittels's book which Freud chose to leave uncorrected, make for a whole story in itself. Furthermore, by 1933 Wittels had had a change of heart, and he published an article called "A Revision of a Biography."[4] By then Wittels was securely back in the orthodox psychoanalytic fold. In 1931 Wittels had published an almost unreadably dull book called *Freud and His Time*,[5] long out of print. Scholars would also note that Wittels left a memoir called "Wrestling with the Man: The Story of a Freudian," which is in the A. A. Brill library at the New York Psychoanalytic Society. The historian Edward Timms has written an article about Karl Kraus, Wittels, and Freud.[6] Thus, for Young-Bruehl to have completely left Wittels out of a chapter purporting to be a history of Freud biographies gives some idea of how sectarianism unfortunately still persists. Wittels has been rendered by Young-Briehl as simply a nonperson; untutored readers might easily miss the full significance of this striking omission. Such incompetence from the accomplished author of several books of her own should give some idea about how appalling biases in this field have been allowed to go unquestioned.

Those who are interested in following up what Young-Bruehl considers the "nadir" of the history of Freud biographies might like to consult a few of the exact words of my 1992 introduction; the full text also contains Fromm's original laudatory remarks. I cite a vivid and amusing account by Puner of her having dinner at the home of Kurt Eissler, which was the occasion of an unexpected inquisition by Eissler in his study. Among other general points I maintain that Wittels's 1924 biography, the first about Freud, remains "still well worth reading today." Young-Bruehl ought to have been obliged at least to deal with Wittels, instead of so arrogantly sweeping aside work she evidently disagrees with. Her "A History of Freud Biographies" is also muddled about when the Sigmund Freud Archives was set up in New York City, she failed to explain its relation to the Freud Collection at the Library of Congress, and she does an inadequate job of recounting Eissler's complex relationship to Jones. Young-Bruehl is also mixed up about a variety of other aspects of my own research, although she is self-confident enough to refer to the supposedly "slip-shod scholarship" of my *Freud and His Followers*. Independent readers can decide for themselves.

John Forrester's contribution to *Discovering the History of Psychiatry* is in a different category from that of Young-Bruehl. Forrester, one of Jacques Lacan's translators and a historian of science at Cambridge University, has a special interest in French psychoanalytic matters. I would, however, want to contest his claim that "the most accomplished of psychoanalytic histories to date" is Elisabeth Roudinesco's "monumental" study of the French Freud. Forrester, although one cannot be absolutely certain on this point, does not seem to realize what a sick joke it is that there could be at least seventeen different French translations of the four pages that make up Freud's 1925 paper "On Negation." Kenneth Piver concludes Part III with an essay about Philip Rieff's work that is, for my taste, too arch. Rieff, who did so much to advance the reception of Freud within the social sciences, deserves to be placed within the context of the work of earlier pioneers like Harold Lasswell and David Riesman, neither of whose names succeeded in making it to the index. Talcott Parsons, Edward Sapir, and other social scientists are also unfairly missing. But I found nothing in any section of *Discovering the History of Psychiatry* to match Young-Bruehl's unfortunate high-handedness.

Part IV, Historical Themes and Topics, starts off with a remarkable chapter by a Dutch theologian, Patrick Vandermeersch, on myths of the origins in the history of psychiatry. It is a thoroughly sophisticated exercise in intellectual dialectics and a sign of a truly original mind at work. Dora Weiner dissects the specific myth about Phillipe Pinel, who, it turns out, by no means deserves to be remembered for having supposedly liberated the insane from their chains; Weiner, however, is not engaged in debunking but conscientiously tries to examine the sources of a persistent legend that has often been repeated as well as notably painted on a huge and prominent canvas. Gerald Grob, the eminent Rutgers historian, has a fine discussion of his personal reflections on the history of the asylum in America. Grob is writing neither in order to celebrate progress, in the vein of the Whig historians, nor to share the opposite belief that institutional psychiatry is in itself an abuse. And Grob places his own work in the context of his contemporaries. Geoffrey Cocks is another historian who does a thoroughly professional job, pursuing Cocks's own special area of expertise—psychiatry, psychotherapy, and psychoanalysis in Germany during the Nazi period. This subject has to be a special ethical minefield if only because the Nazis relied on psychiatrists in the sterilizing and murder of mental patients; furthermore, after World War II some of these same practitioners flourished in the era of the Bonn Republic. Julie Brown concludes this section with a chapter about heroes and nonheroes in Russian-Soviet psychiatry. Although I would have liked to learn even more—if only she had written at greater length—one can look forward to further enlightenment from this distinguished sociologist.

Part V concludes with a lengthy and interesting section on Critics of Psychiatry. The opening chapter, by Richard Vatz and Lee Weinberg, discusses—with fairness—the contribution that Thomas Szasz has made, as they distinguish his work from the apparently similar theses of another original thinker, Ronald D. Laing. Gary Cutting undertakes to examine the work of Michel Foucault, which makes a good introduction to a provocative, difficult, but rewarding thinker. Nancy Tomes does an especially fine job of discussing feminist histories of psychiatry. There is a lot to learn from Tomes, as she finds texts "reversing the usual Whig logic that science has brought nothing but benefit to its recipients." *Discovering the History of Psychiatry* ends on a strong note, with two excellent discussions: Jacques Postel and David Allen writing on antipsychiatry in France, and Norman Dain examining the same subject in America.

Anyone even remotely interested in the broad range of topics covered in this book should find it a genuine feast. It is wonderfully satisfying to realize that such a splendid amount of research has been going on and can be expected to bear fruit in the future. Porter and Micale, even if they might have been more sensitive about the persistent insidious dangers of psychoanalytic sectarianism, have done a superb job of helping to move this whole field in a positive direction.

## Notes

1. Mark S. Micale and Roy Porter, *Discovering the History of Psychiatry* (New York: Oxford University Press, 1994).
2. Henri Ellenberger, *The Discovery of the History of the Unconscious: The History and Evolution of Dynamic Psychiatry* (New York: Basic Books, 1970).
3. Fritz Wittels, *Sigmund Freud* (New York: Dodd, Mead, 1924).
4. Fritz Wittels, "A Revision of a Biography," *Psychoanalytic Review*, 1933.
5. Fritz Wittels, *Freud and His Time* (New York: Liveright, 1931).
6. Edward Timms, "Fritz Wittels," in E. Timms and R. Robertson, eds., *Austrian Studies* Vol. 3: *Psychoanalysis in Its Cultural Context* (Edinburgh: Edinburgh University Press, 1992).

# 45

# Dora

Although at a much slower pace, the study of the history of psychoanalysis has also been moving into a genuinely professional phase. Until now, practicing analysts have had a secure hold on the subject, which unfortunately has meant that questions of organizational allegiances and ideological quarrelling have dominated. Recent research among scholars is not bound by the old needs to propagandize (or debunk) psychoanalysis. While within medicine the traditional practice of psychoanalysis has come under substantial new criticism, among academic historians interest in the development of Freud's school has been expanding. It is now clearer than ever that Freud changed the way we think about ourselves.

One subject in particular has recently attracted a special amount of attention: Freud's early case histories. The woman that Freud called "Dora" has over the last generation fascinated literary critics with a concern for feminist issues. Since Freud treated "Dora" in 1900 when she was eighteen years hold, she has also absorbed those with an interest in adolescence. As Hannah S. Decker puts it in *Freud, Dora and Vienna 1900*,[1] Freud's case history of Dora is now "used in the classroom to assess society's attitudes toward women and the roles it sanctions for them, to study the commingling of familiar pathology and broad-scale malaise, and to illustrate how a psychological illness simultaneously reflects social imperatives."

Decker has done a good job of reconstructing facts connected with "Dora," who was born Ida Bauer, the sister of a prominent Austrian socialist. Decker performs a splendid service in placing this patient within her social context. We learn about turn-of-the-century Central European anti-Semitism, as well as the medical concept of hysteria which Freud invoked for "Dora." Also, Decker has been able to track down some of the material connected with her emigration to the United States, where she died in 1945. *Freud, Dora, and Vienna 1900* is an immensely stimulating book and a permanent addition to the literature.

Still, Decker did not satisfy me in describing what this woman was like, or whether Freud might have had any realistic basis for being happy, when she broke off with him, to be rid of her as a patient. Decker is unremitting about

Freud's mistakes, and inclined to see "Dora" only as a helpless victim of social and medical circumstances. This approach takes away from "Dora" the possibility of autonomy which Decker ought to be upholding. I believe that Freud was right in thinking that under almost every social circumstance people are obliged to make choices. Instead of Decker relying on the liberal individualistic strand in psychoanalysis, which would place some responsibility on "Dora" for her destiny, what we get instead is some old-fashioned-sounding psychological determinism, the scientistic side to Freud.

Decker seems to me too confident, based on psychoanalytic reasoning, about the childhood sources from which this patient's adult character stemmed. We are told that at fifteen, for example, "her identity as a maturing, trustworthy adult was crushed" by what her parents did. I do not know the grounds, other than discredited Freudian theology, for Decker to maintain that events in this patient's early adolescence "dictated the inevitability of some emotional dysfunction." Before Decker proceeds to tell us about what she holds to be "the crucial moment for Dora's future emotional health," some added attention needs to be paid to what might be meant by psychological normality.

Thorstein Veblen once wrote a powerful piece "On the Intellectual Pre-eminence of Jews in Modern Europe."[2] Being Jewish led some people to extraordinary success; and there were women of the era of "Dora" who flourished in the same social circumstances. Helene Deutsch in Vienna, and Karen Horney in Germany, were almost exact contemporaries of Ida Bauer's, yet both were immensely successful in their calling as psychoanalysts. One sentence of Decker's seems to me indefensible: "At no point in his career was Freud prepared to recognize women's sensibilities." In fact, although Decker ignores the point, within his Vienna Psychoanalytic Society Freud was in favor of admitting women members over the opposition of young disciples. It should be the task of historical understanding to see Freud in his time and place, and within that context he helped many women with emancipating opportunities. It is possible to believe that human biology leaves men and women with unequal burdens, without such a conviction necessarily entailing any prejudices about inferiorities. Decker does tell us in a note: "Freud did change his mind about some professional women, much later in his life." But she does not try to account for such an alleged change, nor see some of Freud's sexist biases as defensive in nature. But the weak spots that I have highlighted are not intended to obscure what is Decker's thoroughly important contribution.

* * *

The increasingly vast literature about the early days of psychoanalysis has included an upsurge of interest in Freud's five most celebrated case histories: Dora, Little Hans, the Rat Man, Schreber, and the Wolf Man. Sometimes the focus of attention has been on Freud's considerable literary powers of persuasion. For he was such a fascinating writer that we may not notice the specific examples of various rhetorical devices he used in order to make his presentations convincing. Part of Freud's greatness flowed from his having succeeded in constructing narratives that have remained unmatched within the professional psychological literature. One wonders to what extent Freud's stylistic talents were capable not just of propagandizing the "cause" he sought to forward, but also were likely to interfere with his own assessment of what he was talking about. Freud may have been being self-critical about his artistic talents, and how they could be misleading, when in the 1890s he paused to comment: "It still strikes me myself as strange that the case histories I write should read like short stories and that, as one might say, they lack the serious stamp of science."[3]

In addition to attracting the recent attention of literary critics, Freud's most famous case histories have stuck in the minds of succeeding generations of practitioners. The earliest analysts knew Freud almost literally by heart, and they proceeded to teach his ideas on the basis of how he described his own approach to patients. Even when it was privately understood that Freud's real behavior was markedly at odds with the techniques he recommended for others to follow, these case histories were relied upon as illustrations of how a so-called proper analyst should proceed. Orthodox analysts continue to invoke the example of Freud's cases long after multiple dissenting voices have raised questions about the legitimacy of Freud's approach.

By today, when many theoretical models have shifted away from the "classical" psychoanalytic conceptualization, writers have tried to reconsider the implications these changes have for our understanding of Freud's early clinical presentations. For instance, as Heinz Kohut's self psychology gained in prominence, it has seemed plausible to go over each of Freud's five central case histories from a Kohutian perspective. An interesting book, *Freud's Case Histories: Self-Psychological Perspectives*, has been edited by Barry Magid.[4] As analysts strive to establish innovative approaches to the treatment of patients, a reexamination of Freud's key clinical histories has seemed in order.

Meanwhile, old-fashioned historians have for some time now been trying to unearth as much as possible about the people Freud renamed for the purposes of his case-history writing. As a result, a substantial amount of new information is now available about each of Freud's most well-known patients. The Wolf Man is perhaps Freud's best documented case, and we now have not only the Wolf Man's own reminiscences but a series of interviews that he gave to a Viennese journalist. And someday, when the embargoes finally get lifted on the material the Freud Archives of New York deposited at the Library of Congress in Washington, D.C., all that further documentation about the Wolf Man will be examined to supplement and correct what Freud told us. In the meantime, it has been possible to compare and contrast Freud's daily process notes for the Rat Man with what he later wrote up, and scholars have also come up with a lot of new evidence about the family lives of both Little Hans and Schreber.

Freud's Dora, originally written in 1901 but only finally published in 1905, has attracted a special sort of attention. While Freud presented this patient under the heading "Fragment of an Analysis of a Case of Hysteria," his discussion has spawned a whole debate over his view of women, almost all of it unfavorable to Freud. His treatment of Dora was at best a therapeutic stalemate, yet he nonetheless went ahead with providing his account of that analysis. Freud has been widely criticized not just for the technical therapeutic procedure he adopted, but for having shared so much in his era's characteristic outlook on women.

Any independent evaluations of Dora, apart from Freud's own account, would be of special interest. In 1957 Felix Deutsch published a short paper of his own describing his brief medical contact with Dora, supposedly taking place in the late fall of 1922. Deutsch published his findings only after Ernest Jones, in the course of his biography of Freud, reported that she had died.

Considering all the attention that Freud's original case and Felix Deutsch's postcript have aroused, too little attention has been given to exploring the facts of the matter as they can best be reconstructed. In my biography of Helene Deutsch, which first came out in 1985, I mentioned the existence of 1923 remarks about Freud's Dora that occur in letters from Felix in Vienna to his wife in Berlin.

Even now the scholarly literature keeps irritatingly repeating Felix's published year of 1922 for his having seen Dora. Yet when I had to put a date on Felix's letters about Dora to Helene, I decided—based on the stamped outside envelopes in which the letters had been saved—on March 1923. It is conceivable that over the years Helene had sometimes taken letters out and put them back in the wrong envelope. And there were even a handful of occasions when I suspected (and so did Felix) that Helene had never opened some of his letters. Yet for this set of letters bearing on Dora I felt reasonably secure about the 1923 date. Internal evidence indicates that the month itself had to be March.

Although I could be wrong about the 1923 date, it is worth pointing out that in 1923 Freud added a footnote to his case history in connection with Dora's contact with the physician whom Felix later identified as himself. In that 1923 footnote, Freud wrote about the "secret" of Dora's identity having been kept "until this year." As far as I know, no one has noticed the apparent contradiction between that reference of Freud's to the year 1923 and Felix's published reminiscence. I am writing now partly as an experiment to see whether it will ever be the case that Freud's date, coinciding with my own, gets accepted into the literature as opposed to Felix's remembrance.

At the time Felix was writing Helene about Dora, they were in close and regular correspondence. But their marriage was then under a considerable strain, and she was off in Berlin for the sake of having a second analysis with Karl Abraham; earlier she had been analyzed by Freud in Vienna. In those days Felix was not yet a practicing analyst, although he was already a member of the

Vienna Psychoanalytic Society. In April 1923, at a time when Felix was consulting Freud about undergoing an analysis, Freud asked Felix's medical opinion about the tissue growth that later turned out to be his jaw cancer. Felix was by then a secure part of Freud's circle, even if professionally Felix was far less important within psychoanalysis than Helene herself. It is not true, despite what Peter Gay has claimed, that by April 1923 Felix "had been Freud's internist for some time...."[5]

When Felix wrote to Helene, mentioning his contact with Dora, he knew she would not only be keenly interested in what he had to say about Freud's former patient, but I think he was hoping that she would be impressed by Felix's medical standing and how he had conducted himself clinically.

On a Sunday, Felix wrote Helene how he had "today" visited the sister of Otto Bauer, a well-known socialist, having been asked to do so by "Jula." (According to the Deutsch son, "Jula" refers to Dr. Julius Bauer, husband of Helene's intimate friend Dr. Marianne Bauer.) It is noteworthy that despite what Freud wrote about the "secret" of Dora's true identity, Felix did not need, in writing to Helene, to further identify Otto Bauer's sister, except to say that "she was in Freud's treatment 25 years ago, and has nothing good to say about analysis." (Felix was rounding-off the time to a quarter-of-a-century.) When Felix described her to Helene as "a severe hysteric with organic symptoms," about which her physicians "were at a loss to know what to do," Felix probably assumed that Helene already realized that this was Freud's Dora. (When I first knew Helene in the 1960s she easily acknowledged that Otto Bauer's sister Ida was Dora.) Felix wrote to Helene after his first seeing Dora that he faced "a difficult task" but he said he was confident that he would be "successful."

A few days later, on Tuesday, Felix wrote Helene further about this patient, this time identifying her not just as Otto Bauer's sister, but specifically as "Dora." Felix's report provided confirmation to Freud's earlier diagnosis of hysteria. Felix said that he himself (in implicit contrast to Freud) had had a momentous success, i.e., after the utmost resistance she had a complete transference, in which after two hours of persuasion she resolved upon the dismantling of the symptoms which had lasted for four weeks. "The withdrawal...of the illness is continuing, as Otto Bauer told me today on the telephone."

Felix added that "it will be a difficult piece of work to bring her back into analysis—mainly because of Jula." (Nothing further is known about Julius Bauer's attitude toward psychoanalysis.) Finally, Felix wrote to Helene: "You can imagine the effect of the 'success' upon the surroundings," implying—I think—that Freud himself was impressed and pleased with Felix's results.

Nothing in Felix's communications to Helene indicated any dislike on his part toward Dora. A mysterious "informant" that Felix relied on in his 1957 paper for information about her years in America characterized her as "one of the most repulsive hysterics" he had ever met, and this harsh assessment has often been mistaken to be Felix's own view of her. I myself suspect that despite how much she interested Freud, especially for the purposes of a case history, in the end he was delighted to get rid of her. Perhaps such a mixture of feelings on Freud's part would help untangle Peter Gay's own perplexity: "What is astonishing about the case history of Dora is not that Freud delayed it for four years, but that he published it at all."[6]

I think that the central emotional feeling-tone that accompanied Felix's remarks to Helene was the pride he felt in having had a therapeutic triumph. At a time when Felix was angling to assure that Helene eventually came back to Vienna, and he himself was eager to establish his own independent role within psychoanalysis, Dora became a valuable conquest for him. In Freud's own case history she played a part in a number of emotional triangles, notably between her parents and another Viennese couple. At the time she underwent treatment by Felix Deutsch, she was once again more than, and therefore in some sense less than, an individual in her own right.

Felix Deutsch, who knew the tale of Freud's Dora backwards and forwards, was able to use knowledge of the case to good medical effect. Operating on the same understanding as Freud, and seeing Dora as a hysteric, Felix Deutsch accomplished a dramatic therapeutic improvement.

When Felix came to write up his 1957 paper, he would not have consulted the files that could only be unearthed amidst his wife's papers. (I have reason to suspect that he showed her his essay, and it would have been characteristic if they exchanged harsh words about it.) Felix's letters to Helene remained more or less in a gigantic heap until I came to make some order out of them in the late 1970s, while working on my biography of Helene. So when Felix came up with the date of 1922 for his treatment of Dora, he was probably thinking about the paper he had given in the fall of 1922 before an international psychoanalytic meeting, and which naturally had come to Freud's attention. Neither Deutsch owned the Strachey *Standard Edition* of Freud's works, and therefore did not need to ponder the significance of Freud's 1923 footnote referring to Dora's identity having been kept as a secret "until this year." Furthermore, Felix had every reason to dissociate his seeing Dora from his medical consultation about Freud's jaw, since that incident remained lastingly traumatic for Felix.[7]

Understanding psychoanalytic case histories in the light of theories about narrative makes for an enlightening approach. It is certainly an improvement upon the traditional mechanistic approach of cause and effect to look for thematic continuities in clinical material. There is no question that Felix considered, as had Freud, that the diagnosis of hysteria was appropriate for Dora. And Felix felt that, unlike the founder of psychoanalysis, he himself had been able to handle Dora's transference reactions successfully.

But no amount of interpretive understanding of texts should be allowed to put our common sense to sleep. The date of any event, whether Felix saw Dora in 1923 as opposed to 1922, may not be in itself of earth-shattering significance. But it does matter if conscientious historical reconstruction settles on the year 1923, which would also be in accord with Freud's own view, and if the literature then continues to repeat Felix's erroneous published 1922 date. Felix's seeing Dora came at a time when he was being looked on with special favor within Freud's inner circle, which is also how Felix came to function in April 1923, and for a few months thereafter, as Freud's personal physician.

Hannah Decker repeats like others the mistaken 1922 date, and is completely unaware of the nature of Felix's correspondence with Helene. But since Decker's general judgment about the current status of the Dora case history seems to me right on target, there is all the more reason, I believe, for us to be as accurate as possible about what can be known about Felix Deutsch's contact with Freud's famous patient.

The study of the history of psychoanalysis has been maturing professionally. As long as practicing analysts held their monopoly on the subject, questions of trade-unionism and ideological quarreling tendeed to dominate the literature. Recent research among university scholars is not bound by any need to propagandize about psychoanalysis. And the interest of academic historians in the development of Freud's school has been expanding. It is now clearer than ever that Freud succeeded in changing the way we think about ourselves, and therefore every aspect of his career should continue to concern those preoccupied with the course of intellectual history.

The nature of Felix Deutsch's contact with Dora is now, I think, an aspect of the history of ideas. And even mistaken gropings about Dora, to which Felix contributed in his 1957 paper, in the long run should enhance our understanding of the gripping story which is the history of psychoanalysis.

## Notes

1. Hannah S. Decker, *Freud, Dora, and Vienna 1900* (New York: Free Press, 1991).
2. Max Lerner, ed., *The Portable Veblen* (New York: The Viking Press, 1958), "The Intellectual Pre-eminence of Jews in Modern Europe," pp. 467-79.
3. Freud, *Studies On Hysteria, Standard Edition*, Vol. 2, p. 160.
4. Barry Magid, ed., *Freud's Case Histories: Self-Psychological Perspectives* (Hillsdale, NJ: The Analytic Press, 1993).
5. Peter Gay, *Freud: A Life For Our Time* (New York: Norton, 1988), p. 419.
6. *Ibid.*, p. 255.
7. Paul Roazen, *Freud and His Followers* (New York: Knopf, 1975), pp. 463-64; Paul Roazen, *Helene Deutsch: A Psychoanalyst's Life* (New York: Doubleday/Anchor, 1985), pp. 217-21.

# 46

# Schreber

Specialists have arisen about each of Freud's five most extensive case histories. Perhaps the Wolf Man has drawn the most interest, partly because he lived such a long life and contributed his own memoirs and interviews; the Wolf Man's story was composed by Freud as a part of his war with Jung, which has enhanced interest in the case. Only Dora has now become a heroine, as part of the cause of some feminists, and this is so even though I remain tempted to think that Freud was glad (as I have already suggested) to be done with her, once he had enough material for his case history; Dora's partisans are apt to see in Freud's therapeutic conduct only mistake after mistake. The Rat Man, who died so soon during World War I after his treatment was concluded, has also given rise to recent partisanship, since it today seems established that Freud cooked his own evidence to make it appear that the Rat Man was in therapy longer than was actually true, and the therapeutic result sounds more like old-fashioned suggestion rather than the so-called pure gold of analytic insight. As for the fourth of Freud's case histories, Little Hans, other than the fact that Freud chose to ignore the marital break-up which his parents were going through, the charm of Freud's account, the first ever of a child analytic case, has generally succeeded in holding the reader's attention.

Schreber, however, was a source of difficulty almost from the outset of Freud's having composed it. For here he was trying to deal, at second-hand to be sure, with a case of psychosis, and Carl G. Jung had been insisting that Freud's concepts were unsuited beyond the narrow confines of the psychoanalytic theory of neurosis. While with Little Hans Freud at least saw the boy on a few occasions, and knew the parents within his circle, the Schreber case history was constructed by Freud on the basis of a published text by Paul Schreber himself. And for those who had been all along dubious about the extension of Freud's approach to the understanding and treatment of psychosis, Freud's discussion of Schreber has been deemed highly suspect.

Han Israëls's *Schreber: Father and Son*[1] has to be considered a milestone; it first appeared as a Ph.D. thesis in 1980, got privately printed in English in

1981, and only was finally published in 1989. He painstakingly went through the Schreber family records, and reconstructed so much material about Schreber's father (Moritz) that it is unlikely that anyone will ever be able to read Freud's case history in the same light as before. Whereas Freud had interpreted Paul Schreber's emotional problems in terms of Freud's theory of latent homosexuality and its supposed relation to paranoia, Israëls establishes how benign an influence Schreber's father in all probability had been. (An earlier generation of orthodox analysts had tried to support Freud's point of view by claiming that Schreber's father was cruel, and used orthopedic devices to control children; this piece of supposed reality allegedly got transposed into Paul Schreber's psychotic delusions.)

Israëls sees himself as offering no new theories or explanations, but rather as having come up with much new information. Schreber descendants were Israëls's richest source of material. Most readers, I fear, will find Israëls's book tediously detailed, yet he does succeed in eliminating the old psychoanalytic myth that Schreber's father Moritz was some kind of domestic tyrant. (Freud hinted at this possibility in a private letter.) As Israëls rightly points out, the Schrebers were living in "a form of society in which a relatively high degree of inequality was accepted as the normal state of things by all its members...."

Paul Schreber was only nineteen years old when his father died. (Paul's brother was subsequently, sixteen years later, to commit suicide.) Paul married, had a successful career, ran for the Reichstag, and functioned as a jurist. He had two periods of illness, 1884-1885 and 1893-1902. Schreber successfully contested in court his being placed under guardianship. He returned to normal life, and published his memoirs about his nervous illness in 1903. Paul had a third and final period of illness from 1907 until 1911, when he died.

Freud himself had not, unlike some of his later followers, publicly denounced Moritz Schreber's character. Orthodox disciples of Freud's were responsible for linking Paul Schreber's insanity with his father's recommended methods of child-rearing. Even when advocates of a family therapy approach entered the discussion, the antipathies among students of the Schreber case have been such that they ostentatiously fail to mention one another's works in their bibliographies. As Israëls points out, in the midst of all this curious (if sometimes silent) polemicizing, the genetic evidence about schizophrenia gets ignored. Israëls is entirely sound about the dangers of sectarianism in psychoanalysis, and moreover I could not agree more with his objection to "teleology, a process of giving birth to the ideas of today, in which the only interesting educators are those who anticipated the ideas of the period being studied." Like Israëls, I doubt that there can be such a thing as "the idea of progress in education."

Israëls sets for himself what he calls a "quite narrow biographical task," and it is only on this point that I can part company with him. Other early analysts, such as Victor Tausk and Paul Federn, also tried to write about schizophrenia, and they get no mention in Israëls's book. I wonder whether Israëls has not somehow lost a sense of proportion, so that the larger problem of the theory of neurosis as opposed to psychosis, and the general nature of the different approaches of Freud and Jung, get inevitably downplayed. Nowhere does Israëls adequately dissect Freud's early concept of "narcissistic neurosis," and how it later got replaced, in the 1920s, by Freud's final theory of psychosis. But here I am implying that Israëls might have written a different book, when really we should be grateful for just how much debris he has succeeded in clearing away. The extraordinary literary status of all Freud's case histories should not intimidate any of us from coming to different conclusions than early psychoanalysis, even if its means acknowledging a role for biochemical processes which analysts (and some family theorists) have been loath to face up to.

* * *

Some of the most high-powered theoretical writings on psychoanalysis have been conceived in connection with Freud's case history of Schreber. Zvi Lothane's *In Defense of Schreber: Soul Murder and Psychiatry*[2] is unusual not just because of the original historical research he undertook, but also his tolerance and catholicity meant that he was genuinely able to credit a broad ideological spectrum of people who assisted him. While writings about the history of the growth of this discipline usually have been marked by sectarianism and passionately based commitments, Lothane has had no apparent axes to grind. A commitment to serious scholarship is rarer than one might like to think.

Freud's own study of Schreber was involved with Freud's tangled relationship with Jung and Freud's implied hope that, ultimately, psychoanalysis would be capable of helping to understand the great psychoses as well as the neuroses Freud was used to writing about. The distinction between psychiatry, where Jung had his professional beginnings, and neurology, Freud's own initial profession, has been hard for North Americans to keep straight, since the lines between those fields have been far more fluid on this side of the Atlantic than in Europe. The story has been more difficult to follow since in his last years Jung abandoned hospitalized cases for the sake of exclusively training students, and Freud—despite his theories—was capable in his old age of analyzing patients he diagnosed as schizophrenic.

Lothane has sought to go behind Schreber's *Memoirs*, as well as Freud's own account of them, in order to examine the primary evidence that can now be put together. (Freud often erred in treating stories as if they were straightforward clinical documents; he did not think he needed to have seen Schreber to be able to theorize about him.) Schreber's father, Moritz, has been the subject of scholarly debate. He is still remembered in Germany today since, for some time now, we have known that he was a prominent physician, author of books, and proponent of a whole philosophy of education. As I have already mentioned, when the research into Schreber began in earnest, during the late 1950s and 1960s, it seemed an easy option to blame Daniel Paul Schreber's distinguished father for many of his son's problems. Lothane, however, takes pains to demonstrate the reasons for thinking that Schreber's father was neither a sadist nor a child abuser. Lothane has scoured Moritz Schreber's prolific writings and concludes that there are many passages that reflect a loving and humane attitude toward child rearing. Lothane may have gone too far in his revisionary version of Schreber's father, but the pendulum probably needed such a swing because so many others have taken Moritz Schreber's work out of cultural context.

Daniel Paul Schreber was assuredly sick enough to be hospitalized; the biological psychiatrists he encountered—and the errors they made—should make us wary about some of our contemporaries in this profession. Disturbed families can provide therapists with too much medical power. We are now, for example, back in a stage when psychiatry is once again centrally concerned with classification and hereditary. This is opposed to those fleeting periods of humanitarian idealism when psychotics have seemed unique beings—even accessible to environmental therapeutics. Lothane is sympathetic to Schreber's problems with institutional psychiatrists of his day and how medication could cause special and unpleasant side effects. Lothane also raises the key question of the extent to which there was merit in Schreber's efforts to attain release. Lothane examined all kinds of new documents in order to flesh out what could be gathered on Schreber; hospital records were scrutinized and interviews with surviving family were used to hypothesize the possible dynamics behind Schreber's troubles.

Lothane does Schreber the honor of treating him as an interpreter and thinker. Probably only a trained psychiatrist could have this kind of patience in treating Schreber's ideas so seriously. Madness is mainly frightening for most of us, and Freud's own efforts to deal with this psychotic were doubtless colored by his admitted general intolerance of the great mental illnesses.

Lothane does credit Freud with having sought to make Schreber's delusions humanly understandable. But Lothane objects, rightly I think, to Freud's imputation of suppressed homosexuality behind Schreber's symptomatology. In the 1920s Otto Rank was, I think, the first to repudiate Freud's whole concept of latent homosexuality, and Rank proposed that it was a means Freud had for tyrannizing over patients and mankind as well. The notion of latent homosexuality is one of those Freudian principles that would be difficult concretely to disprove. At the same time, therapeutically it has to be an interpretive move that a patient is apt to feel humiliating—if not overwhelming.

Schreber's *Memoirs* reach metaphysical heights, and it seems to me one of the merits of Lothane's study is that he can follow all the arguments between the rival conceptual points of view as he steers a balanced course of his own. Yet the rewards of research in the history of analysis are apt to be thin. Within academic life psychologists are likely to repudiate all of psychoanalysis, and the literary or philosophic interest in the field is apt to be naively committed to one or another embattled strand of analytic thinking. To compound the problem, clinicians' interest in historical matters is usually a hobby rather than something that can stand up to professional scrutiny. Lothane is one of those exceptions whose example helps sustain the rest of us in our own work.

## Notes

1. Han Israëls, *Schreber: Father and Son* (Madison, CT: International Universities Press, 1989), translated by H. S. Lake.
2. Zvi Lothane, *In Defense of Schreber: Soul Murder and Psychiatry* (Hillsdale, NJ: The Analytic Press, 1992).

# 47

# Unorthodox Technique

If one has been following the literature about Freud's clinical techniques that has accumulated over the past few decades, *Unorthodox Freud*[1] by Beate Lohser and Peter Newton will come as a refreshing improvement to the more stereotypical view of what Freud was likely to do in practice. Lohser and Newton do not concentrate on Freud's technical recommendations, although of course they refer the reader to what Freud wrote about that which he thought a proper analysis supposedly consisted in. Lohser and Newton had the splendid idea of looking at some published firsthand accounts put in print by Freud's former patients, and the authors of *Unorthodox Freud* deal with Freud's analyses of Abram Kardiner, Hilda Doolittle, Joseph Wortis, John Dorsey, and Smiley Blanton. Although the bulk of the book gets taken up by separate chapters devoted to each of these cases, and presents the clinical situations from the point of view of patients, some general conclusions about technique do emerge from the material that is recounted.

As far as I could detect, however, neither Lohser nor Newton seems to have had any personal familiarity with the patients they have chosen to write about, and the result is unfortunately on the wooden side. I was myself able to meet and interview Kardiner, Wortis, and Blanton, and had some correspondence with Dorsey; perhaps it is not surprising that *Unorthodox Freud* seems to be humanly disappointing. One might never guess, from the narrative the authors come up with, many of the idiosyncratic traits characteristically associated with the patients in question. To take an extreme example, I recall Kardiner telling me (with his typical pungency) that Hilda Doolittle had been psychotic, whereas all Lohser and Newton concede is that she belongs in today's category of "borderline," an unduly elastic concept as far as I am concerned. Regrettably, nothing that Lohser and Newton describe reminds me of the patients they are writing about, although the authors have conscientiously studied the narrow published texts. Franz Alexander comes up late in *Unorthodox Freud*, as he was a pioneer in challenging the orthodox approach to technique that solidified in America after World War II and was powerful for at least the next generation. No mention gets made of others, like Carl Jung, Alfred Adler, Otto Rank, Sandor Rado, Erich Fromm, or Harry Stack Sullivan, to mention only a few who notably dissented from the dry-as-dust approach promoted by the central American analytic trade unions. For a variety of reasons this orthodox mirage appealed to the American hope that a neutral and scientific method could be used by analytic practitioners, an expectation encouraged by Freud's metaphor that analysis can be compared to surgery. Although so many distinguished thinkers are ignored in *Unorthodox Freud*, the authors prominently cite Kurt Eissler's work on so-called classical technique; it remains my conviction that it is alarming that anybody could take Eissler therapeutic views seriously at this stage of the game.

For some reason, as emancipated as Lohser and Newton are trying to be, they still share the old motto that in the existential dilemmas of clinical work it remains wisest to "stick to the rules." It is precisely because Freud did not want to appease the hunger of beginners for illusory certitude that he was so reluctant to publish further on technique. Future students should be made aware, whenever for instance Freud's case history of the Wolf Man gets mentioned, of all that he published about his treatment with Freud, and not just what Freud's fervent disciples thought it organizationally good to see in print. Also, if one were to write comprehensively about these five analysands of Freud's, it would be wise to consult their other writings as well.

*Unorthodox Freud* is a good solid book that should do some good, and I hope that what I have written does not appear too harsh. For me it is disappointing that the powers-that-be in the legendary "mainstream" have been so reluctant to acknowledge the merits of the central points concerning these five cases that Lohser and Newton are trying to make. Life is short, and I hope it will not be forever that common sense about the history of analysis waits to be acknowledged.

## Note

1. Beata Lohser and Peter M. Newton, *Unorthodox Freud: The View From the Couch* (New York: The Guilford Press, 1996).

# 48

# The Freud Wars

John Forrester's *Dispatches from the Freud Wars: Psychoanalysis and Its Passions*[1] is an interesting collection of essays. Unfortunately, even after over more than a hundred years of debate, it still seems that writers in this field can be classified into those who are "pro" as opposed to those who are "anti." Although one might have thought that by now we should be at a more sophisticated level of discussion, the charge against Freud for having created a "pseudo-science" reached a new kind of ferocity in Frederick Crews's famous 1993-1994 articles in *The New York Review of Books*. Although there were many reasons for thinking that the complacencies of the American psychoanalytic establishment deserved a thorough shaking-up, it is disconcerting (to me at least) that an impression may now be abroad that psychoanalysis deserved to be seen as junk science.

On this score Forrester is, in my opinion, on the side of the angels. He takes Freud seriously as a figure within intellectual history, and in the last chapter of this book Forrester tries to deal with criticisms like those advanced by such writers as Stanley Fish, Adolf Grunbaum, Frank Sulloway, and also Crews. Forrester is in the Department of History and Philosophy of Science at Cambridge, yet he brings to bear on Freud the sensibilities of a literary critic. Forrester rightly sees Freud as part of Western moral thought, a thinker whose ethical practices and preachings deserve close scrutiny.

Forrester is ardently Francophilic, and in this book and in his earlier ones, there are plenty of references to the seminars and essays of Jacques Lacan. For reasons that still escape me, the French have been especially receptive to the ideas of Melanie Klein. Although there is no school of Kleinian analysts in Paris, her writings—even the most speculative—are treated with dead seriousness there. One will not find in Forrester skepticism or humor about the French Freud. British intellectuals have long taken Klein far more seriously than she has been understood in North America, and it is true that Lacan and Klein both had problems with the reigning powers within international psychoanalysis. But one would hope for more lightness of touch in citing Lacan or Klein, yet without falling into the same barrel as Crews.

Fanaticism has dogged the history of analysis from the outset. And intellectuals, especially those like Forrester who do not practice analysis themselves, have been apt to be more devoutly loyalist than experienced clinicians, who know some of the key drawbacks to the inherited traditions of thought.

Although I believe Forrester is on the right track in standing against the crudeness of some of the most recent assaults on Freud, I did not learn as much from his pieces as I might have hoped. For example, one chapter takes off from a couple of sentences in Freud's *Group Psychology and the Analysis of the Ego* in which he infers from the Biblical judgment of King Solomon the idea that envy can be related to justice. "If one woman's child," Freud wrote, "is dead, the other shall not have a live one either. The bereaved woman is recognized by this wish." That seems to be a wicked reading, and also Nietzschean. But Forrester goes on to link it with John Rawls's liberal theory of justice; it is, on Forrester's part, a high-wire trapeze act, but not one of general interest. Rawls should be shaken by Freud's commentary. Forrester uses the term "historiography of psychoanalysis" more than once, but a hot-house interest in Rawls makes for a dessicated argument detached from the organic flow of anything in Forrester's reasoning.

Chapter 2 of Forrester's book had the most interest for me, since it deals with the Freud-Ferenczi letters, and the emotional triangle between Ferenczi, the woman Ferenczi eventually married, and her daughter (Elma), as well as how they all were involved with Freud. Here Forrester is working concretely from the published texts of the first two volumes (out of a total of three) of the Freud-Ferenczi correspondence. In the mid-1960s, however, I interviewed Elma, as well as others who knew the people; and although Forrester is ingenious in reading these letters, it can be alarming how he misses some of the most striking points that would be evident to someone who had even a passing acquaintance with the human beings involved.

There is something in Forrester's tone, a bit caustic and expressing certitude, that I found off-putting. Perhaps it is partly a question of national culture, and Forrester's presence in Oxbridge which accounts for this mannerism. As an American liberal I remain committed to the idea that it is possible to learn from anyone: Jungians, Rankians, Adlerians, etc., have all something to teach. My own pluralistic outlook does not preclude intellectual convictions. Forrester would be more persuasive if he seemed less sure of himself. He sometimes pontificates in his notes. I can appreciate Crews's rhetoric even if I reject most of his conclusions. All around it seems to me a pity that it is not possible to be more generous and tolerant of the points of views of others.

## Note

1. John Forrester, *Dispatches from the Freud Wars: Psychoanalysis and Its Passions* (Cambridge, MA: Harvard University Press, 1997).

# 49

# The Case of Sigmund Freud

Two books by Sander Gilman, *The Case of Sigmund Freud: Medicine and Identity at the Fin de Siècle* and *Freud, Race, and Gender*,[1] succeed in making an important contribution to the pre-existing literature about Freud. One might think that by now the possible lines of interpretation about Freud had started to dry up. Instead, Freud turns out to be such a considerable figure in intellectual history that he appears to be subject to a wide variety of viewpoints as each generation finds something special in his work. In the case of Sander L. Gilman, he has not invented a new Freud for the sake of novelty. On the contrary, from the extensiveness of his bibliographic references one gets the impression that he has read virtually everything relevant that has appeared in print; oddly enough he is stronger on the continental scholarship than the Anglo-American, but that is in its own way helpful for those of us without Gilman's familiarity with European sources. It also seems that he has legitimately emphasized how significant it is that Freud be seen not only as a Jew, but as part of the history of Western attitudes toward Judaism.

Inevitably there is a certain overlap between these two books, and yet they are distinct entities. In *The Case of Sigmund Freud* Gilman begins by discussing the issue of the relationship between medicine and race as it relates to Freud's career. Gilman is obviously an expert on the varieties of anti-Semitism. The debate over the immutability of the Jew as opposed to the "mixed" nature of the Jewish race was well established by the turn of the century. Galician Jews, which include Freud's family's origins, were especially stigmatized, even by their Western brethren. The Jew was seen not only as a special carrier of disease but as a corrupting force within civilization. Fantasies about the biological nature of Jews, including their body and spirit, had to have an impact on the development of the profession of psychoanalysis that Freud created.

For understanding Freud's development, the importance of the period he spent as a young man studying in Paris with Jean-Martin Charcot has long been established. Freud's memorial to Charcot, although Gilman does not make the point, can be seen as a reflection of Freud's own conception of himself. Even

Freud's consulting room may have been modeled after that of Charcot. Now it appears that Charcot was convinced that Jews were especially prone to mental illness. And Gilman relates Freud's sensitivity about his Jewishness to his declared reluctance to be stared at all day long by his patients, which was a reason Freud gave for his preference for using a couch during psychoanalyses. Gilman points out that the disproportionate number of Jews who played a part in the early days of Freud's movement were in fact predominantly from eastern Europe.

The alleged greater incidence of insanity among Jews was commonly related to their inbreeding. The nose of the Jew was considered a telltale sign, which bears on the way in which Freud, as well as his intimate Wilhelm Fliess, thought that by treating the nose various sexual difficulties could be influenced. Freud characteristically sought to universalize as true for all humanity what might otherwise be considered specifically Jewish. Although, unlike others, Freud himself never converted from Judaism, he shared a typical Jewish reverence for the classical world of ancient Greece.

Gilman has a fascinating section on how the limping Jew and the limping devil were treated as interchangeable images at the beginning of the twentieth century. Jewish men from the Austro-Hungarian provinces were considered especially prone to hysteria, and a prominent symptom was impaired gait. Jews were considered especially likely to commit incest and also to have hemorrhoids. In his attack on the mythical concept of "degeneration," Freud "was also protecting his own position as an innovative scientist from the accusation of being merely a clever but degenerate Jew." Gilman explores how "the idea of homosexuality, like that of the feminine, is redolent with qualities ascribed to the inherent nature of Jewish degeneration." Freud insisted that Judaism was a positive source of his strength and the courage of his people.

In *Freud, Race, and Gender*, Gilman continues to examine similar themes, and he begins with the racial models of being Jewish. In Gilman's opinion, Freud transferred his sense of inferiority "to another object, the woman." Here I think that Gilman, too, uncritically accepts current stereotypes about Freud's approach to women. But Gilman discerns how "Freud's comments on the unknowability of the Jew parallel his claims about the unknowability of the feminine." Being Jewish and being perverted "were virtually interchangeable categories at the turn of the century." Gilman has a lengthy section on the significance of circumcision, an issue on which Freud himself dwelt. As Gilman sees it, "central to the definition of the Jew was the image of the male Jew's circumcised penis as impaired, damaged, or incomplete, and therefore threatening to the wholeness and health of the male Aryan." Gilman thinks that Freud's dismissal of the inheritance of mental illness and his "stress on the specific nature of sexual trauma" lay at the heart of his final repudiation of Charcot. In clinical practice, however, I believe that to a greater extent Freud acknowledged the significance of biology and so-called constitution than Gilman likes to think. I believe that Gilman is right, though, in suggesting that Freud's emphasis on trauma as a cause of neurosis was a way of universalizing "the Jewish predisposition to illness." By proposing that Gentile culture fears circumcision as a sign of castration, Freud was saying that "it is the Aryan who suffers from the trauma of the Jew's circumcision."

Gilman's books are stimulating and at the same time immensely learned. Students in the field should be studying his citations and notes for a good while, since Gilman has brought to this field a cosmopolitan scholarship that is richly rewarding.

## Note

1. Sander L. Gilman, *The Case of Sigmund Freud: Medicine and Identity at the Fin de Siècle* (Baltimore, MD: Johns Hopkins University Press, 1993); and Sander L. Gilman, *Freud, Race, And Gender* (Princeton, NJ: Princeton University Press, 1993).

# 50

# Reading Freud's Reading

In 1991 a summer seminar at the Freud Museum in London, funded by the National Endowment for the Humanities and directed by Sander Gilman, was held on the subject of Freud's reading. Twelve Americans met at the museum and read in Freud's library from a variety of perspectives. Some of the results of their work appear in an excellent book, *Reading Freud's Reading*,[1] edited by Sander Gilman, Jutta Birmele, Jay Geller, and Valerie Greenberg. There are thirteen essays here, and two of the best of them come from one of the members of the museum staff.

Before describing what the papers are about and how fine some of them are, a general point ought to be made, for in 1990 the second director of the museum had been removed for ideological offenses that have not been disclosed. At least one member of the scholarly staff was fired. The sources of the American money behind the museum were able to insist that the work being done at the museum was insufficiently orthodox to suit old-fashioned Freudian requirements. I thought it an open question whether anybody respectable in the world of museum directorship could be uncovered to suit the religious purposes of the aging autocrats who still strove to control what went on at the house where Freud died.

Unfortunately, I must report that the bibliographies in these papers are all distorted by conscious or unconscious censorship. There is almost a hundred years now of serious scholarship on the history of psychoanalysis, much of it critical of Freud and his work, but it is not fairly represented here. The name Peter Gay comes up so often as to establish what I had long suspected, that he is now regarded as the official spokesperson for whitewashing Freud's image. It has been my conviction that Freud was great enough to be in need of no such partisanship. The bibliographies are all politically correct, and if scholars are alerted to the fact then this book can serve the purposes of advancing the field of Freud studies and intellectual history in general.

One of the best pieces, "Sigmund Freud and the Sexologists: A Second Reading," is by Sander Gilman. (He ought to know, though, that Hanns Sachs was nonmedical.) Gilman has a masterful understanding of the European history of anti-Semitism, but it is too simple to think, as Gilman evidently does, that Carl Jung ever alleged that there was an actual affair between Freud and his sister-in-law Minna.

Philip McCaffrey has written a fascinating study called "Freud's Uncanny Woman," demonstrating that a good literary critic can teach something unique about a close reading of Freud's text on the uncanny. Jay Geller has an important article on Freud's book jottings connected to his case history of Schreber. Jutta Birmele has also done a first-class job in helping to forward our understanding of how Freud arrived at his theses in his book on Leonardo da Vinci. All of these scholars worked from Freud's underlinings and marginalia. In my opinion, the papers on Freud and the history of science are on the weak side. But Peter Rudnytsky has a sound chapter on Freud's *Gradiva* essay.

Nobody, however, has established to my satisfaction exactly what role Freud took in deciding which of his books went with him from Vienna to London and which were sold. He was old and extremely sick by 1938, yet still in power within the household. Some books were given away in later years by members of his family or were mixed with the library of Freud's daughter, Anna. Still, there is much to be learned from studying *Reading Freud's Reading*. Some of Freud's marginal comments, or underlinings, made me sit up with astonishment.

## Note

1. Sander L. Gilman, Jutta Birmele, Jay Geller, and Valerie D. Greenberg, eds., *Reading Freud's Reading* (New York: New York University Press, 1994).

# 51

# Otto Rank

Otto Rank remains one of the least known among the several disciples with whom Freud had a major falling-out. Rank had started off in 1905 as a loyal follower of Freud's, and Rank came to play an important personal and organizational role in Freud's life. Rank became Secretary of the Vienna Psychoanalytic Society, and editions of Freud's *The Interpretation of Dreams* appeared with Rank's name on the cover, since Freud had allowed essays by Rank to be included in his text.

When the difficulties first began between Freud and Rank, starting in 1923, the origins of the trouble were primarily personal. But Rank was already such a central figure in the psychoanalytic movement that other of Freud's students were eager to stigmatize Rank as a "heretic," disloyal to the creator of psychoanalysis. No matter how anguished Freud may have been, he was unable to hold onto Rank in the face of the pressures from the organized "cause" Freud had created. Intellectual differences also existed between Freud and Rank, but it took a while for the mixture of the private and the theoretical to get put together in order to seal Rank's exit in 1926 from the Freud world.

It may be that a "dissenter" like Rank will turn out in the long run to have added to, rather than subtracted from, Freud's reputation. We are living in a time right now when it seems the fashion to point out all the ways in which Freud went wrong. Few seem to realize that if it has taken this long to spot Freud's mistakes, that makes him all the more commanding a figure within the history of ideas. In reality, Rank was one of the earliest critics of Freud to subject psychoanalysis to a thorough-going reexamination. "Deviants" like Rank were the ones with the most original ideas. Freud deserves the credit both for originally inspiring Rank as well as for having given birth to a school of thought that included Rank as a notable renegade.

It is only within the last ten years or so that Rank has been coming into his own. Unfortunately, there are still texts by Rank that have never been translated into English, and his diary as a young man remains unpublished. In his edition of *A Psychology of Difference: The American Lectures*,[1] Robert Kramer has wisely assembled twenty-two lectures by Rank that he delivered in America but which remained unprinted until now. (Columbia University has a substantial Rank collection.) One of the difficulties between Freud and Rank grew out of Rank's willingness to travel to the States in the mid-1920s, at a time of Freud's ill-health and when America was the most lucrative source of analytic patients. Freud had all along disliked being dependent on American support, and he resented that Rank was able to capitalize on the fascination with psychotherapy among the Americans.

Rank was full of novel concepts, and *A Psychology of Difference* shows how these notions gradually evolved. Rank was one of the first to insist on the central role of the mother in child development, and the lectures here illustrate Rank's formulating the hypothesis of the pre-Oedipus phase long before it got accepted within orthodox psychoanalytic theory. (Jung had said something earlier along similar lines but had not been politic enough to put his point into terminology connected with Oedipus.) Freud's was a complicated theology, and as clever as Rank was, it took him a good while to work his way toward a position of his own. Perhaps the most poignant lecture in this whole collection was given at the First International Congress on Mental Hygiene in 1930 in Washington, D.C. For after Rank had finished an impressive presentation, he was almost immediately punished by being dropped as an honorary member of the American Psychoanalytic Association.

Rank was one of the pioneers in pointing out the flaws in the classical psychoanalytic situation that Freud had constructed. In addition, Rank proposed some of the key ideas that have helped to make possible the coherent practice of short-term psychotherapy. Rank wanted to include the psychology of the here and now, as he looked on the interaction between patient and therapist as one between potential equals. The objective of therapy was, in Rank's view, to mobilize the patient's will; Rank wanted to go beyond Freud's aim of helping the patient to achieve autonomy, in that Rank sought to encourage self-creation. Rank knew better than most the ways in which the traditional psychoanalytic setting implicitly embodied an authoritarian structure. And Rank sought to inject a note of humanitarianism into psychotherapeutic interactions.

Rank was way ahead in seeing psychotherapy as an interpretive activity, as opposed to Freud's quest for causation. Furthermore, Rank emphasized the significance of emotional reliving in contrast to the standard psychoanalytic insistence on rational insight. By the mid-1930s Rank was formulating the idea that neurosis represented a failure in creativity, and his book on artists today gets more and more cited by literary critics.

Although the commonplace has been that differing with Freud paid off in worldly terms, Rank has had an uphill struggle to succeed in getting his ideas across. His premature death in 1939 did not help establish the genuine individuality of his own point of view, but intellectual historians should have the job of explicating just how important Rank's contribution was.

To repeat: Otto Rank remains one of the most talented, and least appreciated, among Freud's followers. Originally he came to Freud as a young student, and Freud encouraged him in every possible way; Rank became an intimate help-mate, and rewarded Freud's confidence by becoming prolific. It was Rank who was assigned the task of keeping the records of the proceedings of the group around Freud in Vienna, and therefore Rank's notetaking became the basis for today's four-volume set of the *Minutes of the Vienna Psychoanalytic Society*. After serving as an editor of a military publication during World War I, Rank returned to Vienna and became a practicing analyst. Other of Freud's disciples were naturally jealous of Rank's unique status. A careful look at the famous 1922 group photograph of Freud and his so-called secret committee, selected to forward "the cause," shows that Rank was the only one, standing immediately behind Freud's throne-like chair, whose eyes are looking in exactly the same direction as the master.

After Freud fell ill of cancer of the jaw in 1923 Rank's rivals had their opening. Rank prepared himself to assume Freud's position, and then Freud rallied and went on to live until 1939. Freud's initial illness, however, became a decisive turning point in the relation between the two men. Freud was naturally none too pleased to read any newspaper articles about Rank's taking over as leader of the "movement." Rank's little 1923 book on the birth trauma was intimately involved in his complex emotional relation to the founder of psychoanalysis; the text, full of original ideas and yet expressed loyally within Freud's framework, was dedicated to Freud, then thought to be in grave physical danger. Freud's initial reaction to the book was positive; but others in Freud's circle, such as Ernest Jones in London and Karl Abraham in Berlin, made things harder as they sniffed signs of psychoanalytic heresy in Rank's innovations. Freud always resented how Jones and Abraham had made things even more difficult for him with Rank. Rank travelled to America for lectures and supervision, and he and Freud attempted a series of reconciliations. Finally Rank moved to Paris in 1926, and a few years later quietly resigned from the Vienna Psychoanalytic Society. Rank had had one of the best theoretical heads among the early analysts, and he was able to develop his own independent ideas in a set of books. Rank, however, never established his own school or acquired passionately devoted followers; his early death in 1939, not long after Freud himself died, cut short Rank's career.

Despite all Rank's multiple talents, it has not been easy to establish his reputation. E. James Lieberman, one of the co-translators to *Psychology of the Soul*,[2] has been outstanding in his efforts to keep Rank's work alive. His 1985 biography of Rank, *Acts of Will*, remains one of the best studies of a pioneering analyst, and an outstanding work on the history of analysis. Rank did have an influence on a school of social work at the University of Pennsylvania, and also a number of artists and writers have picked up his ideas. But Lieberman knows, in presenting this new edition of *Psychology of the Soul*, that he has an uphill struggle in putting Rank's ideas across. Rank was not a terribly clear writer, and unfortunately no one has ever published a special dictionary of his terms; the secondary literature on Rank remains sparse. Yet Rank deserves to remain a major figure in the history of modern depth psychology.

Early on, Rank came to object to the mechanistic-sounding Freudian approach as being misleadingly scientistic, and he pioneered in talking about the nature of the psychoanalytic setting itself, and how what was therapeutic was the rapport between analyst and patient. Now that most psychotherapeutic cases are being seen in the course of short-term treatment, everything Rank had to say becomes more relevant and timely. While Rank suffered the penaltes of excommunication for what once seemed "heresy" within orthodox psychoanalysis, in hindsight he sounds reliably prophetic. Jones, in his official biography of Freud, claimed that Rank had, like Sandor Ferenczi, supposedly suffered from mental illness, and that that accounted for Rank's differences with Freud. Such accusations are more often made behind closed doors, as analysts too often rely on using diagnostic categories on their troublesome colleagues.

One of the outstanding contributions Rank was trying to establish was the degree to which the therapist is engaged in the pursuit of meaning rather than causation, interpreting instead of explaining. Contemporary analysts are unlikely to be well-educated in the history of their discipline, and therefore Rank is rarely credited for the ideas that at the time caused him so much trouble with the then reigning powers in organized psychoanalysis. Rank was, among other points, one of the first to insist on the significance of pre-oedipal problems, although at the time he put forward such ideas he was accused of taking flight, like Jung for instance, from the significance of the oedipus complex. Rank also, for example in his concept of the birth trauma, was trying to talk about separation anxiety, and the significance of the mother as a legitimate object of dependency. (To my knowledge nobody has ever adequately written about the psychological role of servants in families.)

For Rank there was a spiritual dimension to human existence which was critical not just to the practice of psychotherapy but to mankind's hope for reestablishing an equilibrium after the loss of traditional religious faiths. Rank was not ashamed to embrace a humanitarian position, even though this was at odds with Freud's own rooted distrust of mankind. Further, Rank did not endorse Freud's attitude toward so-called resistances, and instead thought that only by a patient's being encouraged to develop his or her "will" could an individual find self-fulfillment. Rank was always interested in the problem of immortality and death, and these themes appeared in his early attempts to understand the problem of the double. All yearnings for group collective meaning received more tolerant understanding in Rank than would have been the case according to classic Freudian theory.

Rank can be read as having constructed one of the most searching critiques of Freudian thinking, alongside the presentation of his own approach. Some of the central features to Freud's theoretical points of view have survived in the theories of even those contemporary thinkers who imagine themselves as emancipated from Freud's mistakes if not downright at odds with Freud himself. Perhaps above all Rank should be honored for the degree to which he made creativity, the struggle for autonomy and self-expression, central to his thinking. Freud talked a lot about the danger of "illusions," as he purported to be a proponent of the therapeutic efficacy and moral significance of the truth. Rank, however, sounds "post-modern" in the extent to which he is skeptical of the truth and receptive to whatever perspectives manage to fit in with the infinite variety of idiosyncratic human needs.

Rank was probably the most philosophically well-educated of the early analysts, and unlike Freud, Rank was fully receptive to what philosophers could teach. The translator's Introduction to *Psychology of the Soul* by Lieberman explicitly tries to relate Rank's ideas to those of others, including Jacques Lacan. Rank does not make for easy reading, but the more one reflects on the ideas he stood for the more appalling the way intellectual historians have felt able to skip over his work. One of the obstacles to understanding Rank's writings is the way in which he reasons in terms which are anthropological-sounding, even though the notion of evolutionary stages in human development has long since gone out of style among contemporary anthropologists. Rank was one of the great intellectuals in the history of Freud's following, and his involvement with Freud ultimately adds credit to the significance Freud has for the history of ideas. Each of Rank's pages are rich in ideas, and repay the attention of both scholars and therapists. As one of the most scholarly of twentieth-century psychologists, Rank's current neglect makes little sense, although it does make it possible for enterprising students of today to find an easy way to make a genuine contribution by perusing his works. Rank knew Freud well enough to make his critiques of classical psychoanalysis well-grounded, and at no time does Rank indulge in the kind of appalling Freud-bashing that seems so popular now. Rank differed from Freud with the most profound respect, as Rank took seriously the injunction that students repay their teachers best by going beyond them.

## Notes

1. Otto Rank, *A Psychology of Difference: The American Lectures*, ed. Robert Kramer (Princeton, NJ: Princeton University Press, 1996).
2. Otto Rank, *Psychology of the Soul: A Study of the Origin, Conceptual Evolution, and Nature of the Soul*, translated by Gregory C. Richter and E. James Lieberman (Baltimore, MD: Johns Hopkins University Press, 1998).

# 52

# Oedipus

It is a pleasure to single out Peter Rudnytsky's *Freud and Oedipus*[1] from the vast, and yet ever growing, literature about early analysis. Rudnytsky is a specialist in English and comparative literature, and he has decided to explore the theme of Oedipus as it comes up during the century and a half before Freud's own founding of analysis. In addition, Rudnytsky touches on a variety of biographical problems in Freud's life, at the same time raising numerous issues in connection with contemporary theorists of literary criticism; he also subjects the cycle of Sophocles's Oedipus plays to sustained scrutiny. In contrast to the tendentiousness that mars so much of the writing in this field, I found Rudnytsky's critical judgment unusually well balanced and sophisticated.

Part I of *Freud and Oedipus* is concerned with Freud's biography, but I am afraid that I found this the weakest portion of the book. In his effort to get at "the biographical determinants of Freud's discovery of the Oedipus complex," Rudnytsky does a serious-minded job of assembling the key features to this story. I never thought that Rudnytsky was deliberately distorting any of the evidence; the book is written without any apparent ideological partisanship. But still I wonder how, at this late stage of the game, it is possible for Rudnytsky to take Freud's own self-analysis at such face value.

It seems to me (but evidently not to Rudnytsky) an open question what in fact really set off Freud's self-analysis. I do not think it sufficient to take Freud at his own word. For all that has been published in connection with Freud's supposed reaction to the death of his father, I am myself inclined to question whether Freud was not indulging here in a characteristic evasion of the present by a flight into the past. Otto Rank, whom Rudnytsky approvingly quotes on a number of occasions, once pointed out that Freud's account of the significance to him of the death of his father was really a cover for Freud's reaction to the simultaneous loss of Josef Breuer. In addition, I think that Freud was shocked by his allowing himself to be taken in by his own fantasies about the significance of childhood seduction in the origin of neurosis, and this helped precipitate sustained self-scrutiny on Freud's part.

But self-analysis, even that of Freud, is necessarily limited, and he engaged in far more self-deception than Rudnytsky seems to allow. I do not think, for example, that it is at all sound to take so seriously what Freud wrote, for example, about his alleged reactions to the early death of his brother Julius. In addition, Freud's dreams, as reported in his texts, and his letters to Fliess, all need to be taken with a good many more grains of salt. Rudnytsky speaks of Freud's being able "to recover so many of his early memories," without Rudnytsky seeming at all to understand that such memories (as Jung pointed out long ago) can be used defensively, as disguises and self-concealments. Although Part 1, "Biography," suffers from the flaws I have suggested, Rudnytsky is consistently reliable in his judgments made in passing about the relevant secondary literature.

Part 2, "Intellectual Biography," seemed to me the best part of the book; for here Rudnytsky surveys the whole literature on Oedipus since the eighteenth century, "in order to study the culminating moment in Freud's self-analysis not as a personal but as a cultural phenomenon." Rudnytsky struck me as persuasive in seeing Freud primarily as "the heir to the movements of German romanticism and idealistic philosophy." Rudnytsky's account of how Voltaire could mock Sophocles, for example, seems to me grounds in itself for disputing those like Peter Gay who would like to trace Freud straight back to the Enlightenment. Rudnytsky is at his best, I think, in his discussions of Schiller, Hölderlin, and Kleist. (Somehow Rudnytsky misses the significance of Schiller's writing on Moses and how this relates to Freud's *Moses and Monotheism*; *Freud and Oedipus* does follow a somewhat narrow track.)

I would have liked rather more on Schopenhauer, whose philosophic stock is curiously low now but in Freud's time was rightly far higher; and despite Rudnytsky's attention to the figure of Nietzsche, as part of situating Freud in the context of nineteenth century thought, I think that Rudnytsky does not adequately appreciate the extent to which both Nietzsche and Freud went so beyond traditional definitions of good and evil as to lead in a direction that is sometimes horrifying even today. The scariest side of Freud could have been highlighted in the course of discussing his indebtedness to Nietzsche.

Part 3 consists of a psychoanalytic exploration of Greek tragedy as exemplified in the dramas of Sophocles. Here, as throughout *Freud and Oedipus*, Rudnytsky is judicious and informative. An interesting appendix to the book deals with some contemporary theorists on the central theme of the legend of Oedipus. Despite my reservations in reading *Freud and Oedipus*, I hope to help welcome to the world of Freud studies a promising scholar.

## Note

1. Peter Rudnytsky, *Freud and Oedipus* (New York: Columbia University Press, 1987).

# 53

# The Psychoanalytic Vocation

Peter Rudnytsky's *The Psychoanalytic Vocation: Rank, Winnicott, and the Legacy of Freud*[1] is an excellent book. In his new text Rudnytsky tries to appreciate developments in psychoanalytic theory which have sought to correct certain striking imbalances within Freud's thinking. In *Freud and Oedipus* Rudnytsky stood out for his independence in appraising Freud's career and thought; now Rudnytsky has continued to approach psychoanalytic ideas without the contraints which orthodoxy so often imposes on students of the history of psychoanalysis.

At the outset of *The Psychoanalytic Vocation* Rudnytsky tells us of his "conversion to an object relations perspective, which entails a rejection of some key principles of classical analytic theory having to do particularly with the nature of the instincts or drives." Rudnytsky has a humanistic orientation, and in pursuit of his objective he explores here the work of Otto Rank and Donald W. Winnicott. Both Rank and Winnicott, who are rarely thought of in the same breath, had challenging things to say about what was lacking in Freud's original approach. Rank became one of the "heretics" in the story of the development of Freud's school, while Winnicott, who unlike Rank had no personal contact with Freud, has been widely honored within psychoanalysis; Rudnytsky is original in linking together Rank with Winnicott, and Rudnytsky has done something important in spelling out the hidden continuities within the development of psychoanalytic thinking.

Yet I remain hesitant about the degree of enthusiasm for object relations theory implied in Rudnytsky's telling us about his "conversion." *The Psychoanalytic Vocation*, though fine in what it does, shows signs of tunnel vision, as it excludes too many other thinkers and perspectives. For example, though Rudnytsky says he is centrally "concerned with mapping the preoedipal realm," since that in large measure has been the tale of psychoanalysis after Freud, the name Ruth Mack Brunswick does not come up even once; she used the term preoedipal two years before Freud. And ideas fostered by someone like Erik H. Erikson, whom Winnicott said he was indebted to, are completely ignored.

Rudnytsky could not of course deal with everyone, and *The Psychoanalytic Vocation* is excellent as far as it goes, but a stronger book would have taken into account a broader range of thinkers.

Rudnytsky is unusual in the extent of his appreciation for Rank's work. Rank is not an easy writer to follow, and Rudnytsky has used his talents for intellectual history in order to understand a difficult thinker. Few have ever seen, as Rudnytsky does so well, how much of contemporary psychoanalysis is foreshadowed in Rank's writings. Someone like Winnicott, for instance, who was not a student of the history of ideas like Rudnytsky, only once cited Rank.

Supposedly, object relations theory, about which Rudnytsky is a little too uncritical for my money, can be legitimized, in terms of tracing it to Freud's thinking, by connecting it to Freud's *Inhibitions, Symptoms and Anxiety*, a book which Freud wrote in order to answer some of Rank's criticisms. Rudnytsky believes like others that in that book Freud abandoned his theory of anxiety as the result of repressed libido; but here I think that Rudnytsky is not enough aware of the extent to which Freud always stuck to his guns no matter what. One patient of Freud's from the 1920s and 1930s maintained to me that despite what Freud's books might lead one to think, as a matter of practice Freud remained wedded to his earlier notion that anxiety was the consequence of distorted libido.

Rudnytsky, even though he occasionally slips up in dealing with Freud's biography, is well versed in the story of the growth of the so-called Middle Group of British analysts, which has notably fostered the object relations school of thought. Therefore Rudnytsky can follow even such a difficult thinker as W. R. D. Fairbain. I wish, though, that the generosity of spirit that leads Rudnytsky to try to overcome so many taboos that are commonplace within orthodox psychoanalytic thinking had allowed Rudnytsky to be a little more open-minded about Rank's last books. For here Rudnytsky suddenly becomes stand-offish, and he adopts the conventional view that Rank became some sort of mystic. Rudnytsky bemoans the "anti-intellectualism" of Rank's final period, and deplores this so-called "irrationalism" as a retreat from the search for self-knowledge.

I myself think that Rank's last books, in which he was centrally concerned with the psychology of artistic creativity, are some of his most important contributions, and literary critics still have the job of appreciating what Rank offered. Rudnytsky is, however, so involved in object relations thinking that he only sees Rank as a precursor instead of looking at Rank in all his rich individuality.

Rudnytsky does show good judgment in focusing so on Winnicott, since he was probably the most outstanding figure of twentieth century British psychoanalysis. Although Rudnytsky tends to isolate Winnicott from various other thinkers, he does specifically compare him to Jacques Lacan and Heinz Kohut. But I am left a little uneasy by Rudnytsky's public acknowledgment of the emotional uses to him of studying Winnicott. Rudnytsky tells us that he is "in one respect announcing" his "search for a figure to whom I can have a transference as intense and satisfying as that aroused by Freud," although I would have thought that such a quest was unseemly for a student of the history of ideas. The theme of masters and their disciples, as Rudnytsky acknowledges when writing about Lacan, looks too prominent, and sometimes silly, when the history of psychoanalysis is taken as a whole. Nonetheless Rudnytsky's discussion of Winnicott is one of the best to have appeared so far. A fascinating interview with Winnicott's widow, which appears as an Appendix to *The Psychoanalytic Vocation*, seems to me in itself almost worth the price of the book.

## Note

1. Peter Rudnytsky, *The Psychoanalytic Vocation: Rank, Winnicott, and the Legacy of Freud* (New Haven, CT: Yale University Press, 1991).

# 54

# Freud Reappraised

Too much psychoanalytic theorizing has been undertaken as a sideline by practicing clinicians who have unfortunately remained amateurs within intellectual life. In contrast, Robert R. Holt, a clinical psychologist by training, has devoted decades to wrestling with the intricacies of metapsychology. He is thoroughly serious and a professional in matters of theory; everything he writes should command respectful attention.

*Freud Reappraised*[1] is a collection of his papers that have appeared over the last thirty years. The book makes for the most demanding kind of reading, since the issues Holt addresses inevitably enter the realm of not just philosophy but the metaphysics of psychoanalysis. By the end of what was a hard read I felt that the book had something important to teach.

The first chapter, "A Personal Introduction," provides us with the background to Holt's later career at New York University. He studied with some of the great figures in American academic psychology, and it is a pleasure to see him remind his psychoanalytic readers of how pioneering a leader Henry A. Murray was at the Harvard Psychological Clinic.

Holt tells us about his three analyses and his participation at the Washington School of Psychiatry, where he found himself "a defender of Freudian orthodoxy" in seminars with Clara Thompson, Erich Fromm, and Frieda Fromm-Reichmann. Holt was repelled by Harry Stack Sullivan's lectures. Evidently, David Rapaport, despite the dry and intellectualized quality of his thinking, was humanly charismatic, and his work on metapsychology became Holt's key starting point.

Chapter 2, "The Manifest and Latent Meanings of Metapsychology," scrupulously looks at the different uses Freud made of the term. Chapter 3, "Freud's Cognitive Style," is a memorable account of Freud's personality and intellect, as well as his notion of science and his use of rhetoric. Chapter 4 is a painstaking examination of Freud's concept of "bound" vs. "free" cathexis. It was the "first skirmish," Holt tells us, of what was to be "a continuing battle with metapsychology." I think that every ounce of history is worth at least (if not more than) an ounce of logic, and had Holt not been so under the sway of Rapaport, perhaps Holt would have spent his time more fruitfully. There are so many interesting problems associated with modern psychotherapy that I cannot for the life of me imagine why anyone would want to tilt at a windmill like bound vs. free cathexis.

Chapter 5 reviews some of Freud's basic biological assumptions, and how they influenced his theories. Here Holt comes back to the recognizable reality of valuable intellectual history. Freud's outlook is put in the context of the teachings of his early mentors. Holt argues that "many of the obscurities, fallacies, and internal contradictions of psychoanalytic theory are...direct derivatives of its neurological inheritance." Holt tells us that he is still working on another book, an intellectual biography of Freud, and some of these essays are an abbreviated version of what he intends to explicate at greater length. I do hope that Holt in that book can stay further away from the kind of abstract theorizing which he admits "numbs the brain."

Chapter 6 deals with Freud's concept of psychic energy. Although at the outset of the book Holt approvingly cites a surprising verbal observation of Erich Fromm's, in Holt's orthodox period he does not seem to have paid any attention to Fromm's dismissal of how anachronistic the notion of psychic energy is. In Chapter 7 Holt reconsiders the theory of instincts, and once again after great labor he is forced to conclude that the classical theory of motivation is sadly wanting. Even now, for all Holt's sophistication about scientific theory, he seems to believe uncritically in the positivistic notion of there being psychoanalytic "facts" or "data of observation." One would have thought it obvious that the question "What is a fact?" remains an open one for psychologists, historians, and philosophers alike.

Chapter 8 deals with "The Past and Future of Ego Psychology," and Holt recognizes that the post-1939 development of ego psychology was a key way of avoiding the blind alley that psychoanalytic theory was in at Freud's death. Yet Holt unnecessarily faults all ego psychology for being fatally mired in metapsychology. Erik H. Erikson, also a friend of Rapaport's and someone whose work is obviously admired by Holt, never allowed himself to ascend so far away from the realities of struggling human beings. Chapter 9 deals with "Ego Autonomy and the Problem of Human Freedom," but once again Holt is stuck in Rapaport's abstract path. Chapters 10 and 11 are both concerned with the theory of "the primary process," and only the most dogged reader can stick with Holt's ruminations about the "sad disarray" he finds.

And then the last three chapters of the book dramatically perk up. I think that Holt is too narrow in his conception of what constitutes science, and too harsh on an interesting philosopher like Paul Ricoeur. Holt believes that "the misfortune of psychonanalysis is that Freud never developed any means of generating and testing predictions," whereas I think that it is enough that Freud be honored for the way he succeeded in forcing us to think in a different way.

Holt tells us now that "it is best not to get too far away from the details of specific people's lives and problems," when that is what he himself has been doing in almost all his own essays. In a chapter on the current status of psychoanalytic theory Holt finally abandons metapsychology because its defects are "intrinsic, not simply products of Freud's personal style of thinking and writing." It sounds to me like a cry from the heart when Holt tells us: "It is anything but a comforting reflection to realize that most of one's career has been devoted to as worthless a theory as metapsychology has proved to be."

Yet Holt persists in praising positivistic philosophy. It may be entirely correct to think, as Holt does, that "psychoanalysts have been living in a fool's paradise, believing that the clinical theory was soundly established when in fact very little of it has been." But then I would suggest that Holt go through his library to find those writers who came to that same conclusion eighty years ago and see how the study of history can have something uniquely valuable to teach. If, as Holt tells us, "the role of whistle-blower does not particularly suit" him, then he could perform a service by helping to describe what all earlier whistle-blowers might have had in mind.

Holt is too hard on "current fads" like object relations theory and self-psychology; there are many roads to the top of the mountain, and Holt's admitted own misdirected efforts do not certify him as a thoroughly reliable guide. For example, he cites Heinz Hartmann without ever a word of criticism, entirely omitting the work of an earlier whistle-blower like Edward Glover who tried a generation ago to explore what a mess he thought psychoanalytic thinking had fallen into. And although Holt mentions more than once the existence of sensory deprivation experiments, he had not succeeded in picking up Erikson's cue that they teach us how unreliable so-called transference reactions can be; emotions in treatment can be a response, as Rank among others knew, to the peculiarities of the setting that the therapist arranges. *Freud Reappraised* is an admirable fresh look at psychoanalytic theory, even if it will not attract as many readers as it deserves.

## Note

1. Robert R. Holt, *Freud Reappraised: A Fresh Look at Psychoanalytic Theory* (New York: The Guilford Press, 1989).

# 55

# The Clark Lectures

Freud's 1909 trip to America, in which he came to Clark University in Worcester, Massachusetts, to accept the only honorary degree he was ever awarded, has become legendary. Saul Rosenzweig has taken this historic visit and in *Freud, Jung and Hall The King Maker*[1] painstakingly reconstructed all the available evidence touching on this noteworthy expedition. Freud was already a celebrity before he came, but the five lectures he delivered at Clark became one of the most widely read introductions to what psychoanalysis is all about.

Freud was accompanied on the trip by Sandor Ferenczi and Carl Jung; Ernest Jones travelled from Toronto to meet them for the journey to Worcester. Although Rosenzweig has unearthed a pack of letters between the entrepreneurial president of Clark, G. Stanley Hall, and Freud, the exact circumstances surrounding Jung's coming over have been impossible to clarify with certainty. Jung received an honorary degree as well, but Rosenzweig is not able to untangle exactly how this came about. At the time, the thirty-four year old Jung was Freud's chosen successor as leader of the psychoanalytic movement. As it happens, Jung and Freud swapped dream material onboard ship as part of a shared analysis. (Incidentally, they were able to travel in first class.) Jung later claimed in his autobiography that Freud's refusal to provide free associations to a dream, on the grounds that for Freud to do so would undermine his authority, was the beginning of Jung's disillusionment with Freud.

For years we have known that Freud never forgot this trip to America and irrationally blamed all kinds of problems on the New World. He not only expected psychoanalysis to be repudiated in the States, but for him the entire brash culture was suspect. As an educated European, Freud was full of prejudices against America. He disliked in particular what he took to be the prudery and puritanism of the States; he considered it barbaric that it was so difficult to find a public toilet, and that there were not street-corner restrooms as on the continent. It now turns out that while in America Freud suffered not just from indigestion, but that he also experienced urinary incontinence, and that Jung tried to treat him therapeutically for this particular symptom.

The Jung family has still not authorized an official biography, and we have touched on how the literature about Jung retains its amateurish character. Additionally, there is that embargoed existence of a full unpublished volume of Jung's autobiography, which, for some reason, the family has withheld from print. Some of the material in the autobiography pertains to Jung's impressions of his 1909 trip to the States, so Rosenzweig's narrative will have to be supplemented in the future; Rosenzweig is, however, writing with the benefit of having had a personal interview with Jung.

Rosenzweig gives us an ample amount of material with which we can relish a day-by-day account of Freud's 1909 trip. By using contemporary newspaper records, Rosenzweig is able to show just what Freud talked about at each of his lectures, which is not always what Freud later chose to put into print. William James, who was then a year away from his death, made a point of coming to Clark to hear what Freud had to say. Although in later years Freud talked about what a good impression James made on him, we have known for a long time that James was not similarly taken with Freud. From James's point of view the most important feature he valued in anyone was open-mindedness; and Freud as of 1909 seemed to James too fixated on certain psychoanalytic abstractions. While James seems to have thought a good deal better of Jung than of Freud, he was most impressed with Swiss psychiatrist Adolf Meyer who was then at Johns Hopkins. Meyer was awarded an honorary degree with Freud and Jung at Clark.

Freud's Clark lectures became his *Five Lectures on Psychoanalysis*. Rosenzweig follows his account with a fresh translation of this work. Although he is completely unblinkered in his approach to Freud and shows no partiality towards psychoanalytic orthodoxy, Rosenzweig does not attempt to rethink Freud's argument at Clark, or to demonstrate any defects in it. Because Freud's Clark lectures became such an influential popularization of psychoanalytic thinking, it is important, I think, to put them in perspective and see where Freud was being tendentious.

Rosenzweig shows how G. Stanley Hall became tolerant of Alfred Adler's "deviant" contributions, which must have helped confirm Freud in the belief that his American welcome was shallow and untrustworthy. Students of the history of psychoanalysis are in Rosenzweig's debt for this important work which sets forth so many of the key particulars of Freud's visit to the States.

## Note

1. Saul Rosenzweig, *Freud, Jung and Hall the King-Maker: The Historic Expedition to America (1909), with G. Stanley Hall as Host and William James as Guest* (Seattle, WA: Hogrefe & Huber, 1992).

# 56

# Why Freud Was Wrong

*Why Freud Was Wrong: Sin, Science, and Psychoanalysis*[1] is a huge book which makes fascinating reading. The reservations that I express about it ought not to obscure my conviction that Richard Webster has accomplished a significant achievement. It is genuinely unfortunate that the immense size of this text probably precludes its being translated into other languages, for Webster's detailed arguments merit the broadest kind of audience. The spaciousness of *Why Freud Was Wrong* allows the author an opportunity to make, sometimes only as asides, original points that deserve to get incorporated into the professional literature.

The title is obviously meant to be provocative, but I am not sure that the sections of the book that follow up on what the reader has been promised represent the best of what Webster has to offer. Part I is called "The Creation of a Pseudo-Science," and Webster takes great pains to show how Freud, out of a kind of messianic ambitiousness, could stack the deck in favor of his own cherished hypotheses. It seems to me naïve of Webster to have expected anything other than what he recounts. I thought that by this stage it went without saying that Freud tailored all his evidence for the sake of promoting his theories. This kind of bias showed up not just in his accounts of patients, but it extended to his comments on predecessors and enemies.

If one approaches Freud solely from the point of view of science, as Freud might have wanted most, there are bound to be disappointments about the value of his concepts. At no point, however, does Webster seems to recognize how remarkable it is that all these years after Freud's death as an old man in 1939 people still seem so absorbed in evaluating his work. Even while Freud was alive he had respectful critics, and the real mystery may be why they failed to obtain adequate attention. I would have thought that Webster, given his convictions, would have preferred to study the ideas of some of those who centrally challenged Freud ages ago.

At no point does Webster seem to me to absorb adequately the full implications of Freud's artistic achievement. Freud's greatness as a writer—who managed to make so many implausible theories convincing – has, I think, meant that someone like Webster himself has taken such extraordinary pains to reexamine the literature. Surely it cannot be the trade-unionism of orthodox psychoanalyis that has held Webster to this task; the self-interest of practitioners, fewer in Britain than the United States, surely cannot account for why Webster has undertaken his critique. Today, philosophers and literary critics are probably more interested in Freud than at any previous time, and I only hope it is not because they think that psychoanalysis has proved scientifically verifiable.

Throughout *Why Freud Was Wrong* I found myself agreeing with many of Webster's conclusions, although it does seem a bit mystifying that he thinks such a tome is now necessary. I would have thought that the time had come when alternatives to Freud, proposed by a variety of thinkers, would be worth examining. My hunch would be that readers could benefit more from being introduced to those theorists who broke with Freud, even if these works should also fall short of the ideal of scientific confirmation that Webster would seem to be championing.

I found Part II, "The Church and the Psychoanalytic Gospel," better thought through than the earlier section. Here is where Webster is able to score some really telling points. My own (positive) attitude toward religion is such, however, that I wish Webster had gone much further in this sort of argument. Freud, as well as his followers, did in fact advance a quasi-religious cause, but I would have thought that Webster, the author of an earlier book on blasphemy, was in an ideal position to point out parallels between Freud's accomplishment and traditional religious practices.

It is, of course, by no means the case that Freud was correct in thinking that religion could be dispensed with. He did, in fact, construct a system of ideas by which people have been able to pattern their lives. I think that it ought to be a major historical objective that we try to ferret out all the hidden moral commitments implicit in psychoanalytic teachings, and how these ideological values got accepted, if it is going to be possible to understand both the sources of Freud's successes and the damage that could result from an uncritical acceptance of his system.

There is really an immense amount to be said on the subject of psychoanalysis as a surrogate religion, and Webster curiously seems to hold back from pursuing this line of reasoning. I would be intrigued, for example, by an analysis of just how the therapeutic setup Freud constructed looks from the point of view of students of religious belief. Webster could make an even more important contribution if he were to specify exactly what aspects of Freud's analytic situation were reminiscent of traditional religious rites and practices. What did Freud's liturgy consist of, and how did his texts function as sacred?

There is also a good deal to be said about which aspects of traditional moral teachings Freud was undermining—as opposed to those ethical principles that he was lending unspoken support to. Webster does not, I think, adequately follow up on the ways in which Freud sought to attack Christian teachings, nor does he explicate the nature of the alternative worldview Freud was proposing. (The notes contain some fascinating material on Freud as a Jew, but his relation to Judaism should be more central to this book as a whole.)

Webster seems on the right track, except that he might take more for granted that others of us share many of his own conclusions. It is precisely because I think Webster's approach is a sound one that I would be eager to learn what else he has to teach us. *Why Freud Was Wrong* does not, for me, go far enough. And I say this not because I believe we need more Freud debunking; instead, the success of psychoanalysis in intellectual history has been such that a broad examination of how and why its teachings can be replaced seems to be of the utmost urgency.

Webster has written a thoroughly serious book, and he has not undertaken any cheap polemics. Even if we can concede the merits of everything that Webster has proposed, that still leaves us with the substantial constructive task of filling in where we are supposed to go from here. Biological psychiatry, for example, may currently lay better claim to scientific status than old-fashioned psychoanalysis; however, this school of thought, newly revived because of advances in psychopharmacology, is as capable of authoritarianism as anything Freud ever advocated. The ethics of power, and how therapeutic authority can be abused, is not confined as a problem just to Freud's practices but extends throughout all the healing professions. The consuming interest in classification and heredity, which is now so fashionable, was tellingly criticized by Freud and his school in the first years of this century, and it may prove as alive and relevant now as then.

## Note

1. Richard Webster, *Why Freud Was Wrong: Sin, Science, and Psychoanalysis* (New York: Basic Books, 1996).

# 57

# Translating Freud

At first glance *Translating Freud*,[1] edited by Darius Gray Ornston, is apt to seem like an academically precious enterprise. For the authors are primarily concerned with correcting a variety of defects in the work which James Strachey oversaw in putting together the *Standard Edition* of Freud's psychological writings. Not surprisingly, Strachey's translation was also an act of interpretation, and it has not been hard to find spots where he went astray. Strachey did not start out alone as a translator, since Ernest Jones had made certain key decisions before him; and Freud was delighted with the work Strachey succeeded in doing, which is bound to make it more than a bit awkward for contemporaries to poke holes in Strachey's achievement. So far the German editions of Freud's writings have relied on Strachey's editorial apparatus, which should be a testimony to what he accomplished.

What is troubling is the kind of alternative the authors here seem to have in mind. They mention how Freud had learned to read with the Philippson Bible, laid out in such a way that the transcript of the original faces a far longer commentary. And the authors also admiringly cite the way Luther's Bible is "set in large type with wide margins that are used for paraphrasing and alternative wording, as well as for cross-indexing and references to historical accounts." The authors seem to mind the way Strachey became "scripture," only because they feel that Freud himself deserves that designation. We are told without embarrassment how "the King James, or 'authorized,' Bible is said to have been put together by a committee...."

Does it not occur to these conscientious scholars that Freud might ever have been wrong? And that his critics, both former students as well as outsiders, may have had valid points to make? We are instead merely told that "Freud was a scientist," although it should be obvious, for example, that Freud's Leonardo essay, discussing the conflict between art and science, was largely autobiographical and revealed tensions in Freud's own work. We are informed by one author that Freud was not "a Romantic," as if such a category were all or nothing.

Perhaps the most dubious part of joining in the authors' assault on Strachey is their simultaneous idealization of the way Jean Laplanche's group has gone about translating Freud into French. One eminent Parisian expert on old Vienna holds that the Laplanche editions of Freud are a catastrophe, and others in Paris share that point of view. Jacques Lacan may have taught that one could rediscover the genuine Freud through "the literalness of his text," but surely that ought not to be taken as the final truth of the matter. Laplanche's team has, I am told, revived the usage of words that have fallen into disuse for centuries. One cannot take these critics of Strachey seriously as long as they insist on repeating the proposition that the new French renditions of Freud consist of "the text, the whole text, and nothing but the text." These French translators believe they have captured the "true" Freud, at the same time that they dismiss the proposition that all translation is a "reading" on the grounds that it "too often leads to justifying any kind of relativism."

What we have here is a curious return to Freudian fundamentalism. No criticism at all is made of the French pretension to have been singularly "faithful to Freud." As long as the French translators get off Scot-free, why should anyone take seriously the indictment of Strachey? As far as I am concerned, the so-called "genius of the French language" does not justify their "use of neologisms."

The authors here have a serious case to make about what they consider the demonstrable tendentiousness of Strachey. And they question whether or not Freud ever can have intended his work to "play the same cohesive role as the sacred writ does for a church." It is therefore regrettable that instead of remembering where Freud might have gone wrong, they have inadvertently been led to treat Freud's writings with more piety than ever. It is true that new manuscript sources, and thousands of unpublished letters, are going to mean that future generations of Freud scholars are going to know lots more than we do. But it is to be hoped that the next era will be flexible enough to realize when Freud's enemies might have been right all along.

It simply will not wash credulously to refer to "the magisterial effort of Jean Laplanche" at the same time that Strachey gets trashed. It should be laughable, but Laplanche and his co-workers propose here "a Freud in French that is...Freudian." Improving on Strachey, a thoroughly worthy objective, should not become identified with abandoning our critical faculties for the sake of reifying Freud's works into Gospel. One legitimate way of fulfilling the aspiration of "being faithful to Freud" is to go beyond him.

## Note

1. Darius Gray Ornston, ed., *Translating Freud* (New Haven, CT: Yale University Press, 1992).

# 58

# Freud's Discourse

Scholarship on Freud remains in an odd situation. On the one hand, there are numerous psychoanalytic journals, in a wide variety of languages, that regularly cite Freud's work. Yet the authors are usually not professional academic scholars, but busy practicing clinicians. Thus, they not only have a special interest in the clinical import of Freud's writings, but also are involved exclusively in the concerns of present-day practice. Knowing what Freud was like historically is a specialized matter requiring immersion in his texts and time. In all the psychoanalytic training institutes that I know of, however, Freud's writings are taught in isolation from the cultural context in which they were originally authored.

As a result of the need of present-day clinicians to find in the past some sanction for how they proceed now, and the desire to link up today's thinking with earlier ideas of Freud, the tendency to be ahistorical has become commonplace in the literature. Thus, we commonly find isolated sentences by Freud being taken out of their original context on behalf of some pressing contemporary issue. To make the scholarly situation even more troublesome, practicing clinicians seldom have the abundant free time necessary for the secure pursuit of genuine scholarly work.

The upshot is that although Freud is quoted profusely in professional articles, from a scholarly point of view all of this citation does not succeed in adding much to genuine historical knowledge. The pursuit of the past needs to be undertaken for its own sake, and by people with a commitment to the impartial search for truth. It should go almost without saying that social scientists need an intimate acquaintance with the clinical side of Freud's teachings; but the value of social science, and of university life as a whole, has something special to contribute to psychoanalysis as well.

The sectarianism that has historically beset psychoanalysis has not helped matters. I can think of no psychoanalytic institute that equips its students to understand those against whom Freud was writing. Yet one of the oldest saws in intellectual history is that to understand any thinker one must take into account the enemies against whom he was laboring. What one is apt to find instead in the psychoanalytic literature is an appalling series of silences: Freudians who know virtually nothing about Jung; so-called controversial figures like Jacques Lacan, who cannot be cited too often in bibliographies, at least in North America, without raising disapproving eyebrows; accounts of the circle around Freud in Vienna that simply ignore the existence of a pioneering figure like Wilhelm Reich; periods when it was unthinkable to include Karen Horney within the history of concepts of femininity; and now a phase when it is again acceptable to cite her (but not others). The result has been a flattening out of the past and an unwilligness to appreciate the full complexities and subtleties of the many interesting controversies in the whole story of analysis.

These preliminary remarks are intended to introduce Patrick J. Mahony's work and to try to explain why his contribution is of so special a value. *On Defining Freud's Discourse*[1] is not a major work; its brevity alone is an indication of how it should be weighed. Nonetheless, Mahony is such an unusual writer within psychoanalysis that everything he produces is worth paying attention to. Even though I disagree with much of what he has to say in *On Defining Freud's Discourse*, my respect for him is genuine.

Mahony is an outstanding exception in the current state of psychoanalytic literature. He is a professor of English at the University of Montreal and therefore is at home within normal academic life; and he is at the same time a practicing psychoanalyst who has found the time to write several books of considerable interest. Although, as far as I am concerned, Mahony is rather too identified with the latest thinking within psychoanalysis and not detached enough from various current viewpoints, I am satisfied that he has proceeded in a genuinely fair-minded way. I have no doubt at all, for example, that if he had published his *Freud and the Rat Man*[2] a generation ago, he would have been denounced by certain orthodox "authorities" for having launched a so-called scurrilous attack on Freud; his work came at a time when enough glass had already been broken by earlier pioneers in the field so that his own surprising findings scarcely caused a ripple of orthodox outrage.

Mahony is a leading critic of James Strachey's translations of Freud. I would like to point out, however, that Freud's own command of English was considerable, and as someone with experience as a translator himself, Freud gave a good deal of latitude to those to whom he gave approval to translate his own works. He picked James Strachey as a translator while Strachey was still in analysis with Freud in Vienna, and there is no evidence that Freud was anything but delighted with how Strachey proceeded.

Strachey's *Standard Edition* was begun only after Freud's death, but it was undertaken with the full support of Anna Freud and Ernest Jones. Jones, who probably played the largest single role in the original choice of the English equivalents for Freud's technical psychoanalytic vocabulary, worked over the years harmoniously with Strachey. (Their letters to each other made interesting reading.) I doubt Strachey was ever paid adequately for all his work as a translator; he may (or may not) have received what was then the normal professional fee. Strachey did his translations out of dedication to "the cause." Strachey worked almost entirely from Freud's published texts and only infrequently consulted the original manuscripts that were available. It would be extremely unfortunate if the inevitable limitations of Strachey's wonderful edition, which Mahony also admires, were to further the fundamentalist quest for the so-called true Freud. It is far more important that our energies concentrate on a mature evaluation of the substance and validity of Freud's ideas themselves.

In his Introduction to *On Defining Freud's Discourse*, Mahony raises the problem of Strachey's translating abilities. As an initial example, Mahony points out that the literal translation for both "The Antithetical Meaning of Primal Words" and *The Psychopathology of Everyday Life* should have in the case of each title been preceded by the word "On." According to Mahony: "In his translations Strachey surppressed the 'on' and thereby eliminated Freud's tentativeness." I have looked through both texts again, and for the life of me I cannot understand what Mahony is quibbling about; I find nothing at all tentative about the content of *The Psychopathology of Everyday Life*, written shortly after Freud had completed his *The Interpretation of Dreams*. As a matter of fact, *The Psychopathology of Everyday Life* contains some of Freud's most distinctive and idiosyncratic convictions, communicated with full authority; the tentativeness of the word "on" suggests a spurious lack of conviction, which would have imputed to Freud an uncertainty that he did not genuinely feel and might have seemed manipulative to his English-speaking readers. In any event, if Mahony wants to strike at Strachey he would do well to select his examples more carefully: both texts in question – "The Antithetical Meaning of Primal Words" and *The Psychopathology of Everyday Life* – were translated, as Strachey indicates clearly, by Alan Tyson and not by Strachey himself.

I agree wholeheartedly with Mahony that "Freud's style remains perennially fresh, more lively and engaging than many subsequent psychoanalytic treatises." That seems to me an understatement of Freud's genius. Mahony goes on to state that "in spite of their up-to-date contents, these later works are vapid in expression and hence short-lived, so that once their contents are surpassed by new observations, they are likely no longer to be read except by historical scholars." Mahony is right, but if that judgment had been made twenty years ago it might have evoked thunderous disapproval from orthodox analysts.

Mahony singles out Freud's "dogmatic kind of discourse," which, he says, "has received tacit, semi-official endorsement from organized psychoanalysis," and contrasts it with Freud's so-called genetic discourse. What Mahony has undertaken is an examination of Freud's rhetoric, how he set out "to convince, to persuade." As a literary scholar, Mahony has studied Freud as a writer before, and doubtless he will continue to pursue this important avenue of inquiry.

Mahony devotes a chapter to the case of Katharina from *Studies On Hysteria*. Mahony considers it "the most charming of Freud's case histories," a judgment I find arbitrary. I myself would have selected Little Hans as "the most charming." Later on, Mahony contends that among the other cases in *Studies On Hysteria*, "Katharina has the most stylistic merit." I do not feel qualified as a literary observer to comment, but it does strike me that Freud's brief contact with Katharina, who was never his patient, ought not to qualify as a case history at all, and instead should be considered an example of Freud's willingness to undertake what he would later dub "wild analysis." As Freud himself wrote at the end of his brief discussion of Katharina, "If someone were to assert that the present case history is not so much an analyzed case of hysteria as a case solved by guessing, I would have nothing to say against him." Mahony misses the woods for the trees and adds more guesswork from today's thinking to Freud's own original hunches. Translating exactitude is one matter, and should not be identified with treating Freud's writings as the Bible.

Mahony's third chapter is a close examination of Freud's essay "Analysis Terminable and Interminable." The links between each of Mahony's chapters hinge on the author's personal decision on what to write about; therefore the book, attractive though it remains, lacks the unity of conceptual urgency. It is, in addition, erroneous for Mahony to maintain that "Analysis Terminable and Interminable" was "the last great text Freud completed," since that judgment would have to exclude the later *Moses and Monotheism,* which I view as a book of considerable significance.

My questioning of Mahony's argument has been undertaken with great respect, and I hope nothing I have written reads captiously. It is a sign of the greater tolerance within today's psychoanalysis that excellent work like Mahony's has been going on, which bodes well for the future of the discipline as a whole.

## Notes

1. Patrick J. Mahony, *On Defining Freud's Discourse* (New Haven, CT: Yale University Press, 1989).
2. Patrick J. Mahony, *Freud and the Rat Man* (New Haven, CT: Yale University Press, 1986).

# 59

# Moses

Even in relatively early autobiographical accounts of his career Freud states that the acceptance of psychoanalysis was hampered by his being the victim of traditional European anti-Semitism. The subject of Freud as a Jew has been a touchy one, likely to arouse passions of an embattled sort. Freud was of course driven from Vienna in 1938 by the Nazi occupation of Austria, and Hitler's regime banned Freud's teachings. But the complications of Freud's Jewishness have only recently come under renewed scrutiny.

For many years it was held, at least by orthodox psychoanalysts, that it was a slight to Freud even to consider the role of Judaism in the construction of his theories. Some historians, like Peter Gay, have promoted the myth that psychoanalysis represents a neutral body of scientific doctrine, one which has to be seen apart from Freud's own religious heritage. Ernest Jones in his authorized biography of Freud minimized the part that Freud's religious origins played in the development of his thinking.

It is true that some of Freud's critics, like Carl G. Jung, used Freud's Jewishness as a way of accounting for some of the defects in early psychoanalytic thinking. But Freud himself took pride in his Jewishness, and after Hitler rose to power Freud asserted his Jewish identity in defiance. Nor can one understand Freud's thesis in *Moses and Monotheism* apart from the author's Jewish background.

Emanuel Rice's *Freud and Moses*[1] is an excellent exploration of Freud's Jewish identity. Rice has firmly established, for I believe the first time, just how seriously Freud's father, Jacob, took his Jewishness. Both of Freud's parents appear to have come from orthodox Jewish backgrounds and were far less assimilated than has generally been thought. Jacob knew the story of Passover by heart; and Freud's mother, Amalia, stayed ritually observant until her death in 1930.

The only surviving writings of Jacob Freud are some inscriptions in Hebrew for the Freud family Bible. This was intended by Jacob for his son on the occasion of his thirty-fifth birthday. Rice does not say why Jacob would have written in Hebrew, when Sigmund's knowledge of that language was as deficient as he claimed it was. Even more puzzling, considering that Amalia never mastered the German language (she spoke a Galician Yiddish), is Freud's written assertion that he had never learned or spoken Yiddish.

Rice does a good job of explaining how sensitive Viennese Jews like Freud were to Eastern European family origins. Rice demonstrates (as part of establishing the nature of Freud's parents' religious affiliations) that when Freud's half-brothers settled in Manchester, England, they affiliated with the Orthodox (not the Reform) segment of the religious population.

Rice also discusses how cremation is absolutely forbidden by orthodox Judaism, and so it is perplexing to me that Rice ignores the fact that Freud arranged for his own cremation. His ashes were placed in an ancient Grecian urn that had been given to Freud by the Princess Marie Bonaparte. Even more striking, it seems to me, is that Freud's wife, who struggled in the face of Freud's secularism to carry on with traditional Jewish practices, also was cremated and put in the same urn as he. (The urn was not quite large enough for both of them, and, following the custom of the crematorium, some of Martha Freud's ashes were scattered.)

Rice makes an extensive effort to use Freud's ambivalence as a Jew to understand the themes of *Moses and Monotheism*. Here I think Rice is less original than he seems to think; there is an extensive literature about that text, and Rice does not seem to be familiar with all of it. But Rice has done a superb job of nailing down Freud's religious background and its powerful influence. "Freud came from a mildly diminished, East European Orthodox milieu, rebelled against it in adolescence and continued this struggle to the very end of his life." It remains for other students of the history of psychoanalysis to delineate how this religious background influenced the growth of the psychoanalytic movement as a whole. Freud succeeded in creating a church as well as a science, which is probably why his most orthodox followers have always wanted to minimize the role that Judaism played in the background to his ideas.

In 1989 Professor Yosef Hayim Yerushalmi of Columbia University published an article about the manuscript draft of Freud's *Moses and Monotheism.* It turns out that Freud had written an introduction to the book, which had hitherto remained unknown, and that he had originally intended for the book to have the subtitle *A Historical Novel.* The five paragraphs from the unpublished Introduction are a powerful statement of his purposes and intentions. Although Yerushalmi does not go into the issue, I think that Freud decided against using these five paragraphs because he was, no matter how speculatively inclined, in a phase of his work when he wanted to insist as much as possible on the "scientific" standing of psychoanalysis.

Later Yerushalmi wrote an elegant little book about Freud as a Jew, *Freud's Moses: Judaism Terminable and Interminable.*[2] This is a subject which has for years been considered off-limits to orthodox analysis. But evidently times have changed, so that Yerushalmi is able to proceed with the backing of a number of traditional sources of support within orthodox analysis. And he has bold remarks to make about Freud. For example, Yerushalmi insists that Freud and the Bolsheviks had "the same end in mind: the destruction of the family." Yerushalmi may go further in this claim than Freud would have approved of, but Yerushalmi does spell out the implications of Freud's Jewishness for even his most puzzling commitments. Freud's Lamarkianism can be understood within the framework that Yerushalmi proposes.

Like others before him, Yerushalmi believes that "Freud's acute worry that psychoanalysis not appear to be a 'Jewish national affair' remained...an abiding concern and source of inner conflict throughout his life." In spite of Freud's conflicted feelings about Jewishness, he can be taken to have held that "Judaism meant cultural, intellectual, spiritual progress." On the other hand Freud could be, as Yerushalmi fails to point out, withering in his skepticism about the existence of any kind of cultural "progress."

We know now that "up to and after the age of seven" Freud "studied exclusively at home, where Jacob Freud was his teacher." Yerushalmi italicizes one sentence Freud added in 1935 to his Autobiographical Study: "My deep engrossment in the Bible story (almost as soon as I had learned the art of reading) had, as I recognized later, an enduring effect upon the direction of my interest." Yerushalmi easily repudiates key features in *Moses and Monotheism*, such as the contention that the original Moses had been killed by his followers. Freud can be taken to have offered a theory about how "national character," as embodied in Judaism, gets transmitted. And Yerushalmi notes that although "the first crime in the biblical narrative was not a parricide but...a fratricide," Freud did nothing with this insight.

It is a bit disconcerting to learn, as I did for the first time here, that in January 1939 Freud had refused a request from Poland for a photograph, a couple of sentences about Polish Jewry, and a brief article about Freud's following in Poland. Freud, within a year of his own death, explained that he felt "sick and tired of propaganda, [sic] would readily hand all such things over to younger powers."

For those who have followed the historiography of psychoanalysis—and Yerushalmi is not strong on acknowledging all his predecessores—it is welcome to find that there is no longer any taboo about establishing the overt links between Jews and psychoanalysis. For Yerushalmi it is "curious" how someone like Peter Gay, in his efforts to supply orthodox analysis with an elaborate backup, could be "essentially ahistorical" in attempting to detach Freud from his religious background. *Freud's Moses* is a beautifully written narrative, and a welcome addition to the available literature.

## Notes

1. Emanuel Rice, *Freud and Moses: The Long Journey Home* (Albany: State University of New York Press, 1990).
2. Yosef Hayim Yerushalmi, *Freud's Moses: Judaism Terminable and Interminable* (New Haven, CT: Yale University Press, 1991).

# 60

# Confrontation in Vienna

The world of old Vienna was one of the high points in Western intellectual history, and therefore memoirs like *Confrontation in Vienna*,[1] by the distinguished psychoanalyst Leopold Bellak, are bound to be of interest. Bellak grew up there after World War I, and was politically savvy enough to see the writing on the wall regarding his future; when the Nazis invaded Austria in 1938, Bellak was already on the waiting list for emigration to the United States. He believes that he was one of the lucky ones, since he and his most immediate family managed to get away, yet he remains bitter about what happened in his early life and outraged by the brutality of the anti-Semitism of his youth.

By 1939 Bellak was already mid-way through his medical studies at the University of Vienna, and committed to becoming a psychoanalyst. His analysis with Ernst Kris was interrupted by the political upheavals associated with the Nazi takeover of Austria. For those of us raised on this continent, it is unfortunate that Bellak did not choose to share more about what was most characteristic concerning Kris's clinical approach, and how it stands up in the light of Bellak's later experience.

Bellak does provide us with a compelling account of the worst sides of Viennese prejudice and barbarity. *Confrontation in Vienna* begins with an invitation to Bellak to attend the fiftieth reunion of his gymnasium class. Bellak knew from the outset that returning to Vienna for such an anniversary would bring him in contact not only with painful memories, but former classmates of his, many of whom were active Nazis, would also have to be confronted. Bellak nonetheless chose to attend.

He took the precaution of arranging to meet with some congenial old friends before the official ceremonies. Bellak was outspoken in public, and refused to accept the handshake offered him by a former tormentor. Bellak's violent feelings were controllable only up to a point, however; in a washroom, upon seeing an old anti-Semitic brute of an enemy, Bellak attacked him. According to Bellak's spare account, he had to plead "temporary insanity" in court for what he did.

*Confrontation in Vienna* makes for a compelling read, even if it leaves many questions unanswered. He seems to be someone proud of his physical fitness, and unashamed at how he decided to fight back. I know other Viennese who simply made up their minds, once they reached exile, never to return to the scene of the crime. It must have been galling to him that one of the worst of his anti-Semitic classmates was the official who issued the welcoming call for the return of Jews abroad for the sake of a class reunion. He tells us about the Viennese custom of drinking coffee with ice cream in it, topped by a generous amount of whipped cream. But one could write a whole treatise about characteristic Viennese hypocrisy, and how under-handed old world manners could be. Once again, from the vantage point of contemporary straight-shooters, Bellak may not realize how much more we would like to know about the mores and customs of the culture he knew so intimately. Perhaps we should just be grateful that Bellak has been willing to put into writing as much as he did, leaving us to draw our own conclusions.

There is no more important political event in the twentieth century than the Nazi rise to power, and Bellak's first-hand account of his upbringing in Vienna and that era is a chilling reminder of the barbarism that was so close to the surface even at the height of Vienna's intellectual glory. It is not surprising that he snapped under the pressures of going back for that reunion. I hope, however, Bellak will understand that his book only whets our appetite to know even more than he has allowed himself autobiographically to disclose.

## Note

1. Leopold Bellak, *Confrontation in Vienna* (Larchmont, NY: C.P.S., 1993).

# 61

# Freud's Answer

Martin Wain's *Freud's Answer: The Social Origins of Our Psychoanalytic Century*[1] is an interesting book, which leaves a fine impression of the author's mind, but it does get off to a slow start; and just because of the excellence of what it ultimately has to offer, readers ought to be warned not to be put off by the opening chapters. For it seems to me unfortunate that Martin Wain begins by hurriedly giving a potted-history of the Western nineteenth century, which seems largely to rely on good books by Peter Laslett and E. P. Thompson. I doubt that the genuine historical setting for the impact of Freud's work can be enhanced by Wain relying on a few such famed secondary sources. Nor does *Freud's Answer* offer original insights into the biographical specifics of Freud's creation of psychoanalysis.

To move to the real strengths of *Freud's Answer*, Wain is most persuasive about the social fit between Freud's work and the culture around him. And Wain is acute about the world which has followed Freud's death. Some such lines of evaluation will surely help make more understandable why psychoanalysis was able to have such an enormous impact over this past century. Wain seems to believe, and I think he is on sound ground here, that in many ways Freud's psychology, despite its emancipatory-sounding slogans, also served to reinforce social controls which relied on psychology's buttressing. The loss of traditional religious beliefs, and other sources of social identities, fed insecurities which psychoanalysis helped alleviate.

There is nothing in *Freud's Answer* which sounds like any of the Freud-bashing which has become so trendy in the English-speaking world. Yet I wonder whether it would not be desirable to at the same time be criticizing some of the alternatives to Freudian thinking, options that lie outside the boundaries of what Wain feels most comfortable considering. Yes, the psychoanalytic worldview, taken in the broadest meaning, did lead to many conformist practices. But does Wain think that the discovery of neurotransmitters, and the recent revival of the diagnostic approach of Kraepelin in the course of the growth of psychopharmacology, are less likely to lead in the direction of reinforcing the powers-that-be? Instead of belaboring old problems within the historiography of psychoanalysis, it may be time to recall just how easily the spiritual dimension to the healing professions can get lost. And whatever inadequacies there might be to the whole psychotherapeutic approach, it is in real danger of getting lost in the midst of the seeming-simplicity of the drugs that have been invented in the last generation.

It seems to me that in many ways we today confront similar issues that were front-and-center a hundred years ago. As I have already mentioned, Jung came to think that an accurate diagnosis of a patient could only be made after the completion of treatment, but that realism might hardly fly in the current enthusiasm for the scientism of diagnostic exactitude. Biological therapists are now apt to be as interested in family history and heredity as would have been the case among clinicians at the turn of the twentieth century, and the anti-humanitarian therapeutic implications of such an outlook remain very much the same. Pigeon-holing people with neat classifications is at odds with the mysteries of real life, and immediate therapeutic help remains distinct from trying to push back the frontiers of scientific knowledge

The nature of the Western impact of psychoanalysis, which is so central to Wain's argument, might have been well highlighted by looking at the comparative reception of Freudian thinking in Asia. The problems in adapting psychoanalytic thinking outside the West tells us something important about what is distinctive in Freud's outlook. For example, in China today, which is still more influenced by traditional Confucianism than Marxism, it is hard for people to think in terms which make sense within the context of Western notions of individualism. Family ties define people in social contexts which make it almost impossible to conceive of the self at odds with intimate family members. And so while we have been trying to amend psychoanalytic egocentricity in a more socially conscious direction, Asians are still typically looking at themselves in terms which exclude the narrow confines of Western definitions of selfhood. To the extent that we acknowledge that psychoanalysis legitimately ought to be concerned with various conceptions of how life ought to be lived and that past psychoanalytic controversies have been over questions of power combined with rival approaches to what the good life might consist in, then approaching psychoanalytic cross-culturally has a lot to teach.

Wain is at his best in relating psychoanalysis to "the European mind," which is why I think his enterprise might be assisted by going outside of Europe itself. But *Freud's Answer* contains within itself a serious reexamination of the ethical implications to psychoanalytic thought. Wain does not seem tied to any ideological orthodoxies, and he is at home with the historical and social literature about the nature of Freud's work. He might have done more to highlight the concessions about the nature of good therapy which have been made recently within the so-called mainstream of psychoanalysis; for they have the implication of rehabilitating the criticisms directed at classical Freudian thinking which were levelled by well meaning analysts whose contributions are still inadequately recognized. (Here I have in mind not only Otto Rank and Sandor Ferenczi, but also Harry Stack Sullivan and Erich Fromm.)

The time seems to have arrived when talking about politics and society in connection with psychoanalysis is no longer considered a form of heresy. Wain's *Freud's Answer* is a sophisticated contribution to the broadest kinds of philosophic inquiry. Pedants will no doubt continue to question the epistemological basis of the specifics of psychodynamic thinking, but intellectual historians should concentrate on establishing the sweep of Freud's achievement, as well as of course his limitations. As it moves into its second century, psychoanalysis does not have to be insecure about its beginnings; but it is obliged, if it is going to retain its vitality, to reconsider the most basic premises of its thinking, to which Wain has made an important addition.

## Note

1. Martin Wain, *Freud's Answer: The Social Origins of Our Psychoanalytic Century* (Chicago: Ivan Dee, 1998).

# Part 9

## New Documents

# Introduction to Part 9

In as over-heated a subject as the history of psychoanalysis, it does help to pause and comment when valuable bits of new historical evidence get offered. Fresh interpretations should qualify every bit as much as documents themselves. And so correspondences, interviews, and biographies can also rank as documentary. Still, there is a place for considering more narrowly defined material. In concluding on this note, I hope the reader will not misunderstand my own historiographical aims: the objective I have tried to fulfill is not to strive for pseudo-omniscience, but to help open up this field for future inquiry and investigation. Hopefully we are at the start of a new era's approach to Freud's whole legacy as defined in the broadest possible way.

# 62

# Freud Without Hindsight

The idea behind *Freud Without Hindsight*[1] is a thoroughly good one: to collect together the reviews of Freud's works which appeared in his lifetime. Although I would ideally have liked to have every such review appear here, even if it took another large volume or two to complete the task, Norman Kiell has performed an important service in what this book offers. He also has an appendix in which he tries to list all the reviews of Freud's works that have ever appeared; here, however, I was able to spot more than one inadvertent omission, for example, the 1963 review of *Totem and Taboo* by Margaret Mead.

The publisher, International Universities Press, has over the years been a spokesman for orthodox psychoanalysis; it is often forgotten that those who have wanted to challenge the official line have not had the publishing support given to writers who endorse the official powers-that-be. The jacket copy for this book is so much more polemical than the text itself that I hesitate to associate the author with the full responsibility for its words. If one gives Kiell the benefit of the doubt, then someone has done him a disservice. We are told on the front-flap that

> Recent studies of Freud's reactions to the initial reception of *The Interpretation of Dreams* indicate his bitter disappointment with their meagerness and quality and suggested he was not justified in these feelings. Bry, Rifkin and Decker's findings, repeated in work by Ellenberger and Sulloway, among others, reinforced this revisionist bit of psychoanalytic history.
>
> Their arguments run counter to new findings in *Freud Without Hindsight, Reviews of His Work, 1893-1939*. This research indicates the earlier work was based on faulty, twisted translations, misreadings, extrapolation, taking material from the reviews out of context, giving emphases to prove a point and omitting other data. *Freud Without Hindsight* corrects this view.

Yet on the first page of Kiell's acknowledgements he tells us:

> I am especially indebted to Dr. Hannah S. Decker. I have drawn liberally on her scholarly *Freud in Germany: Revolution and Reaction in Science, 1893-1907*, as I have from Drs. Ilse Bry and Alfred H. Rifkind's paper, "Freud and the History of Ideas:

> Primary Sources, 1886-1910." Without their original and challenging work, it would have been far more difficult to complete this book. While I am not always in agreement with some of their basic theses or their translations of reviews, I am deeply obligated to them.[2]

The discrepancy between the polemical-sounding front-flap and Kiell's own acknowledgement of some of his predecessors does appear striking, and yet throughout the text there are abundant indications that he is trying to move the public away from more recent historiography, and back to what used to be the established mode of thought more in accord with the traditionalist myths of orthodox psychoanalysis. Nothing in Kiell's book, however, is as belligerent or partisan as the front-flap, and it is a pity that he allowed his book to appear in this unfortunate way.

Kiell does tell us in his introduction of the reception of *The Interpretation of Dreams* that "the majority of the reviews—those which appeared in the lay journals—were favorably disposed." Of course there is more to be said, and Kiell goes on to evaluate the general reviewing state further; but how one evaluates these reviews does depend in large part on one's ideological point of view. Kiell reports that "even though lay journals and newspapers carried extensive reviews of *The Interpretation of Dreams*, it was, quite understandably, unsatisfactory to a man whose life was devoted to science. He wanted recognition from his peers and it was not to be had." I question whether it would be appropriate to describe Freud simply as "a man whose life was devoted to science." All his efforts to create a "psychoanalytic movement," and his passionate devotion to what he termed "the cause," mean that he aimed at something much larger than science; despite his often expressed distaste for philosophy, Freud was also trying to transform our image of human nature. And he knew at least something of the religious nature of the message he was communicating to his disciples.

When Kiell tells us that the "professional reviews" of *The Interpretation of Dreams* were "virtually non-existent," it turns out that he says he is defining "professional" as psychiatric. But Freud, to reiterate a point made earlier, was a practicing neurologist, received little training in psychiatry and never had any standing within that Central European profession. It would seem that almost by definition the bulk of the reviews had to come from those Kiell terms laypersons. When he grades the reviews of *The Interpretation of Dreams*—in terms of being Favorable, Unfavorable, Mixed, or Noncommittal—I myself thought that by "favorable" Kiell was apt to mean blind.

Like others recently, Kiell blames various translations by James Strachey for the unfortunate tendency to reify Freud's concepts. Of course every translation express also a point of view, but I myself would look more to the nature of Freud's followers, and their need to find perfection in the master, rather than to begin by faulting Strachey's excellent English. Kiell himself, for example, modestly says: "the findings unfolded here are not the most world-shattering since the discovery that Freud's vulture might have metamorphosed [sic] into a kite...." But the word "might" is an evasion; Freud's thesis about a "vulture" in his study of Leonardo was founded on sand, since the word Leonardo had actually used referred to a "kite," not a "vulture." Kiell's own pieties are too thoroughly in accord with the conventional orthodox analytic line; he therefore refers in passing, for example, to the "tome, a biography of Woodrow Wilson, written supposedly in collaboration with Ambassador William Bulitt [sic]...." At one time the *Journal of the American Psychoanalytic Association* made it their studied policy not even to refer to the Freud-Bullitt book on Wilson; for many years it was allowed to go out of print in English, and on those rare occasions when it gets cited in professional literature it often appears as the Bullitt-Freud book, reversing the order of the names as they appear on the original text.

*Freud Without Hindsight* is arranged chronologically, and Kiell has provided useful introductory notes to each of the reviewing items. Again and again, however, I wished that Kiell had refrained from his unnecessary editorializing. One 1896 reviewer, for example, is described as someone who was "never a friend of psychoanalysis," and who "found Freud illogical and faulted his evidence...." It deserves highlighting that this reviewer was commenting on Freud's paper tracing adult neurosis to the sexual seduction of children, a position which Freud himself would almost immediately abandon. Many of us, including perhaps the later Freud, would endorse this reviewer's condemnation of "the absurdity of such wildly conjectural, unproved and unprovable conclusions." Also, Kiell objects when an early reviewer accuses Freud of fitting data to theory. Yet from our own point of view today it does sound prescient, to me at any rate, for such a reviewer to have objected that Freud "seeks sexual causes and sexual nexus always and everywhere." I wish more analysts had taken to heart the early reviewing warning that "anyone who can give his questions a suggestive twist, whether done consciously or unconsciously, can obtain from susceptible patients any answer which fits into his system."

We are of course reading all these reviews with hindsight; Freud did succeed in transforming our conception of character and personality. I fully agree with Kiell when he tells us that Freud's "theories have now had a century of trial and the verdict seems secure. The only full-fledged theory of human nature we have is his." But does not the success of the Freudian revolution in the history of ideas make every critical insight into his work that much more valuable? In my opinion some of the earliest reviewers of Freud's work were right on the mark in seeing flaws in his approach. I think this book could have dropped, alas, almost all the reviews by Freud's loyal disciples; they really seem too predictable in what they have to say, as they almost entirely echo Freud's own theories. Once upon a time such propagandizing might have served its purpose, but from today's perspective the unblinkered assessments of Freud by those outside his movement are bound to appear more intellectually interesting.

One of the most striking impressions that emerges from this collection of reviews is that within about ten years of *The Interpretation of Dreams* Freud had already achieved the basic power that enabled him to triumph later in the century. For within that first decade he had succeeded in acquiring his movement of followers, to whom – at least as much as his texts – one can attribute his later influence. It is no wonder that he was so appalled by reviews that were less than wholly enthusiastic; early on he understood the kind of control he would be able to exert, and therefore disdained those who were in any way half-hearted in their admiration. Later reviews of further editions of *The Interpretation of Dreams* have to be read in the light of the growing influence of Freud's whole school, and the natural resentment some of his cruder following aroused.

Reading the reviews of *The Interpretation of Dreams* that Kiell has included here, however, Freud does seem to me unduly sensitive to his reviewers. It is an old adage among authors that the most important feature to any review is its length; Kiell does not seem objective enough in pointing out what kind of free publicity psychoanalysis might have been getting. One review which Ernst Kris called "malicious" is instead judged "stupid" by Kiell; yet to me it seemed a tribute to the extraordinarily high level of culture in old Vienna. Kiell finds "the intellectual follies of so many of Freud's critics" exemplified in these reviews, whereas I thought they all stood up well to the test of time. Kiell does acknowledge, it should be said, that whatever he thinks of the character of these early reviews, Freud's "sense of isolation arose more out of the zest for martyrdom in which he could be triumphant while suffering."

Incidentally, since so large a part of this book is concerned with Freud's approach to dreams, some mention might have been appropriate to what recent scientific thinking has been about dreaming, and how this supports or challenges the criticisms that were early on advanced of Freud. Even if Kiell decided to steer clear of such recent evidence, I could not read some of this material without automatically thinking of how reminsicent it was of some of the characteristic ideas advanced by Carl G. Jung. He challenged Freud in important ways which analysts often forget today. Jung, however, gets slighted by *Freud Without Hindsight*, and is evidently so outside the pale that not even his early review of Freud's little book *On Dreams* gets listed in the appendix. The only reason I can think of for Kiell's ignoring this review is that he failed to look through Jung's collected works. (It is a small bit of carelessness on Kiell's part, but despite what he writes Alfred Adler was not at the Clark conference in Worcester, Massachusetts, in 1909.)

Sometimes Kiell's editorial commentary is, from the point of view of intellectual history, decidedly amateurish. For example, one reviewer, a neurologist named Hans Haenel, observed in the course of a predominantly favorable review of *The Psychopathology of Everyday Life*: "The author quotes numerous example which sometimes give the impression that he has gone beyond reasonable limits in his subtleties." Somehow to Kiell, however, this mild "comment is devastating, destroying the many positive statements Haenel reports both prior and subsequent to it."

I found two contemporary reviews of Freud's case history of Dora especially interesting. When we read Freud's account of her nowadays, it is inevitably with the kind of hindsight which it should be the objective of Kiell's book to help us overcome. But at no point does he seem to realize that 1906 clinical objections to Freud's manner of proceeding might have been fully in order. Reviewers then did not react to Freud's account as a work of art but thought primarily in terms of whether they could approve of his clinical tactics. Kiell is so wedded to defending Freud that he erroneously criticizes a reviewer for locating the scene of a kiss in Dora's life at the age of fourteen, upbraiding the reviewer for not thinking it took place at eighteen, when James Strachey's chronological summary of Dora's case is entirely in agreement with the reviewer's and not Kiell's understanding of the facts.

Since most psychotherapists today, and even many trained analysts, could not agree with Freud's particular technique with Dora, I do not understand why it is not worth paying more attention to the clinical objections of contemporaries. One reviewer acknowledged "the genius and wit of Freud's presentation" even as he argued: "I am afraid that if this method, which by now has become famous, should be accepted without protest, we would be running the risk of having parents prefer their daughters to remain ill for the rest of their lives rather than handing them over to the analyst for a period of up to three years."

A completely uncritical reaction to *Three Essays on the Theory of Sexuality* is described by Kiell as "one of the most level-headed and sane expositions" the book was to get. Even in a review which Kiell considers "unqualifiedly enthusiastic," he points out where the author "waffled." Kiell does not seem to realize that the reviewing expositions by Freud's most loyal disciples are bound to be now boring to our ears, which makes it almost too easy for Freud's earliest critics to steal the show.

A typical example of Kiell's bias comes up in his reaction to the remarks of a Viennese psychiatrist, Erwin Stransky, who introduced the thoughts of an art historian on *Leonardo da Vinci and a Memory of His Childhood*. Kiell stigmatizes the review by the two men as a "*folie à deux*"; Stransky had begun by saying:

> It is truly difficult to take up the cudgels against such a renowned psychologist as Sigmund Freud whose accomplishments will be fully measured only in time to come when friend and foe alike will have fallen silent. But what must be done, must be done; and we must reject this book. Freud's greatness puts him beyond the reach of ordinary means. A simple satire can take care of some of his disciples—not all, let's add quickly, because there are among them some serious scientists who compel respect even from their opponents. But here we want to avoid writing a satire; Freud's accomplishments make it our duty to avoid it.

The short review by the specialist in art was, although more than a bit Victorian, sound and without polemics; it missed the charm of Freud's effort, but then the whole point of Kiell's book should be to see the beginnings of psychoanalysis in their proper historical context.

By and large the Central European response to Freud's work seems to me to have been sophisticated. For example, there is an intelligent review here of *Totem and Taboo* written by Carl Furtmüller, an early member of the Vienna Psychoanalytic Society who resigned over Freud's struggle with Adler. Furtmüller's understanding of some of the central problems with Freud's thesis makes his praise all the more meaningful: "Freud's narration...is totally absorbing. You have to admire not only his sharp wit and astute combinations; beyond its intellectual qualities the text is pervaded with an outright poetical spirit." However naïve the American reaction to Freud's clinical recommendations may appear to have been, *Totem and Taboo* was more than many reviewers in the States could take: the reviews by William McDougal and A.L. Kroeber both bear reading carefully not just for the sake of anthropological understanding but for what they inferred about the rest of Freud's approach.

Kiell does at one point indicate his difficulty with "the florid prose and toadying praise" of one of Freud's American supporters, and Kiell seems to object when he mentions that another American reviewer "could never fault Freud for anything he wrote"; Kiell further notes a disciple's "almost embarrassing, fawning prose." Yet Kiell is also capable of suddenly including an implicitly flattering and lengthy review of *Group Psychology and the Analysis of the Ego*, written in 1974 and therefore completely at odds with the general principle of selection underlying *Freud Without Hindsight*. I found it a dreadful waste of space, especially given the older reviews which were excluded from this volume.

I wish Kiell had been less doctrinaire in his editing so that it would be possible to be more flattering about the commentary that he has provided. But the conception of the book was brilliant, I found it absolutely fascinating reading, and students of intellectual history will be greatly in his debt.

## Notes

1. Norman Kiell, *Freud Without Hindsight, Reviews of His Work* (1893-1939) (Madison, CT: International Universities Press, 1988).
2. Ibid., p. xvii.

# 63

# The Diary

A distinguished European psychoanalyst once wrote me that he considered the *Diary of Sigmund Freud, 1929-1939: A Record of the Final Decade*[1] a fraud, and his intellectual credentials were weighty enough for me to begin here by considering the merits of his point of view. Although this large book is over three hundred pages long, the German text, reproduced here, takes up only five pages. Photographs of the original handwritten entries, combined with translations, consume just under forty pages. Publishers, who one might think were eager for Freud primary material, were intially leery that there was enough, in what the editor calls "a skeletal grid of isolated words," to constitute a real book.

Freud himself called this brief manuscript "Shortest Chronicle." Most days he wrote nothing in it, and when he chose to do so his remarks were highly elliptical. Sometimes only a name indicating by a cross that someone had died, or else paid a visit, gets recorded. It is particularly odd, since Freud was such a great stylist, that no complete sentences appear here, just fragments of his jottings. These were the years when he was increasingly an invalid; he first fell ill of cancer of the jaw in 1923. Despite his doctors' warnings, Freud kept up with smoking his beloved cigars; inevitably, much of the *Diary* has to concern operations and other medical matters.

I have read this book twice; I first saw it in France in 1991, where the galleys were sent for the sake of a French edition, and then again in 1992 when it appeared in English. It may look like the Freud Copyrights were scratching around to find money-making ventures in behalf of Freud's heirs, but the editing of the *Diary* is so exemplary as to make it, I think, a fascinating addition to the available literature. The credit for this achievement should go to Michael Molnar of the Freud Museum in London. He painstakingly annotated all Freud's laconic remarks, and the *Diary* is really Molnar's book. Molnar has filled the post of researcher at the Freud Museum, and he has had access to all sorts of hitherto unpublished Freud correspondence. Molnar has made the *Diary* into an essential source book. Although from an outsider's perspective it might appear like misleading the public to call this material a "diary," from my own point of view Molnar's work has earned him the standing of being one of the world's great Freud scholars.

I know nothing about Molnar's formal scholarly credentials, but, as a fellow worker in the field, I have on occasion helped him answer some queries, and he duly acknowledges the assistance I offered. When I have visited the Freud Museum, located at the house where Freud died, I have stopped off and chatted with Molnar. It has been impressive for me to find a relatively young man, working in what once was Freud's daughter Anna's house, so unencumbered with the ideological blinkers that have so often afflicted research in this field. Molnar sits at the center of a web of intersecting information, and books about the history of psychoanalysis regularly descend upon him. In my opinion he has made excellent use of the unique position he has been in.

At the same time Molnar has been laboring under a fairly obvious set of contraints. The Freud Museum, which first opened in 1986, has as its trustees the New-Land Foundation and the Sigmund Freud Archives in New York City. One director of the Museum relinquished his duties because the trustees objected to the wide range of projects that were being sponsored. The New-Land Foundation was set up with the money of Anna Freud's friend Muriel Gardiner, and the Freud Archives was the creation of Kurt R. Eissler, long a watchdog in behalf of preserving Freudian fundamentalist orthodoxy. Although Eissler fell from power in connection with the curious but short-lived tenure of Jeffrey M. Masson as projects director of the Archives, Eissler's successors have not shown much improvement in opening up material to independent-minded scholars. Eissler was until his death in 1999 still in charge, as Anna Freud's personal representative, of much documentation that she deposited, through the vehicle of the Archives, at the Library of Congress in Washington, D.C. So that when Molnar mentions, in his acknowledgments, "the essential derestriction" of Freud's "Shortest Chronicle," one does wonder what under the circumstances the word *essential* has to tell us. Molnar reports that this "derestriction" is "in accord with the present policy of the Sigmund Freud Archives of derestricting previously classsified documents," even though to my knowledge this amounts so far merely to a pious set of promises for the future.

The notes at the back of the *Diary* are rivetting, and I reread them with the greatest interest. Molnar, for example, quotes from a variety of unpublished Freud letters and cites a wide range of documents that are lodged at the Freud Museum. Yet even Molnar has not gained access to some material that is still restricted by the Freud Archives at the Library of Congress, some of which is sealed until the twenty-second century. Molnar mentions an interview located at the Library of Congress that will not become accessible until 2007.

Although Molnar is on the whole, given his position at the Freud Museum, remarkably emancipated in his editorial remarks, I nonetheless found evidence of the existence of limits on his research. I am not referring to mistakes and omissions, which are bound to occur in a work such as this. It would seem that Molnar showed portions of his work to a relatively small group of people in London, when one would have guessed that the text should have benefited from the widest possible circulation before publication.

The failure to pass around the *Diary* among relevant scholars reflects a degree of hesitancy about just how far it was possible to go in the direction suitable for satisfying the demands of impartial scholarship. For example, certain key matters remain disguised or unspoken. As we have seen, Ruth Mack Brunswick was one of the leading figures in Freud's final decade, and her name comes up in the *Diary* at a number of points. Yet the most explosive aspects of that story are not repeated here. No mention is made of her having become addicted to drugs while under Freud's care. Nor is she credited with having been the analyst of Max Schur, who was Freud's private physician in these last years. Nothing is said of the circumstances surrounding her tragic early death in 1946. The *Diary* does contain an impressive full-page photograph of Ruth holding her child, Mathilda, who was named for Freud's eldest daughter, and Molnar quotes Freud's writing to one of his sons that Ruth "almost belongs to the family." But Molnar is too reticent about the full story connected with Ruth.

Although I suspect that reasons of statecraft, connected with the welfare of the orthodox psychoanalytic movement, lie behind Molnar's reticences about Ruth, the *Diary* takes on a somewhat wooden quality when it concerns certain people whom Molnar never knew personally. The analyst Herman Nunberg, for instance, was notoriously difficult for people to get on with, but because he remained loyal to Freud, there is no hint here of just how eccentric Nunberg was. And Robert Waelder, a theoretician who was divorced from everyday human emotions, gets cited as an authority when one would have thought his opinions were deeply suspect.

The Scribner editor, Robert Stewart, under whose auspices this *Diary* appeared, conducted interviews of his own in the mid-1960s with those loyal to Anna Freud's point of view on child analysis. But Molnar cites that interview material far too much and in an uncritical way. For example, when Stewart asked Anna Freud why the Gestapo had arrested her in 1938, she merely responded: "Oh, but they arrested everybody!" Such a comment, although palpably untrue, would have been suitably safe for a tape-recorded interview with Stewart. But in fact it should be made clear that the Nazis then were primarily interested in investigating the complicated international finances connected with Freud's publishing house. It reads lamely to be told by Molnar that the Gestapo "suspected the International Psychoanalytic Assocition of being a subversive movement directed against them." Molnar correctly notes that the assets of the psychoanalytic press had to be declared and its many affairs liquidated. My own interpretation of Anna's arrest is that it would not be unexpected, or out of keeping with what any intelligent Viennese of the time would have done, if Freud's son Martin, in charge then of his father's finances, had violated formal rules about where Freud's money was being kept. It does seem that Martin blundered in leaving incriminating evidence around of the existence of such foreign assets.

Molnar only mentions in passing that Anna Freud had been personally analyzed by her own father; this is referred to as a "training analysis," although for Freud there never was a substantial difference between therapy and training. Freud's having analyzed his own youngest child meant a violation of all the technical rules that he laid down for others to follow. He had his reasons, and presumably Anna was fully complicit in the undertaking, but something more should have been said here about this. It is also known that in turn Anna Freud analyzed her nephew Ernst, who went on to be an analyst himself; although a good deal about that Freud grandson appears in the *Diary*, there is no mention of who it was who treated and trained him.

Nonetheless the notes are a rich storehouse of unpublished material about Freud. For example, there is a striking quotation there by Julius Tandler, a medical contemporary of Freud's. Tandler persuasively commented about Freud's character and personality in a 1931 private communication:

> The level of the drives is of unprecedented strength in him, this person is never free of his drive. Even in a spiritual state of mind he is not free of drives....A hard person. It is uncanny in such an old man, this vital strength, this sexual strength, this saturation of his vessels with sap. This person is so rooted in his physical being that the intellect has repeatedly to find points of contact with the physical. This must be expressed in intellectual work....He is a person who is only accountable to his own law, who only lives according to its direction and who cannot subordinate himself to rules. He is incapable of adapting to a mould because of his proportions. Without a doubt a person who influences his time. If he were not a Jew he might be Bismarck.

While Molnar would seem, in citing at least parts of this source, to be aware of Freud's forcefulness, somehow he has accepted the myth that Freud stopped attending the meetings of the Vienna Psychoanalytic Society because of the first occurrence of his illness in 1923. In fact, contrary to what Molnar repeats, Freud was not "too ill to take part in full discussions," but Freud did not want to mobilize any further rivalries and emotional transferences by participating too closely in the doings of his followers.

The *Diary* contains some fascinating glimpses, thanks to Molnar's editing, of Freud's view of the various members of his immediate family. One longs to know, however, exactly what Freud wrote about each of his children, and in particular what Freud had to say about his son Oliver, who for a time was analyzed in Berlin by one of Freud's correspondents there. Although we know so much about the various public controversies in Freud's life, Molnar is entirely correct to remind us of Freud that "virtually his entire lifetime was spent within large families."

The *Diary* is strangely naïve, especially considering that this is a Robert Stewart book, about the publishing circumstances under which the Hogarth

Press in London became Freud's publisher. All the evidence indicates that Leonard Woolf was exceedingly parsimonious in doling out money to Freud and that in the end Hogarth made a great deal out of publishing Freud and the other analysts. Molnar somehow tells us that the commitment of the Woolfs at Hogarth represented "a considerable risk and one which the new publishers undertook against expert advice."

Molnar ought to have been a good deal more skeptical not only of how far out people were when they joined up with Freud, and what sort of realistic risks they were running, but he should also have been more on his toes about Freud's penchant for using diagnostic categories for people whose behavior he disapproved of. The Viennese Hans Lampl, married to one of the favorites in Freud's final phase, is said by Molnar to have been "suffering from irrational moods—possibly even psychotic episodes." But the truth of the matter is that Lampl was in a realistic struggle against his wife's consuming involvement with Freud; Lampl wanted a marital partner, and when he protested against how for her everything centered on Freud, the circle around Anna Freud decided that he was paranoid and should get himself analyzed. The emotional links between Anna and her father were such that he, too, shared this conviction. Lampl's analyst, however, concluded that it was sound jealousy on his part and, though he was not a brilliant man, he had known when to assert himself lest dedication to Freud deprive him of a wife.

No doubt I have dwelt too much on the occasional lapses in the editing of this book. The photographs, many of which have never been published before, are well chosen. Only the most painstaking scholarship could take the cryptic words of Freud's "shortest chronicle" and transform it into a document that will be a primary source for years to come. Intellectual historians will be indebted to Molnar's unusually fine work.

## Note

1. *The Diary of Sigmund Freud, 1929-1939: A Record of the Final Decade*, translated, annotated and with an introduction by Michael Molnar (New York: Scribner's, 1992).

# 64

# Felix Deutsch's Letters

In the course of their fifty-two years of married life, Felix Deutsch (1884-1964) and his wife, Helene (1884-1982), inevitably spent periods apart. Their individual careers imposed special demands on each of them. In 1923 Helene left Vienna for a second analysis with Karl Abraham in Berlin; earlier, in 1918-1919, she had been analyzed by Freud. Again, in the fall of 1935 Helene moved to Boston, Massachusetts, where she helped found the new Training Institute of the Boston Psychoanalytic Society; she had been Director of the Training Institute of the Vienna Psychoanalytic Society since its inception in 1924. Felix joined her in early 1936, and they both became prominent teachers of analysis in the United States. In terms of the history of analytic concepts, Felix is best known as one of the earliest proponents of psychosomatic medicine; he also evolved a special interviewing technique. Helene specialized in feminine psychology, and authored a series of famous clinical papers as well.

I am trying to make sure that passages in their correspondence, unquoted elsewhere, do not slip through the cracks and fail to become part of the historical literature. For example, after the January 3, 1923, meeting of the Vienna Society, Felix sent the following account to Helene in Berlin:

> I went with Otto [Rank] to the meeting. Professor [Freud] was exceptionally friendly. Bernfeld brought up your departure; it was noted with regret. Professor then declared that if as always after a speech no one proposed any discussion, he would immediately close the session. This was the situation that almost threatened after a communication from Dr. Fokschaner. Afterwards, a long discussion on Dr. Reich's report about Schilder's lecture on the "unconscious" in the Psychopathological Society. Schilder came out of the debate rather tattered. But Professor was extraordinarily benevolent, even though Schilder's remarks were nothing but...hodge-podge. I brought out some of my memory experiments, about which Professor spoke with me after the session. It interested him greatly. Annerl [Anna Freud] also asked me to let her be present at a hypnosis.[1]

After the January 17, 1923, session, Felix wrote:

> I am writing right after the meeting, because I won't have a chance tomorrow. Professor was very friendly – he asked me about you. I think it would be fitting to send him a card.—Otherwise, the meeting was rather bloodless. A rather blown-up pedagogic report from Bernfeld. A report from Rank about a new dream-book by de Sanctis. And finally, from Reich, the description of the hypnotic-analytic treatment of a tic case. At this point, Professor announced his views on such methods of treatment: an *analyst* can afford such capers, since he is standing on analytic ground. Otherwise such a treatment is unscientific, and should be applied only after fifteen years, or after a generation – until analysis has nothing new to report.[2]

On January 31, Felix surprised Helene by himself lecturing before the Society:

> Now, since I can't keep you from what I have carried within myself for two weeks and not told you: yesterday I gave a lecture at the Society, "Psychoanalytic Illustrations." Bernfeld engaged me, since no lecture had been scheduled. Tola [Rank's wife Beata], representing you, took the dress rehearsal and was very satisfied. The lecture was really good, about ¾ hour. And the discussion lasted even longer – again almost to 12 o'clock. Professor backed me up constantly and in lively fashion against all attacks, and even accepted corrections of his own previous views on the relation of experiences to symptom formations, favoring my views. As for the rest, it was a generally favorable debate (especially Schilder and Federn)—with the exception of Hitschmann, who again was ugly, and as usual, "stick-in-the-mud," and stupid. But my assured position made me conciliatory. For Professor's attitude is one of supreme benevolence.[3]

Felix wrote briefly about the February 28 meeting:

> Last Wednesday Reik held a lecture "The King of Sidon"—full of deep learning but without a nucleus. Professor summed it up: the dead are never dead for us with their death; only when we have withdrawn our libido from them completely and reconciled our guilt feelings, have they really died. This is the reason for many rites.[4]

Felix missed a few sessions that spring, at least one because of a trip to visit Helene (and their six-year-old son) in Berlin.

On May 30, Tola Rank gave her talk entitled "The Part Played by Women in the Evolution of Human Society"; afterward she was elected to membership in the Vienna Society. Felix wrote as follows about Helene's intimate friend: "I have announced your letter to Tolunin. How glad she is! Her lecture was excellent and profoundly analytical. She's quite a woman."

In connection with the June 13, 1923, session, Felix reported:

> Schilder gave a lecture on the sources of psychic energy—it contained nothing new, so far as I can see, but Professor was conspicuous in his praise of it. The old man is battle-weary. His little grandson is dying, and this is a severe blow for him. There are no more sessions taking place.— It is a bitter ending to the semester.[5]

(In 1925 Paul Schilder was to become a professor in Vienna; in 1929 he left for New York City. Freud's four-and-a-half-year-old grandson, Heinz Halberstadt, died of miliary tuberculosis on June 19; his mother, Freud's daughter Sophie, had herself succumbed in 1920 during an influenza epidemic.)

Later, on September 21, 1935, Helene was on her way to the United States; Felix wrote her the following (Paul Federn was Vice President of the Society; Anna Freud succeeded Helene as Director of the Training Institute, while Edward Bibring became the Training Committee's representative at the Society's clinic, the Ambulatorium, headed by Eduard Hitschmann):

> The day before yesterday was an executive meeting: I had to excuse you. At Anna's request I even signed a letter of separation over your name, to Federn, in which you informed him that Anna is in charge of the business of the teaching Institute, and Bibring, of the business of the Ambulatorium.[6]

On October 2, 1935, Otto Fenichel, as a guest of the Society from Prague, presented a lectured entitled "The Symbolic Equation of Penis and Girl." Three days later Felix wrote:

> In the Society on Wednesday there was a talk by Fenichel on the "Phallus Girl." The title was changed on the invitation cards, being thought too offensive. It was quite a good discussion of the psychology of the transvestite. The Society still presents the same picture. The level was high. People were anxious to ask for you. I sat beside Hitschmann, who now speaks nothing but English—his daughter has just arrived from England. Ruth [Ruth Mack Brunswick] nodded understandingly to everyone. Jeanne [Lampl-de Groot] was in Holland. People weren't concentrating too well, because word has just come of the outbreak of the Italian-Abyssinian war.[7]

(Freud no longer came to public meetings of the Society, preferring small private gatherings, every few weeks, at his apartment.)

Later that month Helene wired that she planned to stay indefinitely in Boston. Felix reported on October 13:

> The circle has come into motion, through your decision. The Teaching Institute session came to the decision to propose you, at the General meeting, again as Director of the Teaching Institute, since it is not known how long you will stay. The seminar was divided: a beginner's seminar will be led by Jeanne [Lampl-de Groot], and the actual seminar will be led by Anna together with Edi [Edward Bibring]. I think this quite a good solution.[8]

On October 19 Felix wrote about a couple of slips of the tongue, for which Federn, with whom Helene got on badly, was well-known:

> On Wednesday, Oct. 16, was a General Meeting, at which Federn produced one of his famous bloopers—as I was told, since I arrived late. When he was excusing you at the beginning of the session, he said: "one of our most esteemed members is absent. Frau Doctor Deutsch has gone to America for an indefinite period of time. You all know how much we regret her collaboration." Homeric laughter resounded. Then, trying to patch things up: "This loss, expressed in dollars, relates only to the battles during our work together, not to the present." Again, guffaws! Nevertheless, he was again elected Vice-President. I am enclosing the list of officers.

Afterward, Waelder gave a talk—more of a report—on his exchange lecture in London, which he will deliver…in November. In essence it is against Melanie Klein. Clear, but not always true.[9]

One day after the October 30 meeting, Felix recounted:

Yesterday's session: [Sterba] "On the Theory of Transference." In essence, the question whether transference and object relation are to be distinguished in principle, or whether love and transference-love are the same thing. Polemics against Bergler and Jekels. He quotes you, where you report of a patient that wanted you to leave your husband and son on his account, and when you suggested that you consent to do so, he was horrified. There was a lot of talk: Bergler saying that love for the analyst is always connected with fear, while real love is free of fear. Grete [Bibring] said that the fear comes from the anlaysand's simply not being happily in love—etc. A small excerpt, which should suffice you?—Everyone is kind and nice and asks: "?"[10]

Felix removed the remaining uncertainty by announcing to Helene on November 3 his decision to join her in Boston; their son was to enroll in the Massachusetts Institute of Technology. In a letter (November 18) Felix wrote her about a paper he thought would interest Helene, since it hinted at a revelation about her former protégé Wilhelm Reich:

Annie Reich gave a good clinical talk last Wednesday: "On Paranoia and Paranoid Conditions." It concerned a young man who at the age of sixteen suffered a schizophrenic shove in breaking the habit of masturbation. To protect himself from his persecutor, he has to keep over-eating. (The food is the persecutor, whom he then gets rid of in his stool). She is approaching English views. I am writing about it because I think it will interest you.[11]

(Wilhelm Reich had had a falling-out with his colleagues at the International Congress in 1934, but he and Helene remained on good terms. Annie Reich was his first wife. "English views" was Felix's short-hand for Kleinian ideas.)

In January 1936 Felix set sail for America; his last report (December 1) about the Vienna Society concerned a talk by Jeanne Lampl-de Groot:

Jeanne has held a lecture—really, rather a report on work not suitable for a lecture—about "Narcissism and Inhibitions." She was led to give it, against her intention, by "friends" (Heinz) [Hartmann]. She is of the view that in the psychic sphere it is a matter of quantities and of the strength of the ego. (Do you recall that Professor, at an evening at his place, once spoke about quantities, which, however, we don't control?)[12]

Felix Deutsch's accounts of the Vienna Psychoanalytic Society inevitably reflect his own perspective, and that of his wife; still, in the absence of formal minutes (which stopped in 1918), they communicate a special flavor of the proceedings. Each of the participants was to play a notable part in the future of psychoanalysis.

## Notes

1. Felix Deutsch to Helene Deutsch, 4 January 1923. Tom Taylor is the translator of Felix Deutsch's letters, which have been deposited at the Schlesinger Library for the History of Women in America at Radcliffe College.
2. Felix Deutsch to Helene Deutsch, 17 January 1923.
3. Felix Deutsch to Helene Deutsch, 1 February 1923.
4. Felix Deutsch to Helene Deutsch, 2 March 1923.
5. Felix Deutsch to Helene Deutsch, June 1923.
6. Felix Deutsch to Helene Deutsch, 21 September 1935.
7. Felix Deutsch to Helene Deutsch, 5 October 1935.
8. Felix Deutsch to Helene Deutsch, 13 October 1935.
9. Felix Deutsch to Helene Deutsch, 19 October 1935.
10. Felix Deutsch to Helene Deutsch, 31 October 1935. For Helene's report of this incident with her patient, see Helene Deutsch, "Acting out in the Transference," in *Neuroses and Character Types* (New York: International Universities Press, 1965), pp. 365-66.
11. Felix Deutsch to Helene Deutsch, 18 November 1935.
12. Felix Deutsch to Helene Deutsch, 1 December 1935.

# 65

# Freud's Will

On moving to England, Freud wrote a new will; he arrived in London on June 6, 1938, and the will is dated July 28, 1938. There is nothing surprising in this action, since in a fresh legal jurisdiction he needed a new instrument to take appropriate care of his estate. He was already eighty-two years old and had had cancer of the jaw for more than fifteen years. It does seem to me remarkable that although the will has been readily available since being probated, it was locked away by the Freud Archives. It should be scrutinized by those expertly knowledgeable in such matters if historians are going to understand properly the significance of Freud's last testament.

The current catalogue of the Freud Collection at the Library of Congress in Washington, D.C., indicates that their copy of the will remains sealed until the year 2007. Such a restriction, established by Kurt R. Eissler on behalf of the Freud Archives in New York City and maintained by his successors as head of that organization, makes little sense in that the document is a public record in London.

According to the probate registry filed on December 1, 1939, Freud bequeathed a net estate, after taxes, of some 15,979 British pounds. In addition, before leaving Vienna Freud and his younger brother Alexander (who moved to Toronto) provided their four sisters with the sum of about $22,400.[1] Freud, then, by the end of his life was pretty well off, although it is possible that like other great men he remained relatively unaware of the extent of his personal assets. While still in Vienna, with the help especially of his eldest son Martin, Freud had been prudently (if illegally) keeping money abroad. When on March 22, 1938, the Gestapo arrested Anna Freud and took her away for the day, it is almost certain that their main interest was in questioning her about Freud's finances.

In Freud's letters that have so far been published he always appears at least reasonably concerned about his financial future. For example, when the Nobel Prize seemed to have definitely passed Freud by, he wrote to Arnold Zweig on June 28, 1938:

> Do not let yourself get worked up about the Nobel chimaera. It is only too certain that I shall not get the Prize. Analysis has several very good enemies among the personalities upon whom the award depends, and no one can expect me to hold out till they are either converted or have died out. So the money would have been very welcome after the way the Nazis bled me in Vienna and since neither my son nor my son-in-law is a rich man, Anna and I have agreed that one is not bound to have everything and so we have decided, I to renounce the Prize and she the journey to Stockholm to collect it.[2]

Freud tried to hide whatever disappointment he felt behind the idea that it was merely the money that he missed getting. Even after the Nazis "bled" him in Vienna before his departure (they looted his safe of the equivalent of some $840.00, and there was a ransom that came to almost $5,000.00),[3] he still left a substantial estate.

In London Freud carried on as a practicing psychoanalyst, and he had paying patients until the end of July 1939 (he died on September 23). The whole subject of money in the history of psychoanalysis is an especially sensitive one. It played a role in influencing who Freud's favorite disciples were, since he was concerned about the future of the movement he had founded. As I have earlier suggested, for years he had resented being financially dependent on his predominantly American patients. And money was part of Freud's explanation for the falling out between himself and his student Otto Rank.[4] (Rank, who died a month after Freud, left an estate of less than $3,000.00.[5])

Some of the terms of Freud's will deserve special comment. It is still unknown how the house he later acquired at 20 Maresfield Gardens became Anna Freud's (it is now the Freud Museum). When the will was signed the household was still established at 39 Elsworthy Road in Hampstead. Presumably the Maresfield Gardens property, as an asset, would have gone into the trust he set up for his wife Martha; after her death in 1951 one would have thought that all her surviving children would have shared in inheriting the house. (Freud's small special bequest to her sister Minna, who was herself already in extremely poor health, may raise eyebrows among the prurient.)

One feature of the will meant some future troubles between Anna Freud and her nephews in London. The royalties on Freud's books went exclusively to Freud's grandchildren; Freud wrote in a letter (with false modesty?) that he hoped his publications would provide some "pocket money" for them. But Anna, childless herself, had to feel left out, even though she exclusively inherited his collection of antiques and his analytic library. These were assets she could not think of using, while her older sister Mathilda could in 1973 sell a first edition of *The Interpretation of Dreams* for $1,300.00. (By the late 1990s the price would be much higher.) According to a 1954 letter of Anna Freud's, "under pressure" from her two brothers in England, Martin and Ernst, their father left "a family estate from which my mother could draw at will but which did belong to the whole family." Anna Freud's troubled relationship with her mother is documented, but the will also meant that in later years there would be a conflict of interest between Anna and Freud's grandchildren. For example, when she sought to block the publication of the Freud-Ferenczi correspondence, which her nephews wanted in print, she and they were at loggerheads. She thought she was preserving the dignity and integrity of psychoanalysis. As Anna Freud wrote in 1979 about another of Freud's correspondences, that with his boyhood friend Silberstein: "I can never help feeling that my various nephews and niece who have nothing at all to do with psychoanalysis are really not the right ones to be considered. Unfortunately, due to the testamentary dispositions of my father, this is the law."

I, SIGMUND FREUD of 39 Elsworthy Road Hampstead in the county of London HEREBY REVOKE all former Wills and Codicils made by me and DECLARE that this is my last Will.

1. I APPOINT DR. MARTIN FREUD of Mount Royal W. 1 and ERNST FREUD of 32 St. Johns's Wood Terrace N.W. 8 and ANNA FREUD of 39 Elsworthy Road N.W.3 to be EXECUTORS AND TRUSTEES of this my will.
2. I BEQUEATH the following specific legacies free of legacy duty
   (a) TO my daughter Anna my Collection of Antiques as defined by the Catalogue
   (b) TO my daughter Anna my Collection of Books on Psychology and Psycho-Analysis
3. I DEVISE AND BEQUEATH all copyrights and interests in copyrights to which I am entitled to my Trustees UPON TRUST to retain same and to pay the whole of the net royalties and profits or of moneys in the nature of royalties or profits whether the same be payable by virtue of any agreement made by my Trustees or virtue of any agreement made by me in my lifetime to all the issue of my children who shall be living at my death and attain the age of twenty one years or (being female) marry under that age other than Ernst Halberstadt son of my daughter Sophie and if more than one in equal shares as tenants in common I DIRECT that my Trustees shall have the fullest powers to sell and deal with such copyrights and interests in copyrights including power to grant licenses or rights (whether exclusive or not) of printing publishing selling or performing the subject matter of any such copyright and that any such sale or dealing may be made wholly or partly in consideration of royalties to be paid to my Trustees AND I DECLARE that my Trustees may join with other persons interested in any such copyright in any such sale or dealing as aforesaid
4. I BEQUEATH an annuity free of all duty to my Sister-in-law Minna Bernays of Three hundred pounds during her life by equal quarterly payments the first whereof shall be made three months after my death and I DIRECT my Trustees to appropriate in their names investments of any nature hereinafter authorized of an amount sufficient at the date of such appropriation to answer out of the income thereof for such annuity and I DECLARE that such income shall be the primary fund for answering the said annuity and the capital of the said investments shall form a secondary fund for answering the same in the event of the income proving insufficient and further that after any such appropriation shall have been made my residuary estate or the income thereof shall no longer be liable to provide for the annuity in respect of which such appropriation shall have been made AND I DECLARE that the balance (if any) of the appropriated

fund not required for any year for answering the annuity shall be part of the income of my residuary estate and shall be distributed accordingly

5. I DEVISE all my real estate and I BEQUEATH all the residue of my personal estate to my Trustees and I DIRECT my Trustees to sell call in and convert into money all such parts of my real estate and residue of my personal Estate as shall not consist of investments of the nature hereinafter authorised

6. OUT of the clear moneys to arise from such sale calling in and conversion as aforesaid and out of such investments as aforesaid my Trustees shall pay or provide for my debts funeral and testamentary expenses and annuity and any duties payable thereon and on the said legacies and subject thereto my Trustees shall invest in manner hereinafter authorized the residue of the said clear moneys and stand possessed of such investments and of the residue of such investments as aforesaid which formed part of my real Estate and residue of my personal Estate at the time of my death and of all parts of such Estate for the time being unsold (hereinafter called "my residuary Trust Fund") upon the following trusts:-
   (a) UPON TRUST to pay the income thereof to my Wife Martha during her life and after her death
   (b) UPON TRUST as to both capital and income for all and every my children or my child (if only one) living at my death who being sons or son have attained or shall attain the age of Twenty one years or being daughters or a daughter have attained or attain that age or previously marry and if more than one in equal shares as tenants in common
   (c) PROVIDED NEVERTHELESS that Ernst Halberstadt being issue of my daughter Sophie who has died previously to the execution hereof shall if living at my death stand in the place of my said daughter Sophie and take the same share of my residuary Trust Fund which my Daughter Sophie would have taken if she had survived me and had attained a vested interest

7. I HEREBY DECLARE that notwithstanding the trusts hereinbefore declared in favour of my children it shall be lawful for my Trustees upon the written request of my Wife at anytime or times to raise any sum or sums (not exceeding Two thousand five hundred pounds in any one year and not exceeding Fifteen thousand pounds in all) out of the capital of my Residuary Trust Fund to pay such sum or sums to my Wife for her absolute benefit in addition to the income of my Residuary Trust Fund hereinbefore given her

8. I RELEASE each of my children from any legal liability to pay any debt which may be due from him or her to me at the date of my death but each of my children shall bring into hotchpot against the capital of his or her share such sum and such sum only as I may have debited subsequent to the date hereof against him or in the case of a daughter against her or against her husband in my private ledger

9. I DECLARE that my Trustees may postpone the sale calling in and conversion of any part of my real or personal estate for such period as they may in their absolute discretion deem fit without being liable to account notwithstanding that it may be of a wasting speculative or reversionary nature and that pending such sale calling in and conversion the income (including the net rents and profits of real estate and chattels real after payment of rates taxes rent costs or insurance repairs and other outgoings properly attributable in the opinion of my Trustees to income) of property actually producing income shall be applied

as from my death as income and on the other hand on such sale calling in and conversion or on the falling in of any reversionary property no part of the proceeds of such sale calling or conversion or of such property shall be paid or applied as past income

10. I DECLARE that all moneys liable to be so required to be invested under this my Will may be invested in any one or more of the following modes of investment
    (a) ANY investments from time to time sanctioned by Law for the investment of Trust Funds
    (b) ANY Public Stocks or Funds or Government Securities of Great Britain or of any British Dominion or of any Foreign Government or State
    (c) FREEHOLD or Leasehold Securities (the latter having not less that Forty Five years unexpired at the date of such investment) in Great Britain
    (d) STOCKS Shares or Securities the capital whereof or a minimum rate of interest or dividend thereon is guaranteed by the British Government
    (e) STOCKS Bonds Mortgages or Securities (by whatsoever name they may be called) of any Public Municipal or Local Body or Authority situate in Great Britain or in any British Dominion or in any foreign state
    (f) SUCH Stocks or Securities quoted on the London Stock Exchange as shall be certified in writing by one Member of that Exchange to fall in the opinion of such Member within the description of gilt edged securities
    (g) STOCKS Bond Debentures Debenture Stocks or Mortgages Securities (by whatsoever name they may be called) or any Railway Shipping Canal Dock Harbour Gas Water Electric Light or Power or Wireless Company Transport Grain-Elevator or Oil Company or other Public Utility Company or any Banking or Insurance Company Incorporated by Royal Charter or by Special Act of the Parliament at Westminster or of the Legislature or Government of any British Dominion or of any Foreign State or of the United States of America or incorporated under General Act of any such Parliament Legislature or Government as aforesaid all such investments paying interest or dividends at the date of investment
    (h) THE guaranteed or preference stock or shares of any such Company as aforesaid which has in each of the years immediately prior to the date of investment paid a dividend at the rate of at least Five Pounds per centum per annum upon its Ordinary Stock or Shares of which fact a letter purporting to be signed by the Secretary of the Company or by a Member of the London Stock Exchange or by the Secretary or Manager or Branch Manager of a Joint Stock Bank shall be sufficient evidence
    (i) THE guaranteed or preference or preferred Stock or Shares of any such Company as aforesaid which has in each of the three years immediately prior to the date of investment paid a dividend at the rate of at least five per centum per annum on such stock or shares of which fact a letter purporting to be signed by the Secretary of the Company or by a Member of the London Stock Exchange or by the Secretary or

Manager or Branch Manager of a Joint Stock Bank shall be sufficient evidence

(j) THE Ordinary Stock of any Railway Company as is mentioned in Section 1 (1) (g) or (h) of the Trustee Act of 1925

(k) THE Ordinary Stock or Shares of any such Company as is mentioned in (g) above upon which Stock or Shares there has in each of the Three years immediately prior to the date of investment been paid a dividend at the rate of at least five per centum per annum of which fact a letter purporting to be signed by the Secretary of the Company or by a Member of the London Stock Exchange or by the Secretary or Manager or Branch Manager of a Joint Stock Bank shall be sufficient evidence

(l) ANY share capital or loan capital of any Company registered in England under the Companies Acts and having a capital paid up or credited as paid up of not less that Two hundred thousand pounds

(m) GOLD Silver or other metals provided not more than Twenty per cent of my Residuary Trust Fund is so invested

11. I negative the rule known as the Rules in Howe v. Earl Dartmouth and Allhusen v. Whittell in all their branches

12. NO Trustees of this Will shall be liable for any loss not atttributable

(a) to his own dishonesty

(b) to the wilful commission by him of an act known by him to be a breach of trust and in particular he shall not be bound to take any proceedings against a Co-Trustee for any breach or alleged breach of trust committed by such Co-Trustee

13. THE Statutory Power of Appointment of New Trustees of this my Will shall be exercisable by my said Wife during her life

IN WITNESS whereof I have to this my last
Will set my hand this day of One thousand nine hundred and thirty eight
Signed by the above named SIGMUND FREUD
as his last Will in the presence of us both being
present at the same time who at his request in his
presence and in the presence of each other have
hereunto subscribed our names as Witnesses:-

## Notes

1. Ernest Jones, *The Life and Work of Sigmund Freud*, Vol. 3 (New York: Basic Books, 1957).
2. *The Letters of Sigmund Freud and Arnold Zweig*, ed. E. L. Freud, translated W. D. Robson-Scott (London: Hogarth Press, 1970).
3. Jones, *op. cit.*
4. Roazen, *Freud and His Followers* (New York: Knopf, 1975; New York: Da Capo, 1992).
5. E. James Lieberman, *Acts of Will: The Life and Works of Otto Rank* (New York: Free Press, 1985).

# A Bibliography of Paul Roazen Since 1988

## 1989

*Brother Animal: The Story of Freud and Tausk*. Belgrade: Decje Novine.
*Freud and His Followers*. Herrsching: Pawlak.
*Helene Deutsch: A Psychoanalyst's Life*. Munich: Internationale Psychoanalyse.
*Comment Freud Analysait*. Paris: Navarin.
Edited, with an Introduction, Walter Lippmann, *The Public Philosophy*. New Brunswick, NJ: Transaction.
Edited, with an Introduction, Helene Deutsch, "Technique: The Therapeutic Alliance," *International Review of Psychoanalysis*. Winter 1989.
Edited, with an Introduction, Helene Deutsch, "On Satisfaction, Happiness, and Ecstasy," *International Journal of Psychoanalysis*. Winter 1989.
"Encountering Freud," *Society*. May-June 1989.
"On Intellectuals," *University of Toronto Quarterly*. Summer 1989.
Review of Brownell and Billings, *So Close to Greatness: A Biography of William C. Bullitt*, *The American Scholar*. Winter 1989.
Review of Kenny, *The Passion of Ansel Bourne: Multiple Personality and American Culture*, *The Journal of Interdisciplinary History*. 1989.
Review of Pomper, *The Structure of Mind in History: Five Major Figures in Psychohistory*, *Journal of the American Academy of Psychoanalysis*. Winter 1989.
Review of *Freud/Jung Letters*, ed. McGuire, *American Journal of Psychiatry*. April 1989.
Review of Gay, *A Godless Jew: Freud, Atheism, and the Making of Psychoanalysis*, *Psychoanalytic Review*. Summer 1989.
Review of Young-Bruehl, *Anna Freud: A Biography*, *The Virginia Quarterly Review*. Autumn 1989.
Review of Mahony, *Freud As A Writer*, *The Forum* of the American Academy of Psychoanalysis. Fall/Winter 1989.
Letter, "Erikson's Second Thoughts," *New York Review of Books*. March 16, 1989.
Letter, "Of Sigmund and Minna," *Sunday New York Times Book Review*. April 9, 1989.
Letter, "Re-Translating Freud," *Times Literary Supplement*. August 4-10, 1989.
Letter, "Anna's Analysis," *London Review of Books*. October 26, 1989.

## 1990

*Brother Animal: The Story of Freud and Tausk*, 2nd ed., with new Introduction. New Brunswick, NJ: Transaction.

*Encountering Freud: The Politics and Histories of Psychoanalysis*. New Brunswick, NJ: Transaction.

Edited, with an Introduction, Louis Hartz, *The Necessity of Choice: Nineteenth Century Political Thought*. New Brunswick, NJ: Transaction.

"Tola Rank," *Journal of the American Academy of Psychoanalysis*. Summer 1990. (Translated into French.)

"Freud's Last Will," *Journal of the American Academy of Psychoanalysis*. Fall 1990. (Translated into French and Italian.)

Review, Gay, *Freud: A Life For Our Time*, *Psychoanalytic Books*. January 1990.

Review, Homans, *The Ability to Mourn: Disillusionment and the Social Origins of Psychoanalysis*, *Psychohistory Review*. Winter 1990.

Review, Timms & Segal, *Freud in Exile*, *American Journal of Psychiatry*. April 1990.

Review, Kiell, ed., *Freud Without Hindsight: Reviews of His Work (1893-1939)*, *Journal of the History of the Behavioral Sciences*. April 1990.

Review, Kurzweil, *The Freudians: A Comparative Perspective*, *University of Toronto Quarterly*. Spring 1990.

Review, *The Selected Correspondence of Karl Menninger*, ed. Faulkner & Pruitt, *American Journal of Psychiatry*. June 1990.

Review, Gay, *Reading Freud: Explorations and Entertainments*, *The Toronto Globe and Mail*. June 9, 1990.

Review, Young Bruehl, *Anna Freud: A Biography*, *The Forum* of the American Academy of Psychoanalysis. Spring/Summer 1990.

Review, Caper, *Immaterial Facts: Freud's Discovery of Psychic Reality and Klein's Development of His Work*, *Journal of Nervous and Mental Disease*. July 1990.

Review, Ayling, *Edmund Burke: His Life and Opinions*, *Virginia Quarterly Review*. Autumn 1990.

Review, Mahony, *On Defining Freud's Discourse*, *Psychoanalytic Books*. Fall 1990.

Review, *The Selected Correspondence of Karl Menninger*, ed. Faulkner & Pruitt, *Psychoanalytic Books*. Fall 1990.

Review, Masson, *Final Analysis: The Making and Unmaking of a Psychoanalyst*, *Toronto Globe and Mail*. November 17, 1990.

Review, Stepansky, ed., *Freud: Appraisals and Reappraisals*, Vols. I, II, & III, *Psychoanalytic Psychology*. Fall 1990.

Review, *The Clinical Diary of Sandor Ferenczi*, ed. Dupont, *The American Journal of Psychoanalysis*. December 1990.

Review, Donn, *Freud and Jung: Years of Friendship, Years of Loss*, *Forum* of the American Academy of Psychoanalysis. Winter 1990.

Review, Alford, *Melanie Klein and Critical Social Theory*, *University of Toronto Quarterly*. Winter 1990-91.

Letter, "Hindsight on Review," *Toronto Globe and Mail*. December 28, 1990.

## 1991

Edited, with an Introduction, Victor Tausk, *Sexuality, War, and Schizophrenia: Collected Psychoanalytic Papers*. New Brunswick, NJ: Transaction.

Edited, with an Introduction, Helene Deutsch, *Psychoanalysis of the Sexual Functions of Women*. London: Karnac.

Edited, with an Introduction, Helene Deutsch, *The Therapeutic Procerss, the Self, and Female Psychology*. New Brunswick, NJ: Transaction.

"Jung and Anti-Semitism," *Lingering Shadows*, ed. Maidenbaum. Boston: Shambhala. (Translated into Italian.)

"Psychoanalytic Ethics: Freud, Mussolini, and Edoardo Weiss," *Journal of the History of the Behavioral Sciences*. October 1991. (Translated into French.)

"Nietzsche and Freud: Two Voices from the Underground," *The Psychohistory Review*. Spring 1991. (Translated into French.)

"Preface to Edoardo Weiss's *Sigmund Freud As A Consultant*." New Brunswick, NJ: Transaction.

"Gross and Subtle Freuds: Interview," *The Idler*. July-August 1991.

"Freud and Lytton Strachey: An Uncanny Parallel," *Psychologist/Psychoanalyst*. Summer 1991. (Also in *Los Angeles Psychoanalytic Bulletin*, Fall 1991.)

"Anna Freud Panel," *Journal* of the International Association for the History of Psychoanalysis. Autumn 1991.

"Freud's Patients: First-Person Accounts," in *Freud and The History of Psychoanalysis*, ed. Gelfand and Kerr. New York: The Analytic Press. (Translated into French and Italian.)

Review, Burlingham, *The Last Tiffany: A Biography of Dorothy Tiffany Burlingham*, *Psychoanalytic Books*. January 1991. (Translated into Spanish.)

Review, Khan, *The Long Wait: And Other Psychoanalytic Narratives*, *Psychoanalytic Books*. January 1991. (Translated into French.)

Review, Hirschmuller, *The Life and Work of Josef Breuer*, *Psychohistory Review*. Winter 1991.

Review, Margulies, *The Empathic Imagination*, *The American Journal of Psychiatry*. March 1991.

Review, Heller, *A Child Analysis with Anna Freud*, *Journal of the History of the Behavioral Sciences*. April 1991.

Review, Jardin, *Tocqueville: A Biography*, and Lamberti, *Tocqueville and the Two Democracies*, *Virginia Quarterly Review*. Spring 1991.

Review, Haynal, *The Technique at Issue: Controversies in Psychoanalysis from Freud and Ferenczi to Michael Balint*, *Journal of the American Academy of Psychoanalysis*. Spring 1991.

Review, Reeves, *A Question of Character: John F. Kennedy in Image and Reality*, *The Toronto Globe and Mail*. June 29, 1991.

Review, Sandler, Kennedy, & Tyson, *The Technique of Child Analysis: Discussions with Anna Freud*, *Journal of the History of the Behavioral Sciences*. July 1991.

Review, Israels, *Schreber: Father and Son*, *Journal of the History of the Behavioral Sciences*. July 1991.
Review, Hopke, *A Guided Tour of the Collected Works of C. G. Jung*, *Psychoanalytic Books*. Summer 1991.
Review, Rudnytsky, *Freud and Oedipus*, *Journal of the American Academy of Psychoanalysis*. Summer 1991.
Review, Starobinski, *Jean-Jacques Rousseau: Transparency and Obstruction*, *Forum* of the American Academy of Psychoanalysis. Fall 1991.
Review, Holt, *Freud Re-Considered: A Fresh Look at Psychoanalytic Theory*, *Forum* of the American Academy of Psychoanalysis. Fall 1991.
Review, *Letters of Sigmund Freud to Eduard Silberstein 1871-1881*, ed. Boehlich, *The American Scholar*. Autumn 1991.
Review, Rybcznski, *Waiting for the Weekend*, *The Montreal Gazette*. August 17, 1991.
Review, Cohen, Freud: *The Paris Notebooks*, *Ottawa Citizen*. August 31, 1991. (Also in *Journal* of the International Association for the History of Psychoanalysis. Autumn 1991.)
Review, Bercuson and Cooper, *Deconfederation: Canada Without Quebec*, *Kingston Whig Standard*. August 31, 1991.
Review, Midlebrook, *Anne Sexton: A Biography*, *Ottawa Citizen*. September 14, 1991.
Review, Roudinesco, *Jacques Lacan & Co.: A History of Psychoanalysis in France, 1925-85*, *Virginia Quarterly Review*. Autumn 1991.
Review, Bovoroy, *Uncivil Obedience: The Tactics and Tales of a Democratic Agitator*, *Quill and Quire*. November 1991.
Review, Eribon, *Michel Foucault*, *Toronto Star*. November 2, 1991.
Review, Grosskurth, *The Secret Ring: Freud's Inner Circle and the Politics of Psychoanalysis*, *Ottawa Citizen*. November 16, 1991.
Review, Monahan, *Meech Lake: The Inside Story*, *Ottawa Citizen*. November 23, 1991.
Review, Alexander, *Rough Magic: A Biography of Sylvia Plath*, *Toronto Star*. December 7, 1991.
Letter, "A Good Cause Hardly Justifies Any Means," *Toronto Star*. July 13, 1991.
Letter, "Duluth Wife Abuse Conviction Rate Disputed," *Toronto Star*. July 23, 1991.

## 1992

*Freud and His Followers*. New York: Da Capo.
*Helene Deutsch: A Psychoanalyst's Life*, with new Introduction. New Brunswick, NJ: Transaction; Paris: Presses Universitaires de France.
"The Historiography of Psychoanalysis," in *Psychoanalysis in Its Cultural Context*, *Austrian Studies*, Vol. 3, ed. Timms and Robertson. Edinburgh: University of Edinburgh Press. (Translated into Italian and French.)
"Privacy and Therapy: The Controversy Over Anne Sexton and Her Psychiatric Tapes," *Society*. January-February 1992.

"Interview," *L'Ane*. January-March 1992.
"The Rise and Fall of Bruno Bettelheim," *Psychohistory Review*. Spring 1992. (Translated into Italian.)
"Introduction to Peter Heller's 'Afterword to a Child Analysis with Anna Freud,'" *Journal of the American Academy of Psychoanalysis*. Spring 1992.
"Introduction to Puner's *Freud: His Life and Mind*." New Brunswick, NJ: Transaction.
"America," *La Ragione Possibile*, 1992. (Italian translation of a chapter from *Encountering Freud*.)
"Opinion: Glasnost & Perestroika in Psychoanalysis," *Forum* of the American Academy of Psychoanalysis. Fall 1992.
"Commentary on Nancy Hollander," *American Journal of Psychoanalysis*. September 1992.
"Erik H. Erikson As A Teacher," *Michigan Quarterly Review*. Winter 1992. (Translated into French.)
"What is Wrong With French Psychoanalysis," *Oedipe*. November-Decmber 1992.
"Interview with Philipp Sarasin," *Le Feuillet*. Autumn 1992.
"Storia Della Psicoanalisi: Interview," *La Bussola*. December 1992.
Review, Sayers, *Mothers of Psychoanalysis: Helene Deutsch, Karen Horney, Anna Freud, and Melanie Klein*, *Toronto Star*. February 22, 1992.
Review, Stevens, *On Jung*, *Psychoanalytic Books*. January 1992.
Review, Petot, *Melanie Klein, Vol. I, First Discoveries and First System*, *American Journal of Psychiatry*. May 1992.
Review, Weissman, *His Brother's Keeper: A Psychobiography of Samuel Taylor Coleridge*, *Forum* of the American Academy of Psychoanalysis. Spring/Summer 1992.
Review, Decker, *Freud, Dora, and Vienna 1900*, *Social History of Medicine*. Summer 1992.
Review, Alford, *The Self in Social Theory: A Psychoanalytic Account of Its Construction in Plato, Hobbes, Locke, Rawls, and Rousseau*, *Canadian Journal of Political Science*. Summer 1992.
Review, Appignanesi, *Memory and Desire*, *Torontro Star*. May 16, 1992.
Review, Leys and Evans, eds., *Defining American Psychology: The Correspondence Between Adolf Meyer and Edward Titchener*, *Journal of the History of the Behavioral Sciences*. July 1992.
Review, King and Steiner, eds., *The Freud-Klein Controversies*, *Psychoanalytic Books*. Fall 1992.
Review, Roudinesco, *Jacques Lacan & Co.*, *The Forum* of the American Academy of Psychoanalysis. Fall 1992.
Review, Dowling, ed., *Conflict & Compromise: Therapeutic Implications*, *American Journal of Psychiatry*. September 1992.
Review, Rycroft, *Viewpoints*, *Forum of the* American Academy of Psychoanalysis. Winter 1992.
Review, Friedman, *Menninger: The Family and Clinic*, *Psychoanalytic Books*. Winter 1992.
Letter, "Freud's Final Weeks Filled with Torment," *Toronto Star*. May 23, 1992.

Letter, "J. Edgar Hoover's Files," *Sunday New York Times Book Review*. September 13, 1992.

## 1993

*Meeting Freud's Family*. Amherst: University of Massachusetts Press.

Edited, with an Introduction, Oskar Pfister, "The Illusion of a Future: A Friendly Disagreement with Prof. Sigmund Freud," *International Journal of Psychoanalysis*. June 1993.

"Felix Deutsch and the FBI," *Psychologist/Psychoanalyst*. Winter 1993. (Also in *Bulletin*, Center for Psychoanalytic Studies, Kent, 1993.)

"Presence de Victor Tausk dans la correspondence Freud-Ferenczi," *Etudes freudiennes*. September 1993.

"Introduction to the 2nd edition of *Brother Animal*," *Revue Internationale d'Histoire de la Psychanalyse*. 1993. (Translated into French.)

"Introduction, Anna Freud panel," *Revue Internationale d'Histoire de la Psychanalyse*. 1993.

Harvard College, *Class of 1958, 35th Reunion Report*.

Review, *Diary of Sigmund Freud*, ed. Molnar, *The American Scholar*. Winter 1993.

Review, Boyer, *Direct Democracy in Canada: The History and Future of Referendums, Toronto Star*. January 30, 1993.

Review, Kennedy, *Preparing for the Twenty-First Century, Toronto Star*. March 6, 1993.

Review, Willis, *Leonard and Virginia Woolf as Publishers, Virginia Quarterly Review*. Spring 1993.

Review, Robinson, *Love's Story Told: The Life of Henry A. Murray, The American Scholar*. Spring 1993.

Review, Rice, *Freud and Moses: The Long Journey Home, The Forum* of the American Academy of Psychoanalysis. Spring/Summer 1993.

Review, Clarke, *In Search of Jung, Psychoanalytic Books*. Spring 1993.

Review, Jamison, *Touched with Fire: Manic Depressive Illness and the Artistic Temperament, Ottawa Citizen*. May 1, 1993.

Review, *The Complete Correspondence of Sigmund Freud and Ernest Jones*, ed. Paskauskas, *Ottawa Citizen*. August 21, 1993.

Review, Rosenzweig, *Freud, Jung, and Hall the King-Maker, Forum* of the American Academy of Psychoanalysis. Fall 1993.

Review, Rudnytsky, *The Psychoanalytic Vocation: Rank, Winnicott, and the Legacy of Freud, History and Philosophy of the Life Sciences*. Fall 1993.

Review, Kerr, *A Most Dangerous Method: The Story of Jung, Freud, and Sabine Spielrein, Toronto Star*. October 9, 1993.

Review, Heller, ed., *Anna Freud's Letters to Eva Rosenfeld, Bulletin of the History of Medicine*. Fall 1993.

Review, *The Complete Correspondence of Sigmund Freud and Ernest Jones*, ed. Paskauskas, *Psychoanalytic Books*. Fall 1993.

Review, Coles, *Anna Freud: The Dream of Psychoanalysis, Forum* of the American Academy of Psychoanalysis. Winter 1993.

Letter, "Henry A. Murray," *The American Scholar*. Autumn 1993.

## 1994

*Brother Animal: The Story of Freud and Tausk.* Buenos Aires: Agalma.

"The Old Encounter," *Queen's Quarterly.* Fall 1994.

"Algunos apuntes para conocer a la familia de Freud: Interview," *La Capital.* Rosario, Argentina. April 17, 1994.

"Los Limites de la Razon: Interview," *Brecha.* Montevideo, Uruguay. June 3, 1994.

"Transmission: Tausk, Erikson, and Helene Deutsch," in *Le Cadre de l'Analyse*, ed. Delbary. Paris: Editions L'Harmattan.

Review, O'Brien, *The Great Melody: A Thematic Biography of Edmund Burke, Virginia Quarterly Review.* Winter 1994.

Review, Appignanesi and Forrester, *Freud's Women, Forum* of the American Academy of Psychoanalysis. Spring/Summer 1994.

Review, Brabant, ed., *The Correspondence of Sigmund Freud and Sandor Ferenczi*, Vol. I, *The American Scholar.* Spring 1994.

Review, Masters, Johnson & Kolodny, *Heterosexuality, Toronto Star.* July 16, 1994.

Review, Sayers, *Mothers of Psychoanalysis: Helene Deutsch, Karen Horney, Anna Freud, Melanie Klein, Psychoanalytic Review.* Summer 1994.

Review, Fullbrook and Fullbrook, *Simone de Beauvoir and Jean-Paul Sartre: The Remaking of a Twentieth Century Legend, Toronto Star.* February 5, 1994.

Review, Whitrow, *Julius Wagner-Jauregg, The History of Psychiatry.* March 1994.

Review, Douglas, *Translate This Darkness: The Life of Christiana Morgan, Psychoanalytic Books.* 1994.

Review, Haynal, *Psychoanalysis and the Sciences, American Journal of Psychiatry.* October 1994.

Review, Gilman, ed., *Reading Freud's Reading, Bulletin of the History of Medicine.* Fall 1994.

Review, Haynal, *Psychoanalysis and the Sciences, American Journal of Psychoanalysis.* September 1994.

Review, *The Complete Correspondence of Sigmund Freud and Ernest Jones*, ed. Paskauskas, *Journal of the History of the Behavioral Sciences.* October 1994.

Review, Yerushalmi, *Freud's Moses: Judaism Terminable and Interminable, Forum* of the American Academy of Psychoanalysis. Fall 1994.

Review, Gilman, *The Case of Sigmund Freud: Medicine and Identity at the Fin de Siecle, Bulletin of the History of Medicine.* Winter 1994.

Review, Gilman, *Freud, Race, and Gender, Bulletin of the History of Medicine.* Winter 1994.

Review, Micale, ed., *Beyond the Unconscious: Essays of Henri Ellenberger in the History of Psychiatry, Forum* of the American Academy of Psychoanalysis. Winter 1994.

Review, *Arendt-Jaspers Correspondence 1926-1969*, ed. Kohler & Saner, *The Queen's Quarterly.* Winter 1994. (Translated into French.)

Review, Lamm, *The Idea of the Past: History, Science, and American Psychoanalysis*, *Canadian Journal of Psychoanalysis*. December 1994.
Letter, "Crossing Swords: Janet Malcolm," *Sunday New York Times Book Review*. April 17, 1994.
Letter, "Freud and Incest," *Saturday Night*. May 1994.

**1995**

*How Freud Worked: First-Hand Accounts of Patients*. Northvale, NJ: Aronson.
*Heresy: Sandor Rado and the Psychoanalytic Movement*, with Bluma Swerdloff. Northvale, NJ: Aronson.
*Brother Animal: The Story of Freud and Tausk*, 2nd ed. Rio de Janiero: Imago Editora.
Edited, with an Introduction, Walter Lippmann, *Liberty and the News*. New Brunswick, NJ: Transaction.
Edited, with an Introduction, Louis Hartz, *The Necessity of Choice: Nineteenth Century Political Thought*. Paris: Presses Universitaires de France.
"Reflections on Psychoanalysis, Creativity, and Jackson Pollock," *American Journal of Psychoanalysis*. March 1995.
"An Interview with Lacan's Brother," *Le Coq-Heron*. December 1995. (Also in English.)
"Introduction to Menaker's *Misplaced Loyalties*." New Brunswick, NJ: Transaction.
"Preface and Roundtable," *A.E.P.A. Proceedings of Collalbo Conference*. Buenos Aires: Editorial Almagesto.
Review, Bjork, *B. F. Skinner: A Life*, *Psychoanalytic Books*. Spring 1995.
Review, Boyer and Giovacchini, eds., *Master Clinicians on Treating the Regressed Patient*, Vol. II, *American Journal of Psychiatry*. May 1995.
Review, Cooper, *Speak of Me As I Am: The Life and Work of Masud Khan*, *Psychoanalytic Books*. Spring 1995. (Also in French.)
Review, Rice, *Freud's Russia*, *Forum* of the American Academy of Psychoanalysis. Spring/Summer 1995.
Review, Shorter, *From the Mind Into the Body: The Cultural Origins of Psychosomatic Symptoms*, *Psychoanalytic Books*. Fall 1995.
Review, Hughes, *From Freud's Consulting Room: The Unconscious in a Scientific Age*, *Bulletin of the History of Medicine*. Fall 1995.
Review, Cocks, ed., *The Curve of Life: Correspondence of Heinz Kohut*, *Journal of the History of the Behavioral Sciences*. October 1995.
Review, Eissler, *Three Instances of Injustice*, *Forum* of the American Academy of Psychoanalysis. Winter 1995.
Review, Micale & Porter, *The History of Psychiatry*, *Psychoanalytic Books*. Winter 1995.
Review, Paris, *Karen Horney: A Psychoanalyst's Search for Self-Understanding*, *Psychoanalytic Books*. Winter 1995.
Review, *Between Friends: The Correspondence of Hannah Arendt and Mary McCarthy*, and Ettinger, *Hannah Arendt/Martin Heidegger*, *Queen's Quarterly*. Winter 1995.

Letter, "*Returning to the Work of Tausk*," *American Journal of Psychiatry*. September 1995.

## 1996

*Meeting Freud's Family*. Paris: Seuil.
"Fromm's Courage," in *Fromm*, ed. Mauricio Cortina. Northvale, NJ: Aronson.
"The Freud-Jones Letters," *International Forum of Psychoanalysis*. October 1996. (Also in *Behind the Scenes*, ed. Mahony, Bonomi, & Stennson.Oslo: Scandinavian University Press, 1997.)
"Paul Roazen Chez Sigmund Freud: Interview," *Le Monde*. February 2, 1996.
"The Political Psychology of Paul Roazen," *Clio's Psyche*. March 1996.
"Interview: The Library of Congress," *L'Ane*. Spring 1996.
Review, Bellak, *Confrontation in Vienna*, *Psychoanalytic Books*. Winter 1996.
Review, Frank, *Dostoevsky: The Miraculous Years*, Vol. IV, *Virginia Quarterly Review*. Spring 1996.
Review, Haynal and Falzeder, eds., *One Hundred Years of Psychoanalysis*, *Journal of the American Academy of Psychoanalysis*. Spring 1996.
Review, Noll, *The Jung Cult: Origins of a Charismatic Movement*, *Canadian Journal of Psychoanalysis*. May 1996.
Review, *The Complete Correspondence of Sigmund Freud and Ernest Jones*, ed. Paskauskas, *Psychoanalytic Quarterly*. July 1996.
Review, Herman, *The Romance of American Psychology: Political Culture in the Age of Experts*, *Psychoanalytic Books*. Summer 1996.
Review, Ettinger, *Hannah Arendt/Martin Heidegger*, *The American Scholar*. Summer 1996.
Review, Lohser and Newton, *Unorthodox Freud: The View from the Couch*, *Journal of the American Academy of Psychoanalysis*. Winter 1996.
Review, Goetz, Bonduelle, and Gelfand, *Charcot: Constructing Neurology*, *Canadian Bulletin of the History of Medicine*. 1996.

## 1997

*Erik H. Erikson: The Power and Limits of a Vision*. Northvale, NJ: Aronson.
*Meeting Freud's Family*. Rome: Erre emme edizione.
"Philosophy and Psychoanalysis: Wittgenstein and Althusser," *Queen's Quarterly*. Spring 1997.
"Helene Deutsch," in *Jewish Women in America: A Historical Encyclopaedia*. New York: Routledge.
"Elma Laurvik, Ferenczi's Step-Daughter," *Journal of European Psychoanalysis*. Spring-Fall 1997.
"Finding Oneself in Exile," *Queen's Quarterly*. Fall 1997.
"A Disturbing Mix of Psychiatry and Politics," *The Toronto Globe and Mail*. August 29, 1997.
"A Plea for Toleration," *Clinical Studies*. Spring 1997.
Review, Lothane, *In Defense of Schreber: Soul Murder and Psychiatry*, *Psychohistory Review*. Winter 1997.

Review, Cushman, *Constructing the Self, Constructing America*, *American Journal of Psychiatry*. May 1997.

Review, Moore and Fine, *Psychoanalysis: The Major Concepts*, *American Journal of Psychiatry*. May 1997.

Review, Forrester, *Dispatches from the Freud Wars: Psychoanalysis and Its Passions*; Warme, *The Psychotherapist: Use and Abuse of Psychological Influence*; and Hagen, *Whores of the Court: The Fraud of Psychiatric Testimony and the Rape of American Justice*, *The Toronto Globe and Mail*. June 28, 1997.

Review, Hale, *Freud and the Americans*, and Hale, *The Rise and Crisis of Psychoanalysis in the United States*, *Psychoanalytic Quarterly*. July 1997.

Review, Webster, *Why Freud Was Wrong*, *Psychohistory Review*. Fall 1997.

Review, McLynn, *Carl Gustav Jung*, *The Toronto Globe and Mail*. October 11, 1997.

Review, Smith, *The Wounded Jung: Effects of Jung's Relationships on His Life and Work*, *Psychoanalytic Books*. Fall 1997.

Review, *Companion Encyclopedia of the History of Medicine*, eds. Bynum & Porter, *Psychoanalytic Books*. Fall 1997.

Review, Pollak, *The Creation of Dr. B.: a Biography of Bruno Bettelheim*, *Boston Book Review*. September 1997.

Review, Mullan, *Mad to Be Normal: Conversations with R. D. Laing*, *Forum* of the American Academy of Psychoanalysis. Winter 1997.

Review, Kahr, *D. W. Winnicott: A Biographical Portrait*, *International Forum of Psychoanalysis*. 1997.

Review, Fursenko and Naftali, *"One Hell of a Gamble": Khrushchev, Castro and Kennedy: 1958-64*, *Boston Book Review, World Wide Web*. 1997.

Letter, "Soft-Hearted Hannah," *The American Scholar*. Winter 1997.

## 1998

*Canada's King: An Essay in Political Psychology*.Oakville, Ontario: Mosaic Press.

*Freud and His Followers*. Giessen: Psychosozial; Torino: Einaudi, with new Introduction.

*How Freud Worked*. Barcelona: Paidos.

"The Enigma of Canada's Mackenzie King," *Clio's Psyche*. March 1998.

"Arendt and Goldhagen on the Holocaust," *Journal for the Psychoanalysis of Culture and Society*. Spring 1998. (Also *Queen's Quarterly*.)

Harvard College, *Class of 1958, 40th Reunion Report*.

Review, Falzeder, ed., *The Correspondence of Sigmund Freud and Sandor Ferenczi*, Vol. 2, *Psychohistory Review*. Winter 1998.

Review, Rank, *A Psychology of Difference*, ed. Kramer, *Journal of the History of the Behavioral Sciences*. Winter 1998.

Review, Ferris, *Doctor Freud: A Life;* Rand and Torok, *Questions for Freud: The Secret History of Psychoanalysis*; Forrester, *Truth Games: Lies, Money, and Psychoanalysis*, *The Toronto Globe and Mail*. February 7, 1998.

Review, Rosenblatt, *Coming Apart: A Memoir of the Harvard Wars of 1969*, *Queen's Quarterly*. Spring 1998.

Review, Muckenhaupt, *Sigmund Freud: Exploring the Unconscious*, *Psychoanalytic Books*. Spring 1998.

Review, Ornston, ed., *Translating Freud*, *American Journal of Psychoanalysis*. June 1998.

Review, Forrester, *Dispatches from the Freud Wars: Psychoanalysis and Its Passions*, *Journal of the History of the Behavioral Sciences*. Summer 1998.

Review, Brunner, *Freud and the Politics of Psychoanalysis*, *History of Political Thought*. Fall 1998.

Review, Oremland, *The Origins and Psychodynamics of Creativity: A Psychoanalytic Perspective*, *American Journal of Psychiatry*. October 1998.

Review, Masters, *Fortune Is a River: Leonardo da Vinci and Niccolo Machiavelli's Magnificent Dream to Change the Course of Florentine History*, *The American Scholar*. Fall 1998.

## 1999

*Freud: Political and Social Thought*, 3rd edition, with new Introduction. New Brunswick, NJ: Transaction.

*How Freud Worked*. Rome: Erre emme edizione; Giessen: Psychosozial.

"Freud's Analysis of Anna," in *The Death of Psychoanalysis: Murder, Suicide, or Rumor Greatly Exaggerated*, ed. Prince. Northvale, NJ: Aronson.

"Helene Deutsch," "Ruth Mack Brunswick," "Sandor Rado," "Hanns Sachs," *American National Biography*. New York: Oxford University Press.

"Freud in Perspective: The Problem of Seduction," *Committed Uncertainty in Psychotherapy: Essays in Honor of Peter Lomas*, ed. Lucy King. London: Whurr.

"Introduction," *Martin Buber on Psychology and Psychotherapy*, ed. Judith Agassi. Syracuse, NY: Syracuse University Press.

"Tragedy in America," *Clinical Studies*. In press.

"Interview," *O Globo* (Brazil), September 19 .

"What Is A Fact? Eva Rosenfeld and Historiography," *Psychotherapy Review*. October 1999.

Review, Etkind, *Eros of the Impossible: The History of Psychoanalysis in Russia*, *Psychoanalytic Quarterly*. Winter 1999.

Review, Geissmann and Geissmann, *A History of Child Psychoanalysis*, *Psychoanalytic Books*. Winter 1999.

Review, Book, *How to Practice Brief Psychodynamic Psychotherapy: The Core Conflictual Relationship Theme Method*, *American Journal of Psychiatry*. February 1999.

Review, Ignatieff, *Isaiah Berlin: A Life*, *The American Scholar*. Spring 1999.

Review, *The Psychology of the Soul*, *Journal for the Psychoanalysis of Culture and Society*. Spring 1999.

Miller, *Freud and the Bolsheviks*, *Psychoanalytic Quarterly*. Spring 1999 .

## 2000

*Oedipus in Britain: Edward Glover and the Struggle Over Klein*_(New York, Other Press; London, Karnac)

*Political Theory and the Psychology of the Unconscious* (London, Open Gate Press) 'Psychoanalysis," *The Encyclopedia of Stress* (Academic Press)

"Women and History," *Psychologist/Psychoanalvst,* Spring 2000

"Edward Glover: An Outsider on Wimpole Street," *Journal of the British Association of Psychotherapists,* Summer 2000

"William Bullitt," "Felix Deutsch," "Helene Deutsch," "Childhood and Society," "Erik H. Erikson," "Ego Identity," "Sandor Rado," "Ruth Mack Brunswick," "Erich Fromm,"

"Horace W. Frink," *International Dictionarv of Psvchoanalvsis*, ed. Alain de Mijolla (Paris, Calmann-Levy)

"The Correspondence of Edward Glover and Lawrence S. Kubie," *Psvchoanalvsis and History,* in press

"Notes on Leonard and Virginia Woolf," *New Analysis,*_in press

"Secret Spaces," *Michigan Quarterly Review,*_in press

"Fromm's *Escape From Freedom and His Standing Today," Fromm-Forum*, in press

"Interview with Lynn Greenwood," *Psvchotherapv Review,*_in press

"What Is Wrong With French Psychoanalysis?," in *Jacques Lacan and the Cultural*

*Unconscious,* ed. Jean-Michel Rabate (New York, Other Press), in press

Review of *Ideas and Identities: The Life and Work of Erik H. Erikson,*_ed. Wallerstein & Goldberger, Psvchoanalvtic Psychology, Winter 2000

Review of Cremerius, ea., *The Future of Psychoanalysis, Psvchotherapv Review*, February 2000 (also *The Psychoanalytic Review*, April 2000)

Review of Ruszczynsky & Johnson, eds., *Psychoanalvtic Psvchotherapv in the Kleinian Tradition, Psychotherapy Review*, April 2000

Review of Brockman, *A Map of the Mind: Towards a Science of Psvchotherapv, The American Journal of Psvchiatry*, in press

Review of Saunders, *The Cultural Cold War: The CIA and the World of Arts and Letters, Sewannee Review*, in press

Review of Harrison, *Bion. Rickman. Foulkes, and the Northfield Experiment, Psvchotherapv Review*, in press

Review of Szaluta, *Psvchohistorv: Theory and Practice, Psychoanalytic Quarterly,* in press

# Index

www.ingramcontent.com/pod-product-compliance
Lightning Source LLC
LaVergne TN
LVHW011102300926
849160LV00008B/259
* 9 7 8 1 1 3 8 5 1 6 0 5 2 *